RUSSIA
The Soviet Period and After
Fourth Edition

Woodford McClellan

University of Virginia

PRENTICE HALL, Upper Saddle River, New Jersey 07458

Library of Congress Cataloging-in-Publication Data

McClellan, Woodford.
    Russia : the Soviet period and after / Woodford McClellan. — 4th
ed.
        p.   cm.
    Includes bibliographical references and index.
    ISBN 0-13-646613-3
    1. Soviet Union—History.   2. Russia (Federation)—History—1991–
I. Title.
DK266.M357   1998
947.084—dc21   97-14284
                                                        CIP

Editor-in-Chief: Charlyce Jones Owen
Editorial/production supervision: Joe Scordato
Copy editor: Brian Baker
Manufacturing buyer: Lynn Pearlman
Cover design: Bruce Kenselaar
Cover photo: Blagoveshchensky Sobor (Cathedral of the Annunciation), 1484–1489, with apses (1562–1564), the Kremlin, Moscow. (Photo by Woodford McClellan.)

This book was set in 10/12 Baskerville by The Composing Room of Michigan, Inc. and was printed and bound by Courier Companies, Inc. The cover was printed by Phoenix Color Corp.

To Irina

© 1998, 1994, 1990, 1986 by Prentice-Hall, Inc.
Simon & Schuster/A Viacom Company
Upper Saddle River, New Jersey 07458

Printed in the United States of America

10   9   8   7   6   5   4   3   2   1

ISBN 0-13-646613-3

Prentice-Hall International (UK) Limited, *London*
Prentice-Hall of Australia Pty. Limited, *Sydney*
Prentice-Hall Canada Inc., *Toronto*
Prentice-Hall Hispanoamericana, S.A., *Mexico*
Prentice-Hall of India Private Limited, *New Delhi*
Prentice-Hall of Japan, Inc., *Tokyo*
Simon & Schuster Asia Pte. Ltd., *Singapore*
Editora Prentice-Hall do Brasil, Ltda., *Rio de Janeiro*

CONTENTS

PREFACE

Events in Russia continue to astonish: The implosion of the USSR; economic collapse far more severe than the West's Great Depression of the 1930s; the 1991 "Vodka Putsch"; millions of genuine and bogus Saul-on-the-road-to-Damascus stories; the 25-month confrontation between Soviet-era parliament and Russia-era president; the terrifying September–October 1993 brush with civil war; a dying president surrounded by unscrupulous pretenders. Russia's reaction to NATO expansion should surprise no one.

The "free" market and the fragile democracy remain at the mercy of the new *nomenklatura*, an officially sanctioned looter-entrepreneurial class, and organized crime, and no more than anyone else do I have a clear view of Russia's salvation. The nation that bested both Nazis and Communists has the capacity to create democracy and truly free enterprise, but whether it can withstand the gigantic wave of vulgarization sweeping in from the West and Japan remains to be seen.

To incorporate a survey and analysis of the recent past yet keep the book the same length, I have completely revised the entire manuscript. Balance and perspective inevitably shift with the march of history, and I have done my best to be sensitive to that. The core remains intact, in part through condensation of the discussion of internal Bolshevik party history. Two new chapters on events between September 1991 and June 1997 appear under the rubric "Time of Troubles" (*Smutnoye Vremya*), which I explain at the beginning of Chapter 25. Beyond the fine secondary literature, only a fraction of which can I list at the end of each chapter, this book rests on research in the Russian archives, where I have been concentrating on the 1923–1982 *nomenklatura* and on the Comintern.

With the question *Ridentem dicere verum quid vetat?* (Horace) in mind, I have tried to write the kind of history students can read for pleasure as well as insight and understanding. To whatever extent the effort has succeeded, credit is due my teachers long ago in the public schools of Tacoma, Washington: Zelda Gellenbeck, Isabel Cooper, William Lemmon, Alice Fraser, Genevieve Wilcox, Ruth Price,

Max DuBois, Evelyn Forbes, Ralph Christie, Howard Carr, and the late G. W. Kennard. Staige Blackford and Steve Dalphin have influenced this book greatly, and Steve Forman gave me unforgettable biblioarchitecture lessons. At the end of Chapter 25 I identify some of the courageous people who were my best sources for the most recent developments.

New edition, new debts, and old ones—especially to my student, the late John Henley; to O. Makarii of Optyna Pustyn; the extended Zarechnak family; Vladyka Vasilii Rodzyanko; O. Dmitri Grigoriev; George and Zosya Halstead; Lawrence and Margaret Williams; Harlington and Cathryn Wood; O. Viktor Potapov; Walter and Content Sablinsky and the Sablinskys of Yerakhtur; Rabbi Gedalyah Engel and Marilyn Engel; the Gogolian O. Valentin Dronov; George and Branislava Brozak; Martin and Jane Davis; William Suggs; Jim and Meg Trott; my children Wendy, Mark, Charles, and Lena (who took two of the photographs); Sandra and Glenn McIntosh; Kathleen Miller, Lottie McCauley; Bonnie Rittenhouse; Elizabeth Stovall; Ella Wood. I extend my warmest thanks to my editor at Prentice Hall, Jennie Katsaros; to Joseph Scordato and his superb production staff; to History Editor Sally Constable; and to my friend Dan Pellow. I wish also to record my gratitude to the outside readers for this edition, Pasquale E. Micciche of Fitchburg State College, J. Lee Annis, Jr., of Montgomery College, and Norman Saul of the University of Kansas.

My greatest debt is to Irina McClellan, to whom this book is dedicated.

W. M.
Alexandria, Virginia
wdm@virginia.edu

RUSSIA
The Soviet Period and After

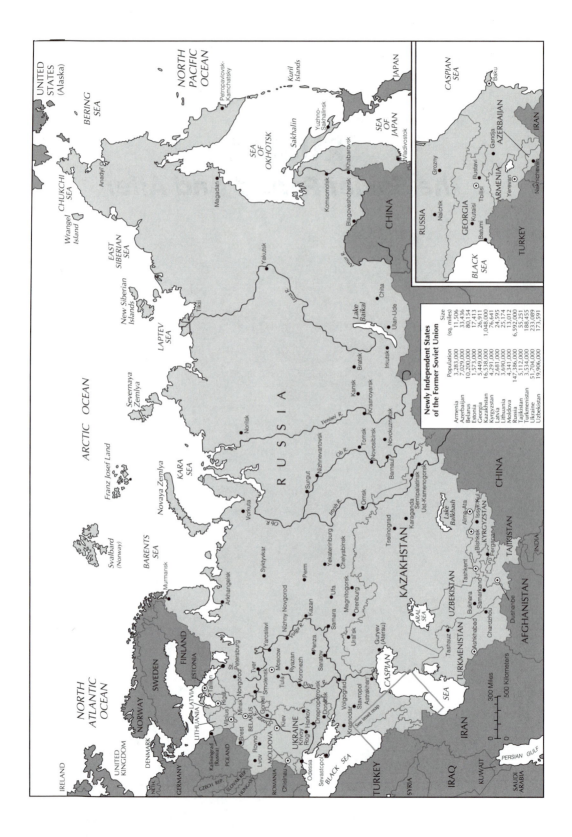

**Newly Independent States
of the Former Soviet Union**

	Population	Size (sq. miles)
Armenia	3,283,000	11,506
Azerbaijan	7,029,000	33,436
Belarus	10,200,000	80,154
Estonia	1,573,000	17,413
Georgia	5,449,000	26,911
Kazakhstan	16,538,000	1,048,000
Kyrgyzstan	4,291,000	76,641
Latvia	2,681,000	24,595
Lithuania	3,690,000	25,174
Moldova	4,341,000	13,012
Russia	147,386,000	6,592,000
Tajikistan	5,112,000	55,251
Turkmenistan	3,534,000	188,455
Ukraine	51,704,000	233,089
Uzbekistan	19,906,000	173,591

1

TOWARD OCTOBER

Russia has always been a puzzle to the West in no small measure because the West is not familiar with the history of the Byzantine or "Eastern Roman" Empire and thus knows little of Eastern Orthodox Christianity. Ukraine, Russia, Serbia, Bulgaria, Romania, and some other lands adopted Christianity from Byzantium, which survived more than a thousand years after the Visigoths sacked and burned Rome. Heir to the glories of ancient Greece and Rome, and largely impervious to the changes that reshaped Christianity in the West, Byzantium had no rival in the first nine centuries of its existence. But it suffered from the piratical expeditions called "Crusades," and in 1202–1204 its capital, Constantinople or New Rome, fell to the swords and axes of the Fourth Crusade. Byzantium never fully recovered from these Western Christians, who left it defenseless before the Muslim Ottoman Turks. After Byzantium finally collapsed in 1453, a small East Slav principality, Moscow, assumed the dignity and burden of leading the Eastern Orthodox Christian community. In time, some clerics would claim that God had designated Moscow the Third and Final Rome and its prince the Defender of the True Faith. That guaranteed that the Fourth Crusade would not be the last.

OLD RUSSIA

Toward the close of the tenth century, the pagan East Slavs from whom the Russians are descended began to embrace the Christianity preached by Eastern Orthodox priests-missionaries sent by the Patriarch of Constantinople. According to legend, clergy from Rome did not compete for souls, but Middle Eastern Islamic mullahs (religious scholars) did, along with rabbis from the only state other than Israel ever to make Judaism its official religion, Turkic Khazaria on the lower Volga. When the eastern and western branches of the Universal (Catholic) Church split in 1054, the newly Christianized East Slavs remained faithful to Eastern Orthodoxy. Rome and Constantino-

ple swapped excommunications, anathemas, denunciations. The wounds still fester.

Because of the schism, the East Slavs—modern-day Russians, Ukrainians, and Belarusians—and other Eastern Orthodox communicants including Bulgarians, Greeks, Romanians, and Serbs would not experience the Renaissance, Reformation, or Counter Reformation. They would not know St. Thomas Aquinas, Blaise Pascal, or Erasmus of Rotterdam. They benefited only belatedly and to a limited extent from the Scientific Revolution and the Enlightenment.

Founded by Scandinavian adventurers-traders and native Slav princelings in the eighth century, the first East Slav state, Rus, the fortified Dnepr River town of Kiev, and its hinterland, grew into a thriving principality. Byzantium accorded it diplomatic recognition, and Hungary and France contracted dynastic marriages with its rulers. In the eleventh century, Rus's religious institutions integrated into those of Eastern Orthodoxy.

Then came the Mongol invasion. Already in decline because rivalry among various princes—and in some areas proto-democratic institutions—thwarted development of a monarchy, early in the thirteenth century Kiev Rus perished under the weight of these last, most powerful conquerors from inner Asia. Part of the population abandoned the steppes (prairies) for the forests of the northeast—the mesopotamia of a triangle bounded by the Volga and two tributaries, the Moscow and the Oka.

Refugees from Kiev Rus blended with indigenous Finnic peoples and others to forge the modern Great Russian ethnic group. Those who remained in the Dnepr basin became the modern Ukrainians; those west of the mesopotamia and east of medieval Poland became the Belarus or "White Russians."

In the northeast the people built a principality around a settlement named after its river, the Moskva (Moscow). Toward the end of the fifteenth century that principality finally shook off the last vestiges of vassal status vis-à-vis Chinghis Khan's descendants. A succession of capable rulers warded off threats from various foreign enemies including powerful Poland-Lithuania, and in the second half of the sixteenth century Ivan the Terrible extended Muscovite territory eastward from the Volga. Muscovite explorers and settlers oozed into vast Siberia.

By 1613, when a new dynasty began its reign in Muscovy, Europeans who lived west of the Oder, the Morava, and the upper Danube knew more about the Western Hemisphere than about the kingdom on the Moscow River. This had not changed when the Romanov dynasty fell 304 years later.

Social and economic relations in Kiev Rus differed from those of contemporary Western Christian principalities and kingdoms only in being more progressive. The hallmark of the citizen was freedom rather than serfdom; the capitalist market developed normally. Rulers vied for power with an aristocracy descended from ancient princely retinues and—especially in the rich sub-principalities Novgorod and Pskov—with unruly town councils.

The Mongol invasion and protracted rule over the East Slavs changed all this. Individually and ultimately collectively, the tiny successor principalities—Moscow being one of several dozen—inexorably plummeted into the vortex of centralized power. From commoners and aristocrats alike, the central authorities collected tribute due the Great Khan. Commoners who could not pay their share of these and other—purely local—levies found themselves reduced from freeholders to serfs of the state or of private landlords. Aristocrats fallen on hard times attached themselves to a prince, agreeing to become his vassals in return for protection and recognition of their social standing vis-à-vis the free peasantry, minuscule free population of the towns, and growing serf class.

As Mongol power stabilized, became complacent, and weakened, the central authority in some principalities organized military operations aimed at establishing independence. A decisive victory came in 1380, the final rout of Mongol forces a century later; princes from Moscow led both campaigns. By the late fifteenth century Muscovy had subdued most Central Russian principalities.

Mongol rule foreclosed continuation in Muscovy of the Kiev Rus tradition of limited princely power checked by aristocracy and free commoners. A quarter millennium of submission to a foreign conqueror forged a system out of the Byzantine-Mongol heritage. Byzantium knew no form of government other than autocracy, the Mongol Horde only the

Great Khan's despotic rule; Moscow would follow suit. The Romanovs, whose dynasty began in 1613, were personalistic rulers whose decisions outweighed all law and brooked no counterclaim. At a time when Western Europe hovered on the verge of intellectual developments that would topple divine-right monarchs, Muscovy was putting the final touches on an autocracy based on the submission to the Crown of a serf-owning aristocracy.

MODERN RUSSIA

Russia entered the modern world an Eastern Catholic country. She would never know a genuine bourgeois-capitalist stage of history because she would not know Protestantism; Martin Luther and John Calvin mean no more to Russia than did Nil Sorsky and Joseph of Volokolamsk to the West. This is not to say that Russia would not be part of the Eurasian capitalist economy. Kiev Rus had participated in that economy; after the colossal dislocations of the Mongol period, Muscovy resumed the process in the sixteenth century. But not until the twentieth century would Russia achieve a wholly articulated capitalist mode of production.

The Muscovite tsar (or czar, from "caesar") was First Landlord as well as ruler; that made him or her First Capitalist, land being the chief form of capital. Peter the Great, under whose rule (1682–1725) Muscovy became the Russian Empire, retained the political attributes of his predecessors but tried to revolutionize society and the economy. He realized Russia could not compete on the world market by playing the role of colony, exporting agricultural and forestry products and importing manufactured goods. But as he set out to develop manufacturing, Peter, rather than permit native entrepreneurs free rein, made himself First Businessman. The state, not private capital, financed the establishment of nearly a hundred factories during Peter's reign, at the end of which only 191 such enterprises existed in the country. Moreover, Peter created "something unprecedented in history, a serf working class." Previously, only the Crown and private landlords could own serfs. Peter extended that right to factory owners, along with credits and technical expertise in the form of hired foreign specialists.

Peter's successors extended the state's financial and bureaucratic interference in the economy. With an assured supply of labor and capital that normally guaranteed profits, manufacturers had no incentive to modernize, seek innovations, or expand. With the state protecting them from the vagaries of domestic and world markets, such entrepreneurs could no more carry out an industrial revolution than Russia's serf-owning landlords could replicate the productivity of Western farmers. Matching British iron output ton for ton in the late eighteenth century, Russian producers doubled production in the next 50 years—but the British increased tonnage 2,900 percent. Bureaucracy's heavy hand stunted the growth of the economy and prevented modernization.

RED HORIZONS

Paradoxically, class conflicts worsened in Russia after the formal emancipation of the serfs in the period 1861 to 1863. Juridically free, millions remained economically bound to the land they worked, obligated to pay the state, which had compensated the landlords for the serfs' freedom. The peasants detested the obligation and despised the government bureaucrats who assumed police and fiscal functions from the landlords. Still loyal to the "good" tsar in St. Petersburg, the peasants coveted the vast lands of the Crown and the Russian Orthodox Church.

Tsar–landlord rule generated sporadic peasant convulsions that produced bloodshed rather than social reform; it was the threat of such violence that led to the Emancipation. The liberation of the serfs brought great changes, though in many important respects the peasants merely exchanged one set of masters, the landlords, for another, the bureaucratic state.

These historical patterns and the absence of industrial capitalism made Russia the despair of Western Marxists. Toward the end of his life Karl Marx himself, pressed by his handful of Russian disciples, toyed with the idea that agrarian Russia might somehow leap the gulf separating it from industrialized Europe and America and become the first nation to make a socialist revolution. He never worked out a coherent position on the issue, however, and he insisted that revolution in Russia could not survive absent simultaneous upheavals in the West.

The leader of the Russian Marxists, Vladimir Ilich Ulyanov, known to history by his revolutionary name, Lenin, refused to believe that revolution in Russia was generations away. Basing his projections on an optimistic assessment of the strength and political consciousness of the Russian proletariat and a creative reading of Marx's musings, he concluded that revolution could erupt in the not-too-distant future. A strong party could prepare the way through propaganda, education, agitation, and political leadership. History itself would supply the critical complex of events—economic depression, war, breakdown in government—that would force a crisis.

Lenin was born at Simbirsk on the Volga on April 10, 1870, which was April 22 in the West (Russia used the old Julian calendar until 1918). He was one of six children of a middle-level state bureaucrat. His mother was German-Jewish, his father mixed Kalmyk (Mongol) and Tatar (Turco-Mongol). In May 1887 the Russian government hanged Lenin's older brother, Aleksandr, and four associates for plotting to assassinate Tsar Aleksandr III. Lenin never recovered from the trauma. Enrolling a few months later at Kazan University, he read law, philosophy, and, on his own, the works of Karl Marx. By 1890 he had become a Marxist bent on revolution. As such, he had to ignore his brother's execution because history moves in majestically impartial ways indifferent to the fate of individuals. But as a human being he could not banish the hanging from his mind. As some historians believe Chingis Khan's enormous conquests constituted revenge for the ill treatment of his family and clan, so some specialists regard Lenin as having been obsessed by a desire to avenge the death of his brother.

In 1892 Lenin took and passed the bar examination by correspondence, and a year later he went to St. Petersburg to begin a clerkship with an attorney. He practiced law but expended most of his prodigious energy on the study, discussion, and propagation of Marxism, convinced that only revolution and class war could end the misery, juxtaposed alongside prodigious wealth, that he saw around him.

Lenin clung to the illusion that the teachings and practical experience of the terrorists might be useful to a Marxist party. But nothing Marx ever said or wrote dovetailed with the kind of terror practiced by some of the Russian revolutionary populists; Lenin confused the style with the goal. Single-minded dedication to a cause, secrecy, tight organization, irresistible élan—*these* were the qualities he wanted in a revolutionary party, and the party he forged between 1903 and 1917 would display these in good measure. Before he created it, however, he changed his position and expressly rejected individual acts of terror as useless and un-Marxist. If the removal of a few officials could undermine society, one could hardly maintain that that society had been produced, and could be destroyed, only by impersonal historic forces.

Following the 1905 Revolution, Lenin would discover "revolutionary class terror" consonant with Marxism. He would also maintain that the peasants, millions of whom supported the Socialists–Revolutionaries, or SRs, one of whose factions preached terror, could play a revolutionary role in history. Marx always considered the peasantry hopelessly reactionary. It was neither the first nor the last display of Lenin's ideological flexibility. He often promoted new and qualitatively different products under reliable old labels; his post-1905 career showed he would modify theory when tactical considerations demanded.

Earlier, the authorities had arrested Lenin (1895) for revolutionary and strike activity, and two years later they exiled him to a remote Siberian village. The isolation gave him a peaceful, productive interlude. He married Nadezhda Krupskaya; carried on a wide political correspondence; wrote *The Development of Capitalism in Russia;* hiked, hunted, and fished; did some minor legal work for the locals; took the name Lenin, which means "Lena River Man." By 1905 he had worked out a strategy that called for an alliance between workers and poor peasants. Less than a decade later, millions of such people would be fighting and dying for a tsarist regime that could offer them no better fate; they would forge that alliance.

New and potentially more dangerous class antagonisms developed when capitalism blossomed in the 1890s. Peasants seeking work fled to the cities, where they encountered poverty and degradation worse than that of the "hungry village," which Russian writers eloquently depicted. Having tolerated landlord rule and privilege for centuries, only occasionally rising up in short-lived insurrections, many peasants found themselves transformed into angry industrial workers.

Unlike its counterpart in the industrialized West, the Russian working class did not experience two generations of essentially leaderless development at the mercy of the entrepreneurs and the state. Influenced by professional revolutionaries, Russian workers were singularly disinclined to submit to management. The resettled peasant had become an aggressive rebel who regularly showed his hatred of the 11½-hour working day—a frequently ignored legal maximum—by beating up foremen, wrecking machinery, and going on strike. His refusal to submit to capital and state the way his ancestors had kowtowed to the landlords provided fine grist for the socialist mill. In the 1905 Revolution, 93.2 percent of all enterprises suffered one or more strikes. The proletariat had matured; some of the Socialists correctly gauged its revolutionary potential.

The Marxists preached class struggle and revolution, exhorting workers to rise up and seize not only factories but political power. Hostile or indifferent to the peasantry, as Marxist parties were, the Russian Social-Democratic Labor party (RSDLP), founded in 1898, split five years later into two factions. The aggressive, impatient wing broke with the gradualist elements to form the Bolshevik (Majoritarian) faction. Cautious Russian Marxists formed the Menshevik (Minoritarian) faction.

When the tsar's troops massacred peaceful, loyal, working-class demonstrators in St. Petersburg on January 9(22), "Bloody Sunday," the Revolution of 1905 began. In that great upheaval, the two RSDLP factions won the allegiance of the urban workers but had little impact on the countryside. Russia experienced enormous turmoil as a shocked population demanded reform. Except for the very rich, most urban elements voiced discontent. Some factory owners, determined to secure state concessions to business and industry, continued to pay striking workers. Finally, in October, an 11-day general strike—the most massive work stoppage in modern history—brought the regime to its knees.

His back to the wall, Tsar Nicholas II established a parliament, extended the franchise, and guaranteed civil liberties. The entrepreneurs won assurance of an improved climate for capitalist development. The tsar's "October Manifesto" blunted the revolutionary impetus and split the opposition. The middle class accepted the promises at face value and affirmed its loyalty. The workers, their illusions shaken, remained hostile, and late in the year they launched armed uprisings in Moscow and several other cities. More than a thousand people died.

Workers' councils, or soviets, emerged as a key element in the 1905 equation. These spontaneous creations of working-class despair were quickly seized and shaped by Socialists, and they appeared in many cities. The most famous and important, the St. Petersburg Soviet, acquired immense authority in the capital and beyond. For several weeks it was the only authority hundreds of thousands of workers recognized. Its chief spokesman and later chairman was Leon Trotsky, born Lev Bronstein.

The tsarist regime survived, and by 1914 it appeared that Nicholas's reforms—sharply curtailed after the crisis passed—had succeeded in shoring up tsarism and capitalism. Marxist leaders despaired of living to see another upheaval.

RUSSIA AND THE GREAT WAR

When Austria-Hungary resolved to avenge the June 1914 murder of Archduke Franz Ferdinand in Bosnia by invading Serbia, whom she suspected of supporting the Bosnian Serb assassins, Nicholas II and his circle perceived an unacceptable threat to Russian national interests. They would not tolerate an invasion of Orthodox Serbia, Russia's Slavic ally. The long series of humiliations had to end somewhere: The Crimean War, the Congress of Berlin, the 1908 Austrian annexation of Bosnia-Herzegovina—these and other defeats had stained Russia's honor. Nicholas and his advisers decided to go to war despite the certainty that Russia would have to fight not only the Habsburg Empire but also its ally, Germany.

The outbreak of the Great War (World War I) signaled the beginning of a catastrophic era. Russia could hold her own against Austria-Hungary but could not compete on equal terms with the armed might of Germany. After enormous losses in East Prussia in August and September 1914, it was, we see in hindsight, all over. The Russians did not have commanders of the caliber of Hindenburg and Ludendorff, the leading German generals. Worse, they had nothing worth fighting and dying for.

THE FEBRUARY REVOLUTION

Demonstrations against the government and its war shook Russia on the 1917 anniversary of Bloody Sunday. In a portent of things to come, the demonstrators protested the lack of food. The largest protest occurred in Petrograd, as St. Petersburg was renamed in 1914, where 150,000 workers went on strike. Serious interruptions of production and street marches struck Moscow, Baku, Harkov, Nizhny Novgorod, and other cities. More protests followed on February 23 (March 8), 1917, and the next day 200,000 Petrograd strikers marched down Nevsky Prospekt shouting "Down with the war!" and "Down with the autocracy!" They sang revolutionary songs.

Nicholas, Tsar of all the Russias and Autocrat—his title—was at General Staff Headquarters at Mogilyov (Grave) in White Russia. His beloved wife, the empty-headed Alexandra, wrote him that all would be well if only the Duma, the parliament the 1905 Revolution created, behaved itself. The tsar ordered General S. S. Khabalov, commander of the Petrograd Military District, to suppress the "inexcusable" disturbances. Nicholas had learned nothing; it might have been Ivan the Terrible announcing his will in Red Square.

The turmoil showed no sign of abating, and for lack of a better policy Nicholas ordered the dissolution of the Duma. But the Petrograd citizenry and men under arms revived their soviet (council), then marched on the Tauride Palace to demand that the deputies certify the existence of a new order. No one knew what it was, but hundreds of thousands knew beyond any doubt that the *old* order had died.

A Temporary Executive Committee of the Soviet of Workers' Deputies immediately invited the capital's workers and soldiers to elect deputies to the Petrograd Soviet and scheduled the first meeting for that evening. Military units were already creating other soviets. Conservative deputies formed a Provisional Committee.

With the rebirth of the Petrograd Soviet and formation of the Provisional Committee, disorder became revolution; no one could reverse the flow of events. Frantically trying to do *something,* General Khabalov called on one unit after another to crush the protests, but the soldiers refused to leave their barracks. On the night of February 27–28 (March 12–13), Khabalov and perhaps 2,000 loyal troops took refuge first in the Winter Palace, then the Admiralty, and then finally just drifted away.

In Moscow the best-organized radical party, the Mensheviks, spurred formation of a Provisional Revolutionary Committee open to everyone who supported the revolution; several Bolsheviks joined it the next day. Demonstrations and protest meetings took place all over the city and were especially noisy and well-attended in working-class districts. Armed workers and soldiers seized the prisons and released political prisoners. A Moscow Workers' and Soldiers' Soviet came into existence.

Born by spontaneous revolutionary generation, soviets sprang up all over Russia. By late spring there were 600, most controlled by some combination of Mensheviks, Trudoviks, and SRs. The Mensheviks projected a calm, reasoned message to the workers. The SRs and Trudoviks were agrarian Socialist parties that appealed to peasants. The Bolsheviks ran fourth but had strong positions in many of the factory committees, a major source of delegates to the soviets.

The rest of Russia followed revolutionary Petrograd's lead. In many areas the pent-up pressures of nationalism blended with and helped shape political and class trends, especially in Finland, the Baltic region, and Ukraine. The Turkic and Iranian Muslim peoples of Central Asia stirred, and the ancient Christian civilizations in Georgia and Armenia found new hope for deliverance from colonial status.

On March 2 (15), telegrams poured into the imperial train's communications center. Generals who had proclaimed loyalty to the tsar now advised abdication. Late in the evening, two deputies from the old Duma arrived to plead with Nicholas to step down, and finally he agreed.

The news became public the next day: The Romanov dynasty had fallen. The tsar went to Tsarskoe Selo near Petrograd and rejoined his family, now under house arrest.

THE PROVISIONAL GOVERNMENT

The Petrograd Soviet Executive Committee approved formation of a Provisional Government composed chiefly of politicians of the middle-class Kadet and Octobrist parties. Prince G. E. Lvov was to be prime minister. Several cabinet members were big landowners or industrialists; a Socialist, Aleksandr Kerensky, was minister of justice.

History has judged the Provisional Government harshly, but it evolved over the spring and summer of 1917 as more Socialists entered it, and it was never merely the servant of the upper classes. Anxious to please everyone, it tried to reconcile peasant and landowner, worker and capitalist, soldier and officer, rich and poor. This was impossible, but freedom confused everyone. Those who had power sometimes did not recognize it; no one knew where it came from, how long it would last, whether it bore any resemblance to power as Russia had always known it. Was democracy the babble of disorganized street mobs? Polite debate in the Duma? Raucous worker–soldier committee wrangling? In the first few months after the February Revolution most social sectors supported the Provisional Government; all Socialist parties and most soviets backed the new regime. Even the Bolsheviks cooperated.

But the Provisional Government would come to grief over the war. Had it carried out a land reform and acceded to all of labor's demands it would have fallen anyway. It refused to abandon the war, unable to understand that Russia could fight no more.

ORDER NO. 1 AND "DUAL POWER"

No Provisional Government decision or act was valid unless the Petrograd Soviet approved it; this was "dual power." The government represented a link with the tradition of more or less orderly administration of state affairs, whereas the Soviet embodied the elemental popular forces that had overthrown the old order. Establishing itself as a kind of inspectorate-general, the Soviet pursued an ambivalent line that wavered between demanding democratic reforms and meekly going along with policies manifestly against the interests of workers and soldiers.

An urgent problem facing authority was the proper care of the thousands of soldiers roaming the streets. The Duma Provisional Committee had ordered them to return to their barracks and obey their officers; many soldiers took this as a move to restore the old order. After discussion, the Soviet Executive Committee produced a document. Order No. 1, death warrant of the old army, appeared during the night of March 1–2 (14–15). It provided for election of soldiers' committees and representatives to the Petrograd Soviet; soldiers' control of weapons; and civil rights for soldiers. Soldiers were to obey the government's Military Commission only if its orders did not conflict with the Petrograd Soviet's.

Order No. 1 made it impossible for any authority other than the Petrograd Soviet to control the soldiers. Nothing in existing law or tradition gave it any legality, but it spoke with the clarity and force of the revolution itself. The troops welcomed it deliriously. The officers were horrified. When a few days later the new government announced its intention to continue "vigorous" prosecution of the war, the confusion knew no bounds. After the democratization of the army, would each unit vote on the wisdom of an order to attack? The logic of Order No. 1 made this not such a farfetched possibility. Soldiers won the right to dismiss "undesirable" officers. This was no longer an army, but Russia had ceased to be a nation. It was a matter of sorting out the strongest waves in the revolutionary tide. In early March 1917, the clear winner was the Petrograd Soviet.

THE BOLSHEVIKS

According to their own suspect figures, the Bolsheviks then had 24,000 members. In the party were professional revolutionaries who could put several times their number into the streets in peaceful or violent demonstrations. This discipline gave the Bolsheviks strength beyond their numbers, and their audacity would increase dramatically after Lenin's return. In an incredible period when hundreds of thousands of people went into the streets every day just to see what was going on; when political speeches and harangues resounded on every street corner for the first time in Russian history; when people addressed each other as "comrade"; when the hated "pharaohs" (police) gave way to earnest young men and women with red armbands; when democracy and equality were in the air and the war seemed distant and surely soon to end—when all this was going on, it was a good time to be a Bolshevik. Membership surpassed 100,000 before the end of April 1917.

Lenin was in Zürich. He wanted to return to Russia via neutral Sweden, but at first the Germans would not give permission. The negotiations ended, however, with a journey in a "sealed" train across Germany to Sweden. In late March, Lenin and his wife, along with Grigory Zinoviev, Karl Radek, and several others, left for Petrograd. It was in Germany's interest to have an antiwar politician on the scene; archival evidence has established Lenin's acceptance of German financial assistance but does not reveal him as a German agent.

At 11:10 P.M. on April 3 (16), 1917, Lenin alighted with his entourage at Petrograd's Finland Station and greeted the "victorious Russian Revolution"—the first shock, he promised, of the social earthquake that would rock all capitalist countries. World revolution was at hand. The speech prefigured one several hours later at Bolshevik headquarters in which he castigated the party. It was time, he said, to make the bourgeois-democratic revolution socialist. The scolding stunned Bolsheviks still drunk with freedom.

Three days later Lenin declared in his "April Theses" that Russia must simply lay down her arms. The imperialist war remained that, no matter what the Provisional Government called it. A "revolutionary war" in defense of Russian territory would be permissible if political power first passed to the soviets, which would renounce annexations and indemnities. Workers, peasants, and soldiers must withdraw their support from the government and support the transfer of all power to a "republic of soviets" with no police, army, or bureaucracy. A popular militia would replace the army; it was not clear what would fulfill other state functions. Lenin would nationalize land, which local soviets would distribute to the peasants. He called on the Bolsheviks to rename themselves Communists. This harsh line disoriented most Bolsheviks and led others to call Lenin insane, a traitor, an enemy of freedom. The sympathies of the Petrograd mob were clearly not with him.

The Bolshevik Central Committee had already angered Lenin by supporting the Provisional Government even to the extent of accepting its war policy; now it challenged him again by rejecting his "April Theses." But membership continued to grow, and Lenin was confident the public too would come around.

THE "KERENSKY" OFFENSIVE

In the wake of a crisis over war policy, the Provisional Government reorganized in April 1917; four more Socialists joined Aleksandr Kerensky in the cabinet. Defenders of the government, including its Menshevik and SR ministers, insisted the revolution had ended. They charged that attempts to continue it aided Russia's enemies.

With a Menshevik–SR majority, the First All-Russian Congress of Soviets of Workers' and Soldiers' Deputies convened in Petrograd on June 3 (16); it approved a resolution backing the regime's foreign policy, and gave carte blanche for a military offensive "if strategic considerations warrant." The majority supported the resolution; a substantial Bolshevik-led minority vehemently opposed it. Having planned to take their campaign to the streets, the Bolsheviks backed off when the Congress forbade them to do so.

The Mensheviks and SRs scheduled a pro-government demonstration for June 18 (July 1). It took place on schedule—infiltrated by marchers carrying banners and placards reading "All Power to the Soviets!" and "Down with the 10 Capitalist Ministers!" That was not what the organizers had in mind.

An offensive on the southwestern front early in July 1917 saw Russian forces repulsed and thrown back. The Germans had to withdraw eleven divisions from France, and the Austro-Hungarian command pulled three divisions out of Italy. It is impossible to count the British, French, and Italian lives spared, or the Russian lives lost.

The 58,000 battle casualties, including more than 7,000 killed, in the nine-day offensive—22,000 *per month* had been the 1916 average—flooded the villages of Russia with yet another wave of unbearable sorrow. As they performed that most unnatural human act, burying the young, Russian widows, orphans, and parents fixed their hatred on their leaders.

The misbegotten offensive sealed the fate of Russia in 1917. Approving it, the Petrograd Soviet lost its original character and became an adjunct of the Provisional Government, confirming Lenin's analysis of the situation and paving his way to power. The Menshevik–SR Soviet proved incapable of managing events.

Lenin in disguise, summer of 1917. (Bolshevik party photo)

JULY DAYS

Before its close on June 24 (July 7), 1917, the All-Russian Congress of Soviets elected a Central Executive Committee (CEC) of 123 Mensheviks, 119 SRs, 58 Bolsheviks, and 30 representatives of splinter factions. Like the Petrograd Soviet, this CEC became an ally of the government, now so strong the Bolsheviks could not overthrow it. On July 3 (16), soldiers from a machine-gun regiment organized

an antigovernment demonstration and demanded the Soviet and the CEC seize power. Lenin's propaganda had succeeded beyond his dreams; he had repeatedly warned against getting too far ahead of the masses. The realization of his slogan "All Power to the Soviets!" would benefit the SRs and Mensheviks, enemies who still controlled these organizations and the CEC. Furthermore, by July many soviets had become more conventional political bodies. Recuperating from a minor ailment in the Finnish countryside near Petrograd, Lenin called the machine-gunners' revolt the mistaking of the fourth month of pregnancy for the ninth.

February had belonged to Petrograd, but not July; the rest of the country had not caught up with the capital. Lenin's colleagues worked through the night of July 3–4 (16–17) but could not calm the situation. Lenin went to the Finland Station in mid-morning on July 4 (17) and saw a sea of banners proclaiming "Down with the Provisional Government!" and "All Power to the Soviet of Workers' and Soldiers' Deputies!" When he met a group of supporters at Bolshevik headquarters he was unusually quiet, and no wonder: Half a million people were in the streets of Petrograd offering him what he had long been asking for. Speaking to the most zealous Bolsheviks, the Kronstadt sailors, he said the slogan "All Power to the Soviets!" was correct and claimed it "must and will win despite all the zigzags along the historical way." If an exhortation to seize power, this was well disguised.

The CEC stalled, waiting for reliable troops to reach the capital. Unable to cancel the July 4 (17) demonstration, Lenin went to the Tauride Palace, where thousands of demonstrators—whose mood oscillated dangerously—had gathered. The possibility of a major insurrection hung heavily in the unstable air.

Loyal troops finally arrived and dispersed the mobs. Because the Petrograd Soviet had joined the Provisional Government in summoning them, their appearance should not have come as a surprise; but about 400 people were killed. The July Days produced the greatest political confusion and the most bloodshed yet.

The CEC had supported the government; under the circumstances that was tantamount to surrendering to it. The Menshevik–SR coalition, its July victory notwithstanding, had foreclosed its options. It was now an agent of a regime determined to stop the revolution. The government closed down the Bolshevik press and issued an order for the arrest of party leaders. Lenin went underground, and on July 10 (23), 1917, he fled to a hideout in Finland.

It was not clear who was fighting whom or for what reason. Because of the almost unanimous acceptance of the February Revolution, appeals to support the government now fell on receptive ears. The citizenry approved the suppression of the Bolsheviks despite ignorance of the real case against them. It was enough for the ministers and Soviet leaders to call the Bolsheviks enemies of democracy. Russia's fickle mood favored the government. August would be unlike July.

KERENSKY AND KORNILOV

When he replaced Lvov as head of the Provisional Government on July 7 (20), 1917, Kerensky supervised the suppression of the Bolsheviks and put the capital under martial law. He ordered the breakup of political organizations in the Petrograd garrison, restored the death penalty and courts-martial at the front, and withdrew recognition of Finland's autonomy. To sweeten all this he offered anew what his predecessor had promised early in March—the summoning of a Constituent Assembly to decide the permanent form of government, settle the land question, formulate new labor legislation, draft a Constitution, and hold elections in mid-September (they were postponed until November). On July 24 (August 6), Kerensky announced his new cabinet. He himself would continue as prime minister and minister of war and navy empowered to deal with "counterrevolution." He had the right to employ measures such as arrest without warrant, exile, and suspension of civil rights. Unsanctioned meetings and assemblies were forbidden. Kerensky appointed General Lavr Kornilov commander of the armed forces and gave him vague general instructions to fight the enemy "wherever he might appear." That referred to "counterrevolutionaries"— the Bolsheviks.

With the fall of Riga to the Germans on August 21 (September 3), the moment arrived: Kornilov decided to march on the capital, crush the Bolsheviks, and oversee formation of a new regime. Telegrams of support poured in from the Union of the Russian People and the Black Hundreds—right-wing, violently anti-Semitic organizations—and from many financiers, industrialists, and landlords.

A dumbfounded Kerensky received the news that troops were marching on Petrograd and wired for an explanation. Kornilov replied that the purpose of the action was to "restore order." Kerensky demanded that the general rescind his commands. Kornilov refused. Kerensky relieved him of his post, but Kornilov declined to comply. At this point the prime minister believed he had to make temporary peace with the Left, including the Bolsheviks. He emptied the jails and appealed for the "defense of the revolution."

The Bolsheviks immediately put 25,000 Red Guards armed with government-supplied weapons on duty across the southern approaches to the city. From his hiding place Lenin wrote, "We are going to fight against Kornilov. We are not supporting Kerensky but exposing his weakness." The Bolsheviks never returned the weapons.

The Red Guards, soldiers, Baltic Fleet sailors, and railway workers had established a strong defense perimeter. The commander of the Kornilov advance forces lost control of his troops, who were unenthusiastic about attacking their comrades in Petrograd, and committed suicide. Other units rebelled and refused to continue their march. Officers loyal to Kerensky arrested Kornilov. The Bolsheviks again demanded what they had sought in April, namely transfer of power to the soviets and a government of SRs, Mensheviks, and Bolsheviks.

The Kornilov affair exposed the Provisional Government as unscrupulous, antidemocratic, and, worst of all, incompetent. The Bolsheviks posed as saviors of Petrograd. Their new, positive image promptly found reflection in the political arena: On August 31 (September 13) the Petrograd Soviet went over to the Bolshevik side, and five days later the Moscow Soviet followed suit. "All Power to the Soviets!" took on a new meaning.

TWILIGHT OF THE PROVISIONAL GOVERNMENT

That workers began to flock to the Bolsheviks in great numbers was not surprising, but, in a new development, many peasants now inclined toward Lenin. For months the peasant-oriented SRs had held considerable power in the local soviets and the Provisional Government. That had not improved the lot of the peasants, who saw no reason to hope for better from the Constituent Assembly. No longer in a tarrying mood, they responded when the Bolsheviks incited them to seize the land and debate legality later. The impatience became all the greater when, bombarded by Bolshevik propaganda, peasant soldiers hungry for land began returning to their villages. The authorities lost count of property takeovers. Russia would abide no further postponement of land and justice.

The centrifugal forces that would destroy the Kerensky regime included breakaway movements among some minority peoples. The Provisional Government had resigned itself to the loss of Russian Poland, but that was the limit of its concessions. It insisted that Finland remain under Russian control, informed Romania it did not recognize the loss of Bessarabia, denounced calls for Ukrainian independence, and rejected the Baltic peoples' demands for freedom. When separatist movements materialized in Transcaucasia and Central Asia, the Provisional Government warned it would not cede a meter of territory. The Kerensky regime eschewed compromise with national-independence movements and refused to consider accommodation with the Bolsheviks. This ensured the hostility of many non-Russian minorities and led Lenin's party to concentrate its efforts, from mid-September, on preparation of an armed uprising.

Believing he could outflank the Bolsheviks with gestures, Kerensky established a "Directory" (or "Council of Five") that nominally ruled Russia for the first three and a half weeks of September 1917. It proclaimed a republic, announced the dissolution of the Duma, promised that Constituent Assembly elections would take place as scheduled, and called a "Democratic Conference" to create a new coalition government.

The Bolsheviks would not be in the coalition; indeed, the regime restricted their participation in the "Democratic Conference" itself. Kerensky, the Kadets, the Menshevik–SR "compromisers," and most middle- and upper-class citizens in Russia meant to keep the Bolsheviks isolated. In that they succeeded, but they could not stave off disaster.

SUGGESTED ADDITIONAL READINGS

FIGES, ORLANDO. *A People's Tragedy: The Russian Revolution.* New York: Viking, 1997.

KAZHDAN, A. P., ed. *The Oxford Dictionary of Byzantium.* New York: Oxford University Press, 1991.

KEEP, JOHN. *Last of the Empires: A History of the Soviet Union, 1945–1991.* New York: Oxford University Press, 1995.

KORT, MICHAEL. *The Soviet Colossus: History and Aftermath,* 4th ed. Armonk, NY: M. E. Sharpe, 1996.

MACKENZIE, DAVID, and MICHAEL W. CURRAN. *Russia and the USSR in the Twentieth Century,* 3rd ed. Belmont, CA: Wadsworth, 1997.

SABLINSKY, WALTER. *The Road to Bloody Sunday.* Princeton, NJ: Princeton University Press, 1976.

SERVICE, ROBERT. *Lenin: A Political Life: Vol. 1. The Strengths of Contradiction.* Bloomington: Indiana University Press, 1985.

WILSON, EDMUND. *To the Finland Station.* Garden City, NY: Doubleday, 1953.

2

THE BOLSHEVIK COUP D'ÉTAT

In the autumn of 1917 the Provisional Government had no plan for feeding the cities, providing fuel, provisioning the army, or resuscitating the economy. Industrial production was off 36.5 percent in comparison with 1916, which was not a good year. Inflation ran wild: 1917 prices stood 248 percent above those of 1913, and real wages had fallen 57.4 percent in the same period. Virtually the only people who still supported the government were those little affected by this inflation. Few in number, the fact that they existed at all meant the real burden fell on the poor even more heavily than the figures indicate.

The summer and early autumn of 1917 was a time of overwhelming social anxiety in Russia. Everyone sensed the country racing toward an abyss: Humiliating defeat and German rule? Restoration of the tsarist-landlord-capitalist regime? Military dictatorship? Anarchy? The February Revolution that had begun with such promise and briefly made Russia the "freest country in the world" had failed to bring forth the promised millenarian harvest.

The Sixth Congress of the Bolshevik party, which had not yet adopted Lenin's advice to rename itself Communist, met in Petrograd July 26–August 3 (August 8–16) and shelved the "All Power to the Soviets!" slogan; those bodies had capitulated to the government. Nevertheless, the party increased its efforts to win control of the soviets; in control of the factory committees since the spring, it was well-positioned to do so. Directing the Congress's work from his hideout, Lenin demanded that the 267 delegates work for the "complete liquidation of the counterrevolutionary bourgeoisie." The Congress reaffirmed the long-standing call for nationalization of industry, "workers' control" of production and distribution, land to the peasants.

Enforced isolation in Finland freed Lenin to concentrate on strategy. In early September he concluded that the Bolsheviks must prepare for an armed insurrection. But independently of anything that the party did or did not do, the citizens of Petrograd and Moscow, and the mobs of soldiers and sailors in those cities, were becoming radicalized. These people had become aware of their power and were willing to use it. Military units daily came over to the soviets, and pacifist sentiment soared after the ill-fated Kerensky offensive. The countryside was in the grip of a land war and the Provisional Government was incompetent.

By the end of April, February's handful of Bolsheviks had grown to more than 100,000, and the delegates to the Sixth Congress represented roughly 200,000 members. That there were many bandwagon-jumpers among the new recruits mattered little because enough new Bolsheviks were enthusiasts who would distribute leaflets, bring crowds into the streets, monitor demonstrations, form noisy claques for Bolshevik orators, jeer speakers of other parties, use weapons. There was wide disagreement in the party on this last issue. Many Bolsheviks with what Lenin called a "Menshevik mentality" opposed an armed uprising, genuinely believing in "All Power to the Soviets!"

When the Petrograd and Moscow Soviets came over to the Bolsheviks, Lenin believed he could seize power. The Kornilov affair, Kerensky's inept handling of the aftermath, and the Menshevik–SR refusal to back the Bolsheviks' demand for transfer of power to the soviets nationwide had convinced him. He churned out articles for the Bolshevik press and for Socialist newspapers all over the country, arguing that the working class's revolutionary consciousness and ardor had matured to the point where a seizure of power was entirely possible. Once again his fellow party leaders and the rank-and-file disagreed. They were no less devoted to Marxism and believed he had gone over to insurrectionism. Lenin threatened to quit the Central Committee.

THE BOLSHEVIKS PREPARE

The Petrograd and Moscow Soviets had narrowly voted to adopt Bolshevik resolutions on the war, on land, and on worker control of industry. A more meaningful test took place in the Petrograd Soviet on September 9 (22), 1917, when Trotsky engineered a no-confidence vote against Kerensky, which the Bolsheviks won 519–414. The military deputies who provided the victory margin had lost confidence in the prime minister and would henceforth, per Order No. 1, follow only their own leaders and the Petrograd Soviet and its dynamic new chairman, Trotsky.

Events in Moscow also favored the Bolsheviks, who won 350 of 710 seats in the October municipal elections. The change in their fortunes in the old capital between July and October was dramatic, as shown by the following table:

| | Change in Total Vote | |
	July–October	*Percentage Change*
SRs	−320,511	−85.5
Mensheviks	−60,520	−79.2
Bolsheviks	+122,911	+263.0
Kadets	−7,675	−7.0

The total vote dropped steeply, but not nearly at the rate of decline in support for the SRs, who, with the Mensheviks, had thrown in their lot with Kerensky. The Kadet vote in Moscow stayed about the same; many people who had earlier supported the party had left the city.

The Bolsheviks offered a haven for the hungry, the poorly housed, the underpaid, inflation-gouged workers, and for every malcontent and bearer of real or imagined personal grievances in Russia. Beyond that, many lower-middle-class individuals—foremen and straw bosses, white-collar workers, retail clerks, professional people, intellectuals—found Lenin's party attractive. In Moscow they flocked to his banner in such numbers that he considered launching the insurrection there.

But the Moscow party organization was less insurrectionist than its Petrograd counterpart; its relatively moderate image accounted for its success. The Moscow workers were a different kind of proletariat. Paid less than their heavy-industry counterparts in Petrograd, they labored in textile factories, other light industry, and food processing. Moscow workers were not quite so badly housed, and—their December 1905 uprising notwithstanding—their strike record was not as impressive as that of the Petrograders.

The Bolsheviks had created a special military organization to disseminate propaganda and to organize the Petrograd garrison and Baltic Fleet. The success of this outfit led to the July Days. That fiasco proved a temporary reverse; the military organization resumed its work. Now, in early October 1917, the Bolshevik-dominated Petrograd Soviet decided, at *Menshevik* initiative, to create its own Military Revolutionary Committee (MRC) under Trotsky's leadership.

The MRC could adapt to "every change in the mood of the revolutionary masses." It stressed programmed action and bureaucratic discipline, but it could also lead a revolution. It had 48 Bolsheviks, 14 Left SRs, and four anarchists; moderate Socialists disdained it. The MRC's main task was to coordinate Petrograd Soviet political work with that of the garrison and the Baltic Fleet, and to provide liaison between the Petrograd Soviet and the 40,000 Bolshevik Red Guards. The MRC constituted the general staff of the 150,000-man garrison, 80,000 sailors, and 25,000 or so working-class irregulars.

Fear of losing the moment induced Lenin to return secretly to Petrograd. The Bolshevik Central Committee voted on October 10 (23) to make "an armed insurrection the order of the day." Only Grigory Zinoviev and Lev Kamenev opposed Lenin in the 10–2 vote. Ten members of the full Central Committee were absent, and three later declared opposition. More dissent surfaced when party activists and the rank-and-file learned of the vote. Concerned with the practical problems of insurrection, the MRC denounced the plan; even those who sided with Lenin had no idea he would abruptly push them into a revolt. It was one thing to place an insurrection on the agenda, another to issue marching orders. Their votes would haunt Kamenev and Zinoviev the rest of their lives, but in fact they had expressed the majority will.

Most party members wanted to wait until the Second All-Russian Congress of Soviets—

scheduled for October 25 (November 7)—to plan for the future. The Congress would be the most democratic and truly representative body yet, and the majority of workers, soldiers, sailors, and non-Bolshevik Socialists in Petrograd looked to it for direction. But Lenin could not wait. In the sometime Menshevik Leon Trotsky—until July 1917 the most influential critic of the Leninist political line— Lenin had found a field commander who could translate his strategy into victory.

TROTSKY IN OCTOBER

Until *glasnost-perestroika,* Communist accounts ignored Trotsky's contribution to the Bolshevik seizure of power. Right after the event, however, Joseph Stalin wrote in the party newspaper *Pravda* (Truth),

The entire labor of the practical organization of the insurrection was placed under the immediate direction of the president of the Petrograd Soviet, Comrade Trotsky. It can be stated with certainty that the party owes the rapid coming over of the garrison into the camp of the Soviets and the skillful work of the Military Revolutionary Committee above all and essentially to Comrade Trotsky.

The remarks do not appear in Stalin's *Collected Works.*

Trotsky backed Lenin's call for an armed uprising when it was hard to find another Central Committee member who really wanted one. Trotsky directed the MRC and the Bolshevik military organization; he formulated the tactical plan; and he steered the debates in the Petrograd Soviet.

After hearing Trotsky speak on October 21 (November 3), the garrison's regimental committees passed a resolution calling for the All-Russian Congress of Soviets to "take power into its own hands and guarantee the people

Leon Trotsky. (National Archives)

peace, bread, and land"—the too-good-to-be-true Lenin program. The same day, the Petrograd Military District commander refused the MRC's demand for the right to countersign orders. Trotsky screamed that "The General Staff has broken with the revolutionary garrison and the Petrograd Soviet . . . thus making itself the tool of counterrevolutionary forces. . . . The Revolution is in danger!"

The Provisional Government no longer controlled the garrison; units stationed in the suburbs signed oaths of loyalty to the Petrograd Soviet. When the government ordered front-line troops to Petrograd, the men refused to move. The railwaymen's union warned that it would physically block any assault on the capital. Most of them older veterans and reservists, the soldiers of the Peter-Paul Fortress refused to recognize the MRC's authority. Vladimir Antonov-Ovseyenko wanted to storm the fortress, but Trotsky merely went over, talked to the troops, and swung them around. The MRC took command of the fortress without firing a shot and seized 100,000 rifles.

AT THE CROSSROADS

Unable to dissuade the Central Committee, which considered a deal a deal even though they did not like it, on October 18 (31), 1917, Kamenev and Zinoviev leaked the Bolshevik plans. An apoplectic Lenin demanded the party oust them as traitors. His colleagues refused, content to accept Kamenev's resignation from the Central Committee and to order him and Zinoviev to obey party decisions.

Lenin feared publicity would thwart his plans; in reality it helped ensure victory by forcing his party's hand. The Bolsheviks could not have survived another July Days crisis. That had been a false opportunity; the situation had changed drastically by October, when a much stronger Bolshevik party faced weaker opponents.

Since early September, when the party obtained weapons for a fight against Kornilov that did not materialize, there had been talk on the street of a Bolshevik coup d'état. Kerensky told the Pre-Parliament on October 20 (November 2),

I must inform you that a part of the Petrograd population is in a state of open insurgency. . . . I have proposed that judicial investigations be started immediately and I have also ordered arrests [protests from the Left]. Yes, yes, because at the moment, when the state is imperiled by deliberate or unwitting betrayal and is on the brink of ruin, the Provisional Government, myself included, prefers to be killed and destroyed rather than betray the life, honor, and independence of the state [ovation from all but the Left]. All those elements of Russian society, all those groups and parties which have dared raise a hand against the free will of the Russian people . . . are subject to immediate, final and definite liquidation.

The right-wing delegates cheered this, Kerensky's swan song. Facing an imminent insurrection, the government could rely only on some military academy cadets, a battalion of women, a few Cossacks, and bombast. So pitiful was this force that it remains a mystery how anyone could have believed Kerensky intended to attack.

Desperately afraid his own party and the Petrograd Soviet would miss the wave, Lenin repeatedly warned his colleagues not to delay even for the Congress of Soviets. A political sixth sense told him there would be no second chance.

OCTOBER 24–25, 1917

Trotsky plotted, and the Bolshevized soldiers and sailors prepared. The Red Guards—disciplined squads of energetic, excited young men and women—checked weapons, adjusted armbands, gulped "victory tea," wolfed down bread and sausage of uncertain provenance, slept an hour or two a day, waited for orders. They could not sustain the tension indefinitely.

Late in the evening on October 24 (November 6), the day before the Congress of Soviets was to convene, Bolshevik units took up positions around Petrograd, firing a few shots and being fired at. The city went about its routine. Bursting with the special stress that can afflict the usually unemotional, about midnight Lenin put on a workman's cap and walked over to party headquarters, now at the Smolny Institute. He was in disguise and did not know the password. Unsure whether he was a spy, panhandler, or a simpleton claiming to be Lenin, the guards finally let him pass. As the news began to come in, he surely permitted himself a smile.

At about 2:00 A.M. on October 25 (November 7), the Central Committee learned that Bolshevik units had seized the central telephone exchange, telegraph office, main post office, and the railway stations. Soldiers, sailors, Red Guards, and deputized workers held positions on the bridges, key intersections, power stations, and the State Bank. They encountered little resistance. Remaining in government hands at daybreak were the General Staff building, a few government offices, and the Winter Palace, to which Kerensky had foolishly—given its symbolic significance—transferred his headquarters.

At 10:00 A.M., the Petrograd Soviet Military Revolutionary Committee issued Lenin's hastily drafted proclamation:

TO THE CITIZENS OF RUSSIA!

The Provisional Government has been overthrown. State power has passed into the hands of the organ of the Petrograd Soviet of Workers' and Soldiers' Deputies, the Military Revolutionary Committee, which stands at the head of the Petrograd proletariat and garrison.

The cause for which the people have struggled—the immediate proposal of a democratic peace, the elimination of landlord estates, workers' control over production, the creation of a Soviet government—the triumph of this cause has been assured.

Long live the workers' and peasants' revolution!

By coincidence the scheduled opening of the Congress of Soviets was only hours away when the Bolsheviks telegraphed this document around Russia. The idea was to present the Congress, to which they themselves claimed to look for leadership and legitimacy, with a fait accompli.

It was an eerily unrevolutionary revolution. Trams continued to run; cafés and restaurants remained open. The bustle in the streets was perhaps a little subdued, but there was no general atmosphere of momentous events. At 2:35 P.M. Trotsky gave an accounting to an emergency meeting of the Petrograd Soviet. Then Lenin arrived to an enthusiastic welcome and said, "Comrades, the workers' and peasants' revolution has come to pass, the revolution which the Bolsheviks have long shown to be necessary." He stressed the critical link between Russian workers and the "world labor movement." He concluded, "In Russia, we must now devote ourselves to the construction of a proletarian socialist state. Long live the socialist world revolution!"

There was an odd calm to this, one of the modern world's decisive moments. After Lenin spoke, people would not live their lives in the same way. The course of history was changing, and not for the better. The other elements in the October equation hesitated, debated, waited—a cautious posture that even many Bolsheviks preferred. But for a brief moment an iron-willed political strategist prevailed.

The government cast about frantically for loyal troops; none responded. Disguised not as a worker but in a dress, Kerensky slipped away with help from the American legation. His ministers won a few extra hours in office when sailors from Kronstadt failed to arrive on time to arrest them; the sailors finally showed up late in the evening. Moored across the river, the cruiser *Aurora* fired some shells to encourage a rapid decision; the ministers did not know they were blanks. A little after midnight a Winter Palace telephone operator contacted Deputy Prime Minister Aleksandr Konovalov and told him a "delegation" was approaching.

Vladimir Antonov-Ovseyenko and a Bolshevik platoon simply walked through the gates. There was no storming of the Winter Palace; the post-tsarist regime died without even a whimper. The platoon found the ministers, and Antonov-Ovseyenko read out the MRC order for their arrest. Konovalov replied, "The members of the Provisional Government yield to force, and surrender to prevent bloodshed." Nothing became them in office so much as the leaving of it. Antonov-Ovseyenko's men escorted them to cells in the Peter-Paul Fortress. The Red Guards restrained sailors and workers who were bent on violence.

There were no recorded lynchings. Across the city there was only a handful of casualties—too few for a cataclysm, but too many for a routine changing of the guard. There was some doubt whether a revolution had actually taken place.

LENIN TAKES OVER

At 10:40 P.M. on October 25 (November 7), 1917, the Second All-Russian Congress of Soviets convened in Smolny Institute, headquarters of both the Petrograd Soviet and the Bolshevik Central Committee. With 300 of the 670 delegates, the Bolsheviks dominated the Congress, charged now with legitimizing the insurrection. Supported by Left SRs, they prevailed on all questions. Fourteen Bolsheviks, including Lenin, Trotsky, Antonov-Ovseyenko, Aleksandra Kollontai, Kamenev, and Zinoviev, were elected to the presidium, along with seven Left SRs and one Ukrainian Socialist.

The Mensheviks, Martov's Menshevik Internationalists, the regular SRs, and members of two small Jewish parties announced opposition to the "military plot and seizure of power" and walked out, saying they would not be tainted by complicity with Bolshevism. Later they would claim to have tried to precipitate the collapse of the Bolsheviks.

A dilemma confronted the anti-Bolsheviks: They could not endorse the insurrection, much less confirm a government of insurrectionists, but the Bolsheviks controlled the Congress. What could the "antis" have done? Down to October 25, the only option was to form a group and call it a government. Every party had this opportunity but only the Bolsheviks took advantage of it.

At 3:10 A.M., October 26 (November 8), the Congress received word that the Winter Palace had fallen and that except for Kerensky the ministers were in custody. An hour later a Bolshevik read aloud Lenin's manifesto "To All Workers, Soldiers and Peasants," which proclaimed the transfer of power to the Congress.

Land was now the property of "peasant committees"; the workers controlled industry. The Petrograd Soviet would immediately propose a "democratic peace to all nations and an armistice on all fronts." The manifesto provided for a "revolutionary army" to be raised by "requisitions from and taxation of the propertied classes." It promised aid to soldiers' families, for whom no previous regime had lifted a finger. The document warned of counterrevolution.

The Congress approved the manifesto with two votes against and twelve abstentions. Russia had passed the point of no return. The Military Revolutionary Committee (MRC) took over police functions and began organizing municipal life. The shops were open; public transportation ran more or less on schedule and the utilities functioned normally. Opera lovers went to the theatre that evening to hear Fyodor Chalyapin. Fashionable cafés and restaurants on Nevsky Prospekt had unlimited delicacies and French champagne for rich customers.

Lenin and his colleagues, Petrograd, late 1917. (National Archives)

Over at the Smolny Institute, the Bolsheviks constructed a government. What to call the heads of departments? They ruled out "minister" because of its "capitalist" connotations, but what about "commissar"? All agreed—commissars in charge of commissariats. The new government would be called the "Council [Soviet] of People's Commissars," or "Sovnarkom."

Lenin became chairman of the new government, Trotsky Commissar of Foreign Affairs. Military Affairs went to the MRC leaders Vladimir Antonov-Ovseyenko, Nikolai Krylenko, and Pavel Dybenko. Joseph Stalin (Dzhugashvili), an Ossete from Georgia, got the minor post of commissar of nationalities. Subcabinet slots went haphazardly; the new State Bank director had, as his qualifications, attendance at a few lectures at the London School of Economics.

Just before 9:00 A.M. on October 26, Lenin arrived at the Smolny Institute to preside over the Congress. He read his "Decree on Peace," then went on to the "Decree on Land," which surprised everyone: It was the SR program. The Bolsheviks abolished private landholding without compensation but pledged not to confiscate the "land of ordinary peasants and Cossacks." All citizens had the right to the land they themselves worked. It was forbidden to hire labor. The land would be periodically redivided—an ancient custom in some areas—to reflect population changes and new agronomic methods. The Constituent Assembly would legitimize all this.

The final item involved composition of the regime. Trotsky called for it to be exclusively Bolshevik; other speakers, including some Bolsheviks, wanted an all-party government. The Bolsheviks offered cabinet posts to the Left SRs, who had by now declared themselves an independent party, only to be rebuffed. Finally, the Congress approved the all-Bolshevik list. The Sovnarkom became the de facto government.

OUTSIDE PETROGRAD

In Moscow, 20,000 well-armed men were poised to suppress a leftist uprising, and the city fathers expected reinforcements from the Southwestern Front and from Cossack units in southern Russia and Ukraine. The 30,000-man local garrison, if not wholly reliable, was less infected by the Bolshevik virus than its Petrograd counterpart; nevertheless, the officers locked up the weapons. The Moscow City Duma formed a Committee of Public Safety.

Bolshevik hopes for success rested on the central industrial region around Moscow, which had nearly half the country's three million workers. If those workers linked up with revolutionary Petrograd, the heartland would be secure.

Lenin's assessment of their revolutionary zeal notwithstanding, the Moscow Bolsheviks were not anxious to fight. The Bolshevik chairman of the Moscow Soviet, Viktor Nogin, who had opposed the insurrection, now urged cooperation with the Sovnarkom, calling it a bulwark against the "counterrevolutionary" Provisional Government. The Moscow Soviet's Mensheviks and SRs disagreed; the full body voted to support Lenin. The Moscow Soviet then formed a Military Revolutionary Committee of Red Guards and workers. Opposition within local Bolshevik ranks remained strong.

Fighting erupted in Moscow on October 27 (November 9). Loyalist military academy cadets seized the Kremlin and dealt savagely with the guards, who had gone over to the Moscow Soviet. The Committee of Public Safety secured the central part of the city and awaited reinforcements. Those came first to the Moscow Soviet, however, in the form of Red Guard detachments from Petrograd and elsewhere. That tipped the balance; a cease-fire went into effect on the morning of November 2 (15), and the Moscow Soviet seized control of the city. More than a thousand people had been killed.

Fighting continued elsewhere in the central industrial region until spring 1918; Tula, Nizhny Novgorod, and Kaluga saw especially intense action. By June 1918 the Bolsheviks controlled most of the region.

After the Petrograd-Moscow axis and the industrial center, the Bolsheviks set highest priority on Ukraine with its million workers, more than 650,000 of them concentrated in the Donbas and Harkov and Yekaterinoslav provinces. About 30,000 Bolsheviks had been agitating for months in the Donbas; that heavily industrialized sector came under Lenin's control in November 1917. Another 15,000 Bolshevik activists scattered around Ukraine were no match for the separatists, not to mention other contenders for power such as anarchists, bandit gangs, and private Cossack armies. Not until February 1918 did the red flag fly over Kiev, and then not for long. A short-lived independent Ukrainian Central Rada succeeded in taking power, only to yield to a German-sponsored puppet government. The fighting did not end nor the political situation stabilize until the mid-1920s; Stalin would never forget this.

War with Poland complicated the situation not only in Ukraine but also in Belarus, Lithuania, and Russian Poland. The new Polish state incorporated part of western Ukraine and Belarus as well as the Polish territories of the Russian Empire. Lithuania, Latvia, and Estonia all won independence. In the southwest, Bessarabia, which Alexander I had seized from the Ottoman Empire in the war of 1806–1812, proclaimed its independence, then agreed to incorporation into Romania. Although two-thirds of the population was Romanian, the Bolsheviks refused to accept the loss of the province.

The fertile North Caucasus slowly came under Bolshevik sway. The region had dozens of different nationalities, most of whom—the Chechens and Ingush were exceptions—had for decades been politically passive. To the south, in Georgia, Armenia, and Transcaucasia, a no less heterogeneous population was far more active. The Bolsheviks did not succeed in taking Georgia and Armenia, both of which established independent regimes. The Turkic Azerbaijanis (Azeris) generally deferred to their feudal landlords and mullahs, but nearly 60,000 oilfield workers—Russians, Ukrainians, Azeris—at Baku acknowledged Bolshevik authority. With the help of a British expeditionary force, the SRs would overthrow the Baku Bolsheviks later in 1918.

In Central Asia, economically and politically mired in feudalism, the Muslim populations—Turkmen, Uzbeks, Kyrgyz, Tajiks, and others—had traditionally submitted to the rule of landlords, religious leaders, and latterly the Russian conquerors. They were unlikely to find the atheist Bolsheviks more attractive. In fact, only in Tashkent, the Uzbek capital, did a few thousand Russian workers employed on the railroads present a potential Bolshevik constituency. After some violence, Tashkent and the surrounding region came under shaky Soviet control.

By February 1918 the ancient cities along the "Marco Polo" road to China—Samarkand, Ashkhabad, Krasnovodsk, Merv, Pishpek, Kushka, Ferghana—had come into the Bolshevik camp. But not until 1920 did Lenin's regime take the Khanate of Khiva and the Emirate of Bukhara, and much of Central Asia would be bedeviled by antisoviet armed gangs for several more years. The members of these units saw themselves as Islamic warriors fighting the atheistic Communists. The Bolsheviks called them *basmachi*—"bandits."

Islam had a relatively weaker hold on the Turkic Kazakhs of the vast, thinly populated Kazakh steppe. Feudal barons dominated the social and political life of these nomads, who had opposed Russian colonial rule for generations and—often in alliance with the Turkic Bashkirs—had frequently rebelled. In 1917 a nationalist party, Alash, challenged the Russian claim to Kazakhstan and tried to establish an independent state. Fighting between Alash and Bolshevik forces continued until the Red Army victory in January 1919.

Siberia and the Far East then had only about 9.5 million people, including 325,000 workers, in an area almost twice the size of the United States. Most people eked out an existence on the land and in the forest. Some workers on the Trans-Siberian Railway, and others in scattered factories and plants, sympathized with the Bolsheviks, but the vast distances made concerted action difficult. Attempting to take key towns and cities along the railroad line, the Bolsheviks encountered strong resistance from monarchist and SR forces.

In the Far East, the Japanese and Americans intervened in force in 1918. The Bolshevik regime did not fully control this area until the mid-1920s.

Finally, the six million men still technically on active duty in the Imperial Russian Army were crucial to Bolshevik plans. As the Provisional Government continued to drift aimlessly, disillusioned soldiers increasingly looked to Lenin's party for deliverance. There was no possibility of victory at the front, no government worth defending in the rear. Not all soldiers came over to the Bolsheviks, but few still in uniform actively opposed them.

THE OCTOBER DISASTER

The people of Russia saw the Bolsheviks as variously agents of soviets, of the Germans, of the international proletariat, of Freemasonry, of international Jewry, of Satan. A small minority regarded Lenin as a savior, a greater number saw him as the Beast of the Apocalypse.

In the autumn of 1917 it was by no means clear that the Bolsheviks would survive. Jacobins of the Russian Revolution, their coup d'état infuriated and energized their enemies.

Any attempt to translate their radical program into action would alienate still more millions. Sophisticated Petrograd politicians and intellectuals assured each other that this party of radical crackpots would disintegrate.

On the great questions of war, social and political organization, and the organization and control of production, the Bolsheviks held positions that were easily understood and superficially attractive. They preached a Western ideology but in many respects remained true to Russia's Byzantine-Mongol-Muscovite tradition, which did not know compromise. The "people" must overthrow the state. Workers must rise up against capitalists. Peasants must take the land.

The monarchists, Octobrists, and other right-wing parties had no program. Forgetting they were dealing with Russia, the Kadets extolled middle-class parliamentary democracy. The SRs would give the land to the peasants, whose greatest hope was to be left alone. The Mensheviks excelled at endless debate. These weak, pessimistic parties had talked and quarreled away the opportunity to take power. They bear enormous responsibility for the catastrophe.

The Bolsheviks snatched power in the name of the poor, the oppressed, the weak, the hungry, the people without hope. The possessing classes of Europe and America proclaimed this messianic movement false, branded it anathema, and called for a new Crusade aimed at its destruction—and incidentally at the taking of some territory, and lots of loot.

SUGGESTED ADDITIONAL READINGS

CHAMBERLIN, W. H. *The Russian Revolution, 1917–1921,* 2 vols. Princeton, NJ: Princeton University Press, 1987.

PIPES, RICHARD. *A Concise History of the Russian Revolution.* New York: Knopf, 1995.

SERVICE, ROBERT. *Lenin: A Political Life: Vol. 2.*

Worlds in Collision. Bloomington: Indiana University Press, 1991.

SHKLIAREVSKY, GENNADY. *Labor in the Russian Revolution.* New York: St. Martin's Press, 1993.

VOLKOGONOV, DMITRY A. *Lenin.* New York: Free Press, 1994.

VOLKOGONOV, DMITRY A. *Trotsky.* New York: Free Press, 1996.

WADE, REX A. *Red Guards and Workers' Militias in the Russian Revolution.* Stanford, CA: Stanford University Press, 1984.

3

CIVIL WAR
AND INTERVENTION

In the spring of 1918 the task of constructing a stable political regime and restoring order seemed beyond Bolshevik capabilities. Only in the new seat of government, Moscow, and in Petrograd and some other cities of north and central Russia, did the population recognize their rule. Regular military units and armed mobs terrorized the cities and laid waste to the countryside.

The Octobrists, Kadets, SRs, Mensheviks, and others fought back with everything from assassinations to military campaigns across vast fronts. Foreign powers financed these operations and sent troops. A disastrous peace treaty with the Central Powers amputated the Russian industrial and agricultural heartland.

THE TREATY OF BREST-LITOVSK

The day after the coup d'état, Trotsky asked the Allied ambassadors to relay to their governments the Sovnarkom's proposal to accept the "Decree on Peace" as the basis for an armistice and peace negotiations. The diplomats ignored him; this confirmed Bolshevik suspicions that the Allies were not interested in peace. A few days later the British government announced it would not recognize the new regime; other powers followed suit.

If the Allies would not join them, the Bolsheviks would go it alone. On November 13 (26), 1917, their emissaries crossed through German lines under a white flag of truce and arranged for peace negotiations to begin six days later at the town of Brest-Litovsk.

The Germans and their allies presented an ultimatum: 150,000 km^2 of Russian territory, a large indemnity, the right to station troops on

Russian soil. The Bolsheviks now split. The "Left Communists" wanted to wage a revolutionary war, counting on uprisings of the German, Austrian, and Polish workers. Lenin led a peace group that demanded Russia stop fighting immediately.

Trotsky took charge of the negotiations in January 1918. Unwilling to surrender on German terms, he knew Russia could fight no longer. He believed revolution imminent in Germany. To gain time, Trotsky adopted a stance unique in diplomacy: "Neither peace nor war." Russia was disbanding her armies and would not fight—but neither would she sign a peace treaty.

The Germans pondered this briefly, then returned to the attack, which soon threatened Petrograd. The Bolsheviks had to choose between capitulation and annihilation.

Failure to accept the German ultimatum, Lenin warned, would lead to the overthrow of the regime. Seven Central Committee members voted with him, four against, and four abstained. Under the rules the majority of those voting carried the day. Trotsky resigned. A second-level official signed the Treaty of Brest-Litovsk on March 3, 1918.

Compared to Brest-Litovsk, the harsh settlement the Allies would impose on Germany at Versailles was magnanimous. Russia lost a million square kilometers of territory, 34 percent of her population, 32 percent of her farmland, 89 percent of her coal fields, 54 percent of her heavy industry. She had to accept the German puppet regime in Ukraine and the loss of Latvia, Estonia, Lithuania, Russian Poland, and part of Belarus.

Russia was now more helpless than at any time since the founding of the Romanov dynasty; but the regime gained a breathing space without which it could not have survived. Four days after the humiliation, Lenin told his dispirited colleagues—many of whom regretted not opting for a revolutionary war—that the Sovnarkom had neither illusions about nor respect for the treaty and was already supplying the Finnish Communists with weapons and ammunition. Lenin anticipated either a proletarian uprising in the West or a German defeat. To his surprise, the latter came first. When the Armistice in the West went into effect on November 11, 1918, the Sovnarkom immediately annulled the Treaty of Brest-Litovsk.

ALLIED INTERVENTION

Belatedly recognizing the Bolsheviks' seriousness of purpose, Allied governments swung into action, spreading rumors that Lenin's people were German agents and Jews who, unless wiped out, would invade the West to "communize" women, sequester private property, stable their mules in churches, devour Christian children.

With defeated Russia's resources at Ger-

Lenin speaking at the unveiling of the temporary Marx-Engels monument, Moscow, November 7, 1918. (Sovnarkom photo)

many's disposal, the Allies feared the tide of battle in the West would shift. Enough German divisions to offset the flow of American aid would move out of Russia and into France. The Allies naturally wanted those German divisions tied down in Russia, and they wanted to keep control of Caspian Sea oil, and protect munitions depôts at Murmansk, Archangel, and Vladivostok.

The Bolshevik repudiation of the tsarist debt, confiscation of private property, and shrill advocacy of world revolution struck fear into middle-class hearts everywhere. With wary eyes on their own working classes, Western capitalists pressured their governments to intervene in Russia. In December 1917 Britain and France secretly agreed to partition Russia. Such was the international morality of the day, and a Bolshevik Russia was unlikely to elevate it.

Ironically, Trotsky and Lenin had some hope for *aid* from the West, particularly America. President Woodrow Wilson seemed less hostile than French and British leaders; one of his Fourteen Points called for evacuation of foreign military personnel from Russian soil and an international guarantee of Russia's right to determine her own destiny.

Intervention and Civil War, 1918–1920.

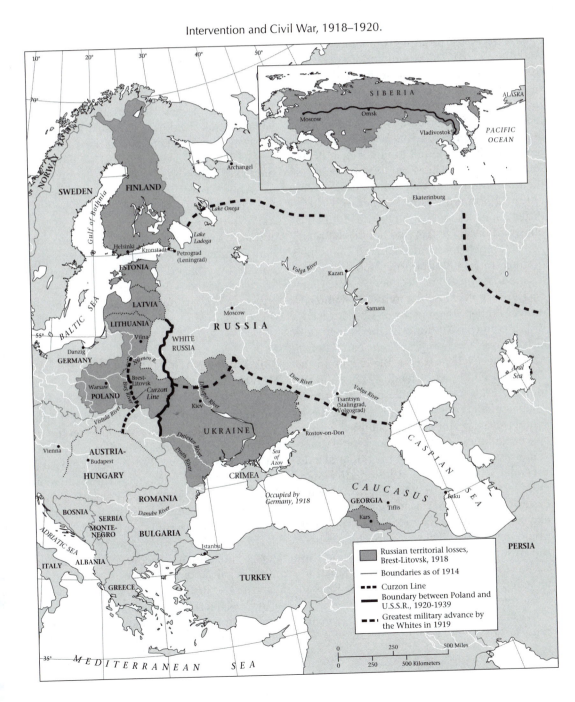

Some influential British politicians including Winston Churchill urged armed intervention, but Prime Minister David Lloyd George hesitated. Unlike Churchill, he cared nothing for the Russian monarchy or aristocrats; he refused to sanction massive intervention because the British public would not stand for it, and anyway the British Treasury could not pay for it. And there were no more generations to be lost.

The British government authorized a series of neither-fish-nor-fowl operations. It spent more than £100 million (nearly $500 million) in 1918–1919 to protect the flow of Caspian oil and find a leader to rule Russia in London's best interests. The oil flowed briefly after a British force helped local anti-Communists overthrow the Bolshevik Baku Commune, but the execution of 26 commissars in September 1918 inflicted a long-lasting scar on British–Soviet relations, and Britain had to find her oil elsewhere.

The French government shared Churchill's hostility toward Bolshevism. Both President Raymond Poincaré and Premier Georges Clemenceau—who was also war minister—wanted to protect French investments in Russia. Like its British counterpart, however, the French public had no stomach for war against an "enemy" so recently a valiant friend. Bled white in the Great War and beset by terrible morale in the military, France could not undertake a new campaign. She could send only small forces to southern Russia and hope for a miracle.

The Japanese were the most eager interventionists. Overcrowded in the home islands, they had seized Korea and lusted after Manchuria, the Russian Maritime Provinces, and eastern Siberia; many leaders believed such expansion a matter of national survival. Japan would never have a free hand in China, where the West had first claim; a disintegrating Russia was the perfect victim. Imperial Japan intervened in force and remained on Russian territory for several years.

Wilson opposed Tokyo's aggression because he genuinely believed in the right of self-determination. As for Lenin and company, Wilson agreed with John Maynard Keynes that Bolshevism was "bred by the besotted idealism and intellectual error of the sufferings and peculiar temperaments of Slavs and Jews." Wilson sent American forces to protect the munitions depôts, and, not incidentally, to restrain Japan.

In all, 15 countries intervened in this new Crusade. The Turks moved into Transcaucasia. Romania took Bessarabia. Newly reconstituted Poland moved to settle some ancient accounts. Even the Greeks and Persians intervened. The Czechoslovak Legion, composed of Austro-Hungarian prisoners of war, became involved.

The Russian Civil War of 1918–1920 pitted the "Reds" (Bolsheviks) against the "Whites" or "White Guards"—loosely, all domestic anti-Bolshevik forces. The White movements took shape in the spring and early summer of 1918 and were scattered all across the defunct Russian Empire. The Bolsheviks then controlled only an oval-shaped area, with Petrograd and Voronezh at the poles of the long axis, Smolensk and Yarolavl opposite each other on the short axis.

BREAKAWAY NATIONALIST MOVEMENTS

Among the first to declare independence from Russia were some non-Slav peoples on the periphery. Their national-liberation movements put the Bolsheviks, who advocated the right of self-determination, in an awkard situation. Their own propaganda had convinced them that the poor would always choose a Communist regime; *nowhere* did that happen.

The Finns left first. An autonomous Grand Duchy, Finland had become restive under the harsh Russification policies of the last two Romanovs. The first Provisional Government had acknowledged Finland's right to independence; the Bolsheviks had no choice but to go along.

The Estonians, Latvians, and Lithuanians

likewise established their own states. Literate and industrious, they were fully capable of maintaining themselves as viable political entities. Some poor peasants in Latvia and Lithuania supported the Bolsheviks, but by and large the populations detested communism.

When the puppet regime in Ukraine fell after the Armistice of November 11, 1918, the German General Staff issued orders for the withdrawal of its troops, who might well be needed to control the working class at home. After the German pullout came a nightmare that saw control of central Ukraine change hands ten times in 23 months. Simon Petlyura, last leader of the independent Central Rada, now rejoined the struggle for power at the head of a motley crew of Cossacks, deserters, brigands, and nationalists. Another major contender for power was Nestor Makhno. Unfurling the black flag of anarchism, Makhno proved a popular guerrilla chieftain who fought Germans, Petlyura, Bolsheviks, and anyone else who needed to be fought. In 1919 he joined the Communists, left them, rejoined them, attacked them. Another swashbuckling Ukrainian warlord, Nikifor Hryhoriv, terrorized vast areas with an army of 15,000 partisans. Allied with the Bolsheviks early in 1919, by summer he had changed his mind. Makhno killed him in July.

The Romanian majority in Bessarabia proclaimed independence early in 1918, then opted for union with Romania. Claiming the Romanian military had forcibly annexed the province, the Bolsheviks swore to retake it.

Armenia and Georgia declared themselves free early in 1918. There were then few Armenian Bolsheviks but many Georgians, including the commissar of nationalities, Stalin, a Georgianized Ossete (the Ossetes are an Iranian people) fast becoming more Russian than the Russians. The loss of Georgia to the anti-Bolshevik camp—Mensheviks playing a major role—galled Stalin personally and drove his party up the wall.

In poorly defined and badly led attempts to win their freedom, the Muslim peoples of Transcaucasia and Central Asia also sought to break away. This would be a protracted process that in the beginning enjoyed almost no support from ethnic kin and co-religionists across the frontiers in Turkey and Iran.

TSARIST AND PROVISIONAL GOVERNMENT FORCES

Disbanded in November-December 1917, the tsarist General Staff remained a potent source of anti-Bolshevik intrigue. Kerensky and General Krasnov commanded a comic-opera operation near Petrograd, which the new regime easily suppressed. General Kaledin, the Don Cossack commander, took the field against the Bolsheviks but resigned after failing to take Rostov-on-Don. His successor, Kerensky's erstwhile comrade-in-arms General Krasnov, assembled an army and attacked on two fronts in the summer of 1918. Former tsarist officials formed various "governments" and "commissions," trying unsuccessfully to conceal the foreign strings.

The Czechoslovak Legion, consisting of 40,000 former prisoners of war spread across Siberia in 60 troop trains, entered the fray in May 1918. The Bolsheviks had agreed to let them leave through Vladivostok. Incited by the Whites, the Legion rebelled against its escorts and began assembling in western Siberia, encountering little opposition: The Whites had overthrown the Bolsheviks in Irkutsk, Omsk, Tomsk, and other Siberian cities. In June the Legion helped create a Committee of Members of the Constituent Assembly (KOMUCH) in Samara and a Provisional Siberian Government in Omsk. In August it captured Kazan and seized the half of the Imperial Russian gold reserve stored there.

Pressure from the Czechoslovak Legion

gave the Bolsheviks an excuse to massacre the royal family, whom they had moved to Yekaterinburg in May 1918. The area became a combat zone, and in mid-July the local Communists warned Moscow that the town was in imminent danger of falling.

After midnight on July 16–17, 1918, a guard awakened Tsar Nicholas and his family and told them they had to go to the cellar for their safety. Sleepy, terrified, and utterly helpless, the family complied. A dozen secret police suddenly burst in, revolvers in hand. The leader, Yakov Yurovsky, hastily read an order. The executioners fired at point-blank range.

The assassins took the bodies to an abandoned mine, dismembered them, drenched them with sulfuric acid, and set them on fire. They later scattered the ashes in the nearby forest.

In April 1989 Yakov Yurovsky's son Aleksandr and the writer Geli Ryabov revealed their discovery of the Romanov family's remains, including the tsar's skull. The interior ministry confirmed this and acknowledged that Lenin and the Sovnarkom ordered the slayings. The dramatic find struck down the long-standing Communist assertion that the SRs had massacred the royal family to discredit the Bolsheviks.

Having made common cause with the Provisional Government in 1917, in 1918 the SRs joined the opposition to the Bolshevik regime. They organized and led major anti-Bolshevik uprisings in several cities, notably Moscow and Yaroslavl. These rebellions failed, but the SRs retained wide support in the countryside, particularly along the Volga.

Responding to an August SR revolt in Penza, Lenin ordered individuals suspected of treason put in concentration camps, thus setting in motion a process that would take—as Aleksandr Lebed said in November 1996—"scores of millions of lives" in Russia. (There was a precedent: In the Boer War, British forces interned 120,000 Boer women and children into such camps, where more than 20,000 died.)

By autumn 1918 the Allies, Whites, and other anti-Bolsheviks controlled three-quarters of the old Russian Empire's territory.

FIRST ANTI-BOLSHEVIK COALITION: KOLCHAK

Having finally achieved some harmony in the matter of Russian policy, the Allies recognized Admiral A. V. Kolchak as the White leader, hoping the various factions would unite around him. Sir Samuel Hoare, the British military attaché, advised London that a military dictatorship would be the best solution for Russia; he described Kolchak as the "nearest thing to an English gentleman" in that country. The attractiveness stemmed largely from Kolchak's willingness to pay the tsarist debt: He now controlled that part of the Imperial Russian gold reserves—651.5 million rubles worth—the Czechoslovak Legion had seized at Kazan.

With massive aid from the Allies paid for with Russia's gold, late in 1918 Admiral Kolchak put an army of 250,000 in the field—but the "field" was more than 20 times the size of Western Europe. The admiral without a navy controlled only a thin line along the Trans-Siberian Railway. Everything depended on local support and continued Allied assistance. Kolchak alienated the Siberian peasantry by attempting to introduce the old landlord system, never fully operative in Siberia. He and the other White commanders offended President Wilson by spurning peace talks, which Lenin had accepted. The Whites' refusal did not end Allied aid but did strengthen Wilson's sense that intervention was a mistake.

With the Red Guards as a nucleus, the Bolsheviks created the Workers' and Peasants' Red Army (RKKA) in January 1918, the Red Fleet a month later. In September they formed a Republic Revolutionary Military Council (RMCR) under Trotsky with responsibility for military operations. The Bolsheviks declared martial law on September 2.

The Sovnarkom planned to put three million men in uniform. The men were available—but not officers, weapons, food, or supplies. Over the objections of many Communists, Trotsky pressed thousands of ex-Imperial Army officers into service, assigning political commissars to all units. As added insurance he held the officers' families hostage. By early 1919, some 29,000 tsarist officers and 166,000 noncommissioned officers were serving in the Red Army. They led about 1.2 million men, many of whom, however, were in noncombat units. In the spring of 1919 the Reds put 450,000 men in the field to face a slightly smaller White force.

The multipronged but poorly coordinated attack began on March 4, when Admiral Kolchak, having regrouped over the winter, sent troops westward toward the Volga. Simultaneously, General Anton Denikin marched a French-supported army northward against Harkov, Kiev, Voronezh, and Oryol. Those cities fell one after the other, although the Communists soon retook Oryol. General E. K. Miller—Russian despite the name—launched a more or less simultaneous attack at Archangel. Miller had support from British and American forces and also ample supplies. In Estonia, General N. N. Yudenich could not move until October, but until then he harassed the Bolsheviks with hit-and-run raids.

The White attacks dwarfed Napoleon's 1812 invasion and in geographic scale eclipsed Chingis Khan's expedition. The fronts now

Olga Ovchinnikova and her Red Army artillery unit in the Urals, 1920. (Yuri N. Zhukov)

stretched from Archangel to the Aral Sea, the Caspian to the Don, and the Sea of Azov to Riga and Tallinn. There was heavy fighting along the Trans-Siberian Railway and in the vicinity of Vladivostok. Surrounded, without friends, industry and agriculture in ruins, the population demoralized, the Russian Republic should have fallen.

The Whites made impressive advances. The Kolchak forces crossed the Urals and swooped down on European Russia but failed to establish a position on the Volga. In Ukraine, General Denikin's troops brushed aside opposition—leaving behind devastation and an embittered population. When the Whites approached Petrograd, Zinoviev, the local leader, panicked and called for reinforcements. The RMCR sent Stalin. His arrival, a 1960s Soviet source noted, "didn't change anything." The Whites took Pskov on May 25. At two forts on Petrograd's western defense line, the garrisons rebelled against the Communists.

At that point Trotsky and Lenin rushed reserves to the Petrograd sector and stabilized the situation. General Yudenich then mounted a new strike—several British tanks alongside his infantry—that took him to the gates of Petrograd by mid-October. When the RMCR sent more reinforcements, Yudenich withdrew.

Lenin declared that the "most critical moment" in the war had arrived. General Denikin ordered an offensive against Moscow in July 1919. At the cost of enormous casualties, the Red Army beat back the attackers and saved the capital. Denikin regrouped and again moved north in September, his men competing for the million-ruble prize that rich Ukrainians offered to the first regiment to fight its way into Moscow.

The prize went unclaimed. Their lines stretched taut across hostile territory, the Whites could not advance north of Oryol. The RMCR threw every available unit against Denikin and again turned him back. The First

Soldiers of the 3rd Battalion, 3rd Horse Artillery Division of the Red Army. Left to right: Mikhail Chumachek, scout; Daniil Strichko, forward observer; Ivan Dubrovsky, communications chief. (Yuri N. Zhukov)

Cavalry—it took its name after the battle—of S. M. Budyonny played an important role in the successful counterattack, as did the Eighth Army. Harkov came back under Soviet control on December 12, Kiev on December 16. Early in January 1920, the Red Army recaptured Tsaritsyn and Rostov-on-Don.

Contemplating Kolchak's defeats, the Western Allies concluded that their protégé had not lived up to expectations; their support began to waver. The French troops in Russia suffered severe morale problems although they saw almost no combat. Britain and France began withdrawing their forces.

Knowing a sinking ship when he saw one, Admiral Kolchak resigned as "Supreme Ruler of All Russia" on January 4, 1920. His good friends, the Czechoslovak Legion, seized him in Irkutsk and turned him over to the Bolsheviks, who executed him on February 7. Those in power in the West did not mourn; Kolchak had already sent the Imperial gold.

WAR WITH POLAND

Kolchak was gone, Yudenich was gone, Miller had fallen back to the White Sea, and Denikin was on the run. Knowing that and nothing more, one might conclude that the Communists had victory within reach. Enter the Poles.

The reborn Poland of 1918 had enormous grievances against the three powers that had partitioned her out of existence in the eighteenth century. Austria and Germany had just gone down to defeat; Russia had simply disintegrated. The time seemed ripe for Poland to regain her historic frontiers and maybe more: Some Poles dreamed of "reestablishing" a nation stretching from the Baltic to the Black Sea, from Smolensk to Berlin's eastern approaches. No such Poland had ever existed, and the Ukrainians, Belarusians, Russians, Lithuanians, Germans, and Czechs rejected Polish historical and ethnic cartography, not

to mention political aspirations. The Germans and Czechs had little to fear; the Allies would not permit any armed aggression against them.

But those same Allies cynically welcomed Poland's assault on Russia. Polish attacks to the south and east began early in 1919 as hit-and-run raids, but when Warsaw's forces took Minsk the war began in earnest. By late 1919 the Poles had put together an army of 200,000 men. France supplied 350 airplanes, 2,800 machine-guns, more than 300,000 rifles, and a corps of military advisers—including Captain Charles de Gaulle—under General Maxime Weygand.

On April 25, 1920, General Joseph Pilsudski struck southward with 80,000 Polish troops. He drove 200 kilometers into Ukraine in six weeks, seized Kiev on May 6, and proclaimed Polish sovereignty over the entire right (west) bank of the Dnepr.

Trotsky and the RCMR designed a counterattack. Budyonny's First Cavalry pushed southwest toward Kiev, while units under G. D. Gai and M. N. Tukhachevsky moved west against Brest-Litovsk. Polish Communists formed a "Temporary Revolutionary Committee" at Bialystok and invited the Red Army to "liberate" Poland.

Kiev fell to the Reds on June 12. Tukhachevsky tore through the Polish forces in Belarus and continued into Poland proper; by mid-August his forces were approaching Warsaw and Lwów. Among those anxiously watching the advance was the papal envoy, Achille Ratti, the future Pope Pius XI.

At this point the RMCR representative on the Southwestern Front made a series of crucial mistakes. Stalin grossly underestimated the threat from the south, where the last important White commander, Baron Peter N. Wrangel, menaced Red forces trying to push the Poles back across the Dnepr. Having assured the RMCR that all was under control, Stalin prepared to detach three units, including the First Cavalry, and send them to aid

Tukhachevsky, who seemed poised to take Warsaw.

Trotsky and Lenin assumed these tactics were sound. But when Wrangel defeated Budyonny's First Cavalry before it could disengage, Stalin's plan collapsed. The Tukhachevsky forces, ready to install a red flag atop Warsaw City Hall, scurried back to Moscow.

Having failed to find a Russian who could defeat the Bolsheviks, London would try a Pole. On July 21, 1920, Lloyd George announced that Great Britain and France would help Pilsudski rebuild his armed forces. The Poles soon had half a million men under arms.

SECOND ANTI-BOLSHEVIK COALITION

It was not difficult to arouse Lloyd George's sympathy for the Poles. To be sure, Poland had attacked Soviet Russia, and not the other way around, but somehow the British prime minister's advisers misplaced that fact. Having sold him a shoddy bill of goods about making the Crimea a new Gibraltar or Hong Kong, the advocates of intervention unveiled one last White general.

Baron Peter Wrangel had served under General Denikin in the Great War, and after the Bolshevik Revolution he commanded an anti-Communist Volunteer Army in the Caucasus. Transferring operations to Ukraine, he quickly clashed with Denikin over military and political strategy. Denikin exiled him to Constantinople.

With Denikin's defeat early in 1920 the remnants of his forces, and some anti-Communist units defeated in Transcaucasia, gathered in the Crimea to await evacuation. The leaders of these troops deposed Denikin and with Allied approval installed Wrangel in his place. A British warship brought Wrangel from Constantinople and deposited him at Se-

vastopol on April 2. Two days later the "Black Baron"—from the exotic uniforms he designed and wore—took command.

Wrangel differed from previous White commanders in having something he called a political and social program. Where his predecessors never went beyond anticommunism and anti-Semitism, Wrangel proposed to nationalize landholdings above 600 desyatins (1,620 acres); permit the peasants to buy this land over a 25-year period; and establish agencies of rural self-government (*zemstvos*). He promised to defend labor's interests.

Wrangel equipped his army with British and French arms. In the spring of 1920 he moved out of the Crimea into Ukraine and northwest Transcaucasia, his advance greased by Stalin's blunders. In August 1920 the RMCR decided to concentrate on destroying Wrangel, but again it entrusted the bungling Stalin with responsibility. After his forces suffered heavy losses, Stalin was recalled to Moscow. M. V. Frunze took charge and the Red Army gradually pushed Wrangel back.

The final, decisive battles took place November 7–17, 1920, on the Perekop and Chongar isthmuses between the Crimea and the mainland. At a cost of 10,000 casualties, Frunze's troops decisively defeated Wrangel. French and British warships evacuated 80,000 White troops, camp followers, and civilians to Turkey, Bulgaria, and Yugoslavia.

END OF THE WAR AND INTERVENTION

A few weeks before the final battles in the Crimea, the Poles agreed to a truce. Once again, zealots wanted to fight on and establish a Communist regime in Poland, but Lenin admitted having overestimated the "revolutionary readiness" of the Polish workers. Russia and Poland signed the Treaty of Riga on March 18, 1921. It fixed the border between

Poland and Russia east of a line recommended earlier by British Foreign Secretary Lord Curzon, who detested the Bolsheviks. The treaty deprived Poland of some coveted Lithuanian territory but gave her sizable areas in Belarus and Ukraine.

With the collapse of Wrangel's army, the signing of the Russo-Polish armistice, and withdrawal of the Allied forces, the Civil War came to an end, though the Japanese remained on the mainland for another year. Still ahead lay the fierce uprisings at Tambov and Kronstadt. So-called bandit gangs kept Ukraine, part of the Volga Valley, and the populated strip along the Trans-Siberian Railway in turmoil, but dealing with them involved mopping-up operations. Central Asian *basmachi*—both Islamic guerrillas and ordinary bandits—constituted an annoyance.

The Red Army had won a victory inadequately described as astonishing. Why were Britain, France, the United States, and a dozen other nations, plus hordes of domestic anti-Communists, unable to defeat the infant regime?

The Communists had a number of practical advantages, notably control of the Central Russian heartland. Under martial discipline, they contained their own internal friction and received or coerced the allegiance of the workers. Having secured communications and supply lines, they found good field commanders, Stalin not among them. To a remarkable degree they were able to exploit the infrastructure of the tsarist war effort—war industry committees, supply committees, civilian auxiliary organizations, *zemstvos*, and so forth. They called for a free, independent, and socialist Russia. Their enemies matched them atrocity for atrocity. The Bolsheviks had proved at Brest-Litovsk they would sign anything to get out of the war.

The Western populations had no stomach for intervention: The Great War had drained Britain and France of blood and treasure and

spirit. The United States had little reason to intervene at all, especially on the side of a White movement unlikely to help make the world safe for democracy. The Whites had no unity, no coherent program, inadequate military forces. Like the postrevolutionary French aristocrats who had learned nothing and forgotten nothing, most White commanders yearned for the revival of the old landlord–tenant system. They wanted either a military dictatorship or the restoration of the monarchy. They never won support among exhausted populations that wanted peace above all. Many people in Russia detested the Whites for responding to the West's call for a new Crusade.

IMPACT OF THE CIVIL WAR

Beginning as an armed contest for political supremacy, the Russian Civil War became a great class conflict. Institutions disintegrated in the months after the Bolshevik coup d'état, and social relations degenerated into an elementary struggle for survival that crowded out ideology. As in all civil wars, people had to choose between disasters. Families broke apart.

The social conflict quickly reached the point where peasants could no longer be persuaded, let alone coerced, to fight for the interests of the upper classes. The peasants of 1918–1920, whose ancestors had periodically burned and slaughtered in great jacqueries, observed the death agony of the landowners and aristocrats without emotion. The workers, who were peasants transplanted into the cities, fought the landlord-military-foreign counter-revolution and intervention with a passion that transcended ideology.

The Bolsheviks-Communists became militarized as no political party in history. In 1918–1920 they were front-line soldiers who knew the commanders of the White forces had decreed the death penalty for them. A party so forged would not be generous toward enemies or tolerant of internal dissent. Of all Bolshevik party members in 1927, a third had joined between 1917 and 1920, 1 percent before 1917. The fight for survival destroyed the elements of their program and tradition that had linked the Bolsheviks to European party politics. Already imbued with Russian revolutionary terrorism, they succumbed to it root and branch, and killing became their preferred weapon.

The West presented the newborn Bolshevik regime with a powerful psychological weapon. From 1918 on, Soviet leaders rallied public support for an aggressive foreign policy and the suppression of internal dissent by raising the specter of "capitalist encirclement."

Against overwhelming odds the Workers' and Peasants' Red Army defeated all enemies. On November 17, 1920, Russia knew peace for the first time since July 31, 1914. She had been at war for 2,301 consecutive days.

SUGGESTED ADDITIONAL READINGS

BENVENUTI, FRANCESCO. *The Bolsheviks and the Red Army, 1918–1922.* New York: Cambridge University Press, 1988.

BROVKIN, VLADIMIR N. *Behind the Lines of the Civil War: Political Parties and Social Movements in Russia, 1918–1922.* Princeton, NJ: Princeton University Press, 1994.

———, ed. *The Bolsheviks and Russian Society: The Revolution and the Civil Wars.* New Haven and London: Yale University Press, 1997.

DEBO, RICHARD K. *Survival and Consolidation: The Foreign Policy of Soviet Russia, 1918–1921.* Montreal: McGill–Queen's University Press, 1992.

FIGES, ORLANDO. *Peasant Russia, Civil War: The Volga Countryside in Revolution (1917–1921).* Oxford: Oxford University Press, 1989.

PEREIRA, NORMAN G. O. *White Siberia: The Politics of Civil War.* Montreal: McGill–Queen's University Press, 1996.

PIPES, RICHARD, ed. *The Unknown Lenin: From the Secret Archive.* New Haven, CT: Yale University Press, 1996.

WHEELER-BENNETT, J. W. *The Forgotten Peace: Brest-Litovsk, March 1918.* New York: W. W. Norton, 1971.

4

BUILDING COMMUNISM

Tsarism had gone noiselessly into the night and the Provisional Government had killed itself. Although the Civil War had necessitated some unpleasant measures, rank-and-file Bolsheviks believed that the natural instincts of the proletariat, whose "dictatorship" the conflict had installed, would now produce a just and equitable society. The Old Bolsheviks knew that this was nonsense. Ideology had meant something when they were seeking power. Now that they had won it, nothing mattered but power itself.

THE CONSTITUENT ASSEMBLY

Millions of ordinary citizens thought that a Constituent Assembly, which the Left intelligentsia had been calling for since the 1860s, would define and shape the new society, but the Provisional Government had stalled in calling it, eliminating any possibility of success. Kerensky finally set the elections for November 12 (25), 1917.

Having long claimed to favor an Assembly, the Bolsheviks now said it smacked of peasant-oriented populist socialism and would only be a vehicle for middle-class parliamentary democracy—which the Bolsheviks detested. Lenin and his people knew the country would return a strong SR (Socialist–Revolutionary) majority; whatever its weakness in the cities, the SR party dominated rural politics. Lenin had defined a "republic of soviets" as the state form of the proletarian dictatorship.

The Bolsheviks seized power 18 days before the balloting, but they were weak and the appeal of a Constituent Assembly strong. Lenin could not cancel the elections; the parties had already published lists of candidates and had begun the electoral campaign.

Voting took place in unsettled conditions; in only 39 of 79 electoral districts did the election proceed on the day scheduled. Other districts voted in December and January. In all, 45 million of 90 million eligible voters cast ballots:

SRs	40.0%
Bolsheviks	24.0%
Kadets	4.7%
Mensheviks	2.6%

Other voters supported religious and national parties—Muslim, Polish, and so on—or splinter groups.

The Bolsheviks never ceased to disparage the vote, which on a "one citizen, one vote" basis manifestly reflected the will of the people. Russia was rural; Bolshevik strength was in the cities. In Petrograd, for example, the Bolsheviks out-polled the SRs 45 percent to 16.7 percent; in the surrounding rural areas their margin was 49 percent to 25 percent. In Moscow City, Lenin's party won 50 percent to 8 percent for the SRs, and in Moscow Province—50 to 26 percent. It won large majorities among soldiers on the Western and Northern Fronts and the Baltic Fleet sailors, but in the army as a whole the SRs—peasants in uniform—prevailed.

What would the Bolshevik regime do, now that the voters had returned an SR plurality, which was really a decisive majority counting SR allies? The opposition helped make the decision. In December 1917 the regular SRs, Popular Socialists, and some Mensheviks and Kadets formed a "Union for the Defense of the Constituent Assembly" (UDCA). Active in Petrograd, Moscow, Odessa, and Samara, it called for the immediate summoning of the Constituent Assembly under the slogan "All Power to the Constituent Assembly!" Lenin did not see the humor. The UDCA organized conferences, published broadsides and proclamations, and agitated against the Bolsheviks.

On November 28 (December 11) Lenin outlawed the Kadet party and declared he would not tolerate the Constituent Assembly. The majority had voted for other parties, he admitted, but Bolshevism represented the working class, the soldiers, and the "poorest stratum of the peasantry." These people had returned Bolshevik majorities in the soviets (councils)—that "higher form of democracy."

With some trepidation, 410 of the 715 Constituent Assembly deputies convened in Petrograd's Tauride Palace on the evening of January 5 (18), 1918, entering the building through a phalanx of Bolshevik secret police and a hostile mob. With Bolsheviks and Left SRs constituting a noisy opposition block of 155, the SR majority elected Viktor Chernov chairman. He read a good democratic speech. Yakov Sverdlov, Bolshevik chairman of the Congress of Soviets' Central Executive Committee (CEC), spoke on behalf of the Sovnarkom—which the majority of Constituent Assembly delegates did not recognize—and moved the adoption of a "Declaration of the Rights of Toiling and Exploited Peoples" cribbed from the French 1789 Declaration of

the Rights of Man. This spelled out Bolshevik promises and prefigured the first Soviet Constitution. The delegates rejected it by a vote of 237 to 146.

The Bolsheviks then walked out; the Left SRs remained a while longer before leaving. In the galleries, sailors picked their teeth with bayonets, pointed their weapons—some of them unloaded—at deputies, squeezed triggers, jeered, whistled, guffawed, made rude noises. Shortly before 5:00 A.M. the new masters cut this contrived madness short and ordered the delegates out.

The Constituent Assembly never met again. Russia seemed largely indifferent to the fate of what was, until the spring of 1989, the only freely elected deliberative body in her history.

FIRST STEPS OF THE NEW REGIME

The Bolsheviks had to contend with the hostility of other parties and vigorous dissent within their own ranks. Five Central Committee members resigned to protest the Sovnarkom's exclusion of members of other parties. But Lenin was still negotiating with the Left SRs, who did in fact enter the government in December, and no other party accepted the Bolshevik stand on the war.

The Sovnarkom gushed decrees, orders, directives, proclamations, and guidelines. Early in 1918 the municipal councils, *zemstvos* (rural councils), and other tsarist agencies and institutions gave way, on paper, to a hierarchical network of soviets. In practice the establishment of the new system would take years, during which the soviets would degenerate into Bolshevik campaign-patronage headquarters.

Lenin's regime abolished estate distinctions and civil ranks. The workers, peasants, merchants, townspeople, gentry, and the déclassé became simply citizens of the Russian Soviet Republic, equal before the law except—George Orwell would later note—some were more equal than others. Most people who were not from the lower classes were in fact not equal at all—except for such Bolsheviks as Lenin, Trotsky, Zinoviev, Kamenev, Bukharin. These, the new rulers, were sons of the middle class. Alongside them stood a single representative of the lower classes, Stalin, offspring of a drunken cobbler.

Women received full rights, again on paper, and in November 1920 Russia became the first nation to decriminalize abortion. But women would long be relegated to "suitable" positions in the cultural and educational sphere, retail trade, farm labor, factory work. Lenin's wife, Nadezhda Krupskaya, was no exception. Aleksandra Kollontai, the only woman on the Central Committee, had almost no influence in 1917 and none thereafter. As always, men controlled laws, politics, the economy, social relations, the established ideology.

Early in 1918 it became possible for either party to a marriage to end it on demand; this would change several times over the Soviet years, as would family law in general. Church marriage—the legally binding tsarist-era norm for Christians—became a matter of private preference having no force in law; even a civil ceremony was optional. In the freewheeling atmosphere wedlock lost its role as a social regulator. The law prohibited discrimination against children born outside registered marriages.

Early in 1918 the Sovnarkom proclaimed separation of church and state. Having earlier nationalized lands of the Russian Orthodox Church, the state now seized its buildings, and those of other faiths. Churches, synagogues, and mosques could hold services, but the Commissariat of Justice, which was responsible for religious affairs through 1923, ordered them to make the premises available for secular purposes. The Communist party converted some church buildings into antireligious museums and set up a horrendous pornographic display—one of many—in Petrograd's Kazan Cathedral. It abolished parochial and other religious schools and forbade the teaching of religion. The clergy had to pay higher taxes and rents; their children could not attend state schools above the elementary level. The July 1918 Constitution stripped clerics of most civil rights. As disfranchised persons they received no food-ration cards, or cards of the lowest category. Communist party officials, the armed forces, and workers received highest-category cards permitting purchase of about 2,700 calories worth of food per day.

On the chaotic economic front, the new regime worked through the Congress of Soviets' Central Executive Committee, which in November 1918 adopted the Rules of Workers' Control: Workers would exercise undefined workplace "control" through trade unions, councils of elders, and other worker-elected groups. This was a sham. The Communist party controlled everything.

A Supreme Economic Council had responsibility for economic planning; that meant nationalization, which proceeded on an ad hoc basis. Foreign trade became a state monopoly; the Bolsheviks took over the banks.

Distribution of land presented the most vexing dilemma for the rural soviets. The Bolsheviks had promised to give the land to those who worked it, with local soviet authorities supervising the transfer. But many soviets themselves were still badly organized, and in practice the peasants themselves divided the spoils.

On the last day of January 1918 the regime solved the calendar confusion in the only possible way, adopting the Gregorian calendar used in the West: Russia went to bed on January 31 and woke up on February 14. In March 1918 the Sovnarkom moved the capital back to Moscow for the first time since early in the reign of Peter the Great. The dangerously exposed location of Petrograd justified this, but the relocation also made psychological sense. Peter's "window" always had too much of the West about it for old Moscow's taste; better to return to the heartland, away from corrupting foreign influence.

THE NEW GOVERNMENT

The Military Revolutionary Committee could not serve as the administrative vehicle for achieving Lenin's goals of "precision, discipline and accountability in government." Indispensable in October 1917, its "organic" character was thereafter an anachronism. Maintaining order, and supplying the cities and the armed forces, required creation of a formal body with a fixed mandate, established procedures, legal responsibilities—a bureaucracy.

To a certain extent the Congress of Soviets' Central Executive Committee (CEC), which Lenin maintained spoke for the revolutionary people, for "soviet democracy," had constituted an alternative. But after June 1918 the CEC met irregularly and in 1919 ceased to exist. Chiefly responsible was the confusion in the soviets (the councils), which could not make the quick, coordinated decisions the Civil War demanded; the Congress was no more capable than its constituent elements. The struggle for power had bred a unity that wartime centrifugal forces tore apart. Democracy died in embryo as Lenin's regime rushed to concentrate decision making in the Politburo. Vestiges of traditional politics did survive, and Bolshevik officials sometimes resigned on matters of principle. Six Left SRs served briefly in the government before leaving to protest Brest-Litovsk. The Bolsheviks had freely debated that treaty, "war communism," and the 1921 New Economic Policy (see below), and of course the plans for the coup d'état. Such debates ended.

Exercising state power on behalf of the party Politburo (Political Bureau), the Sovnarkom was superficially analogous to modern European cabinets, but in fact it served as the executive agency of a political party that claimed exclusive rights to and total control of the state, its property, and its citizens. At its head stood Lenin, immensely powerful head of a political organization free to legitimize its whims. He and his successors could make Russia dance to their tune.

Two Sovnarkom standing committees became specialized arms of the executive power. In the Civil War, the Defense Council—sometimes Labor and Defense Council—mobilized the country's "human and material resources . . . in the interests of defense." Because it had unlimited powers its decisions had the "immediate and unqualified force of law." Lenin, Trotsky, Stalin, and two others served on it. The other new committee, the "Little Sovnarkom," dealt with administrative routine.

The Sovnarkom did not always mesh with the Politburo, which after the Civil War became the sole repository of power. By that time Lenin held his party colleagues in contempt, and from the spring of 1922 until his final, incapacitating stroke a year later he tried to reverse course and strengthen the state apparatus at the expense of the "partocracy." Having lost both his physical powers and his political touch, he could not disassemble that which he had constructed.

State and party structures existed alongside each other, like medieval Europe's religious and secular institutions. Leading party officials held state offices roughly corresponding to their party rank; they insisted that party and state interests were identical.

FIRST CONSTITUTION

Revolutionary rhetoric and decrees had had their day. Like any other state, Bolshevik Russia required a coherent set of general principles expressing the sources of its legitimacy and aspirations, a basic law, or constitution. In January 1918 the Third Congress of Soviets established a constitutional commission.

On the basis of their reading of Lenin's *State and Revolution,* some Bolsheviks dreamed of a revolutionary "commune state" with no police, army, or bureaucracy. Nikolai Bukharin and his allies regarded communism "less as a commitment to actual policies than to a vision of the new order as the antithesis of the old." But Lenin, drunk with power, pressured the commission to retain the coercive agencies and invest the state with enormous authority. On July 10, 1918, the Fifth All-Russian Congress of Soviets confirmed a new Constitution, which reflected the leader's revised views. A few days later the Bolsheviks excluded the regular SRs and Mensheviks from all soviets; several days after that they murdered the Romanovs.

Part I of the Constitution of the Russian Soviet Federated Socialist Republic (RSFSR), a "Declaration of the Rights of Toiling and Exploited Peoples," called for world revolution, the overthrow of capitalism and imperialism, and a dictatorship of the soviets. It warned that "he who does not work does not eat" (from 2 Thessalonians 3:10). Supreme authority resided in the All-Russian Congress of Workers', Peasants', Cossacks', and Red Army Soviets, a body of more than 1,100 deputies that was to meet twice a year. A 200-member Central Executive Committee (CEC) would be constantly in session to attend to day-to-day business.

The Sovnarkom could legislate by decree, and only in theory were its decrees subject to CEC review. Village, town, city, district, and provincial soviets, through their own executive committees, were to carry out the decisions of the central authorities. The Communists always dominated the soviets and soon they outlawed all other political parties.

Remembering the Constituent Assembly elections, the framers of the Constitution made one urban elector equal to *five* rural electors. The makers of the "proletarian revolution" renounced the principle of "one citizen, one vote"; peasant Russia lost its voice. The Constitution specifically disfranchised about 3 percent of the adult population: Those who hired labor or who lived on interest, rents, or dividends ("exploiters"); businessmen; clergy and mullahs; ex-policemen; the Romanovs; the insane; convicted criminals; "enemies of the people."

THE CHEKA

Early in November 1917 the Military Revolutionary Committee (MRC) posted "forty sober men" to guard the Winter Palace wine cellar. Drunkenness, disorder, and common street violence had gotten out of hand; the new regime had to restore discipline. The tsar's wine went into the Neva River and the MRC arrested hordes of drunks and "hooligans." Blaming the Kadets for the lawlessness and "counterrevolutionary" agitation, the Sovnarkom outlawed the Kadet party.

Early in December the Sovnarkom disbanded the MRC and created an "All-Russian Extraordinary Commission for Combating Counterrevolution and Sabotage" (acronym "Cheka"). Over the years the name became variously GPU, OGPU, NKVD, NKGB, MGB, MVD, KGB, FSS. The organization itself has never changed, and only rarely has it been, as Anna Akhmatova noted, "vegetarian." Under the leadership of the first director, the fanatical Polish Bolshevik Feliks Dzerzhinsky, the Cheka became the first twentieth-century secret political police.

In an administrative decision with fateful consequences, the Bolsheviks attached the Cheka not to the Congress of Soviets' Central Executive Committee, which had at least a partial democratic mandate, but to the Sovnarkom, the executive agency. When the Communist party Politburo eclipsed the Sovnarkom, the Cheka became an auxiliary government responsible only to the individual or faction controlling the Politburo. In time it would become a "state within a state."

In the beginning the Cheka was authorized to employ only "soft measures": Confiscation of property, eviction, deprivation of ration cards. It published lists of "enemies of the people." Interpreting his instructions liberally, however, Dzerzhinsky ordered the shooting without trial or investigation of "enemy agents, counterrevolutionary agitators, speculators, organizers of uprisings." The Cheka had license to shoot anyone except Communist party officials. That would change.

The Bolsheviks claimed they did all this to combat terrorism, political and economic sabotage, and speculation in valuables and state property. An SR murdered a prominent Petrograd Bolshevik in June 1918. In July some Left SRs assassinated the new German ambassador, hoping to provoke renewal of the war with Germany and topple the Bolsheviks. The assassins, some of whom were Cheka agents, kidnapped Dzerzhinsky and bombarded the Kremlin. The Left SRs launched an uprising in Yaroslavl that inspired similar revolts elsewhere. On August 30, the Petrograd Cheka boss fell to an assassin and an SR member shot and severely wounded Lenin. In the midst of all this and the Civil War, some militantly Bolshevik Latvian Riflemen put down the Left SR uprising in Moscow; the Cheka freed Dzerzhinsky and executed the kidnappers.

Early in September 1918 the Bolsheviks declared martial law and unleashed their "Red Terror." Two days later the Sovnarkom newspaper *Izvestiya* (*The News*) printed an order to all soviets to take hostages and conduct "mass shootings." Lenin complained at one meeting, "We're not shooting enough professors!" (Twenty-one years later, one of Lenin's admirers ordered that "All representatives of the Polish intelligentsia are to be exterminated." He was Adolf Hitler.)

The Communists lashed out at individuals and the social groups from which they came, notably the middle class, and authorized the Cheka to bludgeon the population into sub-

mission. The Bolshevik rule was to condemn any number of innocents to ensure that not a single guilty person escaped. At Lenin's direction, with the enthusiastic sanction of Trotsky, Bukharin, Stalin, Zinoviev, Sverdlov, and Kamenev, the Cheka began a terror compaign that continued until 1987 and took, at a conservative estimate, 40 million lives. To this day, the Russian secret police proudly call themselves "Chekists."

WAR COMMUNISM

To understand why the creators of the Cheka embarked on "war communism," we need to examine three sets of figures:

Industrial Production	*Area under Cultivation*	
(1913 = 100)		
	Average	
	1909–1913:	83 million desyatins
1917: 74.8	1920:	63 million desyatins
1918: 33.8	1921:	58.3 million desyatins
1919: 14.9		
1920: 12.8		

	Gross Yield of Crops	
	pre-1914 average:	3,850,000 poods
	1920:	2,082,000 poods
	1921:	1,689,000 poods

one *desyatin* = 2.7 acres
one *pood* = 36 lbs. (one bushel)

These figures suggest that Russia suffered the worst economic depression ever to hit an industrialized or semi-industrialized country. The Communists now proceeded to compound the disasters of war, foreign intervention, and Civil War by declaring war on the productive elements of society.

Life in the cities, increasingly difficult after August 1914, became a grim daily struggle for survival under Bolshevik rule. Moscow and Petrograd lost nearly half their populations, those who could not find work or food. In Moscow's Sukharevka Market one paid 500 rubles for a lump of sugar in 1918. Milk cost 1,800 rubles a mug; 50 cigarettes—6,000 rubles. The Bolshevik writer Ilya Ehrenburg remembered that people lived on "hope and rations." The Communists tried—in Andrei Platonov's words—"to transform hope into matter." Meanwhile, "unhusked millet was turning over in people's stomachs." They burned furniture, shade trees, wood molding, doors—anything combustible—to keep warm. People dressed in fantastic getups: old uniforms, draperies, tablecloths, canvas, gunnysacks, even newspapers. Russian newspapers in 1919 were printed on blue paper made from sawdust: The reading eye's pressure on the page, people said, made it disintegrate. Everyone ate and dressed and got warm, or tried to, in this way. They said they would divide the shortages equally among all the comrades.

Millions of urban dwellers fled to the villages only to find life there horrible. And it would get worse before it got still worse than that. Although the majority voted against the Bolsheviks, the peasants had supported—or passively accepted—radical change. When they realized that Lenin's "reform" brought each farmer only an additional *desyatin* (2.7 acres) or so, they reverted to their customary hostility toward authority. They tried to sell their surplus at a good price. Failing that, they stored it against better conditions, or kept it for their own needs. Currency had lost its value, and anyway the cities no longer produced anything the countryside could use. The peasants began refusing to supply the cities. The deadly downward spiral terrified everyone except those who profited from it.

To combat these trends, in May 1918 the authorities introduced "war communism," a militarization and extreme centralization of the economy. The name constituted a tribute to the "Kriegssozialismus" General Erich F. W. Ludendorff had introduced in Germany during the Great War. It involved state control of the means of production, universal labor

service, the equalization of wages, primitive barter. In the first few months the Sovnarkom nationalized only 72 large factories and plants; Red Guards and workers seized 750 more. A June 1918 decree regularized worker seizure and ordered it for all large-scale enterprises. The state imposed labor conscription for some categories of production in January 1919 and for all categories a year later; it "militarized" labor.

Although a November 1920 decree nationalized all industry, thousands of small-scale individual and family enterprises, and many larger ones that slipped through the net, remained in private hands. Some December 1920 decrees authorized free food for workers and officials and free provision of "necessities" (fuel, clothing) to all "productive citizens." In January 1921 the Bolsheviks abolished rents and utility charges for workers and the poor.

War communism nearly destroyed the economy, not solely because of mismanagement, of which there was a superabundance. The working class—large sectors of which already detested Bolshevism—responded to the new policy by simply staying off the job or showing up and not working. In 1919 such job actions eliminated two-thirds of the potential working-days.

With the cities and the Red Army threatened with starvation, in January 1918 the Sovnarkom had decreed nationwide requisitioning of foodstuffs. In theory the state would take grain from the peasants and give matches and kerosene in return. But there were no matches or kerosene. Squads of armed men went into the countryside and seized grain from the peasants and charged those who resisted as "enemies of the people."

Composed of armed workers, the food-requisition detachments encountered fierce opposition. Knowing the receipts for grain to be worthless, the peasants fought with fists, axes, clubs—anything that came to hand—and when they could not conceal their grain they burned it. This was Bolshevik-instigated war, and in the beginning the peasants held their own. By October 1918 they had killed 7,300 of 36,000 men in the food-requisition detachments. In the end they were no match for the food-requisition detachments, but they remained defiant. A popular ditty went:

I'm sittin' on a barrel,
A barrel of flour.
Don't think, you sonofabitch,
That Russia's in *your* power!

If the detachments found the barrel of flour they took it, and more often than not shot the peasant who had hidden it.

In the summer of 1918 the Sovnarkom created Poor Peasants' Committees, compounding intraclass war with class war. The Committees had instructions to assist the food-requisition detachments; that gave them an incentive to ruin the more prosperous people, called "kulaks" or tight-fisted (better-off) farmers. To unscrupulous or shiftless poor peasants, that meant almost everyone.

As dictatorships will, the Communists ruled by decrees enforced by a secret police. They smothered the population with rules, regulations, ordinances, decrees, and directives,

Tossing out decree after decree like
    horseshoes—

Right in the eye, in the face, the brow or the
    groin.

So wrote Osip Mandelstam. People quoted this quatrain:

I'll be in trouble, that I know,
Goin' to the privy, no pass to show.
I'd gladly get one, but, alas,
There's no one around, to issue a pass.

They greeted each other with "Nothin' to eat, but life's a treat!" As always in the villages, they said there was plenty of everyone for food.

SUGGESTED ADDITIONAL READINGS

EHRENBURG, ILYA. *People and Life, 1891–1921.* New York: Knopf, 1962.

LEGGETT, GEORGE. *The Cheka.* New York: Oxford University Press, 1981.

MALLE, SILVANA. *The Economic Organization of War Communism.* New York: Cambridge University Press, 1985.

PIPES, RICHARD, ed. *The Unknown Lenin: From the Secret Archive.* New Haven, CT: Yale University Press, 1996.

SERVICE, ROBERT. *Lenin: A Political Life: Vol. 3. The Iron Ring.* Bloomington: Indiana University Press, 1995.

5

REVERSING COURSE
New Economic Policy, 1921–1927

As the conflict with the Whites and the foreigners wound down, new threats emerged. Peasant disorders erupted in Tambov province in the summer of 1920. An obscure artisan named A. S. Antonov cobbled together an army of 40,000 men that battled the Red Army for more than a year. In March 1921 the Baltic Fleet sailors at Kronstadt, long Bolshevism's staunchest defenders, believing themselves the vanguard of a movement that would recapture the lost freedoms of 1917, rebelled against Communist rule. They counted on the Petrograd workers, then on strike, to come to their aid, but the Cheka and local party boss Grigory Zinoviev had clubbed those workers into submission. Red Army troops under M. N. Tukhachevsky attacked on March 16, crushed the rebellion, and exacted barbaric vengeance. Seventy-three years later, Boris Yeltsin revealed the details.

Lenin telegraphed congratulations to Tukhachevsky and War Commissar Trotsky. No sooner had he done that than, citing the Kronstadt and Tambov uprisings, he urged the Tenth Party Congress to accept a new program of major concessions to the peasants and petty entrepreneurs. Many Communists believed this to be heresy.

DIMINISHING RETURNS OF TERROR

Later cast as martyrs, Trotsky and Tukhachevsky executed most Kronstadt survivors who could not escape to Finland. The Bolsheviks retaliated no less severely against the rebellious Tambov peasants: They sent two thousand to firing squads, many more to concentration camps.

The chief architect of terror began to have doubts. Russia seemed ready for another great peasant rebellion, a nightmare that frightened Lenin as much as it had his crowned predecessors. He had to placate the peasants and "reestablish" their "alliance" with the workers, to end the tension between town and countryside. Industrial production had virtually ceased; unless the peasants agreed to supply food, the nation would collapse. The peasants needed a fair price for that food; they could not be paid in currency so inflated that the equivalent of 100 American dollars in 100,000-ruble notes weighed a kilogram (2.2 pounds).

The previous year, Trotsky, never known for tenderness, had called for an accommodation with the peasants. Lenin sided with Bukharin and the Left Communists in advocating continuation of war-communism terror, but finally even they understood that it could not revive production. Lenin never ceased to believe in terror as a powerful tool requiring frequent application, but with the country at an economic standstill he now accepted the need for flexibility.

THE 1921 FAMINE

Conditions necessary to produce Russia's worst catastrophe yet were in place by the time the Bolsheviks' Tenth Congress endorsed Lenin's call for an "economic breathing-space." The peasants in European Russia were winding down their rebellion; grain and seed stocks were dangerously depleted; nearly a million peasant-soldiers had not yet returned to the villages. And in the spring and summer of 1921, no rain fell in the Volga Valley.

American officials in Constantinople intercepted Sovnarkom-Radio warnings of the danger to public health and order from the famine along the middle Volga. People were already eating grass, leaves, bark, and clay. Tree bark was selling for 40,000 rubles a *pood* (about a bushel), bitter dock (horse sorrel) for 50,000. The Volga River was so low that men and animals not yet slaughtered could wade it near Saratov; May–September temperatures stayed well above normal. Starving people wandered about aimlessly, looking for food that was nowhere to be found. There exist nauseating photographs of traffic in human flesh.

The poet Vladimir Mayakovsky asked,

Cast your gaze upon the Volga:
Isn't this starving inferno,

This peasant desolation,
The ass-end of your wars and blockades?*

The official Soviet famine relief agency, Pomgol, put the number of those affected at well above 25 million. It may have been half that again; approximately five million people starved to death.

The Intervention had made it impossible for the Sovnarkom to appeal to the West for aid. When Maksim Gorky issued a dramatic cry for help, "To All Honest People," Anatole France donated the money from his 1921 Nobel Prize for Literature, and George Bernard Shaw, Albert Einstein, Theodore Dreiser, and other prominent world figures raised funds. The Norwegian explorer Fridtjof Nansen directed a massive relief campaign in Western Europe. President Warren Harding's secretary of commerce, Herbert Hoover, who had organized relief for Belgium during World War I, headed a major American rescue effort. By the spring of 1922 his American Relief Administration (ARA) had distributed more than $20 million (450 million 1997 dollars) worth of food and seed. To show their gratitude the Bolsheviks accused Hoover of dumping supplies "stockpiled for the imperialist war" on hapless Russia, and in 1923 they expelled the ARA.

Pomgol's own relief measures involved sending a special "agitprop" (agitation and propaganda) train to the stricken districts. Equipped with loudspeakers, films, printed matter, agitators—everything but food—the train rolled through the Volga Valley demonstrating Communist impotence. The Cheka and the Red Army moved in to help control—sometimes by shooting into the crowds—the millions of refugees.

Eventually the rains came. Aid poured in

---

*Vladimir Mayakovsky, "Moya rech na Genuezskoi konferentsii," in *Polnoe sobranie sochinenii*, vol. 4 (Moscow: Gos. izdat Khudozhestvennoi literatury, 1957).

from the West; spring and autumn brought good harvests in 1922. The horror subsided.

NEW ECONOMIC POLICY

Speaking *before* the famine, Lenin told the Tenth Party Congress that drastic changes were in order:

In this backward country, the workers, who have made unprecedented sacrifices, and the mass of peasants, are in a state of utter exhaustion after seven years of war. This condition borders on complete loss of working capacity. What is needed now is an economic breathing-space.

War communism had failed. To replace its "primitive" food requisitioning Lenin proposed a tax in kind. Over Left–Communist opposition, the party approved this and fixed the new tax at 60 percent of the tonnage collected at gunpoint in 1920. This was the cornerstone of the New Economic Policy, or NEP.

Having argued passionately for war communism, the Bolsheviks now embraced its opposite. The increasingly influential Stalin went along with the "general line" but unlike his colleagues had sense enough not to talk too much. The party touted NEP as merely a different route to communism. Three agencies directed it: The Supreme Economic Council had overall responsibility, and two new planning bodies, the State Commission for the Electrification of Russia (Goelro) and the State Planning Commission (Gosplan), came into existence.

The peasants could now own land, and private individuals could own small—never conclusively defined—enterprises. Worst of all, to true believers, the state permitted the hiring of labor—"New Exploitation of the Proletariat"? But it seemed that only the marketplace offered a way out of the economic ca-

tastrophe, and the Communists adopted the slogan "Learn to trade!" They permitted essentially free trade in grain; encouraged but did not force the peasants to join producer cooperatives; and abandoned attempts to herd people into collective and state farms.

The regime kept its monopoly on political power, communications, and education, and it retained control over the economic "commanding heights" of heavy industry, financial and credit institutions, transportation, foreign trade. It organized nationalized industries into vertical or horizontal "trusts" and required them to make a profit. The Bolsheviks glibly explained that profits extracted from labor's hide would benefit the proletarian state.

Out went efforts to equalize wages, to pay the hod carrier the same as the plant manager; "to each according to his work" replaced the utopian "to each according to his needs." Engineers and other specialists—except medical and educational personnel—received good wages. The salaries of party and state bureaucrats remained low, but a system of special perquisites, combined with the deference always accorded power, allowed those who so desired to prosper.

This added up to a mixed public–private economy. The state controlled most industry, but nearly all agriculture was now in private hands. In theory the peasants could get a fair price for what they sold. A steady supply of food enabled the workers to resume production; that in turn provided the manufactured goods the peasants needed. The regime reintroduced a money economy and stabilized the currency.

Agriculture recovered quickly. With sufficient grain supplies on hand, free-market prices began declining in the autumn of 1922. Industry did not rebound so rapidly. Production could not meet demand, and monopolistic practices enabled managers to set artificially high prices. Good harvests drove down the purchasing power of agricultural products and forced the peasants to sell more grain to obtain, for example, steel plows. The makers of those plows could sell fewer because the price for each was high. In the autumn of 1923 the state aided the peasants with subsidies and reduced prices on some farm-oriented manufactured goods.

In 1922, industrial production reached 35 percent of 1913 levels; this rose to 73 percent in 1925. In the latter year Russia produced only three-fourths of what she had manufactured before World War I, but that represented an *increase* of more than 500 percent over 1920. The record in agriculture was even better despite poor 1921 and 1925 harvests. Grain production reached prewar levels.

Seeking to learn from the despised capitalists, the Lenin regime granted wide concessions to foreign entrepreneurs. The pro-Soviet American businessman Armand Hammer received the first, to mine asbestos in the Urals and organize foreign trade. Royal Dutch Shell won the Caspian Sea oil concession. Swedish Nobel interests obtained mining rights in Ukraine and the Ural Mountains. Henry Ford supplied motor vehicles worth 300 million gold rubles, technical assistance, and invention–use rights. By the end of 1928, dozens of foreign individuals and firms had come to do business, everyone ignoring the Bolshevik pledge to hang all capitalists. Lenin even invited foreign governments to invest.

THE GOVERNMENTAL SYSTEM

The 1918 Constitution attempted to mix oil and water, providing for both a federal structure and national self-determination. Lenin believed the minorities should have rights far greater than those of the states comprising the United States. He said, but in fact did not believe, that larger minorities—e.g., the Ukrainians—should have their own political-adminis-

trative bodies and their own foreign policy. On December 30, 1922, the Russian, Ukrainian, Belarus, and Transcaucasian republics merged to form the Union of Soviet Socialist Republics, or USSR. By that time Lenin had abandoned his dream of a free association of sovereign and independent states, but he wanted to incorporate the fiction into the Constitution, along with a wide degree of cultural autonomy, also a sham.

Stalin headed a commission charged with revising the Constitution to reflect the administrative changes. He had adopted Russian culture as his own and the Russophobia exposed in the Civil War infuriated him. Ignoring Lenin, he proposed a highly centralized state under firm Moscow control, with no concessions to the minorities.

Adopted shortly after Lenin's death in January 1924, the new Constitution recognized the constituent republics as sovereign and independent nations entitled to join and leave the union; but citizenship resided in the federal union, not in the republics. The union controlled defense, foreign relations, the general economic system and economic planning, the national budget, monetary and credit systems, transportation, and communications, with "everything else" left to the republics. The Constitution guaranteed freedom of speech but did not provide for a secret ballot. The citizenry exercised sovereign power through the All-Union Congress of Soviets. Workers continued to enjoy favored status at the ballot box, one worker vote equalling that of five peasants. Direct elections took place only at the local level. Each district, province, republic, and union congress elected the next higher one; this constituted a system of hierarchical electoral colleges.

The amended Constitution was as meaningless as its predecessor. In the winter of 1924–1925 the writer Mikhail Bulgakov noted in his diary, "Nothing is moving at all. All has been devoured by the hellish maw of Soviet red tape. Every step a Soviet citizen takes, every movement he makes, is a form of torture that uses up hours, days, and sometimes months."

THE COMMUNIST PARTY

In March 1918 the Bolshevik faction of the Russian Social-Democratic Labor party (RSDLP [b]) changed its name to the Russian Communist party (RKP) (b)—the "b" for "Bolsheviks," and late in 1925 the name became the All-Union Communist party (VKP [b]). When the Civil War ended, the Communists could look back on a series of victories. They were concerned about events in Tambov province and at Kronstadt, but they saw their party as an agent of dramatic, positive change.

Admission into the Communist party required sponsorship of three members who had known the applicant for a year or more in the workplace, enterprise, or military unit, and could swear that he or she was not an "exploiter." If certified as to class origin and ideological reliability, the applicant became a nonvoting probationer (candidate) for a year, then a full party member. But between 1920 and 1924 the Communist party was not trying to increase its numbers. After the Civil War Lenin ordered a purge of "rascals, bureaucrats, dishonest or wavering Communists," and "radish" Communists—red outside, white inside. Membership fell from 567,000 in 1921 to 350,000 in 1924. If all 165,000 candidates in 1921 had become full party members, this would have amounted to a decrease of about 382,000.

On the death of its leader, the party announced a "Lenin Enrollment" that doubled membership in two years, to a million-plus. The drive concentrated on industrial workers, peasants, and the military. At the start, only 18.8 percent of the membership were working-class; three years later that had risen to 39.4.

Peasant membership, 8.3 percent in 1924, rose to 13.7 in 1927. Nevertheless, in January 1927 only 8.4 percent of all industrial workers and only 0.6 of the peasants were party members. Fourteen percent of Red Army soldiers were Communists.

By 1927 more than a quarter of a million workers-party members had been promoted to white-collar jobs or to other positions—the military, college studies—that removed them from the proletariat. In the same year, fewer than 1 percent of party members had a college degree; another 7.9 percent had finished secondary school.

The basic Communist political unit, the primary party organization ("cell"), could have as few as three members or several hundred, as in a large mill or factory, which would have several large cells. Those with 300 or more members, and all higher levels, had their own full-time, salaried employees in bureaus and secretariats. The next higher organization, the municipal or county conference, amalgamated local cells. Every local conference was under the authority of the provincial conference, which had a central committee and a secretariat. The provincial conferences sent delegates to the republic party congress, which elected a central committee and a secretariat. From the mid-1920s, the Politburo and its Secretariat in Moscow *appointed* top party officials in the republics.

On paper, the All-Union Congress, to which the republic congresses elected delegates, had supreme authority. It met annually through 1925; after that year, the Stalinist faction summoned the Congress when it was in the mood to do so. The All-Union Congress elected a Central Committee, which in the summer of 1917 had 21 full members, 18 candidate members. By 1923 there were 40 members and 17 candidates; a year later—53 members and 34 candidates.

Designed to be constantly in session or on call, even the Central Committee proved to be too large. Since October 1917 it had had a smaller decision-making body, the Political Bureau* or Politburo, an ad hoc body until the March 1919 Eighth Party Congress legitimized it. The Eighth Congress ordered the Central Committee to establish (1) an Organizational Bureau (Orgburo) composed of five Central Committee members, and (2) a Secretariat under a general secretary, who had to be a Politburo member, and five technical secretaries.

Always in session, its members residing in Moscow, the five-member Politburo was the chief executive agency and policy-making body. Lenin, Trotsky, Stalin, Lev Kamenev, and Nikolai Krestinsky served on the original body. True to Russia's tradition of extreme centralization, the Politburo did not limit itself to major issues but decided such minutiae as the precise amounts of individual subsidies to sympathetic foreign journalists and businessmen; the itineraries of cinematographers allowed to travel abroad; which collective-farm bulls to castrate. The Politburo members knew the animals' names.

Charged with "all party organizational work," the Orgburo met three times a week. Like the Politburo, it made biweekly reports to the Central Committee. When Krestinsky lost his seat on the Orgburo, Stalin transformed that body into his own personal staff and became its only link to the Politburo.

By 1923 Stalin, who was the Communist party's leading authority on organizational-personnel questions, controlled both the Orgburo and the Secretariat; the vague definition of the latter's mission suited him. Appointed general secretary on April 4, 1922, he made the Secretariat a wholly controlled Orgburo subsidiary. As its head, the general secretary coordinated the work of party commissions,

---

*The Politburo came into de facto existence on October 23, 1917, and was legitimized by the Eighth Party Congress.

committees, agencies, and departments, and reported to the Central Committee. Bent on expanding their more glamorous fiefdoms, Lenin's other lieutenants failed to understand the enormous power inherent in the general secretary's control over the flow of information to the Politburo and the Central Committee.

The Secretariat's Organization-Instruction Department disseminated Central Committee decisions and orders and had investigatory functions. Stalin controlled it. Another important Secretariat department was Records and Assignments, where Stalin and his trusted aides reviewed party personnel files. By 1924, Stalin knew everything, or enough to make it seem he did.

At the 1921 Tenth Party Congress, Lenin pushed through a resolution banning factions and factionalism in the party. Once a decision had been taken, compliance was incumbent on all members, who, having grown accustomed to military-administrative procedures in the Civil War, liked it that way.

THE STRUGGLE FOR POWER

Lenin suffered a stroke in May 1922. He made some improvement over the summer, and his physicians issued a guardedly optimistic prognosis to reassure the public. In October Lenin returned to the Kremlin and a full work load; two months later a second stroke removed him from active politics.

It was axiomatic that no one individual could succeed him. His colleagues would share power, but the party and the public speculated as to who would emerge first among equals. The head of the Moscow Communist organization, Lev Kamenev, was an Old Bolshevik, member of the Politburo, and deputy chairman of the Sovnarkom. He passed as an intellectual. In a country with a long history of anti-Semitism, his Jewishness and marriage to

Trotsky's sister were liabilities. He had betrayed the plans for the October 1917 armed uprising.

Grigory Zinoviev, also a Jewish-Russian Old Bolshevik, was politically closer to Lenin than anyone until October 1917. He headed the Leningrad party organization and the Communist International and sat on the Politburo. A stirring orator, he found demand for fiery speeches slack after the Civil War. Zinoviev showed cowardice in the defense of Petrograd, extraordinary cruelty in his ruthless suppression of the 1920–1921 Petrograd strikes and the Kronstadt Rebellion. He had joined Kamenev in leaking plans for the coup d'état.

Nikolai Bukharin, the youngest Old Bolshevik, liked to think he was a thinker. Lenin disparaged his intellect but called him the "party's favorite." Bukharin edited *Pravda*, sat on the Politburo, and argued in favor of the Red Terror. He frequently opposed Lenin. His ability to reverse himself, and argue eloquently in favor of that which he had previously denounced, said something about his character.

A vain little dandy, he publicly boasted of his romantic prowess.

Joseph Vissarionovich Stalin was not the favorite of any first-rank leader other than himself, but he was the candidate of hundreds of key bureaucrats who owed their jobs to him. He had long been constructing a political apparatus, quietly and unobtrusively. Not unshakably loyal to Lenin, he had supported the Provisional government and had disobeyed military orders in the Civil War. This might have cost other men their careers, but the Bolsheviks protected each other; colleagues shielded Stalin at every turn. No such favor would go unpunished.

Stalin praised Trotsky so lavishly that the man's shortcomings cried out for attention. He semi-defended Kamenev and Zinoviev for their October 1917 betrayal, then called in that debt during the 1923–1924 jockeying around Lenin's deathbed. He urged leniency for opponents of Brest-Litovsk, understanding of comrades hostile to war communism, patience with those who disliked the NEP. He

Lenin and Stalin at Gorky, late summer 1922. This is a fake photo, made to suggest a closer relationship than actually existed. (Sovnarkom photo)

could be the soul of moderation; and he knew how to identify an adversary's weakness.

Stalin sat on the Politburo and the Org-buro; briefly directed the Workers' and Peasants' Inspectorate (Rabkrin); and was first commissar of nationalities. On the surface merely the perfect bureaucrat who performed routine but essential work, he was in reality an extraordinarily clever politician with nerves of steel. His conscience seems never to have caused him anguish.

Leon Trotsky had come late to the Bolshevik camp. His vituperative attacks on Lenin, especially those between 1903 and 1912, filled the public record. But all was forgiven in the heady days of 1917 when his organizational genius translated Lenin's will into action. He opposed the Treaty of Brest-Litovsk but quickly returned to the fold and built the Red Army, which did not lose the Civil War. Until the Kronstadt Rebellion he was the second most respected and popular figure in the country.

Russia would not forget his maniacal call for blood. And the jealous Old Bolsheviks hated him with a passion.

TWELFTH PARTY CONGRESS

In December 1922 a document ostensibly dictated by Lenin complained that Stalin had accumulated too much power as general secretary and was too "rude." The comrades needed to "find a way to remove ... [him] from that position and appoint a man who is ... more patient, more loyal, more polite." Praising Trotsky's "exceptional ability" and calling him the "most able man in the present Central Committee," the document also noted his "too far-reaching self-confidence" and love of the "purely administrative side of affairs."

The latter comment more accurately described Stalin, administrator par excellence. Eyebrows were raised: Did Lenin really dictate

From right: Lenin; Krupskaya; Lenin's nephew, Viktor; Lenin's sister, Anna Yelizarova-Ulyanova; unidentified child, August 1922. (Sovnarkom photo)

this "testament"? By late 1922, degenerative neurosyphilis had so affected his ability to communicate that only his wife, Nadezhda Krupskaya, could interpret his distorted speech and scribbling—or so she claimed.

Brought low by years of stress, depression, and hyperthyroidism, Krupskaya had reason to be displeased with Lenin. He had infected her with syphilis, ignored her pleas for a meaningful political role after the coup d'état, and taken Inessa Armand as a lover.

The party Secretariat under Stalin supervised Lenin's medical treatment. Stalin detested Krupskaya and she despised him; but he knew the secrets. She had every reason to cut him down to size, and the incapacitated Lenin was her only weapon. It was probably she who wrote the "testament," with the aid of Lenin's secretaries.

The document embarrassed Stalin but did not destroy him. Krupskaya urged Trotsky to use it at the April 1923 Twelfth Party Congress, the first without Lenin, but he declined to do so. His followers have always cited his fear of being seen as a Bonaparte, a military man riding in to steal political victory after battlefield triumph, to explain his refusal to exploit the "testament," but he was suspicious of it from the beginning.

Delegates who backed Stalin for the party leadership controlled the Twelfth Party Congress. They were not privy to the deathbed intrigue around Lenin; had Trotsky chosen to exploit the "testament," they could not have ignored him. Trotsky remained silent.

"PERMANENT REVOLUTION" VS. "SOCIALISM IN ONE COUNTRY"

Engrossed in his theory of "permanent revolution," Trotsky showed little interest in mundane governmental affairs. Arguing that the proletariat had no fatherland, he refused to believe in the ebb of the revolutionary tide; he interpreted every street fight in Germany as the beginning of a cataclysmic upheaval and argued that socialism could not triumph in Russia unless the working classes in the West rebelled. A socialist island could not long exist, he wrote, in a capitalist sea; it would lose its identity. Building and maintaining a strong national defense would necessitate coercing the population, and would engender state capitalism—which is what Lenin had called NEP. In Trotsky's view, the Soviet workers should subordinate their own interests to those of the world proletariat, be midwife and nurse to revolutionary movements.

Himself no theorist, Stalin counterposed Bukharin's "socialism in one country": Russia *could* go it alone. If revolution did not come in the West, Soviet Communists would make Russia the bastion of socialism.

In an essay entitled "The October Revolution and the Tactics of the Russian Communists," Stalin called "permanent revolution" theoretically flawed and politically seditious. Why had Trotsky so little faith in the Soviet Communists' ability to construct a socialist society without outside help? Also relying on Bukharin's ideas, Stalin had earlier discussed the possibility that capitalism had stabilized and that revolution was no longer imminent. To preserve and eventually expand the gains of the Bolshevik Revolution throughout the world, he now said in response to Trotsky, it was necessary to build "socialism in one country." Part of the world proletariat was already committed to defend the Soviet Union through the Comintern (Communist International). It was the duty of Soviet Communists to shelve their hopes for world revolution and concentrate on strengthening their own country. These arguments prevailed, not only because Stalin was by far the better politician but also because they made more sense.

Stalin had quickly fallen into step on Brest-Litovsk; Trotsky clung to illusions about revolution in the West. Stalin had approved war communism; Trotsky lagged behind. When it was time to turn to the NEP, Stalin had supported Lenin, while Trotsky argued that Communists should not abandon war communism. Temporarily allied with the party's Right (conservative) wing, Stalin championed the NEP to the end. Trotsky and the Left, always wary of compromise with capitalism, had called for "unequal exchange" between town and country—exploiting the peasantry to finance industrialization.

Some second-level leaders attacked Stalin in an October 1923 "Letter of the 46" that urged reforms. Trotsky did not sign the letter, but the Stalin faction knew the "46" had his support. The Central Committee suppressed the letter and lashed out at Trotsky, whom it charged with planning a military coup d'état on Lenin's death—which was obviously only weeks away. Trotsky's vigorous denial served only to publicize the wholly false accusation.

Rumors and innuendoes swirled about in ever-widening circles. Having no personal political organization, Trotsky resorted to the old socialist tactic of appealing directly to the proletariat. He toured factories and workshops in Moscow and Leningrad, attempting to explain his criticism of the party–state bureaucracy. This was to walk a thin line: At what point did disagreement become factionalism and violate the 1921 ban? He who had so recently used naked power to such advantage now appealed to reason. Like the others who stood in Stalin's way, he had dug his own grave.

THE DEATH OF LENIN

On Sovnarkom orders, in March 1923 the attending physicians—among them German and Swedish specialists—declared Lenin's recovery possible. That was for public consumption; in fact, there was no hope. Whether Lenin's syphilis was hereditary or acquired is unknown, but it had ruined several vital organs and his central nervous system. The then-standard treatment with arsphenamine—doctors had given up on mercury—had only worsened his condition. Lenin suffered strokes and arteriosclerosis, and large sections of his brain were ossified. The end came on January 21, 1924.

As he had supervised the medical treatment, so General Secretary Stalin arranged the funeral. Attendants placed the body on a bier and laid flowers and fir branches around it. The Central Committee decreed five days of official mourning and approved Stalin's motion to embalm the corpse and put it on display in a mausoleum to be erected in Red Square.

This further outraged Krupskaya, who had lost what little leverage she had when Trotsky declined to use the "testament." She and other Old Bolsheviks opposed glorification of individuals and thought it monstrous to show off a mummified body.

And yet Stalin knew the Russians, most of whom continued to profess their faith, if less openly. He calculated that a people who had nothing needed to believe in something. A cult of Lenin would provide the spiritual sustenance the peasants and workers ached for. It would serve as a unifying force, an agreed-on myth. A priesthood of interpreters and keepers of the mysteries would be needed; one was already in place.

In the midst of a winter that even Muscovites considered severe, hundreds of thousands of citizens queued patiently, 24 hours a day, to pass the open coffin in Union House on Hunters' Row in the city center. Cases of hysteria, shock, and frostbite swamped medical personnel. Bonfires burned at street corners as people congregated to share their grief and fear. On January 26 the Politburo renamed Petrograd, which became Leningrad.

On the morning of January 27, Stalin, Zinoviev, and six workers carried the open coffin from Union House to Red Square. There, the next contingent of pallbearers took over and bore the coffin across the square to a temporary wooden crypt. At 4:00 P.M. every siren, factory whistle, ship's horn, motor vehicle horn, and other noise-making device in the country sounded from Vladivostok to the Polish border. Thousands of artillery guns fired salvo after blank salvo.

When he delivered the main funeral oration the previous evening, Stalin, the former seminary student, employed the cadences and rhythms and language of the Russian Orthodox Church. The speech grated on the nerves of Communist party members but helped calm fears and reassure millions of ordinary citizens.

STALIN'S EMERGING VICTORY

Russia's grief was real. As the peasants had for centuries believed in a "good tsar" who did not know of their distress and was not to be blamed, so Lenin seemed remote from the harsh conditions and commissars of war communism. Few people associated him with the Red Terror or concentration camps. The country's recovery under NEP was his doing. Life was easier; it was possible to hope again. One could get a little ahead through hard work, sharp practices, thrift.

When Lenin died, Trotsky was in the south, recuperating from an illness. Stalin had deliberately delayed the telegram to him, and it arrived too late for Trotsky to rush back to Moscow to participate in the funeral. His absence had less political significance than his followers claimed; but it did not go unremarked.

The crucial stage of the struggle for power was at hand. The people who huddled around the bonfires that cold Moscow January never suspected that the outcome would doom them to decades of horror, as Stalin built on Lenin's strong foundation.

SUGGESTED ADDITIONAL READINGS

BALL, ALAN M. *Russia's Last Capitalists: The Nepmen, 1921–1929.* Berkeley and Los Angeles: University of California Press, 1987.

COHEN, STEPHEN F. *Bukharin and the Russian Revolution.* New York: Oxford University Press, 1980.

DANILOV, V. P. *Rural Russia Under the New Regime.* Bloomington and Indianapolis: Indiana University Press, 1988.

DAVIES, R. W., ed. *From Tsarism to the New Economic Policy.* Ithaca, NY: Cornell University Press, 1991.

GILL, GRAEME. *The Origins of the Stalinist Political System.* Cambridge: Cambridge University Press, 1990.

SIEGELBAUM, LEWIS A. *Soviet State and Society Between Revolutions, 1918–1929.* New York: Cambridge University Press, 1992.

6

LIFE IN THE 1920s

Millions of ordinary citizens welcomed the age of "Communists but no communism." The intoxicating revolutionary communism of 1917–1921 disappeared as entrepreneurs restarted the capitalist machine. Peasants could own land, sell their produce on the free market, hire labor. There were at least a million unemployed workers. In September 1921 cinemas and theatres, formerly free, began charging for tickets. In October, the free distribution of newspapers and magazines ended.

Workers were the social group most affected by the imposition of charges for reading matter, theatres, concerts, and other cultural events. Hundreds of thousands of rank-and-file party members who believed in communism began to wonder whether one of history's greatest revolutions had been in vain. They wanted a strong leader.

It soon became obvious that no social or cultural revolution would take place under the New Economic Policy (NEP); the Communists were in retreat. Was it a classic case of "plus ça change, plus c'est la même chose"?

URBAN LIFE

Nothing could ever be the same, if only because of the demographic disaster. In 1926 the RSFSR population was about 30 million fewer than it should have been. The losses included approximately four million victims of wars and revolutions; about 1.5 million deaths in the worldwide influenza epidemic of 1918–1919; five million in the famine of 1921. Twelve million inhabitants of the old Russian Empire were now citizens of other countries. Seven to eight million children had not been born because of these developments.

The work force and the military, to say nothing of science, education, and the arts, suffered irreparable harm, and the statistics do not tell the whole story. We cannot determine how many people were lost to society because of psychological wounds associated with war, revolution, famine, and other calamities. Emotional disorders, alcoholism, domestic violence, indifference to social norms including work, and crime all rose dramatically between 1914 and 1921.

Moscow lost half its population and more than ever resembled, as the humorists Ilf and Petrov wrote, a "large, badly planned village." No one would mistake regal Petrograd for a village, but more than half its inhabitants had left, and hunger and fear stalked its streets.

The NEP began to turn the situation around. People came out of hiding, returned to their homes, and life improved. Crucial here was the *nepman* (an acronym), the petty entrepreneur of NEP. He was a wheeler-dealer, a fixer, an intermediary. He could bring buyer and seller together and learned more quickly than anyone the limits of Communist toleration. He knew which laws and regulations the regime enforced and which it winked at. He spotted the bribable and the incorruptible, alcoholics and drug addicts, girl- or boy-chasers, holders of grudges, skeleton-hiders. Everyone had a price; the *nepman* could find it.

In an economy neither capitalist nor socialist but an untidy blend, the *nepmen* proved indispensable because they understood production. They ran the grain market, ensuring the feeding of the cities, and they got factories going. In 1926–1927 there were about 75,600 *nepmen*, who with their families numbered about 209,000 people. (There were in the same period 339,000 "servants"—another social category incompatible with communism.) Communists who had destroyed the old society's political superstructure detested those who were restoring the old economic base.

The *nepmen* hardly constituted an élite, yet their role in the economic recovery—for which they were amply rewarded—made them the premier urban element. Then came Communist party officials and government bureaucrats, of whom there were, by 1927, 3.65 million.

Lenin had a "nationalized" Rolls-Royce but otherwise lived modestly, as did Stalin. Trotsky, Bukharin, Zinoviev, Kamenev, Mikhail Kalinin—first "president" of the RSFSR—and other leading officials enjoyed a luxurious existence.

At the lower levels, idealism survived, the NEP compromise with capitalism notwithstanding, and many officials labored honestly to build the new state and society. They were paid 250 to 300 rubles per year, the same as skilled workers. As always, opportunities for corruption existed, but relatively few bureaucrats appear to have succumbed, if only because the punishment was so severe.

Party officials rarely had any technical skills, and thus the regime had to hire nonparty specialists (*spetsy*); tensions arose between these "former people" and the new masters. In April 1922 the Supreme Revolutionary Tribunal convicted four zealots of hounding the director of the Moscow waterworks—a distinguished engineer and university professor—to suicide; they did not want non-Communists in responsible positions. Lenin declared that the party would employ a Communist to oversee Moscow's water supply when it could find one. Until then the *spetsy* would serve the state and receive its protection.

The social class in whose name the Bolsheviks had seized power did not attain the promised exalted status. By 1927 the number of workers had grown to 4.5 million, up from 3 million in 1917. Industrial workers—the core proletariat—numbered 2.56 million. Skilled workers received higher wages than did semi- and unskilled workers. Technicians, engineers, and specialists earned more money than did skilled workers, foreign specialists more than anyone.

Huge billboards proclaimed GLORY TO LABOR! The poet Vladimir Mayakovsky and the odious rhymster Demyan Bedny exalted work in verse; artists produced posters and paintings of workers in heroic poses; songwriters extolled the proletariat. Whatever this may have done for labor's morale, it did not improve labor's standard of living.

The nationalization of private property put thousands of urban dwellings at the regime's disposal. They went to Communist party and government officials, specialists, and workers—in that order. As residents streamed back into the cities and demobilized soldiers looking for work joined them, officials redivided and repartitioned housing space many times. Communal apartments, in which two or more families shared cooking, bath, and toilet facilities, became the accepted norm. People routinely divided a room by hanging a sheet from the ceiling. Russian has no word for "privacy." (In 1992 and after, this would provide ammunition for opponents of "privatizatsiya.")

Overcrowding plagued urban life for

decades, sapped morale, and adversely affected production. Many workers, however, considered a cramped communal apartment an improvement over filthy doss houses, which were gradually converted into apartment dwellings.

Still more serious was the food problem: Unfed workers could not produce. Between 1918 and 1921 the party had assigned workers first priority after the Red Army, and the NEP did not change that. The state provided subsidies to hold down the cost of staples. Workers could not compete with free-spending *nepmen* and *spetsy* for tables at expensive restaurants or at a Moscow food shop unambiguously called The Stomach, but after 1921 they had ample traditional fare of bread, cabbage, and potatoes. Fresh vegetables and fruit were always in short supply from September until May.

In the educational and cultural sphere, the party moved to bring workers out of the morass of illiteracy in which the old regime had kept them. It initiated *rabfaks,* special schools for adult workers with little or no education. The first opened in February 1919. A factory political committee or party cell had to certify that the applicant (1) belonged to the worker or peasant class and had never exploited the labor of others, and (2) supported "soviet power." Usually attached to existing colleges or universities, the *rabfaks* educated several hundred thousand workers prior to World War II, among them Nikita Khrushchev. The state began phasing them out in 1933 and closed the last in October 1941. As late as 1939 only 8.2 percent of the proletariat had seven or more years of education; this was about the same as in the United States.

From an ideological standpoint, unemployment and the private hiring of workers were both unthinkable. With an undetermined number of workers employed in small—never defined, but usually fewer than a hundred employees—private enterprises, and a million workers without jobs in 1926–1927, the Communist utopia seemed more remote than

ever. A primitive welfare system provided a marginal subsistence for the jobless, but Communists gagged at the spectacle of workers laboring for private employers and others depending on the dole.

Party members could scarcely contain their hatred of the *nepmen* who danced the tango, shimmy, and black bottom—more Western imports—at expensive clubs and restaurants. The women with the *nepmen* were sometimes prostitutes, whose numbers in Moscow had dropped from a wartime high of 28,000 to 3,000 in 1928. The figures for other large cities were roughly proportionate; but the existence of *any* amount of prostitution was politically unacceptable. This lament resounded on Odessa streets:

Comrade, comrade, my wounds hurt,
Comrade, comrade, what did we fight for,
Why did we shed our blood?
The bourgeoisie are feasting, the bourgeoisie
Are gloating.*

And once again people chanted the war ditty,

Eat pine-apple,
Gorge on grouse.
Your last day is coming,
Bourgeois louse!*

Criminals infested the cities. It was a time when, as one writer observed, the laws were unsettled and it was easy to find the road to jail. For confirmed lawbreakers, social instability meant enhanced opportunity, and desperation drove many normally honest people to crime; newspapers and contemporary fiction reveled in describing their transgressions. The most common offenses were robbery, assault, drug trafficking, breaking and entering, pilfering, and "banditry."

---

*From Ilya Ehrenburg (Erenburg), *Sobranie sochinenii,* vol. 8 (Moscow: Izdat. "Khudozhestvennaia literatura," 1966). English translation by W. M.

Not a little crime was the work of roughly six million *besprizorniki*, homeless children who wandered around European Russia and Ukraine throughout the 1920s. Children aged five and older organized gangs and terrorized the cities, committing crimes ranging from petty thievery to drug-dealing, prostitution, and murder. Unable to cope, the police and civilian vigilantes sometimes formed "death squads" and simply raked the child gangs with gunfire.

In January 1919 Lenin fell into the hands of robbers in the Moscow suburbs. The highwaymen knew who he was; they took his wallet containing his identification card with photograph. They also lifted and no doubt treasured more the small Browning automatic he carried outside the Kremlin. The robbers permitted Lenin, his companions, and his chauffeur—who related this story—to go free but took the vehicle. A police patrol found the Rolls-Royce the next day; a policeman and a Red Army soldier who had apparently stopped it lay nearby, murdered. The criminals escaped.

MANNERS AND LEISURE

The Communist party attempted to organize the leisure time of workers, most of whom were interested, after work, only in rest. The workers sometimes went to soccer or hockey matches, but in the 1920s mass spectator sports remained undeveloped; games between even the most popular teams rarely drew 15,000 spectators. Organized gymnastics, cross-country skiing, ice-skating, swimming, and hiking would become popular activities only after the Second World War.

At the end of their 10-hour shift, the workers gathered in clubs and beer halls and on street corners to drink Volga Hawk, Zhiguli, or Tip-Top beer and nibble at black (rye) bread

Rehabilitation of prostitutes, Moscow, late 1920s. (National Archives)

and dried *vobla* (a fish). To Communist distress they perpetuated the old custom of "wetting" a young worker's first pay packet with alcohol. They smoked Kavkaz (Caucasus) *papirosy,* a kind of cigarette with a long hollow mouthpiece and a short tobacco end, and Cannon, Sappho, Our Mark, Beach, and Boxing cigarettes. If unable to afford those, they smoked *mahorka,* a cheap, coarse tobacco rolled in newspaper.

They celebrated "red weddings" at factories, bride and groom standing next to some machinery and pledging loyalty to the Communist state, and to each other. A party official performed the ceremony.

The workers rarely discussed politics, which was reserved for Communists, but popular wit produced telling commentary such as

Chicken roasted, chicken steamed,
Just to live, the chicken dreamed.
Ain't no Kadet, ain't no Red Star,
I'm just a chicken comm-iss-ar!
Didn't cheat, didn't shoot,
Just pecked a little grain
With my snoot.*

This popular ditty said it all:

My dad's a drunk, for the shot-glass he pines,
He lies, he blusters, he whines.
My brother's a crook, sister's a whore,
Ma took up smoking—I can't stand any
    more!*

The workers could always get *samogon* (firewater) if they looked hard enough, but it was illegal, and if improperly made, fatal. At the very least, the suppliers said, it would remove all your doubts. To combat abuses connected with home-distilled liquor and garner the enormous revenues of a liquor monopoly, the

state ended the 10-year prohibition on "hard" liquor in 1924 and put 30-percent vodka on the market. This "infant's drink" did not satisfy thirsts, especially in Russia and Ukraine. A year later, 40-percent vodka appeared. The state treasury and the thirsty public rejoiced; the stronger drink sold at a higher price and produced euphoria more quickly. But Russia again saw the alcoholism rate soar. Production declined and accidents multiplied. Domestic violence and crime increased sickeningly. The All-Union Council of Anti-Alcohol Societies promoted temperance but had no high-level support.

The workers went to public baths; washed with Hammer & Plow soap; and even after reimposition of a charge for tickets sometimes went in Moscow to the Bolshoi Theatre, Tchaikovsky Conservatory, the Moscow Art Theatre. Much more often they went to the cinema, especially to Douglas Fairbanks, Rudolph Valentino, or Charlie Chaplin films. They attended cultural events dressed in the only clothes—other than work clothes—they had. An aggressive grungy look became fashionable among white-collar workers and bureaucrats trying to dress like "hegemon," the worker.

From the standpoint of the literary language of the nineteenth century, Russian itself suffered terribly under Bolshevism. This involved more than a mere reaction against upper-class vocabularies and accents: The new regime created its own cant and especially liked acronyms: Sovnarkom, Cheka, Goelro, NEP, *nepman, rabfak, sovhoz, kolhoz, Piatiletka* (Five-Year-Plan), and so on. Poorly educated people thrust into responsible positions went overboard with the new terminology. A satirist wrote of the bureaucrat who began speaking in acronyms: In Sovietese, *Privzhendet,* which in "English" might be "Helwichi," was "Say hello to your wife and children." People derisively referred to the Soviet Union as "Sovdepia" (Soviet of Deputies) after an acronym then in wide use. Tormenting the language debased

---

*From Ilya Ehrenburg (Erenburg), *Sobranie sochinenii,* vol. 8 (Moscow: Izdat. "Khudozhestvennaia literatura," 1966). English translation by W. M.

thought: Dialectical materialism, hegemony of the proletariat, dictatorship of the proletariat, soviet democracy, enemy of the people—all this was sheer nonsense.

The times in general were coarse. Everyone was rude, and so no one noticed; polite conduct was a middle-class and aristocratic affectation out of a Tolstoi novel. Shop signs warned, FINISH YOUR BUSINESS AND GET OUT. The admonition BY YOUR VISIT YOU ARE DISTURBING A BUSY MAN hung on bureaucrats' office walls. Almost no one said "thank you" or "please."

People talked and acted tough, but socialism was nowhere in sight. The failure of equality and abundance to materialize overnight perplexed many Communist dreamers. The capitalists had departed; but supercilious *nepmen* and bureaucrats paraded their contempt for the masses. Everyone knew one's place and kept to it. Ilya Ehrenburg recorded this scene: In 1921 an elderly peasant woman mistakenly entered a first-class compartment on a train. The conductor yelled, "Where d'you think you're going? Get out! This isn't 1917!" And one of Mikhail Zoshchenko's characters says to someone unsuitably clad at the Bolshoi Theatre, "It's not 1919 now. You can't sit in a theatre in your overcoat."

RURAL LIFE

About 122 million people lived in 25 million village households. Roughly 70,000 village soviets, with an average 1,750 members in 350 families, acted as administrative agencies.

The country folk were divided into kulaks (well-off), average (or "middle"), poor, and landless. In 1927, 750,000 kulak households embraced about 5.25 million people, who employed about a million landless peasants as farmhands. All told about 2.3 million peasants had no land; those who did not work for kulaks worked for the state or peasant associations or existed on charity.

The kulaks produced 15 percent of Russia's grain on 4 percent of the arable land. A 1927 survey showed that each had two or three cows, up to 10 hectares for sowing, and an annual income of 240 rubles per family member. The kulak was thus considerably better off than a rural official, whose annual salary was 297 rubles, and earned twice as much as a middle peasant in European Russia's grain-growing districts. Kulaks owned one-third of the country's agricultural machinery and draft animals.

The vast majority of peasants belonged to the middle and poor categories, with many internal gradations. A poor peasant who lived in an area blessed with mild climate and good soil—North Caucasus, for example—was usually better off than middle peasants in Central and North Russia. Middle and poor peasants produced 83 percent of the grain.

The *kolhozes* (collective farms) and *sovhozes* (state farms; in effect, agricultural factories) still in existence from war communism produced 2 percent of the grain. By any test save the political, they had failed.

After the horrors of 1914–1921, life in the villages tended to resume familiar patterns. The peasants again fed the country and paid onerous, but not ruinous, taxes. The most revolutionary change they experienced was the coming of electricity. By 1931 about 15 percent of farms in European Russia and Ukraine, 6 percent nationwide, had electric power. Andrei Platonov subtly revealed this progress through deprivation of freedom in a short story entitled "The Motherland of Electricity."

As they had for nearly a thousand years, peasant women in the 1920s attended church services several times a week, the men much less often. Peasants tipped the priest for performing rites and at holidays; the clergy baptized and married and buried. Attempting to discourage this, the state demanded that couples have their unions legitimized at a registry office (ZAGS); few peasants did. Urban zealots taught children to taunt priests, but in the villages the clergy retained considerable standing even though the village priest, like many of his parishioners, was often all too fond of vodka. The pointlessness and ennui of rural life, along with tradition, conspired against them all.

Naturalistic traditions in sexual relations did not change. Aside from the question of morality, such carefree attitudes kept the venereal disease rate high; the syphilis that felled Lenin was endemic in many parts of the country, especially along the middle Volga.

The village remained terribly isolated, connected with the towns and each other only by dirt roads nearly impassable in spring and autumn. Radio, in the form of a simple receiver-loudspeaker mounted on a pole in the center of the village, commenced in 1924, but it would be three decades before mass communications brought the majority of the peasants into regular contact with the outside world. The occasional appearance of a portable film projector caused a sensation.

EDUCATION

In 1897, year of the last tsarist census, the aggregate literacy rate stood at 30 percent, and most of the literate were in the cities and towns. To enlighten the village, the Communists established "circles for the liquidation of illiteracy," *rabfak* analogues. The RSFSR aggregate literacy rate rose to 51 percent in 1926. Female literacy more than doubled, to 37 percent; that of males rose from 43 to 66 percent.

The Communist party set itself the goals of universal literacy and elimination of the class character of education, sometimes contradictorily called the "proletarianization" of education. The hostility of most teachers toward communism complicated the revamping of the system, but teachers had few options: Leave the country, work as common laborers,

make peace with reality. Most chose the third course.

New "unified labor schools" were to give students an "active, mobile, creative acquaintance with all that is most useful in life." The schools leaned heavily toward vocational training.

Higher education witnessed striking excesses. In 1918 a Sovnarkom decree gave every citizen not of the "exploiting classes" the right to enroll in any university whether he or she had a high school diploma or not. This reflected a sense of righteous retribution; the universities had always been instruments of class rule.

The authorities abolished tenure for university faculty in October 1918, did away with the "bourgeois" practice of examinations, and prohibited the "bourgeois" lecture method of teaching. All classes became "laboratories"—political discussion groups.

Dozens of "universities" sprang up around the country, but as early as 1922 even the Communists understood the absurdity of all this. Revolutionary passions were cooling, and officials pondered the consequences of allowing people ostensibly trained as physicians and civil engineers to practice without any certification of their abilities. The "open admissions" policy deluged institutions with hordes of well-intentioned but unqualified people who disrupted the educational process. In 1922 the state ordered registration of all students; those who lacked a high school diploma could enter only a *rabfak* or a rural "circle." The schools reintroduced rigorous examinations and awarded only earned diplomas. Most new "universities" shut their doors.

THE YOUNG GENERATION

Addressing the youth problem in general, the Communist party established some important agencies. Children aged 7 to 10 had to enroll in the Octobrist organization, where they learned traditional nursery rhymes, games, and songs and new paeans to Lenin and the Communist party. The Leninist Young Pioneers, a highly structured mass organization for children 10 to 14, came into existence in 1922–1924. It had the task of inculcating good citizenship, proper personal and public manners, reverence for Lenin and—after 1928—Stalin. The Pioneers learned rudiments of close-order military drill.

The Russian Communist Youth League enrolled young people ages 14 to 28. About 25,000 members fought in the Civil War, and the League participated in reconstruction. It became the All-Union Leninist Youth League, or Komsomol, in 1926, when it had 1.25 million members. Originally an elite organization, by 1941 its ranks had swelled to 10.3 million. Failure to join meant social ostracism and great difficulty in finding work. The Komsomol developed cadres for the Communist party.

WOMEN

Women had been active in the revolutionary movement, but the ease with which they moved in those circles had been atypical. Even in the cities of European Russia, in tsarist times women had been at best second-class citizens. In Russian and Ukrainian rural areas, men all too often treated them like beasts of burden. Among the Uzbek, Kazakh, Kyrgyz, Tajik, Turkmen, Azerbaijani, and other Muslim peoples, only the favorite wives and concubines of rulers—or famous outlaws—had any historical existence at all. The situation in Estonia, Latvia, and Armenia was, if far from ideal, more progressive.

Although the Communist leaders treated women with contempt, the first Constitution did guarantee women's rights and it forbade discrimination on the basis of gender. This opened the way to education and jobs, and millions of women took advantage of the opportunity. The party created special women's sections, only to dissolve them in 1921.

By the mid-1920s women constituted the substantial majority of students in pedagogical institutes, but teaching, never well-paid, was now less respected because the Communist authorities diminished the teacher's authority. There were almost as many females as males in higher education in general. Women made enormous strides in medicine—also not a prestigious occupation—but only as general practitioners. Men dominated engineering and scientific-research institutes.

No woman attained political power above the district level. Increasing numbers participated in local and district soviets, where all officials did as they were told. Women occupied positions as directors of registry offices, ran post offices, became apartment-building superintendents, and the like, but few headed factories or construction projects. As always, women performed heavy physical labor on NEP-era private farms, and in the cities they worked, as always, as common laborers. They drove trolleys and buses; and nearly all clerks in the socially despised retail-trade sector were women.

Wife-beating remained a common crime, official denunciations notwithstanding. Few men saw any reason to overturn traditional roles in which women performed all household chores, including the enervating tasks of standing in line (queuing) for everything, and child-rearing. Those who had no moral objections saw the legalization of abortion as a step in the emancipation of women, but this extreme form of organized birth control, an urban phenomenon, had scant impact on peasant women.

Finally, Bolshevik rule brought women rough equality in one unexpected area: Many went to prison. In the 1920s thousands of upper-class women fell afoul of authority, usually for the crime of not being of worker or peasant origin. In later years they would be charged with various crimes against the state on a nearly equal basis with men and would help populate the Gulag Archipelago, the vast network of concentration camps.

RELIGION

The Communists made the USSR history's first officially atheist state. In the spring of 1922 the regime convicted several Moscow Russian Orthodox leaders of refusing to turn over valuables to the famine relief agency (Pomgol). Five clerics received the death penalty, a dozen others prison sentences. A month later, a trial in Petrograd rendered a similar verdict against several dozen people: The court sentenced ten defendants to death, of whom four, including Benjamin, Metropolitan (Archbishop) of Petrograd, were actually shot. The GPU arrested Patriarch Tikhon, head of the Russian Orthodox Church, and held him without charge or trial for more than a year.

Thus began a campaign that proceeded at varying tempos over the next 66 years, until the celebration of the millennium of Christianity in Russia in 1988. After 1922 the state usually did not resort to mass trials but persecuted and sometimes executed members of the religious community including nuns and monks. The Communist authorities denied thousands of priests the right to minister to their congregations. They stole, profaned, or reduced to rubble the priceless treasures of Russian–East Slavic culture, and destroyed, padlocked, or converted to secular use—often as taverns or dance halls or breweries—thousands of churches and chapels. Among the scores of monasteries the Communists used as concentration camps and torture palaces were the Solovetsky Islands monastery, the Danilovsky Monastery in Moscow, and the Optina

Pustyn Monastery that Fyodor Dostoevsky—his "Father Zosima" lived there—made famous. (Lev Tolstoi paid a difficult personal visit to Optina Pustyn.)

The Communist League of Atheists—later Militant Atheists—preached "scientific atheism" and produced pornographic antireligious displays and such films as *Judas* and *Opium*. Millions of people continued to worship in defiance of the regime, but under relentless and often violent persecution the number declined steadily after 1928.

Other faiths did not initially suffer quite such persecution. The churches of the Baptists, Mennonites, Lutherans, Uniates, Roman Catholics, and other Christian sects did suffer extensive vandalism, as did synagogues, but the clergy fared a little less badly. The Communists allowed a Baptist Youth Union (Bapsomol), a Baptist organization infelicitously called Christ-o-Youth (Khristomol), and a Mennonite Youth Union (Mensomol) to operate within strict limits.

In the Caucasus and Central Asia, Muslim peoples endured inhuman torment. Seeking to destroy the organic link between faith and everyday life that characterizes Islam, the Communists razed more than 85 percent of all mosques and religious shrines, arrested and frequently executed the mullahs, and banned the Holy Koran and the *hajj*. This brought religion and nationalism together, and violence racked Central Asia. Especially bloody clashes involved Uzbek, Kazakh, Kyrgyz, Turkmen, and Tajik *basmachi* (bandits), but the Red Army captured the last important rebel leader, Ibrahim Beg, in 1931.

CULTURAL LIFE

A few talented writers initially supported the Bolsheviks. The Symbolist poet Aleksandr Blok produced two enduring poems, "The Twelve" and "The Scythians." In the first, 12

Honor guard at funeral of Viktor Nogin, Moscow, May 1924. (National Archives)

Red Guards patrol Petrograd in October 1917, ruthlessly destroying everything and everyone in their path that does not serve the Revolution. They do not recognize their leader, Jesus Christ. In "The Scythians," Blok warned the West to accept not merely the fact of Bolshevik rule but also its spiritual importance.

Vladimir Mayakovsky joined the Bolsheviks in 1908 at the age of 15 and was a founder of the Futurist movement. After 1917 he wrote plays, patriotic verse, and lyrical poems, but within a few years he regretted his saccharine panegyrics to Bolshevism. When the Russian Association of Proletarian Writers (RAPP) attacked him in 1930 for "betraying" communism he lost his emotional balance: He had given it his all, even denouncing a writer of far greater talent, Boris Pilnyak. Mayakovsky committed suicide at age 37.

The "peasant poet" Sergei Yesenin eulogized the Russian village. Born in the Meshchera (Ryazan Province), when the Bolsheviks came to power he moved to Moscow and fashioned a new public image. He married the American dancer and free spirit Isadora Duncan; among their accomplishments was the trashing of hotel rooms in Europe and America. When this marriage disintegrated, Yesenin married Sophia Tolstaya, granddaughter of Lev Tolstoi. In his "tavern verses" Yesenin humanized crooks and prostitutes and revealed his disappointment with communism. He wrote a poem in his own blood and committed suicide in 1925, when he was only 30.

The collapse of the old regime and the harsh ways of the new bewildered the poets Osip Mandelstam, Anna Akhmatova (Gorenko), Boris Pasternak, and Marina Tsvetayeva, all previously devotees of various avant-garde trends. Pasternak's collection of poems, *My Sister, Life,* conveyed the excitement of 1917 and won him great fame. In 1912 Akhmatova wrote *Evening,* an exposé of the crisis in Russian Symbolism. She wrote *Anno Domini MCMXXI* in agony: The GPU had shot her husband, the poet Nikolai Gumilyov, as a "White Guardist." Tsvetayeva sided with the Whites and emigrated in 1921. She returned on the eve of the Second World War only to realize that her life, like old Russia, had ended; she committed suicide. Mandelstam published two major collections in 1922, *The Stone* and *Tristia,* then, in despair, fell silent.

In the late tsarist period, Maksim Gorky wrote the realistic *Childhood* and *Among People,* then completed the trilogy in 1923 with *My Universities.* His play *The Lower Depths* enjoyed great success, and for a time he was the Communists' favorite writer; he preferred order over freedom and detested democracy. Gorky helped a few writers in trouble but conspired in the destruction of others, including some of Russia's greatest talents. He glorified the Stalin White Sea–Baltic Canal, knowing the secret police built it with slave labor.

The first major novelist to portray the dictatorial regime was Yevgeni Zamyatin, whose *The Cave* depicted war-communism Petrograd as an outpost of a dying civilization; a terrifying ice age loomed. Zamyatin's masterpiece, *We* (1924), attacked "primitive, spiritually empty 'barracks' socialism." It was the source of many ideas erroneously attributed to George Orwell (*1984*) and Aldous Huxley (*Brave New World*). Harassed unmercifully, Zamyatin emigrated, the last of the great writers given the privilege.

In Mikhail Bulgakov's hilarious *Heart of a Dog,* a surgeon transplants a dog's heart into the body of a petty crook and comes up with a Soviet bureaucrat who spouts unintentionally comic Sovietese in expressing lunatic views. No academic history ever came, or could

come, so close to the truth. The central theme of Bulgakov's tragi-comic masterpiece, *The Master and Margarita,* unpublished during his lifetime, is the eternal clash between the sacred and the profane. Communists loathed Bulgakov; he knew them all too well.

This was, paradoxically, a golden age of comedy. The writers I. A. Fainzilberg and E. P. Katayev, who wrote as the team of "Ilf and Petrov," poked fun at the NEP in *Twelve Chairs* and *The Golden Calf.* Mikhail Zoshchenko's short stories and vignettes lampooning the new society were all the more powerful for their brevity and realistic language.

Isaak Babel wrote meticulously crafted short stories. His *Odessa Tales* dealt in a sympathetic yet detached and often merry way with the city's vibrant Jewish community. Babel's *Red Cavalry* stands as some of the finest writing on the Russian Civil War.

Second- and third-rate writers embraced communism. The Stalinist Mikhail Sholokhov wrote a banal Civil War novel, *Quiet Flows the Don,* which enjoyed enormous popularity in Russia, Europe, and the United States. Dmitry Furmanov, Aleksandr Fadeyev, and Fyodor Gladkov—whose *Cement* was the "first proletarian novel"—wrote trash that did not travel but pleased the Communists.

The Bolsheviks silenced the talented writers and brought the practitioners of cinematography into line. Sergei Eisenstein portrayed the masses as collective hero in films such as *Strike, Battleship Potemkin,* and *October;* such was his genius that the films succeeded as art despite the massive propaganda content. Denis Kaufman ("Dziga Vertov") produced the technically interesting *Forward, Soviet!* and *A Sixth Part of the World.* V. I. Pudovkin's *Mother* and *The End of St. Petersburg* pleased Soviet censors, as did the Expressionist film *New Babylon,* which Grigory Kozintsev and Leonid Trauberg directed and for which Dmitri Shostakovich later wrote a musical score.

Because it was less severely censored, at least

in the 1920s, the legitimate stage flourished. Konstantin Stanislavsky (real name Alekseyev) created "method" acting. The brilliant director-producer Vsevolod Meyerhold, who would come to a horrible end at Stalin's hands, staged innovative productions of Gogol's *The Inspector General* and the works of Aleksandr Ostrovsky. Later he produced Mayakovsky's *The Bedbug, Mystery-Bouffe,* and *The Bathhouse.*

Music, the least political of the arts, also felt the paralyzing Bolshevik sting. Nikolai Rimsky-Korsakov's most talented pupil and a giant among composers was Igor Stravinsky, who emigrated before the Great War. He held the Bolsheviks in contempt, and Russia would not hear his music again until 1960. The music of Sergei Rakhmaninov (Rachmaninoff), who emigrated in 1917, embodied the lyric harmonies of Russian folk music and the haunting melancholy of Russia herself. For decades the Bolsheviks pretended Rakhmaninov did not exist. Sergei Prokofiev left Russia in 1918 but returned 14 years later to compose popular symphonic works. He also wrote film scores, including a magnificent one for Eisenstein's *Aleksandr Nevsky*—one of the greatest propaganda films of all time.

After Stravinsky, the giant among twentieth-century Russian composers was Dmitri Shostakovich, pupil of Aleksandr Glazunov. Shostakovich's *First Symphony* premiered in 1925. Two years later the *Second Symphony,* commissioned by the government for the anniversary of the Revolution, became an instant political as well as artistic success because of the industrial sounds incorporated into the score.

Music-hall tunes celebrating the Bolshevik seizure of power and Civil War victory enjoyed a vogue, but "Lenin, Our Lenin," "Song of the Brick Factory," "Mine No. 3," and "Give Us a Ride on the Tractor, Pete!" and the like were for Communist true believers alone. Folk music survived in the villages, and in the side-street cafés and taverns in towns, and in private dwellings.

Avant-garde art briefly flourished. At first such talented people as El Lissitsky, Kazimir Malevich, Vasili Kandinsky, Aleksandr Rodchenko, Vladimir Tatlin, Marc Chagall, Ivan Puni (Jean Pougny), and others thought the USSR would become a paradise for artists. Chagall and Kandinsky returned from France to help build the new society; Chagall founded and briefly directed the famous Vitebsk school in Belarus. Unable to tolerate the Communist regime, he returned to France in 1922. His successor at Vitebsk, Malevich, participated in creating a Supremacist school that tried to go beyond Cubism and Futurism to depict non-visible reality.

The artists soon found their works denounced as decadent, obscene, incomprehensible, antisocialist, pornographic. The Communists declared those works inaccessible—bureaucrats could not understand them—and therefore unworthy of support or even toleration.

THE LULL

Before the claws and tentacles of the Communist dictatorship tightened their deadly grip, Russia had a few brief years when life was reasonably good—"like cheese in butter," as Russians say. Anyone who had the cash could buy French champagne and Western clothes, Singer sewing machines, Ford vehicles. Westinghouse sold Russia elevators and air brakes. Royal Dutch Shell sent hydrocarbons experts; American geologists and mining engineers began planning to extract Siberia's mineral wealth; the Swedes advised the Russians how to exploit their forests with less waste.

All this activity affected impoverished Russia relatively little. Mikhail Bulgakov noted in his diary for December 20–21, 1924, that Moscow had very few trams and only eight motorized buses. Public transport was practically nonexistent—and Moscow was far better served than any other city. The Volga provincial town of Samara had two functioning trams; the sign on the first proclaimed its destination as REVOLUTION SQUARE–PRISON, the second, SOVIET SQUARE–PRISON. Mikhail Kalinin, the titular head of state, roamed the countryside in a horse-drawn carriage looking for girls.

In their pursuit of happiness and the good life, few people gave much thought to the future. Serious Communists understood, however, that politics rested on an unstable economic base. A party dedicated to a planned economy based on heavy industry could not continue to compromise with free farmers. Communists made poor managers of a quasi-capitalist economy; to go along such a path would be to lose power.

The Communists looked to the post-Lenin leadership to end this apotheosis of the peasant proprietor. A majority counted heavily on Joseph Stalin to show the *nepmen,* prostitutes, *spetsy,* and foreigners the broad open road to doom.

SUGGESTED ADDITIONAL READINGS

BALL, ALAN M. *And Now My Soul Is Hardened: Abandoned Children in Soviet Russia, 1918–1930.* Berkeley: University of California Press, 1994.

EDMONDSON, LINDA, ed. *Women and Society in Russia and the Soviet Union.* New York: Cambridge University Press, 1992.

HOLMES, LARRY E. *The Kremlin and the Schoolhouse: Reforming Education in Soviet Russia, 1917–1931.* Bloomington: Indiana University Press, 1991.

KENEZ, PETER. *Cinema and Soviet Society, 1917–1953.* New York: Cambridge University Press, 1992.

SHENTALINSKY, VITALY. *Arrested Voices: Resurrecting the Disappeared Writers of the Soviet Regime.* New York: Free Press, 1996.

STITES, RICHARD. *Russian Popular Culture: Entertainment and Society Since 1900.* New York: Cambridge University Press, 1992.

TARUSKIN, RICHARD. *Stravinsky and the Russian Traditions: A Biography of the Works Through "Mavra,"* 2 vols. Berkeley: University of California Press, 1996.

7

FOREIGN POLICY
IN THE 1920s

In the 1920s the Soviet Communists tried to persuade the proletariat of other
countries—especially Germany—that the time was ripe to overthrow capitalism.
Only a small fraction of the world's workers shared that view, and the few
revolutionary uprisings that did take place came to grief. This necessitated a
reexamination of Soviet dreams. Communist outrages in Germany and Hungary
had alienated governments and peoples in Europe and America; it would be
difficult to establish normal diplomatic relations. Acknowledging that the capitalist
system had stabilized, the Kremlin began shaping a nationalist foreign policy.

SOVIET INTERNATIONAL ORGANIZATIONS

The Communists founded a number of organizations that reflected both their ideology and Soviet national interests. The most prominent, the Communist International, or Comintern, came into existence as a "counterintervention," a crusade against the latest Crusade. Fifteen nations invaded Russia in an attempt to topple the Communist regime; that regime would send agents to destroy those nations from within.

In 1920 the Comintern established 21 conditions for membership, among them a requirement for strict obedience to the political line as the Comintern Executive Committee defined it. Member parties had to maintain rigorous internal discipline, give unquestioning support to the USSR, and establish underground sections. There was no mention of improving the lives of the workers or the poor.

By late 1921 communism seemed a failure everywhere, including Russia, and there, circumstances forced the Communists to retreat. Two basic assumptions had proved erroneous: The collapse of capitalism was not imminent, and the world proletariat was not ready to revolt. The Communists insisted that time was on their side. Obliged to deal with reality, however, they cooked up the idea of a "united front." Under certain conditions, Communists would unite with other leftist parties, sometimes "from above" in a semi-private understanding with leaders of Socialist parties, sometimes "from below"—an alliance between Communist and Socialist rank-and-file.

In July 1920 the Soviets established the Red International of Labor Unions (RILU, or Profintern) as a counter to the International Federation of Trade Unions ("Amsterdam International") and International Labor Office (ILO) of the League of Nations, and charged it with infiltrating existing unions and founding Communist ones. It had some success in Europe and the United States but proved useless in the struggle against nazism and fascism; Stalin disbanded it in 1937.

The Communists cared nothing for the peasants as long as they produced food. Thus a Peasant International or Krestintern came into being only in October 1923 to counter the International Agrarian Bureau, or Green International, a clearinghouse for agrarian parties. The Peasant International had no status outside Russia; the Soviets soon discarded it.

The organizing congress of the Communist Youth International (KIM, the Russian initials) took place in Berlin November 20–26, 1919. Twenty-nine delegates claimed to represent 219,000 members of youth organizations in 13 countries. Meant to promote harmony and solidarity among young people, advance the struggle against militarism, and protect Soviet national interests, KIM survived until 1943, when Stalin liquidated it and the Comintern.

In 1921 the Soviets founded the Communist University for the Toilers of the East (KUTV) in Moscow to train cadres for party and government service in the eastern republics and provinces. The institution's mission quickly expanded, however, to embrace the schooling of revolutionaries from East and Southeast Asia and elsewhere. Half the students came from the Soviet east, the rest from Japan, China, Indonesia, Indochina, the Arab lands, and Africa. In 1930–1931, KUTV established a secret "Manchurian School" to train guerrillas, saboteurs, and political officers to fight the Japanese invaders of Manchuria. Nearly 400 Russian, Mongolian, and Chinese students who passed through the school later saw combat in Mongolia and the Soviet Far East.

Sun Yat-sen University for the Toilers of China opened in Moscow in 1925 with 600 students. Two years later the first rector, Karl Radek, lost his job to Stalin's China expert, Pavel Mif, who was as ignorant of China as Stalin himself. Mif formed a group of Chinese students who became known as "Stalin's China Section" and the "28 Bolsheviks." The idea was to create ties between the Chinese students at KUTK and those at the Soviet-sponsored Whampoa Military Academy. That proved impossible after the Guomindang, the party of the warlord Chiang Kai-shek, conducted the "Shanghai Massacre." In 1929 Sun Yat-sen University became the Communist University for the Toilers of China, or KUTK.

THE MUSLIM EAST

In July 1920 the Comintern summoned the "Enslaved Peoples of Persia, Armenia, and Turkey" to attend a congress in Baku to plan the "liberation of the Near East." Nearly 1,900 delegates assembled in Baku in September and spent a week listening to speeches in languages that no one other than the speaker and his compatriots understood. Somehow they managed to agree that they were in favor of the destruction of colonialism. The Russian Communist delegates then committed the blunder of calling on the delegates to launch a holy war—*jihad*—against their own faith. This dampened the enthusiasm but set the tone for the Kremlin's policy toward Muslim peoples.

A few weeks after the Baku fiasco, Stalin and Sergo Ordzhonikidze organized an Extraordinary Congress of the Peoples of Dagestan. Most of the several dozen ethnic groups of Dagestan were Sunni Muslims. It would have been impossible for a party of European atheists to win their allegiance, but Stalin did somehow persuade them to shun the anti-Soviet movements in Transcaucasia. Vigorously denying any intention to ban the *shariat,* the canonical law of Islam that governs secular as well as religious life, on November 13, 1920, Stalin announced creation of the Autonomous Soviet Socialist Republic of Dagestan. He promised that the Kremlin would grant Dagestan's

Muslims the same autonomy already enjoyed by those in Soviet Turkestan, Kyrgyzia, and Tatarstan. Dagestan became part of the RSFSR on January 20, 1921.

TREATY OF RAPALLO

The Imperial Russian debt, calculated in 1918 at 18.496 billion gold rubles, complicated the Communist regime's relations with the West. The European nations had failed to restore their economies to prewar levels, and some politicians hoped to finance reconstruction with repayment of the tsarist debt. They began to rethink the wisdom of excluding two of the largest and most populous continental states, Germany and Russia, from the European economic system. Both had been good customers of France and England, and Russia had been a major supplier of raw materials.

Early in 1922, French and British officials invited Germany and Russia to attend a general economic and financial conference in Genoa the following April. Calling the invitation tantamount to diplomatic recognition, the Kremlin accepted. Russia's isolation began to break.

Commissar of Foreign Affairs Georgi Chicherin headed the Soviet delegation. On the way to Genoa, the delegates stopped off in Berlin, where in secret negotiations with the German government they agreed on, but did not formally conclude, the diplomatic bombshell they would toss a few days later. At the first session in Genoa, Chicherin asked the conference to discuss disarmament first, then economic recovery. French Foreign Minister Louis Barthou objected that disarmament was not on the agenda; Lloyd George persuaded Chicherin to concede the point.

A battle of claim and counterclaim ensued. The Allies told the Communists they could expect normalization of relations once they settled Russia's debts. Chicherin answered that

the USSR would indeed acknowledge tsarist obligations and pay compensation for nationalized foreign property—*after* the West compensated Russia in the amount of 39 billion gold rubles for the blockade and Intervention.

The conference remained bogged down for a week, then, on Easter Sunday, the German and Soviet delegations announced that they had concluded a bilateral treaty at the nearby Italian resort town of Rapallo. They would restore diplomatic and consular relations immediately. Germany renounced all claims on Russia; the most-favored-nation principle would govern commercial relations. The two countries would provide each other "mutual assistance for the alleviation of their economic difficulties."

The Rapallo Treaty, which constituted total expunction of the Treaty of Brest-Litovsk, astonished and divided the Western Allies. Barthou signed a note condemning Germany but refused to put his name on a virtually identical note to Russia. This was accounting and emotion, not logic: France and her ally Belgium had been tsarist Russia's two biggest creditors, not to mention her wartime allies. Having failed to recoup her losses through the Intervention, France would try diplomacy. After a week of bickering, the Allies agreed the new treaty was acceptable insofar as it did not violate existing agreements. Put another way, there was nothing they could do about it.

Having assembled at Genoa hoping to get another pound of flesh from Russia, the Western Allies found themselves outmaneuvered. The most sensible comment from the Allied camp came from British Prime Minister Lloyd George, who warned of the danger posed by a "hungry Russia equipped by an angry Germany." Military collaboration did not figure directly in the Treaty of Rapallo, which did, however, lay the groundwork for German–Soviet cooperation in many fields. Weimar Germany would soon obtain Soviet assistance in surreptitiously building up its armed forces. In the 1920s the Germans developed and tested weapons forbidden them by the Versailles settlement, and they trained military cadres in Russia.

RECOGNITION

The Rapallo Treaty ended the isolation of Germany and Russia and made potential enemies think twice about attacking either nation. When the French occupied the Ruhr in 1923, they prepared contingency plans in case Moscow sent troops to support Germany. The eastern anchor of the French alliance system was a *cordon sanitaire* around Russia's western frontiers; France now shored up her ties with Czechoslovakia, Poland, and Romania.

One crisis followed another in 1923. As Germany struggled with inflation of unimaginable dimensions, Communist and right-wing uprisings erupted in Hamburg, Berlin, and many other German cities. The Comintern had a clumsy hand in the Communist affairs, which the Social-Democratic German government put down. How any government could have failed to suppress armed insurrection is unclear.

The Soviet Communists concluded that all Social-Democratic parties were their worst enemies, even though those parties had been born Marxist and remained at least quasi-Marxist. The Kremlin would deal with the German Social-Democratic government because it had no choice, and indeed it did not dare put newly restored relations at too great a risk. But thenceforward the Soviets would, if it came to that, cooperate with extreme right-wing German parties such as the National Socialists (Nazis), and the Fascists in Italy, and would not lift a finger to help any Social-Democratic party anywhere.

In 1921 Chicherin negotiated a commercial agreement with Britain. It did not involve formal recognition; Britain's first Labour govern-

ment took that step three years later. Benito Mussolini's Italy followed in February 1924, France in October. Japan recognized the USSR in January 1925 and agreed to withdraw its forces from the northern half of Sakhalin Island. Only the United States refused to establish normal diplomatic ties.

Diplomatic relations between the USSR and Great Britain collapsed within months. Four days before the October 1924 British elections, the Conservative party published a letter allegedly from Zinoviev, the Comintern chief, directing the British Communist party to increase its revolutionary activity and infiltrate the British Army. There was no time for the Labour government, which had been severely criticized for recognizing Russia, to mount a defense. The Conservatives won overwhelmingly.

Russian émigrés had forged the "Zinoviev letter," duping British Foreign Office officials who had close ties to the Conservatives. Britain's master spy "Sidney Reilly," in reality a Russian Jew named Sigmund Georgievich Rozenblum, received a sort of finder's fee. Later in 1924, the Bolsheviks caught him trying to cross the border and executed him. The Conservatives had earlier financed planning of Reilly's scheme to parade Lenin and Trotsky nude through the streets of Moscow. With such sponsors, who would later fabricate documents besmirching Edward VIII's lover (the "Shanghai File"), there was no need for a market survey. In 1928 an emissary collected £5,000 "on behalf of X"—Reilly-Rozenblum, after whom Ian Fleming patterned "James Bond"—from the Conservatives.

Two weeks after taking office the Conservative government broke the diplomatic and commercial treaties its Labour predecessor had negotiated with Moscow; relations remained suspended for several years. The Conservatives even manufactured a "war scare" in 1927, claiming once again that the Kremlin was interfering in British internal affairs.

Labour returned to office in 1929 and reestablished ties.

DISARMAMENT AND COLLECTIVE SECURITY

The 1919 Versailles settlement produced an armistice rather than peace. France and Germany remained extremely wary of each other. Every new state in Eastern Europe had grievances with one or more of its neighbors; the whole world detested Soviet Russia. No nation was prepared to lay down its arms, but none could afford to maintain its forces at existing levels, let alone increase them.

In 1922 the Kremlin began an effort to negotiate arms control agreements. The Soviet delegation to Genoa had stopped not only in Berlin but also in Riga (Latvia), where Chicherin obtained the signatures of Latvian, Estonian, and Polish officials to the Riga Protocol, an innocuous document that simply called on nations to reduce arms stockpiles. At the Moscow Conference of December 1922, Latvian, Estonian, Finnish, Polish, and Soviet representatives discussed arms limitation, but the Baltic states remained deeply suspicious of Russia, and both Poland and Finland claimed Soviet territory. The Poles had no interest in an agreement requiring reduction of their forces stationed in eastern Poland.

When the Moscow Conference ended in failure, Warsaw charged that the Soviets had staged it as a propaganda exercise. There was some truth to that, and anyway it was unthinkable that Poland would disarm. Nevertheless, the Soviets tidied up their propaganda position, and in some quarters their moral standing, by posing as the only nation sincerely interested in disarmament.

The search for collective security involved lengthy talks in Paris, Berlin, and London. Those seemed to bear fruit at the Locarno Conference in October 1925: France, Germany, Great Britain, Belgium, Poland, and Czechoslovakia signed a series of agreements that guaranteed Germany's western frontiers and assured Poland and Czechoslovakia that France would come to their aid if Germany attacked either. The press promptly gave birth to a "spirit of Locarno" that seduced public opinion and for a few years sustained the illusion that goodwill ruled international relations; so desperate was the desire for peace that millions of people believed this. Excluded from Locarno, the USSR denounced the agreements and noted that failure to declare Germany's *eastern* frontiers fixed and inviolable proved indifference toward German aggression in the East. Moscow saw the Locarno accords as the West's invitation to Germany to look eastward. And indeed, in February 1935 Britain and France would propose an "Eastern Locarno" to Adolf Hitler. In return for his guarantee of the security of Czechoslovakia, Poland, and Soviet Russia, they would permit Germany to rearm. The politicians in London and Paris thought they had tricked everyone: Having read *Mein Kampf* at long last, they were sure Hitler would use his weapons against Russia no matter what he signed.

Germany became a member of the League of Nations in 1926, but the Western powers did not permit Soviet Russia to join or even to participate on the Preparatory Commission for a Disarmament Conference, the first meeting of which took place in May 1926. The Commission did include the United States, which had previously rejected cooperation with League agencies. The United States approved of the exclusion of the USSR.

The opposition finally softened, however, and in November 1927 Maksim Litvinov, Chicherin's deputy, came to Geneva to represent the Soviet Union on the Commission. In his first speech, Litvinov called for complete and immediate disarmament. Western diplomats dismissed this as a stunt, but Litvinov pointed to the Soviet record: Riga Protocol, Moscow Conference, treaties of nonaggression and neutrality with Turkey (1925) and Iran (1927).

Having had no interest in disarmament proposals that threatened either their hegemony in Europe or their overseas possessions, France and Great Britain declined to be instructed by Communists in the ways of peace. No nation, their diplomats loftily observed, could lay down its arms against unverifiable assurances others would do likewise. They simply could not believe that Moscow might be sincere.

Convinced that history was on their side, the Soviet Communists had in fact calculated that they had nothing to lose from disarmament. The march of capitalism would inexorably deepen class contradictions and lead to revolution. Disarmament was thus ultimately irrelevant, but worth working for in the short term if only as an economy measure.

Western governments could not ignore the public clamor for peace. The American Secretary of State, Frank Kellogg, and Foreign Minister Aristide Briand of France negotiated a Pact of Paris Concerning the Renunciation of War as an Instrument of National Policy (Kellogg-Briand Pact). On August 27, 1928, representatives of 15 nations—the USSR was again blackballed—signed the agreement, which merely called on nations to renounce war. There were provisions for sanctions. Humiliated, the Kremlin denounced the pact, only to ratify it two days later. The hypocritical game placed no limits on the number that could play.

The original agreement was not to become operative until ratified by a majority of the original signatories. Once more the Kremlin seized the initiative with the Moscow (or Litvinov) Protocol of February 9, 1929, according to which the USSR, Poland, Romania, Estonia, and Latvia agreed to put the Kellogg-Briand Pact into force immediately. Turkey, Iran, and Lithuania swiftly followed. At the League of Nations later in the year, a majority of member nations accepted Litvinov's proposal to implement the Kellogg-Briand Pact by providing for conciliation and arbitration in international political disputes.

CHINA

Shortly after taking power, the Bolsheviks renounced tsarist concessions in China, pledged support for Chinese independence, and declared implacable hostility toward imperialism everywhere and specifically in China. They hinted at a willingness to renegotiate the treaties through which the tsars had ripped huge territories out of the Chinese Empire. The Chinese, especially educated young people embittered by the West's despoilation of their country, welcomed Lenin's gestures. In an incredibly arrogant riposte that harked back to eighteenth-century attitudes, the Western allies announced at Versailles that Germany's colonial holdings in Shandong (Shantung) would not be returned to China but would be given to Japan. It was small wonder that many young Chinese saw a beacon of hope in Moscow, not Paris or London.

The Comintern sponsored the First Congress of the Toilers of the Far East in Moscow in January 1922. The 150 delegates included a 16-member Japanese contingent consisting of nine Communists, four anarchists, and three without specific party affiliation. More than 80 Chinese and Koreans attended, as did several Mongolians, and some RSFSR Yakuts and Kalmyks. Grigori Zinoviev delivered the opening address. Taking time out from his amours, Mikhail Kalinin also spoke, as did Sen Katayama, leader of the Japanese delegation. All insisted on the need for the peoples of the Far East to overthrow Western and Japanese imperialism. Zinoviev and Kalinin proclaimed support for national independence movements—even bourgeois ones—throughout Asia. This line would lead to the Shanghai

Massacre. Preposterous on its face, the attempt to reconcile proletarian internationalism with nationalism became official Comintern policy. This was the chief result of the Moscow meeting, which also led to the formation of the Japanese Communist party.

A. A. Joffe, a negotiator at Brest-Litovsk and a top Soviet diplomat, went to Beijing (Peking) in August 1922 to establish relations with the Chinese government. But Beijing's writ did not run very far, and nothing came of this. A secessionist regime in Guangzhou (Canton) had a broader if still limited mandate. Joffe journeyed south to meet its leader, Sun Yat-sen, who sent a delegation to Moscow a year later, but no meaningful accord resulted. In September 1923 the Comintern despatched its best organizer, Michael Borodin (Gruzenberg), to Guangzhou to help Sun prepare a political-military offensive and seize control of all China. A few months later the Red Army sent General Vasili Blücher to plan the military operations.

Borodin and Blücher reorganized both the fledgling Chinese Communist party and its mortal enemy, the Nationalist party or Guomindang (Kuomintang), and helped both raise and train armies. The Soviet military mission established the Whampoa (Huangpu) Military Academy under the Guomindang's Chiang Kai-shek (Jiang Jieshi). The deputy head of the Academy's political department was a young Communist, Zhou Enlai.

Following negotiations with Joffe, in January 1924 Sun Yat-sen urged the Guomindang to unite with the Chinese Communist party on the basis of his Three Principles of the People: Nationalism, livelihood, and democracy. The parties would fight jointly for the national liberation and unification of China and for broad reforms. Sun's program included reorganization and revitalization of the villages to alleviate the misery of the peasant.

Comintern China policy reflected the Soviet struggle for power. Stalin knew little about foreign affairs and nothing about China. Nevertheless, citing Lenin's sagely uninformed remark that China was on the verge of a bourgeois revolution, Stalin declared it necessary to support a "united front" between Chinese Communists and the Guomindang. At its first All-China Congress in January 1924, the Guomindang officially accepted alliance with the Chinese Communist party and called for close ties with Russia.

Trotsky remained skeptical, arguing that there was no need to cooperate with the bourgeoisie because the situation in China replicated the Russia not of 1905 but of 1917. The time was ripe for a Chinese proletarian revolution. Or if it was not, Trotsky would help the process along.

Stalin won on this issue as on all others where he clashed with Trotsky. As Sun Yat-sen's health declined in late 1924, Stalin and his then ally, Nikolai Bukharin, backed Chiang Kai-shek as the new Guomindang leader. Opposing cooperation with Chiang, Trotsky urged establishment of a soviet system in China.

On May 31, 1924, the Soviet plenipotentiary in Beijing signed an agreement "On the General Principles for the Regulation of Questions Between the USSR and the Chinese Republic." It annulled all "conventions, agreements, accords, contracts and so forth" between tsarist Russia and China. The Soviets declared "null and void and without force" all treaties the tsars had concluded with any third party or parties that infringed on China's rights and sovereignty. The Kremlin recognized Outer Mongolia as part of China. The Soviets and Chinese agreed not to interfere in each other's internal affairs, and to regulate navigation on waterways that constituted any part of their borders. The complicated matter of the Chinese Eastern Railway, in which the tsarist government had part ownership, was subject to further negotiation. The Soviets renounced extraterritoriality, the tsarist share of the Boxer Rebellion indemnity, and "all special rights and privileges" conferred by treaty on Russia.

When it signed this accord, the Kremlin—at the time that meant Stalin, Kamenev, and Zinoviev—seems to have intended to honor Lenin's promise and restore the territories the tsars had seized from China. But the situation in China was unstable, however, and Russian nationalism began reasserting itself after the failure of Communist uprisings in Europe. Not until November 1996 would the two sides agree to make significant cuts in troop levels along their border.

Also on May 31, 1924, the Soviets signed a series of bilateral declarations that further defined the basic accord; provided for the disposition of tsarist and Russian Orthodox Church property in China; and regulated the status of Soviet citizens on Chinese soil. A separate agreement established a board of five Soviet and five Chinese members to oversee joint operation of the Chinese Eastern Railway until resolution of the ownership dispute. (The Chinese later seized control of the railway in July 1929 and imprisoned thousands of Soviet employees. The USSR broke diplomatic relations. Late in July 1929 a protocol signed at Khabarovsk restored joint ownership and reaffirmed the international frontiers; diplomatic relations resumed only in December 1932.)

When Sun Yat-sen died early in 1925, Chiang Kai-shek succeeded him. The following year Chiang confounded Borodin, then on a secret mission to Beijing, by swooping down on Chinese Communist party headquarters in Guangzhou (Canton) and arresting party leaders. Isolated and denied access to Guomindang leaders, Borodin returned to Moscow for consultations. General Blücher remained the Guomindang's chief military adviser; Chiang needed his expertise for the Northern Expedition, the July–October 1926 military campaign in which Guomindang forces conquered and united most of China south of the Yangtze River.

These developments stunned Moscow, and there were those in Stalin's own entourage who shared Trotsky's distrust of Chiang. Stalin did not, however, change his mind, and the united-front policy remained in effect. He sent Borodin back to China to ensure that the Chinese Communists followed Comintern orders.

By the spring of 1927 Chiang had extended his control still farther north and set up his capital at Nanjiang (Nanking). He defeated some of the most powerful warlords and with Soviet assistance created a huge army. He now turned on the Communists. Guomindang street fighters—the Blue Shirts—attacked in the Communist stronghold of Shanghai on April 12, 1927, and slaughtered every Communist they could find, killing more than a thousand. Over the following 13 months, something like 318,000 Chinese revolutionaries—including 18,000 of 58,000 members of the Communist party—were massacred.

Stalin responded to the "Shanghai Massacre" by radioing some bizarre instructions to Borodin, who was to arm and equip 20,000 Chinese Communists; create a 50,000-man army in Hunan and Hupeh provinces; confiscate all landlord properties in those provinces; pack the Guomindang Central Committee; and put "reactionary" officers of Chiang's army on trial. He might as well have ordered the construction of a second Great Wall by the end of the month. Stalin was speaking to the Soviet Communists, who knew he had erred disastrously. Trotsky's reading of China was no less wrong, but in a different way: He was not in power.

Soviet China policy lay in ruins. Reinhold Glière's *Red Poppy* ballet, which celebrated Soviet–Chinese friendship, had its première at the Bolshoi Theatre in June 1927. A modest artistic success, it was a bad political joke.

In China, the decimated Communists struck back in three unsuccessful attempts in 1927 to challenge the growing might of the Guomindang. Zhou Enlai and Zhu Deh were among the leaders of the Nanchang Uprising in August and September. In September, Mao Zedong commanded the Autumn Harvest Uprising in the Hunan–Jiangxi border area, which saw the birth of the Chinese Workers' and Peasants' Revolutionary Army. A minor Communist revolt took place in Guangzhou in December.

The Communist-Guomindang alliance had been a "Right" (conservative) policy that reflected some temporary cooperation between Stalin and Bukharin. After the 1927 disasters, the Chinese Communists moved toward the "Left," that is, they began laying the groundwork for the seizure of political power by the revolutionary peasantry.

The Sixth Congress of the Chinese Communist party met in Moscow in June–July 1928 and reaffirmed the leftward reorientation. Increasingly preoccupied with domestic Soviet policy, Stalin had even less time to devote to Chinese affairs. He accepted the practical necessity of protracted guerrilla warfare.

A DECADE OF PROLETARIAN DIPLOMACY

Soviet foreign policy remained officially predicated on world revolution throughout most of the decade after 1917, and no real change could take place until Stalin elaborated the policy of "socialism in one country." The post-Lenin leaders took their time in learning to distinguish between an ideological and a pragmatic foreign policy. They saw no contradiction between supporting Communist parties dedicated to the overthrow of governments and conducting more or less normal diplomatic relations with those same governments. The Kremlin insisted on the fiction of the Comintern as an independent agency with headquarters in Moscow and—mere coincidence!—many Soviets among its top officers.

The great fear of Soviet leaders was that the USSR would be attacked by a capitalist power or group of powers before it had built a strong industrial and military base. Because the state was so weak, Soviet foreign policy became ever more conciliatory and defensive. The Soviets supported the concept of collective security and adhered to pacts aimed at establishing it. From 1927 on they repeatedly spoke out for immediate, universal, and complete disarmament. It would be incorrect to dismiss this as mere propaganda.

The Soviet stance on disarmament and impassioned defense of collective security made a favorable impression on millions of people around the world. In the titanic clash between communism and fascism that loomed on the European horizon, the Soviets would have friends among the populations of many countries but not a single ally among the various nations.

SUGGESTED ADDITIONAL READINGS

EUDIN, XENIA, and H. H. FISHER, eds. *Soviet Russia and the West, 1920–1927.* Stanford, CA: Stanford University Press, 1957.

EUDIN, XENIA, and R. C. NORTH, eds. *Soviet Russia and the East.* Stanford, CA: Stanford University Press, 1957.

KENNAN, GEORGE. *Russia and the West Under Lenin and Stalin.* Boston: Little, Brown, 1961.

KENNAN, GEORGE. *Soviet Foreign Policy, 1917–1941.* Westport, CT: Greenwood Press, 1978.

McDERMOTT, KEVIN, and JEREMY AGNEW. *Comintern: A History of International Communism from Lenin to Stalin.* New York: St. Martin's Press, 1997.

O'CONNOR, TIMOTHY E. *Chicherin and Soviet Foreign Affairs, 1918–1930.* Ames: Iowa State University Press, 1987.

ROSENBAUM, KURT. *Community of Fate: German–Soviet Diplomatic Relations, 1922–1928.* Syracuse, NY: Syracuse University Press, 1965.

ULAM, ADAM. *Expansion and Coexistence.* New York: Praeger, 1968.

8

STALIN'S REVOLUTION, 1924–1932

Joseph Vissarionovich Stalin bullied the dying Lenin, insulted and threatened Lenin's wife, Nadezhda Krupskaya, and treated his colleagues now with contempt, now with effusive goodwill. His sense of humor lacked sophistication and tended toward the scatological. He treated women crudely, and after his second wife's death he led an infrequently interrupted ascetic life. In their childhood he treated his daughter affectionately, his two sons as strange brats.

Stalin never forgave an insult and frequently invented insults not to forgive. Short and stout, he was self-conscious about his slightly withered left arm, a birth defect. His Georgian accent and high-pitched voice grated on the ears of native speakers of Russian. Chicken pox permanently scarred his face before he was 10. Smiling contentedly, he often listened to a recording of a coloratura singing against a background of howling dogs.

Intelligent, moody, quick to blame other people for his own errors and shortcomings, Stalin was a true psychological isolate: No one ever came close to knowing him, at least no one who lived to tell the story. Aside from his personal servants, whom he treated kindly, few people liked him, but he loved himself enough, the Moscow and Leningrad sophisticates whispered, to make up the difference. He never fully trusted anyone. Outside his family, he had what can be described as personal relations only with Vyacheslav Molotov, Kliment Voroshilov, Lazar Kaganovich, and, for shorter periods, a few others. He ate, drank, caroused, gossiped, and did party and

state business with these men, who agreed with everything he said and did; instantly got to their feet when they saw him about to rise; smiled and laughed a microsecond after he did; agreed with and even countersigned his orders for the arrest of their closest relatives and friends on blatantly preposterous charges. Such were the Stalinoids at the top of the Soviet bureaucratic machine.

CONSOLIDATION OF THE DICTATORSHIP

In the summer of 1924 Stalin turned on his partners of convenience, Kamenev and Zinoviev, drastically curtailing their authority and ousting their chief aides. He smiled benevolently on party conservatives (the "Right") and appealed for the continuation of the NEP—the position of Aleksei Rykov, Mikhail Tomsky, and of Nikolai Bukharin, who was promoted to Lenin's Politburo seat.

Politically disoriented after Lenin's death, and unable to judge the life expectancy of the

Stalin-Zinoviev-Kamenev triumvirate, Trotsky returned to the struggle for power in autumn 1924 and stumbled badly. He publicly assailed Kamenev and Zinoviev for wavering during the Revolutionary year. Those two, who had misjudged their own prospects and had begun to fight back against Stalin, now rushed to return to his forgiving embrace. Anyone but Trotsky, they said.

Stalin mobilized his forces, which now included nearly all the Soviet leaders. Dismissed as commissar of military and naval affairs early in 1925, Trotsky submitted meekly, thinking his capitulation would lay to rest the charge of "Bonapartism." Kamenev and Zinoviev proposed to excommunicate him from the party. The magnanimous Stalin objected. Today Trotsky's head, tomorrow whose? Let us be gentle and forgiving, he said.

In the winter of 1924–1925, Zinoviev decided to make a move against Stalin. He still had a base in Leningrad, some power as head of the Comintern, and he could sway not only Kamenev but also—suppressing his disgust—Trotsky and maybe Lenin's widow, Krupskaya, as window-dressing. Zinoviev gave several speeches attacking the NEP's generosity to the peasants. That might have flown in proletarian Leningrad, but the rest of the country wanted nothing to do with a new war communism.

Stalin struck back quickly. He dismissed more key Zinoviev aides in the Leningrad party and Komsomol organizations, undermined Zinoviev in the Comintern, and cut off his access to the Kremlin. Stalin joined his good friends of the moment, Bukharin and Rykov, in a vigorous defense of the NEP.

A British specialist remarked that the December 1925 Fourteenth Party Congress "marked the lowest ebb of political morality . . . the party had yet reached." Stalin and his allies handpicked most of the delegates. Zinoviev expressed outrage at the prolonged jeers and catcalls that greeted his attempts to speak. The Armenian Stalinist Anastas

Mikoyan ridiculed him, saying, "When Zinoviev is in the majority, he is for iron discipline; when he is in the minority, he is against it." The Stalin faction shouted Zinoviev down and—on a signal from their leader—insulted Krupskaya. His political capital exhausted, Trotsky remained silent. Kamenev behaved with surprising courage: "I have come," he said, "to the conclusion that Comrade Stalin cannot fulfill the role of unifier. . . . We are against the doctrine of one-man rule, we are against the creation of a leader." The Congress erupted into a cacophony of shouts, curses, whistling, and general disorder.

Stalin let this go on for some time, then brought it to an abrupt halt with a slight wave of his hand. He spoke soothingly. Of course we must have collective leadership, he said. The party must have leaders of the stature of Rykov, Bukharin, Tomsky, Kalinin, Molotov: "It is impossible to lead the party other than collectively. It is stupid to think of any other way after Lenin." But Stalin and his people would not tolerate "anti-party activity," which they alone would define.

Betrayed by hubris, Trotsky, Zinoviev, and Kamenev awakened at last and attempted to reconcile their differences. Zinoviev and Kamenev now agreed with Trotsky that the Stalinist bureaucracy was dragging the revolutionary masses down to defeat. The Kronstadt sailors whom Trotsky massacred had said the same thing, but that was then.

By 1926 Stalin controlled the bureaucracy; only the truly daft would attack him and his support system at their strongest point. He had only to quote his rivals to prove that all three had supported the line they now attacked, and had consistently opposed not only him—Stalin—but also Lenin.

Trotsky and Zinoviev sponsored a series of street demonstrations and meetings in October 1926; a few thousand of their supporters demanded the restoration of party democracy. The bureaucracy responded with an attack designed to isolate and destroy them. It forbade them to address the workers in factories and shops and denied them access to the media, which attacked both viciously. Suddenly aware of the danger, Trotsky, Zinoviev, and Kamenev publicly renounced their own activities, admitting they had violated the ban on factionalism and promising to behave. This cowardly recantation, which could not save them, deprived their followers of all hope of protection. The Stalinists ousted Trotsky and Kamenev—a candidate member—from the Politburo and removed Zinoviev from the Comintern leadership. The Central Committee dismissed Trotsky and Zinoviev.

In October 1927 the oppositionists again tried to stage factory meetings and street demonstrations, only to encounter bored indifference. The following month the Communist party expelled Trotsky, Kamenev, and Zinoviev. After groveling, Kamenev and Zinoviev won conditional reinstatement. The OGPU—as the Cheka was renamed in 1923—escorted Trotsky into exile in Alma–Aty, Kazakhstan, early in 1928, and a year later they frog-marched him across the border into Turkey. Kamenev and Zinoviev shouted approval.

THE SITUATION IN AGRICULTURE

The power struggle directly involved only a few top officials and their aides. The political role of the 1,236,190 rank-and-file Communist party members in December 1927—including 348,957 candidates—consisted of carrying out Moscow's orders. The rest of the Soviet population, 146.5 million people, were simply concerned with making ends meet.

The Communists had not abandoned their dream of creating a planned, crisis-free economy. They acknowledged that the New Economic Policy's free market had brought about the recovery but remained committed to ending the "tyranny" of the market.

After the catastrophic 1921 famine, over the following two years agriculture regained pre-1914 levels, but the peasants were not fully participating in the market. More food and grain were remaining in the countryside, and supplies in the cities were barely adequate. The major grain-producing regions—middle Volga Valley, North Caucasus, Ukraine—had little margin for shortfalls.

Backward, inefficient, wasteful farming remained the norm. In many areas the village commune periodically redistributed the land among the peasants, determined which crops to sow on which parcels, and set the dates for plowing, sowing, and harvesting. A strip-farming system gave each peasant some decent land here, a mediocre parcel there. After 1921 these ancient customs were more or less standardized throughout European Russia. Russian yields of wheat and rye were seven to nine centners (1 centner = 100 kg) per hectare—lower than those of fourteenth-century French estates and not half those of Germany in the 1920s. Unable to subsist on their own allotments, millions of peasants hired themselves out.

There was all too little animal power, not to mention machinery. In the Russian Republic, 28.3 percent of peasant households had no draft animals in 1927. On the 31.6 percent that *had no plows*, human hands did every bit of the work. Barely 15 percent had horse-drawn agricultural implements. Between 1928 and 1939 the urban population increased by 18.5 million; much of the increase was due to peasants leaving the farms for the city factories. Fewer peasant producers thus had to feed more people. A major and clearly visible crisis loomed just ahead.

THE INDUSTRIALIZATION DEBATE

In the short term, the task was to supply the Red Army and the cities with food. But over the long term, the regime had to transform agricultural Russia into a modern industrial society. How was that to be accomplished? How could Russia accumulate the necessary capital? How to raise the growth rate so that Russia could catch up with capitalist states? How could the people, living reasonably well because they spent everything and saved nothing, be made to tighten their belts?

Gosplan (State Planning Commission) and the Supreme Economic Council concluded that Russia had to squeeze agriculture to finance industrialization. The peasants had to deliver more grain and get less for it. Moreover, they, and the urban population, would have to consume less—and pay more because of the artifically created shortages. The state needed a food surplus to sell on the world market. Soviet Russian grain competed with more efficiently produced—therefore cheaper—American, Canadian, and other foreign grain. But for Russia, making the sale was a matter of life and death. She would if necessary sell below cost, so desperately did she need foreign currency with which to purchase machines, certain raw materials, technical expertise and designs, and so forth.

The party debated. A "Right" faction personified by Bukharin, Rykov, and Tomsky favored the "go-slow" policy of maintaining the NEP. The free market—a distasteful necessity—could produce the surplus grain needed to finance industrialization, which like collectivization of agriculture would have to wait; this was the price of Russian backwardness. Trotsky was no longer a player, but the "Left" of which he had been spokesman insisted that the USSR could not postpone industrialization and survive. The only way to control the peasantry was to collectivize private farms, at least initially through nonviolent persuasion. Stalin kept his own counsel, but he seemed to favor the Right if only because it was not the Left.

Neither wing anticipated an early demise of the NEP. The Fifteenth Party Congress in December 1927 adopted a Bukharinist scheme for a Five-Year Plan; it called for collectivization on a partial, voluntary basis. Stalin agreed, giving no hint of his impending 180-degree reversal.

1928 CRISIS

In the mid-1920s the Russian workers were employed, fed, and left alone. Having no choice, they passively accepted Communist rule.

After the best harvest of the decade in 1926, all seemed well. But rumors of plans to resume war-communism grain requisitions raced through the villages in August–September 1927, when news leaked from Moscow that farmers had sold the state only about half as much grain as the year before. Requisitions did not materialize, but grain deliveries again fell short in 1928, when weather conditions that occur once every 30 to 40 years cut the harvest sharply. Some district authorities forced the peasants to sell their crops at a fixed price. Confronted by artificially low prices, many peasants began switching to industrial crops. There would not be enough grain to feed the cities at pre-1927 levels.

Early in 1929 the state introduced bread rationing, first in Leningrad and Moscow, then everywhere else. Officials mixed inferior grains into wheat and rye held in granaries and stockpiles, and lowered the milling standard.

Stalin repeatedly labeled the very idea of forced collectivization absurd. The small private farm, he said in April 1929, would be the mainstay of agriculture indefinitely. But in private he was now attacking the call by the Right to continue NEP and leave collectivization voluntary.

In April 1929 the Sixteenth Party Conference approved Gosplan's Five-Year Plan, which envisioned collectivization of 20 percent of peasant households by 1933. The party swung into action: Within four months it created 57,000 collective farms by amalgamating more than a million private farms. On the whole, this took place peacefully; the Communists built the first *kolhozes* out of the handful left over from war communism, marginal farmsteads, and lands that already belonged to the state. They spent huge sums to make them attractive to poor peasants.

But this was not even a good beginning, and after the inferior 1929 harvest, Stalin and the Politburo decided to push for all-out collectivization. Because resistance was certain, they did not announce the decision publicly. They ordered special urban party cadres, the Red Army, and where necessary OGPU troops to force the peasants into collective farms. These forces swooped down on the countryside like angels of death and systematically destroyed private farming in Russia.

Ignoring weather and history and every other standard index, Stalin and his men decided that, because the peasants were infected with a "kulak mentality," they had deliberately produced the grain shortage, withholding stocks to drive up the price.

On November 7, 1929, *Pravda* published "The Year of the Great Change," in which Stalin called collectivization a huge success. The Communists had solved the problem of accumulating capital so as to finance industrialization. The peasants were flocking enthusiastically into collective farms. This was not a statement of fact but a warning to the collectivizers to obtain results—or face the consequences.

Five days later Bukharin, Rykov, and Tomsky publicly confirmed Stalin's boasts. A November 1929 Central Committee meeting recorded the Right's capitulation and expelled Bukharin from the Politburo.

The "great change" marked the beginning of the Stalinist nightmare. The hit-or-miss requisitions of war communism, terrible though they were for those whom they struck, offered

no real precedent. Stalin and the Stalinoids had launched a war against their own nation.

THE PUSH FOR TOTAL COLLECTIVIZATION

A nightmare ensued as the Soviet Communist state moved with overwhelming force toward total collectivization. Peasants branded "kulaks" or "enemies of the people" had no defense: Local party bosses interpreted the terms as they wished. If they failed to meet the quotas of human beings set by Moscow, they would join the ranks of the doomed. And so they confiscated the property of the condemned ones and threw men, women, children, and the elderly into unheated, overcrowded freight cars bound eventually for forced-labor camps in the far North or Siberia.

Some far-sighted individuals who saw what was happening began selling off their grain surpluses, agricultural implements, livestock, and other movable property in 1928. This "self-dekulakization" became a criminal offense. You had to wait for the state to destroy you.

Many went meekly, but others attacked the collectivizers with pitchforks, axes, clubs, rocks, bare fists. The cattle-herders called in the Red Army, but that Army was a cross section of peasants and workers and thus effective only up to a point. Then, OGPU troops took over. These were the ones who would kill as ordered.

A peasant war convulsed Russia in the winter of 1929–1930. There were nearly 3,000 armed attacks on the collectivizers by peasant mobs in European Russia in the first three months of 1930. The peasants buried their grain trying to save it, or burned it, or dumped it in creeks and rivers. In February and March 1930 they slaughtered 14 million head of cattle and killed 4 million horses. The slaughtered animals were left to putrefy. Stalin obligingly published these figures in January 1934:

	Millions of Live Animals	
	1929	*1933*
Horses	34.0	16.6
Cattle	68.1	38.6
Sheep and goats	147.2	50.6
Swine	20.9	12.2

This had a ripple effect. Russia lost animal power, the slaughter reduced drastically the amount of organic fertilizer, and crops dwindled. Were they not documented by the authorities themselves, the excesses would be unbelievable. Squads of state terrorists swarmed into villages in the Smolensk region, confiscated clothing off people's backs and "nationalized" their food and drink. The thugs smashed religious icons and broke everything they could not carry away.

At bayonet-point, they drove the peasants who survived the initial swoop to the railhead, whether nearby or 200 kilometers away. In winter the trains frequently remained on sidings for days or even weeks at a time. The Communists had not foreseen, let alone planned for, the physical problems of transporting millions of people to distant, uninhabitable regions. Uncounted numbers of helpless, fear-crazed peasants froze to death or starved or went out of their minds in the trains, sometimes within sight of their villages.

Agriculture hovered on the brink of disaster. In the absence of some surcease, the country would collapse, the regime with it.

"DIZZY WITH SUCCESS"

The break came with the publication of Stalin's article, "Dizzy with Success: Problems of the Kolhoz Movement," in *Pravda* on March 2, 1930. The author of the insanity blamed local Communist party officials. What kind of lunatics, he asked, were collectivizing agriculture by ripping the bells from churches? Who could have doubted this was a *voluntary*

operation? He condemned the zealots for providing "grist for the mill of Right opportunism."

The peasants interpreted the article as commutation of a death sentence and paid high prices for that issue of *Pravda*. They stood in rutted village streets reading it aloud over and over, voices increasingly slurred as vodka oiled the great celebration. The writer Andrei Platonov viewed it differently in *For Future Use*: "In March 1930, a certain man, feeling unfortunate, got onto a train and left the city of Higher Command far behind." When this story appeared in 1931, Stalin read it and, according to Platonov's wife, scribbled the word "Bastard!" on the title page. Never again would the writer know peace.

The timing was no accident. The optimum period for spring plowing had arrived in the southern grain districts, and plowing would have to commence immediately in Ukraine and the Volga Valley if 1930 were to yield any crop at all. There ensued a mass exodus from the collective farms. Of 14 million households—70 million people—forced into *kolhozes* down to March 1930, five million remained in May. By the summer of 1930 only 24.6 percent of all peasant farms were still collectivized.

Dazed party cadres gaped in the direction of the Kremlin. They had carried out orders, only to have Comrade Stalin denounce them for doing so. In the wake of Stalin's article, special boards tried and convicted about 4,300 "Left deviationists"—providers of grist to the "Right"— on various charges, shot a quarter of them, and dismissed or demoted another 22,000.

Spring plowing took place a little behind schedule, but as it happened no harm was done. The peasants worked harder than ever, thinking that might prove good faith, and save them. The 1930 Sixteenth Party Congress noted tranquillity in the countryside, again blamed the winter excesses on local cadres, and called for increased aid to the *kolhozes*.

About this time, the last article critical of Stalin and the Central Committee appeared in *Pravda*.

RESUMING SPEED

The 1930 harvest produced a record grain delivery of 22 million tons, six million more than 1929 and double that of 1928. The farms recovered more quickly than anyone could have foreseen. But the Communists did not believe in miracles. Convinced that the harvest showed what the peasants could do *every* year, they now knew for certain that the "kulaks" had manufactured the shortages of 1927–1929.

In October 1930 the Central Committee ordered resumption of collectivization on a massive if less frantic scale. Class warfare resumed as the peasants, who could have no doubts as to what lay in store for them, fought Red Army and OGPU troops ferociously. The "red rooster crowed" as the villagers set fire to fields and grain stores and destroyed their homes to keep them out of Communist hands. Their ancestors had greeted Napoleon this way in 1812. They poisoned wells, slit their animals' throats, lynched officials, and committed suicide.

It was no contest. By January 1931 the state had collectivized 26.1 percent of all peasant households; 42.0 percent by April; 52.7 percent by June. In the latter month, 65 million people in 13 million peasant households were toiling on 211,000 collective farms. Officials spoke confidently of building tractors and mechanizing agriculture. In 1933 they put only about 200,000 tractors with an aggregate horsepower of 3.1 million into the countryside. This was a small fraction of the power provided by horses and oxen before the slaughter.

The 1931 harvest yielded 21 percent less grain than that of 1930. The shortfall outraged the Kremlin, which needed ever more grain for the foreign market. The state sold foreign consumers 2.6 million centners in 1929; 48.4 million in 1930; 51.8 million in 1931. These sales provided a major share of the financing for industrialization. No one in authority paid attention to the effect on the grain producers.

It did not occur to Stalin and his colleagues to enquire whether the quotas were unrealistically high, or whether unfavorable weather conditions in 1931 might explain the poor harvest—hardly the first in Russian history. The Central Committee again sent troops and the OGPU into the countryside to seize reserves, including seed grain, reorganize local party organizations, purge official cadres, and conduct "mass repressions" against "enemies of the people."

Agricultural output declined. Where 1928 equals 100, production stood at 81.5 in 1933. Nevertheless, the state made money on domestic sales by charging consumers up to 40 times the procurement price for wheat flour. By the end of the first Five-Year Plan, the Communists had collectivized 61.5 percent of all peasant households. This represented 70 percent of the crop area; in the major grain-producing areas the percentage ranged from 68 to 90 percent. In this way, Bolshevism came to the Russian village.

Archival revelations constantly push the estimate of the number of people who perished during the collectivization of agriculture upward; the 1997 consensus placed the figure at about 13 million. If foreign invaders had killed the entire 1935 populations of Norway, Denmark, Finland, Portugal, and Bulgaria, they would have shed less blood. Yet Stalin and his headsmen had not even begun the Great Terror.

FIVE-YEAR PLAN IN INDUSTRY

The Stalinists could partially conceal their political bankruptcy behind strident propaganda, and camouflage military weakness behind the façade of a large standing army, but they could not hide Russia's industrial and technological backwardness. Russia lagged behind the United States, Britain, and Germany, and in several crucial areas France, Belgium, and even Holland outproduced her. In 1926 Russia had no machine-tool industry, a tiny chemical industry, no turbine or generator factories, no high-grade steel or ferrous alloys, no aircraft-manufacturing plants. Europeans had sneered since the time of Peter the Great that the Russian precision tool was a sledgehammer.

Russia had to industrialize, but where was the money to come from, after every kernel of grain had been sold and Russians were going hungry? Foreign credits or loans were out of the question. Weimar Germany, neither friend nor enemy, had enormous financial problems of its own, and other capitalist nations certainly would not help. Russia had no colonies to milk, and Marxism-Leninism forbade the plundering of the people. Thus the only solution was to abandon Marxism-Leninism.

Gosplan produced both baseline and optimum variants of the Five-Year Plan, and the Central Committee opted for the latter. It called for investing 24.8 billion rubles in industry, especially *heavy* industry. That was far beyond Russia's reach, and collectivization disrupted the country still further as workers left the factories to enforce it. The food supply was perilously low; undernourished workers produced less.

The Great Depression that began in 1929 had repercussions in the world's only socialist state. The price of raw materials dropped, and grain was already selling below the cost of production. After 1929 suppliers had to export more to obtain the same returns, but the market could not absorb a significant increase in any commodity, certainly not Russia's chief export, grain. The fact that imported machinery and other goods now cost less did not offset the reduction in income.

About 45 percent of the Soviet industrial budget went to 60 giant projects. The Communists planned to build huge hydroelectric complexes, immense automotive factories, enormous new cities.

A notorious example of this gigantomania, the Stalin White Sea–Baltic Canal, stretched 227 kilometers from Lake Onega to the White Sea through swamps, bogs, marshes, creeks, rivers, lakes, and forests. What better agency to carry out this awesome project than the OGPU, which had a vast reservoir of cheap labor? The labor came from the concentration camps, and was not just cheap but free and inexhaustible. The authorities had only to arrest more people. With no machinery available, the state called in the OGPU.

Like the slaves who constructed the Pyramids, Russian prisoners built the canal by hand, their only tools shovels, picks, and wheelbarrows. The waterway opened with great fanfare in 1933, Stalin and some of his associates cruising along in style. They only went part way, however, in a shallow-draft vessel; the canal was not deep or wide enough for larger boats and barges. Rebuilt in the 1960s, it remained useless. Maksim Gorky, putative friend of labor, praised the OGPU and its work, but neither he nor the press mentioned the 300,000 OGPU prisoners, 15 percent of them women, who died building Stalin's folly. Daring souls told this joke:

Q: Who built the Stalin White-Sea–Baltic Canal?
A: The left bank by people who asked such questions, the right bank by those who answered truthfully.

The Turksib Railway linking Central Asia and Siberia proved more successful; the tracks also lay on the bones of OGPU prisoners. The Dnepr River hydroelectric complex at Zaporozhye—relatively little prisoner labor was involved because foreign specialists were present—proved successful despite its incred-

"Greetings to the factory's shock-workers from us, the little children!"
Young Pioneer demonstration, 1931. (National Archives)

ibly high cost. The construction of metallurgical complexes at Sverdlovsk, Magnitogorsk, and Kuznetsk figured in the industrialization drive, as did huge automotive plants at Stalingrad, Harkov, and Cheliabinsk.

There would not be a second "Dizzy with Success" article. At the Sixteenth Party Congress, Stalin proposed to *increase* the optimum goals of the plan: Seventeen million tons of pig iron instead of ten million, 170,000 tractors instead of 55,000, and so on. All this to the tune of the slogans "Let's fulfill the Plan in four years!" and "Five in four!"

Hundreds of thousands of young people flocked to the industrial sites. They lived in tents while building new plants and cities such as Magnitogorsk for pay that was as meager as their diet. They worked overtime without extra pay, Saturdays for no pay, suffered deprivations, sickened, and died. Everyone complied with "decree time" (daylight-saving) in March 1930 and advanced the clocks one hour, and no one protested when the Kremlin ignored its promise to revert to standard time in October. (The state returned the lost hour in March *1991.*) The Communists failed, however, to institute a 10-day week, a French Revolutionary idea whose time had not come even in Stalinist Russia.

The state introduced rationing for all basic foods and many industrial products in 1929, but the privileged few could buy still scarce goods in "commercial" stores. From 1928 to 1930, the nominal wages of industrial workers rose 18 percent, but the cost of food rose 89 percent. The first Five-Year Plan did not reverse the decline in real wages of blue- and white-collar workers. Wages rose only during the second Five-Year Plan, stood at 60 percent of the 1928 level in 1940, and regained the 1928 level only in 1963.

RESULTS OF THE FIRST PLAN

The shortcomings, blunders, and brutality notwithstanding, Soviet Russia made great strides forward during the first Five-Year Plan, achieving a growth rate of about 13.8 percent. The Supreme Economic Council and Gosplan had foreseen a 280 percent increase in gross industrial output between 1928 and 1933. As it happened, output had just about doubled by the end of 1932; but heavy industry increased by 270 percent. The overall performance of the economy fell short of the planners' goals but was nevertheless remarkably good. The following figures reflect the performance:

	1928	*1932*	*[Planned]*
Pig iron	3.3 million tons	6.2	[10]
Steel	4.3 million tons	5.9	[10.4}
Rolled metal	3.4 million tons	4.4	[8.0]
Tractors (units)	1,300	50,600	[170,000]
Cement (barrels)	11 million	22.4	[41]
Superphosphates (tons)	182,000	612,000	[8–8.5 million]
Cotton cloth (meters)	2.678 billion	2.694	[4,588]
Woolen cloth (meters)	86.8 billion	88.7	[270–300]
Electricity (kwh)	5.0 billion	13.5	[22]
Automobiles (units)	800	23,900	—
Leather shoes (pairs)	58 million	86.9	—

May Day in Red Square, 1932. (National Archives)

Agricultural production suffered a net decline at a time when fewer farmers had to feed more people, and when the state was exporting huge supplies of grain. Reflecting more the influx from the countryside than natural increase, the urban segment grew from 17.9 percent of the total population in 1928 to 24 percent in 1932. This worsened the lot of a people with the lowest standard of living of any industrialized nation.

There had to be some dramatic signpost to mark the extraordinary journey on which the country had embarked: In January 1933 Stalin announced fulfillment of the Five-Year Plan after four years and three months. What had begun as an overly ambitious plan became, in 1930–1931, a crash program that paid almost no attention to rational allocation of scarce resources. But the Communists had laid the foundations of a mighty industrial base.

For a brief moment it appeared that Stalin might not be around to broadcast the momentous announcement. At a November 9, 1932, private dinner in the Kremlin, Nadezhda Alliluyeva, his second wife, raised the forbidden topic of the famine then raging across Ukraine and southern Russia, and she talked about the OGPU terror. She had embarrassed her husband in front of guests before; now she provoked a violent outburst that made her flee the room. Within moments she was dead.

The Communist party claimed that Nad-ezhda Alliluyeva shot herself with a Walther automatic while of unsound mind. Was it in fact true, as many people then and later suspected, that Stalin killed her? We shall probably never know; no dinner guest left any record. Stalin, Molotov, and Voroshilov immediately destroyed the physical evidence.

At the next meeting of the Politburo, a shaken Stalin offered his resignation. After a long moment of uncomfortable silence, the chief lackey, Molotov, assured him that he retained the party's confidence.

SUGGESTED ADDITIONAL READINGS

Davies, R. W. *The Socialist Offensive: The Collectivization of Soviet Agriculture, 1929–1930.* Cambridge, MA: Harvard University Press, 1980.

Gill, Graeme. *The Origins of the Stalinist Political System.* Cambridge: Cambridge University Press, 1990.

Hughes, James. *Stalin, Siberia, and the Crisis of the New Economic Policy.* New York: Cambridge University Press, 1991.

Hunter, Holland, and J. M. Szyrmer. *Faulty Foundations: Soviet Economic Policies, 1928–1940.* Princeton, NJ: Princeton University Press, 1992.

Merridale, Catherine. *Moscow Politics and the Rise of Stalin.* New York: St. Martin's Press, 1991.

Shearer, David R. *Industry, State, and Society in Stalin's Russia, 1926–1934.* Ithaca, NY: Cornell University Press, 1997.

Volkogonov, Dmitry A. *Stalin: Triumph and Tragedy.* New York: Grove Weidenfeld, 1991.

9

THE GREAT TERROR

Late in December 1917, Feliks Dzerzhinsky, head of the newly established Cheka, asked the Sovnarkom to create concentration camps to hold "violators of labor discipline, parasites, and people suspected of counterrevolutionary activity against whom we do not have sufficient evidence to punish through the legal process and whom even the strictest court would almost certainly acquit." Lenin and all the top Bolsheviks wholeheartedly endorsed the request. With the outlawing of the Kadet party the same month, the dissolution of the Constituent Assembly in January 1918, and the formation of the food-requisition detachments, this launched the Communist Terror.

In the spring of 1922 Lenin ordered a "proper soviet trial" of some SR party members for "counterrevolutionism." The verdict preordained, the court levied death sentences on the 15 defendants and the OGPU arrested their families as "relatives of enemies of the people." Even Maksim Gorky protested.

The Genoa Conference had just concluded. In a bid for respectability, the Kremlin did not immediately execute the condemned innocent, who sat in Moscow's Butyrka Prison until 1925. Then Stalin, one of Lenin's two best pupils (the other was Hitler), had them shot. The fate of the families is unknown.

Many such spectacles followed: The 1928 trial of "wreckers" in the Shakhty mines; the 1929 case of "saboteurs" in the transportation system; the 1930 trial of members of a mythical "Industrial party"; the 1933 case of the British Metro-Vickers engineers employed in Russia. Every political trial in Soviet history was a star-chamber farce.

SEVENTEENTH PARTY CONGRESS

When the Seventeenth Party Congress met in Moscow in January–February 1934, Stalin boasted that the Communist party had routed its enemies: There was "no one to fight." Molotov and Valeri Kuibyshev outlined the second Five-Year Plan's progress in glowing terms and received ovations.

But the delegates to this "Congress of Victors" knew the truth, or some of it. The human cost of collectivization and industrialization, and the 1932–1933 Ukraine–South Russia famine, had been beyond comprehension. Many Communists considered Stalin's own wife one of the victims; there was cautious talk of ousting him as general secretary. In guarded conversations in the corridors and on the streets, groups of delegates discussed replacing him with Sergei Kirov, the Leningrad party boss. Under Kirov they could relax, initiate reforms, perhaps revive the NEP. At a meeting in Sergo Ordzhonikidze's apartment several senior officials urged Kirov to declare his candidacy. He not only refused but at the next session lauded Stalin's leadership.

All was not lost; the rules required a separate vote for each Central Committee member. Of the 1,225 delegates with voting rights, 292 cast ballots against Stalin. That left him with fewer *positive* votes than anyone. Nervous electoral commission members consulted Central Committee Secretaries Molotov and Lazar Kaganovich, who decided to burn all but three negative ballots; there had been three against Kirov.

Unable to account for all 1,225 votes, the credentials committee simply reported without explanation that only 936 delegates had cast ballots. But those who had voted against Stalin, plus the 41 electoral commission members, Molotov, and Kaganovich—nearly 350 people—knew the extent of the protest. Stalin did not yet have the confidence to stage a trial and find 292 randomly selected delegates guilty of treason, nor could he simply order the OGPU to shoot that many and some more for good measure. But he always thought ahead.

Of the 1,961 Congress delegates (736 nonvoting), 1,108 would perish in the 1936–1938 purges, as would 33 electoral commission members. By early 1939 the secret police had arrested 110 of the 139 Central Committee members and candidate members elected at this Congress. Of those 110, it would execute 77. The rest, and many Congress delegates, would never emerge from the concentration camps. The well-known victims—who merit less sympathy than the forgotten ones—included Nikolai Krylenko, a great champion of terror; G. K. Ordzhonikidze; Valeri Kuibyshev; V. A. Antonov-Ovseyenko; A. I. Rykov. Also among those who perished were Generals Yan Gamarnik, M. N. Tukhachevsky, and V. K. Blücher. Nikolai Bukharin, who failed to speak out against terror when his voice might

have counted, would be a member of this doomed "Class of 1934." Mikhail Tomsky committed suicide on the eve of his arrest. Two chief executive officers of the Great Terror, NKVD (People's Commissariat of Internal Affairs, the secret police's new name) Commissars Genrikh Yagoda and Nikolai Yezhov, served on the "Congress of Victors" Central Committee, and they would soon fall, sacrifices to the horror they had served with pride.

THE KIROV MURDER

The first and most famous victim of the Terror was Sergei Kirov, the consensus—save for Stalin's dissent—heir-apparent. Many Communists saw him as a reformer. Born in 1886, he joined the Bolsheviks in 1904. He was a dynamic, flamboyant, true believer, the kind of man on whom the Bolsheviks pinned their hopes. He compiled a good record between 1917 and 1920 and became a full member of the Central Committee in 1923. To the delight of everyone save Zinoviev, he replaced Zinoviev as Leningrad party leader in 1926.

Kirov's rough proletarian demeanor was one key to his success. He associated with working-class people, drank vodka with uncomplicated pleasure, loved and understood machinery. That he was a Russian—his real name was Kostrikov—counted heavily with people who detested Stalin. It would not be easy to arrange Kirov's murder. Happy in Leningrad, where he thought he was safe, he rejected Stalin's unctuous entreaties to come to Moscow.

The first attempt on Kirov's life took place shortly after the Seventeenth Party Congress (1934). OGPU agents pulled two common criminals from prison, drove them to Kirov's apartment building, and promised to free them on delivery of Kirov's corpse. The men failed, and were executed—a fate that would also have awaited them had they succeeded. A second attempt also miscarried.

General Secretary Stalin lost patience. Apparently without consulting him, Stalin announced that Kirov would move to Moscow early in December 1934. That was intended to heighten the drama: On December 1, a nonentity named Leonid Nikolayev assassinated Kirov.

The police knew Nikolayev well. He had publicly expressed grievances against the party, and twice the police had apprehended him near Kirov carrying a concealed, loaded revolver. On both occasions they released him, obviously not on their own authority. No country had stricter gun-control laws or guarded its top officials more closely. Kirov never went anywhere without at least two bodyguards yet was alone when he was murdered. Contrary to standard procedure, there were guards only on the ground floor of party headquarters; the murder took place on the third floor. Higher authority had to have ordered removal of the guards from the upper floors; "higher" was Stalin.

At the Twentieth Party Congress in 1956, Nikita Khrushchev acknowledged that the Kirov murder demanded investigation, and five years later he said that one was under way. But the secret police, knowing Khrushchev's own bloody secrets, blackmailed him. He filled in only a few relatively minor blank spots before falling from power in 1964. His successors reclosed the books.

Contemporaries had no doubts. A famous *chastushka*—humorous verse—went:

Oh my cukes,
And tomatoes evermore,
Stalin nipped Kirov
Down by the cor-ri-dor.*

---

*From *Nepodtsenzurnaia russkaia chastushka* (New York: Russica Publishers, 1978). Used with the permission of Russica Publishers. English translation by W. M.

THE FIRST PHASE

Notified within minutes of Kirov's death, Stalin gathered up Molotov, Voroshilov, and Andrei A. Zhdanov—newest member of the inner circle—and left for Leningrad. Before boarding his special train, Stalin decreed a new procedure—text prepared weeks earlier—for the "adjudication" and disposition of political crimes. The investigation of persons accused of terrorism would be accelerated. Those found guilty and sentenced to death would not have the right to appeal. The NKVD would carry out death sentences immediately. The decree had no standing in law, even in Communist Russia. It was Stalin's personal order; he did not even hold a government position. Nevertheless, as Robert Conquest has written, it constituted a "Charter of Terror."

Within hours of the murder the chief of Kirov's bodyguard detachment died violently in what the death certificate described as a traffic accident. The pathologists who performed the autopsy revealed years later that the man had suffered severe head blows from a blunt metallic object. Khrushchev made this public at the 1961 Twenty-second Party Congress—and added that the assassins themselves had been killed soon thereafter.

The interrogation of Nikolayev—of whose guilt there is no question—was perfunctory. Stalin allegedly asked, "Why did you kill such a nice man?" Nikolayev and 13 NKVD agents who "failed to protect" Kirov were tried *in camera* on December 28, convicted, and shot.

To "avenge" Kirov's murder, the NKVD had already executed 37 "White Guards" in Leningrad, 33 in Moscow, 28 in Kiev. Mass deportations to Arctic camps and to Kolyma in the far northeast began in January 1935. Within a few months, more than 40,000 Leningrad residents disappeared into the camps, accused as "Trotskyites" and "rotten liberals" linked to the Kirov murder. In January 1935 a military court tried Zinoviev, Kamenev, and other "members" of a "Moscow Center" on charges of complicity in the assassination.

Andrei Vyshinsky prosecuted. As a Kerensky-regime official and Menshevik in 1917 he had ordered the arrest and trial of the "German spy Vladimir Ilich Ulyanov [Lenin]." In the 1920s, now a Bolshevik, he orchestrated the judicial persecution of many Mensheviks.

Kamenev declared on the stand that he had never heard of a "Moscow Center" but agreed that, insofar as it might have existed, he might have been responsible for it. Zinoviev made a similar nonsense plea; the Soviet press did not dare print a verbatim transcript. The court found the two guilty but awarded Zinoviev only ten years, Kamenev five. That amounted to exoneration; Prosecutor Vyshinsky prepared to die. As it happened, however, Stalin needed a lawyer who, though incompetent, had no scruples and no conscience.

THE OMINOUS LULL OF 1935–1936

The bungled "Moscow Center" case necessitated reevaluation of NKVD procedures and called for construction of a rationale for what Stalin had in mind. The anticipated wave of public revulsion over Kirov's murder had not materialized; thus it was not yet feasible to kill hundreds of thousands of enemies and deport millions to the Gulag—the Soviet concentration camps—without explanation. If demand did not exist, it would have to be manufactured.

The international situation complicated matters. The Soviet Communists were initially contemptuous of their close moral kinfolk, Hitler and the Nazis, who came to power in Germany in January 1933. After a few months of such lunatics, Stalin and his associates reasoned, the German people would sweep out the Nazis and bring in the German Communists, who were on the Kremlin payroll. That

remained a fantasy, and German domestic and foreign policy began to take on increasingly menacing hues which would, in turn, color the Stalin Terror.

That other Lenin pupil, Adolf Hitler, set an example for Stalin. In the July 1934 "Night of the Long Knives" Hitler personally supervised the murder of 77 of his main enemies, including some top Nazis.

TRIAL OF THE "TROTSKYITE–ZINOVIEVITE UNITED CENTER"

After the 1935 Kamenev–Zinoviev comedy (no blood was spilled), a special security commission that included Stalin, Zhdanov, Vyshinsky, and Nikolai Yezhov—NKVD boss as of September 1936—furiously rewrote the script. Then the Soviet state re-indicted Zinoviev, Kamenev, and 14 others for complicity in the Kirov murder; plotting to kill Stalin and other leaders; conspiring with foreign powers; and assorted other crimes. The NKVD held the accused incommunicado.

The charade began in Moscow on August 19, 1936. Some independent foreign observers were present, but the Soviet "spectators" were NKVD employees. Prosecutor Vyshinsky and the judges badgered and humiliated the defendants, denied them the right to have counsel or to cross-examine witnesses, and allowed them to communicate only with interrogators and jailors.

The evidence consisted of pretrial depositions and the defendants' confessions in open court. Only one minor glitch disrupted Vyshinsky's progress: A former Trotskyite denied membership in an organization that did not exist, only to have his fellow defendants contradict him.

Save for scriptwriters and performers, the apparently uncoerced admissions of guilt shocked everyone. Having no uncensored information, many Soviet citizens believed the confessions genuine. Outside the USSR, some well-meaning but hopelessly naive observers allowed as how, although the facts did not accord with the testimony, the defendants were no doubt guilty of *something* and had confessed in order to earn lighter sentences. Communists who loved Lenin but hated Stalin said the accused were performing a last, heroic service to Bolshevism.

No one seems to have suspected torture, but NKVD interrogators deprived the defendants of sleep for days and even weeks. Invariably effective, this left no marks; the jailers were not to blame if the prisoners refused to sleep. If even that failed, the interrogators could almost always obtain a confession by threatening to harm a defendant's family. And the NKVD had perfected new pharmacological combinations.

The spectacle ended on August 24 with guilty verdicts. Within hours, deep within the cellars of NKVD headquarters on Moscow's Lubyanka Square, executioners shot the condemned men in the back of the head, a Soviet Communist trademark; France and Germany preferred decapitation. A ghoulish chorus of approval welled up, Stalin's foreign apologists joining in.

TRIAL OF THE "PARALLEL CENTER"

In the second infernal circus, 17 "members" of a "Parallel Center"—or "Anti-Soviet Trotskyite Center"—stood in the dock in January 1937. Least significant of the trials, it was designed as a reminder. Four defendants were well known. Karl Radek, who had denounced Zinoviev and Kamenev, now stood accused of making common cause with them. Grigory Sokolnikov had accepted the defeat of Trotsky, his idol, and had subsequently served in high-level posts. State Bank Director Grigori Pyatakov had also

sided with Trotsky; the party expelled and then readmitted him after he recanted. The former Trotskyite Leonid Serebryakov had been a Central Committee secretary.

Prosecutor Vyshinsky served up the familiar charges of sabotage, "wrecking," conspiracy to assassinate Soviet leaders, plotting with foreign governments. The prominent defendants had no defense counsel, and the lawyers who "represented" the others took their cues from Vyshinsky. The accused testified against themselves. Promised lenient treatment, Radek confessed to all charges and added colorful details, none true. This made the state's case against Radek himself, his co-defendants, and scores of people still at liberty.

With the eager cooperation of Radek and Pyatakov, Vyshinsky established a link between Trotsky and Rudolf Hess, a member of Hitler's inner circle. The prosecutor said this proved that they had conspired to divide the USSR among Germany and Japan. Vyshinsky demonstrated to the court's satisfaction that the defendants had indeed organized the acts of "wrecking" and sabotage to which they had confessed. He introduced into evidence a letter to *Pravda* published on January 28, 1937, the next to last day of the trial: A young railway switch operator claimed to have lost her legs averting a train wreck the defendants tried to stage.

At 7:15 P.M. on January 29, the judges retired to deliberate. They returned to the courtroom at 3:00 the next morning and sentenced Pyatakov, Serebryakov, and 11 junior defendants to death. Sokolnikov, Radek, and one other received 10-year sentences. The last of the small fry got 8 years. Radek glanced at his fellow defendants, grinned foolishly, and shrugged his shoulders as if to say, "You never know!" His feelings about his daughter's arrest shortly before his own trial remain unknown. The NKVD sent her to the Gulag as a "member of the family of a 'repressed' person."

Radek's own term in an Arctic camp ended in 1939 with his death in unexplained circumstances.

THE DECAPITATION OF THE MILITARY

On June 1, 1937, the Red Army reported the suicide of General Yan Gamarnik, party Central Committee member, head of the Red Army political administration, editor of the newspaper *Red Star*. Gamarnik had lost his job as first deputy commissar of defense three weeks earlier, and *Pravda* claimed he killed himself because he had become "entangled ... with anti-Soviet elements and evidently feared that he would be arrested."

On June 11 the Kremlin revealed the arrest of eight senior commanders on charges of treason. The next day, the press reported their trial, conviction, and execution.

Even Hitler had shot only a couple of generals and Captain Ernst Röhm. Stalin's unprecedented assault on the Soviet officer corps became an unimaginably bloody purge. About 55 percent of the uniformed-services officers would be imprisoned during the Terror; thousands would be executed in 1937–1938. The mass killing did not end until the June 1941 German invasion, and even then an occasional trial showed who was boss.

Believing himself threatened by the senior officers, especially Marshal M. N. Tukhachevsky, Stalin tore the heart out of the armed forces. In stark contrast to Stalin's criminal blunders and insubordination in the Civil War, those who fell in the 1937 purge had good or even distinguished records. Several were first-class strategic planners, others excellent tacticians. But Stalin and his mediocrities claimed they had conspired with the Wehrmacht— German armed forces—to enthrall the Soviet Union. A culpably naive Prague government sent the Kremlin some documents that Stalin's

Marshal Tukhachevsky and his wife, Nina. (Tukhachevsky family archives)

own agents had forged. The papers "proved" Soviet commanders were plotting with Trotsky to weaken Soviet defenses and pave the way for a German invasion.

As even a cursory glance at *Mein Kampf* revealed, every day Hitler remained in power increased the risk of an armed conflict between the USSR and Germany. Belatedly realizing that the Nazis would not fall under the weight of their own filth, Stalin sent a personal envoy to Berlin in December 1936.

Stalin proposed an insanely high-risk deal. The Soviet Union would continue to supply Germany with raw materials at low cost, and would refrain from undertaking any defense measures that might appear to threaten Germany. Specifically, the USSR would not build up its western defenses. Sworn to defend the country, many Red Army commanders indeed opposed this policy. None, so far as we know, conspired with Germany.

TRIAL OF THE "RIGHT TROTSKYITE CENTER"

The Great Terror ended with the March 1938 trial of 21 defendants. Included were the top Old Bolsheviks Nikolai Bukharin, Aleksei Rykov, and Nikolai Krestinsky. Also in the dock was a minor Old Bolshevik, Genrikh Yagoda, who had headed the NKVD at the time of the Kirov assassination—in the wake of which Stalin had accused the organization of being four years behind in its work. The last well-known defendant was Christian Rakovsky, a Bulgarian in the Soviet diplomatic service. Among the obscure officials on trial were a couple of Uzbek Communists, the first non-Europeans to appear in these charades. Three apolitical physicians rounded out the group.

Stalin and his people now jammed the last pieces of the puzzle into place. Though leaders of the former "Right" opposition, Bukharin and Rykov had once made common cause

with Trotsky and the "Left" and were thus guilty on both counts, or "deviations." And Radek's testimony tied them to the Tukhachevsky–Nazi "plot."

All the accused entered guilty pleas until Krestinsky said, "I am innocent." This was not according to the script Prosecutor Vyshinsky and Chief Judge Ulrikh had written and Stalin had edited. Questioned about his confession, Krestinsky acknowledged it; he was withdrawing it. Prosecution and judges called a recess.

When the proceedings resumed 20 minutes later, Vyshinsky turned to a minor defendant and elicited testimony incriminating Krestinsky. The latter promptly reaffirmed his innocence and said he had lied during the interrogation because "If I were to say what I am saying today—that [my confession] was not in accordance with the facts—my declaration would not reach the leaders." The judges ordered him to sit down.

The next day, Vyshinsky dealt with other defendants in the morning session. Following the afternoon break, he asked Krestinsky whether he would cease playing games, tell the truth, and reaffirm his confession made during the pretrial investigation. Krestinsky did so. Why then had he lied in court? A "mechanical" declaration of innocence growing out of shame. At long last facing up to the error of his ways, he confessed to "treason and treachery." Western observers thought Krestinsky listless, but he bore no visible marks of mistreatment. The jailers had warned him that he was placing his family in grave jeopardy. He was now tame.

Rykov confessed to most charges, lulling the prosecution into a false sense of security. By accident or design, however, Lenin's successor as Sovnarkom Chairman began to confuse details, and that threw Vyshinsky off stride. Rykov denied knowing anything about "wrecking" in the livestock industry and refused to admit specific acts of espionage and sabotage.

The best-known actor, Bukharin, needed no physical persuasion. Facing Vyshinsky on March 5, he believed he understood what Stalin was doing. He may even have realized that he and his fellow Old Bolsheviks were reaping exactly what they had sown. He had agreed before trial to plead guilty to all charges, but on reading the script he changed his mind. He denied plotting to assassinate Lenin, nor had had he committed sabotage and espionage. Like Rykov, he accepted general responsibility for "opposition": By failing to commit himself without reservation to Stalin, he had encouraged opposition movements and lent them respectability.

When Bukharin denied knowledge of plans to assassinate Kirov, Vyshinsky blundered in turning to Genrikh Yagoda for assistance. Yagoda admitted having "given instructions" about Kirov to a high-ranking Leningrad NKVD official. Was the "Bukharin–Rykov bloc" involved? Yagoda requested permission not to answer; they had not rehearsed this. Vyshinsky dropped it too late: Yagoda had shed some light on the Kirov murder. Such "instructions" could only have come from Stalin.

Vyshinsky then tried to rehabilitate the charge that Bukharin had schemed to kill Lenin, calling two SR party members as witnesses. But not everyone could master the required theatrical techniques, and non-Communists were at a special disadvantage because they had never been subject to party discipline. The SRs repeatedly stumbled over the truth as they remembered it. There had indeed been a plot to kill Lenin, but no one ever mentioned Bukharin.

The Bukharin-Rykov-Krestinsky trial involved so many defendants accused of so many fantastic crimes that Solomon himself would have been hard-pressed to sort it all out. Espionage, "wrecking" in food-processing and transportation, treason, espionage, conspiracy to murder, and other bizarre allegations were all mixed in together. The NKVD charged the

three physicians with the murders of Kuibyshev, Vyacheslav Menzhinsky (Yagoda's predecessor at the OGPU-NKVD), Maksim Gorky, and Gorky's son—all on Yagoda's orders. As the circus neared its climax, Vyshinsky called for 19 of the 21 defendants to be "shot like dirty dogs!"

Stalin slept during the day and worked at night; that is why the verdicts came in at ungodly hours. At 4:00 A.M. on March 13, the judges filed back into the courtroom. They found all 21 defendants guilty on all counts. They sentenced 18, including Lenin's old comrades-in-arms Bukharin, Rykov, and Krestinsky, to death. On March 15, 1938, *Pravda* announced the executions.

Lenin's party had devoured its personnel. Leninism lived on in its offspring, Stalinism.

THE GREAT TERROR IN RETROSPECT

Responsible historians agree that General Secretary Stalin was neither "ill" nor "mad." He does, however, seem to have been afflicted by *paranoia,* which the World Health Organization defines as

a rare chronic psychosis in which logically constructed systematized delusions have developed gradually without concomitant hallucinations or the schizophrenic type of disordered thinking. The delusions are mostly of grandeur, persecution or somatic abnormality.*

Wrapped in his carapace of insecurity, Stalin fashioned bits and pieces of reality into a distorted image that only he understood. Accidents did not happen in his world: A crop fail-

---

*Mental Disorders: Glossary and Guide to Their Classification in Accordance with the Ninth Revision of the International Classification of Diseases, Geneva: World Health Organization, 1978, p. 31, cited in Anthony Storr, Feet of Clay. Saints, Sinners, and Madmen: A Study of Gurus, New York: Free Press, 1996, p. 170.

ure, machinery breakdown, mine explosion, train derailment, tank gunner's miss, typographical error, a badly-suppressed cough at an official function—nothing was inadvertent. Stalin alone could interpret hidden meanings, determine motive, get to the bottom of the situation. He invariably found treachery.

Incapable of surrounding himself with psychologically healthy people, he sought out men—he and Hitler had all-male entourages—whose pathology enabled them to bear and even take pleasure in his excesses, to suffer whatever fate he decreed and thank him on their way down. He arrested many of his own relatives, those of his two wives, and his closest colleagues. He watched like a hawk for signs of disloyalty on the part of those whose loved ones his secret police snatched away. The former seminary student put his disciples to the test of Abraham: Would they flinch? To a man they did not. Some even applauded when their family members were taken away and rushed to disown them. Would such men not betray *him* at the first opportunity? He detested them and planned to slaughter every last one.

Nothing lies beneath the lowest depths. It was not enough, the satirists Ilf and Petrov wrote, to love Soviet power: *It* had to love *you.* Soviet power was Lenin and Stalin and Bukharin and all the Old Bolsheviks plus the other genius of 1917, Trotsky. Together they created the system, the machine, that Stalin perfected and guided to peak performance. How many did they kill one way or another? The Holocaust in Russia antedated the one in the Third Reich and took as many as 40 million and perhaps as many as 60 million lives.*

SUGGESTED ADDITIONAL READINGS

CONQUEST, ROBERT. *The Great Terror: A Reassessment.* New York: Oxford University Press, 1990.

RAZGON, LEV. *True Stories: The Memoirs of Lev Razgon.* Dana Point, CA: Ardis, 1997.

SUDOPLATOV, PAVEL, and ANATOLI SUDOPLATOV. *Special Tasks.* Boston: Little, Brown, 1994.

SHENTALINSKY, VITALY. *Arrested Voices: Resurrecting the Disappeared Writers of the Soviet Regime.* New York: Free Press, 1996.

SOLZHENITSYN, ALEKSANDR. *The Gulag Archipelago, 1918–1956,* 3 vols. New York: Harper & Row, 1973–1978.

VAKSBERG, ARKADY. *Stalin's Prosecutor: The Life of Andrei Vyshinsky.* New York: Grove Weidenfeld, 1990.

---

*For a much lower estimate of the number of victims, and a different view of Vyshinsky, see Robert W. Thurston, *Life and Terror in Stalin's Russia, 1934–1941,* New Haven, CT: Yale University Press, 1996, pp. 5–9, 107–11, 119–21, 125, 137–40, 138–50. Thurston concludes (p. 227) that "Stalin was not guilty of mass first-degree murder from 1934–1941 and did not plan or carry out a systematic campaign to crush the nation."

10

THE OTHER RUSSIA
OF THE 1930s

In Russia in those years they divided people into three categories: Those who had
been in prison; those in prison; and those who would go to prison. The Terror
grabbed even workers who did their jobs and kept any doubts to themselves, and
peasants who had gone docilely into the *kolhozes*. If such people were in less
danger than others it was only because there were more of them. The Communists
exalted them in propaganda but forced them to work long hours in wretched
conditions for miserable wages and live in squalor. People whispered that VKP—
initials of the "All-Union Communist Party"—stood for *Vtoroye Krepostnoye
Pravo*, "Second Serfdom." No one said this aloud. It was a time, Anna Akhmatova
wrote, when they would interrogate your shadow.

THE FAMINE OF 1932–1933

No one joked about the famine. The 1931 autumn harvest was meager, that of spring 1932
sparse. In the summer of 1932 the situation approached catastrophe in parts of the country,
notably Ukraine, the North Caucasus, and the
lower Volga. But many grain-producing areas
enjoyed more or less normal conditions, and
the state reserves destined for export, or long-
term storage, could have compensated for the
shortfall. The Kremlin, however, refused to intervene. Far from reducing the quotas, it *increased* them. And there would be no aid for
the worst-hit areas of the country.

Molotov, Kaganovich, and other high-ranking officials conducted punitive expeditions
into the affected regions. On their orders the
OGPU summarily executed scores of local
party bosses, *kolhoz* managers, and peasants
whom informers and local secret police agents

had singled out as troublemakers. This often
meant that they had begged for food for their
districts. The state had contracted to supply
foreign purchasers with grain; failure to deliver cost Russia substantial hard-currency revenues. That would impede industrialization,
and so Stalin and his associates decided to continue exporting even as Soviet citizens were
starving to death. Had this threatened to become a disaster on the 1921 scale, it would
have been impossible to keep it secret, and
markets for Soviet grain would have softened.
But the authorities recognized the dimensions
of the problem and predicted it would ease in
1934. The OGPU restricted travel into the
famine areas, allowing in only citizens who had
legitimate business.

Almost nothing appeared in the foreign
press, but some journalists suspected a cover-
up. One American correspondent who visited
Ukraine in October 1933 after travel restric-

tions eased estimated the death toll from starvation at five million to six million. Publication of his belated report caused a sensation; Western governments asked questions. Mikhail Kalinin, the figurehead president, responded angrily: There was no famine, and the millions of Ukrainians said to have died, he insisted, had never existed.

In 1934, the first spring vegetables eased the crisis, and August–September brought a good harvest. Once again Stalin had been proved right; his reputation for infallibility soared. In a poem that would be published only decades later, Osip Mandelstam immortalized the victims of modern history's first human-made famine in a poem that concludes,

On the felted land starving peasants
Stand at the gate, but do not touch the latch.

SECOND FIVE-YEAR PLAN

The Seventeenth Party Conference of January–February 1932 ordered Gosplan to give capitalism the coup de grâce: The country had to complete collectivization, accelerate the technological revolution, achieve faster growth in heavy industry. The 1934 "Congress of Victors" approved the Gosplan project, one of the most grandiose in history.

Somehow they did it. By 1937 more than 80 percent of industrial production came from factories and enterprises that were new or rebuilt since 1928. Investment in capital projects of all types jumped from 50.5 billion rubles in the first Five-Year Plan to 137.5 billion in the second. The figures are even more impressive for investment in industry: 25 billion rubles in the first Plan, 65.8 billion in the second. In the second Five-Year Plan the state invested 53.4 billion rubles in heavy industry; approximately 4,500 new factories went into production. There was, people said, all the steel you could eat.

	Percentage increase		
	1932	*1937*	*1932–1937*
Pig iron (millions of tons)	6.2	14.5	235
Steel (millions of tons)	5.9	17.7	300
Rolled metal (millions of tons)	4.4	13.0	295
Coal (millions of tons)	64.4	128.0	199
Hydroelectric energy (billions of kwh)	13.5	36.2	270

Russia's historic backwardness, and the tense international situation, relegated the consumer-goods sector to a distant second place in the first two Five-Year Plans. Usable resources were scarce, capital limited, skilled labor in short supply, technology inferior. To compete, the USSR had to extract more natural resources faster; produce steel; build machine-tool, armaments, chemical, and automotive industries; manufacture agricultural implements. There would be little left over for food-processing, textiles, or housing. Russia might go hungry, her people wear rags and live in impossibly crowded conditions, but she would produce steel or die.

The Communists collectivized 93 percent of the farms by 1937, and as a result gross annual crop yields were substantially lower than those of 1913. Grain production declined, meat production remained at low levels, and vegetables and fruit were scarce.

On April 1, 1937, Stalin proclaimed the second Five-Year Plan fulfilled. Despite incredible hardships and sacrifice, Russia had indeed achieved many of the most important goals and tasks the party laid down. Peasant Russia was on her way to becoming a great industrial power.

STAKHANOVISM

During a 5-hour, 45-minute shift in the Donbas on the night of August 30–31, 1935, a worker named Aleksei Stakhanov allegedly mined 102 tons of coal, 14 times the norm.

With the USSR in the middle of a Five-Year Plan whose success depended on a dramatic increase in labor productivity, the Communist party pounced on Stakhanov's feat to justify the extremely high quotas it had set.

Stakhanov used a specially built pneumatic drill and had several helpers, and party officials and the press were present to witness and record the event—a sure sign there was less to it than met the eye. But Stalin quickly launched a campaign to raise labor-productivity goals still higher. A "Stakhanovite movement" took shape overnight and a conference of "Stakhanovite workers" took place in November 1935. Addressing it, Stalin ordered Soviet workers to emulate Stakhanov, never mentioning the special conditions of the "record." He accused bureaucrats of stifling worker initiative—this was ominous—and the planning agencies of setting industrial goals too low. Up went the quotas.

The aggressive support for "Stakhanovism" reflected shifting values and priorities. Having come to power on a wave of leveling and egalitarianism, the Communists now reintroduced competition and rewards. Stakhanovite collective farmers raised more crops, locomotive engineers increased the average speed of their trains, steelworkers produced more steel, teachers taught more students better, fishermen caught more fish. Officialdom and the media exhorted the work force to emulate the superachievers. Stakhanovites received highly publicized cash awards.

The propaganda machine called these workers exemplars of the "new Soviet man," an unselfish, heroic worker. In fact, fellow workers often beat up and sometimes even killed the zealots, because of whom they all had to work harder, longer, and for lower wages. A famous joke was set at a *kolhoz* awards ceremony: For her exemplary service, a milkmaid won a trip to Moscow. Polite applause from the *kolhozniks*. A tractor driver got a new suit for putting in 100-hour weeks at harvest-time.

Languid clapping. The *kolhoz* boss who directed these efforts received an autographed set of Stalin's works. After an uncomfortable silence a voice called out, "Serves the sonofabitch right!"

A character in one of Mikhail Zoshchenko's short stories demands, "Sleep quickly—somebody needs the pillow!"

Sham notwithstanding, labor productivity increased. The Communists claimed an 82 percent jump—they had projected 63 percent—over the Five-Year Plan's four years and three months. Western experts set the annual rate at 8 to 10 percent, but that was a feat no capitalist country matched.

THIRD FIVE-YEAR PLAN

Moscow mocked the West's Great Depression, which appeared to ease only in Germany after the Nazis came to power and began preparing for war. The Soviets advertised in the West for technicians, engineers, skilled and even unskilled workers. They made a special effort to reach African-Americans, a few hundred of whom actually went to the Soviet Union. There was no unemployment in the land of communism, the advertisements declared, no bread lines, no plowing under of crops or slaughtering of animals to raise farm prices; nor any mention of the 1932–1933 famine in Ukraine.

At their Eighteenth Party Congress in March 1939, the Communists promised to invest more in the consumer-goods sector during the third Five-Year Plan. They allocated funds to construct 35 million square meters of living space, but even doubling that figure would have left the Soviet people the worst-housed in Europe. Nadezhda Mandelstam, a writer and the wife of the poet Osip Mandelstam, recalled how people would commit crimes for those "wonderful, precious twelve and a half square meters of living space."

Lenin had decreed that minimum. In the five largest cities in 1939, people did not have half that.

The regime continued to place overwhelming emphasis on heavy industry. Production of pig iron and steel once again increased dramatically, and the Soviets took more ore out of the mines. The chemical and automotive industries developed in a series of great leaps, but because the starting point had been so low the country remained undersupplied. The explosive international situation diverted funds and resources from the civilian economy to the military from 1936 onward. The outbreak of war in 1941 interrupted the third Five-Year Plan.

The armaments industry took precedence over all others, but the Terror slowed progress even here. On the Kremlin's orders, the NKVD continued to imprison and sometimes execute key engineers, designers, production managers, technicians, and others on trumped-up charges. A few prominent prisoners—including the airframe designer Andrei Tupolev and the jet propulsion pioneer Sergei Korolyov—labored in minimum-security prisons called *sharashkas*.

THE 1936 CONSTITUTION

By 1935 the public sector had almost totally replaced the private. Only a statistically insignificant number of private farms remained in operation, and nonagricultural private enterprise had almost ceased to exist. Everyone worked for the Communist party's state.

Stalin wanted a new Constitution that would reflect "socialism's victory." A 31-member commission presented a draft in the spring of 1936; already marked—as he knew—for elimination, Nikolai Bukharin wrote the section on civil rights. The leadership invited public discussion; millions of citizens "debated." It was another mass comedy.

The Eighth (Extraordinary) Congress of Soviets unanimously approved the "Stalin Constitution" on December 5, 1936. The architect of the Great Terror boasted that Russia had the "most democratic Constitution in the world." On paper that may have been true, but the paper might just as well have been sand: The vaunted civil and human rights simply did not exist. Through his personal extended staff and the NKVD, Stalin ruled as an autocrat. His word was law.

As empty as the civil and human rights provisions was the Constitution's guarantee of the right of secession to the 11 constituent republics: Russia, Ukraine, Uzbekistan, Belarus, Tajikistan, Kazakhstan, Georgia, Armenia, Turkmenistan, Kyrgyzstan, Azerbaijan. Entering against their will after the Soviet conquests of 1940–1941 were Karelo-Finlandia, Latvia, Estonia, Lithuania, and Moldavia or Moldova.

THE MISSING CENSUS OF 1937

In 1926 the first reliable Soviet census put the population at 147,028,000. According to demographic projections, by 1937 it would exceed 180 million; but the January 1937 census counted barely 150 million. It provided a photograph of human shadows no one cast, a trace of the millions of victims of collectivization and famine and Terror through December 1936, when the Great Terror had barely begun.

No one had questioned the 1926 census, and so, if the Kremlin were to release the 1937 count, the world would know that the rumors of millions of deaths during collectivization, the famine of 1932–1933, and the Great Terror were true. Communist rule could not have survived such a disclosure. On September 26, 1937, *Pravda* charged that "extremely crude violations of the most elementary principles of statistical science" rendered the January survey invalid. There would be a recount. Fifteen officials of the Central Statistical Bureau, and hundreds of minor bureaucrats and census-takers, took the "Stalin Road" to the Gulag.

In 1939 the terrified bureaucracy concocted a sham count and reported a population of 170.2 million. An increase of 18 million to 20 million people in two years was not, in the normal course of events, possible. Not even Stalin could orchestrate that kind of activity. But capitalist enemies had to understand that Russia had a large and rapidly growing population.

It was questionable whether the world would accept Stalin's statistics as gullibly as it did his verdicts. But he had the power to attack the low Soviet birthrate. When Communist Russia decriminalized abortion in 1920, only a few obscure specialists pondered the potential effect on industrialization and national defense. But analysis of the 1926 census data—long before the horrors of 1929–1938—had shown that trouble lay ahead, and in 1928 the state imposed certain restrictions: Women had to fill out a detailed questionnaire that touched on personal conduct and pay a small fee for the abortion. The birthrate did not rise.

In May 1936 *Pravda* published the draft text of a law banning all save therapeutic abortions. In response to the newspaper's call for a nationwide discussion, letters came in criticizing women who regarded the "issue of child-bearing as a personal matter." But other citizens raised objections to a ban on abortion. Many women of child-bearing age complained of the housing situation, the lack of day-care centers, and fathers who decamped.

Enraged by the bold criticism, the Communist party-state terminated discussion and promulgated the new law on June 9, 1936. The birthrate soared in 1937 and remained high until the war. The numbers of illegal abortions and deaths from such procedures shot up; the country experienced an increase in chronic female diseases and secondary sterility.

EDUCATION AND SCIENCE

In the 1920s and 1930s, the Communists made considerable progress in education. The aggregate literacy rate, 51 percent in 1926, rose to 81 percent in 1939. The increase among females, reflecting the special attention paid rural areas and Muslim lands, was particularly striking.

At the start of the period there was a shortage of teachers. Primary and secondary education was not a glamorous field, and only a tiny minority of university graduates—whose diplomas carried greater prestige than those awarded by the teachers' colleges—entered it. Between 1934 and 1938, 55 percent of Moscow University graduates went into industry; 10 percent into the Commissariat of Agriculture or related agencies; and 17 percent into primary and secondary education. The remainder went elsewhere in the bureaucracy, higher education, and research.

Disparaged by sophisticates, the teachers' colleges in fact provided a good—if in the social sciences and humanities tendentious—education and splendid professional training. By the mid-1930s the colleges had produced thousands of young teachers who, though they were indoctrinated in Marxism-Leninism, could nevertheless educate children. In the natural and physical sciences, and mathematics, they had only to nod politely in the direction of official ideology; that was yet another reason why those fields were popular with the best pupils. In the humanities and social sciences, ideologues rewrote textbooks, monitored teachers closely, and followed extremely strict hiring procedures.

What was true in the schools held in higher education and research. Entire disciplines—economics, history, sociology, anthropology, political science—deteriorated. In these and many other fields, the Great Terror dealt the universities and research institutes a devastating blow because the Stalinists, not without reason, considered them hotbeds of opposition: Trotsky, Zinoviev, Radek, Bukharin, and some other anti-Stalinists had been especially popular among professors and students. In May 1935 Stalin set up a special commission to review higher education. Under Zhdanov's leadership, the commission conducted a massive purge and sent thousands of people to the Gulag. It closed many institutes and laboratories.

A turning point came in 1935. Until then the party-state had given more support to genuine scientists than to impostors known chiefly for obedience. The second Five-Year Plan awarded the Academy of Sciences—the least "bolshevized" professional group—a 676 percent budget increase and earmarked the 63.765 million rubles for genuine research. But in 1935 the purgers began to apply an ideological test not merely to individuals but also to disciplines. A severe assault caused enormous damage in biology and the agricultural sciences and destroyed genetics. Many prominent scientists, some of world caliber, vanished into the Gulag.

The main culprit—never forgetting who captained the ship—was Trofim Lysenko, a Ukrainian tinkerer with a spotty education, awesome ignorance in every field he touched, and the good fortune to be available when the Communists needed a crackpot. Lysenko was to science what Andrei Vyshinsky was to justice; he argued that acquired characteristics are heritable. If the environment produces a change, the offspring of the species in question will reproduce it. Properly controlled vernalization, for example, could turn winter wheat into spring wheat. Lysenko promised to turn rye into wheat, pine into spruce.

The Communists jettisoned the genetic theories of heredity worked out by Gregor Mendel, August Weismann, and T. H. Morgan. They turned the clock back to J.-B. Lamarck, who had claimed that changes undergone by an individual as a result of its habits or environment could be passed on to its offspring over time. Science had long since abandoned this position, but the Soviets were determined to demonstrate communism's ability to control the environment, and to reshape humankind.

Lysenko was not uniformly successful. Some of his own supporters ended up in the Gulag, and the state did not silence all his critics. But one of his most prominent adversaries suffered a tragic fate: Nikolai Vavilov, world-renowned director of the Genetics Institute, lost his position, then his freedom, and perished in the Gulag in 1943.

THE ARTS

Dmitri Shostakovich composed his somber Fifth Symphony in 1937. At the first performance in Leningrad, the city that had suffered more than any other from the Great Terror, many people in the audience wept openly. A few may have thought of Franz Kafka's words: "There is infinite hope, but not for us."

Shostakovich was fortunate to be alive to compose that musical tribute—as he later acknowledged—to the victims. Early in 1936, Stalin attended a performance of Shostakovich's opera *Lady Macbeth of the Mtsensk District* and did not like what he heard. On January 28 a *Pravda* editorial, "Muddle Instead of Music," attacked the opera and accused Shostakovich of being an "enemy of the people." People so labeled usually disappeared. The inquisitors hurled the fatuous charge of "bourgeois formalism" at Shostakovich and other composers, writers, sculptors, choreographers, and painters, and assailed them for their "insincerity." But even after the arrest and execution of his friend M. N. Tukhachevsky, Shostakovich survived.

The Soviet Communists invented a literary genre and gave it the nonsensical name "socialist realism." Calling the Stalin dictatorship "socialism," they ordered writers to glorify it. Heroic characters had to be Communists or occasionally non-party people who owed their good qualities to "soviet power." The writers were to depict all socially unacceptable behavior—first and foremost, independent thinking—as a relic of tsarist times.

Under these circumstances, little literature of lasting merit appeared in print, but a treasure trove piled up in the NKVD archives. The secret political police came for the poetic genius and clairvoyant Nikolai Kluyev on February 2, 1934. As he told the investigators in between torture sessions, his "Burned Ruins" expressed his horror at collectivization's destruction of the "foundations and beauty of that Russian popular life of which I was the bard." In the "Song of Gamayun," Kluyev foretold the destruction of the Aral Sea, the ruination of Ukraine, and the desecration of the North. In chillingly powerful verse, he prophesied the polluting of the Irtysh and Yenisei rivers and Lake Baikal. Like a latter-day Nostrodamus he penned his vision—more than 50 years before the event—of the Chernobyl catastrophe: "Then the Star Wormwood [Chernobyl] fell."

In 1934 the Russian-Jewish poet Osip Mandelstam wrote a devastatingly witty caricature of Stalin and read it at a private gathering. It quickly made its way around Moscow and Leningrad in typescript. The NKVD arrested Mandelstam, interrogated him, then placed him under house arrest—in the town of Voronezh in south-central Russia, where his wife voluntarily joined him. Having no means of support and forced to rely on handouts from friends, the two sometimes went to Moscow and Leningrad and remained there several days. The NKVD thus had a pretext to rearrest the poet.

Not knowing of the caricature, Nikolai Bukharin had made official enquiries when Mandelstam was first arrested, but when he became aware of the ramifications he washed his hands of the matter. On May 1, 1938, a few weeks after Bukharin's execution, the NKVD again took Mandelstam into custody. He died in the Gulag in eastern Siberia on December 27, 1938.

The state-sanctioned murder of such people as Kluyev, Mandelstam, and Boris Pilnyak, together with the silencing of Boris Pasternak and Anna Akhmatova and Marina Tsvetayeva, set back civilization in Russia. These were only a few of the well-known victims.

The new barbarism demanded conformity rather than talent. The most popular conformist was Nikolai Ostrovsky, a personally decent man whose polyarthritis kept him confined to his bed; his banal *The Tempering of the Steel* sold five million copies. The hero, Pavel Korchagin, overcomes wounds and illness to participate in the building of a socialist society. As his native town survives war, foreign invasion, civil war, banditry, and the wanton violence of nationalist gangs, so Korchagin triumphs over cruel circumstance.

Typical of "socialist realism" was Mikhail Sholokhov's portrayal of collectivization in *Virgin Soil Upturned.* An unworthy successor to *Quiet Flows the Don,* the new work did catch some of the spirit of the time. Other popular but eminently forgettable collectivization novels were Fyodor Panferov's *Whetstone* and Vladimir Stavsky's *Running Start.*

Leonid Leonov's *Soviet River* revolves around attempts to construct lumber camps and paper mills on a pristine northern river. As in the capitalist nations, the goal is to industrialize as rapidly as possible, ignoring the damage to nature. Struggling against provincial hostility and obscurantism, as well as the elements, Leonov's young Communists emerge victorious.

In *Time, Forward!* the writer Valentin Katayev tried to integrate technology into fiction.

An underequipped, badly housed, wretchedly fed labor brigade trying to build a steel plant in the Urals undertakes a crash program to set a new construction record. The friendly race is ostensibly against a Harkov brigade. The real message was that Russia had to catch up with her capitalist enemies.

The cinema, which had flourished in the 1920s, now produced little but propaganda. An early sound film was Nikolai Ekk's *Road to Life* (1931), which dealt in a technically interesting but overly sentimental manner with the homeless waifs (*besprizorniki*) of the 1920s. The first real commercial success was the 1934 film *Chapayev*, a fictionalized biography of a minor Civil War hero. Mosfilm (Moscow Film) released *We Are from Kronstadt* in 1936, Lenfilm (Leningrad Film) did *Baltic Deputy* in 1937, and Kievfilm produced *Shchors* in 1939. Kievfilm also commissioned a film on the Komsomol and assigned the screenplay to Yuri Olesha, one of Russia's finest writers. Olesha's *A Severe Young Man* turned the film into—in Vitaly Shentalinsky's words—"an indescribable lampoon" of the young Reds. It was never shown.

For the twentieth anniversary of the Bolshevik coup d'état in 1937, Mosfilm offered *Lenin in October*, which featured Stalin. This film was a quantum step backward from Sergei Eisenstein's 1927 film *October*, in which Stalin figured marginally—a fair index of his role.

By now Stalin was an expert in all branches of science, agriculture, military strategy and tactics, linguistics, history, poultry farming, forestry, oceanography, and cinematography. His personal interference in the two-part film *Peter the First* wrecked it. But in 1938 he allowed release of Eisenstein's *Aleksandr Nevsky*, the story of the thirteenth-century Russian triumph over the invading Teutonic knights. Like *Professor Mamlock* of the same year, it was meant as a warning to the Germans. *Nevsky*, however, for which Sergei Prokofiev wrote a fine score, transcended propaganda to become a classic. Not remotely in that category but nevertheless amusing were *Volga Volga!* and *Circus*.

Sergei Eisenstein created the ill-fated *Bezhin Meadow*, which was based on a true story. At the frantic peak of collectivization in 1932, a 14-year-old boy, Pavlik ("Paul-Boy") Morozov, denounced his father for sabotaging the harvest. The OGPU arrested the father, whose infuriated friends and neighbors promptly lynched Pavlik. The party commissioned a film. Trying to depict Pavlik as an heroic, Christ-like figure, Eisenstein failed miserably. Even Stalin admitted that the public would not stomach such blasphemy; he forbade release of the film and ordered the destruction of all prints.

In the summer of 1989, the Moscow International Film Festival showed a print of *Bezhin Meadow* partially reconstructed from fragments Eisenstein's widow had preserved. It reveals little of Eisenstein's genius, much about the depravity of the era.

In a strange sense the 1930s were the decade of the artist. We have already noted the fate of some writers. Mikhail Bulgakov, one of the best Russian novelists of the century, lived in fear of his life and could not publish his masterpiece, *The Master and Margarita*. Isaak Babel, who had tried to collaborate with Eisenstein on *Bezhin Meadow*, which they both hated, was arrested in May 1939, shot in January 1940. He had been a lover of Yevgeniya Yezhova, wife of the infamous head of the infamous "Iron Commissar" Nikolai Yezhov; they charged Babel and Yezhova with espionage. The NKVD arrested Lev Gumilyov several times and finally sent him to the Gulag. He was not even a writer but the son of the poets Anna Akhmatova and Nikolai Gumilyov.

On her son's first arrest in 1935, Akhmatova began to write the cycle *Requiem* in which she sought to express the anguish of mothers and wives whose loved ones dematerialized into the Gulag. The NKVD arrested and shot the husband of the writer Lidiya Chukovskaya, who merely had the same surname (Bronstein) as Trotsky. Vsevolod Meyerhold looked on helplessly as the party-state closed down his theatre in 1938. Two years later the NKVD subjected him to inhuman tortures, then shot him as an agent of Japan, with which he had no connection. For good measure they murdered his wife.

LIFE IN THE 1930s

Death and putrefaction hovered over the Soviet heart: In 1930 the regime opened the huge granite and marble Lenin Mausoleum in Red Square. There, under glass, was the founder's embalmed corpse bathed in an odd orange-blue light. For the rest of the century, millions of people from every nation would come to see the relics.

In 1931 the Communists dynamited the Cathedral of Christ the Savior near the Kremlin, destroying the view from the apartment of Boris Pasternak's parents. Built a century earlier to commemorate the victory over Napoleon, the Bolsheviks leveled it to make way for a Palace of Soviets, a 320-meter monstrosity atop which a 100-meter statue of Lenin was to perch.* Fortunately for the world, the porous soil could not support the weight and the party dropped the project. A swimming pool occupied the site for several decades. In 1996, the Patriarch of Moscow presided over the dedication of a new cathedral, construction of which continues at stupendous cost.

The Moscow Water and Canal Company began test-drilling in December 1924 for the construction of an underground rail system, but because of lack of funds work began only in 1932. Lazar Kaganovich and Nikita Khrush-

chev kept sharp party eyes on the political aspects of the tunnels; in May 1935 the initial 11.5-kilometer line went into service. The 11-kilometer Berlin subway had been six years in construction; building 20 kilometers took New York seven years; Tokyo built its base four-kilometer subway in four years.

In the Soviet fashion, the party originally named the system the L. M. Kaganovich Moscow Metro. Private citizens showed their gratitude for the bounties of communism by saddling their daughters with such names as Stalinka and Oktyabrina (from *October*); they called their sons by the acronyms Vladlen or Vilen, or Vil (Lenin's initials), sometimes Ninel (Lenin backward). This fad blossomed in direct proportion to the growth of Stalin's dictatorship. No one knows how many male infants were named Melsor (Marx, Engels, Lenin, Stalin, October Revolution), shortened to Melor after the 1956 demythologization of Stalin. A colorful coinage was Parlikder, an acronym for a Communist slogan, "The party face-to-face with the countryside." Redema stood for "revolutionary youth day." During the Five-Year Plans people sometimes named children Traktor, Turbina, and Renat (an acronym for Revolutsiya, nauka, trud [Revolution, science, labor]). Some children suffered as "Five-Year-Plan-in-Four." Uneducated people who misunderstood party slogans occasionally went overboard. In Soviet Armenia some parents gave their offspring such names as Embrion (Embryo), Vinegret (Vinaigrette), and even Dizenteriya (Dysentery).

Municipalities with perfectly respectable old names became Stalinabad, Stalingrad, Stalingradsky, Staliniri, Stalinka, Stalino (seven of these), Stalinsk, Stalinsky, Stalinskoye, Stalinogorsk. When Zinovievsk proved embarrassing, officals went back to the original Yelizavetgrad, only to rename it Kirovgrad. Kamenevsk and Yezhovsk fell by the wayside. Ordzhonikidze, Frunze, Kuibyshev, and other municipalities kept their new names even after Stalin en-

---

*The Swiss–French architect Charles le Corbusier won the 1932 design competition, but the structure Stalin approved did not follow his project.

L. M. Kaganovich (second from right) and N. S. Khrushchev (third from right) with workers tunneling for the Moscow Subway, 1935. (ITAR-TASS)

gineered the eponyms' murders. All cities named after Stalin, along with the Molotovs and Voroshilovgrads, would bear the designations until the last, Stalingrad, became Volgograd in 1961, then reverted to the original Tsaritsyn in 1990.

An internal identification-document system went into effect in December 1932. At age 16, urban dwellers had to obtain a "passport" valid only inside the country. It required renewal every five years; because it listed place of residence, it constituted permission to live there, and only there. One had to present it on demand to the police, NKVD, and hotel clerks; in ration lines and in the workplace; and in other civil situations. Each time a citizen applied to the police for a new five-year stamp, that individual was interrogated. When Nadezhda Mandelstam renewed her passport in 1938 she lost the right to live in Moscow: The police simply refused to validate the document for

residence in the city. She waited 28 years for a new stamp.

The fifth line in the passport listed nationality, meaning not "Soviet" but ethnic group. One could fudge this, and for many reasons uncounted non-Russians listed themselves, or were listed by indifferent officials, as Russian. Those whose passports listed them as Jews frequently encountered discrimination, especially in the workplace and in educational institutions.

The peasants did not receive these passports and thus could not leave the *kolhozes* or *sovhozes* without special permission. This was a hallmark of serfdom. The Soviets wanted to ensure a stable agricultural labor force at a time when the state itself was recruiting many peasants to work in the cities. Only in 1976 did the regime begin issuing passports to peasants.

The Romanov doubled-headed eagles remained on the Kremlin spires until 1937, when, on the twentieth anniversary of Bolshevik October, they gave way to heavy glass, illuminated red stars. The change of public symbols accelerated the introduction of innovations in private dwellings. Devout Communists, and people superstitiously trying to ward off evil, substituted a "red" or "Lenin" corner for the Russian Orthodox icon corner in their homes. A photograph of Lenin, after 1927 accompanied or replaced by one of Stalin, took the place of the icons on a small, cloth-covered table; a candle burned when guests were expected. One of Stalin's works also lay on the table, many passages piously underlined. Such displays no more deterred the NKVD than did the defacing in books and encyclopedias of the portraits of purged Communists with the words "enemy of the people" and even "superenemy of the people" (*obervrag naroda*), the latter considered particularly appropriate for Trotsky.

People withdrew into themselves. It was dangerous to trust the neighbors, who might be plotting a denunciation in the hope of obtaining one's room or apartment. The famous case of Pavlik Morozov, who had denounced his father, demonstrated the unwisdom of counting even on one's children, who learned in school to recite, "Thank you, dear Stalin, for our happy childhood." At social gatherings people protected themselves from informers by offering the first toast "To those who have given us such a happy life!" This was one of the few jokes one could make in public, and even then it was best not to smirk. The wonder is that there were any jokes at all; life was so very grim, and the thick, sticky fear never went away. The Communist motto was "Persuade by propaganda, coerce by terror." What hope could there be for a regime that smiled approvingly when schoolchildren chanted hate ditties?

A bad kulak, *he's* our foe,
A good kulak?—The *same*, don'cha know!

Only fear and work remained. Above the gates of some of the Gulag's camps was inscribed "Work is honorable, glorious, valiant, and heroic." This sounded exactly the same tone as the *Arbeit macht frei!* (Work liberates!) of Nazi concentration camps. A German Communist poet, Erich Mühsam, a guest in one of Hitler's camps whose wife was in the Gulag, called Stalin just "Hitler plus Asia."

SUGGESTED ADDITIONAL READINGS

CONQUEST, ROBERT. *The Harvest of Sorrow: Soviet Collectivization and the Terror-Famine.* New York: Oxford University Press, 1986.

FITZPATRICK, SHEILA. *Stalin's Peasants: Resistance and Survival in the Russian Village After Collectivization.* New York: Oxford University Press, 1994.

RUBENSTEIN, JOSHUA. *Tangled Loyalties: The Life and Times of Ilya Ehrenburg.* New York: Basic Books, 1996.

SCOTT, JOHN. *Behind the Urals.* Bloomington: Indiana University Press, 1973.

SHENTALINSKY, VITALY. *Arrested Voices: Resurrecting the Disappeared Writers of the Soviet Regime.* New York: Free Press, 1996.

TUCKER, ROBERT C. *Stalin in Power: The Revolution from Above, 1928–1941.* New York: W. W. Norton, 1990.

11

FOREIGN POLICY
IN THE 1930s

The dream of a world proletarian revolution faded as Soviet Russia tried to build
"socialism in one country"—the overarching issue on which Stalin defeated
Trotsky. The Stalinists concluded that "proletarian internationalism" had no
practical significance until the construction in the USSR of an invulnerable
industrial-military base.

When the Great Depression struck in 1929, stock markets around the world collapsed, governments fell, factories closed, unemployment reached unprecedented levels. Predictions of total collapse appeared frighteningly believable. Nations that had weathered domestic aftershocks of the Bolshevik victory in Russia braced for radical new demands for economic and social change.

Great Britain muddled through the crisis with political institutions intact, as did France, where the institutions were weaker. The poorest major nation, Italy, had been Fascist but calm since 1922; the Italian Communists hailed Mussolini's persecution of the Socialists. The United States undertook a series of economic and social innovations. Only in Germany did an extremist political party, the Nazis, come to power.

The 1929 economic collapse caught the Communists by surprise, their prognostications notwithstanding. Preoccupied with internal problems, the USSR let the most propitious moment in history for international communism slip by.

SIXTH COMINTERN CONGRESS

After the "Shanghai Massacre" and the ensuing catastrophe in China, the Kremlin reviewed its foreign policy, some premises of which had proved false: There would be no worldwide uprising of the proletariat, and cooperation with bourgeois parties was dangerous. The USSR had no reliable friends. At the Comintern's July 1928 Sixth Congress, first since the settling of the Soviet succession, the Soviets unveiled a new line that owed more than they admitted to Trotsky. Stalin had supported the New Economic Policy until 1927–1928, when he reversed himself completely. The rise of tensions in Europe appeared to justify abandoning the NEP in favor of rapid industrialization; this had been Trotsky's position. Stalin had favored cooperation with bourgeois parties abroad. Events in China shattered the latter policy—which Trotsky had assailed from the beginning.

In the summer of 1928 Stalin turned the Comintern sharply to the left, away from cooperation with non-Communists, in favor of a "united front from below." Communists would cooperate with the rank-and-file of other leftist parties but continue fighting the leaders of those parties. Insisting it saw no difference between Fascist dictatorship and bourgeois democracy, the USSR would not defend any democratic regime even against a Fascist takeover.

Such a threat appeared remote. Italy was already Fascist, and a few smaller nations were headed in the direction of authoritarianism, but the major powers seemed stable. In 1928 Hitler's Nazis held only 12 of the nearly 500 seats in the German Reichstag. Moscow vilified the world's oldest Marxist party, the German Social Democrats, as the German proletariat's worst enemy.

GERMANY

This foolish reading of German politics stemmed from the Marxist-Leninist determinism that had produced disaster in China—the view that history operated according to discoverable laws, and that all industrialized or industrializing nations would follow the Russian pattern. Thinking all perverts more or less alike, Stalin saw Hitler as a kind of German Rasputin, his Nazi party the analogue of the jaded old-regime Russian politicians. Stalin and his men—not to mention hordes of Western observers—fatally underestimated the revolutionary nature of Nazism. Not even Hitler's respectful tip of the hat to Stalin, in the form of the Nazi "Four-Year Plans," awakened the dreamers.

It took Stalin a year to come to his senses about Hitler; most Westerners needed more time. In 1933–1934 the Soviet leader was more concerned about the Japanese menace than the German, and he wanted diplomatic recognition from the new Roosevelt Administration in Washington. The two apparently unrelated phenomena were in fact closely linked; both

Russia and the United States were concerned about Japanese expansion.

The Soviets had signed a nonaggression accord with Poland in 1932. When Warsaw made a similar deal with Germany in January 1934, Kremlin alarm bells rang. The agreement also stunned France, whose alliance system began to collapse. Adolf Hitler had repeatedly written and said that Germany must extend her frontiers eastward. The Berlin–Warsaw agreement raised hopes for a nonviolent solution of the Polish Corridor dispute; and that spelled trouble for Russia.

The Versailles peace settlement had given Poland access to the Baltic via a strip of land through German territory (the Polish Corridor). Both the Weimar Republic and its Nazi successor deeply resented this. Looming over a peaceful solution to this problem, however, was the specter of German–Polish cooperation against the USSR. In Poland, the ruling military junta would not allow the Russo–Polish nonaggression pact to stand in the way of a Warsaw–Berlin deal to march eastward together. Poland would regain her "lost" territories; Nazi Germany would have its *Lebensraum* (living space).

Germany replaced Great Britain, who became a potential ally, as the major threat to the USSR. The search for collective security continued.

THE LEAGUE OF NATIONS AND THE APPEASERS

Rejected by the United States, the League of Nations had excluded Soviet Russia. Later, when the League offered admission in return for concessions, Moscow spurned the overture and called the organization a capitalist creation whose goal was to overthrow the Soviet regime. Hitler's accession to power changed attitudes.

In September–October 1932 the League

had declined to brand Japan the aggressor in Manchuria. A special commission did call the action "not an act of self-defense" and recommend against recognizing the puppet "Manchukuo" (Japanese for "Manchuria") regime. Japan quit the League and stayed put in Manchuria. Hitler took Germany out of the League in the autumn of 1933.

The Soviet Union joined in September 1934. The League was then holding an International Disarmament Conference of 63 nations. When he withdrew from the League in 1933, Hitler also left the Disarmament Conference, ensuring its failure. Represented by Commissar of Foreign Affairs (since 1930) Maksim Litvinov, the Kremlin called on the League to work for immediate and total disarmament. This merely aroused scorn. Litvinov then proposed that the League at least define *aggression*. That too failed; but in October 1935 a few delegations joined the Soviets in denouncing the Italian attack on Ethiopia.

Words were one thing, oil another. The West refused to impose an oil embargo against Italy and blocked other sanctions. Italy annexed Ethiopia in May 1936; two months later the League abandoned all pretense of indignation; it was business as usual. An organization powerless to stop Italy could not dream of disciplining Germany, which in March 1936 sent troops into the demilitarized Rhineland. Hitler declared that the just-concluded mutual assistance treaty between the USSR and France threatened German security. The League and the world looked on indifferently as Hitler's soldiers trampled the Versailles settlement—which for all its faults was international law—into the dust. Western politicians argued that Versailles had dealt too harshly with Germany, which had legitimate security needs. Who could reasonably expect Germany not to post armed forces along the Rhine, her main economic artery? No one mentioned the Treaty of Brest-Litovsk.

Alone among the leaders of major nations,

Stalin saw the German move as a grave threat to peace. As he knew, the action was indeed Hitler's last geographic demand—in the West.

Western politicians now approached the point of no return on the road to appeasement and lacked the courage to admit to themselves, let alone the public, that they were gambling. British Prime Minister Neville Chamberlain and the French leaders Pierre Laval and Édouard Daladier banked everything on appeasement. If that failed, all would be lost.

The Kremlin claimed that the appeasers wanted Hitler to satisfy his appetite at Soviet expense. Some observers have scoffed at this, arguing that, contemptuous of the USSR, the West had no reason to work for its destruction. Presumably the West was no more interested in overthrowing the Bolsheviks in the 1930s than it had been in 1918–1920.

European conservatives praised Hitler for coping successfully with the Great Depression, restoring Germany's dignity, and suppressing the Communists. Between 1933 and 1939, Hitler was almost as popular in the West as he was in Germany. He was unknown to the vast majority of the Soviet public, but the Comintern's decade-long flirtation with the Nazis had helped pave the way for Hitler's accession to power. When the Kremlin finally recognized the Nazi threat, it appealed for an alliance of anti-Nazi and anti-Fascist parties—a "Popular Front."

THE SPANISH CIVIL WAR

In Spain, a Popular Front of Socialists, Syndicalists, Communists, and assorted friends of the republic—and opponents of the Spanish monarchy—came to power in February 1936. This was the first such government; the French Popular Front followed four months later. The conservative Spanish parties, the military, and the Catholic Church united against the leftist alliance. When some key army commanders rebelled in July, the revolt spread; a Junta of National Defense came into existence at Burgos.

Spain became a testing ground. In the autumn of 1936 the German, Italian, and Japanese governments concluded a series of bilateral agreements known collectively as the Anti-Comintern Pact. The "Axis" powers (Germany–Italy–Japan) pledged to combat communism at home and abroad. Berlin and Rome interpreted this as a license to send aid to the Spanish Falange (a Fascist party). Hitler and Mussolini despatched thousands of "volunteers" to fight under Generals Francisco Franco and Emilio Mola.

Expressing a timid wish to limit the conflict, Britain and France, whose governments preferred a Falange victory, banned the shipment of war matériel to the democratically elected Spanish government. If meant to set an example, the signal came too late: Berlin, Rome, and Moscow were already involved.

The Soviets would have preferred to stay out, but the German and Italian action, and the prejudicial inaction of France and Britain, gave them little choice. Refusing to permit Soviet citizens to fight, they shipped large stocks of weapons and ammunition, and military-political advisers, from Odessa to Barcelona and other ports. Counterintelligence, censorship, and communications quickly came under Soviet control.

First skimming some off the top, the Madrid government sent Spain's gold reserve, then valued at more than half a billion American dollars, to Russia for safekeeping. The Kremlin promised to return the gold after the cessation of hostilities—minus the cost of Soviet aid. In 1936 and early 1937, Soviet intervention saved the Spanish Republic. The assistance declined abruptly, however, after February 1937, when domestic problems distracted Stalin. He ordered the arrest of Bukharin, Rykov, and Krestinsky.

The NKVD would link these prominent victims and many others to Trotsky and "foreign imperialism." Along with young idealists—including George Orwell—who had no real politics, several thousand Trotskyites from Europe and the United States fought in volunteer units in Spain, the Americans in the Abraham Lincoln and George Washington Brigades.

Stalin feared the virus of Trotskyism had infected the Soviet advisers and the Western Communists who professed loyalty to Moscow. The NKVD conducted a savage purge on Spanish soil, and in the USSR after the men were recalled. This did not help the Spanish Republic, in which Stalin had lost interest.

Some historians maintain that Stalin backed away from the Loyalist cause when he saw it was doomed. Whether he was so prescient is open to question; in any event the Great Terror figured most prominently in his calculations. He backed off, and Hitler and Mussolini redoubled their efforts. Democracy and socialism died in Spain when the Falange triumphed in the spring of 1939 and began its own terror. Even after Franco's death and the ignominious collapse of his military–Church–landlord regime decades later, not an ounce of Spain's gold ever came back from Russia.

MUNICH

Stalin wagered that the fall of the Spanish Republic would not interfere with his alliances in the West. Proving him right, the French parliament, encouraged because the Soviets had signed a similar pact with Czechoslovakia, ratified the Franco–Soviet mutual assistance accord of May 1935. But the Soviet–Czechoslovak covenant had this provision: Moscow would come to Prague's aid only jointly with France.

There seemed no doubt in 1936 that France would honor her commitments in Eastern Europe: The Popular Front government was solidly anti-Nazi and anti-Fascist. France had acquiesced in the reoccupation of the Rhine-land and did nothing to save democracy in Spain but would not let Czechoslovakia go under without a fight. Or such was the myth.

Germany menaced Czechoslovakia on several fronts. The Versailles negotiators had given the new Czechoslovak state a defensible frontier along the ridge of the Sudeten Mountains. This served the larger Allied purpose of weakening Germany. Hitler came to power in no small measure because he convinced so many compatriots of the absolute necessity of uniting all Germans. Nearly three million "Sudeten Germans" lived in western Czechoslovakia.

Hitler had to handle Czechoslovakia carefully; Austria presented fewer problems. After years of Nazi subversion, propaganda, and violence, Germany annexed Austria on March 13, 1938. In an April 10 plebiscite, 99.75 percent of the Austrian voters approved the annexation (*Anschluss*). It appears to have been a reasonably honest vote count; Hitler's popularity diminished the need for fraud.

Having repeatedly violated solemn treaty obligations without penalty, Hitler seemed invincible. His moves mesmerized politicians all over Europe: The more reckless his actions, the louder the applause. In the summer of 1938 he demanded that Czechoslovakia be dismembered. There was almost no doubt that he would succeed. But what would Stalin do?

Stalin was still preoccupied with the business that had sapped his will in Spain, but he would not have intervened in the Austrian situation anyway. Russia had not been a party to the Versailles settlement that created modern Austria; and like most politicians Stalin believed Hitler had the right to unite the Germans. The Bukharin-Rykov-Krestinsky drama ended on March 15, 1938.

Britain's Neville Chamberlain and France's Édouard Daladier, who was Premier from April 1938, actually believed annexation of the Sudetenland Hitler's "last territorial demand in Europe." Stalin knew better. There were many ethnic Germans in Poland or surrounded by Polish territory in the Free City of Danzig and the Polish Corridor; Hitler was certain to turn to Poland after getting what he wanted in Czechoslovakia. And after Poland?

There were 2.3 million ethnic Germans in the USSR, descendants of colonists whom Peter the Great and Catherine the Great invited to Russia. Neither Stalin nor anyone else expected Hitler to attack Russia for the sake of these "Volga Germans." He would make war because the Reich needed *Lebensraum,* food, raw materials, cheap labor, resorts for high-ranking Nazis and ordinary citizens, glory, amusement.

Concentrating on the Great Terror and the concomitant reorganization of party, state, and military cadres, and paying rather less attention to the Nazi menace, Stalin could only hope the Western democracies would deal forcefully with Hitler. But Hitler sensed they would not. In the spring of 1938 he ordered the Sudeten Germans, who had long demanded autonomy, to up the ante and to raise their voices.

Mindful of their treaty obligations but fearful of having to fight alone, the French asked Britain to extend a guarantee of aid to Prague. Neville Chamberlain declared that his government neither knew nor wanted to know anything about Czechoslovakia. And incidentally, Britain did not have enough aircraft. The Establishment newspaper, *The Times,* refused to publish anything that might conceivably offend Hitler. The ardently pro-Nazi ambassador in Berlin, Nevile Henderson, urged Whitehall to pressure the Czechoslovaks into accepting Hitler's demands. A British mediator went to Prague in August to convey that message to Prime Minister Eduard Beneš of Czechoslovakia, who continued to beg Paris and Moscow for help.

In response to large-scale German maneuvers west of the Rhine, in September 1938 the

French government did call up about a million reservists. In England, the Admiralty prepared for a display of British naval power. Faced with rebuilding the officer corps he had gutted, Stalin bided his time.

On Hitler's instructions, the Sudeten Germans broke off negotiations with Beneš early in September. In a Nürnberg speech on September 12, Hitler demanded not autonomy but the right of self-determination for those Germans. As he finished speaking, Nazi-orchestrated violence was erupting all over Czechoslovakia. The moment of decision was at hand.

The risk of a general war in Europe was greater than at any time since 1918; Hitler had made it clear that he would fight if his demands were not met. Beneš's government, certain its army could hold off the Germans long enough to give France and the USSR time to come in, refused to help liquidate the country. Prague found it hard to believe that, if Czechoslovakia's very survival were in question, the French and British would continue appeasing Hitler. And if France and Britain stood sturdy, the USSR was treaty-bound to follow suit.

On September 29 Chamberlain and Daladier flew to Munich to meet Hitler and his Foreign Minister, Joachim "von" Ribbentrop, with Benito Mussolini present. No one represented Czechoslovakia.

The conferees came to hear Hitler pronounce sentence. The *Reichskanzler* knew that Britain and France would not fight, and that French refusal to honor treaty commitments relieved the USSR of its obligations. Shortly after midnight the parties signed the agreement, which satisfied Germany's every demand. Poland and Hungary were to receive some coveted Czechoslovak territory. Only then did the signatories deign to tell Prague what they had done.

Back in London, Chamberlain bragged that the Munich agreement spelled "peace in our time." Let Czechoslovakia go under, he said; the rest of Europe would survive. By an overwhelming margin the British public agreed; Winston Churchill's constituents in the working-class London suburb of Woodford nearly recalled him for opposing the agreement. All France hailed the peacemakers.

To Stalin, "Munich"—synonymous with appeasement—proved the democracies were maintaining the policy of giving Hitler carte blanche in Eastern Europe. Disdainful of the West's weakness, Stalin boasted of Soviet readiness to aid small nations in danger. Had it not been for the refusal of the Polish and Romanian regimes to permit passage of Soviet troops across their countries, he said, Russia would have sent troops to Czechoslovakia despite France's perfidy. Did he speak the truth? The question is moot; but the USSR had the most to lose from Nazi aggression.

JAPAN

Because most of the population and three-quarters of industry were in the Cisuralian part of the USSR, Soviet foreign policy in the 1930s concentrated heavily on Europe. By far the larger part of the territory itself, however, lay in Asia, where Japan was on the march.

The Japanese won concessions in China late in the nineteenth century, and in 1910 they annexed Korea. Tokyo sent large forces to the Soviet Maritime Provinces after the Bolshevik coup d'état and pulled out of Vladivostok only under American pressure in October 1922. Japan recognized the Soviet regime in January 1925; ten weeks later, the last Japanese forces left Sakhalin.

The Tokyo militarists were determined to extend their empire on the Asian mainland. Discounting the high risk of conflict with Soviet Russia, they decided to take Manchuria, China's largest single source of raw materials and home of her biggest industrial complex.

The tsarist government had built the Chinese Eastern Railway across Manchuria; it provided direct access to the great port of Vladivostok and great savings in time, distance, and money. After the Intervention, the European powers and the United States attempted to force Moscow and Beijing to internationalize the rail line. The Soviets and Chinese successfully resisted this and agreed to operate it jointly. The Beijing government that signed the accord, however, only nominally controlled Manchuria, where a shifting coalition of warlords held power. In October 1929 some of those warlords attacked the Chinese Eastern Railway in an attempt to seize it from the Russians. A force of 70,000 Russian White Guards augmented the 300,000 warlord irregulars.

Several months earlier, the Soviets had created a Special Far Eastern Army under General Vasili Blücher, who had helped the Guomindang's Chiang Kai-shek build the largest warlord army of all. Blücher had only about 100,000 men to send to Manchuria, but that well-equipped, highly trained, and disciplined force faced a rabble that excelled chiefly at robbery and the slaughter of unarmed civilians. General Blücher routed the Manchurians and White Guards and secured the 1,000-kilometer Chinese Eastern Railway.

What the Manchurian bandits could not accomplish, someone else could. Japan attacked Manchuria in September 1931, and by the following February all but guerrilla resistance—the leaders trained in Moscow's top-secret Manchurian School—had ceased. The Japanese proclaimed the independence of "Manchukuo." Tokyo at first permitted the Soviet Union, technically still in partnership with China, to continue operating the Chinese Eastern Railway. Negotiations for the transfer of the line began in May 1933; two years later the Kremlin sold its interest to Japan.

Three armed Soviet–Japanese clashes occurred late in the decade. The first two took place in July–August 1938 at Lake Khasan and at Changkufeng Hill in the Soviet Maritime Provinces south of Vladivostok, at the point where the frontiers of Manchuria, Korea, and Russia meet on the Tumen River. Probing Soviet frontier defenses, the Japanese attacked with a small force toward the end of July. The Special Far Eastern Army under Blücher—recently promoted to the rank of marshal—repulsed the attacks; the fighting ended on August 11.

Three months later, the NKVD executed Blücher as an "agent of Japanese imperialism." Only if he had withdrawn his forces entirely could Stalin, who ordered the execution, have done more to harm the Soviet defense posture.

The third violent confrontation took place in Mongolia, virtually a Soviet protectorate since the mid-1920s; Red Army troops were stationed in the country under the terms of a 1936 mutual defense treaty. Japanese forces stormed across the Khalkha River on May 28, 1939, again testing Soviet reactions, and drove deep into Mongolia without encountering much resistance. Only the overextension of supply lines prevented them from reaching the capital, Ulaan Baatar ("Red Hero"). Late in July the Kremlin rushed two Red Army groups under General Georgi Zhukov, then a corps commander, to Mongolia. Zhukov had at his disposal 35 rifle battalions, 500 tanks, about 500 aircraft, 350 armored cars, and some heavy artillery. A tiny Mongolian army—heir to the tradition of Chingis Khan—was badly equipped and untrained for modern warfare.

The invasion along a 70-kilometer front centered on the tiny settlement of Nomon-Khan-Burd-Obo on the Khalkhin Gol (Khalkha River), which marked the Mongolian–Manchurian frontier. The Japanese struck with 182 tanks, 500 heavy artillery guns, 300 to

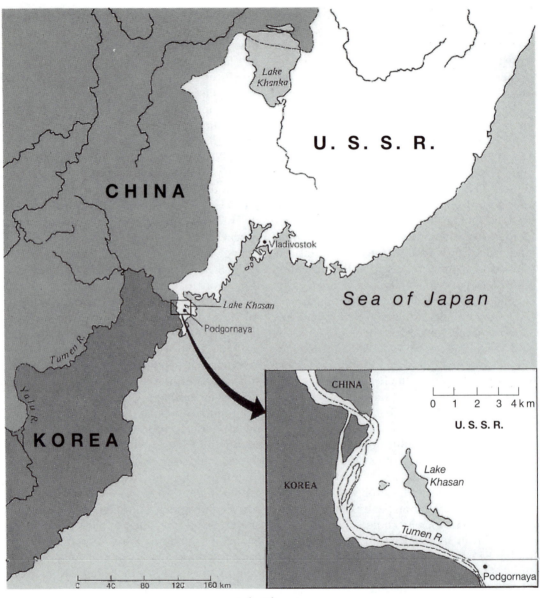

Lake Khasan.

350 airplanes, and a dozen infantry divisions; thus the sheer size of the armies made this one of the major undeclared wars of the period. The battle of Khalkhin Gol lasted from August 20–31, 1939. Zhukov's forces chased the Japanese back into Manchuria, inflicting heavy casualties. The two sides signed an armistice on September 16, 1939. Nine months later a tripartite commission fixed the Mongolian–Manchurian frontier.

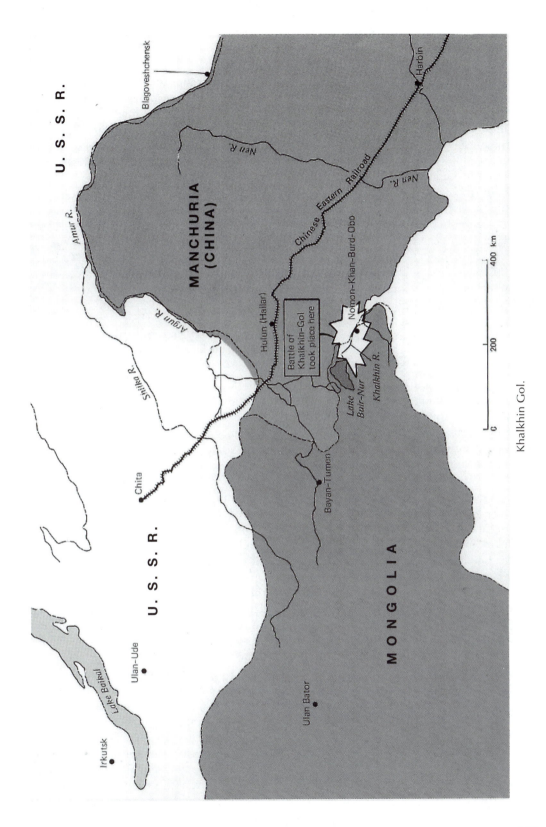

Khalkhin Gol.

117

CHINA

The survivors of the 1927 Shanghai Massacre split into two camps. One looked to Moscow for guidance, while the other advocated a uniquely Chinese revolution. The former was under the leadership of Wang Ming and Po Ku, members of "Stalin's China Section," the 28 Chinese Communist students loyal to the Soviet dictator. In 1930 Wang,* Po, and several associates went secretly to Shanghai's International Settlement, where the Guomindang (Chinese nationalists) normally could not touch them. On Comintern orders they worked to prepare a proletarian uprising. In a peasant country this was sheer folly, but Stalin did not always learn from his mistakes.

In 1931 the Chinese Communists proclaimed a "Soviet Republic of Ruijin" in Jiangxi province. The first Congress of Soviets of Workers' and Peasants' Deputies took place in the city of Ruijin on November 7. Mao Zedong and other "peasantists" among the leadership, however, continued to insist that the revolution would hinge on developments in rural China. In bitter internecine quarrels Mao began to prevail over people such as Wang Ming, whom he would later call a "left adventurist," that is, an advocate of urban insurrection—the Stalin line.

The Guomindang undertook a series of "encirclement and suppression" campaigns against the Communists in Jiangxi; the fifth, in 1933–1934, destroyed the "Soviet Republic." The Communists then began the famous Long March that covered 10,000 kilometers and lasted 368 days. The trekkers crossed 18 mountain ranges and 24 rivers in 12 provinces before reaching sanctuary in Shaanxi.

Events since the Bolshevik seizure of power had convinced most Chinese Communists to pursue an agrarian revolution, and in January

---

*The Chinese, Hungarians, and many other peoples usually write the surname first, e.g., Smith John.

1935 they recognized Mao's leadership. China would follow its own path.

The "years of confrontation" between Communists and the Guomindang halted temporarily in 1937, when both shifted attention to the struggle against the foreign invader, Japan. The Japanese had suspended military operations after annexing Manchuria, but now their attempt to conquer all China resumed. The Chinese Communist Army undertook a long guerrilla campaign against the invaders. Avoiding the Japanese, Chiang Kaishek's Guomindang concentrated on plundering China.

PRELUDE TO THE DIPLOMATIC REVOLUTION

The Munich accord tucked away, Hitler pronounced himself satisfied: He and the appeasers had shaken hands over a corpse. Britain entered into negotiations to grant a huge loan to Germany.

Two clouds dimmed the horizon. His Ethiopian conquest having proved less of an economic and theatrical success than he had hoped, Mussolini decided he too needed territory in Europe. The question of where he would strike obscured the diplomatic scene: Nice? Monaco? Dubrovnik? The deceptively peaceful European landscape also itched from the pen and tongue of Winston Churchill. Then merely a member of Parliament, he had good press contacts and a gift for making people wonder whether the appeasers had been quite so clever after all. Earlier, Churchill had expressed admiration for Hitler's—and Mussolini's—economic performances. After the reoccupation of the Rhineland he warned against trusting the Nazis.

The Wehrmacht suddenly marched into and occupied western and southwestern Czechoslovakia (Bohemia and Moravia) on March 15, 1939. Native Fascists friendly to Germany took control of Slovakia. A week later, Hitler seized the port of Klaipeda (Memel) from Lithuania. Less than six months after Munich, he had broken his pledge to refrain from further expansion. He also demonstrated that a disinclination to limit his acquisition of new territories to German-inhabited lands.

Then the Spanish Civil War ended, having cost about a million lives—a toll to which German, Italian, and Soviet Russian intervention contributed enormously. The delighted Hitler offered congratulations to Franco; Spain joined the Anti-Comintern alliance.

Mussolini annexed Albania on Good Friday, April 7, 1939. Because Albania had been an Italian satellite, this did not have much practical significance. But in a world where the toleration of violence bred still more of it, the annexation fueled the flames.

As Hitler prepared to carve up rump Czechoslovakia, the Soviet Communists' Eighteenth Party Congress met in Moscow March 10–21. Stalin and Kliment Voroshilov explained to the more than 2,000 cheering delegates that the state murder of thousands of military officers had strengthened the national defense. The comments were as predictable as they were incredible. Both Soviet and foreign observers reacted in disbelief, however, to Stalin's March 10 speech warning that the USSR would not be drawn into a conflict with Germany in order to "pull Western chestnuts out of the fire." He aimed this at some Western politicians who were now hinting at a pact with Stalin to stop Hitler and Mussolini.

In an extraordinary gesture, Hitler repeated these words in an April 1 speech at Wilhelmshaven: "He who declares himself ready to pull the chestnuts out of the fire for . . . [Poland and Romania] must realize he will burn his fingers."

At the time, there seemed no danger that any Western politician anxious to deal with Stalin would ever be in power. Firmly ensconced at No. 10 Downing Street, Neville Chamberlain declared unequivocally that he would resign rather than seek an alliance with Soviet Russia. But on the last day of March 1939 the Prime Minister told a hushed House of Commons that the British government was extending a unilateral guarantee of aid to Poland. Should Poland be attacked by Germany, Britain would go to her aid. Chamberlain gave a similar guarantee to Romania. Having signed democratic Czechoslovakia's death warrant, he and his government made sweeping commitments to reactionary regimes in Poland and Romania. Be that as it may, this constituted an assurance to Russia and a warning to Germany. If the latter attacked Poland *and* the USSR, Germany would face Bismarck's nightmare—a war on two fronts.

The convoluted diplomatic ramifications of Chamberlain's declaration were obvious, but Stalin understandably remained suspicious. What about the January 1934 German–Polish nonaggression pact? In view of the cozy Warsaw–Berlin relations, it was not unreasonable to assume that the Poles might permit German forces to cross their territory to attack Soviet Russia. The German–Polish romance was rapidly cooling, but hatred of Russia tended to reconcile differences between Central European nations.

On April 28, 1939, Hitler unilaterally abrogated the treaty with Poland. But in announcing the decision he departed from custom and did not refer to the "Bolshevik menace."

Chamberlain had asked the Kremlin to extend its own unilateral guarantee to Poland; the Soviets demanded a two-way pact. If attacked by Germany, they wanted Poland to come to their aid. The Poles rejected this proposal, and Romania later followed suit. Warsaw and Bucarest would welcome a Soviet declaration of war on Germany should that country attack either of them, but further they would not go. Later, when the Soviet government asked whether Warsaw would permit the

Red Army to cross Polish territory to fight Germany, the answer was again negative. Refusing to make any commitment, the Poles promised only to examine the question of troop passage *if war came*. Moscow broke off negotiations.

On April 3, 1939, the Chief of the German High Command issued a secret order calling for an attack on Poland on September 1. The British guarantee to Poland *preceded* this by three days. Any doubt the Germans might still have had as to whether an invasion of Poland would lead to war with Britain arose from their faulty reading of unmistakable signs. Some historians charge the USSR with precipitating the Second World War by signing a nonaggression pact with Germany. War was inevitable no matter what the Soviets did.

THE NAZI–SOVIET PACT

When he ousted Maxim Litvinov as Commissar of Foreign Affairs on May 3, 1939, Stalin signaled his readiness to deal with Hitler: Litvinov was Jewish. Short of publicly beheading him in Red Square, the Soviet dictator could not have made his intentions clearer. Vyacheslav Molotov, Chairman of the Sovnarkom and a Russian, replaced Litvinov.

Unaware that Chamberlain was already doing a splendid job, Hitler hoped to sabotage the Anglo–French–Soviet negotiations. His plans could be compromised by such a tripartite alliance, and so he had to assume—as Chamberlain refused to do—that Stalin was negotiating in good faith. Hitler had earlier been confident of bringing about his next great *coup,* the conquest of Poland, without reference to Moscow. But the persistence of Soviet signals, and Ribbentrop's machinations, won him over to the idea of parleying with Stalin.

August 1939 was a tense month in an anxious year. The USSR and Japan were fighting a major battle in Mongolia. Already in control of

vast areas of China, the Japanese were extending their domination south and west. Great Britain and France were frantically rebuilding their arsenals. The Soviets asked for transit rights across Poland in the event they needed to aid Czechoslovakia. Warsaw refused; and no one could blame the Poles for not wanting the Red Army on their territory. But the arrogant colonels who ruled Poland displayed irresponsible judgment in believing they could hold out against a German attack long enough for the British to enter the conflict and tip the balance in their favor. Britain had nothing with which to enter. The Poles kept the Red Army out, ensuring that the Wehrmacht and the SS would come in. The Red Army and the NKVD would follow.

On April 17, 1939, Soviet diplomats proposed a treaty to London and Paris: The contracting parties would provide aid, including military assistance, should any be attacked by Germany. Two months later the Soviets proposed to extend this agreement to Belgium, Poland, Latvia, Estonia, Finland, Greece, Romania, and Turkey. Neville Chamberlain dispatched a low-ranking mission on a slow boat to Leningrad. The junior diplomats and officers were at sea for nearly three weeks. When they finally arrived in the USSR, they lined up with a nervous group of Red Army colonels for some photographs. One can read the apprehension in the faces of the Soviet officers: What better evidence of collaboration with foreign agents? The British officials, none of whom knew precisely what he was to do, did not receive a cordial welcome. Another delegation had arrived in Moscow.

August 20 saw three crucial developments: The battle at Khalkhin Gol got under way. The USSR and Germany announced a trade and credit agreement. Danzig's Nazi mayor declared that the city's hour of deliverance from the Polish oppressor was at hand.

Rumors that Germany and Soviet Russia would conclude a nonaggression treaty flashed around the world. Someone in the German government leaked the news that Berlin had accepted a Soviet draft agreement in principle; Ribbentrop would fly to Moscow.

Until lately a vendor of wine, Ribbentrop and his aides met with Stalin and Molotov for three hours late in the afternoon of August 23. They took a recess around 7:00 P.M.; the Germans returned to their embassy. Ribbentrop cabled Hitler for final instructions.

At dinner that evening, the pact was sealed. Ribbentrop swore the Anti-Comintern Pact was aimed not at the USSR but at the Western democracies. Stalin agreed, noting that it had frightened The City (London's Wall Street) more than anyone else. Ribbentrop told his hosts a Berlin joke: "Stalin may *join* the Anti-Comintern Pact!" Stalin responded with a toast: "I know how much the German nation loves its Führer. I should therefore like to drink to his health." Molotov complimented the guests on their keen understanding of Stalin's March 10 "no chestnuts" speech.

History records few such fantastic episodes.

The world learned the details of the Soviet–Nazi nonaggression pact on August 24. It would remain in effect for 10 years. The two High Contracting Parties would neither attack each other nor "participate in any grouping of powers whatsoever that is directly or indirectly aimed at the other." Should either country suffer attack from a third, the other would "in no manner lend its support."

The astonishment that greeted this news would have been even greater had the Secret Additional Protocol leaked out: The dictators agreed to divide Eastern Europe. The Soviets would take Estonia, Latvia, Bessarabia, and—a later addition—Lithuania. The two parties would divide Poland along the line described by the Narew, Vistula, and San rivers. They postponed discussion of whether any Polish state at all would exist.

Thus did Hitler and Stalin slice up Eastern Europe. Hitler could now resolve the "Polish question," with Russia taking a huge chunk of Polish territory. The Soviets could strengthen their position on the Baltic, push the Finnish frontier back from Leningrad, and take Bessarabia. Nor was this all. Stalin's "no chestnuts" speech, and the recent history of relations between the USSR and the Western democracies, indicated that Stalin would not object to anything Hitler did in the West.

Bent as they were on giving Hitler everything he wanted, the Western appeasers had excluded the USSR from their calculations. The cry of anguish that now arose from London and Paris rang false.

To be sure, Western politicians faced a choice between Nazi evil and Soviet evil. They regarded Stalin as likely to reduce the world to barbarism. Whether one liked it or not, Hitler on the other hand was a son of the Western world who hated "non-Aryans" and pledged to destroy "Jewish Bolshevism."

At Munich, the West chose Hitler, making the question of Stalin's insincerity in pursuit of collective security moot. The Western powers ignored overtures from the Soviet dictator, who desperately sought to shore up his own country's security. Unsubtly, they suggested to Hitler that he look east for future conquests.

Having ordered the mass murder of his officer corps, Stalin undermined the Soviet defense system and thus bears responsibility for millions of wartime casualties. Frantically seeking time, he entered into the surpassingly cynical agreement of August 23–24, 1939.

SUGGESTED ADDITIONAL READINGS

BRENAN, GERALD. *The Spanish Labyrinth.* New York: Macmillan, 1943.

CHURCHILL, WINSTON S. *The Gathering Storm.* Boston: Houghton Mifflin, 1948.

HAIGH, R. H., D. S. MORRIS, and A. R. PETERS, eds. *Soviet Foreign Policy, the League of Nations, and Europe, 1917–1939.* Totowa, NJ: Rowman and Littlefield, 1986.

HASLAM, JONATHAN. *The Soviet Union and the Struggle for Collective Security in Europe, 1933–1938.* New York: St. Martin's Press, 1984.

HOCHMAN, JIRI. *The Soviet Union and the Failure of Collective Security, 1934–1938.* Ithaca, NY: Cornell University Press, 1984.

ORWELL, GEORGE. *Homage to Catalonia.* New York: Harcourt, Brace, & World, 1952.

PAYNE, STANLEY G. *A History of Fascism, 1914–1945.* Madison: University of Wisconsin Press, 1995.

12

THE GREAT FATHERLAND WAR

Having eviscerated the Soviet military, Stalin began to ponder the consequences. The third Five-Year Plan for 1938–1942 doubled defense spending and provided for the relocation of hundreds of factories from European Russia to Transuralia and Siberia. But it did not provide for the strengthening of the western defense perimeter. Like Neville Chamberlain, Stalin did not wish to offend Adolf Hitler.

THE WAR BEGINS

German troops crossed into Poland at dawn on September 1, 1939. The European phase of the Second World War thus began eight years after the Japanese initiated the Asian phase by invading Manchuria. Poland fell in less than a month. Like the "enlightened despots" Frederick the Great, Catherine the Great, and the tearful Maria Theresa of Austria, Hitler and Stalin partitioned the country. In the Baltic, Soviet Russia made puppet states of Estonia, Latvia, and Lithuania.

Now it was Finland's turn. In 1939 the Finnish frontier was only 32 kilometers from Leningrad. The Soviets demanded that Helsinki exchange most of the Karelian Isthmus for a larger but essentially worthless territory in the north; this would have pushed the frontier 20 to 30 kilometers farther away from Leningrad. The Finnish government refused even to consider this. On November 30, 1939, fifteen Red Army divisions attacked at several points along the 1,500-kilometer frontier.

The Red Army soldiers did not fight well under their poorly trained new commanders.

The Finns resisted valiantly until overwhelming numerical superiority wore them down. The peace treaty signed on March 12, 1940, cost Finland more territory than Moscow had demanded earlier, but Finland preserved her honor.

On June 26, 1940, Vyacheslav Molotov summoned the Romanian ambassador and presented an ultimatum: Bucharest had 24 hours to cede Bessarabia and the northern part of the Bukovina. The Romanians capitulated.

The Soviets increased production and tightened labor discipline. Factories operated 24 hours a day, 7 days a week; the Red Army frantically trained officers and enlisted men; a new, qualitatively different layer of fear hung in the air. Stalin continued to send raw materials and food to Germany, and he did not act to shore up Russia's western defenses.

In April 1941 Japanese Foreign Minister Matsuoka and Soviet Foreign Minister Molotov signed a Neutrality Pact, but Japanese forces continued to make violent probes and feints—more than 100 in 1942 alone—into Soviet territory, forcing Stalin to keep large military units in the Far East. Between June 1941

Molotov signing documents incorporating Finnish territory into the USSR, December 1939. Standing from left: Zhdanov, Voroshilov, Stalin, Otto Kuusinen. (National Archives)

and late 1944, the Japanese navy sank or detained more than 170 Soviet merchant vessels. Tokyo pressed ahead with the conquest of China and Southeast Asia.

British and American intelligence learned in February 1941 that the Germans would soon invade the USSR; the Western leaders informed Moscow. About the same time, Stalin's chief spy in Japan, Richard Sorge, pried the details out of the German ambassador. From the middle of March, ominous troop movements took place in German-occupied Poland and in the satellite states of Slovakia, Romania, Hungary, and Bulgaria. Between April 10 and June 21, German reconnaissance aircraft violated Soviet airspace along the new frontier—formerly Poland—about 200 times, often flying 150 kilometers into Russia.

On May 6, 1941, Stalin replaced Molotov as Chairman of the Sovnarkom. Thus for the first time in many years Stalin held a government post.

A soothing June 14 communiqué from TASS, the Soviet news agency, denounced rumors of an impending German attack and declared that the Germans were adhering to the Non-Aggression Pact. The troop movements along the Soviet frontier were, "one must suppose, prompted by motives which have no bearing on Soviet–German relations." The

USSR itself was not, TASS said, preparing for war; Red Army maneuvers did not imply hostility toward Germany. Stalin personally edited this statement.

At 3:30 A.M. on June 22, 1941, the German ambassador requested a meeting with Molotov. At the Foreign Commissariat two hours later, the ambassador read a statement from Hitler accusing the Soviet Union of "gross and repeated violations" of the Non-Aggression Pact. This was a declaration of war after the fact.

JUNE 22, 1941

Germany had attacked at 0400 hours, June 22, Moscow time. The two largest and most powerful armies ever assembled collided along a 3,000-kilometer line from the Barents Sea to the Black Sea. The Germans had 183 divisions. The Red Army had 170—54 percent of its total strength. The Soviets had quantitative superiority in tanks and aircraft, but much of the equipment was of inferior quality. The old tanks were insufficiently armored; only 27 percent were in working order and many tank crews had only 90 to 120 minutes of actual experience in the vehicles. Red Air Force planes were outmoded, their maintenance badly organized. Pilots sometimes had only four hours' training in the air; the Luftwaffe and the British Royal Air Force required 135 to 150 hours. Soviet airfields in eastern Poland, Belarus, and northwest Ukraine were virtually unprotected. Within three days, the Luftwaffe destroyed three-fourths of the Soviet aircraft on the ground and controlled the skies.

When Red Army officers radioed that they were under attack, their superiors berated them for not transmitting in code; wishful thinking extended all the way up the chain of command. But it was quickly established that an invasion was indeed taking place. At 6:00 A.M., Radio Moscow's chief announcer, Yuri Levitan, read the brief official announcement. What Russia would call the Great Fatherland War had begun.

At noon on June 22, the dazed citizenry heard not Stalin but Molotov broadcast a more detailed statement. Where was the Leader? Profoundly shaken and humiliated, Stalin did not, as historians previously assumed, sink into depression or give way to panic, nor did he leave strategic decision making to subordinates. Archives released in 1992–1993 indicate that, contrary to his lifelong habits, Stalin began work early that morning and remained at his Kremlin desk throughout the day, meeting with Politburo members, military commanders, and other high-level personnel. He simply chose to remain out of sight.

Stalin did not speak publicly for 11 days. In that time, the Germans advanced 150 kilometers into Russia. Only on July 3 did he finally address the nation on radio: "Comrades! Citizens! Brothers and sisters! Warriors of our army and navy! I turn to you, my friends!" The enemy was rapidly advancing, he said. Soviet losses had been severe. Although the Red Army was resisting heroically, the country was in mortal danger. Reminding his listeners of Napoleon's fate, Stalin defended the pact with Hitler, claiming it had bought time to build the defenses. That did not explain anything.

Stalin ordered the destruction of everything of potential use to the enemy in battle zones and called for the forming of partisan (guerrilla) units behind enemy lines. He announced creation of a State Defense Council with himself at the head. Great Britain and the United States had offered aid. He closed with, "All the strength of the people must be used to destroy the enemy! Forward, to victory!"

The words and the tone electrified the country and stiffened the national spine Stalin had done so much to break. By the end of July the Germans controlled an area inside the Soviet Union more than twice the size of France.

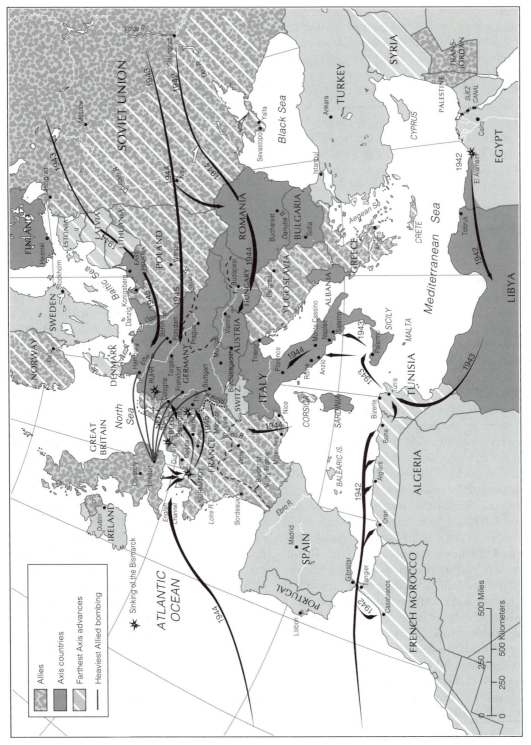

European Theatre of World War II.

Allies
Axis countries
Farthest Axis advances
Heaviest Allied bombing
★ Sinking of the Bismarck

SOVIET UNION

FINLAND
NORWAY
SWEDEN
DENMARK
GREAT BRITAIN
IRELAND
Dublin
Coventry
London
ESTONIA
LATVIA
LITHUANIA
EAST PRUSSIA
POLAND
GERMANY
RUHR
Cologne
BELG.
NETH.
FRANCE
NORMANDY
Paris
Bordeaux
SPAIN
Madrid
PORTUGAL
Lisbon
FRENCH MOROCCO
Casablanca
Tangier
Gibraltar
Oran
ALGERIA
Algiers
TUNISIA
Tunis
Bizerte
Bone
LIBYA
EGYPT
El Alamein
Tobruk
PALESTINE
SYRIA
TRANS-JORDAN
SUEZ CANAL
Cairo
CYPRUS
TURKEY
Ankara
GREECE
Athens
CRETE
BULGARIA
Sofia
ROMANIA
Bucharest
YUGOSLAVIA
Belgrade
HUNGARY
ALBANIA
ITALY
SICILY
Palermo
SARDINIA
CORSICA
BALEARIC IS.
MALTA
Rome
Anzio
Monte Cassino
Naples
Salerno
Florence
Trieste
AUSTRIA
SWITZ.
Vienna
Berchtesgaden
Munich
Stuttgart
Frankfurt
Prague
Torgau
Berlin
Potsdam
Königsberg
Danzig
Hamburg
Odel R.
Vistula R.
Warsaw
Kiev
Dnieper R.
Dniester R.
Don R.
Volga R.
Stalingrad
Moscow
Leningrad
Helsinki
Stockholm
Oslo
Sevastopol
Yalta
Istanbul
Black Sea
Aegean Sea
Mediterranean Sea
ATLANTIC OCEAN
North Sea
Baltic Sea
English Channel
Loire R.
Seine R.
Rhine
Maginot Line
Vichy France
Bordeaux
Vichy
Marseilles
Nice
Ebro R.
Budapest
Danube R.

1943
1942
1944
1945
1946

500 Miles
500 Kilometers
250
250
0

126

BATTLE OF MOSCOW

In a three-pronged offensive, Field Marshal Leeb's Army Group North marched on Leningrad. Army Group Center under Field Marshal Bock struck toward Moscow. Field Marshal Rundstedt's Army Group South raced toward Kiev, then veered in the direction of the Crimea and the North Caucasus. Snatching at body parts, Germany's allies joined in the frenzy. Romania struck north toward Odessa; Slovak and Hungarian units fought alongside—or rather accompanied—Bock and Rundstedt. Finland retook her lost territory. Currying favor with his idol, Hitler, Spain's Francisco Franco sent the hapless "Blue Division" to Russia.

German aircraft bombed Moscow in the early summer; by October, artillery fire made it difficult to sleep in the capital. The regime had already moved some Moscow factories east of the Volga and evacuated more than two million people, half the residents. As the artillery grew louder, the Kremlin ordered relocation of defense laboratories and institutes and transferred many government offices to Kuibyshev.

The flight of the petty bureaucrats—always the first to run—sapped civilian morale. Something approaching panic ensued and peaked on October 16, 1941. The authorities went to extraordinary lengths to reassure Muscovites: the State Defense Council under Stalin, the *Stavka* (General Headquarters) of the Supreme Command, and a core cadre of senior officials remained in the city, toward which Red Army reinforcements were rushing. The pilots who defended Moscow performed as heroically as their RAF counterparts over London, sometimes simply ramming enemy planes after exhausting their ammunition.

Moscow very nearly fell. The Germans reached to within 50 kilometers before halting to regroup. The Wehrmacht invested the city along a semicircular, 300-kilometer front from the Volga town of Kalinin (Tver) in the north to the headwaters of the Don River in the south. Reinforcements detached from Army Group North (Leeb) enabled Bock to resume his progress. By November 23, the Germans had dug foxholes and gun emplacements 23 kilometers from the Kremlin.

On December 6, a hundred divisions under General Georgi Zhukov—hero of Khalkhin Gol—counterattacked. Hitler had not known of the existence of this force, which was equipped with better tanks than the ones that had failed to hold the western frontiers. Stalin had not totally wasted the months between August 1939 and June 1941. Zhukov threw the Germans off stride and fatally compromised their timetable.

Replacing the aged Semyon Timoshenko as commander of the central front, Zhukov built a force composed of regular units rushed from the Far East, and reserves from European Russia and Central Asia. Unusually cold weather favored the defenders, who were armed with weapons designed to function in the cold and outfitted with heavy coats, mittens, felt boots. Wehrmacht equipment frequently malfunctioned at low temperatures, and lengthy supply lines were vulnerable to partisan attack. Certain the war would end by Christmas, Hitler had clad his troops in uniforms designed for the climate of Western Europe.

The Red Army regrouped psychologically. On the anniversary of the Bolshevik seizure of power, Stalin spoke in Red Square to some Red Army units literally moments before they left for the front lines. He invoked the great military heroes—Aleksandr Nevsky, Dmitri Donskoy, Suvorov, Kutuzov—in exhorting the soldiers to be worthy of their heritage.

In a startling departure from all that was Soviet, Stalin had appealed the previous evening to national pride. Lingering over the revered—by all save the Communists—names of Pushkin, Tolstoi, Tchaikovsky, Glinka, Chekhov, he asked people to defend not communism but *Russia*. Easing restrictions on the Russian Orthodox Church, he exalted the old values: Russian nationalism-patriotism, Orthodoxy, *sobornost* ("communityness").

From this time forward the Red Army went into battle shouting "*Za rodinu i Stalina!*" (For the motherland and Stalin!). The "Vozhd"—Leader, akin to Duce and Führer—was beyond mere popularity. Stalin was the commander-in-chief, embodiment of the nation he had so tormented, and—this required a leap of the imagination—chief defender of the faith.

SIEGE OF LENINGRAD

On August 28, 1941, Nazi forces severed the rail line to Mga, 40 kilometers *east* of Leningrad, cutting Russia's second city off from the outside world. Only when Zhukov took over from the incompetent Voroshilov on September 11 did the situation stabilize.

A September 9 air raid had obliterated the food warehouses, a heavier blow than putting a hundred antiaircraft guns out of action. Hitler had Leningrad in a stranglehold. Municipal authorities evacuated hundreds of thousands of residents including almost all the children. About half the prewar population of 3.85 million remained. Rationing began early in the war. On November 20, officials reduced the daily bread ration to 250 grams for manual workers, the highest category, and 125 grams for white-collar workers, the lowest. By Christmas, air-dropped supplies permitted an increase to 350 and 200 grams, respectively, but there were no vegetables or fruit. A foreign journalist reported a jelly made from 2,000 tons of sheep intestines. When the winter food supplies were almost gone, the authorities issued this as food.

From November 1941 to October 1942, about 630,000 Leningrad residents died of starvation. That was equivalent to the entire population of San Francisco. People died in the streets, at work, in dark, unheated apartments. Survivors often lacked the strength to put corpses on sleds and tow them to a collecting station. As the ordeal deepened, in many families no one survived. Toward the end of the winter, officials conducted a meticulous search to collect unburied bodies.

When Lake Ladoga east of Leningrad froze to a thickness of about two meters, the Red Army and the civil defense authorities built a "road to life" across the ice to the eastern shore. The Germans bombarded it incessantly with artillery and, when weather permitted, from the air. Truck convoys carrying supplies raced across the ice twice a day, but many vehicles never made it. There would be an explosion and a gaping black hole would open up. Military police would mark the spot quickly with flags on long poles and reroute traffic. The "road to life"—actually three separate routes—resembled a 37-kilometer slalom. People who made the run described how drivers would dodge the holes and try to stay between the flags. They would curse Hitler and erupt into maniacal laughter when a shell or bomb burst nearby and showered their vehicles with ice but did not impede their progress toward the opposite shore. The last convoy before the spring thaw made it safely on April 8, 1942.

In all, a million people died—victims of starvation and military action—in the siege, which lasted nearly 900 days. Their collective heroism, and that of the survivors, has no equal in the annals of warfare. Never in history had a city of that size been under siege for so long, or paid such a price. The siege and blockade did not officially end until January 27, 1944. The lovely city had seen the last of the Nazis. The Communists would remain several decades longer.

The first post-Soviet mayor, Anatoli Sobchak, confirmed that Communist officials had received regular shipments of fresh vegetables, fruit, meat, and other food throughout the siege. In 1992, Leningrad residents voted overwhelmingly to restore the city's original name, St. Petersburg.

BATTLE OF STALINGRAD

Despite its failure to take either Moscow or Leningrad, in the spring of 1942 the Wehrmacht seemed to be in command of the Eastern Front. It had fortified positions 135 kilometers east of Leningrad; it controlled Moscow's northern, western, and southern approaches; it occupied Ukraine and would take the Crimea in July. This territory had provided the USSR with two-thirds of its coal and pig iron before the war, 60 percent of its steel and aluminum.

But the war had not gone the way the Führer had promised. Blitzkrieg (lightning war) had degenerated into a protracted campaign, and the problem of supply became critical as the Red Air Force and partisan units blew up trains and truck convoys. Industries in German-occupied territories operated at only 10 percent of capacity. Food from the Ukrainian "breadbasket" went to feed the Wehrmacht; little reached Germany.

Soviet defenses along the Leningrad–Moscow line had not broken, but south of Moscow the situation was precarious. After mopping up the remnants of resistance in the Crimea, the Germans prepared for an assault on Stalingrad. Code-named "Kremlin," the plan rested in part on a "disinformation" scheme designed to show that the main German campaign in 1942 would be a second assault on Moscow. Most Red Army generals expressed skepticism, but Stalin transferred men and matériel to the Moscow region.

As Zhukov, Vasily Chuikov, and other commanders had warned, the Wehrmacht struck at Stalingrad. Stalin's ignorance of strategy, first revealed in the Civil War, returned to

haunt Russia, and to cost her hundreds of thousands of lives.

Stalingrad lies on the Volga's west bank at the point closest to the Don, which flows into the Sea of Azov. Originally called Tsaritsyn, it took Stalin's name in 1925. It was home to the Stalin Tractor Works, largest in the world, which in 1940 converted to tank production. The population was then about half a million.

The Germans attacked on June 28, 1942, aiming to drive the Red Army out of the territory west of the Don loop. In four weeks they advanced 150 to 400 kilometers and on August 23 reached the Volga north of Stalingrad, which suffered a heavy Luftwaffe bombardment that day. By September 4 there was fighting in the suburbs, and nine days later the battle inside the city began. The authorities proclaimed a state of siege on August 25 and evacuated all nonessential residents. On September 12 the 62nd Army under General Vasily Chuikov and the 64th Army under General M. S. Shumilov took over the defense. Having failed to see the blow coming, Stalin now ordered Stalingrad held at all costs. Hitler ordered the Wehrmacht to take it.

The city stretched 28 kilometers along the river on the north-south axis but was only five kilometers wide. The peculiar banana-shaped layout presented unusual problems for attacker and defender, but the Red Army artillery positioned on the high eastern bank of the Volga had an enormous advantage. The guns were protected, and the Nazis could not encircle Stalingrad.

The greatest battle ever fought *inside* a major city began on September 13, 1942. The Germans dictated the pace for nine weeks, then, on November 19, the tide shifted. In the Red Army counteroffensive, forces under Generals Nikolai Vatutin and Konstantin Rokossovsky broke through German lines northwest of the city. The next day, another army under General Andrei Yeremenko tore through the Wehrmacht perimeter south of Stalingrad.

The jaws of the pincers began to close; several encircled Romanian divisions handily surrendered. Forbidding the commander of the doomed German Sixth Army, General Friedrich von Paulus, even to consider negotiating, Hitler promoted him to field marshal: No German commander of that rank had ever surrendered. There were fortified German positions 40 kilometers west, but Paulus did not try to break out.

The Red Army kept up a round-the-clock artillery and aerial bombardment. Fresh troops under the best generals bore down relentlessly. On the shortwave frequency the Wehrmacht used, the Red Army broadcast a monotonous, terrifying message in German: "Stalingrad—[tick, tock, tick, tock]—Massengrab!" ("Stalingrad—is a mass grave!—Stalingrad . . . "). What little German morale was left vanished.

The battle ended on February 2, 1943. The Red Army took Field Marshal Paulus, 24 generals, and 91,000 soldiers prisoner. The Germans had earlier evacuated nearly 50,000 wounded. The Red Army buried 147,000 enemy dead. Soviet military and civilian casualties exceeded that number.

BATTLE OF KURSK

The Red Army now raced westward and seized the industrial center of Harkov, the former capital of Ukraine. His prestige sullied on the Volga, Hitler ordered his forces to retake the city. The Germans dislodged Soviet forces on March 15, 1943; but it was a hollow victory. There was no reason to hold Harkov if the Wehrmacht was prepared to stake everything on recapturing it. Reduced to rubble, it had no strategic or even tactical value.

Harkov was scant compensation for Stalingrad. Hitler searched for a different theatre, there to stage yet another grand spectacular.

He settled on Kursk, 330 kilometers southwest of Moscow. An important center on the Moscow–Simferopol railway line, Kursk had 120,000 inhabitants in 1939. With food processing its major industry, it had no intrinsic strategic importance. An enemy could cut the railway line at a dozen other points and do more harm. The Red Army had reoccupied Kursk during the post-Stalingrad counteroffensive. When intelligence reports indicated an attack likely, Generals Zhukov and Aleksandr Vasilevsky prepared partially disguised defensive positions.

Hitler knew about the Kursk defenses, and he knew Zhukov and Vasilevsky knew that he knew. This was the way Hitler thought, as General Paulus should have known. The Red Army would not expect an attack. Therefore, the World War I corporal—Hitler fought bravely—reasoned, that was exactly the right move. He would snip off the Kursk salient.

Powerful new Tiger and Panther tanks, Focke-Wulf 190 and Henschel 129 fighter planes, and the huge "Ferdinand" mobile gun would obliterate the Red Army. This "Operation Citadel" would be under two new field marshals, Hans Kluge and Erich von Manstein. The old aristocratic German officers had failed; Hitler would show the world what real Nazi commanders could do.

What they could do was lose. One of the war's largest engagements began on July 5, 1943, with a massive assault on the Red Army defense line, now converted into a gigantic trap. The balance of forces favored the defenders, who had large reserves. The Germans broke through the defenses but could not penetrate the salient deeply anywhere. The Red Army lines held.

This was the largest tank battle ever fought; 2,700 Wehrmacht and 3,598 Red Army vehicles were engaged. On the evening of the first day, Yuri Levitan announced on Radio Moscow that the Red Army had destroyed 586 Ger-

German soldiers surprised by a survivor, southern Russia, 1942. (National Archives)

man tanks. That convinced the Soviet people as nothing before, not even victory at Stalingrad, that they would win the war. As they had done on the ice of Lake Chud (Peipus) 700 years earlier under Aleksandr Nevsky, Slav bested Teuton. The Soviet T-34 tank and the *katyusha* (multirail rocket projector) outperformed German technology.

The Battle of Kursk ended on August 23. Once again German losses were staggering. The Red Army paid a high price to shatter the myth that the Wehrmacht was invincible in summer, but Kursk was Hitler's last attempt to recapture the initiative in the East.

WARTIME DIPLOMACY

Since June 1941 the Kremlin had pressed Britain and later the United States to open a second front against Hitler. Stalin dismissed the fact that the British had fought alone from the fall of France to the Nazi invasion of the USSR, thought the Allied campaigns in North Africa and Italy paltry, and had no interest in the war in the Pacific. He maintained that the USSR was bearing most of the burden in the struggle against fascism.

High-level discussions took place in 1942 and 1943. Roosevelt and Churchill informed

Stalin that it was physically impossible to invade the European continent until they had built up the huge force required for what would be by far the greatest amphibious assault ever. The agony of Moscow, Leningrad, Kiev, Stalingrad, Harkov, Kursk, and countless Russian, Ukrainian, and Belarusian villages, however, did not inspire a sober appreciation of such explanations. It seemed to Stalin and his advisers, and to millions of Soviet citizens, that the West hoped Hitler would bleed Russia to death.

The "Big Three" met at Tehran (Iran) November 28 to December 1, 1943, to discuss the proposed Allied landing in France, and postwar cooperation. General Dwight Eisenhower, the Allied Commander-in-Chief, had scheduled the invasion for May 1944; it actually began on June 6. Stalin expressed satisfaction but continued to grumble.

The leaders took each other's measure. Stalin decided he liked Roosevelt better than Churchill, and Roosevelt conceived a certain admiration for the Soviet dictator. Roosevelt and Stalin agreed in principle to divide Germany into occupation zones to ensure against future aggression. Churchill preferred to isolate Prussia and allow the South German states to join Austria and even Hungary in a "peaceful confederation." Such a union would certainly be hostile to the Soviet Union—as would, of course, "isolated" and independent Prussia. Stalin rejected this.

Soviet Women's Land Army, 1943. (National Archives)

The Allies also discussed aid to the USSR. Britain and the United States had sent massive amounts of military supplies in 1942 and 1943, contributing greatly to the Soviet victories. By late 1943 the American Lend-Lease program had provided more than 7,000 aircraft; 215,000 motor vehicles; and huge quantities of steel, machinery, and food.

KATYN

Russia's security against invasion from the West hinged on Poland. For centuries all Polish regimes had been anti-Russian; in the interwar period the anti-Communist military junta opposed any accommodation with the USSR. The events of the Second World War only complicated a dilemma that persists to this day.

Poland had reason to fear Russia. In April 1943, the Wehrmacht found mass graves of Polish soldiers and officers near the Russian city of Smolensk. Documents on the bodies, and other evidence, placed the atrocity in 1940, when the USSR controlled that part of Poland where the victims had been taken prisoner. A team of forensic scientists sent by the International Red Cross concluded that Soviet forces had committed the atrocity. The puzzled Western leaders thought at first that Hitler was up to another monstrous trick. On direct orders from Churchill and Roosevelt, Allied military authorities refused to discuss the matter. There could be no interference with the war effort.

Nearly 26,000 Polish officers and soldiers were "missing," and the Free Poles in London—politicians in exile—had repeatedly tried to learn their fate. They had simply disappeared when the Soviets invaded in 1939, and the Kremlin ignored requests for information. When news of the atrocity became public, Moscow blamed the Germans, accusing them of attempting to split the Allies. In 1941–1943, Germany had indeed controlled the area where the mass graves were located, and no atrocity was beyond the SS. But the killings took place in 1940. When the Red Army retook the Smolensk region in September 1943, Moscow sent in its own forensic specialists but denied outside experts access. Again the USSR pronounced the Germans guilty.

Soviet forces had invaded and occupied Eastern Poland in September–October 1939. Early the next year, the Red Army and the NKVD moved the interned Polish soldiers and officers to Katyn Forest near Smolensk. In the summer of that year, NKVD death squads under the personal direction of Commissar of State Security Lavrenti Beria executed 21,857 Poles at Katyn and other holding areas. Stalin received regular reports on the operation, the general outlines of which were known to all his top associates.

The Katyn martyrs lay in unmarked graves. For four decades, the Polish Communists slavishly parroted Kremlin lies. In 1981, the unofficial labor-political movement "Solidarity" erected a memorial. The Communist government destroyed it, then in 1985 unveiled its own monument in Warsaw. The inscription read, TO THE POLISH SOLDIERS—VICTIMS OF HITLERITE FASCISM ON THE SOIL OF KATYN. Only in February 1989 did Poland's Communists admit that the NKVD perpetrated the atrocity. This came more than a year after creation of a bilateral Soviet–Polish commission to investigate what Mikhail Gorbachev called "blank spots" in relations between the two countries. In April 1990 the Kremlin itself acknowledged Soviet responsibility for "one of the gravest crimes of Stalinism." The Gorbachev regime released documents that detailed the NKVD's planning and execution of the Katyn operation. There is now an appropriate monument at Katyn, and free access to it. The question of Polish membership in NATO hangs in the air.

BABI YAR

When the Red Army retook Kiev on November 6, 1943, it discovered another wartime outrage, this one the work of the German SS. Most of the victims were Jews, and the Kremlin compounded the horror by keeping silent.

Kiev had fallen to the Germans on September 19, 1941. A few days later, delayed-action mines and bombs leveled the city's central district. The day after the explosions, *Einsatzgruppe C* (special-duty troops) reached full strength. After conferring with the German military governor, the SS commander accused Kiev's Jews of sabotage. Placards went up all over the city ordering the remaining Jews— 75,000 had already fled—to assemble near the Hebrew cemetery at 8:00 A.M. on September 29, 1941, bringing personal documents, money, valuables, warm clothing. Those who disobeyed would be shot. The rumor went around that the Germans were sending all Jews to Palestine.

The cemetery lay near a gash in the earth known as Babi Yar (Crone Ravine). Kiev's Jews arrived there as ordered. Troops of *Sonderkommando* (special commando) *4A,* a division of *Einsatzgruppe C,* herded them—mostly women, children, and elderly men—into several narrow lanes. At a point where the lanes turned, the soldiers ordered the people to take off their clothes and place them in one pile, the food and other items they had brought for their journey on another. Those who balked were savagely beaten and stripped by the *Sonderkommando*'s Ukrainian helpers. As the naked, bleeding, terrified people were pushed violently into ever narrower lines, many went into shock and began screaming, jumping up and down, befouling themselves. The behavior of the doomed people, the shouts of the guards and their helpers, the barking of the police dogs, the sound of wooden truncheons and rifle butts striking human flesh—all was pandemonium. Soldiers despatched small groups up a slope and around to the other side of the hill. People were shoved onto the ledge overlooking Babi Yar until there was no more room, then the machine guns opened fire. The victims collapsed into the ravine. At regular intervals the Ukrainian assistants climbed down to ensure no one survived.

In two days, *Einsatzgruppe C* killed 33,771 Jews. This set a record; even Auschwitz could kill only 6,000 a day. The murders at Babi Yar continued throughout the Nazi occupation. In all, more than 100,000 people died there during the 750 days the swastika flew over Kiev.

Not until 1976 did the Soviet regime build a war memorial at Babi Yar. The inscription at the foot of the monument read, "Here in 1941–43 the German fascist invaders executed more than 100,000 citizens of the city of Kiev and Soviet prisoners of war." There was no mention of the fact that most were Jews.

CAMPAIGNS OF 1944–1945

Every piece of regained territory testified to the might of the Red Army, which recaptured Novgorod in January 1944 and stood at the prewar Russo-Polish frontier a few weeks later. It liberated Odessa on April 10 and soon reached Romania. A month later the Crimea and Ukraine came under Soviet control. Having slashed through Belarus and the eastern part of the Poland of 1919–1939, on August 1 the Red Army halted 60 kilometers east of Warsaw. Both the Polish underground and the Western Allies believed the Kremlin would order the taking of the Polish capital.

Determined to liberate as much Polish territory as possible and earn the right to deal with the Soviets as equals, the Polish underground had long planned the uprising it launched on August 1, 1944. The leaders believed they could overthrow the Nazis on their own despite the fact that the Germans had five

On the home front: teaching high school students to shoot. (National Archives)

divisions in Warsaw, and intact supply lines. The Poles claimed to have several divisions; in reality they had only about 2,000 men under arms.

The Red Army did not budge, and Stalin refused to let British and American planes use Soviet airfields. Denied air drops and Red Army support, the Polish uprising collapsed after 63 days. On October 11, 1944, Hitler ordered Warsaw razed. The Poles blamed the Red Army for the calamity, which cost 200,000 mostly civilian Polish lives. The Soviets saw the situation differently. The Red Army had advanced 600 to 700 kilometers in the 40 days before August 1. Anticipating a counterattack, it needed to rest, regroup, and resupply. The Polish underground made no serious effort to coordinate its efforts.

The Katyn massacre story had broken the previous year. The anti-Communist Poles understandably beat the Soviets with that stick until Churchill finally restrained them. Nothing would bring the Katyn dead back; only the

Red Army could drive the Germans out of Poland. Too late did the Poles realize that the Soviets, who had earlier suggested that an uprising might be in order, never had any intention of assisting. The anti-Communist Poles miscalculated. The Soviets would not agree to restoration of the interwar frontiers or creation of a truly independent Polish government. If Stalin did nothing else, he would make sure that postwar Poland offered no threat to the USSR.

The Red Army marched through ruined Warsaw on January 17, 1945—five and a half months after the uprising began.

YALTA AND THE END OF THE WAR

All the Polish tragedies figured in the February 1945 Yalta Conference. Some loomed larger than others; the Katyn Forest massacre was banished entirely. The end of the war in sight, Stalin demanded and received the con-

Molotov and Soviet officers greeting President Roosevelt on his arrival in the Crimea, February 1945. (Department of Defense)

sent of Roosevelt and Churchill to shift the Polish frontiers 200 to 300 kilometers west. Thus the postwar Russo–Polish border would roughly follow the Curzon—or Curzon-Ribbentrop-Molotov—line. West of it the population was predominantly Polish. To the east were some Poles but also Belarusians, Ukrainians, Lithuanians, a few surviving Jews, and Russians. The Poles had rejected that line and had fought in 1920 to move it east. Soviet Russia now pushed back, "compensating" Poland with historically German territory in the west.

Stalin did not originate this scheme. Early in the war, Polish General Wladyslaw Sikorski, foreseeing Stalin's war aims, proposed substantially the same settlement. He stood virtually alone.

Stalin won the Western leaders' grudging approval of his plan to install the Communist-dominated Lublin Poles as the nucleus of the postwar Polish government. He promised "free and unfettered elections" in which the anti-Communist London Poles could participate.

Contemptuously dismissing Red Army control of Poland, European and American conservatives charged that Roosevelt sold that country to Stalin for small and sordid coin. But in 1945 there was no sentiment in the West for fighting the USSR. Under the circumstances, Roosevelt and Churchill got the best deal they could.

Given the sensitivity of Polish issues, Germany was almost a secondary consideration at Yalta. The Allies agreed on occupation zones; at Churchill's insistence one of those would be French. Germany would remain divided indefinitely, and the victors would ensure she could not again threaten peace. The major Nazi leaders would stand trial.

The USSR agreed to enter the war against Japan soon after Germany's defeat. In return it would gain the southern half of Sakhalin and the Kurile Islands from Japan. The Allies recognized the Soviet sphere of interest in Manchuria.

In February 1945 American strategists estimated that the war against Japan would continue for a year and a half after victory in Europe and cost a million casualties. Only a few of the planners knew of the attempts to develop the atomic bomb, and those privy to the secret had no idea whether it would prove the awesome engine of destruction predicted. Russian assistance in the Pacific was vital.

Finally, the Yalta conferees agreed to establish a United Nations, making Woodrow Wilson's dream of international cooperation a reality. Stalin was given three UN votes—the USSR, Ukraine, Belarus. That made no sense; but the extra votes did not alter the course of history.

About the time of the Yalta Conference, the RAF and the U.S. Army Air force conducted some of the war's heaviest bombing raids. In Dresden, 135,000 Germans perished. This compared with Hiroshima and Nagasaki, where atomic bombs took a total of 114,000 lives. The Dresden raid made little strategic sense. The war in Europe was about to end. The city did have defense industries, but there were other, closer targets. The Allies could have crippled the German war effort more severely, at less cost to themselves. But the German cities hit so hard in January–April 1945 were in the planned Soviet occupation zone.

On March 7, 1945, the American First Army crossed the Rhine at Remagen; there was henceforth little organized German resistance in the West. American forces soon reached the Elbe River and linked up with Red Army units on April 25. Advance parties of the Red Army fought their way into the German capital on April 20. The Battle of Berlin, a week of in-

Churchill, Roosevelt, and Stalin at Yalta, February 3, 1945. Standing behind them are Eden, Stettinius, Molotov, and Harriman. (Department of Defense)

tense house-to-house fighting, began on May 1. On the German side, only the true fanatics were left. Hitler had set the stage for the *Götterdämmerung* but had not the courage to attend the finale. Along with the wife he had just married, Eva Braun, he committed suicide in his bunker beneath the *Reichskanzlei* on April 30, 1945.

Franklin Roosevelt had died 18 days earlier. Harry S Truman, his successor, and British Prime Minister Winston Churchill, proclaimed the end of the war in Europe on May 8. Stalin waited until the German generals had completed the formalities of surrender before declaring victory the next day.

The Soviet Union entered the Pacific war on August 8, two days after the bombing of Hiroshima. The Japanese surrendered on August 14. The USSR was already on the move in the Far East, and so was the Yalta controversy.

THE WAR AND THE SOVIET PEOPLES

Approximately 58 million people, half of them civilians, were killed or died of causes directly related to the fighting in the Second World War. At least 27 million were citizens of the USSR, one-eighth of the nation's population. Only Yugoslavia—in particular, Serbia—gave proportionately more blood.

In Soviet Russia, everyone lost someone and many lost everyone. In addition to the dead there were uncounted numbers of physically and psychologically wounded; no nation ever had so many mutilated veterans as living reminders of its agony. The death—it will go unrecorded—of the last Soviet World War II veteran around the year 2025 or 2030 will not close the book of sorrow.

The material damage, which unlike the human could be repaired, was on a monumental scale. West of the Leningrad-Moscow-Stalingrad line the destruction was almost total; cities, towns, and villages lay in ruins. The

peasants had lost their homes, barns, sheds, and other property to the invaders, who also destroyed dams and canals, blew up bridges, clogged waterways, poisoned wells. The USSR lost 31,850 factories and other industrial enterprises, not counting small plants; 1,876 *sovhozes;* 2,890 machine-tractor stations. Of the 200,000 collective farms, 98,000 in the most fertile part of the country were ravaged. It is said that no one who saw European Russia, Ukraine, or Belarus in 1945 could dread Hell.

The Soviet people drew several conclusions from the war, notably that there must never be another. The Communist regime declared that no power or combination of powers would be permitted to threaten the security of the USSR.

The Soviet Union emerged from the conflict a great power, but the atomic bomb threw the postwar military-political equation into confusion. Poised in the spring and summer of 1945 to dominate Eastern Europe, and northeastern Asia, the USSR and the world suddenly had to contend with weapons of mass destruction on a scale where "mass" had a hitherto undreamed-of meaning. It would soon become possible to pack into one bomb an explosive force greater than all the firepower on all fronts in World War II. Warfare, diplomacy, and human psychology would never be the same.

SUGGESTED ADDITIONAL READINGS

BARBER, JOHN, and MARK HARRISON. *The Soviet Home Front, 1941–1945.* White Plains, NY: Longman, 1991.

CHURCHILL, WINSTON S. *The Second World War,* 6 vols. Boston: Houghton Mifflin, 1948–1953.

MASTNY, VOJTECH. *Russia's Road to the Cold War.* New York: Columbia University Press, 1979.

WERTH, ALEXANDER. *Russia at War, 1941–1945.* New York: Dutton, 1964.

WRIGHT, GORDON. *The Ordeal of Total War.* New York: Harper & Row, 1968.

13

THE COLD WAR

On August 6, 1945, an American military aircraft dropped an atomic bomb on the Japanese city of Hiroshima. Two days later the USSR declared war on Japan and invaded Manchuria. A second American nuclear weapon destroyed Nagasaki on August 9. Japan sued for peace the next day.

General Douglas MacArthur accepted the formal Japanese surrender aboard the U.S. battleship *Missouri* on September 2, 1945. There would be no invasion of the home islands. The Second World War, which began when Japan seized Manchuria in 1931, had come to an end.

Thus the West interpreted events, but Stalin and his entourage saw it differently. In their view, the capitalist nations had fought among themselves for colonies and markets until June 1941, when Germany marched east to achieve the universal capitalist goal—destruction of the world's only Socialist state. Although Britain and the United States declared themselves Soviet Russia's allies, they in fact, the Stalinists believed, worked for a German victory by delaying the opening of a second front in Europe for three years.

Uninformed about and indifferent to events in Asia, Western public opinion had regarded the war in Europe as a contest between good and evil. But in the 1920s and 1930s some Western politicians had repeatedly called for a Crusade against the Communists. Many openly expressed admiration for nazism and fascism; not a few were willing to let Hitler lead the Crusade. Kremlin suspicions were thus not entirely without foundation.

Franklin Delano Roosevelt thought he could reach a postwar modus vivendi with Stalin. Less sanguine, Winston Churchill regarded the wartime alliance as a disagreeable necessity. During the war the British Prime Minister had called for an Anglo-American invasion of Europe's "soft underbelly" near Trieste and Venice. The idea was to push into the European heartland to defeat Hitler and deny the Soviets territory west of the Warsaw-Budapest-Bucarest line. Roosevelt and Stalin vetoed the idea.

The alliance of convenience seemed certain to collapse after Hitler's defeat. Voices in the West spoke of a "Cold War," a condition of confrontation between two heavily armed camps, possibly a Third World War. The Soviets read post-1945 developments as a new phase of the conflict between capitalism and "socialism"—cynical code word for "police state governed from Moscow."

THE POTSDAM CONFERENCE

The "Big Three" leaders—France not represented—met in the relatively undamaged Berlin suburb of Potsdam on July 17, 1945, to work out a German settlement and refine the Yalta agreements. Some Americans believed an untested U.S. president, Harry S Truman,

Stalin, Truman, and Churchill at Potsdam, July 1945. Visible over Truman's left shoulder is Clement Attlee, Churchill's successor. (Department of Defense)

would be no match for either Stalin or Churchill, and their fears intensified when the British voters, thinking Churchill too hostile to Russia, did not reelect him. The Labour party won the British election of July 26; its leader, Clement Attlee, immediately replaced Churchill at the negotiating table. Attlee thought communism merely a variant of democracy. Fortunately, the new Foreign Minister, Ernest Bevin, once head of the Scottish dockworkers, had no such illusions.

Midway through the Potsdam Conference, Truman informed Stalin and Attlee that the United States had successfully tested a weapon of unimaginable destructive power. The Soviet dictator seemed strangely indifferent.

Secretary of War Henry Stimson had told President Roosevelt early in 1945 that the Soviets probably knew of the "Manhattan Project." Moscow had indeed been receiving detailed reports from spies about the American effort to develop an atomic bomb, and Stalin

had established his own crash nuclear-weapons program, placing it under control of the Butcher of Katyn, NKVD Chief Lavrenti Beria.

The Potsdam Conference confirmed the division of Germany into four—later five—occupation zones. An Allied Control Council with headquarters in Berlin would provide coordination but had a vague mandate: Each occupying power could do as it liked in its own sector. The Allies called for reunification after a suitable period. Moscow was determined to ensure that Germany would never again be capable of aggression. The Germans would have to pay $20 billion in reparations, half of it to the USSR. At least 10 percent of the military-industrial equipment of the Western occupation zones, where most German industry was located, would go to Russia.

The Allies pledged to eradicate nazism and militarism and authorized the trial for "crimes against humanity" ("war crimes") of the surviving Nazi leaders. Berlin, 150 kilometers inside the Soviet occupation zone, was to be under four-power administration pending a general peace settlement. The newly created Council of Foreign Ministers would negotiate peace treaties with Italy, Bulgaria, and Romania before dealing with Germany. The Potsdam Conference tacitly established a fifth (Polish) occupation zone: The Polish–German frontier would follow the line of the Oder and Neisse rivers. The Western powers formally agreed only to Polish "administration" of historically German territory *east* of the Oder–Neisse line but raised no serious objections to the expulsion of nine million German citizens. This was a settling of accounts; the German people would pay for what their Führer did in their name. The most casual reading of the Yalta accords would have shown that Polish administration would swiftly pass from occupation to outright annexation.

Having taken part of interwar Poland, the Soviets also seized much of East Prussia. They renamed Emmanuel Kant's Königsberg "Kaliningrad" after the satyr Mikhail Kalinin, who would die in June 1946. Poland received the German cities of Danzig and Stettin.

The Japanese surrender obviated the need for a military campaign in Asia but did not prevent the Soviets from occupying or annexing the areas that Yalta and Potsdam assigned to them. The United States did, however, deny Moscow participation in the occupation of Japan.

The Yalta Conference had agreed on the repatriation of military and civilian prisoners of war. The Western Allies had liberated a million Soviet POWs and civilians employed in German slave-labor enterprises, and they controlled areas where there were roughly 10 million "displaced persons" from Eastern Europe, including inhabitants of the de facto Polish zone of Germany. The Red Army liberated about a million of their own POWs and Soviet civilians from the German camps. As many as 50,000 of the military prisoners had joined the so-called Russian Liberation Army (RLA). Commanded by General A. A. Vlasov, who defected to Hitler, the RLA fought against the Soviet Union. There could be no question about the fate of Vlasov and his men.

The other POWs, dragooned Soviet civilians, and refugees, were another matter, or should have been. Moscow demanded the return of all—except for the Germans—who fled from the territory now part of Poland; Stalin particularly insisted on getting his hands on the POWs. The Red Army had standing orders to shoot its own wounded when the enemy closed in, and thus in Stalin's view there could be no prisoners of war. Anyone who surrendered was guilty of collaboration, as were, no matter what the circumstances, civilians who had served the Germans.

In an action with the sinister code name "Keelhaul," the Western Allies forcibly repatriated almost two million Soviet "citizens," by which Stalin understood not merely bona fide USSR residents but also Estonians, Latvians, Lithuanians, and Poles whose homes lay east of the new 1945 Soviet–Polish frontier. Few if any of these people wished to live under Soviet rule. The Western Allies sent them back, however, ostensibly to ensure humane treatment of the 25,000 of their own POWs whom the Red Army had liberated. A second, less publicized goal was to secure postwar Soviet cooperation. Hundreds of terrified prisoners were killed and thousands injured in clashes with American and British troops. They knew that the fate of Vlasov's men also awaited them.

Many Soviet and other East European collaborators found refuge in the West, where American and other authorities recruited many—forgiving Nazi and even Gestapo and SS backgrounds—to fight the Cold War. Hundreds of major war criminals would escape prosecution for several decades, in many cases with official assistance or the aid of some Christian sects.

EASTERN EUROPE

At the end of the war, the Red Army controlled Poland, Czechoslovakia, Hungary, Romania, Bulgaria, and the eastern third of Germany. Stalin withdrew his troops from Yugoslavia, now ruled by the ardent Croatian Stalinist Josip Broz ("Tito"). Another Stalin disciple, Enver Hoxha, was master of Albania. In the Near East, the Red Army pulled out of northeastern Turkey, which it had occupied since late 1941. It remained in northern Iran, where Stalin had established a puppet government.

The only new areas in Europe physically absorbed into the USSR were some districts of northern Finland, the Carpatho–Ukraine (formerly part of Czechoslovakia), and parts of East Prussia. The so-called regained territories included the Baltic states, eastern Poland, Bessarabia, and the Bukovina.

Given postwar realities, Soviet actions were more restrained than might have been expected. Moscow would no more permit reestablishment of independent anti-Communist regimes in the strategically important Baltic states than the United States would allow Communist regimes in Latin America. The territory taken from Poland had long been the subject of dispute; the population included not only Poles but also Belarusians, Lithuanians, Ukrainians, Russians, and Jews. (The 200,000 Jews residing in the areas of Poland that the Soviets took in September 1939 were the largest group to survive the Holocaust.)

The overwhelming majority of all Eastern European populations passionately opposed the Soviet-sponsored Communist regimes. Only in Czechoslovakia, Yugoslavia, and Bulgaria did genuine friendship for the USSR exist, at least in the initial postwar period, and there it soon faded.

The postwar political contest in Eastern Europe did not, however, pit democracy against communism. Democracy had never existed anywhere in Eastern Europe save partially in Czechoslovakia, where the Slovak minority had valid grievances against the dominant Czechs—grievances that would, after the fall of communism, lead them to secede. Most parties paid lip service to democracy but had few qualms about suppressing their opponents. Corrupt politics ran the gamut from military dictatorship to degenerate monarchy. As in occupied France, there had been a great deal of sympathy for fascism throughout the interwar period and enthusiastic collaboration with the Nazis during the war in Croatia, Bosnia, Slovakia, Hungary, Romania, and Bulgaria.

Political agents who rode into Eastern Europe in the Red Army baggage train generally began bringing a country under Soviet control by directing the domestic Communist parties—ranks purged repeatedly on Soviet orders—to enter coalition "governments of national unity." Western observers sometimes monitored the elections such regimes held in 1946–1947, but the real supervision came from Soviet officials. Nowhere did the Communists come close to winning a parliamentary majority, but they invariably took such key ministerial posts as interior—control of national police forces—and justice, communications, and the media. Non-Communists might hold the premiership and the foreign ministry but their freedom of action was severely limited.

Once in control of the police, courts, and media, the Communists would move to isolate and discredit influential non-Communists by any means available. Prewar politicians, Resistance heroes, intellectuals, and professional people suffered harassment, physical violence, and often death. The Communists charged them with being stooges of the Nazis or agents of "Western imperialism."

After eliminating all but a few tame non-Communist political figures, a third step involved holding new elections under a bloc system. Each political party received a per-

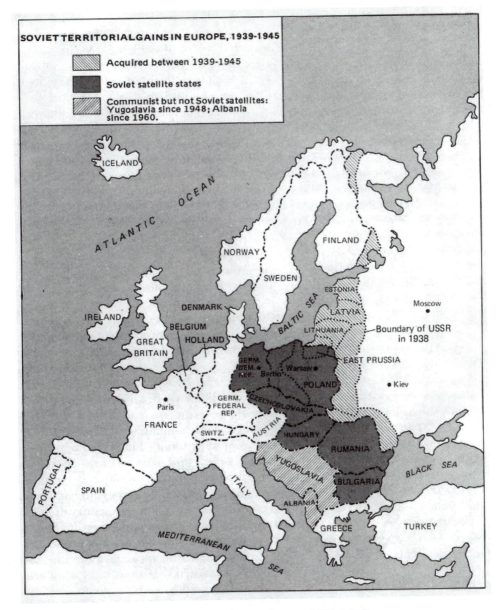

Soviet territorial gains in Europe, 1939–1945.

centage of seats in parliament based on a complicated formula weighted in favor of urban working-class constituencies, poor peasants, bureaucrats, soldiers—but never officers—and others believed well-disposed toward communism. Under this system the Communists would take a majority of seats no matter what the size of their vote, which never exceeded 34 percent in a free election. They would then proceed to enact Moscow-dictated legislation, enabling acts that gave them carte blanche. Like the courts and the media, the legislature became an arm of the executive branch, which Moscow controlled.

This pattern was typical, and by early 1948 every country in Eastern Europe save Yugoslavia had come under Soviet control. Yugoslavia differed only in that native Stalinists insisted on running their own country and conducting their own terror.

With a strong nudge from British Foreign Minister Bevin, in the spring of 1947 President Truman marshalled American forces to meet the Soviet challenge. Congress approved massive economic and military aid to Greece and Turkey with the aim of helping them withstand Communist pressure. Washington accepted the role of policeman in areas deemed vital to American national security and promised to send money, arms, military advisers, and even troops to any threatened nation.

The new Truman Doctrine offered a defense against armed aggression but was not designed to deal with economic chaos. Some prominent Americans reasoned that the abysmal state of the European economy made communism attractive. Put Europe on its feet, they argued, and the threat would diminish. In June 1947 Secretary of State George C. Marshall proposed that the United States finance Europe's economic recovery with a program of loans, capital investment, grants, and other aid (the Marshall Plan).

A few days later the Soviet delegation walked out of a Paris meeting of foreign ministers called to respond to the American offer. Stalin had toyed with accepting, but when Washington insisted on supervising the use of loan funds he abandoned the idea and compelled Czechoslovakia, which had jumped at the aid, to follow suit.

With American assistance, Western Europe surpassed 1939 industrial production levels in mid-1951—by almost 45 percent. There was virtually full employment, the living standard was rising, and food rationing ended everywhere save in Britain. The leftward political drift ceased. Communist strength among French and Italian voters peaked at 27 to 33 percent and was much less elsewhere.

East and West accused each other of base conduct. The Soviets tried to subvert legitimate governments and institutions. The United States supported resistance in Eastern Europe with money, propaganda, and night drops of arms, equipment, and Western-trained agents. It infiltrated free trade unions and some segments of the media in the attempt to mobilize public opinion against the Communists. Claiming that the "world proletariat" marched at its side against the "American imperialists," the USSR organized massive protests against the American presence in Europe, strikes, "peace" marches and rallies, and propaganda campaigns.

THE IRON CURTAIN

Tensions rose dangerously after March 1946. Churchill spoke of an "iron curtain" running across Europe from Stettin to Trieste, prompting Stalin to compare him to Hitler. On July 13, 1949, Pope Pius XII, who had declined to condemn the German attempt to exterminate the Jews, excommunicated Catholics who voted for or supported Communists. He even denied the sacraments to those who read Marxist or Communist literature—the first such mass malediction since the twelfth century.

In 1947 the Soviets sought to counter the American economic initiative with their own "Molotov Plan," a structural framework for integrating the economies of the USSR and its satellites. Designed to mask Soviet exploitation of Eastern Europe, this was the forerunner of the Council on Mutual Economic Assistance (CMEA, or Comecon), which came into existence in January 1949. The Kremlin view of economic cooperation envisaged the importation of satellite countries' raw materials into the USSR, which would export manufactured goods to those countries. As the Poles explained, Poland would supply the USSR with coal, and in return the USSR would take Poland's steel. The Soviets set the prices for the raw materials and the manufactured goods—which they frequently could not provide.

Part of Moscow's effort to parry the Truman Doctrine involved establishing a Communist Information Bureau, or Cominform, with headquarters in Belgrade. It was to replace the Comintern, which Stalin formally dissolved in 1943, and had representatives from the USSR, its East European puppets, Yugoslavia, and the Italian and French Communist parties.

Under intense Western pressure the USSR withdrew from northern Iran in the spring of 1946. That represented the Kremlin's first retreat.

Worsening relations rapidly dimmed the West's memories of wartime cooperation. This was particularly true in the United States, which experienced almost no fighting on its own territory and had suffered fewer casualties than most other combatants. For the first time the rich and powerful United States now assumed responsibility for defending the West, which then had only one potential military enemy, Soviet Russia. From both the strategic and the psychological political standpoint, Germany was crucial to that defense. The Soviets ruled the eastern third of Germany, the British, French, and Americans the western two-thirds. No amount of propaganda, and no artificially created barriers, would be able to conceal the stark contrast between East and West Germany.

Despite internal disagreements, especially in France, the Western Allies rejected various schemes for transforming Germany into an agrarian nation without war-making potential. That had been Moscow's goal. The West decided not only to rebuild but also to rearm Germany. In December 1946 the Americans and British agreed to fuse their occupation zones as a step toward reunification. They invited France and the Soviet Union to follow suit and bring their sectors into "Bizonia."

France hesitated to cooperate because anti-German sentiment stemming from two world wars and now a massive Communist propaganda campaign ran high. The Kremlin refused to go along and insisted on immediate payment of the $10 billion in reparations promised at Potsdam. Eventual reunification remained the public Soviet position, but Stalin would not allow free elections in the Soviet zone or anywhere else in the new Soviet empire. The Kremlin believed each step toward unifying the Western sectors threatened its rule in East Germany and Eastern Europe.

Developments in Yugoslavia, where the brutal Tito regime continued to resist Moscow's colonization efforts, temporarily overshadowed tensions in Germany. No Communist was more devoutly Stalinist than Tito, but he saw no contradiction between Yugoslav independence and loyalty to Moscow. In 1947 the Yugoslav Communists purged their ranks of thousands of Stalinists; Moscow protested vigorously as Tito tried some top Yugoslav officials as Soviet agents.

In March 1948 the Soviets recalled their military and technical advisers. Three months later, the Cominform expelled the Yugoslav party and thus smashed the myth of a monolithic Communist bloc.

BERLIN BLOCKADE

The Yugoslav crisis, which seemed to portend a Soviet invasion to overthrow Tito, gave way to a more serious one in Germany. Moscow manufactured a major confrontation in Berlin in an effort to pressure France to steer clear of "Bizonia," protest the West's plan to reform the currency in its occupation zones, and force the West out of Berlin itself. The Kremlin was determined to prevent the creation of a West German state hostile to the USSR.

Ostensibly to repair it, Soviet authorities closed one of the Autobahns leading from the west into East Germany and Berlin on June 15, 1948. Within a week all highway, rail, and river traffic halted. Only three 30-kilometer-wide air corridors linked Berlin to West Germany. The city's western sectors had a population of more than 2 million that daily required about 3,000 tons of supplies in summer, 4,000 in winter.

On June 26, an American C-47 transport aircraft landed at Berlin's Tempelhof Airfield with its maximum load—three tons—of food, milk, and medical supplies. Four days later the first of the 10-ton capacity C-54s touched down. Eventually 225 C-54s, plus scores of RAF and French transport aircraft, would take part in the Berlin Airlift. On July 26, the three air forces landed 3,028 tons of supplies.

The Western Allies were to make more than 250,000 flights. They transported more than 2.3 million tons of supplies, including hundreds of thousands of tons of coal, into West Berlin.

The Soviets harassed the supply planes by sending up fighter aircraft to "buzz" them. They shone spotlights to blind the pilots, raised barrage balloons along the air corridors, and occasionally peppered the Western planes with small-arms fire. But they always stopped short of major violence. Eventually 39 British, 31 American, and 5 West German pilots were killed in air accidents, nearly all due to adverse weather or pilot error.

Early in the blockade, the Allies considered and rejected a plan to send an armored column into East Germany; that would have constituted an invasion. President Truman calculated that

the airlift could achieve Allied objectives. The gamble succeeded. Unable to force the West out, the Soviets backed down in mid-May 1949 and reopened the surface corridors. The West appeared to have won an impressive victory. Berlin remained under four-power control, and France decided to link her occupation zone to "Bizonia." This set the stage for creation of an independent West German state, and the currency reform went forward.

On the surface it seemed Stalin had lost face. But later, when East–West relations had deteriorated still further, some observers wondered whether he too might have gained something from the Berlin crisis. Had he not established that the West would not go to war, even when provoked? Stalin's victims in Russia had learned that the time to watch him most carefully was when he seemed at his most conciliatory.

The unfolding of the Berlin crisis had ramifications around the world. Led by the charismatic Ho Chi Minh, who had studied and taught at KUTV (Communist University of the Toilers of the East) and the Lenin School, the Vietnamese Communists stepped up the guerrilla war against French colonial rule in Indochina that had begun in 1947. A divided public opinion in France sapped the French Army's morale and hampered political prosecution of the war. In the 1950s the United States tentatively began to shoulder some of the burden. The USSR provided only limited support to Ho, but many people in the West saw the confrontation in Vietnam, and in Cambodia and Laos, as a Cold-War testing-ground. Korea would be another.

NATO, CHINA, KOREA

The North Atlantic Treaty Organization (NATO), a mutual defense pact between the United States and 11 allies, came into existence in 1949, four years after the fall of Berlin. In a future war in Europe, the USSR would confront a united West. The Soviets did their best to block NATO. In Italy, the Communists of Palmiro Togliatti—who had sold his own comrades to the NKVD—kept the country in an uproar during parliamentary debates over adoption of the treaty. The French Communist leaders Jacques Duclos and Maurice Thorez sought to sabotage negotiations. Spies and "agents of influence"—students, intellectuals, journalists, businessmen—worked to achieve Kremlin objectives.

Ignoring vehement Soviet protests, in May 1949 the West fused its occupation zones to form the quasi-independent Federal Republic of Germany, which it planned to incorporate into the Western alliance. Stalin continued to call for reunification and neutralization, but the West insisted on free elections and renegotiation of the temporary frontiers established at Potsdam. Moscow rejected this because West Germany, with its powerful industrial base and unshakably anti-Communist population—swollen by the refugee influx—posed a huge menace. Frustrated in their attempts to block formation of West Germany, the Soviets created a dummy "German Democratic Republic" (GDR) in their occupation zone.

In September 1949, TASS announced that Soviet scientists had successfully tested a nuclear weapon. With more than a little help from Western spies, Moscow had broken the American atomic monopoly, and the unbalanced military equation began to level. The West still had superior delivery capability, but its lead in weapons research and development shriveled. In at least one sphere, Russian was backward no more.

A month after the world learned about the Soviet atomic bomb, Mao Zedong and the Chinese Communists paraded through the streets of Beijing in triumph, having routed Chiang Kai-shek and the Guomindang. The USSR had given Mao Zedong little aid. Reconstruction of the USSR had first priority, but it was also true that Stalin had again miscalculated the Chinese Communists' chances. Mao and his deputy, Zhou Enlai, resented this, but in general they admired Stalin, and they needed his aid. In February 1950 Mao flew to Moscow to sign a 30-year Treaty of Friendship, Alliance, and Mutual Assistance.

Powerful as they were, the Western democracies believed the new Sino–Soviet accord endangered their security. Communists now ruled a third of the world population, and the Soviet Union had the atomic bomb. An armed clash, most likely in Berlin, seemed inevitable.

The fighting erupted in Korea. Inspired by Mao's victory, Communists throughout Asia redoubled efforts to seize power. A provisional postwar settlement had divided Korea into North and South, and between 1947 and 1950 sporadic clashes had kept the artificial frontier aflame. The North Korean Communist leader, Kim Il Sung, repeatedly asked Soviet permission to attack the South in force; Secretary of State Dean Acheson had unwisely declared South Korea outside the American defense perimeter. The American stooge Syngman Rhee suffered a setback in the May 1950 elections.

Stalin decided he had nothing to lose in Korea. With his encouragement, North Korea struck southward on June 25, 1950. As in the Spanish Civil War, the USSR sent supplies, technicians, "advisers," and pilots to the North Koreans, but it did not provide ground troops.

Communist forces drove the South Koreans and a small American contingent to the sea; by early September Kim Il Sung's triumph seemed imminent. Then the UN branded North Korea the aggressor and authorized what Washington would call not a war but a "police action." American, South Korean, Australian, British, Turkish, and other forces counterattacked and drove the invaders to the Chinese–Korean frontier on the Yalu River.

Against the urgent recommendation of the UN commander, General Douglas MacArthur, Washington and the United Nations ordered those forces to halt there. The UN would not move into China. Mao Zedong and the Chinese Communists rejoiced; in power barely a year, they did not want war with the United States. Stalin, however, insisted that Mao send "volunteers." Still in awe of the man in the Kremlin, Mao reluctantly complied. Hundreds of thousands of Chinese troops entered the conflict, drove the UN forces back to the 38th parallel, which marked the border between the North and South zones, and the conflict became a war of attrition.

In March 1951 the United States conducted thermonuclear tests on the Pacific atolls of Eniwetak and Bikini. That prompted the Kremlin, where caution was again in vogue, to call for a cease-fire and negotiations. Talks began on July 8, 1951, and continued with frequent interruptions for two years.

When the United States did not use nuclear weapons against the Chinese and North Korean armies, Mao and Kim Il Sung denounced the United States as a "paper tiger." But Stalin was already having some second thoughts about his war by proxy. Truman proved much tougher than anticipated, and the November 1952 election of General Dwight D. Eisenhower as president increased the Soviet dictator's uneasiness. Fighting to the last North Korean and Chinese cost Stalin little, but he was not prepared to risk destruction of the USSR. In December 1952 he hinted he would welcome a meeting with Eisenhower.

It did not take place; Stalin died on March 5, 1953. The North Koreans and Chinese agreed to terms in July 1953 after President Eisenhower bluntly informed them he was prepared to use nuclear weapons in Korea. The deterrent had not deterred, but when couched as an ultimatum it produced the desired effect.

THE WEST AND RUSSIAN SECURITY

Stalin had defined the political and philosophical conflict of the postwar period in terms and categories pragmatic Westerners found difficult to fathom. He denounced Western "imperialists" and "warmongers," threatened to annihilate nations, risked catastrophe in Berlin and Korea, and boasted that the future belonged to communism. Yet he regularly proclaimed his hope for peaceful cooperation with the West "in spite of the difference of economic systems and ideologies" and declared such cooperation "unconditionally necessary in the interests of general peace."

Reasonable people found this confusing, but the West likewise did not always speak with one voice. Once the wartime honeymoon ended, high-ranking U.S. officials sometimes hinted broadly at the possibility of destroying the USSR with nuclear weapons. The way the 1948–1949 Berlin crisis unfolded made that mere bluff, but at what point would Washington decide that enough was enough? And how far would Stalin go to find out? The uncertainty made it difficult to defuse crises such as the one in Korea, which cost two million lives.

Attempts to fix blame for the Cold War persuade only the already convinced and inflict today's politics on yesterday's dilemmas. East and West both contributed to the tensions; neither side had a monopoly on virtue or perfidy. In the final analysis, however, the West represented democracy and its promise of peaceful resolution of antagonisms. The USSR, China, and North Korea stood for the dictatorial police state.

The Soviets erred tragically when they not only failed to capitalize on but actively spurned the West's postwar goodwill. In America, Britain, France, Italy, Scandinavia, and elsewhere, public opinion recognized and paid homage to the suffering and heroic resistance of the Soviet people. Not even a political giant like Churchill could prevail against the postwar tide, which ran heavily in the USSR's favor. But when Stalin opted for confrontation, the West had no choice but to fight fire with fire.

Usually fickle in matters of foreign policy, Western public opinion shifted abruptly after the first few confrontations. The West too had mourned the deaths of millions of soldiers and defenseless civilians, but Soviet Russia's casualties matched those of the West and Germany combined, and for every Western victim of the war, there were 32 Soviet dead.* The memory of all that faded as the West prepared for yet another Crusade.

The Soviet obsession with security was not negotiable. The formulation of a kind of "Stalin Doctrine," a policy of building an invincible defense that leaned heavily toward offense, was the inevitable result of the invasions of 1914, 1918–1920, and 1941.

SUGGESTED ADDITIONAL READINGS

BEREZHKOV, VALENTIN. *At Stalin's Side.* Secaucus, NJ: Carol Publishing Group, 1994.

BOROVIK, GENRIKH. *The Philby Files: The Secret Life of the Master Spy Kim Philby.* Boston: Little, Brown, 1994.

GLEASON, ABBOTT. *Totalitarianism: The Inner History of the Cold War.* New York: Oxford University Press, 1995.

GONCHAROV, SERGEI N., JOHN W. LEWIS, and XUE LITAI. *Uncertain Partners: Stalin, Mao, and the Korean War.* Stanford, CA: Stanford University Press, 1993.

HOLLOWAY, DAVID. *Stalin and the Bomb.* New Haven, CT: Yale University Press, 1994.

MODIN, YURI, WITH JEAN-CHARLES DENIAU and AUGIESZKA ZIAREK. *My Five Cambridge Friends: Burgess, Maclean, Philby, Blunt, and Cairncross, by Their KGB Controller.* New York: Farrar, Straus and Giroux, 1994.

PARISH, THOMAS, ed. *The Cold War Encyclopedia.* New York: Henry Holt, 1996.

ZUBOK, VLADISLAV, and CONSTANTINE PLESHAKOV. *Inside the Kremlin's Cold War: From Stalin to Khrushchev.* Cambridge, MA: Harvard University Press, 1996.

---

*One writer cautions against the "pseudo-science of comparative victimology—who suffered the worst, at whose hands." Norman M. Naimark, *The Russians in Germany: A History of the Soviet Zone of Occupation, 1945–1949,* Cambridge, MA: Harvard University Press, 1995, p. 7.

14

THE LATE STALIN YEARS

The Red Army commanders had won a brilliant victory. Russia inscribed the names Bagramyan, Chuikov, Konev, Rokossovsky, Tolbukhin, Vasilevsky, Sokolovsky, Vatutin, and Zhukov in the temple of her war heroes alongside those of Aleksandr Nevsky and Dmitri Donskoi, Aleksandr Suvorov and Mikhail Golenishchev-Kutuzov.

The Red Army's prestige eclipsed that of the Communist party, and that was the trouble. The Communists had always feared the soldiers; that is why Trotsky had initiated the practice of planting "political advisers" in all military units. In the Red Army, political indoctrination had the same priority as did military training. That did not sit well with professional officers, whose job it was to defend the country.

The 1937 purge of the military had removed what Stalin considered a challenge to party leadership. That nearly cost Russia the war. In 1945 he moved again to cut the military down to size, albeit in less bloody fashion. In February 1946 he renamed the Worker–Peasant Red Army, which had defeated all enemies, the "Soviet Army." There was too much in a name. Stalin demoted Marshal Georgi Zhukov, commander of Soviet occupation forces in Germany, to a lesser position, then later dropped him down another notch.

FOURTH FIVE-YEAR PLAN

Nine million demobilized Red Army soldiers joined the urban work force, which in 1950 numbered almost 39 million. Production declined in the initial postwar period as many industries reconverted to peacetime: The 1946 gross industrial product was 17 percent less than that of 1945 and only 75 percent of the 1940 level. But the situation began to improve as new natural gas pipelines to Leningrad, Moscow, and Kiev made industrial expansion possible. After capital repairs, hydroelectric power again flowed from the giant Dneproges station, which in 1950 produced more electricity annually than all pre-Revolutionary Russia had consumed. Coal production was 57 percent higher in 1950 than in 1940, 75 percent above that of 1945. In all, 6,200 major industrial enterprises became operational during the fourth Five-Year Plan of 1946–1950. By its end there were 400,000 engineers in the work force.

The state moved to restore the chemical industry, always a weak link. In 1937, the total Soviet chemical production had been only one-tenth that of the United States; by 1950 the gap had narrowed to one-sixth. The machine-tool industry also registered considerable progress. The 1940 production of 58,400 units had dropped to 38,400 in 1945, but by 1950 it reached 70,600. The early postwar period saw little innovation; Soviet engineers simply copied or adapted foreign models. Lend-Lease had provided American machine tools during the war, but the Cold War brought the cancellation of contracts and the cessation of trade.

Stressing production volume over innovation, the Soviets patterned design and development on old foreign machine tools. On the eve of history's latest technological revolution, this portended disaster. But as long as Stalin lived, innovation remained risky. Believing pure research "anti-Soviet," a cover for the essential laziness of the intellectuals, he populated the *sharashkas* (minimum-security prisons) with scientists.

History, tradition, and the technological lag forced the USSR to continue assigning priority to heavy industry; thus it continued to shortchange the consumer-goods or "light" industry. Between 1946 and 1950, the state built or restored 100 million square meters of living space in the cities and provided 1,119,000 new or restored dwellings in the countryside. Though impressive, this was a fraction of what was needed.

The new Five-Year Plan aimed unrealistically at a 27 percent increase over prewar production levels for grain, 25 percent for industrial crops. Only in 1953 did the farms yield as much as they did in the record year 1926. The agricultural work force was barely half the size of 1940's, and the number of able-bodied *men* had declined even more dramatically. War deaths, and the settling of nine million demobilized peasant-soldiers in urban areas, accounted for this.

The 1945 harvest was only 40 percent of that of 1940. The war obviously played an important role, but the 1946 disaster also had natural causes: The most severe drought in 50 years struck grain-growing districts from the lower Volga to the Romanian frontier. The regime accused *kolhoz* managers and regional

party officials of "inept management" and sent thousands of urban Communists into the countryside to help with the 1947 planting. The Kremlin released 2.5 million temporarily employed peasants to return to the *kolhozes*, established a Collective Farm Council, and revised the Collective Farm Statutes. The official in charge, Andrei Andreyev, reported to Georgi Malenkov and Nikita Khrushchev.

The state continued to fleece agriculture to build industry. The farms sold their produce to earn money for taxes. The sole buyer, the state, paid artificially low prices. This constituted yet another tax on the peasants. On the retail market, the state kept prices low for staples—flour, bread, cabbage, potatoes, milk—but high for meat, dairy products other than milk, fruit, and other items—a tax on consumers.

This was the police-state capitalism the Soviets called "socialism." The peasants who financed it were poorly paid and badly housed. They had grossly inadequate medical, educational, and recreational service. They remained psychologically numbed by the war, and the state did next to nothing to help them.

Nikita Khrushchev had built a controversial reputation in agriculture. Briefly demoted as a scapegoat for the 1946 drought—that was Stalin's way—and the terrible harvest, he survived to make a comeback. Under his direction the number of privately owned cattle reached 30 million in 1949, highest since the introduction of the NEP. The peasants now owned 26.5 million sheep and goats, 7.2 million hogs, about 350 million fowl. Assailing this trend, fundamentalist Communists called Khrushchev a heretic; more than a few wanted his head, and Stalin smiled enigmatically.

A second, less successful innovation involved reducing the number of collective farms:

1937	1940	1950 (Dec.)	1953	1959	1962
243,500	236,900	126,000 (approx.)	93,300	54,600	40,500

Equating size with efficiency, Khrushchev merged many failing or marginal *kolhozes* with more successful ones, rewarded good managers, punished the unsuccessful, and shuffled party cadres in an attempt to find the right combinations. But larger farms produced less. Peasants were still more alienated in bigger collectives. The mergers broke up teams in which the members, for better or worse, knew each other and had evolved a modus operandi. A change in crop rotations after the amalgamations also adversely affected production, which by 1950 had barely reached prewar levels.

POSTWAR POLITICS

Some national and local Communist leaders—notably the Leningrad bosses during the Siege—had had a safe, comfortable war, but not even their enemies accused rank-and-file Communists of cowardice. So many were killed—more than three million—that it was necessary to relax membership conditions. There had been 3.87 million party members in February 1941. That increased to 5.8 million by July 1945, but more than three quarters of the 1945 roster had joined since 1941. Between a third and a half were under 35, and three-quarters were under 45. The percentage of women increased from 14.9 in 1941 to 19.2 in October 1952.

The membership was young, the leadership middle-aged. Excluding Mikhail Kalinin, who died in 1946, and Stalin, at the war's end the average age of Politburo members was nearly 62. These lackeys had been with Stalin for two decades.

The two most ambitious courtiers were Georgi Malenkov, second in command in the party, and Andrei Zhdanov, a Central Committee secretary. Seeking to discredit his rival, Zhdanov accused Malenkov of neglecting ideology. Early in 1946 Stalin removed Malenkov from the Secretariat and authorized a housecleaning; in 1947 Malenkov found himself in Kazakhstan wondering what had gone wrong. Now in control of the entire Soviet ideological network, Zhdanov appeared to be Stalin's heir apparent. He put men he trusted into positions in the bureaucracy and on the party's chief ideological journal, *Bolshevik*; its newspaper, *Pravda*; and the Propaganda and Agitation Administration (Agitprop, formed in 1938).

In March 1946 the Council of People's Commissars became the Council of Ministers. This came a month after the disappearance of "Red Army" and provided further evidence of Stalin's determination to eradicate the Leninist past. The days of "Politburo" and "Bolshevik" were numbered. In 1946 the NKVD, which had been divided into two Commissariats in 1943, became the MVD, or Ministry of Internal Affairs. The NKGB, as the secret police was known between 1943 and 1946, became the Ministry of State Security (MGB).

ZHDANOVSHCHINA

The postwar cultural-ideological purge became known as the *Zhdanovshchina* ("Zhdanov business"). The humorist Mikhail Zoshchenko and the poet Anna Akhmatova came under fire: Andrei Zhdanov pronounced their works "ideologically harmful" and "steeped in the venom of savage enmity toward Soviet power." The Writers' Union expelled Akhmatova and Zoshchenko, who thus could no longer earn a living.

Zhdanov accused many film directors of

ideological shortcomings and forced a humiliating confession of "error" from Sergei Eisenstein. Talent yielded to sycophancy: In M. E. Chiaureli's *The Vow* (1946), the actor who played Stalin sported a halo. Composers felt the lash as Zhdanov denounced the "bourgeois decadence" of Shostakovich, Khachaturyan, Prokofiev, and others. "I want," Stalin said, "music I can hum."

Stalin kept the inner circle off balance. Late in 1946 he criticized G. F. Aleksandrov's *A History of Western European Philosophy* for failing to condemn Western philosophy and taking the "un-Marxist and anti-Soviet" position that Western philosophy influenced Russian thinkers. A Zhdanov protégé, Aleksandrov headed Agitprop and monitored the Writers' Union.

Zhdanov had ignored the Russian proverb, "Don't dig somebody else's grave": Malenkov was in exile, but he was not dead. He returned from Kazakhstan and—in an alliance of convenience with Lavrenti Beria—charged Zhdanov with ideological shortcomings in the Aleksandrov affair. Too late, Zhdanov replaced Aleksandrov with the grim mystagogue M. A. Suslov at Agitprop. Suslov's rise spelled Zhdanov's fall and thus, so it seemed, Malenkov's resurrection near the top.

An affair in academic-party economics had still more serious repercussions. In 1946 the leading Soviet economist, Yevgeni Varga, published a book entitled *Changes in the Economy of Capitalism as a Result of the Second World War,* which generated a controversy pitting the Zhdanovites—themselves prehistoric—against super-fundamentalist Communists. Varga argued that capitalist governments had not surrendered the control over their economies acquired during the war and were thus moving in a Socialist direction. That made them less threatening to the USSR. Varga also suggested that capitalism might not always suffer periodic crises.

Nikolai Voznesensky, another Zhdanov protégé, headed Gosplan and had just been pro-

moted to full membership on the Politburo. In October 1947 he fired Varga as director of a major research institute, and in December he closed down Varga's economics journal. In the spring of 1949, after Zhdanov's death, the state forced Varga to admit "errors of a cosmopolitan character." Voznesensky seemed triumphant; then suddenly he lost all state and party positions.

THE LENINGRAD CASE

The spectacular reversal in the fortunes of Zhdanov and his men astonished everyone but those who engineered it. Zhdanov suffered a further setback, one that grew out of the break with Yugoslavia. In 1947 he and Malenkov represented the USSR at the Cominform's birth in Belgrade. Already suspicious of the Yugoslav leaders, Stalin ordered Zhdanov and Malenkov—then between stays in Kazakhstan—to keep an eye on them. Zhdanov believed he had to have some contact with the Yugoslavs to do so.

The ex-Comintern leader Georgi Dimitrov of Bulgaria had proposed the merger of his country and Yugoslavia in a Balkan federation. Delegations from Yugoslavia and Bulgaria came to Moscow early in 1948 to discuss this. Stalin opposed the idea, leaving little to discuss. Tito had tentatively approved but declined to come to Moscow: He had been there in the 1930s and knew what often happened. About this time, the Yugoslavs respectfully declared they would no longer permit the USSR to exploit their natural resources. The Yugoslav delegates visited Leningrad, where Zhdanov—who had been the local party boss—arranged a warm reception, thinking he was doing the Lord's work. Stalin would later accuse him of being cozy with the Titoists.

Belgrade and Moscow continued to disagree on key issues. When in late June the

Cominform expelled Yugoslavia, the chief Soviet representative, M. A. Suslov, wrote the resolution. Zhdanov attended the meeting and was never seen in public again. He died in August; whether with or without help remains unclear. Most historians believe his death to have been natural, but key documents have disappeared, and others have been altered.

Zhdanov's sudden fall from grace and mysterious death stranded the many high- and mid-level officials who had tied their careers to his. The man who seemed to have lost most when Zhdanov was in the ascendant, Malenkov, was now back in Moscow for good, determined to avenge his humiliation. Acting on his orders, early in 1949 Minister of State Security V. S. Abakumov—a Beria protégé—indicted Zhdanov's chief associates on various charges, including treason.

The rubber-stamp Supreme Soviet abolished the death penalty in 1947. At Stalin's order, it restored it in 1950 for "spies and traitors." This was designed expressly for the main victims in the "Leningrad Case," as the Malenkov–Beria operation against the Zhdanovites became known. Khrushchev revealed in 1954 that Malenkov, with Beria's excited encouragement, had concocted the entire affair and sold it to an eager buyer, Stalin.

The most prominent victim, Nikolai Voznesensky, had won a Stalin Prize in 1948 for work in economics that included a proposal for some modest reforms. In some eyes, he was winning too much favor too quickly. Malenkov persuaded Stalin he was disloyal; Voznesensky lost his posts in March 1949. Obeying Malenkov–Beria orders, Minister of State Security Viktor Abakumov brought Voznesensky to trial on a charge of mishandling state secrets, then suddenly dropped the charges without explanation.

It had dawned on Beria that Malenkov was getting ahead of him in the race for favor. They had cooperated to destroy the Zh-

danovites, but they despised each other. A pawn in Beria's game, Voznesensky remained at liberty, worked on a new book, and even dined with Stalin in the Kremlin in October 1949. The next day the secret police took him to the Lubyanka. They held him incommunicado for nearly a year before executing him without trial on September 30, 1950.

Another highly placed Leningrad victim, A. A. Kuznetsov, had gone to Moscow with Zhdanov in 1946 to replace Malenkov as the Central Committee secretary charged with overseeing the ministry of state security—which Kuznetsov's friend Abakumov headed. After Zhdanov's death, Malenkov persuaded Stalin to test Abakumov by ordering him to do away with Kuznetsov. A loyal Communist and Chekist, in February 1949 Abakumov arrested Kuznetsov and shot him.

Aleksei Kosygin, Kuznetsov's relative by marriage, had held several important Leningrad, RSFSR, and national posts. A full member of the Politburo since 1948, he served as both deputy premier and minister of finance. In October 1948 Beria ordered Kosygin's arrest. Although he cared nothing for Kosygin, Malenkov also knew how to use pawns: He prevailed on Stalin to cancel the order.

Partial "rehabilitation" of the Leningrad Case victims began under Khrushchev, and it continued, more slowly, after his fall. One of Khrushchev's successors was Aleksei Kosygin, who became chairman of the Council of Ministers (prime minister). Kosygin remained indifferent to the fate of those who had not had his good luck. In the spring of 1988 the Communist party posthumously reinstated Voznesensky, Kuznetsov, and two dozen other leading Zhdanovites. The survivors received letters of apology.

Malenkov suffered a setback in late 1949, when Stalin excluded him from security matters. This was a victory for Beria, and there was more. Stalin transferred another Malenkov rival, Khrushchev, from Kiev to Moscow. Khrushchev became a Central Committee secretary and head of the Moscow party organization. Suddenly, Malenkov, the mastermind of the Leningrad Case, appeared no more secure than anyone else.

TROFIM LYSENKO

For a decade a preposterous debate over biology and genetics had been unfolding not in scientific conferences and journals but in philosophical journals and *Literaturnaya gazeta* (*Literary Gazette*), voice of the arch-reactionary Writers' Union. The Beria–Malenkov faction, or rather shaky alliance, took control of this publication and through it intervened in matters far removed from belles lettres. The philosopher B. M. Kedrov, a mediocrity but an opponent of the fundamentalists, had published a book on Engels and natural science. Party mystagogues attacked him for failing to recognize a "Soviet science" superior to that of the West. The leading representative of "Soviet science" was Trofim Lysenko.

Lysenko and his crowd were mired in an absurd dispute over Lamarckism and the "political significance" of the discoveries of the Russian plant breeder Ivan Michurin. Correctly reading the postwar political climate, they put forward a "two biologies" position in which the "bourgeois" variety stood in opposition to "Michurinist, Soviet" biology. Lysenko labeled unpatriotic and pro-Western those Soviet scientists who believed in the existence of genes and the chromosome theory of heredity.

One of the most sinister pseudo-scientific meetings of modern times took place in August 1948 at the Lenin Agricultural Academy in Moscow. The president of the Academy, Lysenko, delivered his report, then sat back and let his opponents hang themselves. When the genuine scientists attacked him, he sprang his trap: Stalin and the Central Committee had already sided with him.

In 1948 Lysenko contented himself with having his opponents barred from all scientific work. Two leading scientists were arrested; hundreds of professors, senior researchers, and graduate students lost their jobs; but there was no blood purge. Genetics research ended; the Lysenkoites even destroyed the fruit flies used in laboratory experiments. Biology and medicine suffered the same fate, as did agricultural institutes.

THE DEPORTATIONS

Some observers question whether, after the war, there were any Russians left at all, for so many had perished in the two world wars, the Civil War, famine, and the Lenin–Stalin Terror. The people called "Russian" were a mélange of many nations. They gave Stalin no trouble. Peoples on the frontiers were another matter.

The Soviet party-state had forcibly resettled several minorities in the 1930s, but the most extensive deportations came toward the end of the war. The Karachai are a Turkic-speaking people who had their own Autonomous Region in the North Caucasus. Nine thousand died in the first five days of the Nazi occupation, and by 1943 almost all able-bodied adult male Karachai were serving in the Red Army. Nevertheless, because a handful had collaborated with the Germans, in November of that year the NKVD deported all 70,000 Karachai to Kazakhstan and Central Asia. A month later the NKVD removed the 95,000 people of the Kalmyk Autonomous Soviet Socialist Republic (ASSR) in the northeastern Caucasus to Central Asia and Siberia. Some Kalmyks—a Mongol, Buddhist people—had worked for the Germans, but the overwhelming majority were loyal. That did not save them.

The largest deportation involved the 250,000 Crimean Tatars. Descendants of Chingis Khan's hordes, they are a Turkic–Mongol people who have lived in the Crimea since the thirteenth century. Under the Soviet system they had their own Autonomous Soviet Socialist Republic (ASSR). During the war, some among them collaborated with the Germans in the hope that the German flirtation with the pan-Turkic movement would lead to an independent Crimean Tatar state. But most Crimean Tatars were patriots. In May 1944, however, the Soviets abolished their ASSR and deported about 200,000 people to "special settlements" in Central Asia and Kazakhstan. Into the Crimea came thousands of new settlers, mostly Russians and a smaller number of Ukrainians. The peninsula was part of Russia until 1954, when the Kremlin grandly transferred jurisdiction to the Ukrainian SSR to mark Russian–Ukrainian unification three centuries earlier. This was yet another sowing of dragon's teeth.

The 400,000 Chechen and Ingush, Caucasian-speaking peoples of the Checheno-Ingush ASSR in the southeastern Caucasus, suffered forcible exile in 1944. The same fate befell most of the 145,000 Kabardinians (Caucasian-speaking) and 38,000 Balkars (Turkic-speaking) of the Kabardino-Balkar ASSR in the southern Caucasus.

As boss of Ukraine 1938–1947, Nikita Khrushchev persecuted the Ruthenian, Polish, Romanian, and Jewish minorities. He did not like to talk about that, but in 1956 he lamented the mistreatment of the Karachai, Balkars, and Kalmyks as "crude violations of the basic Leninist principles of nationality policy." The deportations, he admitted, had no military or political justification. The Germans were retreating at the time, and Soviet lines were secure. The Soviet state eventually dropped charges of treason and collaboration against the deported peoples and permitted most to return to their homelands. The Crimean Tatars and Volga Germans, however, have yet to regain full civil rights even in post-Soviet, democratic Russia.

LIFE IN THE LATE STALIN ERA

After the disastrous harvests of 1945 and 1946, good weather brought excellent crops in 1947. Food rationing ended in December of that year.

Many consumer items remained in short supply. The Communists tried to disguise the shortages with a brutal device that fooled no one. Simultaneously with the end of rationing, the state undertook a "currency reform" that exchanged old rubles for new at a ratio of 10:1. This would, the Kremlin claimed, wipe out the ill-gotten gains of speculators, reduce the amount of money in circulation, and eliminate notes the Germans had counterfeited. Reducing the money supply was perhaps a laudable step. But no one explained how speculators could have flourished under Stalin, and the amount of counterfeit money was insignificant. The "reform" wiped out the savings of millions of people. To sweeten the bitter medicine the state reduced food prices by an average 10 percent, thus continuing to subsidize urban consumers at the expense of the peasants. The shortages remained.

The price reductions lent substance to the Kremlin boast that national income rose 64 percent between 1940 and 1950, and that fourth Five-Year Plan productivity increased substantially. More dramatic "confirmation" came with the February 18, 1950, decree putting the USSR on the gold standard: The ruble would henceforth be worth 0.22168 grams of pure gold. This was pure propaganda; the ruble was not convertible.

Except for the steel mills, the defense establishment, the MGB (ex-NKVD, ex-Cheka, etc.), and the Moscow subway, it was difficult to find anything that functioned, and even the exceptions cited here were far less efficient than anyone outside the top Soviet circles knew. Retail stores were a nightmare of surly clerks serving up meager supplies of poor-quality merchandise. Old apartments badly needed repair; poorly constructed new ones were slums before anyone moved in. The clothing industry turned out garments more suitable for storing potatoes or bricks; shoes often disintegrated after a few wearings. Even in Moscow and Leningrad it was difficult to find a laundry or dry cleaner. Most restaurants were just overcrowded, unsanitary places to eat unappetizing food—but at low cost.

Before and during the war, only high-ranking civilian and military officials and a few privileged people in the arts and the scientific-technological establishment had automobiles. In 1948 the state began to produce a small Volkswagen-like Pobeda (Victory) for a target market of plant managers, *kolhoz* managers, and assorted minor functionaries. Middle-level officials drove the ZiM (Molotov Factory). Members of the Politburo and others at the very top, the "servants of the people," rode in splendid comfort in the ZiS (Stalin Factory) limousine, styled after American Packards of the 1930s. The people called this vehicle a "membermobile" (*chlenovoz*). Because of the poor roads, climate, and the Russian propensity for size and rough design (cars, factories, rockets, hydro- and later nuclear-power plants, etc.), the ratio of weight to horsepower of Soviet automobiles always significantly exceeded that common in the West and later Japan and Korea.

The state had always assigned a low priority to the production of consumer goods, and this did not change in the fifth Five-Year Plan of 1951–1955. That kept the standard of living low, and most Communists shared it. Only on promotion to mid-level or higher positions did party officials begin to enjoy the good life. There was little run-of-the-mill venality in Stalin's time; even petty thievery could earn the culprit five to ten years in prison.

The urban population increased from 60.6 million in 1941 to 71.4 million a decade later. To house it, the fifth Plan provided for construction of 102 million square meters of new living space (9.5 m^2 per person). But because the prewar housing shortage had been so great, and so many dwellings destroyed or damaged in the war, the situation remained desperate. Three generations of one family often lived together in cramped quarters. As often as not, divorced couples continued to share a room in a communal apartment because there was no alternative.

A massive construction program in Moscow only slightly alleviated the crowding because so many people kept moving to what was far and away the most favored city. Several enormous "Stalin gothic" (or "wedding-cake") structures went up. One housed Moscow University, another the foreign ministry; some were deluxe apartment houses. The government newspaper *Izvestiya* compared these buildings to those in the United States:

Our tall buildings have nothing in common with foreign skyscrapers. The American skyscraper is the unnatural grimace of a capitalist city, the monstrous expression of hopeless contradictions, the naked symbol of private, animal egoism. On the other hand, the multi-storied buildings of Moscow are the highest expression of our planned city construction and the free, rational development of our cities.

The state tried to monitor and shape people's lives through decrees and regulations. To spur population growth, replace wartime losses, and provide the labor force of the future, a July 1944 decree nullified common-law marriages and made divorce more difficult. The authorities assumed that, as good citizens, couples who were merely living together would formalize their union. In fact, many fathers exploited the confusion of 1941–1951 to abandon their partners and families. In 1950 the press discussed the worsening problem of men who avoided paying child support, which was set at 25 percent of the father's wages for the first child, 50 percent for two or more children.

Labor being scarce, factory managers often hired workers with personal documents open to various interpretations. As in Nazi Germany, the law mandated inspection of one's work history at each change of employment. When the postwar economy stabilized, the party-state cracked down on managers who failed to enforce regulations, and the problem abated.

The postwar tax on single adults, and childless married couples, complicated matters. The state encouraged marriage and childbearing; unhappy couples sought divorce. Almost always granted custody, mothers demanded financial support from ex-husbands. The ex-husbands, in turn, tried to avoid child-support payments. Not a few fathers gave themselves away by presenting a child's birth certificate to avoid paying the "childless tax."

To improve discipline, which had eased during the war, and enforce Stalinist prudery, the state tried in 1943 to abolish coeducation in primary and secondary schools. Single-sex education proved unpopular. Ninety-eight percent of letters to *Literaturnaya gazeta* in 1950 favored coeducation, which in practice remained the norm. The schools were terribly overcrowded; most operated two shifts, and except in Moscow, Leningrad, and Kiev, few even tried segregation by gender. The experiment ended in 1954.

Neglected in the first three decades of Soviet rule, special education for the handicapped improved only slowly after the war. The conflict had added several million people to the ranks of the physically mutilated and the psychologically tormented. The state's inability to cope reflected not only lack of funds but also a nearly universal tradition. People with shattered bodies or minds who had no family to care for them were simply warehoused in hospitals or left to roam the streets and roads and often to die.

The state could not produce prostheses in sufficient number, and the ones it made often did not fit. A common sight for three decades after the war was double amputees who affixed casters to a small wooden platform on which they propelled themselves by pushing gloved hands against the ground. The plight of the handicapped received almost no attention in the media, which reported only good domestic news of the sort the state decided people should read and hear. Press, radio, and soon television did, however, report incessantly on unbearable conditions in "imperialist" nations.

In 1950, 7,700 newspapers had a combined circulation of more than 33 million. Those who staffed them were not journalists but state publicists and propagandists. Not one uncensored word could appear.

In the spring of 1950, the first television station provided service to 7,845 TV sets in Moscow for a few hours a day, four days a week. Television came to Leningrad in 1951, Kiev the following year. By 1963 the number of stations had grown to 418; TV sets were widely available if only marginally more reliable; they often simply blew up.

WOMEN IN THE POSTWAR PERIOD

The state did little to improve the lot of women, on whom enormous practical as well as psychological burdens fell as a result of the war. In 1949 the Kremlin proudly announced that more than 100,000 women in *kolhozes* were brigade (team) leaders and managers. Behind the statistic, however, lay the harsh truth that women ran the *kolhozes* because the men had been killed. The absence of males, the lack of machinery, and tradition obliged women to continue the same kind of backbreaking labor they had performed since Russia began to till the soil.

Female construction gangs and road crews remained a common sight even after the end of Soviet rule. Women routinely did heavy labor in the factories; they drove trucks, laid bricks, and worked in the mines. Most women, whether blue- or white-collar, worked 48 hours a week. Married women did housework, shopped, and cared for children—men shunned these tasks—in their "spare" time.

By 1949, 700 women had won the highest civilian award, Hero of Socialist Labor. Another 237 had received the Stalin prize in various fields. About 44 percent of white-collar workers with a higher education were female; the percentage was greater among those with only a secondary education. In the medical profession, 75 to 80 percent of general practitioners were women, but most specialists and surgeons were male. Men dominated research institutes, certification boards, hospital administrations, and the Ministry of Health. That accounted in part for the failure to address birth control in an enlightened manner; also significant, however, was the official desire to increase the birthrate. Women who did not wish to carry a pregnancy to term were left to their own primitive devices. Even women physicians devoted little attention to the problem of contraception. The population rose slowly following the war, but the "boom" the state had good reason to hope for did not occur.

Almost no one even thought about women's practical needs. Dresses were badly cut, the colors drab. It was extremely difficult to find a pair of shoes in the right size, impossible to find anything attractive. Coarse-fabric underwear came in two sizes, small and extra-large. No one had heard of sanitary napkins or tampons. Cosmetics were few and of poor quality. After Stalin's death there arose a lively black market in the manufacture and sale of cosmetics, and at least one "lipstick king" would be executed.

Of 1,339 delegates elected to the Supreme

Soviet in February 1946, only 177 were women. By 1949, a total of 1,700 women were serving in the Supreme Soviets of the Republics and the ASSRs; half a million were members of local soviets. Real power remained with the party hierarchy, which men dominated.

"ROOTLESS COSMOPOLITANS" AND THE "DOCTORS' PLOT"

Stalin decided to deal with the Jews. Christianity had taught him anti-Semitism, and many of the Old Bolsheviks whom he had slaughtered were Jews. Some members of Stalin's family—notably his daughter Svetlana—gravitated toward Jewish artists and intellectuals. The Soviet representatives in the UN had backed the creation of Israel, but as Cold War temperatures dropped, and his personal attitudes hardened, Stalin thought this a mistake.

During the war, the director and noted actor of the Moscow Jewish Theatre, Shlomo Mikhoels (Vovsi), had become a leader of the state-sponsored Jewish Anti-Fascist Committee, one of whose members was Polina Zhemchuzhina, Molotov's wife. Along with the poet Itzik Feffer and others, Mikhoels visited the United States to raise funds. In 1948 the security organs accused him of being an agent of the Joint Distribution Committee, an American Jewish organization whose mission was to resettle the surviving European Jews. The order for Mikhoels's execution bore Stalin's signature. Posthumous "rehabilitation" came a month after Stalin died.

Early in 1949 the Soviet press excoriated an "anti-patriotic group of theatre critics" as "rootless cosmopolitans." This instantly became a code term for Jews and especially Zionists. In August 1952, a secret military tribunal convicted two dozen leading members of the Anti-Fascist Committee—poets, writers, actors, and intellectuals—of treason and sentenced them to 25 years in the Gulag. They did not even reach that destination. They had fought loyally for the USSR on many fronts, but their crime was to be exemplars of Russian Jewish culture: Itzik Feffer, David Hofshteyn, Leyb Kvitko, Peretz Markish, and others fell to the Communist anthropophagi in the Lubyanka cellars. Kvitko had written in the poem "Day Grows Darker,"

Let him at least note,
That my heart was bloody young,
That strong, like fear, was my will to live,
Strong and crazed,
Like my final day.

Next came the "Doctors' Plot," which like the "Industrial Party" and the "Moscow Center" and so on never existed outside someone's twisted imagination. In 1948 a radiologist in the Kremlin Clinic named Lydia Timashuk sent a letter to Stalin accusing some of her colleagues of having misdiagnosed Zhdanov's illness and thus of complicity in his death. The letter simply went into the files.

In July 1951, Semyon Ignatyev replaced Viktor Abakumov as minister of state security. It was usually the first priority of any new appointee to discredit his predecessor. That was all the more pressing in this case because Beria and Malenkov wanted to ruin Abakumov, who knew too much. And Ignatyev's existence depended on Beria, or Malenkov, or both. Ignatyev and one of his investigators, Colonel Mikhail Ryumin, now retrieved Dr. Timashuk's 1948 letter from the files. Zhdanov remained safely dead; Ignatyev and Ryumin could rearrange the manner of his passing to suit Beria and Malenkov's present purposes.

Ignatyev arrested nine Kremlin Clinic physicians and charged them not only with having murdered Zhdanov but also with planning to kill Stalin. He took into custody the wives of the accused and ordered their children expelled from the Komsomol. Seven of the original accused—three more were added later, for a total of 12—were Jewish. The MGB claimed the Joint Distribution Committee and the CIA had masterminded the plot.

As in the 1930s, MGB inquisitioners obtained "confessions" through torture. Timashuk received the Order of Lenin and a 100,000-ruble award to console her for the loss of her husband, who was one of those she accused. The USSR broke diplomatic relations with Israel in February 1953.

NINETEENTH PARTY CONGRESS

In an ominous rebuke to Beria, who controlled the MGB although he did not actually head it, *Pravda* criticized the secret police for not exposing the "Doctors' Plot" earlier. Other top leaders felt Stalin's fixed gaze, as did members of his own family and the families of his late wives. Molotov meekly acquiesced in the arrest of his wife on trumped-up spy charges. Kalinin, Andreyev, Semyon Budyonny, Anastas Mikoyan, and Aleksandr Poskrebyshev—chief of Stalin's personal secretariat—cringed, smiled, and nodded assent when their own loved ones went off to the Gulag.

The Nineteenth CPSU Congress, first in 13 years, met in Moscow in October 1952. It was a dispirited meeting. Two-thirds of the delegates had won their jobs when the Terror eliminated their predecessors, and now they realized that Stalin's axe was about to fall again.

Stalin had delivered the main report at every Congress since 1924. Now 72 and a relic of his former self, this time he sat alone in the first row behind the rostrum, a gray-haired old man on whom every eye focused in a combination of worship and dread, maybe more dread. The great mystery was how a creature grotesquely engorged with the blood of at least 40 million human beings could be so insignificant. Here was a repository of total evil, in such a small package.

Having been restored at least temporarily to power, Malenkov was the only man at Stalin's right hand in both party and state. He gave the main speech outlining the Communist party's accomplishments and its plans for the future. The USSR, he announced, had solved the problem of grain production. The protracted agricultural crisis had come to an end. A lie like that had to come straight from Stalin.

The Congress rid the party of more names from its past. The All-Union Communist Party (Bolsheviks) became the Communist Party of the Soviet Union (CPSU), and *Bolshevik* disappeared from the political lexicon. New party statutes renamed the Politburo the "Presidium," which would have 25 full members and 11 candidates. This fourfold increase would swamp Stalin's cronies, all of whom he had marked for extermination. An enlarged Central Committee would have 125 full members and 111 candidates. The statutes abolished the Orgburo and transferred its functions to the Secretariat. The office of general secretary was redesignated "first secretary." The Control Commission, which monitored compliance with party directives, would report directly to the Central Committee.

Stalin spoke only at the last session. Welcoming the delegates of foreign Communist parties, he informed them that the bourgeoisie had abandoned the fiction of democratic freedoms and national independence. The world was divided into two camps, Socialist and the monopoly-capitalist. He sat down.

The ex-seminary student had always seen politics and life in stark colors. As he neared his end, the forces of darkness loomed ever larger, the one threat against which violence and intrigue were useless. All his life he had sought isolation; now, we may suppose, he realized that fate had cursed him by granting his wish. He would die alone, but only after slaughtering the traitors. He would defy Machiavelli's dictum that no man ever killed his successor.

DEATH OF AN IMMORTAL

On December 21, 1952, Stalin celebrated, or at least pondered, his seventy-third birthday in private. Only a brief mention appeared in the press, nothing like the sickening adulation of 1949.

Rumors of an impending purge filled the air as Muscovites speculated on the longevity of Beria, many of whose hirelings in Georgia—his homeland—had fallen from grace earlier in the year. January 1953 saw the arrest of Poskrebyshev and General Nikolai Vlasik, commander of both the Kremlin guard and of Stalin's personal security. Beria told Molotov in February he believed Stalin would "rub us all out."

On February 7, 1953, the Argentinian ambassador met with Stalin and afterward reported nothing out of the ordinary about his appearance or demeanor. Ten days later the Indian envoy found Stalin sketching wolves. Russian peasants, he said, knew how to deal with wolves: They killed them. The wolves knew this and conducted themselves appropriately.

Three daily shifts, each with about 275 men, guarded Stalin's *dacha* (cottage) in the Moscow suburb of Kuntsevo. When he was alone there, no one had authority to disturb him. On Saturday night–Sunday morning, February 28–March 1, 1953, he drank and dined at the *dacha* with Malenkov, Beria, Khrushchev, and Bulganin. The guests departed at 4:00 A.M.

At 6:00 P.M. Sunday, a guard reported that Stalin had not rung for his dinner. His office was dark. At 11:00 P.M., two duty officers and a servant went through the *dacha* and found Stalin lying alive but motionless on the floor in the small dining room. He was dressed in a nightshirt and pajama trousers. It was later determined that he had suffered a cerebral hemorrhage.

The guards called Malenkov, who refused to move without Beria's approval. Beria was both drunk and incommunicado with a new female conquest; it took several hours to find him. When he and Malenkov finally arrived at the *dacha,* Beria insisted that Stalin was merely sleeping soundly and at first refused to call for medical assistance. Only at 9:00 A.M. the next day did some physicians arrive, along with the full Presidium.

The first public announcement came on March 4: Stalin was gravely ill. The prognosis was uncertain. Ten physicians led by the minister of public health twice applied leeches; their ministrations were in vain. He regained consciousness a couple of times, but Stalin was paralyzed and could not speak. He died on March 5 at 9:50 P.M.

The attending physicians—all Russians—signed the death certificate. The Presidium's Secretariat telephoned political and military leaders around the country. Only then, at 4:00 A.M. on March 6, did the second best-known voice in the USSR, that of Radio Moscow's Yuri Levitan, broadcast the communiqué, which skimped on grief. The Presidium insisted on "high political vigilance" in the "irreconcilable struggle against domestic and foreign enemies." It decreed three days of mourning; there had been five for Lenin. State radio played funeral music, interrupting it only to broadcast tributes.

They took the body to Moscow, embalmed it, then transferred it to the Hall of Columns in Union House. Lenin had lain in state there 29 years earlier, and the great circus trials had taken place in Union House.

The communiqué had warned against "disorder and panic," but only Beria among the top officials had tried to position himself to seize power, and he who had personally shot handcuffed Polish officers and others in the back of the head now lacked courage. Thousands of regular police and army troops proved no match for the millions of citizens who tried to reach the center of the city. Many people sobbed uncontrollably; hundreds were trampled to death in the densely packed throngs that stretched 10 to 15 kilometers in all directions.

It is a measure of the other leaders' political obtuseness that they named Khrushchev to organize the funeral, one of the three or four most important events in Soviet history. Stalin's body, which after further treatment would be placed on permanent—until 1961—exhibition in the mausoleum next to Lenin, was dressed in a military uniform bedecked with medals. The slightly canted coffin rested on a raised, flower-engulfed bier. A uniformed honor guard rotated on the half hour.

On March 9, pallbearers Malenkov, Beria, Molotov, Kaganovich, Voroshilov, Khrushchev, Mikoyan, and Bulganin, assisted by soldiers, carried the body the few hundred meters to the Lenin Mausoleum. The first three delivered funeral orations. Only Molotov displayed emotion.

Stalin reposed next to the man whom he had succeeded three decades earlier. For nearly two of those decades he had wielded more power than anyone in history. No one could count his victims, yet even in the Gulag many prisoners mourned, convinced Stalin had not known of the horrors perpetrated in his name. He was a giant who had removed the uncertainty from life, and millions praised him.

For a variety of historical reasons, Russian society had failed to evolve a constitutional system that could calm a collective fear of chaos. In the centuries after the disintegration of the Kievan state, a catastrophe followed by the 250-year Mongol occupation, Russia equated salvation with the rule of a powerful prince. None was more powerful, nor more terrible, than the Russified Georgian Ossete who held a great nation in thrall for a quarter of a century.

SUGGESTED ADDITIONAL READINGS

MOLOTOV, VYACHESLAV M. *Molotov Remembers: Inside Kremlin Politics.* Transcribed and edited by Feliks I. Chuev. Chicago: Ivan R. Dee, 1993.

RAPOPORT, YAKOV. *The Doctors' Plot of 1953.* Cambridge, MA: Harvard University Press, 1991.

RAZGON, LEV. *True Stories: The Memoirs of Lev Razgon.* Dana Point, CA: Ardis, 1997.

SUDOPLATOV, PAVEL, and ANATOLI SUDOPLATOV. *Special Tasks.* Boston: Little, Brown, 1994.

VOLKOGONOV, DMITRY A. *Stalin: Triumph and Tragedy.* New York: Grove Weidenfeld, 1991.

15

THE THAW

No healthy political organism could grow in Stalin's shadow, which was so
enormous as to raise doubts as to whether it was a shadow at all. After him came
nothingness. In the satire that cost him his life, Osip Mandelstam wrote that Stalin
surrounded himself with "thin-necked bosses . . . semi-humans." The bosses were,
as the historian Lewis Namier said of a pro-Nazi British ambassador to Germany,
"obtuse enough to be a menace and not stupid enough to be innocuous."

The Stalin-less Presidium proclaimed collectivity the "highest principle of party leadership." Stalin had said the same thing in 1924. The new ruling *troika* (trio) had Malenkov as Chairman of the Council of Ministers (prime minister), Beria as minister of state security, and Khrushchev as Communist party first secretary.

Malenkov ached to succeed Stalin but had made too many enemies in the Purges, the Leningrad Case, the Doctors' Plot, and other murderous ventures. His porcine appearance—he was not at the top when Mandelstam wrote—made him the subject of ridicule, and exposure of his trickery eliminated him as a viable contender: He published a fake photo of himself alongside Stalin and Mao in *Pravda*.

Within hours of Stalin's death the new leaders, fearing mass disorders, combined the Ministries of Internal Affairs (MVD) and Security (MGB) under Beria. They hoped that he who shrank from nothing would save them from everything. But there was no appreciable violence in Moscow; Beria was left with troops and tanks and no one to massacre. It remains unclear whether he actually drew up contingency plans for a coup d'état. That he wanted power is certain; so did Malenkov and Khrushchev. But Beria was the most detested man in Russia, and once the others ceased to need him, or to think they did, he was finished.

Khrushchev's emergence occasioned surprise because he had had sharp differences with Malenkov, Beria, and Molotov. That he became party leader, the post from which Lenin and Stalin had derived their power, indicated not only the dim-wittedness of the other leaders but also strong support from the party apparatus and the Central Committee. As for the others, the icy Molotov, who had no feeling in any vital organ, deserved the "finest file clerk in Russia" label Lenin had pinned on him. Lazar Kaganovich's only talent was obedience to Stalin. The cleverest man on the Presidium, Anastas Mikoyan, did not bid for power. No one considered the others—Bulganin, Pervukhin, Saburov—anything but ciphers.

THE NEW REGIME'S FIRST STEPS

The "amnesty" of March 27, 1953, bore the name of Kliment Voroshilov, titular head of state, and was thus appropriately a fraud. There were then 2.6 million people both in the Gulag and "regular" prisons, millions more "enemies of the people" in exile in remote regions, and several million children of prisoners in state orphanages. Fewer than 4,000 political prisoners won their freedom, among them Polina Zhemchuzhina, Vyacheslav Molotov's wife and a fanatical Communist.* She did not blame her husband for failing to defend her when she was arrested on trumped-up charges; Stalin took that into consideration when he added Molotov's name to his final list of victims. When they met Polina at the railway station, Beria gave her some flowers and a box of chocolates, and Molotov cried.

Fatally compromised in the political race, Malenkov remained chief economic spokesman in his capacity as prime minister. Seeking to salvage something, he gambled on wooing public opinion. On April 1 the state lowered prices for potatoes, cabbage, and fruit by 50 percent; by 10 percent for bread, flour, cereals, rice, and legumes; 15 percent for meat and meat products. In the name of the Council of Ministers, Malenkov also announced price cuts for clothing, shoes, and other consumer goods that would save citizens 46 billion rubles annually.

In his last published work, *Economic Problems of Socialism in the USSR*, Stalin had justified the postwar emphasis on defense spending and heavy industry. He had executed the would-be reformer Voznesensky. Malenkov could hardly challenge Stalin's teachings, but he could try to carve out a "middle way" that would allow the country to maintain the pace in heavy industry and defense yet produce more consumer goods.

Only the incorrigible "steel-eater" Molotov opposed the April 1953 price rollbacks. The normally garrulous Nikita Khrushchev, though he too was a champion of heavy industry, concentrated on agriculture and let Malenkov do

the talking. A strong advocate of the new, milder approach was Beria, who supported Malenkov's economic arguments, smiled benignly, and bragged of being the "father of the Soviet atomic bomb."

On April 4 the Communist party declared the "Doctors' Plot" a hoax and released the physicians. This sent a signal to party cadres that there would be no purge and served to warn Beria and Malenkov that other manufactured scandals, obviously including the Leningrad Case, were under scrutiny.

FALL OF BERIA

On April 6 a *Pravda* editorial blamed the Doctors' Plot on Semyon Ignatyev and his deputy Mikhail Ryumin, both Stalin's men. Beria moaned with relief, certain that a notice on another page did not concern him:

Nobody will be permitted to violate Soviet law. Every worker, every collective farmer, and every Soviet intellectual can work confidently and in peace, knowing his civil rights are reliably guarded by Soviet socialist law.

The citizen of the great Soviet state can be confident that his rights, guaranteed by the USSR Constitution, will be solemnly preserved and defended by the Soviet government.

Russia, land of words, was accustomed to such empty talk. But official publication of the news that the Soviet secret police, and not imperialist agents, had manufactured the Doctors' Plot—that hinted at a purge of the *purgers*. Would the party at last bring the security organs to heel?

Beria had succeeded in restoring some friends to their posts in the Georgian party–secret police bureaucracy; that enhanced his sense of security. He was confident he had either hidden his tracks or could eliminate anyone who uncovered them.

---

*When they informed her she would be liberated, Polina asked, "How's Stalin?"

His own hands about as bloody as Beria's, Nikita Khrushchev wanted to eliminate the security chief, reasoning that, while Beria was a monster, he, Khrushchev, had merely obeyed orders. Khrushchev maneuvered the chastened Malenkov, who anyway loathed Beria, into supporting him. The lesser lights on the Presidium (formerly Politburo) either favored Beria's arrest, would not oppose it, or—Molotov, Mikoyan, Voroshilov—did not act in time to save him. On June 26, 1953, General K. S. Moskalenko, Marshal Zhukov, and other officers arrested Beria at an unscheduled Presidium meeting.

The Kremlin did not immediately publish this news. The leaders waited several days, anxious lest Beria's disappearance automatically trigger an MVD-MGB attempt to free him and install him as dictator. No such attempt materialized.

At a secret Central Committee session early in July 1953, Khrushchev and his allies denounced Beria as an "enemy of the party and the state" who had acted illegally and arbitrarily, sabotaged the food supply, tried to place his ministry above the party and government, and interfered in the economy. They called him a "bourgeois-nationalist deviationist" who had incited ethnic groups against each other, a "bourgeois degenerate and agent of international imperialism." The Central Committee voted unanimously to try him on all charges; the press published the indictment on July 10. The "degeneracy" got lost in the indictment but the Presidium, and the families of the victims, knew what it meant. The syphilitic Beria constantly cruised the streets of Moscow or Tbilisi or wherever he happened to be in his black *chlenovoz* ("membermobile"), curtains drawn, preying on young women. There was no escape.

Several high-ranking MVD-MGB officials went to prison, as did some of their counterparts in the Soviet republics. An investigation uncovered an avalanche of information about the Gulag, and Beria's personal crimes. It con-

firmed what Khrushchev and the other new leaders already knew—but lacked the courage to reveal—about the Katyn Forest massacre. Like the Germans who never heard of the Nazi death camps, Khrushchev and the rest of Beria's colleagues professed shock at the news.

The state tried Beria and six close associates in December 1953 under Stalin's personal 1934 decree ("Kirov Law"), which excluded defendants and defense counsel from the proceedings, ruled out appeals, and provided for the immediate execution of death sentences. Marshal Ivan Konev, who had assisted in concocting the Doctors' Plot, presided. The media reported only that the accused had made use of "strictly forbidden methods of conducting investigations" and had "falsified court proceedings and accused completely innocent persons of state crimes." The bill of particulars did not mention that the accused had acted on orders from Stalin and the Communist party. On Christmas Day the government announced the conviction and execution of the defendants.

AFTER BERIA

Stalin had left the scene but remained a presence in Soviet politics. The media constantly hailed him as the "great continuer of Lenin's cause" and so on. On the first anniversary of his death, *Pravda* praised his war record and management of the purges. It went unnoticed that, six weeks earlier, speaking on the anniversary of *Lenin's* death, Khrushchev had not mentioned Stalin.

In July 1954 a military court tried, convicted, and shot the pathetic stooge Mikhail Ryumin for his role in fabricating the Doctors' Plot. In December, former Minister of State Security Abakumov and five associates went before another tribunal. Charged with hatching up the Leningrad Case, they were found guilty. Abakumov and three others were shot;

the remaining two got 25 and 15 years. Testimony in the Abakumov trial implicated only the late Beria among the higher-ups, but it was impossible to conceal Malenkov's role.

Khrushchev had led the Central Committee faction that successfully argued for putting Ryumin and Abakumov on trial. Malenkov and Molotov had taken the opposite line, pleading the shopworn case against washing dirty linen in public. The latter argument prevailed in the Presidium, but Khrushchev won a majority in the Central Committee.

At Andrei Vyshinsky's funeral in November 1954, Molotov said over the corpse of the Soviet Torquemada,

His brilliant speeches in defense of Soviet legality and his accusations, which we all remember, against the enemies of the Soviet state, against saboteurs and subversive foreign agents and against traitorous groups of Trotskyites and right-wingers, were a great and unforgettable service to the Soviet people.

Despite some attempts in Russia and the West to rehabilitate him, Vyshinsky would indeed long be remembered, but not in the way Molotov suggested. The Abakumov trial, the very existence of which constituted an indictment of all that Vyshinsky and Molotov stood for, went forward as Khrushchev and his supporters—confident they could cover *their* tracks—had demanded.

AGRICULTURE AND POLITICS

In the spring of 1953 Khrushchev persuaded the Presidium to change the way the state taxed the peasants. Money payments replaced levies in kind on privately owned cattle and other farm animals, fruit trees, beehives, and so forth, and the state agreed to purchase the private-sector products at fair prices. With these incentives, the peasants responded dra-

matically; morale improved and with it the food supply.

A September 1953 Central Committee plenum reduced taxes on individual gardens and farm animals still further and abolished the tax on cows and pigs. It allowed blue- and white-collar workers to have household plots and small gardens, which could not exceed 0.25 hectare (0.6 acre); they could keep a cow, two pigs, a goat, fowl, beehives. The private sector flourished and was soon supplying the cities with most of their fresh vegetables; the relaxation of controls helped avert a crisis in 1954. But the private plots—barely 2 percent of the arable land—alone could not solve agriculture's problems. The government injected large sums of money into the countryside: It raised the prices paid *kolhozes*, increased purchases, cancelled old debts. Peasant-family income increased almost 400 percent 1953–1954, bringing the tillers of the soil up to the level of the lowest-paid industrial workers for the first time since the NEP.

Kolhoz managers used the infusion of funds to increase wages and provide bonuses; the party disliked this but tolerated it. Meat production rose by 32 percent; milk, 61 percent; eggs, 44 percent; wool, 36 percent; sugar beets, more than 200 percent. Grain yields increased an average of 7 to 11 centners per hectare. All this enhanced Khrushchev's stature, but his earlier 1951 scheme to establish "agrotowns" had failed. These were large rural population centers from which the peasants commuted to the fields; Khrushchev considered this the logical next step after *kolhoz* amalgamation. Malenkov and Beria had opposed him, and Stalin had sided with them. The Central Committee declined to revisit the issue.

Khrushchev had more success in developing the "virgin lands" in northern Kazakhstan and the Altai. In December 1953 *Pravda* noted that six million hectares of arable Altai land were being used as pasture, and for hay. The following March a Central Committee "Decree on Virgin and Idle Lands" ordered the planting of about 2.3 million hectares of wheat, 10.7 million in 1955. By 1958, more than 30 million hectares were sown to grain, principally wheat but also corn—which could not grow in that climate in those latitudes. Hundreds of thousands of volunteers came from the traditional agricultural regions and the cities to help out, and in 1954 almost the entire production of the agricultural implements industry went to the virgin lands: 50,000 15-horsepower tractors, more than 6,000 trucks, 10,000 mower-threshers, thousands of other implements. The first results were discouraging. The new lands yielded only three million tons of grain in 1954—two million short of the goal.

The Khrushchev faction's attempt to reform agriculture had major political repercussions. Maintaining and even increasing the levels of heavy industry and defense while committing vast sums to revitalize the *kolhozes* and develop the virgin lands ruled out any increase in the supply and quality of consumer goods. Khrushchev stuck to the "hard" line, backed by the military leadership, Molotov, Bulganin, and Mikhail Saburov. Taking the "softer" approach were Malenkov, Mikoyan, Kosygin, and Minister of Agriculture Ivan Benediktov.

An acrimonious debate in the Presidium and the Central Committee ended with Malenkov's defeat late in 1954, on the eve of the Abakumov trial. Confident of victory, Khrushchev issued an ultimatum: Malenkov would acknowledge defeat on the "guns versus butter" issue and resign as prime minister or face exposure as architect of the Leningrad Case. Malenkov not only resigned but accepted blame for the 1950–1953 agricultural failures—*Khrushchev's* area of responsibility.

To give the impression of an orderly transfer of power, the party did not announce the resignation until February 1955. Malenkov retained his seat on the Presidium.

Nikolai Bulganin became prime minister. Innocent of any qualities, he had been a member of the Central Committee for 20 years, of the Presidium for six. He had worked with Khrushchev in Moscow in the 1930s; the two had remained friendly. Khrushchev masterminded Bulganin's elevation to the top government post and placed men loyal to himself in other ministries, notably Interior and Agriculture. Marshal Zhukov received the ministry of defense as a reward for his role in the elimination of Beria.

The government changes accompanied a major reorganization of the Communist party apparatus. Two years after Stalin's death, Khrushchev had become the most powerful man in the USSR without resorting to violence, except in Beria's case. But in the summer of 1955 it appeared he might lose everything. Weather conditions in the virgin lands were miserable; the harvest failed. Malenkov, Kaganovich, Molotov, and others blamed Khrushchev and argued that funds and manpower should have been spent in the traditional grain-growing districts.

Despite dry conditions in some areas, the USSR brought in its best harvest ever in 1956. Kazakhstan alone gathered in 16 million tons of grain. In all, the collective and state farms produced 125 million tons and temporarily saved Nikita Khrushchev. But in the long run, much of the "virgin lands"—until Khrushchev a sea of grass unchanged for millennia—became an ocean of dust, useless even for grazing.

NEW LOOK IN FOREIGN POLICY

Proclaiming Kremlin foreign policy fixed and immutable, the new leaders at once began to alter it. In May 1953 they abolished the Control Commission through which they had ruled their sector of Germany and appointed a single high commissioner. Such a system had been effective in the Western sectors and had simplified efforts to create an independent West German state. The East German puppet regime instituted a series of reforms but also tightened labor discipline and ordered a 10 percent rise in production quotas, which were already high and were in reality crudely disguised reparations. On June 16, 1953, thousands of East Berlin residents took to the streets in protest, calling for a general strike. Soviet military authorities sent in tanks; the world's news agencies published photographs of Berliners attacking the vehicles with rocks and fists.

These events helped galvanize the anti-Beria conspiracy in Moscow. Many Central Committee and Presidium members blamed Beria for letting the situation in Germany, where the Soviet secret police were present in force, get out of hand. In 1963 Khrushchev revealed that, on Stalin's death, Beria and Malenkov had urged German Democratic Republic (GDR) leaders to mute their propaganda so as not to offend the West.

The Soviet-GDR regime quelled the protests, rescinded the production-quota increase, and made other concessions. Officials removed restrictions on travel between East and West Berlin, and on July 11 they lifted martial law. The first of the foreign tremors traceable to the Kremlin power struggle thus ended in partial victory for the East German people. Unimaginable under Stalin, this greatly increased the likelihood of other upheavals.

Stalin's major postwar defeat had come at the hands of Josip Broz Tito, whose successful defiance had made Yugoslavia a second capital of world communism. The Chinese Communist seizure of power added a third, further undermining Soviet hegemony. As the new leaders pondered how to deal with Tito and Mao, indications of a thaw came in November 1953 with publication in the USSR of Tito's congratulations on the anniversary of the Bolshevik coup d'état.

Stalin misjudged Tito and the Yugoslavs as he had Chiang Kai-shek and the Guomindang. He had backed Chiang, who, to express his gratitude, had slaughtered every Communist he could find in Shanghai and elsewhere. The Chinese Communists never forgave Stalin; but in 1949 they needed allies. Two months after seizing power, Mao flew to Moscow for talks with Stalin. No longer a guerrilla chieftain living in filthy Shaanxi caves but leader of a nation of 600 million, Mao expected to be received as an equal. He was not. After the public embraces and expressions of respect, the Soviets dealt with him condescendingly and dragged out the negotiations for nine weeks. In February 1950 they finally gave a modest $300 million in economic assistance over five years. Moreover, Stalin forced China to agree to a number of border rectifications favoring the USSR and to recognize the independence of Mongolia, now a Soviet puppet but long subject to China. Stalin also asked for concessions in return for helping develop China's natural resources. Mao said that getting anything out of Stalin was "like taking meat from the mouth of a tiger."

Mao signed the humiliating agreement. Politically isolated and economically ruined after generations of European, American, Japanese, and Russian plundering, and soon to be mired—at Stalin's insistence—in a war in Korea, China had no hope of aid from any other source. Beyond that, an American-backed invasion by Chiang's forces—now on Taiwan—seemed a strong possibility. The Chinese invested the crumbs Stalin gave them in armaments, and Moscow sent 3,000 military advisers to begin modernizing the Chinese People's Liberation Army.

Mao's statement on Stalin's demise described the man responsible for the Shanghai Massacre as the "greatest genius of the present age . . . known for his ardent love of the Chinese people." Soviet–Chinese relations appeared to take a turn for the better in 1953, not least because the Korean War had drained China's meager resources and postponed industrialization. Mao would after all emulate the Soviet pattern of development, exploiting the peasant masses to build heavy industry. In September 1953 the Kremlin agreed to undertake 141 major construction projects in China and provide money, equipment, technology, and experts.

In the face of implacable American opposition, the USSR argued that the People's Republic of China should replace Nationalist China (Taiwan) in the United Nations. At the 1954 Geneva Conference on Far Eastern Affairs, the Soviets again championed the Chinese. The conference formalized the Korean Armistice and reviewed the agreement by which France had left Vietnam.

As part of his Yalta commitment to enter the Pacific war, Stalin had sent troops to Port Arthur, Manchuria, in the late summer of 1945. By that time they were not needed against Japan, but they remained there to protect the Liaodong Peninsula against American invasion, or so the Kremlin said. Stalin promised to withdraw them by 1952 but did not. When Khrushchev went to Beijing in 1954 for the anniversary of the Chinese Communist victory, he and Mao announced that Soviet forces would leave Port Arthur by the end of May 1955.

Welcoming Khrushchev to Beijing, Mao offered him a thousand divisions to crush the United States. Khrushchev retorted that American atomic bombs would incinerate them and asked instead for a million lumberjacks. Offended, Mao replied that China would not supply coolies. Hoping to have Mao's moral support in the impending showdown with Malenkov, the first secretary tried to atone for his blunder with an offer of increased military and economic aid. Mao accepted the aid but never forgave the insult. When Khrushchev began speaking in 1955 of "peaceful coexistence" between Communist and capitalist states, he made Mao his enemy.

The still-jelling Khrushchev regime—it was that because he headed the party—carried its campaign for the relaxation of tensions to the West, suddenly agreeing in April 1955 to sign a peace treaty with Austria. Only Molotov opposed this. Two months later, Marshal Zhukov sent a cordial message to his former comrades-in-arms in the United States, and in July Khrushchev and Bulganin traveled to Geneva to meet President Dwight Eisenhower, Prime Minister Anthony Eden of Great Britain, and Premier Edgar Faure of France. Holding no state or government post, First Secretary Khrushchev was merely "attached" to the Soviet delegation.

The Geneva "summit" conference, the first since Potsdam nearly a decade earlier, dealt with German reunification, arms control and disarmament, and European security. The two sides had sparred over Germany since 1945, and hopes for reunification sank in May 1955 when the Federal Republic ("West Germany") won independence and joined NATO. The Soviets responded with the Warsaw Pact, a military alliance with their East European satellites.

East and West had long debated arms limitation. In the spring of 1955 each presented proposals to the UN, where there was some accord on the size of the armies the major powers could have: 1.5 million each for the United States, the USSR, and China; 650,000 each for Britain and France. The issue of atomic and thermonuclear weapons remained deadlocked. Both sides professed horror of nuclear war; neither would concede anything. Confident of the huge American lead in nuclear weapons and delivery systems, notably the B-52 bomber, Eisenhower proposed "open skies": Each side could photograph the other's territory from the air to monitor compliance with a prohibition on deployment of new weapons of mass destruction. Existing arsenals would remain in place pending further negotiations. Knowing their nuclear and general strategic inferiority, the Soviets would not agree to halt development of weapons, and Khrushchev rejected "open skies" as a scheme to legitimize American espionage.

The two sides agreed to initiate cultural and commercial contacts. To some unknowable extent this fostered mutual understanding; thus the Conference did not fail, but it made no progress on substantive issues. Nevertheless, some Western commentators wrote wistfully of a "spirit of Geneva." With their ill-fitting suits and bumbling public manners, the goateed, *faux-raffiné* Bulganin and the crude, roly-poly Khrushchev seemed rather different from Stalin. The journalists who dreamed up the "spirit of Geneva" did not mention that these two had signed death warrants for untold thousands of human beings.

Rarely had the world seen such diplomatic theatre as Khrushchev and Bulganin proceeded to stage. After Belgrade—they apologized for Stalin's tactlessness—and Geneva, they traveled to India, Burma, and Afghanistan. Prime Minister Jawaharlal Nehru of India and Prime Minister U Nu of Burma had impeccable anti-imperialist credentials of great interest to the Kremlin.

This circus had both the West and China in its sights. The Communist seizure of power in China did not alter the balance of nuclear forces, which heavily favored the West. The post-Stalin Soviet commitment to help the Chinese modernize might have strengthened the Communist "bloc" had one existed; Khrushchev and Mao knew that it did not. Moscow–Beijing relations deteriorated dangerously after 1955 because on many issues the national interests were diametrically opposed. The Chinese detested the Russians as imperialists. The Soviets feared an aggressive China that would one day have nuclear weapons.

Moscow courted India, Burma, the Arab lands, Latin America, and Africa with an anti-imperialist, anti-colonialist campaign. NATO and China would probably never be Russia's friends. Building a coalition of nonaligned nations plus the USSR was within the realm of possibility.

HARBINGERS OF DE-STALINIZATION

The conduct of foreign policy turned on the still unresolved situation in the Communist party. Khrushchev held the Leningrad Case sword over Malenkov's head, but the weapon had two edges. Everyone on the Presidium and the Central Committee knew that Malenkov played the major role in the bloody 1949–1951 purge that cost so many Zhdanov supporters their lives, but revealing that publicly would stir up the hornets' nest already abuzz from the Abakumov trial—and exposing Malenkov might well lead to exposure of the whole sordid history of the party. They would *all* go down. Malenkov knew as much about Khrushchev as Khrushchev knew about him.

Monthly and quarterly journals featured Stalin prominently through the spring of 1954, newspapers and radio—shorter lead-times—rather less so. In 1955 the media rarely mentioned him. In June the Supreme Soviet promulgated new regulations for the office of public prosecutor. Article 4: "The USSR prosecutor general and the prosecutors subordinate to him . . . must take prompt measures to eliminate all violations of laws, regardless from whom these violations proceed." This reaffirmed the April 1953 "new legality"; other articles embodied a warning to security and Gulag officials. Article 33 obliged prosecutors to make regular inspection visits to all places of detention; halt illegal practices; and try those suspected of misprision in a court or before an administrative board. Incredibly, in the Soviet context, Article 34 required the prosecutor to "free immediately all those unlawfully arrested or detained illegally in places of detention."

No one could calculate the consequences of opening the Gulag gates. Even the admission of the Gulag's *existence* would indict Stalin and the Communist party, notably the present leadership, which was not about to plead guilty to complicity in the death of 40 to 60 million Soviet people. The prospect of releasing even one innocent prisoner terrified these Communists. History offered no precedent, except this: The Revolution had devoured its young in the 1930s, and now history was presenting the bill. Every party leader over 40 had been involved in the Terror one way or another; all owed their present comfortable circumstances to that Terror. The idea that they would ask to be relieved of their posts and indicted was simply counterintuitive.

The new regulations for the prosecutor's office appeared about as meaningful as the Soviet Constitution. The state released only a few people from the Gulag, but conditions there slowly became a little less awful. No one could staunch the flow of hope. More than a few administrators and guards began to hedge bets against the future.

THAW

In 1953, Ilya Ehrenburg published a mediocre novel titled *The Thaw*. The plant manager-protagonist, basically decent, pollutes his character trying to conform to the system. He is determined to fulfill the plan and increase production, if need be at the expense of worker welfare. He loses touch with normal people and surrounds himself with sycophants, one of whom tries to frame a senior engineer by spreading the rumor that he has a daughter in capitalist Belgium. The manager connives out of habit, but the plot backfires when the locals sympathize with the innocent engineer. Disgusted by her husband's callous behavior, the manager's wife leaves him. The engineer keeps his job; there is change in the air. One minor character, an artist, sees he has wasted his talent painting "socialist realism." Another artist, who had suffered for insisting on high standards, receives acclaim and reward. After a long winter, the thaw is coming. There would be no new Leningrad Case.

This political journalism had an immediate impact. Reform-minded officials—there were some—praised it, while fundamentalists attacked the portrayal of corruption. Was Ehrenburg advocating "bourgeois" values, placing the individual above the state?

Six weeks after Stalin's death, the poet Olga Berggolts publicly defended personal expression in lyric poetry; in other words, it was all right to write about human emotions whether or not they had anything to do with tanks and tractors and reverbatory furnaces. If Berggolts—a minor talent—could get away with this, Anna Akhmatova and Boris Pasternak and other geniuses might produce something earthshaking. Vera Panova's novel *The Seasons* dealt with the negative side of Soviet life and attacked plump, pompous functionaries. Leonid Sorin's play *The Guests* depicted political and moral corruption. In December 1953 the writer and critic Vladimir Pomerantsev assailed the Communist party's control of literature through the Writers' Union—the literary police.

The party struck back. Aleksei Surkov, mediocre poet, secretary of the Writers' Union, party member Class of 1925, lashed out at Pomerantsev, Ehrenburg, Panova, and Sorin. The authorities suddenly closed down *The Guests,* which had been playing to packed houses for months. Surkov demanded enforcement of censorship; by the time his article appeared in May 1954 that had already taken place. The timid flirtation with a retreat from Stalinism had terrified the Communist party, to which ideas presented a greater threat than Nazis.

LIFE WITHOUT STALIN

Unless the consumer was the secret police, Presidium, or Army, the Soviet system could not make decent consumer goods. In 1953 a newspaper reported that a toy rabbit manufactured by the Moscow Haberdashery Cooperative was made of coarse dark-colored material and had a hippopotamus head; such a toy, the article observed, "excites only fear and aversion." *Izvestiya* declared that a certain doll carriage could serve to grate cabbage, or perhaps hew logs. A poorly constructed metal doll for sale in state stores could easily double as a wolf trap. A cartoon in one of the humor magazines showed a mother warning her child, "Behave or I'll buy you a toy!"

In July 1953 a Moscow newspaper claimed that ordinary working people were buying ZiM automobiles in considerable numbers. No worker in all the wide USSR could ever hope to buy one. A *Pravda* reader wrote that he had ordered bicycle parts and some film from Mail Order House, sending 160 rubles. Four months later he received the film and 131 rubles' worth of phonograph records. A note informed him that the bicycle parts were unavailable but they thought he might like records instead. A July 1954 letter reported that imitation silk stockings made at Aurora Mills in Riga and Leninakan Stocking and Knitwear Mills in Yerevan developed runs on the second or third wearing. They came in one size, "very large," an "unpleasant yellow color," and cost 20 to 25 rubles. It was that or nothing.

Publication of such letters indicated official willingness to allow in a few rays of sunshine. The light began to shine on crime, alcoholism, and juvenile delinquency in the workers' paradise. In the context of a discussion of public drunkenness, a July 1954 letter to *Literary Gazette* (*Literaturnaya gazeta*) said: "You go into . . . these dives and all around there is dirt and drunken people rolling on the floor in their own vomit." The writer charged that many officials accepted bribes.

Kommunist called for critical discussion of Lysenko's theories. This followed a letter to *Pravda* from a Moscow University biologist who accused Lysenko of forcing his department to grant a doctoral degree to a candidate ignorant of biology: "Academician Lysenko, with his customary sharpness, called all reviewers who had spoken negatively of the dissertation . . . Weismannists [after the German biologist August Weismann]." After a party investigation, the university rescinded the degree, and *Pravda* so reported. In 1955 the *Botanical Journal* revealed that the "engendering" of soft wheat into hard was "nothing but the result of hybridization and the subsequent branching out in the descendants of hybrid individuals." Further, Lysenko's claim that a hornbeam had engendered a hazelnut collapsed under scrutiny. But Lysenko retained considerable authority because Khrushchev persisted in thinking him a genius.

The leadership continued to support charlatans in science, and in many areas the scientific-technological gap between the USSR and the West widened. Premier Bulganin declared that the way to increase labor productivity was to "raise the level of party guidance."

We make take this asininity as the beginning of the end of Soviet communism.

Honest officials in low- and mid-level positions—they could not rise higher—acknowledged semi-publicly that the party had not always intervened to good advantage in science, military affairs, and the arts. The astonishingly ignorant Presidium and Central Committee, however, almost always sought to remedy shortcomings by sending out more Communists to put the situation right.

The party permitted publication of *The Thaw* and—briefly—the staging of *The Guests,* but it also commissioned a symphonic poem, "Pavlik Morozov," based on the life of the boy

who betrayed his father during collectivization. The Communists allowed publication of
some appeals for a free art yet condemned the
vaudevillian Ruzhena Sikora for such "vulgar
and even fascist" songs as "Besamé mucho."
Their spokesmen assailed the "obscene witti-
cisms" of the hugely popular comedian Arkady
Raikin, whose routines never went beyond
mildly suggestive commentary. Fundamentalist Communists rejoiced when an arts journal
commented that the "constantly rising culture
of Soviet man is setting lofty standards in
love."

For all its vacillation and confusion, the
party was changing, if only because the generations had changed. The leaders patched up
some old quarrels, began speaking haltingly of
an accommodation with the West, did away

with some of the shackles. They put the Gulag
on short rations. This was not yet reform, but
as the Russian proverb says, "In a place with no
fish—the crawfish is a fish."

SUGGESTED ADDITIONAL READINGS

KEEP, JOHN. *Last of the Empires: A History of the Soviet Union, 1945–1991.* New York: Oxford, 1995.

KNIGHT, AMY. *Beria: Stalin's First Lieutenant.* Princeton, N.J.: Princeton University Press, 1993.

RUBENSTEIN, JOSHUA. *Tangled Loyalties: The Life and Times of Ilya Ehrenburg.* New York: Basic Books, 1996.

SUDOPLATOV, PAVEL, and ANATOLI SUDOPLATOV. *Special Tasks.* Boston: Little, Brown, 1995.

TOMPSON, WILLIAM J. *Khrushchev: A Political Life.* New York: St. Martin's Press, 1997.

16

THE GREAT REFORM

Khrushchev
and De-Stalinization

The Stalinist fundamentalists worried that their own party would succeed where their enemies had failed: Nikita Khrushchev and his allies seemed determined to destroy Communist rule. Having grudgingly accepted some modest reforms and condemned Beria, the Stalinists wanted to call a halt. If there had been errors, if Stalin had sometimes acted harshly, there was no need to rehash all that now. The party could not survive the dismantling of its myths. For nearly 40 years the principle of its infallibility had gone unchallenged; but that was about to change.

THE TWENTIETH PARTY CONGRESS

The first post-Stalin Party Congress convened in Moscow on February 14, 1956. So far as the 1,349 delegates and several hundred foreign Communist guests knew, it met merely to accept the sixth Five-Year Plan for 1956–1960. Following a series of glowing reports, the delegates approved the Plan unanimously, as always. Khrushchev then spoke on foreign policy and stressed the USSR's adherence to "peaceful coexistence." Wars were no longer inevitable—that was a clue to what was coming—but the ideological struggle would continue.

Reporting on the Central Committee's work, Khrushchev mentioned Stalin only once, noting that he was dead. Most people already knew that. The chief ideologist, M. A. Suslov, spoke of restoring the "norms of party life and principles of party leadership worked out by Lenin and frequently violated prior to the Twentieth Congress." Suslov was as Stalinist as anyone. The delegates found his comment puzzling, and they were utterly bewildered when he used a phrase not heard since Marx had coined it nearly 80 years earlier: "Cult of the individual." Suslov said it had flourished too long.

Anastas Mikoyan, a member of the Presidium and deputy prime minister, stepped across the line into heresy. Claiming that "collective leadership has been established in our party," he admitted that the "cult"—instant euphemism for Stalin's dictatorship—had existed for "about 20 years" with "an extremely negative effect." Jurisprudence, legislation, and trial procedures had suffered. Mikoyan attacked Stalin's *Economic Problems of Socialism in the USSR* and condemned the dictator's disdain for the "treasury of Leninist ideas." The reactionaries desperately looked to Molotov, but he who had found it inexpedient to defend his own wife could do more than praise Stalin with faint condemnation: The "cult," he conceded, had not always been helpful in conducting foreign policy.

Khrushchev did not address this matter during the regularly-scheduled sessions, which were to end with the election of party officers. The Central Committee reelected him first secretary on February 24. It was his prerogative to move the adoption of the party's list of candidates for the Presidium, but the Congress adjourned before he could do so that day. The motion and the voting were mere formalities, but until they took place he was technically the sole leader in office.

Shortly before midnight on February 24, couriers dashed around Moscow collecting delegates and bringing them back to the Kremlin for a special secret session. Once they were assembled—there were no foreign guests or press—Khrushchev delivered a report "On the Cult of Personality and Its Consequences." The Stalinists sensed catastrophe.

Saying not a word about the *scores of millions* of non-party victims, Khrushchev told of the illegal arrest, imprisonment, torture, and execution of thousands of innocent Communist party members. Stalin himself had signed many orders for these acts; so had Khrushchev and every other member of the Presidium, but that went unreported. Khrushchev blamed Stalin for the battlefield reversals of 1941–1942 and charged him with taking all the credit for the later victories. Stalin had ordered the mass deportation of peoples falsely accused of collaborating with the Germans; "violated the norms of revolutionary legality and ignored all norms of party life"; coined the term "enemy of the people"; elevated himself "above party and nation"; cooked up the conflict with Yugoslavia. And that was the good news.

Six years later, Khrushchev revealed that party leaders had discussed whether to place the matter of Stalin's crimes on the agenda. Molotov, Kaganovich, Malenkov, and Voroshilov had been "categorically opposed." Molotov defended Stalin and predicted that reprisals against innocent persons might again be required in the pursuit of "enemies of the people." Khrushchev might be one of them. Though they differed on the details, all the leaders wanted to cut the party's losses, and save their own hides.

Dazed, the delegates returned to their hotels for a few hours early in the morning of February 25, then came back to the Kremlin to elect party officers and wind up the Congress. Khrushchev's "secret" speech was the talk of Moscow and soon the entire world was reading it.

Riots erupted in Tbilisi on March 9. The Georgians, who had suffered as much as any ethnic group, would not permit an attack on "their" Stalin. Violence struck many cities and some Gulag locations in the spring and early summer as both free citizens and prisoners seized the opportunity to vent grievances. Only in Tbilisi did the mobs defend the late dictator.

Having gone on "ready alert" status at the start of the party Congress, security forces in all the major cities and the Gulag easily suppressed the demonstrations. But the unrest at home and abroad—especially in Poland and Hungary—led the Central Committee to forbid mass publication of Khrushchev's speech. Party officials did, however, read numbered copies—for which they were strictly accountable—aloud at public meetings.

DE-STALINIZATION

Set in type earlier, attacks on the "cult of personality" in monthly and quarterly journals indicated a carefully planned campaign was underway. The leading history journal hinted in

March that the regime would soon exonerate of all charges several executed military officers. These "rehabilitations" constituted partial payment to Marshal Zhukov, who had backed Khrushchev against Beria and now at the Congress. *Pravda* declared that, although Stalin had "rendered great services to our party," in the latter part of his life the "cult of the individual and the leadership practices which developed under its influence . . . did much harm." The party newspaper disavowed the odious official party history (*Short Course*) and the no less odious official biography of Stalin. It admitted that "many of our films, books, and paintings, especially those dealing with the war, are dedicated chiefly to the praise and glorification of Stalin." The first public mention in 32 years of the "Lenin testament" appeared in the Komsomol newspaper in May, the text in June.

In June 1956 the Soviet press published the Central Committee resolution "On Overcoming the Cult of the Individual and Its Consequences." Whining over the exploitation in Western political circles of the revelation of Stalin's crimes, the resolution paid tribute to Stalin's services and referred to some of his atrocities as "mistakes." The Communist party had simply "not known" the full extent of the abuses until Beria's arrest. The "Leninist core" had always remained intact. It would have been impossible to remove the dictator "under conditions then prevailing." The Soviet people would never have supported anyone who spoke against him. There was unfortunately much truth to that claim.

Though the Communists refused to admit the Gulag housed a single innocent soul, the dismantling of the far-flung Archipelago—as Aleksandr Solzhenitsyn named it—constituted the party's most pressing task. The cautious, mostly unpublicized "rehabilitations" of 1953–1955 had resulted in the liberation of only a handful of high-ranking Communists

like Polina Zhemchuzhina. Khrushchev's "secret speech" had implied that reviews of questionable legal proceedings would affect only party members, at least initially. But "de-Stalinization" generated its own logic and momentum. Bowing to irresistible public pressure, the Communists grudgingly freed about eight million non-party prisoners (*zeks*) by the end of 1957. A year later "only" a million innocent people remained in the camps. The acronym *Gulag* disappeared from the official lexicon; no one could erase it from history.

The regime gave special treatment to former Soviet POWs whom Stalin had sent to the Gulag after the war. Marshal Zhukov announced that military personnel who had died in the Gulag had in effect fallen on the battlefield. Their widows and orphans would receive monetary "compensation" and preferential treatment for housing and jobs, with lifetime pensions for the widows and handicapped children. The Communists now exonerated and restored full civil rights to people forced to work for the Germans.

Making an exception in the case of the Crimean Tatars and two other groups, the Communists cleared the minority peoples of all charges of collaboration and permitted them to return to their homelands. The Crimean Tatars remained in limbo; the party needed the Crimea for itself.

The sudden reappearance in society of all those innocent victims had an enormous impact. Broken in body and spirit, some returnees simply lived out their days quietly, but millions demanded restoration of their rights and their honor, and punishment of those who had stripped them of everything. The Communist leadership refused the demands. Sooner or later, however, accountability for Stalin-era crimes would come to rest at the doorsteps of all who had served Stalin in high posts and survived—fattened—on blood, certainly including Nikita Khrushchev.

FURTHER REFORMS

Local, regional, and Union republic courts had been insignificant appendages of the power-mad center under Lenin and Stalin. Attempting to end the grotesque centralization of judicial powers, in June 1956 the regime abolished the USSR ministry of justice and transferred its functions to the republic ministries. At least on paper, justice by administrative fiat ended with revision of the Code of Criminal Procedure. Article 7: "No person may be considered guilty of having committed a crime and subjected to criminal punishment save by the sentence of a court." This was no writ of habeas corpus, which has never existed in the Russian legal tradition. But it would, if honored, be a step forward. In April 1956 a legal journal assailed the Vyshinsky–Stalin theory of evidence according to which a confession constituted proof of guilt. April 1957 decrees forbade police and prosecutors from tricking suspects into incriminating themselves.

In 1962 the chief prosecutor declared that his office was strictly observing the new Criminal Code, specifically the prohibition against nonjudicial arrest and punishment. But that same year a Moscow prosecutor defended the Vyshinsky contention that anyone bound over to a court for trial was guilty: A court's sole function was to determine the "objectivity" of police conclusions. In practice, this interpretation had prevailed in all "political" cases since 1920 and it would continue to do so until 1985. The number of such cases after 1953, however, was a fraction of what it had been under Lenin and Stalin. The state—here meaning secret police, regular police, courts, and Communist hierarchy—accused fewer citizens of "anti-Soviet" behavior; when it made the charge, however, it almost invariably found the accused guilty.

The public welcomed Khrushchev's assurance that the Communist party would no longer allow the secret police to run amok. The words were neither empty nor wholly sincere: Despite some shuffling of personnel, the overwhelming majority of guards, interrogators—even the most notorious—and clean-hand administrators remained on the job or retired with honor on comfortable pensions. Ivan Serov, a Beriaite who had become head of the MGB in 1954, did not immediately leave office. He had earned a reputation for brutality supervising the wartime deportations—a job Mikhail Suslov also performed to satanic perfection—and kept his position because he knew where to find the skeletons, including those from Khrushchev's service in Ukraine.

After a decent interval, Serov accepted a demotion. Aleksandr "Iron Shurik [Alex]" Shelepin, a career party bureaucrat, replaced him. The KGB (ex-Cheka, GPU, OGPU, etc.) thus came under Communist party control for the first time. Having taken enormous pains to cover some of his own misdeeds and to collect evidence against those whom he was about to sack, in 1963 Khrushchev stripped a number of present and former high-ranking KGB officials, including Serov but excluding Suslov, of medals won for conducting the deportations.

A few days after "Iron Shurik" replaced Serov, safeguards against extrajudicial punishment and curbs on secret police powers came into effect. Six months later the Soviet Supreme Court directed lower courts to de-emphasize punishment in favor of reeducation and preventive measures and to work to eradicate the social causes of criminal behavior. This read far better than it worked in practice, but the situation did improve.

Dealing with Stalin in the teaching and writing of history posed vexing problems; the official Soviet encyclopedia was replete with errors. Acknowledging the falsification of Stalin's Civil War record, military journals charged him with numerous costly errors as commander-in-chief. It was impossible to revise textbooks before the 1956–1957 school year, but something had to be done. Late in August 1956 *Pravda* provided vague guidance: "While giving credit to J. V. Stalin's merits and showing his role as organizer and theoretician, the teacher must at the same time throw light on the very grave errors he committed." This was an invitation to political analysis; countless people had died for even thinking about that, or being so accused. Publication of a "de-Stalinized" party history in 1959 finally gave teachers some reliable guidance.

Real and paper reform embraced all aspects of civic life. Legal liability of workers who left the workplace without permission ended in April 1956. A September 1957 order retroactively halted the naming of places, enterprises, and organizations for living persons. Not until 1961, however, did Stalingrad become Volgograd; and all efforts to style the great clash the "Battle on the Volga" proved unsuccessful. Stalin Prizes reverted to the Lenin Prizes they were until 1935. In 1958 the press admitted the idiocy of calling Shostakovich and other composers, writers, and artists "antipopular" and "formalist." Such evaluations, *Pravda* confessed, "reflected J. V. Stalin's subjective approach."

"REHABILITATIONS"

The revelation of Stalin's crimes made it imperative for the CPSU to exonerate and "rehabilitate" hundreds of thousands of persecuted party members as quickly as possible. This was an exceedingly delicate matter: Was it necessary to accept—posthumously, of course—Bukharin, Zinoviev, Kamenev, and Trotsky back into the ranks? Even anti-Stalinist Communists shuddered. The Kremlin announced there would be no review of the judicial proceedings against, let alone rehabilitation of, these people.

But public exoneration of lesser fry began in *Pravda* while the Twentieth Party Congress was in session: The newspaper praised the Hungarian revolutionary Béla Kun—not mentioning his execution in 1937. The same issue disavowed the dissolution—really a super-purge—in 1938 of the Polish Communist party, which, according to NKVD reports at the time, "enemy agents" had infiltrated. Moscow now admitted that "this accusation rested on materials falsified by subsequently exposed provocateurs." The "provocateurs" had acted on Stalin's orders.

Over the next several years the press published the names of hundreds of prominent Communists now cleared of the charges that had sent them to their doom between 1936 and 1952. The courts and prosecutors exonerated thousands of rank-and-file party members. Not until the late 1980s, however, did the CPSU complete the *party* rehabilitations, and only then did it begin to pay serious attention to the millions of others.

In October 1955 the party secretly cleared General Yan Gamarnik of all charges. Fifteen months later the state prosecutor rescinded—also in camera—the June 1937 guilty verdicts against Tukhachevsky, Kork, Yakir, Uborevich, Eideman, V. P. Primakov, and B. M. Feldman. Later, A. I. Yegorov and V. K. Blücher won posthumous acquittal. But only in 1988 would the Communists *publicly* acknowledge these rehabilitations.

The 1956 anti-Communist, anti-Soviet violence in Poland and Hungary gave Khrushchev an excuse to forbid public discussion of his own speech. Review of the "repressions" continued but was limited to CPSU members and a few prominent outsiders. Most former *zeks* (Gulag prisoners) simply returned to the factories and collective farms on parole. Complete, official rehabilitation had to follow established judicial procedure including the time-consuming cross-examination of witnesses and presentation of documentary evidence. Such cases inundated the courts; it usually took years to reach a decision. Millions of potential litigants were forced simply to trust the new regime and hope the old one would not return.

THE "ANTIPARTY GROUP"

As many as 500,000 Communist party and secret police officials had a keen personal interest in halting the revelations about the Stalin era, and many Communists uninvolved in the Terror or even victims of it felt threatened by the challenge to their faith. Returning *zeks* were filing thousands of petitions, complete with affidavits demanding the arrest and trial of their tormentors. Like any bureaucracy, the regime could sidetrack pleas from obscure citizens indefinitely, but Khrushchev's own brief against Stalin had set an irreversible precedent. The leaders had to do something to calm the country.

Conservatives argued that *everyone* had been a Stalinist, and everyone but he and his relatives admitted that Khrushchev's hands were as bloody as anyone's and bloodier than most. Many Communists resigned their posts to wait out the storm. The pseudoscientist Lysenko was the most prominent example; he left the Agricultural Academy chairmanship in April 1956, only to regain his political influence the following year. A few officials involved in the Terror killed themselves when threatened with exposure. That was the path chosen by Aleksandr Fadeyev, secretary-general of the Writers' Union. Some fanatics decided that only the elimination of Khrushchev could restore order.

Various plots to assassinate the first secretary failed; a political maneuver aimed at deposing him almost succeeded. While Khrushchev and Bulganin were on a state visit to Finland in June 1957, the Stalinists struck. Summoned to a Presidium meeting the day after his return, Khrushchev found himself voted out of office. Only Suslov and Mikoyan among the full members supported him. With his own vote, that meant three against eight—Molotov, Kaganovich, Malenkov, Voroshilov, Saburov, Pervukhin, Kirichenko, and traveling companion Bulganin. Among the six candidate members, Khrushchev had the support of all save Shepilov; but of the five others only Marshal Zhukov could be of immediate service.

Only the full Central Committee could legally elect or depose a first (or general) secretary. Khrushchev insisted that the Presidium follow the rules. The conspirators, however, had taken steps to prevent Central Committee members from learning of events in Moscow until presented with a fait accompli. Prime Minister Bulganin had posted his own bodyguards inside the Kremlin and at Central Committee headquarters in Old Square; the Presidium majority planned to arrest Khrushchev if he refused to submit.

At this point Khrushchev called in some debts. He had retained Ivan Serov as chairman of the KGB. Serov now sided with him, leaving the conspirators unable to force the KGB to arrest Khrushchev or prevent the convening of the Central Committee. Khrushchev had rescued Marshal Zhukov from oblivion; Zhukov now arranged for military aircraft to fly Central Committee members to Moscow. Frol Kozlov, whom Khrushchev had installed as head of the Leningrad province party organization, rushed to support his patron, as did Leonid Brezhnev, a candidate member of the Presidium with good connections in Ukraine. By June 21, 1957, more than 300 top party leaders, including nearly all the 133 full members of the Central Committee, had gathered in Moscow. Neither Bulganin's bodyguard nor any other agency at the anti-Khrushchev faction's disposal could prevent convocation of a plenary session on June 22–29.

There was no time limit on speeches, and

Molotov, Kaganovich, and Malenkov each spoke twice. They denounced de-Stalinization and rejected the Twentieth Party Congress's decision to expose Stalin and rehabilitate his victims. They assailed the virgin-lands scheme and called for reversal of plans to enlarge the powers of Union republics. Molotov condemned peaceful coexistence, normalization of relations with Japan, reconciliation with Yugoslavia, the peace treaty with Austria, and summit conferences. He and Kaganovich demanded an end to the prosecutions—few though they were—of officials involved in the Terror and restoration as a guide to the past of the *Short Course* in party history, which deified Stalin.

Khrushchev mounted a vigorous defense and had wide support. No one save the conspirators wanted a return to Stalinism. Molotov's prediction that the day would come again when the innocent would "inevitably and unavoidably" be imprisoned in the fight against "imperialist agents and class enemies" sent a Siberian chill through the meeting.

The anti-Khrushchev faction had mustered eight votes in the Presidium. That now fell to four. Voroshilov, intoxicated as usual, broke down and cried, admitting his mistakes. Mikhail Pervukhin and Mikhail Saburov, short on political acumen but aware of the difference between four and 300, recanted with slightly more dignity. Despairing of taking any more trips with Khrushchev but wanting to keep his head, Bulganin backed off.

Only Molotov, Malenkov, Kaganovich, and Shepilov were left in what became known as the "antiparty group," men *Pravda* described as "sycophants and hallelujah-shouters." The Central Committee heard an account of their crimes. Malenkov had assisted Nikolai Yezhov in the purge in Belarus in 1936 and had fabricated the Leningrad Case. Lazar Kaganovich had supervised purges in Ukraine and the North Caucasus. Vyacheslav Molotov liked to write on secret police lists of candidates for the Gulag: "Arrest, convict, shoot." Later the party would learn that he had once ordered innocent people arrested as "terrorists" when his car skidded on the ice.

The session expelled Molotov, Kaganovich, and Malenkov from the Presidium and the Central Committee. It expelled Shepilov from the Central Committee and dismissed him as a candidate member of the Presidium. These relatively lenient measures indicated Khrushchev's shaky hold on power and his own culpability. But the Central Committee that saved him was also determined not to revive the Terror. Molotov became ambassador to Mongolia. Malenkov once again went to Kazakhstan, this time to manage the Ust-Kamenogorsk hydroelectric plant. Kaganovich became manager of a cement plant in Sverdlovsk (Yekaterinburg), where Boris Yeltsin was beginning his party career. Shepilov, who had been foreign minister from June 1956 to May 1957, went to the Academy of Sciences as a junior political scientist.

To convey the impression of a stability and order, three Presidium members—including Bulganin—who had voted against Khrushchev were permitted to remain on that body briefly. Bulganin retained the premiership for nine months, then became director of the State Bank, then director of the economic council of the backwater town of Stavropol, where he made the acquaintance of the young Mikhail Gorbachev. The drunken Voroshilov kept the "presidency" until May 1960, when Brezhnev replaced him. One of Khrushchev's opponents, Mikhail Pervukhin, was demoted to candidate member of the Presidium; Mikhail Saburov went into forced retirement.

The June session elected a new Presidium and increased its membership from 11 to 15. Among the new full members were Marshal Zhukov and Leonid Brezhnev. Khrushchev's allies Aleksei Kosygin and Andrei Kirilenko were among the eight new candidate members.

TWENTY-SECOND PARTY CONGRESS

Victory over the "antiparty group" did not give Khrushchev a free hand. The fact that several of his opponents retained their posts—however temporarily—indicated that the Central Committee controlled the first secretary, not the other way around. The Central Committee meant to keep Khrushchev on a short leash; he and the other leaders were in turn anxious to curb the military commanders. In October 1957 the Presidium expelled Marshal Zhukov from its ranks and dismissed him as defense minister. The media charged Zhukov with exaggerating his role in the war and neglecting ideological work. Professional officers did resent interference in military affairs, and Zhukov had tried to lessen CPSU meddling. After his fall the party instituted a 50-hour ideological training program for military officers. The extent to which this improved efficiency and morale is open to question.

The Central Committee accused Zhukov of "Bonapartism" and of attempting to create his own "cult of personality" with a view to seizing power. It remains unclear whether Zhukov harbored political ambitions. Nothing in his record substantiates the "Bonapartism" charge, but there is a mountain of evidence that attests to the party's fear of a military coup d'état. The Communists suspected the officers and believed the best way to neutralize them was to besmirch the character of their chief. Zhukov disappeared into obscure retirement. The Army, like the party, began to reward mediocrity and conformity.

The charge of inflating his role in World War II was more properly directed against Stalin. Throughout the Khrushchev era the late generalissimo was frequently taken to task for his failure to prepare the nation for war and for his mistakes in the early campaigns. Marking the eightieth anniversary of Stalin's birth in December 1959, *Pravda* repeated the accusations, only to praise him as an "outstanding theoretician and propagandist of Marxism-Leninism."

The militant Stalinist line returned in October 1958, when the Khrushchev regime savagely attacked Boris Pasternak. Intent on fueling anti-Soviet propaganda and incidentally on honoring a writer, the Swedish Academy awarded Pasternak the Nobel Prize for literature. Although he had published little except translations in the Stalin years, Pasternak had been in the front rank of Soviet poets for a generation. On the recommendation of the illiterate wordsmiths who controlled the Writers' Union, in 1956 the censors rejected Pasternak's first and only novel, *Dr. Zhivago*. It was published abroad in 1957. That, more than its fairly banal story line, indicted the Soviet system.

The reactionaries had their case. At their prompting, Khrushchev and the KGB's "Iron Shurik" Shelepin directed a vitriolic campaign against the writer. Rejecting the appeals of opportunist organizations and individuals—who cared nothing for him—to come to the West, Pasternak endured public humiliation, renounced the prize, and begged Khrushchev not to expel him from Russia. The Communists, having gotten their pound of flesh, let him stay. He died less than two years later.

Increasingly on the defensive at home and abroad, Khrushchev did not vary the pace of his innovations. In 1961, his popularity at a low ebb, he summoned the Twenty-Second Party Congress. (The Twenty-First, in 1959, had been devoted to economic matters.) In October nearly 4,400 delegates—the most ever to that time—assembled in Moscow ostensibly to approve a new party program. Khrushchev vilified the "antiparty group" and presented new details about the Terror. He described hideous scenes in Stalin's office when Molotov, Kaganovich, and Voroshilov co-signed orders condemning innumerable innocent people to death: Stalin customarily signed in red ink, Molotov in black, Kaganovich and

Voroshilov in blue. The first secretary outlined Malenkov's concoction of the Leningrad Case and heaped scorn on Bulganin.

Khrushchev hinted at Stalin's involvement in the murder of Sergei Kirov:

Great efforts are still needed to find out who was really to blame for . . . [Kirov's] death. The more deeply we study the materials connected with . . . the case, the more questions arise. . . . A thorough enquiry is now being conducted into the circumstances of this complicated matter.

This could only mean that Kamenev and Zinoviev, shot for inspiring the murder, had been innocent. That left the NKVD, which in December 1934 could not have planned and carried out the murder without Stalin's approval.

In part because he himself moved slowly lest he stub his own toe, Khrushchev fell from power before his investigators resolved the Kirov matter; his successors closed the books. Gorbachev reopened them in 1986, but despite massive circumstantial evidence implicating Stalin, no direct proof has emerged. That is what happens when a regime kills the killers of the killers and so on. In the end, the executioners are merely shooting at designated targets.

Khrushchev proposed that the party erect a monument to Communist victims of the Terror. Wary of Khrushchev but not afraid of him, other speakers at the Twenty-Second Party Congress argued against this, insisting that people who had "deserved" punishment should not be rehabilitated or reinstated in the party. There was no need for a monument. The head of the Control Commission, Nikolai Shvernik, said that the judicial review of questionable convictions was proceeding slowly; fewer than a quarter of those who had applied for reinstatement had been accepted back into the party.

The Congress voted to remove Stalin's body from the Lenin–Stalin Mausoleum and bury it under 10 meters of concrete in the small cemetery for party and state heroes at the foot of the Kremlin's east wall. Khrushchev assured the delegates that the "cult" lay alongside the man who had created it. Many speakers praised Khrushchev himself for all this, making him uncomfortable:

A certain special emphasis is placed on me personally, and my role in carrying out major party and government measures is underlined. I understand the kind feelings which guide these comments. Allow me, however, to emphasize vehemently that everything said about me should be said about the Central Committee of our Leninist party and about the Presidium of the Central Committee. (*Stormy, prolonged applause* [note in official transcript].) Not one measure, not one responsible pronouncement, has been carried out upon anyone's personal directive; they have all been the result of collective deliberation and collective decision. (*Stormy applause.*)

The ideological quarrel with the Chinese, Albanian, and Romanian parties was growing sharper, and the CPSU had other problems. Many officials had been ready to end de-Stalinization, yet Khrushchev continued to wash some extremely dirty party linen in public. This bold move indicated not strength but Khrushchev's precarious hold on power. Behind his back, party grandees quoted the Russian proverb, "When the Devil grows old, he becomes a monk." Had Khrushchev acknowledged his own past, resigned his post, and gone off to manage an obscure collective farm, his fellow citizens would have recognized a Dostoyevskyan syndrome: Sin, repentance, atonement, salvation. But Khrushchev repented Stalin's sins, not his own, and he loved power.

Educated and taught Holy Writ by Russian Orthodox priests, who had thought him a "model pupil," Khrushchev did undertake a kind of surrogate atonement: In 1962 he personally authorized publication of Aleksandr Solzhenitsyn's powerful novel about the Gulag, *One Day in the Life of Ivan Denisovich.* That book, and Khrushchev's own "secret speech," changed history.

SUGGESTED ADDITIONAL READINGS

BURLATSKY, FEDOR. *Khrushchev and the First Russian Spring.* New York: Charles Scribner's Sons, 1992.

FILTZER, DONALD. *The Khrushchev Era: De-Stalinization and the Limits of Reform in the USSR, 1953–1964.* London: Macmillan, 1993.

KOPELEV, LEV. *To Be Preserved Forever.* Philadelphia: Lippincott, 1977.

LINDEN, CARL A. *Khrushchev and the Soviet Leadership.* Baltimore and London: Johns Hopkins University Press, 1990.

MCCAULEY, MARTIN, ed. *Khrushchev and Khrushchevism.* Bloomington: Indiana University Press, 1987.

TOMPSON, WILLIAM J. *Khrushchev: A Political Life.* New York: St. Martin's Press, 1997.

17

REFORM-ERA FOREIGN POLICY

A domestic upheaval on the scale of "de-Stalinization" inevitably had sweeping
ramifications abroad. As Molotov had warned, foreign enemies used Khrushchev's
revelations as a stick with which to beat the USSR and communism. The Soviet
puppet regimes in Eastern Europe waited anxiously for the dust to settle
in Moscow. In Beijing, Chairman Mao listened as Marshal Zhu De, head
of the Chinese delegation to the Soviet Party Congress, gave his report.
Mao could only regard developments apprehensively. For a few months
he went along with Khrushchev, agreeing that Communists should not exalt
any individual; then he changed his mind.

TURMOIL IN POLAND

On June 28–29, 1956, thousands of workers in
Poznan, Poland, disrupted an international
trade fair by marching through the streets carrying banners reading BREAD AND FREEDOM!
and RUSSIANS GO HOME! Humiliated, the authorities sent in the police. Violent clashes ensued; 53 people died. The regime did not call
in the Army, then under the command of Soviet Marshal Konstantin Rokossovsky. A Polish-
born Soviet citizen, Rokossovsky knew the Polish Army to be unreliable. He had contingency
plans to use Soviet troops stationed in Poland,
and reinforcements from East Germany, in the
event the disorders continued.

In October, a few days after a court sentenced the alleged ringleaders of the Poznan
riots to prison, Khrushchev, Mikoyan, Molotov, and Kaganovich flew to Warsaw to meet
with the new Polish Communist party leader,
Wladyslaw Gomulka. It was imperative to

reach an accommodation or crush Poland
quickly: The situation in Hungary was also
threatening to spin out of control. Gomulka
insisted the Soviets accelerate repatriation of
Polish citizens from the Gulag, regularize the
status of Soviet troops in Poland by statute, and
give Poland a fair price for its coal. He also
asked for a share of German reparations.

The negotiators compromised. The Soviets
approved Gomulka as head of the Polish Communist party. Rokossovsky resigned as Polish
defense minister and vice-chairman of the
Council of Ministers and returned to Moscow.
In late autumn the two sides concluded agreements guaranteeing equality in their relations
and regulating the status of Soviet forces.

THE HUNGARIAN REVOLT

Spurred on by U.S. Secretary of State John Foster Dulles's rhetoric, official and semi-official

American media outlets—the CIA's Radio Free Europe (RFE) and the State Department's Voice of America (VOA)—had repeatedly and stridently encouraged the Hungarians to rise up against Moscow. Launched from West Germany and Italy, millions of balloons with propaganda leaflets and instructions on waging guerrilla warfare drifted into Hungary. Secret agents, mostly CIA-trained émigrés, parachuted into the country to make contact with anti-Communists, foment discontent, commit sabotage. The Hungarian regime caught and shot almost all of them. (The Albanian Communist regime killed 100 percent of the agents who landed in that country; the notorious British spy Kim Philby always alerted the Tirana regime when a drop was coming.)

In progress for years, these activities intensified after Khrushchev's "secret speech." Interpreting those revelations as a warning to put their house in order, late in March 1956 the Hungarian Communists announced posthumous rehabilitation of a foreign minister arrested and shot in 1949 on trumped-up charges of "Titoism." Hungarians began returning home from the Gulag. Censorship eased slightly, and more food appeared in the markets. In July Ernö Gerö replaced Mátyás Rákosi as party leader—a change, but not an improvement. The Western propaganda barrage continued. In Budapest the Petöfi literary circle became the focal point of a spontaneous reform movement among intellectuals, journalists, professional people, students, and workers, and *Pravda* took note. Through the Petöfi Circle, it said, "certain elements which oppose the policy of the . . . [Communist] party and which have succumbed to the external influence of imperialist circles have tried . . . to spread their anti-party views." *Pravda* told the Hungarians to remember Poznan.

Imre Nagy, Prime Minister before his ouster in April 1955 for being too weak, resumed the leadership on October 24. The same day, anti-Soviet riots convulsed Budapest and Soviet troops intervened. On October 25 the Hungarian Communist Central Committee consulted with Soviet Ambassador Yuri Andropov and his aide Vladimir Kryuchkov—both future KGB directors—and János Kádár succeeded Gerö.

Secretary of State Dulles's speeches and the RFE–VOA broadcasts had not gone unheard in the Kremlin. Uncertain as to Western intentions in Hungary, the Soviet leadership initially decided not to invade. Indeed, it would negotiate with Imre Nagy for the withdrawal of Soviet troops. But Moscow quickly learned that behind the rhetoric lay more rhetoric. And just as quickly, Hungary's fate became linked to events in the Middle East.

On October 28 the UN voted to discuss the Hungarian situation. The following day, Israeli forces attacked Egyptian positions in the Sinai Desert and advanced on the Suez Canal, which Egypt's Gamal Abdel Nasser had just nationalized. Britain and France rejected an American proposal—which Moscow supported—for an Israeli–Egyptian cease-fire. London and Paris issued an ultimatum to both sides to stop fighting and permit Anglo–French occupation of the waterway. On October 31 French and British planes bombed Cairo and the Canal; Israel continued to attack Egyptian positions. Only on November 6, bowing to intense pressure from the United States, did London accept a cease-fire. Paris and Tel Aviv followed suit. President Dwight Eisenhower won reelection that day.

These events made it possible for the Kremlin to reverse its decision to allow the Hungarians to go their own way. Nagy and Kádár had appealed for order and said they would negotiate the withdrawal of Soviet military forces. The Soviets began pulling out the troops. Nagy promised free multi-party elections and took leaders of a previously outlawed peasant party into his cabinet. The head of the Roman

Catholic Church in Hungary, Josef Cardinal Mindszenty, who had been in asylum in the American Embassy since February 1949, hailed the Soviet withdrawal as the beginning of the end of Kremlin rule.

Nagy summoned Ambassador Andropov on November 1 to enquire about the massive Soviet military buildup in eastern Hungary. The somber Kryuchkov at his side, Andropov swore the troops were merely resting, and would continue their homeward march to the USSR; there would be no invasion. On November 2, a relieved Nagy informed him that Hungary would quit the Warsaw Pact and would henceforward be a neutral nation.

The Soviet Army swung around 180 degrees on November 4 and raced toward Budapest, guns blazing. After 10 days of fighting, the peace of the tank and the machine gun prevailed. Kádár became leader of the new Hungarian regime. Unswervingly loyal to Moscow even though the Stalinists had imprisoned him and subjected him to hideous torture, he supervised the brutal pacification of his country.

Kádár and Andropov had promised Imre Nagy safe conduct out of the country. A waiting Soviet platoon arrested him on November 22 as he left the Yugoslav Embassy. Nagy and the military leader of the uprising, Pal Maléter, were executed at a Soviet base in Romania after a secret trial in June 1958. Andropov and Kryuchkov won promotions.

CHINA

Russia had been resolving problems in eastern Europe by force for two centuries. China was another matter. In his *public* remarks at the Twentieth Party Congress, Khrushchev had carefully praised the Chinese and Yugoslav Communists, whose reaction to the disclosure of Stalin's crimes he had to take into account.

After the Congress, he sent Anastas Mikoyan and an Uzbek official to Beijing to explain that he really had not attacked Stalin, just scolded him.

But quite aside from "de-Stalinization" fundamental political differences existed between China and the post-Stalin USSR. The Soviets had a horror of nuclear war; misreading Washington's restraint in Korea and elsewhere, Chinese leaders jeered at the American "paper tiger." The Soviets were speaking of "peaceful coexistence"; the Chinese, who had enunciated that policy in 1954, reversed themselves and called for "uninterrupted revolutions." The Kremlin accused them of resurrecting Trotsky's "permanent revolution." When the Soviets tried to restore normal diplomatic relations with Japan, China attacked this as trafficking with a "Yankee puppet." In the mid-1950s Moscow announced that it would work with the "national bourgeoisie"—for example, in India. The Chinese condemned this as a "capitulation."

Zhou Enlai's January 1957 peace mission to Moscow failed. Mao himself headed a delegation to the fortieth anniversary celebration of the Bolshevik coup d'état, but he and Khrushchev could not compromise, not least because Khrushchev's criticism of "Talmudists and pedants" and "pedantic quotation-lovers" in the CPSU was obviously aimed chiefly at Mao and his people. Khrushchev jibed that it would be "absurd to comb Marx and Engels for instructions on deliveries of farm products by collective farmers." That referred to a Chinese Communist practice that would be a hallmark of Mao's Cultural Revolution of the 1960s.

Khrushchev and Mikhail Suslov went to Beijing in September 1959 for the tenth anniversary of the Communist seizure of power and received a cold reception. By 1960, relations between the two countries had so deteriorated that only a change of leadership on one side or the other could bring about rapprochement.

FROM SPUTNIK TO BERLIN

In August 1957 the USSR, and Khrushchev personally, seemed suddenly much stronger: The Soviets conducted the first successful test flight of an intercontinental ballistic missile (ICBM). Henceforward, no radar or other warning system, no amount of firepower, could guarantee any nation against attack. Two months later the Soviets put the first artificial satellite, *Sputnik (Companion),* into Earth orbit. Radio signals from the 83.6-kilogram device testified to Soviet capabilities. Then, two days later, the USSR successfully tested a hydrogen bomb. The saber-rattling incited the Americans to undertake more than 30 thermonuclear tests in the Marshall Islands in 1958.

The Soviet "spectaculars" did not produce the capitulation Khrushchev and some of his colleagues hoped for. An American show of force in Lebanon made them hesitate to meddle too blatantly in the Middle East, and they could not compete on equal terms with the Chinese Communists in Asia. NATO was arming West Germany—a step forbidden by the Potsdam Conference. West Germany banned the Communist party. When would the humiliations end, and Moscow get the respect it thought it merited? In November 1958 Khrushchev issued an ultimatum: The West had to leave West Berlin within six months. West Berlin would become a free city, which in effect meant incorporation into the East German puppet state.

The Western powers rejected the ultimatum. To spread joy at Christmas 1958, Foreign Minister Andrei Gromyko spoke publicly of the "growing threat that Berlin may become a second Sarajevo."

The four powers had been unable to agree on a German peace treaty, and the West had come to regard that as an advantage. So long as the German question remained unsettled, the "German Democratic Republic" remained merely a Soviet occupation zone. Determined to force recognition of the GDR, early in 1959 the Kremlin produced a draft peace treaty that recognized the GDR as an independent state and fixed its frontier with Poland along the Oder–Neisse line. The West had never accepted that line and rejected the draft. Khrushchev indulged in more bluster, warned of a new Berlin blockade, then agreed in March that East and West Germany could continue to exist side by side. He pledged not to resolve the German question by force. Once again he had ranted and threatened only to back down. That cost him face in Moscow, not to mention Beijing.

Khrushchev withdrew his ultimatum because he and Eisenhower, attempting to moderate the international climate, agreed in the spring of 1959 to exchange state visits. Khrushchev-style diplomacy saw the Soviets launch a rocket—their second—and land it on the moon the day before he departed for Washington.

The feat heralded a gaudy September 15–27 tour. Only in the last three days did any real accord develop, and then the two leaders merely agreed to continue talking about Berlin and other matters, and to expand the cultural, educational, scientific, and sports exchanges negotiated in 1958. The press featured photographs of the smiling leaders and spoke of a "spirit of Camp David"—the presidential retreat in the Maryland mountains—that had as little in common with reality as the 1955 "spirit of Geneva." Nevertheless, tensions did seem to ease.

THE U-2 AND THE UN

The Kremlin sought to reach an accord on Berlin and perhaps on arms control before the

Khrushchev and Eisenhower at Andrews Air Force Base near Washington, D.C., September 1959. (Department of Defense)

November 1960 American elections. Soviet, American, Soviet, British, and French leaders planned to meet in Paris in May. But on May 1, Soviet rockets shot down an American U-2 high-altitude reconnaissance aircraft near Sverdlovsk (Yekaterinburg), 2,000 kilometers from the nearest international frontier. That sank the meeting. When the leaders arrived in Paris, Khrushchev declared he would not negotiate until the United States apologized, promised to halt the U-2 flights, and punished those responsible. Eisenhower responded that there would be no more flights, but he declined to apologize. The conference concluded before it began. Khrushchev cancelled Eisenhower's visit to the USSR.

Seeking to extend his advantage, Khrushchev came to New York in September for the 1960 session of the UN General Assembly. Several other Communist leaders came along to support him: Castro, Novotny, Kádár, Gomulka, Zhivkov, and Mehmet Shehu of Albania. Also on hand were Tito, Nehru, Macmillan, Nkrumah of Ghana, and Eisenhower.

The conclave of so many egos became a spectacle. Irritated by a UN delegate's speech, Khrushchev removed his shoe and pounded it on his desk, evidently believing this civilized behavior. He and Castro harangued crowds from the balcony of the Hotel Theresa in Harlem and engaged in debates with journalists, spectators, police guards, passersby—anyone who wanted to match wits. About on their level, the New York *Journal–American* urged "all patriotic Americans" to switch off their television sets during broadcast of an interview with Khrushchev. It was General Assembly as Grand Guignol.

KHRUSHCHEV, KENNEDY, BERLIN

Khrushchev pronounced the Monroe Doctrine dead and warned that the Soviet Union would launch nuclear-tippped rockets should the United States try to overthrow the Castro regime. In part because the United States reacted so vehemently to Castro's nationalization of foreign—much of it Mafia—private property, the Soviets and Cubans had drawn closer more quickly than they had planned after Castro took power in Cuba in January 1959. In the 1960 presidential campaign, Richard Nixon counseled moderation, while John F. Kennedy called for "liberating" Cuba. Shortly before leaving office, Eisenhower severed diplomatic relations between Washington and Havana. He had earlier approved plans for an invasion by Cuban émigrés trained, equipped, and financed by the CIA. As president, Kennedy gave the signal to launch the operation. On April 17, 1961, the émigrés attacked—or at least landed on—the beach at the Bay of Pigs. Within three days Castro's forces had captured or killed all the invaders. Following Eisenhower's U-2 precedent, Kennedy accepted responsibility.

The tragic farce gave way to more theatre when Khrushchev and Kennedy met in Vienna on June 3–4, 1961. The grandiosity of the agenda—Germany, disarmament, a test-ban treaty, Southeast Asia—indicated that both sides wanted a public-relations stunt; the leaders simply took each other's measure. There was no accord save for a hypocritical pledge to support a peaceful, independent Laos and respect its neutrality.

The June 1961 "summit" constituted an argument against such meetings, but it had important consequences. Khrushchev said the USSR would sign a peace treaty with East Germany by the end of 1961, with or without the participation of the Western Allies and West Germany. He revived his demand that West Berlin be made a free city and warned that, after the conclusion of the Soviet–East German treaty, the Allies would have to deal with the GDR.

The war of nerves escalated. On August 13 the East Germans closed the border with West Berlin. Two days later they began building a wall between the two sectors. This soon stanched the human hemorrhage that had cost East Germany several million citizens since 1945. The surpassingly unlovely wall symbolized Communist terror and failure.

But Moscow then dampened the 1961 crisis. Khrushchev did not sign a treaty with East Germany, nor did Berlin become a free city. The Soviets waited a year before abolishing the office of Soviet commandant in East Berlin. When they did, the Allied commandant in West Berlin theoretically should have had to deal directly with East German authorities, but in practice that did not happen, and the commandant still met with Soviet Army generals. Khrushchev continued to bluster. In December 1962 he told West German Chancellor Konrad Adenauer that "if the war to which your present political course is leading is unleashed, the Federal Republic of Germany will burn up like tinder in the very first hours." But by this time Khrushchev had become the boy who cried "Wolf!": He shouted too much. In June 1964 he signed a treaty of friendship and mutual aid with the East German regime of Walter Ulbricht, one of Moscow's most faithful henchmen. The limited, basically insignificant accord, Khrushchev's last statement on the issue, highlighted his failure to resolve the German problem.

THE SINO–INDIAN DISPUTE

Khrushchev regularly proposed an international conference that would include India but not China, arguing that Washington's refusal to deal with China presented an insurmountable barrier; it was better to accept half a loaf. The infuriated Chinese Communists, seeking revenge, embarked on a strange adventure in India. China and India had shared a common frontier since 1950, when Chinese forces occupied Tibet. The mountainous, remote border remained quiet until August 1959, when China suddenly moved into the Northeast Frontier Agency territory, which India claimed. Khrushchev was scheduled to visit the United States three weeks later.

The invasion left the Soviets in an awkward position. Supporting the Chinese would cost them the friendship of the nonaligned nations. Backing India would further alienate China and her allies, Albania, North Korea, and the Indonesian and other Communist parties sympathetic to Beijing. And so the Khrushchev regime simply called for negotiations. This displeased the Indians, who saw themselves as victims of aggression. It outraged the Chinese, who insisted *they* were the aggrieved party—no one believed this—and further that it was Moscow's duty to aid a fraternal Socialist country.

A September 9, 1959, TASS statement stressed the Soviet wish for friendly relations with both countries but criticized "those who seek to obstruct the relaxation of international tensions and complicate the situation on the eve of the visits [Khrushchev to the U.S., Eisenhower to the USSR]." This was the first time the Soviets had publicly spoken so harshly against Communist China. Cornered, Khrushchev had no choice but to pursue the logic of his policy and cut off supplies of weapons, spare parts, aircraft, and fuel to China. Beijing accused him of being more interested in having a glass of beer at the White House than in the emancipation of the oppressed.

At a stroke the Chinese achieved two goals of the Indian operation: They embarrassed Khrushchev, and won the right to lead the militant wing of the international Communist movement. A third goal, the discrediting of "neutralism"—John Foster Dulles wanted that too—and its chief voice, Nehru, seemed tantalizingly close. Beijing knew that Nehru had secretly requested American aid but could not produce evidence of a "sellout." Most nonaligned nations continued to support India.

Khrushchev redoubled his efforts to woo India. In September 1959 his regime extended a 1.5-billion ruble credit to that country, and the following February Khrushchev went ahead with his scheduled visit. He even persuaded Nehru to invite Zhou Enlai to New Delhi.

The Sino–Indian border remained quiet for more than three years. Then in October 1962 the People's Liberation Army attacked in force. The Indian Army fled as the Chinese raced southward against token resistance.

A desperate Nehru turned to the Soviet Union, only to find the Kremlin denouncing India's "imperialist legacy" and pledging support for China. Khrushchev was nothing if not inconsistent. Rebuffed by his friend in the Kremlin, Nehru looked on in horror as India's defeated soldiers stumbled down from the Himalayas. Then on November 2 a *Pravda* editorial declared that Moscow would back India with weapons, including MiG-21 fighter aircraft. The stupefying double about-face left the world dizzy and did not calm India's fears. Nehru asked for and received some modest American aid.

At this point the Chinese announced a unilateral cease-fire. Beijing promised to withdraw its forces to the line they had held on November 7, 1959, in the Northeast Frontier Agency. The retreat indeed took place.

The 1962 "Roof of the World" conflict was only superficially a dispute between China and India. The Chinese forced the crisis not to seize Indian territory but to humiliate Khrushchev. Their timing was superb: In October 1962 the Soviet Union was locked in a nuclear confrontation with the United States.

CUBAN MISSILE CRISIS

On August 31, 1962, Senator Kenneth Keating (R–N.Y.) charged that the USSR was installing offensive missiles in Cuba and targeting them on the United States. The Kennedy administration promptly denied this. The next day, TASS warned that an attack on Cuba would lead to war with the Soviet Union. Soviet weapons on the island, the agency declared, were "intended solely for defensive purposes," to prevent another Bay of Pigs. In fact, the missiles were deployed in a "soft"—easily targeted—configuration consistent only with first-strike—that is, offensive—use.

TASS did not reveal that Castro's deputy, Ernesto "Ché" Guevara, was then in Moscow for briefings on the Soviet nuclear-tipped rockets in Cuba. Construction had been under way for some time; the missiles would be aimed at targets on the U.S. East Coast. Had this plan succeeded, the number of nuclear systems able to strike the United States would have increased substantially.

As late as October 14, 1962, Kennedy's national security adviser declared that there were no offensive missiles on Cuba. That same day, U-2 reconnaissance photos showed four launch sites for medium-range devices near completion, two others under construction. Soviet personnel were also assembling Il-28 medium-range Beagle bombers shipped to the island in crates.

When Foreign Minister Andrei Gromyko met Kennedy at the White House on October 18 and again insisted that the only weapons in Cuba were defensive, Kennedy concluded that the Soviet Union wanted a showdown. He set in motion procedures to get the weapons out. In a somber speech on October 22, Kennedy reported the presence in Cuba of Soviet rockets capable of hitting American targets, and said that the United States would not tolerate aggression anywhere, least of all in the Western Hemisphere. He announced a naval "quarantine" of Cuba. This amounted to a blockade—which carried with it the risk of an incident that would nudge the crisis into war. Kennedy warned that he would consider a mis-

sile launched from Cuba against any nation in the hemisphere as "an attack by the Soviet Union upon the United States." He appealed to Khrushchev to "halt and eliminate this clandestine, reckless, and provocative threat to world peace and to stable relations between our two nations."

Nuclear conflict was at hand. With nearly a thousand intercontinental delivery systems, the Americans had an overwhelming advantage. The USSR had only 10 operational ICBMs and 221 long-range bombers. Had war come, the United States would have taken severe blows but would have inflicted enormous destruction on the USSR.

For more than 48 hours the world awaited Moscow's response. Would Khrushchev cave in, or go to war? Capitulation would make his position untenable, but he quickly determined that Kennedy was not bluffing. American forces around the globe went on ready alert, and the Pentagon radioed missile-carrying Polaris submarines an uncoded message ordering them to "put into play" their objectives.

On October 24, the 18 Soviet-bloc freighters bound for Cuba with military cargo stopped dead in the water. Khrushchev would not try to run the naval blockade. Four days later technicians began dismantling the missiles already in place and preparing them for shipment back to the USSR. Construction at new sites halted.

Washington and Moscow had reached a compromise. To allow Khrushchev to save face, Kennedy agreed to state publicly, after receiving unambiguous evidence of Soviet capitulation, that he would not invade Cuba. Further, on October 26 the president's brother, Robert Kennedy, told Soviet Ambassador Anatoli Dobrynin that the United States would remove its missiles aimed at the USSR from Turkey after the Cuban crisis passed. That pledge would later cover American missiles in Italy as well, but it was not a quid pro quo. The weapons in Turkey and Italy were outmoded and vulnerable; Washington had long planned to phase them out.

American officials neglected to specify which offensive weapons the Soviets could not deploy on Cuba, and thus Washington lost some of the advantage gained when Khrushchev "blinked." Kennedy had merely said missiles *then on the island* had to go, leaving the door open to new projects. Eight years later, when the Soviets began constructing a submarine base on Cuba, the Nixon Adminstration searched for records of Kennedy's 1962 understanding—or presumed understanding—with Khrushchev. It found nothing.

At a 1989 Moscow conference of officials who had served Kennedy, Khrushchev, and Castro, the Kremlin bureaucrats reported that half their 42 missiles on the island had been operational and could have been launched within a few hours. Not unreasonably, Castro feared an American invasion and spent the night of October 26, 1962, in a bunker at the Soviet embassy; according to one report he urged Moscow to attack. Khrushchev's son asserted that the Cuban dictator had told his father that he and his comrades "were prepared to die."

THE SOVIETS AND NUCLEAR WEAPONS

The chief lesson Khrushchev and Kennedy drew from the horrifying face-down was to avoid another. They instituted various measures including emergency communication links and guarantees of better diplomatic access to the leadership. The informal correspondence between the leaders, a new phenomenon that grew out of the Cuban crisis, remained hostile and sometimes so rude that aides declined to pass it along, but Khrushchev and Kennedy nevertheless resolved to confront the nuclear weapons issue directly.

The Soviet Union had detonated its first atomic bomb in August 1949, its first U-235 (h–bomb) weapon in 1951. The United States introduced tactical nuclear weapons into Europe in 1952, thus ensuring their use in any violent Soviet–NATO clash. NATO maintained that the substantial Soviet superiority in conventional forces necessitated deployment of this atomic hardware. The Soviet Army and Air Force began incorporating atomic and thermonuclear weapons in 1953. In the ensuing seven years, the Soviets built a huge arsenal of such bombs and delivery systems for them. As the stockpile grew, Khrushchev reduced conventional forces, alienating the military establishment. The number of men in uniform, 5.763 million in 1950, fell to 3.623 million by 1960.

In the spring of 1957 the Kremlin called for a ban on the testing of nuclear and thermonuclear weapons. No one took this seriously; then Khrushchev repeated the proposal shortly after renewing his "absolute weapon" boast. Western intelligence established that he might be ready to deal. The USSR would unilaterally suspend tests, Khrushchev announced, as of January 1, 1958.

This was a response to a domestic disaster. In November 1957 a military reactor that produced plutonium had exploded in the Ural Mountains. The area around the town of Kyshtym, near Sverdlovsk and Chelyabinsk, had long been dangerously polluted because of careless nuclear waste-disposal procedures. Radioactive liquids had seeped into the groundwater, thence into the Techa, a tributary of the mighty Ob River. Further, the plant operators simply pumped the water used to cool the reactor into a holding pond and from there directly into the Techa. Gas containing radioactive particles was expelled through a smokestack; this subjected a wide area to a deadly rain of nitric acid and radioactive iodine-131.

The plutonium plant had been bombarding Kyshtym and its environs with high levels of radioactivity for a decade before the November 1957 catastrophe. The explosion, however, was chemical rather than nuclear, the product of negligent storage of a combustible combination of chemicals. There was considerable loss of life, and thousands of people were exposed to massive doses of radioactivity. Plant and animal life was destroyed over an area of at least 100 and perhaps as many as 1,000 square kilometers. The authorities cordoned off the entire area and constructed dams to halt the contamination. The inhabitants of 44 villages—which disappeared from subsequent editions of Soviet maps—were resettled. They left behind everything but the clothes they wore, and then burned those when they reached their new destinations.

Pravda later noted that the "harmful effects of thermonuclear tests on living organisms are well known in the Soviet Union." Nothing about the events in the Urals in November 1957, however, appeared in the popular press until the *glasnost* era. In the late 1950s, only through scientific journals did some specialists learn what had happened.

The other two nuclear powers, the United States and Great Britain, soon learned about the Kyshtym tragedy, the first nuclear "accident" of such dimensions. They did not cease their own tests until the end of October 1958, after negotiations to limit nuclear arms talks had already begun.

Polish Foreign Minister Adam Rapacki had proposed creation of a nuclear-free zone in central Europe in October 1957. Under this born-in-Moscow plan, no atomic or thermonuclear weapons would be permitted in either of the two German states, Poland, or Czechoslovakia, which together had a population of more than 100 million. The West rejected this as a ploy to get American nuclear weapons out of West Germany—a fixed Soviet goal—and perpetuate the division of Germany.

The West also rejected Khrushchev's 1959 call—aimed at Beijing—for a nuclear-free zone in the Pacific. The Chinese were trying to develop a nuclear capability that would threaten the USSR first and foremost. Khrushchev's proposal met derisive rejection.

At the height of the August 1961 Berlin crisis, the Kremlin announced it would resume thermonuclear testing. The "aggressive actions of the imperialists," *Pravda* declared, necessitated this step, which was accompanied by a decree extending military service "until the signing of a peace treaty with Germany." According to the rules of the deadly game, that gave Kennedy an excuse to order resumption of "safe" tests which—experts swore—produced little or no radioactive fallout. At the end of October the UN General Assembly formally asked the Soviets not to proceed with plans to detonate a 50-megaton hydrogen bomb in the Arctic. The plea went unheeded. The Communists ruined a huge section of the Arctic forever.

Negotiations for a test-ban treaty began early in 1963. Former Ambassador to the USSR Averell Harriman went to Moscow in July for the final stages, and on August 5, 1963, the United States, Great Britain, and the USSR signed a limited nuclear test-ban treaty barring tests—even the "safe" ones—in space, the atmosphere, and under water. The accord did not affect underground tests.

Within a year more than 100 nations had signed this treaty, but China and France refused. Described at the time as a major step in arms control, the accord in fact had a more modest impact. It reduced radioactive fallout and helped prepare the ground for the Outer Space Treaty of 1967, the Non-Proliferation Treaty of 1970, and the Strategic Arms Limitation (SALT I) Pact of 1972.

MOSCOW AND THE KENNEDY ASSASSINATION

The assassination of John F. Kennedy on November 22, 1963, appeared to shock Soviet

Fidel Castro, Nikita Khrushchev, and Marshal Rodion Malinovsky in Soviet Georgia, 1963. The man on the left is Aleksei Leonov, the long-time Soviet Consul in Mexico City who gave Lee Harvey Oswald a visa to enter the USSR. (ITAR-TASS)

leaders as much as anyone. It quickly developed that the alleged assassin was an American citizen, Lee Harvey Oswald, who had once defected to the USSR. Back in the United States, Oswald conceived a passion for Castro's Cuba. Anticipating charges of Soviet–Cuban involvement in the assassination, the Kremlin took the unprecedented step of conveying what it claimed was the complete KGB file on Oswald to the American authorities. No Soviet connection to Oswald after his departure from the USSR was established. The Warren Commission, which investigated the assassination concluded that the killer was a deranged fanatic who had acted alone.

The Warren Commission also dismissed the possibility of a Cuban link, but this angle would prove a tangled mess. The public learned in the 1970s that, after Castro came to power, the CIA concocted a number of plots to assassinate Castro, even negotiating a contract with the crime syndicate, the Mafia. Several CIA-sponsored attempts on Castro's life failed. Critics of the Warren Commission denounced its report for failing to refute the claim that the Kennedy assassination was Castro's retaliation. And if Castro were involved, the critics argued, he had unquestionably consulted his Kremlin masters at every step. The archives continue to hold their secrets.

THE THIRD WORLD

When Egypt's Gamal Abdel Nasser flirted with the Soviet Communists, he brought down on himself the righteous wrath of John Foster Dulles. In July 1956 the United States, obediently followed by the British government, withdrew its offer to finance construction of the Aswan High Dam on the Nile. Then the Suez crisis deepened the rift between Egypt and the West, even though the United States forced the Israeli-Franco-British alliance to halt its aggression against Nasser.

Preoccupied with events in Poland and Hungary, and the stress of de-Stalinization, the Soviets nevertheless stepped into the breach. Moscow pledged unequivocal support for Egypt and took up that nation's cause in the UN. Not until Nasser visited the Soviet Union in the spring of 1958, however, did real cooperation commence. In October 1958 the Kremlin announced that it would lend Egypt—the "United Arab Republic," in the 1958–1961 union with Syria—$100 million toward construction of the Aswan High Dam. Nasser turned the first shovelful of earth in January 1960.

But the Soviets badly misjudged Nasser, and many Western politicians also thought him a malleable nonentity. In fact, Nasser was exactly what he claimed to be, a devout Muslim and Arab nationalist. And he was tough. In January 1961 the Egyptian police arrested 200 leading Communists, and Cairo warned the Kremlin to cease interfering in Egyptian politics. So far as the Egyptians were concerned, construction of the dam, which involved the influx of several thousand Soviet technicians, was strictly a business deal. It did not require political concessions, still less any cozying up to the atheist Communists. Relations between the two countries deteriorated. Anwar Sadat, then chairman of the UAR National Assembly, went to Moscow in May to explain that the government had only arrested people suspected of treason.

Nikita Khrushchev visited Egypt in May 1964 to celebrate completion of the first stage of the dam. Wary of a New York-like spectacle, the Egyptians kept him in a cocoon. When he fell from power a few months later, one of the charges against him was that he had given so much to, and received so little from, Gamal Abdel Nasser.

Elsewhere in the Middle East, the Soviets tried to subvert the American bilateral defense agreements with Iran, Pakistan, and Turkey. Equally to their distaste was the defensive alliance between Iraq and Turkey (Baghdad Pact), to which Britain, Pakistan, and Iran adhered. The Baghdad Pact, renamed the Central Treaty Organization (CENTO) after Iraq's withdrawal, constituted a *cordon sanitaire* against any Soviet move toward the Persian Gulf, the world's richest oil-producing area. Further adding to Soviet problems in the region, American nuclear-tipped missiles in Turkey were pointed at the USSR until their removal in 1962–1963. The U-2 flights over European Russia originated from airfields in Pakistan.

Soviet apprehensions did not lessen when the shah of Iran settled an oil-revenues dispute with the West in August 1954 and took his country into the alliance of Middle Eastern and Western nations. In 1955–1956 the USSR and Iran resurveyed their frontier, one of the most heavily guarded in the world. The tension between the two countries soared when in 1959 the shah unilaterally abrogated a 1921 Irano–Soviet agreement that permitted Soviet troops to enter Iran to counter any invasion of that country, if such invasion also threated the USSR. Moscow did not recognize the shah's action.

In East and Southeast Asia, the Kremlin frequently used domestic Communist forces to achieve Soviet goals. After the July 1954 division of Vietnam into a Communist North and a non-Communist South, the Soviets stepped up military and economic aid to North Vietnam. When the United States increased its assistance to the South Vietnamese regime in the early 1960s, the Soviets expanded their support for both the Viet Cong (South Vietnamese Communists) and the North Vietnamese.

The Vietnamese conflict grew more violent in 1964, and the Americans became hopelessly entangled. The Soviets reacted cautiously, keeping up the flow of aid to the Viet Cong and North Vietnam but seeking to stay out of the actual fighting. Because of its ongoing dispute with Moscow, and the ancient enmity between China and Vietnam, Beijing periodically halted the transhipment of Soviet supplies. This complicated game in Southeast Asia would cost several million lives. History bills the cost to cynical politicians, especially those utterly ignorant about Vietnam.

The Soviet Union fostered Communist and Communist-dominated insurrectionary movements elsewhere in Southeast Asia. The most important were in the Philippines, Malaya (Malaysia), Burma, Cambodia, and Laos. Sizable American and British aid programs helped defeat the Communists in the first three countries, but Cambodia and Laos long remained unstable.

In the largest, wealthiest, and strategically most important nation in the region, Indonesia, a clever thug named Sukarno led the postwar struggle against the Dutch colonial regime. A nationalist with a visceral hatred of colonialism, he believed he could manipulate the large Indonesian Communist party (PKI) and deal with the Soviet Union without compromising his newly independent country. In April 1955 Sukarno hosted a conference of 29 Asian and African states at Bandung, Indonesia. The final communiqué denounced "colonialism in all its forms" but omitted to list the Soviet variety. The USSR had helped organize the Bandung Conference, which also approved the "five principles of coexistence" Zhou Enlai and Nehru enunciated in April 1954; Beijing soon repudiated the entire concept.

Sukarno took Moscow's side in the Sino–Soviet dispute, and his imposition of severe restrictions on the millions of Indonesian Chinese late in 1959 provided an early clue to the depth of the quarrel. Indonesia acted as a Soviet surrogate in Southeast Asia in other ways. It repeatedly launched guerrilla raids against the new Federation of Malaysia, which included Sarawak and North Borneo, both claimed by Indonesia. The PKI, many of whose members were Indonesian Chinese, was loyal to Mao Zedong. Overestimating his own political sagacity, Sukarno thought he could tack between Moscow, Beijing, and the PKI, playing each off against the other. When the Sino–Soviet conflict reached the stage of open hostilities, his efforts came undone.

A year after the ouster of Sukarno's patron, Nikita Khrushchev, the PKI attempted to seize power. The Indonesian Army responded by slaughtering 300,000 Communists—after the 1927–1928 events in China, the largest massacre in the history of the international Communist movement. The Indonesian Army accused Sukarno of complicity in the PKI putsch and ousted him.

The Soviet Union courted leaders in black Africa, among them the mentally unstable Kwame Nkrumah of Ghana, Sékou Touré of Guinea, and Patrice Lumumba of the Congo Republic. Its unswerving anticolonialist policy won Moscow some friends in Africa, and foreign aid likewise purchased a certain amount of temporary affection. But the Soviets underestimated the ability of Western nations to learn from their mistakes. Further, the persistent Soviet refusal to put serious pressure for reform on the racist Republic of South Africa—a major if semiclandestine Soviet trading partner—hurt Moscow's image in Africa, as did the racism African students encountered in the USSR.

The Soviet Union had not paid much attention to Latin America before 1959. When the United States failed to move decisively against the Communist Castro regime, the Soviets plunged into the Caribbean basin. Massive infusions of aid kept Castro afloat, neutralized the American economic boycott, and financed mischief-making. "Ché" Guevara became a favorite of both the Kremlin and Western political illiterates. Through him, Moscow organized a network of revolutionary underground organizations throughout Latin America. In some areas skeleton forces were already in place and needed only guns, money, and hope; elsewhere, Guevara had to build from the ground up. The Soviets did not spare the purse. The Cuban cadres were well financed, and huge amounts of arms flowed into the region through Havana. Thousands of Latin American youths learned guerrilla warfare at special camps in Cuba, Czechoslovakia, and the Soviet Union.

The great crisis of October 1962 momentarily brought the increasingly aggressive Soviet–Cuban revolutionary mission to a halt. The activity resumed in 1963, however, and the pace quickened after 1964.

KHRUSHCHEV'S FOREIGN POLICY: A SUMMARY

Khrushchev was as recklessly audacious as Stalin had usually—we may exclude the Berlin Blockade and the Korean War—been prudent. He subdued the Hungarians by force and the Poles with a few concessions and the threat of force. He undertook a foreign-aid campaign that matched that of the United States.

Soviet philanthropy was designed to serve the political interests of the USSR, but the billions spent in the Third World purchased little goodwill. As a percentage of gross domestic product, Soviet foreign aid greatly exceeded the American figure.

Their own standard of living terribly low, the Soviet people resented the expenditure of vast sums abroad, and even Khrushchev's colleagues questioned the policy. Nasser's harsh treatment of the Egyptian Communists, Sukarno's inability to turn the PKI away from Beijing, and the failure of Communist parties to make significant headway in black Africa led some Soviet leaders to undertake their own cost-benefit analysis of foreign aid. They concluded that the USSR simply was not getting an adequate political return. Castro's Cuba needed a daily infusion of a million dollars in the 1960s, and the 1962 crisis accentuated the vulnerability of the USSR's most distant client state.

A protracted reappraisal of foreign policy began after the Cuban missile crisis. A subdued Khrushchev undertook no substantial new gambles and reduced foreign aid. The Soviet leadership now believed that, because the dams and steel mills and refineries built with Moscow's aid had not noticeably altered the East–West balance of power, Kremlin foreign policy had to concentrate on targets of real opportunity, exploiting unstable situations. Captives of the image they wished to project as defenders of oppressed peoples, the Soviet Communists had often intervened in crises best left alone.

Khrushchev had spoken with increasing frequency of "wars of national liberation" but did relatively little to encourage them. He preferred to concentrate instead on showy, costly construction projects. It was far cheaper, his critics argued, to plunge into an existing conflict with AK-47 assault rifles and military experts than to build roads or construct factories.

In the end, Khrushchev proved an inept manager of revolution. His colleagues would not tolerate that.

SUGGESTED ADDITIONAL READINGS

AUSLAND, JOHN C. *Kennedy, Khrushchev, and the Berlin–Cuba Crisis, 1961–1964.* Oslo: Scandinavian University Press, 1996.

GOLDGEIER, JAMES M. *Leadership Style and Soviet Foreign Policy: Stalin, Khrushchev, Brezhnev, Gorbachev.* Baltimore: Johns Hopkins University Press, 1994.

KULL, STEPHEN. *Burying Lenin: The Revolution in Soviet Ideology and Foreign Policy.* Boulder, CO: Westview Press, 1992.

RICHTER, JAMES G. *Khrushchev's Double Bind: International Pressures and Domestic Coalition Politics.* Baltimore: Johns Hopkins University Press, 1994.

TOMPSON, WILLIAM J. *Khrushchev: A Political Life.* New York: St. Martin's Press, 1997.

18

REFORM ERA INTERNAL AFFAIRS

The U-2 crisis produced dramatic changes in the Soviet leadership. A Central Committee plenary session elevated the Khrushchev loyalists Aleksei Kosygin, Nikolai Podgorny, and Dmitri Polyansky to the party Presidium, and removed A. I. Kirichenko from that body. Three days later, Leonid Brezhnev succeeded Kliment Voroshilov, last Stalin crony still in high office, as titular head of state.

POLITICAL MANEUVERS

Khrushchev led a 14-member Presidium that included seven of his protégés. Yekaterina Furtseva, the first woman to serve at that level, and Nurhitdin Mukhitdinov, an Uzbek and the first non-Caucasian, joined Brezhnev, Kosygin, Podgorny, Polyansky, and Frol Kozlov. Khrushchev believed he could also count on Anastas Mikoyan. For the rest, Nikolai Shvernik, 72, and O. V. Kuusinen, 78, were party hacks interested only in a comfortable ride down life's last hill, and A. B. Aristov and N. G. Ignatov did as they were told. The final member of the Presidium, the blood-stained Mikhail Suslov, had sided with Khrushchev in 1953–1957 against the still *more* reactionary Stalinists. Khrushchev and Suslov agreed that the time for terror had passed, and that the party could coerce conformity with the mere *threat* of violence.

Kosygin supplanted Mikoyan as Presidium economic expert. Brezhnev was a good, not-very-bright Communist politician with—in his circles—a considerable personal charm. Podgorny headed the Ukrainian party organization, Mukhitdinov the Uzbek branch. Furtseva had long served in the Moscow party organization. (The Twenty-First Party Congress would expel Mukhitdinov, Furtseva, Aristov, and Ignatov from the Presidium.) Kozlov headed the Leningrad Province party organization; he opposed the anti-party group in 1957 but soon broke with Khrushchev, whose job he wanted.

The Khrushchev faction pushed through more "de-Stalinization" at the 1961 Twenty-Second Party Congress, the last time it held together. Khrushchev's denunciation of the Albanian Stalinists at that meeting widened the split in the international Communist camp. Zhou Enlai vigorously defended the Tirana regime, then abruptly departed for Beijing, where Mao Zedong ostentatiously met him at the airport.

Fundamentalist Soviet Communists recoiled in disbelief when Khrushchev declared that, "because the construction of socialism has been completed, the dictatorship of the proletariat has fulfilled its historical mission." The Central Committee report and the new party program pronounced the USSR a "state of the whole people—workers, peasants, and intelligentsia." This killed off the "dictatorship of the proletariat" and hinted at full civil rights for the peasants—heresy to hard-core Stalinists. Middle-of-the-road party members disapproved of Khrushchev's prediction that "this generation of Soviet people will live under communism," which smacked of his 1957 boast that the USSR would soon overtake the United States in several categories of agricultural production. It also recalled his taunting Eisenhower that his grandchildren would live under communism.

Khrushchev alienated party cadres by instituting term limitations. At each regular party election, the Communists would replace at least a quarter of the Central Committee and its Presidium; a third of the republic central committees and regional party committees; half the town and district party committees; half the officers of all cells. An escape clause permitted exemptions for "experienced party workers of special merit." The stated motive—new blood—had much to commend it, but was Khrushchev planning a purge?

The Twenty-Second Party Congress marked Khrushchev's last triumph. Thereafter he seemed to lose his political touch and occasionally—as at the UN and in the Cuban missile affair—his grip on reality. One of his advisers revealed in 1988 that it was his *opponents* who persuaded Khrushchev to adopt a crackpot scheme that called for division "on the production principle" of district and province party committees into independent industrial and agricultural sectors. The bizarre move hastened his downfall.

TROUBLE IN AGRICULTURE

The 1957 harvest came up far short of expectations, and that of 1958 was not much better. Their natural nutrients exhausted, the virgin lands yielded a fraction of the 1956 total. Lysenko's shelter-belt forestation program, designed to protect steppe (prairie) topsoil from wind erosion, proved a dismal failure: Farmers planted the seedlings in "clusters," Lysenko having promised that the fittest would survive and prosper. The plowing of vast tracts of open terrain inevitably brought disaster. Pavlodar province alone lost 1.5 million hectares in 1962, and the next year windstorms blew away millions of tons of topsoil in many areas.

Contemptuously dismissing the reality that the virgin lands lie in an area where the May–July probability of drought is 20 to 40 percent, the first secretary produced a Khrushchevian diagnosis and treatment: It was necessary, he said, to rename the region's chief town, Akmolinsk, which in Kazakh means "White Grave."

Akmolinsk became Tselinograd, Russian for "Virgin Land City." The Kazakhs were doubly insulted; nature ignored the change; the harvests did not improve. In 1962 Kazakhstan fell 35 percent short of its grain quotas and could not meet the targets for meat, milk, or wool. The virgin lands could not save Soviet agriculture. In European Russia, the 1961–1964 annual grain production per capita fell below that of 1913.

In 1956 the Communist party began to introduce cost-accounting in the machine-tractor stations (MTS). Established in 1928, these served the *kolhozes*, which until 1956 paid high rates (taxes) for using the machinery. In 1957 there were about 7,900 MTSs, each servicing six or seven *kolhozes. Sovhozes* had their own implements.

The MTS operations bore no relation to crop and livestock yields, and Khrushchev admitted that the cost of MTS services were artificially high. The party decided to abolish the stations and force each *kolhoz* to buy its own machinery. The average MTS had serviced 30 to 35 *kolhozes* before the war, but post-1945 amalgamations created huge enterprises. In 1958 the average Ukrainian *kolhoz* had 3,000 hectares of land, 600 head of cattle, 200 milk cows, 500 pigs, and 640 sheep, exclusive of privately owned animals. Organizations this size and larger—Kazakhstan had 20,000-hectare *kolhozes*—needed their own machinery and repair shops.

Fearing that self-sufficient *kolhozes* might generate delusions of independence, conservatives opposed this step. Khrushchev prevailed, however, and in 1958 the state liquidated the MTSs. It sold their property—32 billion rubles worth—to the *kolhozes,* which had already amortized 18 billion of the sum. Compulsory deliveries and payments in kind came to an end. The stations became repair and technical service centers (RTSs), which performed capital repairs—those the *kolhoz* could not perform—on a cost-plus basis.

Abolishing the MTS proved no more effective than renaming Akmolinsk. Even in the best years, the country could barely feed itself. Foolish theories, political meddling, and natural phenomena—in that order—created this dismal state of affairs. The drought of 1963 forced the USSR to buy 12 million tons of grain on the world market—bitter medicine for a first secretary who had sworn to overtake the United States in food production.

THE SEVEN-YEAR PLAN

The sixth Five-Year Plan of 1956–1960 called for a 65 percent increase in industrial production. The Central Committee claimed at the Twenty-Second Party Congress that the economy had actually achieved a stupendous 80 percent growth rate. This was fantasy, but Vasily Selyunin and Grigori Khanin wrote in 1987 that the 1950s did represent the "most successful period in [Soviet] economic history." It is impossible to give precise figures, but labor productivity and return on assets increased, while material intensiveness declined. After the 12-fold increase of 1928–1950, retail prices fell, and wholesale prices stabilized, between 1950–1955.

In 1957, Khrushchev attributed these achievements to the scrapping of the existing Five-Year Plan for a new Seven-Year Plan. In some important respects, the reorganization represented the largest peacetime social upheaval since reversal of the New Economic Policy. It established 105 economic regions, including 70 in the RSFSR and 11 in Ukraine. Leningrad, with 600 very large enterprises employing about a million people and producing 50 billion rubles worth of goods annually, constituted one region, as did Uzbekistan, Belarus, and so on. In control of each region was a regional economic council or *sovnarhoz* empowered to deal with problems of supply, production, and marketing. Only large enterprises came under *sovnarhoz* purview; smaller ones remained responsible to the appropriate republic-level ministry. Except for those directly involved in defense and nuclear power, all *Union* industrial ministries were abolished, their powers divided among Union Gosplan, republic Gosplans, and the *sovnarhozes*. The boundaries of the new economic regions coincided with provinces or groups of provinces. Because the *sovnarhozes* reported directly to him—no woman had yet attained this rank—the party leader in the province, or the senior leader in a group of provinces, had great economic power.

The goal was to decentralize. To meet its quotas, before 1957 each ministry produced materials and components in its own plants whenever possible, even if that meant going across the country for something available locally—from plants belonging to a competing ministry. The constant striving for quick fulfillment of the plan encouraged production of expensive goods to meet it "in gross," that is, in terms of output ruble value.

The same pressures that impelled the ministries toward self-sufficiency influenced the *sovnarhozes*. Research and development remained under control of Union committees for particular branches of industry. This created a "rupture in the research-production cycle" and vitiated the decentralizing effort.

A new emphasis on the *centralization* of planning had accompanied *decentralization* of management in 200,000 "state industrial enterprises" and more than 100,000 construction sites. Coordinating their activities was like playing chess on a board with 300,000 squares. Computers would have helped; but they were either unavailable—the KGB and the military got them—or when available, too slow. The USSR was suffering from its technological backwardness.

In January 1959 the CPSU admitted that Soviet heavy-industry labor remained only half as productive as its American counterpart, in part because of lack of incentives. Soviet steelworkers received far lower wages, and the party could no longer summon up the specter of war to produce Stakhanovite efforts and sacrifices. Prewar technology prevailed in the USSR, while the Americans, West Germans, Japanese, and others had rebuilt. The backwardness of the Soviet chemical industry, for example, retarded growth. The Kremlin invested 11.5 billion rubles in that area during the Seven-Year Plan and claimed a 240 percent increase in production—an average annual growth rate of 13.6 percent. That would have been astonishing if true—but still below the Japanese figure. The state admitted that output of plastics increased by only 300 percent vs.

a projected 700 percent, that of synthetic fibers by only 250 percent against the hoped-for 1,200 to 1,300 percent.

The party acknowledged in 1961 that reorganization simply was not working. The inefficiency that paralyzed the ministries continued in the *sovnarhozes*. The gap between planning and capabilities had not narrowed. Labor productivity stalled. The state cut the number of economic regions from 105 to 17—dramatic evidence of "creeping recentralization." More proof came in March 1963 with the creation of the Supreme Council of the National Economy to supervise and coordinate among Gosplan, the *sovnarhozes*, Gosstroi (state construction agency), and production committees.

In 1962 the Communists gingerly touched another heresy: *Pravda* published Harkov University Economist Yevsei Liberman's "Plan, Profit, Bonus," which argued that, to make enterprises efficient, the state should make them profitable, and give labor and management a share in those profits. Such common sense sent true Communists into convulsions.

The Khrushchev regime announced plans to reduce taxes in 1960, then postponed the measure until 1962, then deferred it indefinitely. A January 1961 monetary reform exchanged ten old rubles for one new one; this imperfectly disguised the across-the-board price increases that, even with some offsetting measures, raised the cost of meat, butter, eggs, and other consumer items by as much as 50 percent. When demand remained high, the state again raised prices.

Widespread unrest resulted. Violence racked Novocherkassk, a Don River industrial town of 100,000, when officials announced 30 percent wage cuts the same day they raised food prices. Thousands of workers went on strike and held meetings on June 1. The police arrested 48 "ringleaders." The next morning, nearly a thousand people marched on CPSU headquarters. Many times that number of sympathetic onlookers effectively became part of the demonstration. Local officials panicked, but troops of the garrison refused orders to fire. The commander brought in non-Russian soldiers. Aiming over the crowd, the new arrivals shot some small boys out of their perches in trees. (The future presidential candidate Alexander Lebed, then 12, witnessed this.) The outraged crowd surged forward; the troops killed 73 people at point-blank range. Nothing about this "Bloody Friday" appeared in the Soviet press.

Mikoyan and Kozlov flew in and decreed the death penalty for "enemy provocateurs." Mikoyan claimed the unarmed dead had used dum-dum bullets, which were not Soviet Army issue. The verdict in, the trial began. The "court" sentenced seven men to death, two women to 15-year prison terms.

The Novocherkassk tragedy, and confrontations and demonstrations elsewhere, frightened the national authorities, who promptly stocked the affected cities with food. They never explained where it came from, or why it had been withheld. But neither this miracle of the loaves nor the granting of a few timid incentives revived the economy. Party bureaucrats and industrial managers thwarted every attempt at reform. Recentralization gathered momentum; by 1964 the reforms of 1957 were a distant memory. Soon after Khrushchev's fall the party abolished the *sovnarhozes*.

LIFE IN THE KHRUSHCHEV ERA

Though progress was uneven, the standard of living did improve under Khrushchev. Residents of the showcase cities of Moscow, Leningrad, and Kiev were better housed, fed, and clothed than ever, but in all material—not spiritual—respects they lagged far behind London and Paris and Frankfurt. The three urban agglomerations dazzled visitors, although not in the way the Communists intended. New housing was badly constructed. Food stores had adequate supplies of bread, potatoes, and cabbage but rarely meat, vegetables, or fruit. Clothing remained drab and poorly tailored.

Cities were far better supplied than towns and villages, but no matter where one found them, most consumer goods were of wretched quality. *Pravda* admitted in May 1956 that Soviet radio tubes, for example, had a life of only 800 to 1,000 hours; British tubes lasted 10,000 hours. In 1963 the RSFSR Ministry of Trade inspection service tested 12.6 million manufactured items and found fully half defective. A large Moscow shoe store examined 672,000 pairs in 1959 and rejected 50,000.

And often it was difficult to find even this shoddy merchandise. In 1961, visitors to the Black Sea port of Novorossisk assumed it was local custom for men to wear beards; *Izvestiya* learned that the city of 100,000 had no razor blades, nor did Lvov (450,000) or Tbilisi (770,000).

The shortage of telephones provided another index of the quality of urban life. In 1957 there were only 5,000 for Harkov, population one million. Saratov (620,000) had only 3,800 phones, and Stalingrad (Volgograd from 1961), with a population of 600,000, had only 1,300. The few people with telephones went each month to a central office to pay their bills. Payment by mail was unknown.

An extensive black market eased some shortages, as did various survival techniques. After Stalin, white-collar crime flourished and some people made fortunes. Entrepreneurs from the Caucasus and Central Asia would fly to the cities with fresh fruit, vegetables, or flowers; set up shop on a street corner; and quickly make lots of money. The poorly-paid police did not interfere unless some stubborn or naive vendor failed to bribe them. The free market, through which peasants disposed of food grown on private plots, operated with semi-official sanction and provided three quarters of the fresh fruit and vegetables.

The Seven-Year Plan envisioned construction of more than 205 million square meters of housing space, a goal that remained elusive. By 1965 the number of people in communal apartments in Moscow had dropped to three million out of a total 6.5 million. Khrushchev had initially favored prefabricated, five-story apartment houses, which were cheap and easily assembled. Block after block of these eyesores (*khrushchoby* [Khrushchev slums]) sprang up like toxic fungi. City–planning experts warned the 1950s construction rate would lead to the merger of the suburbs of Moscow and Leningrad—600 kilometers apart—before the year 2000. Gosstroi switched to high-rises.

To reduce construction costs, Gosstroi established the standard ceiling height at 2.7 meters and sometimes approved 2.3 meters; previously it had been 3.2. The agency reduced the average area of a one-family apartment—still a luxury—from 41.6 to 28.3 square meters. Gosstroi used prefabricated units whenever possible and introduced lighter-weight materials: New dwellings weighed about 278 tons per 100 square meters as against 315 tons in prewar buildings. The cell-like postwar apartments were flimsy and oppressive. But the urban population had increased from 60.4 million in 1939 to more than 100 million in 1959, and people could not afford to be choosy. Better to have a cubbyhole of one's own, millions of young people thought, than continue living with the older generations.

Housing woes exacerbated social problems. According to the 1959 census, the divorce rate stood at 8.5 percent—17.6 in France, 26.3 percent in the United States—but the figures did not tell the whole story. The rate was always low in the countryside, higher in the cities; in Moscow and Leningrad it exceeded the U.S.

figure. So difficult was it to find housing that untold thousands, perhaps millions, of couples who otherwise would have divorced remained together in barren misery. Overcrowding played a role in child and spousal abuse and the abandonment of families by fathers. The media discussed these problems with increasing frankness; the party-state began levying penalties—including imprisonment—on malefactors.

The centuries-old problem of alcoholism plagued Russia, Ukraine, Belarus, and the Baltic republics. The fact that the left hand knew what the right was doing only made the situation worse: In the 1950s and 1960s the turnover tax—a value-added tax [VAT]—on alcoholic beverages accounted for 10 to 12 percent of state revenue. Alcohol abuse sapped off about 5 to 7 percent of the 1982 national income. The authorities conducted periodic temperance and public-awareness campaigns; they restricted the hours of alcohol sale and raised prices. They established sobering-up stations in Moscow and some other cities; the police charged a fee for the service and informed the culprit's employer. Society seemed increasingly willing to recognize alcoholism as a disease and treat it accordingly. Reporting the suicide of Writers' Union Boss Aleksandr Fadeyev, the media noted he suffered from the "severe and chronic ailment" of alcoholism.

In 1958 Khrushchev announced the state's intention to pass a law limiting customers in bars and restaurants to one drink—but no such law was ever enacted. In 1960 the RSFSR ministry of trade issued an order establishing a limit of 100 grams—three ounces—of spirits per customer but never enforced it. When Khrushchev fell from power, Russia and the other European republics began to drink seriously, urged on by one of the most lethal official campaigns in history.

A tiny percentage of the population, chiefly

in Central Asia and the big port cities, had long known hashish, opium, and cocaine. In the late 1950s, however, a nationwide problem developed. Dealers called "bankers" bought a "plan"—a kilo—of hashish in Central Asia or Afghanistan for sale in European Russia. Cocaine (*marafet*) entered through Odessa and Leningrad, as did opium. Marijuana, indigenous to Central Asia, grows wild in many parts of the Soviet Union. Smoked for centuries in steppe villages, no one had paid any attention to it. In the 1960s it became fashionable in student and artistic circles.

The state continued the Stalinist practice of intruding into the private lives of citizens even in trivial matters. In February 1957 the Komsomol newspaper asked rhetorically,

Who is not familiar with these utterly repulsive young men with their ultra-modish jackets, their ultra-tight and ultra-short trousers and their eccentric neckties in all colors of the rainbow, with an air of self-satisfied stupidity on their faces? Or with the even more disgusting girls, with their coiffures 'à la garçon'—pitiful bristles of cropped hair—and their shoes that remind one of caterpillar tractors?

The newspaper was referring to the *stilyagi* ("the trendy"), young people who—the puritans charged—adored everything foreign, shunned work, and in general failed to behave like disciplined citizens of a Communist state.

Young-generation popular music generated this outburst from Foreign Minister D. T. Shepilov: "All these 'boogie-woogies' and 'rock-and-rolls' sound like wild orgies of cavemen." As music critic, Shepilov remained in favor, but he lost his job as foreign minister. Media attacks on "vulgar"—no one defined this—popular music intensified. The state deputized Komsomol zealots and prigs as morals police, and "music patrols" began in 1960. Members went to restaurants—many had orchestras—to check the music. If they did not like what they heard they stopped it

and called the police if anyone protested. There being no law against music, the perplexed police fell back on "outrage against public morals" or "disturbing the peace." The patrols posted signs in restaurants and clubs: DANCING "IN THE STYLE" IS FORBIDDEN. Only the Komsomol deacons knew what that meant. In 1960 the police arrested some dealers in "rocks and bones"—recordings of forbidden music on X-ray film. Cultural and political fundamentalists believed that the young generation's music, hairstyles, and clothing constituted political opposition. There was some truth to this, but it was almost impossible to do anything about it without sealing off the country. Modern communications had made the USSR west of the Urals another outpost of the global village.

EDUCATION

Despite the successes of Soviet science and technology, the educational system had serious problems. The 1959 census found virtually universal literacy, but only about 30 percent of primary school graduates went on to obtain a secondary education. Only 7 percent of secondary school graduates continued their education in universities and university-level institutes. The percentages were about the same in Great Britain, twice as great in the United States.

Economic factors figured heavily in the Soviet educational profile. The work force was shrinking; the state wanted people to enter it early. The standard of living was so low that every family member had to begin working as soon as possible. Overcrowding forced many city schools to operate double and even triple shifts. Teachers had no time for counseling; many pupils dropped out. Discipline broke down and teenage crime jumped.

Gender-segregated education ended in 1954. The following year saw the introduction of a slightly modified curriculum:

GRADE
(Hours per week per subject)

1955–1956 School Year	1	2	3	4	5	6	7	8	9	10
Russian lang., lit.	13	13	13	9	9	8	6	6/5*	4	4
Mathematics	6	6	6	6	6	6	6	6	6	6
History	—	—	—	2	2	2	2	4	4	4
USSR Constitution	—	—	—	—	—	—	—	—	—	1
Geography	—	—	—	2	3	2	2	2/3	3	—
Biology	—	—	—	2	2	2	3	2	1	—
Physics	—	—	—	—	—	2	3	3	4	5/4
Astronomy	—	—	—	—	—	—	—	—	—	1
Chemistry	—	—	—	—	—	—	2	2	3	3/4
Psychology	—	—	—	—	—	—	—	—	—	1
Foreign languages	—	—	—	—	4	4	3	3	3	3
Physical education	2	2	2	2	2	2	2	2	2	2
Drawing	1	1	1	1	1	1	—	—	—	—
Mechanical drawing	—	—	—	—	—	—	1	1	1	1
Singing	1	1	1	1	1	1	—	—	—	—
Practical work	1	1	1	1	2	2	2	—	—	—
Practicum	—	—	—	—	—	—	—	2	2	2
TOTAL	24	24	24	26	32	32	32	33	33	33

*Six hours first semester, five hours second semester.

This course of study broke no new ground, but it attracted close attention in the West after *Sputnik*. Soviet pupils were generally better educated in mathematics and science than their French, British, and especially their American counterparts. But the Soviet record was uneven. As late as 1962 few graduating chemists had any idea what a polymer compound was. Trofim Lysenko regained a position of authority in the agricultural sciences, biology, and botany; he told the Central Committee that Western scientists who identified DNA as the key to heredity were ignoramuses.

One of Khrushchev's most controversial reforms was his attempt to democratize education. In April 1958 he denounced the "shameful situation" in which the children of influential people were admitted to institutions of higher education regardless of qualifications. The privileged classes and their offspring showed great contempt for Socialist equality of opportunity, superb skill in avoiding work. Everyone knew this, but until Khrushchev no one in authority acknowledged it. A December 1958 decree reorga-

nized the educational system over a five-year period. There were to be eight rather than seven years of compulsory primary schooling, three years of secondary. Admission to secondary schools, institutes (colleges), and universities would be determined by merit. Trade union and Komsomol committees would oversee the competition and give preference to individuals with two years of work experience. Exceptions remained for pupils with special talent in mathematics, the natural and physical sciences, and the arts. A system of advanced technical-vocational schools enabled young workers to continue their education while holding down jobs.

Secondary-school students were to work at a trade for two years. As part of a "from the asphalt to the land" scheme, the state began moving agricultural institutes from the cities to rural areas. It restricted admission to people who pledged to make careers in agricultural production rather than administration. Higher education became the responsibility of the republics in 1959.

By 1963, 80 percent of the places in higher

education went to students with production experience. But the *nomenklatura* and lower-ranking bureaucrats were outraged at Khrushchev's assault on one of their most sacred privileges, and they did not fail to notice that he took good care of his own family and friends. After October 1964 the education reform would go the way of its author.

WOMEN

Khrushchev boasted that Soviet women enjoyed full equality. He appointed Yekaterina Furtseva to the Presidium and made her minister of culture despite her lack of qualifications—except gender—for either job. Furtseva pointed out in 1960 that 27 percent of Supreme Soviet deputies were women, as were 47 percent of the urban work force and 45 percent of industrial workers. More than a thousand women served on the Moscow University faculty—but mostly as laboratory assistants and language instructors. Since 1920, about 1.845 million women had received a higher education.

The devastating impact of the war struck Soviet women with a special fierceness. The following figures are from the January 1959 census:

Number of Men and Women in Various Age Groups as of January 15, 1959 (in thousands)

Age 1959	(Age 1941)	Men	Women
0–24	(2–6)	10,056	10,287
25–29	(7–11)	8,917	9,273
30–34	(12–16)	8,611	10,388
35–39	(17–21)	4,528	7,062
40–44	(22–26)	3,998	6,410
45–49	(27–31)	4,706	7,558
50–54	(32–36)	4,010	6,437
55–59	(37–41)	2,906	5,793
60–69	(42–51)	4,099	7,637
70 and over	(52 and over)	2,541	5,431

Fifteen million women age 30 to 59 had no husbands. Many older women were war widows, and the younger remained unmarried not by choice but because there were not enough men.

In Muslim Central Asia, ancient customs kept women in a state of servitude. In the Kyrgyz and Turkmen republics, men often abducted girls as young as 12 as "brides." Soviet law considered this kidnapping and rape, but sympathetic local officials usually tried to legitimize it with a Komsomol wedding. In any case, the terrified girl had no choice. Once abducted, she could not return to her family except as a married woman. In the Turkmen republic some parents gave underage daughters in marriage in return for "bride money," retaining custody of the girl until paid. Bigamy and polygamy continued at about the same high rate as always in Central Asia and the Caucasus, where the population lived in villages and small towns and despised European customs and values. The people preserved the old ways and lived by the Koran. Moscow charged that their customs constituted "offenses against the personal freedom and dignity of women" but took no action. All things considered, that may have been fortunate. The heavy Kremlin hand would have created more problems than it solved.

ARTISTS AND INTELLECTUALS

Reactionaries and conservatives did not like Ilya Ehrenburg's *The Thaw* (1953), which suggested the end of the long Stalinist winter, and Vladimir Dudintsev's attack on the bureaucracy in *Not by Bread Alone* (1956) outraged them. Khrushchev called the latter "slanderous." In 1958 the troglodyte editor of *Literary Gazette*, Vsevolod Kochetov, hit back at Dudintsev in *The Yershov Brothers,* a "primitive and savage attack on the liberal intellectuals."

With the Boris Pasternak affair behind him, however, Khrushchev could afford to strike a generous pose. In a spring 1959 speech to the Third Congress of Soviet Writers he "rehabilitated" several authors, admitted that Dudintsev "was never our enemy," but demanded that literature serve party goals. Denied access to state publishing houses, nonconformist writers had only the option of silence. In the late 1950s, however, some courageous individuals revived the tradition—which dated from the late eighteenth century—of *samizdat,* or self-publishing, then *tamizdat* (publishing abroad) and *magnitizdat* (tape-recording). Andrei Sinyavsky wrote in *samizdat* as "Abram Tertz," Yuli Daniel as "Nikolai Arzhak." For nine years the KGB hunted for these mysterious writers, analyzing their essays and short stories with the aid of computers. Once again the Soviet state assigned literature the highest priority.

The KGB did not find the writers. It obtained them gratis from the CIA. On the defensive in the court of world public opinion for its intervention in the Vietnamese civil war, the United States tried to divert the spotlight. Knowing the Kremlin would put them on trial and earn some bad publicity for the USSR, the CIA sacrificed Sinyavsky and Daniel. The KGB arrested them in September 1965. After a 1930s-style "trial" the following February, Sinyavsky received the maximum sentence of seven years at hard labor for slandering the state. Daniel got only five years.

This marked the first time writers had been tried for what they had written. The Communists had accused some authors of crimes such as "anti-Soviet agitation" and had "disappeared" many into the Gulag, but not even under Stalin had it actually put anyone on public trial for the alleged political content of literary works.

In one of the deceptions that made it appear as though the party might again relax its control over the arts, in late 1962 *Pravda* published Yevgeny Yevtushenko's poem "The Heirs of Stalin," which suggested the party redouble the guard at the late dictator's grave. In November, publication of Aleksandr Solzhenitsyn's *One Day in the Life of Ivan Denisovich* caused an immediate and sustained sensation.

Hopes for a new thaw quickly faded. The bosses of "socialist realism" tried to destroy the talented young artists who refused to conform to party dictates by tricking them into showing some of their most daring—in the context—works at the December 1962 exhibit, "Thirty Years of Moscow Art." Khrushchev and several other high officials, dazzlingly ignorant about art, attended. Acting as guides, the talentless but officially blessed "artists" noted the "severe" style of the post-Impressionist canvases. The Western media, they told the officials, had praised these works. Thus egged on, Khrushchev, Suslov, and Andropov—none of whom knew art from tire tracks—pounced on the real artists, calling them "pederasts." Three months later, to the accompaniment of organized chants for blood, Khrushchev shook his chubby fist and hurled threats at the mild-mannered poet Andrei Voznesensky.

The fundamentalists rejoiced and stepped up their assault on nonconformist artists, sculptors, and writers. They began a campaign against Solzhenitsyn and denied him a Lenin Prize in 1963. He managed to publish two short stories that year, but the hysterical KGB-fundamentalist war against him culminated in his expulsion from the USSR in 1974.

As in the United States, the fundamentalists-reactionaries worshipped violence and condemned sex. The Moscow watchdogs assailed "naturalistic scenes of intimacy" in such films as *Quiet Flows the Don* and *The Forty-First,* finding the brief glimpses of unclad women and an occasional embrace politically dangerous. More to their liking were straightforward war films—but even those were beginning to change. M. K. Kalatozov's *The Cranes Are Flying* depicted the *civilian* population in wartime. The film had no heroic Communists, and some positive characters had flaws; it won the Gold Palm award at Cannes. Another war film set in the rear, Grigori Chukrai's *Ballad of a Soldier,* made a party-pleasing point about patriotism in order to tell a love story. More evidence of a new approach in cinematography came with the restoration in 1962 of cuts Stalin had ordered 36 years earlier—he excised most scenes depicting Lenin—in Sergei Eisenstein's classic film *October.* The government newspaper *Izvestiya* observed that the "Stalin cult had a ruinous effect on our films."

In December 1962 the party demanded changes in Dmitri Shostakovich's Thirteenth Symphony. Yevtushenko's poem "Babi Yar," which served as a choral interlude, lamented the absence of a monument to those massacred and hinted at official Soviet anti-Semitism. Under pressure, Yevtushenko added four lines noting that Russians and Ukrainians perished alongside Jews. The première took place on schedule. Having learned of the backstage ordeal, the Moscow intelligentsia exploited the concert to express solidarity with the artists. There could be no mistaking the meaning of the prolonged ovation for Shostakovich and Yevtushenko.

The months after Khrushchev's emergence as an art critic were not a period of unrelieved oppression in the arts. Shostakovich's symphony, after all, made its debut on schedule, and the added lines did not dilute Yevtushenko's point about Babi Yar. Further, *Lady Macbeth of Mtsensk,* which earlier had very nearly led Shostakovich to his doom, was restaged as *Katerina Izmailova* in 1963. The same composer's Fourth Symphony, completed in 1936 but withheld out of concern over Stalin's reaction, was first performed to critical and public acclaim in 1961.

The off-again, on-again campaign to suppress nonconformist art and literature confused everyone and made implacable enemies of the Stalinists, to whom one poet or writer or composer was more dangerous than a foreign army. Khrushchev's vacillation would not by itself have tipped the scales against him, but it added another arrow to his opponents' quiver. Communists too prudent to take a stand on political issues without a signal from Moscow rushed to express weighty opinions on art and literature. Many party members condemned writers and artists who did not depict Soviet life in the brightest, most flattering colors.

THE "LITTLE OCTOBER REVOLUTION"

Khrushchev had woven a long rope of errors, making a fool of himself in Cuba, China, Berlin, Albania, Egypt, and India. He disrupted agriculture. He criticized the *nomenklatura's* privileges but constantly increased his own. His proposal for term limits—excepting himself and his cronies—outraged all bureaucrats. His reduction of conventional military forces alienated the officer corps. The public resented his unfulfillable promises, and the intelligentsia despised his crude behavior.

In April 1964 the press celebrated Khrushchev's seventieth birthday with an orgy of congratulations, eleven pages over six days in *Pravda.* A new "cult" was taking shape. But Leonid Brezhnev said surprisingly little, and Suslov and Kosygin were likewise restrained.

In the summer of 1964, Khrushchev sent his son-in-law, Aleksei Adzhubei, who had few qualifications at all and none in foreign policy, on an important diplomatic mission to West Germany. He despatched an insultingly low-ranking delegation to Beijing for the fifteenth-anniversary celebration of Mao's victory. To party leaders deeply concerned over the split with China, this was the last straw.

Pyotor Shelest, who headed the Ukrainian party organization in the Khrushchev years, revealed in 1989 that Brezhnev and Aleksandr Shelepin headed the conspiracy to oust Khrushchev. After making sure of the support of KGB chief Vladimir Semichastny and other key security officials, they approached Suslov, who had become disenchanted with Khrushchev. Shelest and others on the Presidium got on board.

While Khrushchev was vacationing on the Black Sea under Anastas Mikoyan's watchful eye, his opponents summoned the Central Committee to Moscow to hear Suslov read the indictment. Only two or three officials defended Khrushchev. The trial over, the conspirators summoned the defendant back to Moscow. On October 14, 1964, the Central Committee ousted Nikita Khrushchev as first secretary and prime minister. Leonid Brezhnev became party leader, and Aleksei Kosygin took Khrushchev's state post. The media reported that Khrushchev had voluntarily stepped down "because of age and poor health." Presidium members flew around the country to brief officials on the changes.

KHRUSHCHEV'S TOMBSTONE

Nikita Khrushchev became simply another retired bureaucrat with a fine apartment in Moscow and a state-owned cottage in the suburbs. He and his family had use of the Kremlin Clinic, special stores, and a chauffeured automobile. KGB guards ensured that he had no contact with dissidents, journalists, or foreigners. When he died in September 1971, the party denied him burial in the Kremlin wall, which it reserved for its heroes. The Khrushchev family interred him in the cemetery of Moscow's Novodevichy Convent. No ranking official attended; the party Central Committee sent a wreath. A year later an artist who had felt Khrushchev's wrath in 1962, Ernest Neizvestny, sculpted a chillingly appropriate monument in black and white stone.

Khrushchev had apologized to Andrei Voznesensky. He could not make amends to Boris Pasternak, or to the people he had sent to their death as Stalin's faithful henchmen.

A few days after cashiering Khrushchev, the new rulers charged their former patron and colleague with "crudeness, shouting . . . [and] a tone of offensive superiority." They condemned his "bombastic phrases and braggadocio, overhasty conclusions and harebrained schemes divorced from reality":

Even the most authoritative person cannot be permitted to escape the control of the guiding collective, the party organization, or get the idea that he knows everything and can do everything, that he has no need for the knowledge and experience of his comrades.

The first leader to admit that power had corrupted Stalin, Khrushchev admitted to no trace of the virus in himself. To the end he saw himself as a democratically elected leader of a democratic society. He was in fact drenched in blood; but under his leadership the USSR slowly moved away from Stalinism. The state dismantled the Gulag, leaving only three camps as a permanent reminder. After the Twentieth Party Congress, citizens had little reason to fear arbitrary arrest and imprisonment; but it was dangerous to decline a secret police suggestion to have a "friendly chat." Although the licenses were more difficult to obtain, the KGB remained licensed to murder: We may record the names of Anatoli Marchenko, Father Aleksandr Men, Father Jerzy Popieluszko, Georgi Markov . . . and hundreds of others.

If only because his colleagues would not tolerate it, Khrushchev was no tyrant. People made jokes about him: In the 1964 Olympic Games, he won a gold medal for "falling from an unprecedented height." When Stalin spoke, nations trembled. Nations laughed with, and sometimes at, Khrushchev. In dramatic contrast to the mysterious, remote Stalin, Khrushchev was approachable. He met

Soviet and Western journalists frequently in formal and informal interviews, displayed emotion. Crude and scatological though it was, he had a sense of humor.

After October 1964 the Soviet media ignored Khrushchev. But within a few weeks of Leonid Brezhnev's death in November 1982, the party began to reassess the deeply flawed man who had cracked the clay idols.

SUGGESTED ADDITIONAL READINGS

BURLATSKY, FEDOR. *Khrushchev and the First Russian Spring*. New York: Charles Scribner's Sons, 1992.

FILTZER, DONALD. *The Khrushchev Era: De-Stalinization and the Limits of Reform in the USSR, 1953–1964*. Basingstoke, UK: Macmillan, 1993.

McCAULEY, MARTIN. *The Khrushchev Era, 1954–1964*. New York: Longman, 1996.

TOMPSON, WILLIAM J. *Khrushchev: A Political Life*. New York: St. Martin's Press, 1997.

19

TROIKA RULE, 1964–1971

The makers of the "Little October Revolution" congratulated themselves
on restoring "Leninist collective leadership" in the spririt of the Twentieth Party
Congress. Never again, they agreed, would one individual serve simultaneously
as Communist party first secretary and as prime minister. They offered no
timetable for the triumph of communism, hurled no threats. The transfer
of power took place with a minimum of dislocation.

The new Soviet leaders had declined to support Khrushchev's "radicalized anti-Stalinism" at the 1961 Twenty-Second Party Congress and blocked him on other issues. They refused to put Molotov, Kaganovich, or Malenkov on trial, exonerated Voroshilov (blue ink on death warrants), and declined to indict hundreds of thousands of ordinary assassins. They shelved plans to build a monument to the victims of the Terror and slowed the pace of "rehabilitations." Unable to prevent publication of *One Day in the Life of Ivan Denisovich*, they harassed Aleksandr Solzhenitsyn relentlessly. And they overthrew the architect of "de-Stalinization." The fundamentalists anticipated a return of the good old days.

The new leaders halted the assault on Stalin and Stalinism but did not shoot Khrushchev, reopen the Gulag, or attempt a wholesale reversal of the post-1953 reforms. They publicly renounced terror as a political weapon. Denied the right to participate in the manage-

ment of public affairs, the population was as indifferent to the birth of the new regime as it had been to the death of the old.

COLLECTIVE LEADERSHIP

The lead "Troika" (trio) of M. A. Suslov, Aleksei Kosygin, and Leonid Brezhnev had been close to Khrushchev and were remarkable for the uniformity of their political and personal profiles. They were Russians, of worker or peasant descent, had risen through the party-state bureaucracy, and were 8 to 12 years younger than Khrushchev. They had won rapid promotion in the late 1930s when the Terror created vacancies. Too old to constitute a new generation, too young to have much memory of tsarism in peacetime, they were the first leaders whose political consciousness took shape under Communist rule.

Brezhnev was less intelligent than Suslov or

Kosygin, but more conventionally ambitious. He had done party work in the RSFSR, Ukraine, Kazakhstan, and Moldova. He emerged from the war a major general, but the heroics later ascribed to him never took place: He did political work in reserve echelons. After 1945 he supervised reconstruction of Zaporozhe and Dnepropetrovsk, and at the Nineteenth Party Congress he won an appointment to the Central Committee Secretariat, where he worked with Stalin, Malenkov, Suslov, and Khrushchev. A candidate member of the Presidium, he appeared destined for the inner circle.

For a time after Stalin's death, however, it appeared he would fall in the infighting. Because Brezhnev was a Khrushchev man, Malenkov demoted him to a minor defense ministry post. But when Khrushchev outmaneuvered the other contenders for power, his protégés thrived. Brezhnev supervised the Kazakhstan "virgin lands" project and received credit for the exceptional 1956 harvest. That won him a second posting to the Central Committee Secretariat. Along with Suslov and Kosygin, he sided with Khrushchev against the "antiparty group" and became a full member of the Presidium. No one blamed him for the later harvests.

Brezhnev's new duties made him responsible for Communist party oversight of heavy industry, defense, and the space program—a preposterously large portfolio that as early as 1958 marked him as a future first secretary. But an increasingly powerful anti-Khrushchev faction sidetracked him in the shakeup that followed the U-2 incident in 1960. Frol Kozlov, who coveted Khrushchev's job, won the unofficial post of "second secretary" and kicked Brezhnev upstairs to the chairmanship of the Supreme Soviet Presidium—the titular presidency. Although the position carried only ceremonial head-of-state responsibilities, Brezhnev made the most of it. In his 1960–1964 tenure in office—he would resume the post in

1977—he traveled widely, cobbling together modest credentials in foreign policy. In June 1963 he returned to the Secretariat. When a stroke removed Kozlov from politics, Brezhnev again became unofficial heir apparent. In the summer of 1964 he relinquished the "presidency" to plot Khrushchev's ouster.

Until 1971, when First Secretary Brezhnev spoke on foreign affairs and economic policy he did so strictly as party leader in the "collective leadership." Prime Minister Aleksei Kosygin articulated official Kremlin policy. Kosygin directed the effort to reconcile with China and went to the United Nations to present the Soviet view on world developments, especially those in the Middle East and Southeast Asia. He served as impartial mediator between Pakistan and India over Kashmir. Kosygin also bore responsibility for the initiation of a major economic reform.

The third member of the Troika, M. A. Suslov, had the more or less final word in ideological matters. We may describe him as a "strict constructionist" in that he had unsurpassed skill in finding scriptural guidelines and precedents. He did not seek any other kind of power; but what he had was enough to keep the others pure.

THE RESTORATION OF STABILITY

The new leaders abolished the division of Communist party organizations, local soviets, Komsomol, and trade unions into industrial and agricultural sections, then turned to the 1961 term-limitation rule. The turnover of cell secretaries had doubled; this created instability and weakened morale. Sounding the cry of "Leninist respect for cadres!" the leadership abolished the rule. More than three-quarters of the RSFSR regional first secretaries in mid-1965 had held the same job three years earlier. Only 10 percent had fallen to term limitation; the others had won promotion, transferred, gone on pension on schedule, or had died. The same situation existed in the other republics. Party officials who carried out their responsibilities satisfactorily now had job security; even those who got into trouble were rarely disciplined.

This bred contentment and loyalty: Cadres rejoiced that the men in the Kremlin understood their problems. A smug sense of inviolability pervaded every office. When the media occasionally attacked a low-level sinecurist, the critics, not the bureaucrat, usually received a reprimand.

FATE OF THE REFORMS

The Troika undertook one reform Khrushchev had resolutely opposed. Within days of taking power, it authorized a media attack on Trofim Lysenko; by mid-November the entire country was talking about the "Lysenko cult." Agricultural journals revealed that farm production *declined* wherever the charlatan's theories had been applied. Early in 1965 Lysenko lost his job as director of the Genetics Institute. In May *Izvestiya* published an article on Gregor Mendel by the late N. I. Vavilov, Lysenko's most prominent victim, and *Pravda* carried a laudatory article on Mendel in June. Reappearance of the scientific journal *Genetics* completed that discipline's rehabilitation. By 1966, ten new laboratories were functioning within the Institute of Biological Problems, where previously all research had to have the imprimatur "Lysenkoist." The ultimate sanction came in October 1968: Academician B. M. Kedrov—no friend of liberty—wrote in *Pravda* that Lenin himself approved of genetics—as though that had any effect on genetics.

Cessation of Khrushchev's brutal antireligion campaign constituted a second positive signal. Trying to placate the unreconstructed Stalinists, the former first secretary had persecuted clergy, razed still more churches, monas-

teries, mosques, and synagogues, and presided over an atheist propaganda effort as vicious as anything Stalin—ex-seminary student—had undertaken. The Troika ended that. The Communists had not made their peace with religion; they simply considered it unnecessary to continue fighting a war they had won. It became rare for Komsomol and KGB thugs to break up religious services. The pace of architectural destruction slowed and—to attract the tourist trade—a few minor restoration projects were commenced. The clergy still had to report to the KGB, which relaxed its stranglehold just a little.

In 1968, four Muslim minorities expelled from their homes in Georgia two decades earlier as "unreliable" were permitted to return. That left about 500,000 Crimean Tatars, several thousand Koreans transported by the Japanese to Sakhalin Island before 1945, and an indeterminate number of border peoples languishing in exile.

The reestablishment in 1970 of the Union ministry of justice seemed to indicate still more liberalization. Abolished as part of "de-Stalinization" in 1956, the ministry was charged with ensuring the strict observance of "socialist legality." It was to oversee and coordinate the work of the republic courts that had separately exercised its function between 1956 and 1970; correct technical mistakes in court practice; and analyze court statistics. It was to codify existing laws. The ministry did not have the right to protest court decisions.

The new regime liberalized family law. Restrictive wartime rules ended, and unwed mothers won the right to sue to establish paternity. The party-state abolished the legal concept of illegitimacy, made divorce easier, and issued regulations defining the responsibilities of children toward aged parents. The divorce rate increased sharply, leading the media to suggest reinstituting the Russian custom of posting wedding banns six months before the intended marriage. This, the journalists said, would help end the "plague of three-day marriages."

It appeared that the Troika would revert to Stalinist persecution of literature and the arts. It sent Andrei Sinyavsky and Yuli Daniel to the Gulag and frightened many writers into silence. Nevertheless, works critical of Soviet society—but not the Communist party—continued to appear. A modest amount of "Gulagia" issued from the state presses, but only through *samizdat* and *tamizdat* did the uncensored truth reach readers.

For the first time in 40 years the state had to deal with "those who think differently," or dissidents. Some citizens had begun to call on the state to make the civil rights provisions of the 1936 Stalin Constitution reality. Cautiously, at great personal risk, these people tested the regime. In the beginning, the KGB and the police warned them to stop, threatened them with dismissal from their jobs, kept them under surveillance, and beat them up. In the context this amounted to restraint. The Kremlin believed the handful of individuals involved posed no threat; and their very existence demonstrated official tolerance. That would change when Aleksandr Solzhenitsyn and Andrei Sakharov won international fame.

People who sharply criticized the regime and Soviet society, especially if they spoke to the foreign media, received no mercy. The KGB arrested them; the "reformed" courts tried and convicted them of "anti-Soviet activity" and sent them to one of the remaining islands of the Gulag. KGB psychiatrists at the notorious Serbsky Institute diagnosed some dissidents as suffering from "sluggish schizophrenia" or "reformist delusions." They injected their "patients" with mind-altering drugs such as stelazine and thorazine and confined them in special prisons called psychiatric hospitals. Supervising the unspeakable tortures inflicted on these people was Yuri Andropov, ambassador to Hungary in 1956 and KGB director since 1967.

The public rehabilitation of the *Communists* among Stalin's victims continued, at a substantially reduced rate. Nikolai Bukharin's widow and son had launched a public campaign in 1961 to clear his name. Joining them were several Old Bolsheviks, among them Elena Stasova, one of Lenin's associates. The Khrushchev regime opened an investigation, but opposition from party fundamentalists and even mere conservatives stalled it. The case was still pending when the Troika came to power. Thirteen years later the family heard Suslov's decision: The criminal charges against Bukharin remained valid. That stamped Troika approval on the Terror.

TWENTY-THIRD PARTY CONGRESS

In the spring of 1965, *Pravda* suggested a "reevaluation of certain historical figures who have suffered from one-sided treatment." The trial balloon went nowhere. Reformist Communists struck back, publicly attacking Stalin's wartime leadership and lashing out at some of the dictator's henchmen, notably the sinister prosecutor, Andrei Vyshinsky. It was at about this time that Ivan Serov, wartime supervisor of the deportations and later (1954–1958) head of the KGB, lost his job and his medals.

Then came the Stalinist counter-counterattack. Writing in *Pravda* in January 1966, three pseudo-historians pronounced the term "cult of personality" incorrect and un-Marxist, conveniently overlooking the fact that Marx had coined it. A few days later the kangaroo court crucified the writers Sinyavsky and Daniel. The Soviet media complained about the lenient sentences. Mikhail Sholokhov, author of *Quiet Flows the Don,* lamented the absence of the 1920s "revolutionary justice" that would have sent Sinyavsky and Daniel before a firing squad. Sholokhov had received the 1965 Nobel Prize for Literature from a Swedish Academy that hoped to placate the Kremlin for the earlier award to Boris Pasternak. Stalin's spirit lived, and even non-Communist foreigners did its bidding.

Signs that the impending Twenty-Third Party Congress would rehabilitate Stalin inspired some of Russia's most prominent citizens to send a letter of protest to the leadership. Any whitewashing of the discredited past, they warned, would shatter the trust between party and people. Among the 25 who signed were the physicists Pyotr Kapitsa, Igor Tamm, and Andrei Sakharov; the writer Konstantin Paustovsky; prima ballerina Maya Plisetskaya; film director Mikhail Romm; and diplomat Ivan Maisky.

The Troika and the Presidium gave these individuals, and the millions for whom they spoke, what at first seemed a victory. The Party Congress, which convened in March 1966, did not discuss Stalin—directly. But in his report on foreign and domestic developments since the last Congress, First Secretary Brezhnev proposed to restore the old nomenclature: Back came "Politburo," out went "Presidium." The delegates roared approval. The Politburo under Lenin and Stalin had led them through the difficult and glorious years. They associated "Presidium" with the despised Khrushchev even though Stalin himself had made the change in 1952. And one restoration demanded another: "First secretary" reverted to "general secretary."

This move came stealthily, buried among ten insignificant changes in the statutes always routinely approved as a final order of business. Lacking a Stalin, the Troika moved cautiously, uncertain of Russia's reaction. Brezhnev would have Stalin's title but did not appear to be cut from the same cloth. Russia would forever live in the shadow of the only real general secretary, and that was the problem: The Troika was determined to keep Russia in that shadow.

Prime Minister Kosygin did not need to speak Stalin's name in paying homage to the achievements of 1929–1941; no one doubted who had been in charge. The leader of the Moscow Communist party organization signaled the decision to accept the fait accompli of "de-Stalinization" while halting it in place. No one, Nikolai Yegorychev declared, could use the "scarecrow of so-called 'Stalinism'" to discredit the party. The "personality cult" was safely buried; the decisions of the Twentieth Congress continued to guide the party. But it was impossible simply to cross out the Stalin years; even Winston Churchill acknowledged that Stalin found Russia in birch-bark sandals and left her with nuclear weapons.

Fundamentalist and conservative Communists restored the mass murderer Kliment Voroshilov to a seat on the Central Committee. Aleksandr Tvardovsky, the courageous editor of *Novy mir* who had discovered and published Solzhenitsyn, lost his own seat.

After the Congress, some Communists called on the party to put Stalin's body back alongside Lenin's in the mausoleum; others were willing to settle for an heroic statue on his grave beneath the Kremlin wall. A smaller number tried to revive the project to build a monument to the victims of the Terror. Far more complained that the rehabilitations had gone too far.

By 1969, the suppression of the "Prague Spring"* behind them, the fundamentalists had regained the upper hand. A concerted publishing campaign defended Stalin's war record; an article in *Kommunist* pointed to an imminent, total rehabilitation. Then suddenly, in March serious clashes along the Soviet–Chinese border cost a number of Soviet soldiers their lives. Whatever his motives, Mao Zedong had never ceased to praise Stalin, but the times were now inauspicious for the Troika to agree with him.

In December 1969 the fundamentalists staged a lavish funeral tribute—Molotov

---

*See Chapter 21.

emerged from disgrace to participate—to Voroshilov. If *that* inhuman mediocrity merited such praise, the Communist party would surely put the ninetieth anniversary of Stalin's birth a few days later to good use. Under Suslov's supervision, the top propagandists prepared an article so fulsome as to ensure that Stalin would rise to take a bow despite those 10 meters of concrete. *Pravda* would publish it on Stalin's birthday, December 21. Other Soviet newspapers and the foreign Communist press would reprint it on December 22.

A key member of the collective that wrote the article leaked the news. Thus alerted, the Soviet reformers persuaded some key foreign Communist leaders to join them in warning the Troika that publication would generate major and perhaps violent unrest. Brezhnev favored going ahead; Kosygin wanted to rethink the matter. When the arch-Stalinist Suslov opted in favor of caution, the Politburo voted to cancel the article.

But they forgot to call the editor of the Mongolian party newspaper in Ulaan Baatar. On December 22, *Unen* published the article rehabilitating Stalin, noting erroneously but in good faith that it had appeared in *Pravda* the previous day. Ulaan Baatar is eight hours ahead of Moscow time.

The anniversary article *Pravda* did in fact carry sorely disappointed the Stalinists. It reviewed the dictator's career and praised him as an "outstanding theoretician and organizer" and principal architect of the 1945 victory but also noted that he had claimed personal credit for the nation's achievements. It accused him of believing in and insisting on his own infallibility. He had violated legal norms and had condemned innocent people to death. *Nevertheless,* although such "mistakes and perversions" had done some "harm," they had only temporarily sidetracked the USSR's—and the world's—march toward communism.

A revised party history published in January 1970 criticized Stalin and referred to the Terror instead of the gently euphemistic "repressions." In June 1970, the gray granite bust the *original* ninetieth birthday article promised suddenly and without ceremony materialized over Stalin's grave.

THE ABORTIVE ECONOMIC REFORM

The notion that political expertise or at least success is translatable into economic wisdom was as much a pillar of Soviet thinking as the Western belief—rooted in Calvinism—that wealth is synonymous with political sagacity. In the USSR, the enormous crises of industrialization, war, and postwar reconstruction had seen the commissars work wonders with human minds, bones, and blood. But the Soviet "Thirty Years' Crisis" had ended. It was time to modernize, automate, introduce innovations. Heroic, "damn-the-human-cost" measures were as anachronistic as cavalry charges; moreover, the nation would surely not tolerate them. Having built physically the largest if not the most productive industrial base in the world, the people—especially those born after about 1930—were demanding rewards. The penetration of foreign influence—inevitable with modern communications—reinforced the demands.

In June 1965 the economist Abel Aganbegyan told a group of Leningrad editors that, in the preceding six years, the growth rate of the economy as a whole had declined by a factor of three. Spelling out the reasons, he singled out the industrial structure, the "worst and most backward of all the industrially developed countries." So badly organized and equipped was mining, for example, that it cost the state more to extract a ton of raw material than it could earn by selling it abroad. The wood-processing industry wasted half the timber and made only one-third as much use of it as did American industry (one-eighth as much as the Swedish) of the other half. Frequent, often artificial shortages distorted the economy. Some industries had huge stockpiles of unnecessary reserves. Wages increased, heightening demand, but still the goods remained in warehouses. Inflationary price increases failed to halt demand.

Aganbegyan reported that unemployment, which officially could not exist, stood at 8 percent of the work force; in small and medium-sized cities it averaged 20 to 30 percent. He did not mention underemployment: Several million citizens worked for a pittance at menial, often meaningless jobs—for example, as pass-checkers. Employing 30 to 40 percent of the 100 million working people, the defense industry was draining the economy.

The factor of growth-rate decline in agriculture, Aganbegyan revealed, was eight. Agricultural production between 1961 and 1965 was substantially below that of the preceding five-year period; the puny 1963 harvest had forced the importation of 12 million tons of grain. Another crop failure in 1965 again made it necessary to turn to foreign suppliers.

Long after the need for "superindustrialization" had passed, the state continued to ravage agriculture to finance heavy industry and defense. Collective farmers produced a 22-billion-ruble net income. They yielded fully half that to the state through taxes: Farmers received artificially low prices for their produce and paid artificially high prices for machinery. In 1965 a *kolhoznik* could earn only 1.50 rubles a day on the collective farm, 3.50 on a private plot. His only incentive to work on the farm was that he *had* to.

The post-Khrushchev leaders continued to emphasize size over quality. They constructed buildings Andrea Lee described as "like American vegetables—all size and no taste." They enlarged the already unwieldy and unproductive farms. Of the 95,000 collective farms in June 1945, only 20,000 remained in 1987. Quadrupling the size quintupled the problems.

The party blamed "subjectivism," that is, Khrushchev's schemes, for the early 1960s slowdown but admitted to some errors at Gosplan. The problem went deeper. Until about 1940, economists had argued that the "bourgeois" concept of value had no meaning in a socialist society. Prices and money were indexes of bourgeois value, vestiges of capitalism. But then party theoreticians decided that "value" was after all appropriate to socialism "in a changed form." They did not say what the form was. Stalin had advanced bizarre views in his postwar *Economic Problems of Socialism in the USSR* and had set economics back still further.

A September 1965 Central Committee plenum rejected the advice of economists who argued that the rationalization of planning through computerization could help solve economic problems. It opted instead for a complex blend of decentralized economic decision making with a *more centralized* administrative structure. Plant managers were to assume greater responsibility for determining the fair local share of the national plan, then produce it. This was a new departure: The Moscow planners-bureaucrats had always treated managers as obedient executors of orders.

Prime Minister Kosygin revamped the organizational framework, switching from a regional to a ministerial system. He replaced the *sovnarhozes* (regional economic councils) with industrial ministries and state committees organized along pre-1957 lines, but with this difference: The new bodies could not simply dictate to plant, factory, and mine managers, but had to consult with them as partners.

Party conservatives—notably Brezhnev and Suslov—reacted angrily when Kosygin and his reformers announced that *sales and profits* would henceforward be the chief indicators of performance. Gross output had always been the main criterion; the very idea of profits was anathema. But emphasis on output had always led managers to produce without regard for quality or even deliverability. They fulfilled the plan, but no one—least of all the state—profited. There was little innovation; managers stuck with what they knew they could do.

Although the 1965 reform owed some faint debt to Bukharin, Kosygin and his colleagues cited the theories of Yevsei Liberman, whose 1962 *Pravda* article had created a sensation. Liberman's insistence that incentives would make industry more efficient had won few other supporters in the bureaucracy, but Kosygin persuaded the Central Committee to measure efficiency by only seven success indicators—there had been several dozen—of which the most important were sales and profits.

Enterprises could retain some of their profits to establish funds for bonuses for workers and management; for social and cultural facilities and housing construction; and for reinvestment and development. They would have some latitude in the first two areas; the central authorities retained veto power over the reinvestment fund.

The 1965 reform fostered consolidation. Small and medium-sized plants producing identical or nearly identical goods in a given locale united under one management, where possible under one roof. Large factories began merging with satellite suppliers. This tendency accelerated after a September 1968 decree provided for closer links between research-design and production.

These innovations encountered opposition from party fundamentalists (Stalinists) and conservatives (neo-Stalinists), Gosplan, and bureaucrats everywhere. The prospect of having to take responsibility—that was the thrust of consolidation and oversight, not to mention computerization—for plant performance terrified managers. Three years after the Twenty-Third Party Congress made economic incentives official policy, an economist said, "My party conscience does not allow me to vote for profits." But the Moscow party boss reminded the Congress that socialism's watchword was

"from each according to his ability, to each according to his work." Incentives were necessary until the achievement of communism.

Speakers at the Twenty-Third Party Congress bragged of economic achievements but acknowledged glaring shortcomings. Brezhnev reported failure to meet the Seven-Year Plan's output targets for coal, machinery, chemicals, and consumer goods. Gosplan Chairman Nikolai Baibakov spoke of the "extremely slow assimilation" of new assets and called attention to the especially critical situation in ferrous metals and chemicals. Baibakov also admitted sizable cost overruns—a problem usually associated with state contracts in *capitalist* countries. Brezhnev and others assailed bureaucrats and managers for the low shift-index at most plants: Idle factories produced no goods and turned no profits, yet managers refused to introduce a shift system that would keep them operating 16 or 24 hours a day.

The shift-index problem pinpointed a phenomenon lurking in the background for nearly four decades: A labor shortage. Where were the children and grandchildren of all those victims of the Terror when the party-state needed them? Khrushchev, Brezhnev, Suslov, Kosygin, and the others did not ask that question.

The USSR population was only five times that of France, but the Soviet economy was 18 times bigger. Failure to automate and modernize rapidly enough to compensate for the shortage exacerbated the situation Lenin and Stalin had created. Technological advance did not keep pace with the relative decline in the size of the labor force, and it was becoming increasingly difficult to substitute capital for labor. One Thirty Years' Crisis had ended. Another loomed menacingly at the front door.

The 1965 reform did not pursue its initiatives to their logical conclusion. According to inflated official figures, the economy expanded at an average annual rate of 5.2 percent during the eighth Five-Year Plan of 1966–1970. Cost-accounting expanded to embrace a 6 percent charge on capital, but there were exceptions for projects in remote areas, and for most defense plants. Labor productivity barely rose. The chemical, machine-building, ferrous metals, and coal industries all failed to meet output targets. At the Twenty-Fourth Party Congress in 1971, Brezhnev bragged one minute about increased per-capita consumption of meat and other food items, but admitted the next that the farms had not met their quotas: There had been "interruptions in trade." It was frequently impossible to find butter, unprocessed meat, fish, or fresh fruit and vegetables outside Moscow, Leningrad, and Kiev, and often one could not find them even there.

Vodka remained in ruinously bountiful supply. In February 1988, Mikhail Gorbachev revealed that from 1964 through 1984 the Communist state *increased* the already substantial production of distilled spirits in order to swell the state's coffers and enrich the *nomenklatura,* which was plundering the national wealth. Gorbachev did not note in his memoirs that his revered mentor had introduced a cheap vodka that consumers called "Andropovka" or—touchingly—"Crankshaft." Nor did he blame Yuri Andropov for "filling the gap between the enormous money supply and the wretched supply of goods with alcohol." Here was Orwellian *1984*: It was state policy to keep people drunk.

The new attention to sales and profits made prices critically important, but the price structure did not correspond to economic reality. The years of denying "bourgeois" laws and concepts came back to haunt planners now struggling to determine fair market value. A revised industrial wholesale price index went into effect on July 1, 1967, a too-timid step forward. Competition for some undervalued goods produced artificial shortages. Goods in great demand were priced so high as to make it impossible to buy them; this generated production bottlenecks as factories shut down for lack of supplies.

The attempt to decentralize economic decision making while simultaneously recentralizing administration was like sitting on a chair while trying to lift it. The reformers declined to introduce genuine market mechanisms even as they insisted that factories become profitable. Real competition would have threatened central planning, the "main guarantor of defense industry supply priority."

This was a crucial area, not only in terms of national security. Brezhnev noted in 1971 that 42 percent of total defense-industry output went into the civilian sector—civil aircraft, merchant ships, consumer durables, etc. No nation can leave defense to the mercy of the market, but the zany Soviet system made it virtually impossible to incorporate market mechanisms even into the *civilian* sector.

Finally, the bonus system threatened to worsen the already significant problems that wage differentials generated. Worker resentment of the "Stakhanovite" superachievers had created tensions since the mid-1930s. If there were to arise a privileged new group of exceptionally productive and innovative workers, technicians, managers, and research development specialists, there might also come into existence some class conflicts not seen for forty years.

COMMUNISM AND COMPUTERS

Demographers, sociologists, legal experts, other specialists, and Communist party officials were devoting considerable if largely uncoordinated attention to the labor shortage. There was growing concern, but no general sense of urgency. Most experts simply assumed that automation of industry and further mechanization of agriculture would compensate.

Mechanizing and chemicalizing agriculture

proved difficult. The automation of industry and the rationalization of planning and management, however, depended on application of computer technology, in which the USSR lagged far behind the West and Japan. Only in the mid-1960s did the Kremlin, nostalgic for the spirit of 1928–1932, finally heed warnings and jump into the field with a catch-up program.

The Soviet Union trailed in automation first, because Stalinist ideology imposed major restraints until 1956, and second, because, after that year, Soviet-style computerization made no room for decentralized, market-driven forces. In Stalin's time the party had denounced cybernetics as "un-Marxist." The first Soviet cybernetics seminar was held only in 1956; two years later the Academy of Sciences established a special Scientific Council to supervise the field. Still the party hesitated; as late as 1961 its official program devoted exactly one paragraph to automation.

Only in the early 1960s did the party-state try to introduce computers into the defense complex and the economy in general. Political authorities attempted to force computers on potential users who did not want them. Abel Aganbegyan reported in 1965 that the Central Statistical Board itself did not have a single computer and had no plans to get one. Accustomed to commanding, the leadership did not know how to persuade; the attempt to create a market miscarried. The introduction of computers was painfully slow; general improvement became visible only in the late 1990s.

Planners, managers, and even military leaders resisted computers for fear the machines would be used to tighten oversight and control. They had a vested interest in preserving the existing inefficient system. The introduction of data-processing equipment threatened sinecures from which the holders had always attacked the problem of plan fulfillment with imaginative extralegal and illegal measures. Beyond that, creative accounting on old-fash-

ioned adding machines and even abacuses enabled managers to tell Moscow what Moscow wanted to hear.

A March 1966 decree spelled out responsibility for developing automated management systems and for utilizing computers in planning. The ministries, Gosplan, the Central Statistical Board, the Academy of Sciences, the State Committee on Science and Technology, and the State Committee on Standards shared authority; such bewildering division created confusion and waste. Worse still was the failure to establish clear responsibility for organizing a nationwide computer network; both Gosplan and the Central Statistical Board claimed that right. Creation of the Statewide Automated System (OGAS) in 1971 finally resolved the dispute.

Brezhnev referred several times at the Twenty-Third Party Congress to the necessity of making efficient use of automation and computers. This did not, however, constitute a major theme; most delegates dismissed his words as the usual Communist-materialist obeisance to science. The resolution approving the Central Committee's report directed industrial ministries to introduce new technology as rapidly as possible—and gave computers lowest priority.

Senior party officials, military leaders, scientists, economic planners, and managers conferred at exhaustive length. A September 1968 decree called for establishment of four types of research-development and production complexes aimed at creating new processes, developing new products, improving production methods and work organization, and providing research institutes for large industrial enterprises. Computers were at the heart of this new program. During the eighth Five-Year Plan, the output of the computer industry grew 480 percent in value terms, and the record was almost as good in the ninth Five-Year Plan of 1971–1975. But these figures reflected the late start. By 1970 there were about 5,000 computers in the USSR, 20 per 1 million people. In the United States there were 344 computers per million population; in Japan, 96; and in Great Britain, 91. Moreover, the most powerful 1970 Soviet computer operated at one-sixth the level of the most advanced American model. Substantially more than half the American, Japanese, and British computers were third generation; in 1970 no Soviet-manufactured third-generation machine existed. More than 23 percent of all Soviet computers were first generation. Even in late 1975, second-generation devices comprised 83 percent of all Soviet computers.

The technology advanced in gigantic, unpredictable leaps; research and development assumed crucial importance. The West and Japan were not standing still, and the Soviet political, military, and scientific establishments considered it essential to obtain Western and Japanese computers and computer knowledge. Legal, questionable, and blatantly illegal deals brought many electronic items into the USSR. Despite an American embargo the Soviets obtained several dozen second- and third-generation computers before the Nixon administration tightened controls in the early 1970s. Unscrupulous entrepreneurs, espionage agents, and politically naive Western scientists and engineers kept up the "technology transfer."

By the mid-1980s it had become clear that the Western nations and Japan could not keep their computer technology out of Communist hands. In 1984 the Coordinating Committee for Multilateral Export Controls (Cocom)—representing Japan and all NATO countries save Spain and Iceland—recommended abandoning efforts to prevent the sale of microcomputers to the USSR and other Communist countries. Cocom favored concentration on efforts to prevent the transfer of supersophisticated technology with military applications. In 1985 the United States, which had advocated strict controls, bowed to Cocom and relaxed its rules. The USSR immediately began negotiations to buy large numbers of personal computers.

Computer education figured heavily in the April 1984 educational program. A year later the new Gorbachev Politburo decreed that such training would begin in the 1985–1986 school year. More than eight million students would be involved. If the program were to go forward, the USSR would have to purchase tens of thousands of microcomputers, primarily from the United States and Japan. In the end, the Kremlin proved unable to finance these plans.

SUGGESTED ADDITIONAL READINGS

BREZHNEVA, LUBA. *The World I Left Behind.* New York: Random House, 1995.

COOK, LINDA J. *The Soviet Social Contract and Why It Failed.* Cambridge, MA: Harvard University Press, 1993.

HAYWARD, MAX, ed. *On Trial: The Soviet State vs. "Abram Tertz" and "Nikolai Arzhak."* New York: Harper & Row, 1967.

HELLER, MIKHAIL, and ALEKSANDR M. NEKRICH. *Utopia in Power: The History of the Soviet Union from 1917 to the Present.* New York: Summit Books, 1986.

LITVINOV, PAVEL, AND PETER REDDAWAY, eds. *The Trial of the Four.* New York: Viking Press, 1972.

MARCHENKO, ANATOLI. *My Testimony.* New York: Dutton, 1970.

MATTHEWS, MERVYN. *Privilege in the Soviet Union.* Boston: Allen & Unwin, 1978.

20

THE ERA OF
STAGNATION, 1971–1985

**Leonid Brezhnev took care of his hordes of friends and hangers-on, helping along
careers, looking after families, winking at foibles great and small, remembering
birthdays and other special occasions. He dealt severely with challenges to party
authority and gave the KGB wide latitude to deal with dissent. He engineered
the May 1967 appointment of Yuri Andropov, not a career Chekist, to head
the KGB—insurance against former KGB Director "Iron Shurik" Shelepin.**

TWENTY-FOURTH PARTY CONGRESS

A new "cult" blossomed at the March–April
1971 Twenty-Fourth Party Congress. According to the Brezhnev protégé Heidar Aliyev,
leader of the Communist party and the KGB in
Azerbaijan: "In all the work . . . [of] the Central Committee, an enormous role belongs to
Leonid Ilyich Brezhnev . . . who has won universal affection and respect for his tireless activity and constant solicitude for the people's
welfare."

Until now, the Brezhnev core—Suslov,
Kosygin, Nikolai Podgorny, and Andrei Kirilenko—had been a minority on the 11-mem-
ber Politburo. The Twenty-Fourth Party Congress added four seats and approved
Brezhnev's choices to fill them: V. V. Grishin,
F. D. Kulakov, D. A. Kunayev, and V. V. Shcherbitsky. Brezhnev now had a substantial majority. The Central Committee grew from 195 full

members to 241; among the newcomers was
Mikhail Gorbachev.

The general secretary always read the Central Committee's report. In 1971 Brezhnev did
that, but he also, to underscore his new se-
niority, postponed Prime Minister Aleksei
Kosygin's speech on the economy a full week.
He said more about foreign policy and defense
than the responsible ministers, Andrei
Gromyko and Andrei Grechko. Brezhnev
claimed the Communist party was healthy, but
he could not call it proletarian: Only 40.1 percent of the members were workers. Membership had doubled in 14 years, but fulltime staff
had decreased by 20 percent. Brezhnev repaid
the party that had been good to him by engineering the reelection of 81 percent of Central
Committee full members.

To spur innovation, improve efficiency, and
achieve economies of scale, the regime introduced a "territorial production association

movement" that involved creating conglomerate enterprises. An outgrowth of the *sovnarhozes* and the failed 1965 reform, this was yet another attempt to restructure industry. It amalgamated several enterprises in a given industry and territory into a "production association" under a united administration. Directors of the chief enterprise exercised some functions previously reserved for the appropriate ministry in Moscow. The Brezhnevists called the consolidation of all—or as many as possible—stages of a given commodity's production "developed socialism." A latecomer to the computer age, the USSR would have to automate entire industries.

Kosygin echoed Brezhnev's ideas, noting that Gosplan and some other agencies had already begun installing automated management systems. The ninth Five-Year Plan would see the introduction of "at least" 1,600 more systems in which "continuous planning"—constant review from birth of an idea to series production—would be crucial. Modern technology would make possible a substantial rise in the standard of living, but labor would have to do its share. Kosygin predicted that switching to digitally programmed control would increase labor productivity 200 to 300 percent in the machine-tool sector alone.

The USSR needed such a feat. The economist Abel Aganbegyan said in 1965 that the Soviet Union had about the same number—two million—of machine tools as the United States, but only half the Soviet units were in operation at any given time. The rest were "not in use or under repair." This meant underutilized capacity; and crews of out-of-service machines constituted a drag on the economy.

If the USSR could not keep the nonautomated sector working at more than 50 percent, it was unlikely to do much better after automation, at least initially. User resistance to computers intensifed. By the time a factory or group of factories automated, the computers were invariably outdated: "Developed socialism" found it difficult to assimilate new technology. Bureaucratic inefficiency and inertia, and labor's insistence on working strictly according to rule—effectively a permanent slowdown—kept productivity low and stifled innovation. Wary managers spoke of the "dehumanizing" effects of automation.

Spelling out targets for the ninth Five-Year Plan of 1971–1975, Kosygin stressed it would be the first to provide for a faster growth rate in the consumer sector. At last the Soviet people would receive reward for sacrifice.

ECONOMIC DECAY

The new Five-Year Plan made some ambitious assumptions. In percentages, the targets for production and real income differed little from those authorities *claimed* to have achieved between 1966 and 1970; this amounted to an admission that the actual results had been disappointing. The ninth Plan projected an increase in the total nonagricultural labor force of 13 percent vs. 19 percent in the eighth Five-Year Plan, and an increase in the industrial labor force of 6.5 percent vs. 15 percent. The relative decline in the labor pool inspired planners to count heavily on a dramatic increase in labor productivity and on achieving enormous economies in raw materials and energy. The Soviet economy had never performed that way.

The new economic plan recentralized decision making and increased pressures on resources and managers. It had always been safest to defer to Moscow, and Moscow always shouldered the burden. The bureaucracy justified its existence.

The introduction of new technology depended on an uninterrupted supply of Western machines and expertise, and the planners assumed that détente would continue. But there were signs that opposition in the United States might halt the flow or at least attach stricter conditions.

Determined to solve one of its most vexing problems, the Kremlin planned to increase the already huge investment in agriculture. That sector had taken an average of 23 percent of gross fixed capital investment in the latter half of the 1960s; by 1973 agriculture's share reached 26.5 percent and continued to climb.

Midway through the new Five-Year Plan, the fundamentalists who had defeated the 1965 reform renewed their assault on modernization, attacking the Central Economics—Mathematical Institute's econometrics. They denounced systems analysis, economic forecasting, and decentralized decision making as "bourgeois" and condemned the high priority assigned the consumer-goods sector. Had the millennium arrived? Until the world was Communist, they insisted, the USSR must emphasize heavy industry—steel and guns.

The new plan did not come close to meeting its goals, in part because of nature's caprice but more importantly because of party interference and "longer-term retardatory trends in the economy." According to routinely invented official figures, total national income rose by 28 percent between 1970 and 1975, for an average annual growth rate of 5.1 percent. The plan had called for increases of 38.6 and 6.7 percent, respectively. Measured against 1966–1970 performance, agricultural production rose 13 percent in average-annual gross value instead of the projected 21.7 percent. Total industrial production was 43 percent higher in 1975 than in 1970, or 7.4 percent annually; the target figures were 47 and 8.0 percent, respectively. Production of consumer goods rose 37 percent—6.5 percent annually—instead of the planned 48.6 and 8.2 percent figures, respectively.

Western experts estimated the economy's average annual growth rate closer to 4 percent than the claimed 5.1 percent; Aganbegyan re-

ported in 1965 that CIA estimates had been "absolutely accurate." Industrial output could not have reached the published levels, which represented a 97 percent fulfillment of goals.

There were two major crop failures during the period. The purchase of 30 million tons of grain abroad helped overcome this in 1972, but that year's poor harvest was only a taste of what would come three years later, when the USSR had to buy even greater quantities of foreign grain. This depleted gold reserves, but the dramatic rise in oil and natural gas prices after 1973 temporarily softened the blow. As an energy exporter, the USSR had a favorable balance of trade; but history shows nothing so clearly as the cyclical nature of the world economy. Diminishing reserves, and ever-increasing domestic requirements, did not permit the unlimited sale of hydrocarbons.

The 1975 drought and crop failure were the worst since the early 1930s. Grain production fell 76 million tons short of the revised goal of 215.7 million tons. Imports could not take up all the slack, if only because Soviet seaports physically could not handle more than 40 million tons *per year*. Once again consumers, including the farmers who had to have seed and fodder, would have to tighten their belts. An American economist described the 1975 disaster as "possibly the largest single blow suffered by the Soviet economy since the German invasion of 1941."

There were innumerable ripple effects. The dipping into reserve stocks—never large—to provide for human consumption decreased the amount of high-quality fodder, and that in turn forced premature slaughter of many animals including breeding stock. There was a temporary glut of meat, then scarcity; rebuilding the herds was difficult. The slaughter reduced the organic fertilizer available, and *that* increased pressures on producers, transporters, and handlers of chemical fertilizers.

Consumers had no choice but to endure

shortages and lower expectations. The standard of living, which had been improving at a modest rate, went into reverse despite some wage increases. By 1976 the average wage had reached 145.80 rubles per month—126.80 for farm workers, 162.20 for workers in industry. The average family spent less than 40 rubles a month for rent and utilities, 10 to 12 rubles for transportation. Before the 1975 crop failure it spent 40 to 50 percent of its income on food despite massive state subsidies for bread, milk, potatoes, and cabbage. Crop failures raised prices; the state had to intervene to fight inflation and limit political damage. Medical care was "free" in the sense of negligible out-of-pocket costs, but people got what they paid for: Soviet medicine in general remained primitive. The Kremlin Clinic provided excellent care for those at the top, and good KGB clinics and hospitals serviced the Chekists.

TWENTY-FIFTH PARTY CONGRESS

In April 1973 Leonid Brezhnev reorganized the Politburo and expanded it to 16 members. Dismissing Gennadi Voronov and Pyotr Shelest, he promoted Minister of Defense Andrei Grechko, Foreign Minister Andrei Gromyko, and KGB Director Yuri Andropov to full membership. The high-living Leningrad Party Boss Grigori Romanov—no relation, but with Winter Palace aspirations—became one of seven candidate members.

Brezhnev counted on the leaders of the armed forces and secret police, and the foreign ministry, to shore up his personal position and his foreign policy. The new team seemed to function smoothly. In 1975 the general secretary unceremoniously ousted "Iron Shurik" Shelepin from the Politburo. Not without reason, the Brezhnev people suspected Shelepin of wanting to supplant Brezhnev.

When the Twenty-Fifth Party Congress convened in February 1976, Brezhnev spoke in slurred tones and appeared confused as to his situation. He defended détente, blamed the Chinese for the deterioration in bilateral relations, and reprimanded the French and Italian Communist parties for seeking independence. Criticizing the USSR's poor economic performance, he singled out "Group B" (consumer goods) enterprises. He castigated ministerial-level officials for treating consumer goods as "something secondary and ancillary."

That was for public consumption; Brezhnev had no intention of shifting emphasis away from "Group A" (heavy industry). If consumers wanted a higher standard of living, they would have to work harder for the same or lower wages—in other words, there would be no improvement. Brezhnev said little about the production associations but declared it impossible to postpone *perestroika* ("restructuring") of the economy.

Offering up a sacrificial lamb for the 1975 disaster, Brezhnev removed Minister of Agriculture Dmitri Polyansky from the Politburo. The *party* secretary in charge, Fyodor Kulakov, escaped without a public reprimand, but events soon proved he had been compromised. There would be an opening for Mikhail Gorbachev, on whom Suslov and especially Andropov had kept benevolent eyes. Brezhnev said the eighth and ninth economic plans had invested 213 billion of the 320 billion rubles allocated to agriculture since 1917. They fed the problem with money and the country with excuses.

Kosygin called the ninth Five-Year Plan a success despite "problems" in agriculture and the failure of about 18 percent of all industrial enterprises to meet quotas. He boasted of Soviet self-sufficiency in energy—no other major industrial nation could claim that—but noted a decline in proven oil reserves. The USSR would have to rely more heavily on hydroelectric power, nuclear energy, and coal.

Spelling out the tenth plan's goals, Kosygin called for a 24 to 28 percent increase in the national income to be achieved by expanding

"Group A" industrial production by 38 to 42 percent, "Group B" by 30 to 32 percent. Wages would rise 16 to 28 percent for industrial and clerical workers, 24 to 27 percent for collective farmers. The regime would accelerate the automation of industry and the mechanization and chemicalization of agriculture.

At a plenary meeting while the Twenty-Fifth Party Congress was still in session, the new Central Committee sanctioned Polyansky's dismissal from the Politburo and promoted two candidate members, Grigori Romanov and Dmitri Ustinov, to full membership. This brought the number of full members back up to 16. No one called attention to the fact that the inner circle of Brezhnev, Suslov, Kosygin, Grechko, and Gromyko had an average age of 71. The average age of the full Politburo was 66; that of the six alternate members, nearly 60. Heidar Aliyev was the youngest at 52.

The USSR would soon pay a stiff price for this gerontocracy's obsession with power and privilege. The old guard clung tenaciously to power, grew ever more rigid, resisted new ideas and new people, fought change. The untidy infighting that occurs in all political organizations simply ceased after 1971 as Brezhnevian "stability of cadres" defied all the known laws of the political universe.

Brezhnev boasted that he had put "an end . . . to the unjustified reshuffling and frequent replacements of cadres." He was blind to the ossification of those cadres, whose main goal was to remain in office by stifling healthy trends. Between 1964 and 1976, 78 percent of the regional party bureaus in European Russia either kept the same leader or replaced her or him only once. There was a 33 percent "stability index" under Nikita Khrushchev.

THE 1976–1977 POLITICKING

In May 1976 Brezhnev promoted himself from four-star general to marshal of the Soviet Union—the first politician since Stalin to hold that rank. At about the same time, the media revealed that he was president of the Defense Council, the very existence of which had been kept secret. A bronze bust of the general secretary appeared on the main square of his home town and stayed there. In December 1976 *Pravda* devoted a couple of pages to Brezhnev daily between the 11th and the 18th, then on the 19th gave him six of the total eight pages. It was his seventieth birthday. He awarded himself his fifth Order of Lenin and second Gold Medal Hero of the Soviet Union.

But Brezhnev, who suffered from Alzheimer's disease and other ailments, soon became a secondary figure in the building of this new "cult." The laying of every brick was now done by the Brezhnev *machine*, Andropov and Suslov at the controls.

When Marshal Grechko died in April 1976, Dmitri Ustinov became defense minister. Like Brezhnev, he was not a professional soldier, but he was a crony; and so he was promoted to marshal. Yuri Andropov of the KGB and Nikolai Shchelokov, ultra-dishonest—even in those circles—minister of internal affairs, became Army generals. In September 1976 the machine appointed Nikolai Tikhonov, 71, first deputy prime minister—heir apparent to the ailing Aleksei Kosygin. Like many other key officials, Tikhonov had served in various posts in Dnepropetrovsk, where Brezhnev was born and began his career.

The Tikhonov appointment coincided with the ouster of Nikolai Podgorny. A May 1977 Central Committee plenum dropped the 74-year-old Ukrainian from the Politburo; three weeks later the Supreme Soviet dismissed him as chairman of its Presidium—titular president—and elected Brezhnev in his place. The general secretary thus became chief of state, the first Soviet politician to hold both posts simultaneously. Brezhnev declared that this demonstrated the primacy of the Communist party. That had not been in doubt since 1920.

It was awkward for Brezhnev, in a formal sense merely the leader of a political party, to deal with foreign heads of state. Moreover, all Communist countries save Hungary and Poland were ruled by men who held the top position in both party and state. At a time when Moscow's domination of the satellites was increasingly in jeopardy, Brezhnev's technically inferior rank was an unnecessary complication and irritant. "Cult" logic dictated that Brezhnev take the last prize the machine could offer.

There was nothing subtle about the timing. Four days after taking office, Brezhnev paid a state visit to France, where full honors including a 101-gun salute greeted him. He liked the noise.

NEW CONSTITUTION

There was another factor in the 1977 maneuvers. Eighteen years earlier, legal experts had proposed sweeping changes in the 1936 Constitution, ostensibly to bring it into line with the progress of socialism. In reality the document was hateful to the "de-Stalinizers." Khrushchev became chairman of the Constitutional Commission in 1962; Brezhnev replaced him in November 1964.

As the Brezhnev machine consolidated its power its leaders took an ever greater interest in the project; it was a toy. Brezhnev frequently referred to the commission's work, and in 1973 he announced plans to submit a draft to a nationwide referendum. That was not in the script, or at least not in the machine version. The media deleted the reference to a referendum.

The draft was published on June 4, 1977, 12 days before Brezhnev replaced Podgorny at the ceremonial helm—only to find the work too heavy. It was much like the old Constitution. But there were changes, one of which bore on the 1977 politicking: There was to be

a "vice president." A first deputy chairman of the Supreme Soviet Presidium would fulfill routine ceremonial duties previously entrusted to the chairman, freeing her or him for grander tasks. Wanting the chairmanship for himself, Brezhnev offered the lesser post to Podgorny, who declined it.

Submitted to nationwide discussion—but not a referendum—over the summer, the new Constitution's infamous Article 6 stated: "The Communist Party of the Soviet Union is the leading and guiding force of Soviet society, the nucleus of its political system and of [all] state and public organizations. The CPSU exists for the people and serves the people." Article 50 guaranteed the equality of citizens and basic civil and human rights. Article 39, however, declared that the "exercise of rights and liberties by citizens must not injure the interests of society and the state or the rights of other citizens." This constituted the *ultima ratio*: Article 6 made it clear that the party would be the sole judge of injury to the state or the rights of others.

Article 4 recognized each citizen's right to lease a dwelling and a small private plot of land from the state for one's lifetime. An innovative Chapter 4 (Articles 28–30) on foreign policy reflected an attempt to prove compliance with the Final Act of the Helsinki Conference. It emphasized the peace-loving nature of the Soviet state, called for "general and complete disarmament," and forbade war propaganda.

Presenting the slightly revised document to the Supreme Soviet for its approval in October 1977, Brezhnev reacted to the sting of foreign criticism. He named half a dozen Western newspapers critical of the Constitution and hurled a challenge: Did the West boast of guaranteeing the "right" to unemployment, inadequate medical care, neglect of the elderly, racial discrimination, crime, sociopathic values? It was an odd defense.

Like its predecessors of 1918, 1924, and 1936, the new Constitution embodied the antidemocratic values of the Communist party. It made no pretense of seeking political or social equilibrium and did not recognize even the theoretical possibility of CPSU error. It did not sanction political or ideological compromise. Freedom of speech meant freedom to agree with the Communist party.

The Supreme Soviet unanimously approved the "Brezhnev Constitution" in time for the sixtieth anniversary of Bolshevik October. It is unlikely that Lenin, Stalin, or Khrushchev would have objected to a word. In a one-party state, the document was irrelevant.

THE MACHINE WEARS OUT

Veteran diplomat V. V. Kuznetsov became deputy chairman of the Supreme Soviet Presidium, or vice president. Never an insider, he would perform the routine state duties that bored Brezhnev and taxed his deteriorating health. Kuznetsov became a candidate member of the Politburo in October 1977. At 76, he did not bring youth to the position.

Several personnel changes between 1977 and 1980 revealed the inability of the machine's stewards to agree on the succession, let alone a succession policy. Brezhnev promoted an incompetent close friend, Konstantin Chernenko, to the Politburo in October 1977 and made him a full member a year later. Brezhnev's personal choice as the next general secretary, Chernenko was then 66.

Having suffered a cerebral hemorrhage in 1976 and a massive heart attack in 1979, Aleksei Kosygin relinquished his party and government posts in October 1980. Nikolai Tikhonov succeeded him as prime minister. Kosygin's seat on the Politburo went to Mikhail Gorbachev, party secretary in charge of agriculture since Fyodor Kulakov's death in 1978. Gorbachev was 49.

The coalition that had ruled so long began to collapse. Mikhail Suslov remained officially

in charge of ideology, but his own health failed. That left Yuri Andropov alone at the top, but he was seriously ill. American experts regularly flew to Moscow to treat him.

Aleksei Kosygin died on December 18, 1980, but the party he had served so faithfully made no immediate announcement. The machine, and Brezhnev's personal entourage, did not want to spoil the general secretary's birthday on December 19. Brezhnev received lavish tributes, including the Order of the October Revolution. Not until December 21 did the Kremlin inform the world of Kosygin's death.

LAST POST: TWENTY-SIXTH PARTY CONGRESS

Hoping his own kidneys would improve, Yuri Andropov propped Brezhnev up and cast about for ways to take formal control without a fight. By the time the Twenty-Sixth Party Party Congress convened on Army-Navy Day (February 23), 1981, however, it had become impossible to conceal Brezhnev's infirmities. Although they stayed a respectful distance away, television cameras showed the general secretary trapped in decrepit old age.

The nation awaited vigorous new leadership. The economy needed a revolutionary overhaul. Nationalist unrest in Estonia, Azerbaijan, Kyrgyzia, and elsewhere sapped resources and patience. In the wake of the December 1979 invasion of Afghanistan, relations with the West and China plunged to their lowest level since 1962. The Afghan War demoralized both the Army and the people. Brezhnev was largely unaware that these events were taking place.

The Party Congress unfolded in "stability of cadres" fashion: Nothing happened. Save for a wistful call for a meeting with the new American president, Ronald Reagan, Brezhnev's abbreviated remarks had no substance. Barely able to read the speech, he defended Soviet policy vis-à-vis Poland and Afghanistan; otherwise he struck a conciliatory note. He blamed the collapse of détente and the 60 percent drop in bilateral trade on the United States. Soviet foreign policy had remained consistent, he declared, and dialogue could resume on condition it not touch on Poland or Afghanistan.

Brezhnev bragged of an enormous increase in labor productivity, claimed that the territorial production complexes were functioning satisfactorily, and spoke of "truly revolutionary possibilities" created by the development and introduction of microcomputers and industrial robots. But the regime's speechwriters could not ignore the stagnation in industry or the monumental problems of agriculture. Brezhnev called for more discipline, better leadership, and an end to the practice of adjusting plan targets downward. He warned again of the decline in energy reserves and spoke of the economic consequences of an increasingly severe labor shortage.

The eleventh Five-Year Plan of 1981–1985 would place a greater strain than ever on both human and material resources, but the party had no coherent program to deal with the crisis. It continued to advocate half-measures, tinker with the planning mechanism, exhort managers and workers to efficiency.

Brezhnev and Prime Minister Tikhonov demanded a revamping of the economy; how a party that refused to rejuvenate itself would accomplish that remained a mystery. For the first time in post-1917 history there was no change in the composition of the Politburo. The new Central Committee had 319 full members, up from 287. It included 231 holdovers—80 percent—from 1976 and seven members who had taken office after that year. Of the 81 newcomers, 37 had been candidate members. Among the new members were at least five KGB officials, including three who were part of a *KGB-Andropov* machine that had

formed inside the Brezhnevian original: Viktor Chebrikov, Georgi Tsinev, and Semyon Tsvigun. There were nine generals on the new Central Committee; only eight women; eleven genuine workers.

THE ARTS

The cultural avant-garde is always composed of people from marginal or even outcast groups whose personal histories are often irregular. The broad middle classes in the West and Japan have generally followed the lead of such people in popular music, dance, dress, and "lifestyle." The geriatrics who ran the USSR as their personal fiefdom hated these marginal types. Cultural innovation remained unacceptable; the slightest suggestion of moral or political deviation invariably triggered a brutal response. But as happens under repressive and corrupt regimes, the arts enjoyed a renaissance in the Troika-Brezhnev era.

Ever since Karl Marx, Communists had detested the village. Khrushchev and his immediate successors predicted the total urbanization of the USSR by the turn of the twenty-first century and literally did their best to destroy the villages. Thoughtful people warned of the loss of this "spiritual gold mine," a term coined by Fyodor Abramov, a feculent scribbler who claimed membership in the "rural school" of writers. Abramov had been a *Smersh* ("Death to Spies"—akin to SS Death's-head squads) killer in wartime. The school itself won wide respect. Vladimir Soloukhin wrote of the beauty and simplicity of rural life in central Russia. Valentin Rasputin and Sergei Zalygin limned Siberia. Chingiz Aitmatov glorified Kyrgyzia and Kazakhstan. Fazil Iskander popularized Abkhazia as the bucolic home of yoghurt-eating, wine-drinking people whose elders could remember the Crimean War: The Abkhaz have the world's highest proportion of centenarians. Yefim Dorosh wrote stories featuring heroic non-Communist peasant characters.

These writers made the hacks who controlled the Writers' Union writhe in discomfort. In the mid-1970s only the talentless half of the Union's membership of 2,000 were Communist party members. Belatedly realizing that the idealization of the village evoked doubts about Communist values, the CPSU tried to suppress the "rural school."

In 1969 the Writers' Union expelled one of Russia's greatest literary talents of the century, Aleksandr Solzhenitsyn. Protected to some extent by his international fame, Solzhenitsyn lived precariously after winning the Nobel Prize in 1970. Officially silenced, his influence as a writer waned, but he retained considerable moral authority. When his history of the Gulag appeared in the West, the regime sneered that his real name was "Solzhenitsker"—it has Jewish overtones—and denounced him as a traitor. It ignored the question of whether his account was true. The KGB-party-state drove Solzhenitsyn from the USSR in 1974.

Scores of poets, writers, and other artists followed Solzhenitsyn in an exodus resembling the flight from Nazi Germany: Mstislav Rostropovich, Galina Vishnevskaya, Mikhail Baryshnikov, Natalia Makarova, Maksim Shostakovich, Yuri Lyubimov, Joseph Brodsky, Vasily Aksyonov, Lev Kopelev, Georgi Vladimov, Vladimir Voinovich, Ernest Neizvestny, Andrei Tarkovsky, Viktor Korchnoi, Boris Spassky, and many others.

The good writers who remained succeeded in retaining their integrity under terrible conditions. In *The House on the Embankment* and other works, Yuri Trifonov argued that only through honest examination of the past could the country cleanse itself and move forward. Chingiz Aitmatov and Kaltai Mukhamedzhanov pursued this theme in *The Ascent of Mount Fuji.* Yuri Lyubimov, director of Moscow's Taganka Theatre, staged Mikhail

Bulgakov's *The Master and Margarita* in 1977, faithfully preserving the author's indictment of the spiritually desolate Communist system. When Lyubimov went to London in 1984 to stage a play, the "stupid little men" who had damaged Russian culture more than any foreign enemy refused to let him return to Russia.

Vasili Shukshin's *And in the Morning They Awakened,* which dealt with the monumental problem of alcohol abuse, also startled audiences. Aleksandr Gelman's *We, The Undersigned,* presented the "fixers" who wormed their way around production bottlenecks and moral dilemmas in a sympathetic light. Viktor Rozov's *Nest of Wood Grouse* attacked pompous, insensitive bureaucrats.

In 1979 nearly two dozen writers and poets collaborated on a *samizdat* venture titled *Metropol.* Vasili Aksyonov, Fazil Iskander, and three others served as editors. Bella Akhmadulina, Andrei Voznesensky, and the working-class bard Vladimir Vysotsky contributed poems. The collaborators insisted that *Metropol*—only 10 copies were produced—was strictly nonpolitical: It merely demanded the right of free artistic expression.

The Communists denounced the poems in *Metropol* that dealt with the Gulag, the stories of corruption, fictional accounts of sexual adventures, and the drawings of nudes, calling all this "pornography of the soul." The Writers' Union expelled two young contributors and sharply warned the others.

In the same year, the Writers' Union expressed "heartfelt thanks" to Leonid Brezhnev, whose hopelessly banal memoirs had had "an enormous influence on all types and genres of literature." Russia relished the perverse humor.

Seeking to upgrade Khrushchevian art criticism, in September 1974 the Moscow authorities bulldozed an unauthorized outdoor exhibition of "nonconformist" art. When photographs of the episode appeared around the world, the Kremlin dismissed a couple of officials and authorized a new exhibition whose works were no more avant-garde than Impressionism. More modern schools remained proscribed.

Conservatism reigned in classical music, where the Lysenko-like head of the Composers' Union, Tikhon Khrennikov, sought to freeze the clock in 1893—the year of Tchaikovsky's death. Orchestras did perform Shostakovich's works, but they only rarely dared touch the music of the brilliant young composers Edison Denisov, Aleksandr Knaifel, and Alfred Schnitke. Schnitke's *Latin Requiem Mass* finally had its triumphal Moscow première in the spring of 1980, several years after it was first heard in Budapest. Soviet audiences in general, however, became aware of Schnitke's genius chiefly through his many film scores, which rival those of Bernard Hermann. Knaifel and Denisov rarely worked in that medium.

Most of the 150 to 175 films made annually in the Troika-Brezhnev era had little to commend them. The Communists paid handsome commissions for quasi-documentary features like *Lenin in Poland, Lenin in Paris, Lenin Manuscripts, Conversation with Comrade Lenin,* and *The Living Lenin,* none of which left much doubt about the subject matter. Heavy-handed propaganda exercises such as *Our March, Banner Over the World,* and *The Internationale* played to nearly empty houses. With the aging of the heroic generations, the war-film genre was withering away. *Ordinary Fascism* had 479 showings to 118,000 people in Gorky in 1967; in the same year the American film *Some Like It Hot* had 1,037 showings to 268,000 viewers.

An outstanding young director was Andrei Tarkovsky, whose first film, *My Name Is Ivan* (1962), was a conventional portrayal of a young boy orphaned in the war. Its success, however, freed Tarkovsky to make the classic *Andrei Rublev* (1966). Harshly realistic, this study of the great icon painter who died in 1430 portrayed human beings as something other than class-struggle symbols; party watchdogs withdrew it from circulation. Tarkovsky's science-fiction *Solaris* (1972) and stream-of-consciousness *The Mirror* (1975) disappointed his admirers. In 1984, citing frustration over impossible working conditions in the USSR, Tarkovsky sought asylum in the West.

The immensely popular actor, director, and writer Vasili Shukshin composed "village prose" and translated several of the stories into successful films. *The Guelder-Rose* (1974) portrays a criminal who, after completing a prison term, tries to rehabilitate himself by moving from the corrupt city to the countryside. His old gang hunts him down and kills him. Enraptured audiences praised the screen treatment of corrupt Communist officials, bored workers sleeping during political lectures, and devoutly Christian peasants. Shortly before his premature death, Shukshin appeared in Gleb Panfilov's *I Want to Speak* (1976), which dealt with mindless bureaucrats, the painful Stalinist legacy, and spoiled youth. The authorities tolerated these films, but they preferred such trivial comedies as *The Quiet Bride* (1979) and *Moscow Does Not Believe in Tears* (1980).

DISSIDENTS AND "REFUSENIKS"

The failure to demolish the dissident movement in the mid-1960s reflected a peculiar kind of progress. After tormenting Andrei Sinyavsky and Yuli Daniel, the regime eventually allowed them to emigrate. Several individuals who publicly protested the invasion of Czechoslovakia likewise suffered under the blows of the KGB but survived and left the country. Solzhenitsyn escaped the fate of Mandelstam, Bulgakov, and other writers. All this made the lonely fate of people like Anatoli Marchenko and Yuri Orlov all the more agonizing.

In an unprecedented development, thousands of Soviet Jews received permission to leave the country before the collapse of détente sealed the borders. A group of Soviet citizens who demanded the right to monitor compliance with the human rights provisions of the Helsinki Final Act drew world attention to Kremlin hypocrisy. The regime imprisoned several members, accused others of having CIA connections, and silenced them all—but they had made their voices heard.

The Troika exiled Andrei Sakharov, the nuclear physicist who became its most articulate and respected critic, to Gorky (Nizhni Novgorod) on the Volga. Cut off from the outside world, his fate became a source of concern abroad and thus a chronic dilemma for the Kremlin.

There was little cohesion among the dissidents, no agreement on goals. Solzhenitsyn's conservative Russian nationalism and devotion to the Russian Orthodox Church appealed to some oppositionists but by no means all. Sakharov sometimes seemed aloof, and the Moscow and Leningrad intellectuals squabbled among themselves. The KGB penetrated most groups and placed several thousand agents among émigrés and "defectors."

The West, and in particular the United States, bought these KGB plants as eagerly as it had hired Gestapo and SS operatives after 1945. In 1979 more than 5,000 former Soviet citizens had "top-secret" security clearances in the United States, where they worked in the defense industry, the academic world, and on the staffs of some senior politicians.

The real dissidents were few in number. The Soviet public, which knew little of them, remained indifferent and even hostile. The rough suppression of the dissident movement seemed yet another grossly excessive application of force, but the authorities knew better than anyone that numbers often do not reflect the strength of ideas. Unwilling to take chances, the Kremlin moved against the dissidents, and in so doing made martyrs of some of them.

END OF THE BREZHNEV ERA

Leonid Brezhnev had both brought political stability and presided over the final stages of the USSR's ruinously expensive climb to superpower status. He remained in power because the machine he had constructed, though it had safeguards against plots and intrigues like the "Little October Revolution," lacked the ability to replicate itself. So long as it kept running, all was well. But now it had exhausted its fuel.

The last 20 months of Brezhnev's earthly existence were a bizarre collage of intrigue and scandal as the general secretary became an object of public and even Communist party derision orchestrated by Yuri Andropov. In December 1981 the play *Thus We Will Win* opened in Moscow. Set in October 1922, at one point the actor playing Lenin speaks emphatically of the need to curb the general secretary's power. The editors of the Leningrad literary journal *Avrora* (Aurora) dedicated the December 1981 issue to Brezhnev on his 75th birthday, and on page 75 they published a savage satire. An unnamed "wonderful writer" had astonished everyone by remaining alive long after he ought to have died. The narrator of the story reports that his daughter—who loved a joke—delighted him one day with the news that the writer had died, only to deflate him when she confessed the story was false. But the writer would surely die soon! Everyone had been waiting so long. . . .

Brezhnev's ghostwritten memoirs had recently won a Lenin Prize.

All the USSR knew that "stability of cadres" included the covering-up of malfeasance. Mikhail A. Suslov had done his best to limit the consequences, but his death at 79 in January

1982 opened the floodgates. The KGB arrested the passport office director and charged him with selling exit visas; the carefree days were over, at least for a while, at least at that level. On the same day the police seized a Moscow Circus employee and accused him of illegal financial dealings: This "Boris the Gypsy" was a close friend of Brezhnev's daughter.

The nation soon learned that the death six days before Suslov of a KGB official, Semyon Tsvigun, had been a suicide. Tsvigun had clashed with Suslov over the arrest of Brezhnev family intimates; Suslov opposed this step and prevailed. Career ruined, Tsvigun killed himself. It suddenly became clear why Suslov and Brezhnev did not sign Tsvigun's obituary in *Pravda*; Yuri Andropov and all top KGB officials did sign.

In March 1982 a Suslov protégé, Aleksei Shibayev, lost his job as head of the central trade union organization—always a crook's paradise and a job "Iron Shurik" once held. Fourteen months later Shibayev received a humiliating public reprimand for illegal financial dealings. In July an old Brezhnev friend, Sergei Medunov, who headed the Krasnodar party organization, was forced from office. When Brezhnev died, Andropov arrested Medunov on charges of corruption.

As *Thus We Will Win*, the *Avrora* article, high-profile arrests, and other developments indicated, Andropov and the KGB were impatient for Brezhnev to die. At Suslov's funeral, state television—always under strict KGB control—showed a tired, indifferent, disoriented Brezhnev. Two weeks later it focused at length on his uncontrollable weeping at another burial. The machine was not supposed to have, or certainly not to show, emotion.

Brezhnev suffered a stroke in March 1982, but he seemed to revive during his usual long summer vacation. In September, however, the KGB planted rumors that he was about to resign. The rumors gained strength when Brezhnev did not appear in public in October. Then, on November 7, he stood atop the Lenin Mausoleum to review the usual parade. Three days later, TV and radio suddenly, without explanation, interrupted regular evening programming to broadcast stately classical music. At eleven the next morning the CPSU announced that General Secretary Brezhnev had suffered a fatal cardiac arrest.

The party buried Leonid Brezhnev with pomp and circumstance, renamed a Volga River town "Brezhnevsk"—the original name, Riverbank Canoes, has since been restored—and forgot him, or tried to. Four years later, Mikhail Gorbachev would launch a public assault on the entire Brezhnev legacy.

Brezhnev had enjoyed greater uncoerced popularity inside the Communist party than any leader since Lenin, and the years between 1964 and 1982 had seen unprecedented political stability. Brezhnev shunned both Stalinist Terror and Khrushchevian bureaucratic confrontation. Guided by Yuri Andropov, he used the surviving islands in the Gulag, psychiatric hospitals, KGB thugs, social ostracism, and economic sanctions to achieve domestic tranquillity. Gorbachev said in November 1987 that the "process of restoring justice . . . [begun by the Twentieth and Twenty-Second Party Congresses] was actually suspended in the mid-1960s."

The year of Brezhnev's death saw the Soviet economic growth rate reach its lowest postwar level; and the previous year it had produced the smallest grain harvest in two decades. The economy was in shambles. But for the high world-market price for oil and the sale of oceans of alcohol, the Soviet treasury would have collapsed.

The living standard of the poorest stratum of the *working* population did improve, but retirees on fixed pensions subsisted on next to nothing. The *kolhoz* peasantry finally won ac-

Burial of Leonid Brezhnev, November 15, 1982. Pallbearers include Marshal Ustinov and Nikolai Tikhonov on the left, Andropov and Chernenko on the right. (ITAR-TASS)

cess to the state pension system and other social security benefits, and they received the identification papers ("passports") issued to all other USSR citizens.

The Soviet Union moved from military inferiority to parity with its great rival, the United States. The humiliation had ended, but as it developed, only temporarily. The Brezhnev machine had given the nation something that had eluded Lenin, Stalin, and Khrushchev; but its operators disappeared before the bill came due.

ANDROPOV

Who would replace Brezhnev? No mechanism for doing so existed in the Communist party,

which had placed power in the office of general secretary. According to the rules, the Central Committee controlled that office; in practice, the Politburo made a recommendation, and the Central Committee endorsed its choice. When there was a split, as with the 1957 "anti-party group," grave problems arose. Khrushchev had no defenders in October 1964, and harmony had reigned since then.

No KGB chief had ever been a serious candidate for the top post, but Yuri Andropov had begun a move when he delivered the main speech on the anniversary of Lenin's birth in April 1982. In May he joined the Central Committee Secretariat and resigned as chairman of the KGB. His replacement, Vitaly K. Fedorchuk, continued the investigation of shady practices among high officials—except for

Politburo members Grishin, Romanov, Kunayev, and Aliyev.

Andropov installed himself as general secretary-designate in July 1982, when, during one of Brezhnev's absences from Politburo meetings, he simply took the general secretary's chair. Konstantin Chernenko, who had wanted, and been promised, that seat, meekly accepted defeat.

Within 48 hours of Brezhnev's death, the Central Committee approved the Politburo's unanimous choice, Andropov, as the new general secretary. Indelibly stained with Hungarian and Gulag blood, Andropov had been a worthy successor to Dzerzhinsky, Yagoda, Yezhov, and Beria at the KGB. As general secretary, he would be no disgrace to Stalin.

In a "disinformation" campaign begun in 1979, the KGB attempted to portray the chief Chekist as a friend of reform and free speech, patron of the arts, poet, connoisseur of single-malt scotch whiskies. One admirer who fed this line to gullible Western government officials, journalists, and professors, Roy Medvedev, called Andropov "an outwardly urbane and civilized leader, a man of intellectual interests . . . fond of painting and music, fluent in English, German, and Hungarian . . . a good conversationalist."

As the "Dnepropetrovsk mafia's" rampant corruption became an uncontainable national scandal, the morale of the young generation of bureaucrats—junior members of the *nomenklatura*—sank out of sight. Only the military leaders and the truly Neanderthal fundamentalists approved Brezhnev-era economic priorities. Some mid-level officials, including Mikhail Gorbachev, looked to Andropov for reform. They, and Andropov himself, believed passionately in Soviet communism. Andropov knew the extent of bureaucratic improbity better than anyone, and he and his supporters believed that as general secretary he could eradicate it.

These hopes quickly faded. Gravely ill when he assumed power, Andropov cracked down on some Brezhnevian corruption, but his prescription for reviving the economy remained on the Bulganin level: More party intervention. His methods had the merit of openly acknowledging the rule of the KGB.

Irrational economic theory, and the gargantuan military buildup, had distorted the economy beyond recognition. As the economist Vasily Selyunin wrote early in 1988,

truly tectonic shifts toward manufacture of producer goods . . . have put us in a paradoxical situation where accelerated rates of development and more rapid growth in national income have little effect on the standard of living. More and more the economy works for itself, rather than for man.

Noting the USSR's long-standing supremacy in most branches of heavy industry, another observer called in question the need for stupendous quantities of steel and heavy machinery:

What good is it [Otto Latsis asked] that we produce 6.5 times more tractors than the United States? Or 16 times more grain-harvesting combines? You can't eat tractors and combines . . . despite our abundance of combines, we harvest only two-thirds as much grain [as the U.S.].

Decades of "more is better" had yielded an indigestible glut. In 1928, the last year of the NEP, 60.5 percent of output went into consumer goods. By 1985 the figure had fallen to 25.2 percent, and the USSR was supporting a space-age military machine on the back of a Third-World civilian economy. Her manned rockets soared into space, but Russia could not properly feed, clothe, or house herself, let alone provide quality disposable-income items.

Yuri Andropov would be remembered not for genuine reforms—there were none—but for the KGB-police sweeps that struck the cities when he took over. Hunting for people who had left work to attend to personal business, squads swooped down on that fixture of Soviet life, long lines—for everything—and demanded identification papers and authority to be absent from work. The squads crashed into restaurants, cinemas, parks, public baths, sports arenas, barber shops, beauty parlors, department stores, factories, public transportation, and offices in search of shirkers. The raids extended to innocent pedestrians and visitors to maternity hospitals. Another sinister method of flexing secret police muscle resurrected a Lenin–Stalin tactic: In factories, mines, workshops, offices, schools, ships at sea, and schools, "black boxes" appeared. The KGB was inviting anonymous complaints and especially denunciations.

Andropov admirers in Russia and abroad pointed to the shake-up in party and government as evidence of reform. In less than 15 months as General Secretary, Andropov replaced about a quarter of the 150 *oblast* (province) heads and removed 19 of 84 members of the Council of Ministers. The average age of the dismissed: 67.3 years.

Andropov ousted Nikolai Shchelokov as interior minister—in effect the national police chief—and replaced him with KGB Chairman Vitaly Fedorchuk. Notorious for bribe-taking during the Shchelokov years, the police had earned public contempt. The massive KBG investigation Fedorchuk had begun would continue under his successor, Viktor Chebrikov, and hundreds of high-ranking police officials, including Brezhnev's son-in-law, would go to prison.

Andropov cracked down severely on nonconformist artists, dissidents, members of religious sects, and citizens who sought to emigrate. He urged thousands of poor Jews from the Caucasus and Central Asia to leave the USSR. With limited education, many of these people were not equipped to survive the forced expatriation; but the KGB could claim that anyone who wanted to leave the USSR was free to go. In flagrant violation of the Helsinki Accords, the regime refused to allow most educated Jews and for that matter other ethnic groups, especially Russians, to emigrate, even to reunite divided families.

Andropov ordered the terror-bombing of Afghan villages in rebel-controlled areas and the indiscriminate strewing of millions of camouflaged anti-personnel mines—small children were especially vulnerable—over the landscape. Relations with the West deteriorated to the lowest level in three decades, then descended still further in September 1983, when a Soviet fighter aircraft shot down an unarmed Korean Air Lines (KAL) passenger plane, killing 269 Korean and American citizens. Claiming the plane was spying on military installations, the Andropov regime refused to apologize. Soviet Navy divers, however, recovered the flight recorders, which indicated that a navigational error had led KAL 007 off course. In November 1992 Boris Yeltsin formally expressed regret to the South Korean government and the victims' families, but the story would take another bizarre turn. Criticizing his predecessor, Gorbachev, for withholding them, Yeltsin gave the bright orange "black boxes" to the South Korean government. They were empty. Russian officials said they would give the tapes to the International Civil Aviation Organization.

In 1993 the pilot who destroyed KAL 007 admitted, and the Kremlin confirmed, that Soviet commanders all the way up the chain of command had known exactly what they were doing. In November 1996 that pilot told journalists his only regret was that he had received too small a bonus—about 400 rubles (thirty dollars)—for downing the plane.

Responding to the threat of nuclear-tipped Soviet rockets aimed at Western Europe, in the autumn of 1983 NATO deployed cruise missiles—which could strike targets in the USSR—in four of the targeted countries. Andropov immediately broke off bilateral talks aimed at reducing the numbers of these weapons and also of long-range (strategic) missiles. He transferred missiles from Central Asia and Siberia—where they threatened China—to Belarus, and pointed them at NATO's European partners.

Warning of a "runaway" nuclear-arms race, Andropov sped down the track, and President Reagan was also buying weapons at an unprecedented rate. The verbal exchanges between Moscow and Washington grew ever more heated; hopes for the revival of détente disappeared.

Relations with China did not improve. The two sides made no progress on border issues or trade disputes, and Moscow's war in Afghanistan, and support for the Vietnamese incursion into Cambodia, worsened tensions.

In the summer of 1983, Andropov disappeared from public view. His protégé, Mikhail Gorbachev, ran the party and the state for 176 days until Andropov died from kidney failure in February 1984. Roy Medvedev said, "Most of our people will recall . . . [his] death with regret for many years." There were those who believed that.

CHERNENKO

The Communist party buried Andropov between Dzerzhinsky and Kalinin near the Kremlin wall. A few hours earlier, the Central Committee, following the Politburo's recommendation, had elected the nearly comatose Konstantin Chernenko to succeed him.

Born in Siberia in 1911, Chernenko claimed the nationality of his Russian mother rather than that of his Ukrainian father. According to his official biography, he worked as a hired laborer for kulaks during the NEP period, became a Komsomol official, and served in the secret police Border Guards on the frontier with China in the early 1930s. He joined the Communist party in 1931.

Chernenko did not serve in the military during the war, not even as a political officer like Khrushchev and Brezhnev. He sat out the conflict as a petty official in Siberia and then as a student at the Higher School for Party Organizers in Moscow. This profile proved embarrassing when he became general secretary. Trying to inflate his unremarkable Border Guards duty into an heroic saga, the CPSU published glowing reviews of a documentary film that highlighted that episode.

Chernenko became a soldier in Brezhnev's "Dnepropetrovsk mafia" in 1950. When Brezhnev moved to Moscow in 1956, Chernenko went along, and he became head of the CPSU General Department shortly after Brezhnev replaced Khrushchev as first (general) secretary. Newspapers regularly published photographs showing Chernenko at Brezhnev's side lighting his cigarettes, steadying his elbow, straightening his tie, indicating where to sign. Modestly educated and inarticulate, Chernenko peaked as Brezhnev's alter ego, his super-valet. When Brezhnev died, the Politburo chose Andropov to replace him.

That was November 1982. In February 1984, no candidate had enough strength to unseat the Brezhnevists; protracted debate over the six months of Andropov's terminal illness did not produce agreement. The Politburo named Chernenko head of the Andropov funeral commission—general secretary-designate. But over the three days it took to reach this decision, the USSR had no real leader. As in the 1991 "Vodka Putsch," the briefcase with the nuclear-war codes was in the hands of Kremlin guards.

A British physician-politician who met Chernenko at the Andropov funeral detected signs of emphysema. A lifelong cigarette-smoker and more than social drinker, Chernenko suffered from heart disease, cirrhosis of the liver, arteriosclerosis, and other ailments; he often seemed disoriented. Andrei Gromyko, his voice picked up by a microphone, admonished the new general secretary not to remove his hat during the burial ceremony for Andropov.

But the Brezhnevist old guard, of which Andropov for all his power had never been a member, triumphed one last time. It included Chernenko himself, Grishin, Kunayev, Solomentsev, Tikhonov, and Ustinov, and the Ukrainian leader V. V. Shcherbitsky cooperated on major issues. Andrei Gromyko, at 75 the old guard's coeval, had survived as foreign minister since 1957 because he did *not* attach himself to any particular faction; he obeyed orders. The average age of the old guard was nearly 72, then a decade beyond the life expectancy of the average Soviet male. CPSU politicians were not renowned for leading healthy lives, but they were strong enough to block the rise of younger politicians such as Gorbachev, 53, and Grigori Romanov, 61.

Following the pattern established by Brezhnev and maintained by Andropov, Chernenko also became head of state. Military policy in general and conduct of the war in Afghanistan in particular devolved on the aged Defense Minister Dmitri Ustinov, who simply pushed ahead blindly. Ustinov suffered a stroke in September 1984 and died three months later.

Nearly a year passed before Moscow tacitly acknowledged that the emplacement of American medium-range missiles in Western Europe had thwarted its attempt to tilt the balance of power on the Continent. Only in January 1985, with Chernenko manifestly on his last legs, did the USSR agree to resume arms negotiations.

A Moscow joke had subway conductors calling out, "Next stop Chernenko—transfer from Brezhnev to Andropov!" But the train had passed Andropov, and was about to leave Chernenko.

Elevated beyond his capabilities when Brezhnev brought him to Moscow in 1956, Chernenko did not even have the grace to recognize this. Confronted with a problem, he denied its existence or, Bulganin-like, prescribed greater party intervention. Foreign policy consisted of building more rockets and tanks. To deal with the steel glut, produce more steel. If *kolhozes* and *sovhozes* could not feed the country, the state would create more *kolhozes* and *sovhozes* and operate them the same way. If artists and writers and intellectuals clamored for freedom, beat the hell out of them. If some comrades lined their pockets, give them even greater opportunities.

Chernenko paid lip service to Andropov's program to reduce the swollen state bureaucracy but canceled his predecessor's plans to trim *party* staff by 20 percent. "Stability of cadres" policy remained valid, CPSU privileges inviolable.

In November 1984 the enquiry into the Interior Ministry scandal led to Shchelokov's demotion and dismissal. He committed suicide. Normally this would have created a sensation, but the Chernenko deathwatch had begun. Under Mikhail Gorbachev's direction, the Secretariat conducted almost all state and party business.

Chernenko died on March 10, 1985, and the third change of leadership in 28 months finally broke the old guard's back. The Central Committee chose the dynamic young Andropov protégé, Mikhail Gorbachev, to lead the country out of stagnation. Andrei Gromyko said that Gorbachev had a nice smile but "iron teeth."

SUGGESTED ADDITIONAL READINGS

AKSYONOV, VASILY, ed. *Metropol.* New York: W. W. Norton, 1983.

ANDERSON, JOHN. *Religion, State, and Politics in the Soviet Union and Successor States.* New York: Cambridge University Press, 1994.

BREZHNEVA, LUBA. *The World I Left Behind.* New York: Random House, 1995.

GORBACHEV, MIKHAIL. *Memoirs.* New York: Doubleday, 1995.

LOWENHARDT, JOHN, JAMES OZINGA, and ERIK VAN

REE. *The Rise and Fall of the Soviet Politburo.* New York: St. Martin's Press, 1992.

ORLOV, YURI. *Dangerous Thoughts: Memoirs of a Russian Life.* New York: William Morrow, 1991.

SATTER, DAVID. *Age of Delusion.* New York: Knopf, 1996.

VOZLENSKY, MICHAEL. *Nomenklatura: The Soviet Ruling Class.* Garden City, NY: Doubleday, 1984.

21

FOREIGN POLICY, 1964–1985

The Troika leadership and then Leonid Brezhnev accelerated the stupendous expansion of Soviet military that Nikita Khrushchev began. Echoing NATO's justification of its own titanic arsenal, the USSR called the buildup wholly defensive. The Soviets might face two adversaries simultaneously. No matter what the cost, they wanted a war-making capability equal to that of the West and China *combined*.

THE EAST EUROPEAN EMPIRE

In the tradition of medieval Russian churchmen who proclaimed Moscow the "third and final Rome," the Soviets claimed to be sole leaders of the world Communist movement. The 1948 defection of Yugoslavia shook that claim; the break with China destroyed it.

Romanian Communist leaders seized on the Moscow–Beijing quarrel to get out from under Soviet domination. Attempting to mediate between the two giants in 1964, they built an independent foreign policy that the Troika tolerated because it approved Bucarest's domestic Stalinism.

The Communists of Bulgaria, Moscow's ideal satellite, tried to make their country the sixteenth Soviet republic, and the Bulgarian writer Georgi Markov paid with his life for denouncing this betrayal. Oleg Kalugin, a KGB officer who later became another of the West's

darlings, provided the assassin with a ricin-tipped umbrella. Markov, who lived and worked in London, had written that the Bulgarian Communists polluted their country with the "Soviet chemicals of ruthless demoralization and moral corruption."

Hungary's value as an ally diminished after the 1956 revolt. Three years after that heroic episode, Hungarian Communists who had cooperated in the Soviet slaughter experimented with economic liberalization. They labeled their efforts "socialist" and trumpeted their fealty to Marxism–Leninism and Moscow. In 1968 the Hungarian regime installed a "new economic mechanism" designed by young, Western-oriented economists; it abolished the Soviet-style command economy in favor of a decentralized market system faintly reminiscent of the NEP.

The Czechoslovaks did not master the Hungarian method of crooning Marxist–Leninist lullabies while doing whatever was best for Czechoslovakia. This failure doomed the 1968 democratic-socialist "Prague Spring."

Only in late 1967 did Moscow concede that the Prague Stalinists had outlived their usefulness and sanction their dismissal. The forward-looking young Communists who then came to power democratized the party, abolished censorship, and curbed the secret police. They launched an investigation of past abuses and said they wanted a multiparty system. Led by Alexander Dubček, the reformers pledged loyalty to the USSR but were not as convincing as the Hungarians.

The reformers' "socialism with a human face" won widespread sympathy in the West and generated apprehension in Moscow. The Troika feared that the reforms might inspire imitation. As the "Prague Spring" blossomed into summer, the Moscow winter gathered momentum.

The USSR proclaimed the right to intervene militarily in any Warsaw Pact nation where "internal and external forces hostile to socialism" threatened to push that nation "toward restoration of a capitalist regime." Like the American version associated with President James Monroe, the "Brezhnev Doctrine" codified a great power's hegemony. Soviet and other Warsaw Pact forces invaded Czechoslovakia on August 20, 1968. Resistance quickly ceased. In the brutal reincorporation of Czechoslovakia into the Soviet empire, Yuri Andropov, now head of the KGB, played a major role.

Marches and demonstrations protesting the Soviet attack took place in many Polish cities. Unable to quell them, and anyway anxious to distance itself from its own economic catastrophe, the Gomulka regime slunk out of office in 1970. A new crowd under Edward Gierek, a former miner, promised reform and modernization. This necessitated foreign loans: Poland's debt to Western banks leaped

from $1.1 billion in January 1971 to $22.3 billion in December 1982. Gierek seemed to have some success in 1971–1975; the net material product—roughly, GNP minus services—grew at an average annual rate of more than 9 percent, far better than the Soviet performance.

The consequences of living on borrowed money began to catch up with Warsaw, which had not used the funds rationally. Polish Communist party bosses squandered billions on projects designed to enrich themselves, reward cronies, extend fiefdoms, and build technologically backward industrial plants. The growth rate fell below 3 percent between 1976 and 1980; industrial production dropped almost 25 percent 1979–1982.

A sharp increase in meat prices in July 1980 touched off strikes and demonstrations that continued for the next year and a half. Unofficial labor organizations arose all over Poland. In September 1980 they merged into a single national industrial trade union, Solidarity, which had arisen in the Gdańsk shipyards. The "Mother Country of All Workers," the USSR, demanded the regime disband it.

In a decision unprecedented in the Communist bloc, a Warsaw court conferred legitimacy on Solidarity in October 1980. The Kremlin summoned Polish party officials to Moscow and warned them it might intervene. The situation seemed to stabilize, then the strikes resumed in February 1981. *Pravda* accused Solidarity of being funded by the CIA. Late in a tumultuous summer, a Solidarity Congress in Gdańsk demanded free trade unions and free elections throughout Moscow's empire. When Soviet fleet exercises offshore failed to intimidate the meeting, the Kremlin ordered the Polish Communists to take action. General Wojciech Jaruzelski, already prime minister and minister of defense, assumed leadership of the Polish Communist party and prepared for a showdown.

Solidarity and its charismatic leader, Lech

Walesa, posed a threat to Communist domination of Poland and in general to Moscow's hold on Eastern Europe. But as Mark Kramer has noted, recently opened archives indicate that Soviet leaders "were extremely reluctant to use military force . . . and were desperate to achieve an 'internal' solution." An invasion would generate massive protests, not least because a Polish clergyman was now Pope.* And Moscow was bogged down in a costly, confusing war in Afghanistan.

But patience and options had their limits, and General Jaruzelski stepped up the pressure. In December 1981, trade union leaders proposed establishment of a provisional non-Communist regime and free elections. Jaruzelski proclaimed martial law, outlawed Solidarity, and arrested its leaders and thousands of workers, intellectuals, and students.

Though spared the horrors of invasion, Poland was morally shattered. Once again her identity, so thoroughly rooted in Western civilization, threatened to disappear. As it happened, the reprisals involved less bloodshed than in Hungary in 1956 or Czechoslovakia in 1968. For all his unquestioned brutality, Jaruzelski seemed not the worst of Poland's Communists. But then came the barbaric October 1984 murder of a Polish priest associated with Solidarity, Father Jerzy Popieluszko. At their trial, the Polish security agents who beat the courageous Roman Catholic priest to death admitted acting on orders "from a very high level." Like their Bulgarian counterparts, the Polish secret police coordinated in the

closest possible manner with the KGB. At the time, former KGB Director Andropov was now General Secretary of the CPSU; Mikhail Gorbachev almost never left his side.

In April 1989 the Jaruzelski regime agreed to the restoration of Solidarity as a legal organization.

Soviet efforts to build an economic empire in Eastern Europe failed. Stalin had created a Council for Mutual Economic Assistance (CMEA, or Comecon) to mask the colonization, but toward the end of the 1950s the East European countries ceased to be profitable. The upheavals of 1956 led to renegotiation of the one-sided trade agreements. Reciprocal trade among CMEA countries—the East European satellites, Cuba, Mongolia, the USSR, and Vietnam—increased substantially. When the price of oil and natural gas soared in the 1970s, the East Europeans went heavily into debt to Moscow.

To deal with that debt and defuse social unrest, the Kremlin reversed normal imperialist procedure: It now sent cheap raw materials to Eastern Europe and imported manufactured goods from them. The fact that most of the goods were of inferior quality increased this de facto subsidy, which stood at about $1.6 billion in 1973 and increased to $20 billion in 1981. But the subsidy did not offset higher energy prices, and the East European countries were also in debt to the West; that collective debt rose from $6 billion in 1970 to $55 billion in 1984.

MOSCOW AND BEIJING

The Soviet Troika's failure to patch up relations with China proved that the dispute hinged not on ideology but on the power struggle in the Communist movement. Underlying that was the unresolved dispute over huge territories in the Far East, Mongolia, and Central Asia. Lenin had denounced the tsarist

---

*After 1953, the KGB's so-called "wet affairs" (murders) always required top-level sanction. Former KGB General Oleg Kalugin said in 1993 that his superiors at the KGB had ordered him to prepare the poison and the device used to murder the writer Georgi Markov in London in September 1978. It is inconceivable that the Bulgarian secret police would have orchestrated the May 1981 attempt on the life of Pope John Paul II in St. Peter's Square without also turning to the KGB. Only circumstantial evidence links Yuri Andropov directly to these affairs, but like Thoreau's trout in the milk, it is enough.

"unequal treaties" with China, but he and his successors refused to renegotiate them.

The Chinese Communists were determined to settle ancient scores a slice at a time. They did not demand the immediate return of 1.5 million km² they said the tsars had stolen but did insist Moscow acknowledge the treaties as having been imposed by force. They demanded extensive adjustments along the border and declared that Mongolia, a Soviet satellite, belonged within the Chinese sphere of influence. The Soviets responded that they bore no more responsibility for the sins of the tsars than Mao did for those of the Chinese emperors. The Kremlin position was that the treaties were simply part of history, like British rule in Hong Kong. The Mongolian People's Republic, Moscow swore, was independent.

The Soviet and Mongolian frontiers with China extend about 7,500 kilometers. In 1962, thousands of Chinese soldiers and civilians crossed the border at many points seeking to "absorb" sections of territory. More incursions took place in the next two years; the clashes with Soviet Border Guards produced substantial casualties.

The two sides exchanged topographic maps in Khabarovsk in 1964. The Chinese versions showed hundreds of border rectifications in Beijing's favor; some moved the line 150 kilometers into the USSR. Moscow insisted that the Chinese claims had "no juridical foundation whatsoever . . . and do not coincide with lines fixed by . . . treaties." The talks collapsed.

The situation deteriorated. Knowing that the Chinese were about to test a rocket capable of packing a nuclear warhead, the Kremlin revised the 1966 Soviet–Mongolian treaty. Moscow's forces had long been stationed in Mongolia; now the Kremlin despatched more infantry, tanks, and antiaircraft batteries equipped with tactical nuclear weapons. This arsenal was only 600 kilometers from Beijing.

Mao's Cultural Revolution, which began in May 1966, exacerbated the already tense relations between Beijing and Moscow. Moscow police broke up a demonstration by Chinese students in Red Square in January 1967. Red Guards in Beijing retaliated by besieging the Soviet Embassy and forcing the humiliating evacuation of diplomatic dependents. China called the USSR a "most reactionary and savage fascist dictatorship."

In March 1969, violent skirmishes took place on Damyansky (Zhenbao) Island in the Ussuri River 400 kilometers north of Vladivostok. More than 800 Chinese and 60 Soviet soldiers died; threats of war filled the northeast Asian air. The Kremlin accused Beijing of obtaining arms from West Germany and called Mao a "traitor to communism." The Soviet media broadcast American charges that China was selling 8,000 tons of opium a year to earn hard currency. Brezhnev attacked China at the June 1969 International Conference of Communist and Workers' Parties in Moscow. The Romanian, Italian, and other delegations succeeded in muting the final communiqué's criticism.

In late summer 1969 a KGB journalist declared that China was not exempt from Brezhnev Doctrine. It was "common knowledge," he wrote, that Moscow was prepared to destroy the Chinese nuclear weapons center in Xinjiang Province. *Pravda* warned that Beijing was risking nuclear war. General V. F. Tolbuko, a rocket specialist, took command of the Soviet Far Eastern Military District. The Kremlin shifted nuclear missiles from Belarus and Ukraine, where they had been targeted on Western Europe, to Central Asia and the Far East.

After Ho Chi Minh's funeral in Hanoi in September 1969, Aleksei Kosygin stopped in Beijing on his way home. He and Zhou Enlai agreed to negotiate the border dispute and other issues. High-ranking delegations began talks in October; the two sides exchanged ambassadors. But an ominous cloud—in Moscow's view—appeared on the horizon:

Rapprochement between China and the United States.

The situation did not improve after Mao Zedong's death in September 1976. The two sides could not agree on an agenda for the border talks, and Moscow rejected Beijing's demand that it withdraw its forces from the disputed districts. China turned down proposals for a nonaggression pact. In April 1979, shortly after reestablishing full diplomatic relations with the United States, Beijing announced it would not renew the 1950 Sino–Soviet Treaty of Friendship, Alliance, and Mutual Assistance when it expired in 1980.

Calling the USSR the greatest threat to world peace, the Chinese Communists sought a grand alliance with the United States, Japan, Western Europe, and some Third World countries against Soviet imperialism. When in February 1979 China invaded a Soviet ally, Vietnam, the Kremlin condemned the attack. The Soviet invasion of Afghanistan later the same year drove China closer to the United States.

The Soviets banked on President Ronald Reagan's hostility toward Communist China to cool the romance. Brezhnev regularly reminded the Chinese that the USSR had always supported their claim to Taiwan, and he held out the prospect of increased trade and aid. Mongolia agreed in the spring of 1982 to discuss the resurveying of its border with China. A wary Beijing repeated its conditions for better relations with Moscow: Pullback of Soviet and Mongolian forces on the frontiers, withdrawal of Soviet forces from Afghanistan, and cessation of Soviet support for the Vietnamese intervention in Cambodia. Brezhnev, and later Andropov and Chernenko, rejected these stipulations.

THE MIDDLE EAST

The USSR and the United States often confronted each other through unpredictable, reckless surrogates in the Middle East. Neither power had a coherent policy for dealing with Arab nationalism, Muslim religious fundamentalism, or ancient conflicts between peoples and religions.

The decisive Israeli victory in the 1967 Middle East War alarmed and humiliated the Kremlin. Soviet arms proved inferior, Soviet-trained Arab troops performed badly, and no one could blame the disaster on Khrushchev. Moscow had to start again. Arms deliveries to Egypt, Syria, and Iraq increased; the USSR sent matériel and new teams of advisers to rebuild Arab armies.

Egypt's expulsion of 20,000 Soviet military specialists in 1972 slowed but did not halt the rearming. The Arabs gave a better account of themselves in the 1973 October War against Israel, not least because Moscow's new hardware proved a match for U.S.- and French-made Israeli tanks and aircraft. The Kremlin recovered some prestige. In most Arab states, however, the Communist party remained outlawed. Where it was legal, the regimes infiltrated it with spies and restricted its movements.

Syria proved as difficult a friend as did Egypt. When the Baath (Renaissance) party came to power in 1966, Syria began making common cause with the USSR in Middle Eastern politics. After the expulsion of its advisers from Egypt, Moscow built up Syria as a counterweight to Israel. The Syrians, however, suffered more severe losses than did the Egyptians in the 1973 war. The Soviets sent new tanks, a large military advisory group, MiG-23 fighters, and surface-to-air missiles.

Hostile to the Arab League's intervention in Lebanon, the Kremlin withheld arms deliveries to Syria briefly in 1976, only to resume them when U.S. shipments to Israel upset the regional military balance. Syria broke with the Soviet-backed leader of the Palestinian Liberation Organization (PLO), Yasir Arafat, and over strenuous Kremlin objections sided with

Iran in its war with Iraq between 1980 and 1988.

THE PERSIAN GULF

Napoleon had urged the Russians to look south, toward the Persian Gulf and the Indian Ocean, to expand their territory. That would keep them out of the Mediterranean, where France claimed hegemony. And it had the added benefit of bringing them into conflict with Britain. The tsars sometimes followed Napoleon's advice, but they also moved southwest into the Balkans, in the direction of Constantinople.

Agreeing in principle to adhere to a Four-Power Pact with Germany, Italy, and Japan, in November 1940 Moscow stated as a condition "that the area south of Batum and Baku in the general direction of the Persian Gulf is recognized as the center of the aspirations of the Soviet Union." The immediate Soviet object was Iran (Persia).

A 1921 Moscow–Tehran treaty had specified that, "If the Persian Government, having been alerted by the Russian Soviet Government, is not itself able to avert the danger [from a third country], the Russian Soviet Government will have the right to send its forces into the territory of Persia in order, in the interests of self-defense, to take the necessary military measures." Stalin cited this treaty to justify keeping his troops in northern Iran until May 1946. Moscow refused to accept Iran's unilateral renunciation of the USSR's right to intervene.

When the British withdrew from the Persian Gulf in the late 1960s, Shah Muhammed Reza Pahlavi, backed by London and Washington, assumed the role of area policeman. Though suspicious of this megalomaniac, the Arab states welcomed his efforts to eradicate Communist influence. The shah armed Iran with expensive Western weapons and paid for them by raising the price of his oil. Some grand strategic thinkers in Washington had given him permission.

Those strategists played a major role in giving the world the 1973–1974 energy crisis. Petroleum prices soared, and the Persian Gulf became the object of intensified Western and Soviet attention. Kosygin warned in November 1973 that the USSR—the largest oil producer—faced a shortage and might have to increase Middle Eastern and Persian Gulf imports well above 1972's six million tons, or 2 percent of Soviet consumption.

Despite their differences, the Soviet Communists and the shah maintained reasonably cordial relations. Iranian natural gas went to the USSR through a jointly owned and operated pipeline, and Iranian oil fueled Soviet factories and military installations in Central Asia and the Caucasus. The two regimes sometimes cooperated in attempts to bring Kurdish nomads under control and give them the benefits of acquaintance with the KGB and the shah's secret police.

Shiite Muslim fundamentalists led by the Ayatollah Ruollah Khomeini overthrew the shah early in 1979. The Soviets relished the discomfort of the United States, which lost its staunchest regional puppet and suffered the ignominy of having dozens of diplomats held hostage for more than a year. But the Khomeini regime proclaimed itself "Neither East nor West!"

Concern about the effect of the Iranian revolution in particular, and the Islamic revival in general, on the 50 million Soviet citizens of Muslim heritage, figured in the Kremlin decision to invade Afghanistan. Soviet radio broadcasts from Baku hinted that Iran might suffer the same fate. The Kremlin had long wanted to unite the three million Azeri Turks in northwest Iran with the five million in Soviet Azerbaijan, and Moscow had briefly established an "independent" Azeri state in northwest Iran in 1945–1946. In the Iran–Iraq war, the Kremlin's neutral stance outraged Iranian fundamentalists bent on *jihad.*

Still convinced they knew the world's destiny, and that every country's history mimicked Russia's, the Soviet Communists considered Khomeini not Lenin but Kerensky. They groomed the Iranian Tudeh (Communist) party to take control of the revolution. But Khomeini outlawed Tudeh, expelled Soviet diplomats, and stepped up support of the anti-Soviet guerrillas in Afghanistan.

The Kremlin also had to deal gingerly with Iraq, a fiercely anti-Communist country with the most volatile political tradition in the Arab world. Iraq had the region's largest Communist party, but after a 1963 coup d'état the new military rulers imprisoned thousands of party members and executed many others. When Baghdad later sought better relations with the USSR, the ban on the Communist party remained in effect. Moscow sent technicians and engineers to help construct a modern naval base near the head of the Persian Gulf; in exchange for docking facilities, the Soviets sent arms.

Soviet policies appeared to backfire when hostilities erupted between Iraq and Iran. For all its mischief-making, the Kremlin did not want war in an area where American, West European, Japanese, South African, and Israeli interests converged. About 70 percent of Western Europe's oil passed through the Gulf and the Strait of Hormuz, as did 90 percent of Japan's, almost all of South Africa's and Israel's. American imports declined after the fall of the shah, but every American President since Roosevelt had warned that Washington would resist any attempt to block the Gulf.

The Soviet Union declared itself neutral, suspended arms deliveries to Iraq, and tried unsuccessfully to mediate. Only when President Saddam Hussein threatened to mend Iraq's relations with the United States—broken off after the 1967 Middle East War—did the Kremlin resume weapons shipments.

Moscow registered one of its rare long-term successes in the Arab world in Yemen, with which it established cordial relations in 1955. Both Britain and Egypt opposed communism in the Arabian Peninsula, however, and tried to halt its spread. But Egypt's Gamal Abdel Nasser had to withdraw his troops after the 1967 war with Israel, and Britain ended its police mission east of Suez. This enabled the USSR to intervene in the 1967 Yemeni civil war. In the ensuing partition, the extreme left-wing Southern Yemen regime allied with the Soviet Union, which gained the use of the port of Aden and an airfield. The Yemeni-controlled island of Socotra near the entrance to the Gulf of Aden lay at the Soviet Navy's disposal.

AFGHANISTAN

After 1945 the sleepy feudal monarchy of Afghanistan, which borders on the Soviet Union, Iran, China, and Pakistan, found itself swept into the vortexes of Persian Gulf, East Asian, and South Asian politics. The Soviets built roads and tunnels in the high mountains. The Chinese constructed the Karakorum Highway from Xinjiang through Afghanistan to Pakistan. The United States spent huge sums on various major construction projects. None of this did much to improve the lives of the Afghani peoples: Attached to every kilometer of road and cubic meter of concrete were political strings. The Afghani cultural heritage meant nothing to the outside rivals.

Under the monarchy, Western influence dominated the government and the tiny intelligentsia. With the 1973 ouster of King Muhammad Zahir Shah and the proclamation of a republic, however, what had never been a united, coherent nation totally disintegrated. The People's Democratic party (Communist) came to power in an April 1978 coup d'état; it signed a 20-year Treaty of Friendship, Good-

Neighborliness, and Cooperation with the Kremlin. Moscow sent economic and military aid; its advisers and technicians had free run of the country.

But the Soviets were never popular, in part because they spent less than the CIA-subsidized Americans. The formation of a Communist regime in Kabul did not alter that. In the spring of 1979 more than 200 Soviet advisers perished in riots in Herat. Attacks on Soviet personnel induced many to wear "cowboy" garb in the attempt to pass as Americans.

Events elsewhere conspired against Afghanistan. The Soviets feared U.S. military intervention in Iran after the seizure of the American Embassy in Tehran in November 1979. The following month, the NATO Council approved an American plan to install nuclear missiles in Western Europe. The United States Senate seemed poised to reject the SALT II treaty. Also in 1979, Beijing established full diplomatic relations with Washington, announced its intention to terminate the 1950 treaty with the USSR, and briefly went to war against Vietnam, a Soviet ally.

As though the situation were insufficiently complicated, three charismatic national leaders on the southern and southwestern flanks of the USSR fell in fairly quick succession: Sheik Mujibur Ali Rahman of Bangladesh in 1975, Zulfikar Ali Bhutto of Pakistan in 1977, and the shah of Iran in January 1979. Anti-Communist military rulers came to power in Bangladesh and Pakistan; Muslim fundamentalists took control in Iran. Bangladesh and Pakistan had close ties to China. Iran under Khomeini promised to exacerbate the existing instability in the Islamic world—and that included Soviet Tajikistan, Uzbekistan, Turkmenistan, Kyrgyzstan, and Azerbaijan. (Several million other Soviet Muslims, notably the Volga [Kazan] Tatars, did not have their own Union republics.)

In late summer 1979 the Kremlin made the decision to send troops to Afghanistan to crush the anti-Communist guerrillas and strengthen the Soviet military posture in the Persian Gulf. The original timetable broke down when puppet President N. M. Taraki died in September in a clash with his rival, Hafizullah Amin. An erratic journalist-politician, Amin became president despite Soviet suspicions of his coziness with the CIA. Amin launched a ferocious campaign against the guerrillas.

Insisting there was nothing unusual about its buildup of troops and matériel on the Afghan frontier, the Kremlin denied being displeased with Amin but chose an odd way to prove it: On Christmas Eve 1979 the Soviet Army began airlifting four divisions into airports near Kabul, the capital. With the aid of some Afghan units, the invaders staged a coup d'état on December 26–27. Amin was killed after refusing to resign in favor of a Soviet stooge, Babrak Karmal, who became president. The invasion force swelled to more than 110,000 and took control of Kabul and other key points around the country. Appealing for calm, Kabul radio praised Moscow's "fraternal assistance."

The world condemned the invasion, first of its kind in peacetime beyond the frontiers of Moscow's satellites since Lenin tried to Bolshevize Poland in 1920. The Carter Administration withdrew the SALT II treaty from Senate consideration, pulled out of the 1980 Moscow Olympic Games, and suspended shipments of grain beyond those already contracted for. The 1979 Soviet harvest had fallen far short of goals. Ignorant of the siege of Leningrad, Carter decided to use food as a weapon. The United States lifted its ban on military aid to Pakistan and China and several Arab nations increased theirs. After some hesitation, the Ayatollah Khomeini denounced the invasion and promised aid to the Afghan guerrillas.

A broad coalition took shape as the United States, China, Pakistan, Egypt, Saudi Arabia, some of the smaller Arab states, and several Muslim nations rallied to the anti-Soviet cause in Afghanistan. The Japanese—after 1931–1945 wary of foreign military adventures—sent communications equipment through third parties. No nation sent troops. Pathetically small in the beginning and hardly generous later, the aid did enable the fight against the invaders to continue.

Split into four major factions and innumerable smaller ones, the Afghan guerrillas found their own disunity a greater enemy than the USSR. Nevertheless, they controlled at least three-quarters of the countryside. They killed several thousand Soviet soldiers each year, losing four or five of their own for each one. The Soviet Army and especially the Air Force inflicted astronomical casualties on the civilian population. More than a quarter of the prewar population of about 15 million fled to Pakistan, where they lived in Gaza Strip-like misery.

The Soviet media did not note the tragic record set on November 13, 1983: As of that date, the Soviet Army had fought one day longer in Afghanistan than in the Second World War, and there was no end in sight. The Afghan—and the *Soviet*—political situation remained unstable. The Karmal regime was the Kremlin's prisoner, and for several years the Kremlin itself had been a captive of the dying Brezhnev machine. So long as Soviet forces remained the guerrillas could not win; but neither could they be defeated.

Their political goals eluded them, but the Soviets achieved some strategic objectives, among them completion of a bridge across the Amu Darya at Termez in Uzbekistan early in 1982. Soviet forces occupied the strategic Wakhan corridor, a narrow, high-altitude sliver of Afghanistan surrounded by the USSR, China, and Pakistan. The Kremlin announced "border adjustments" in its favor in that corridor. In the west, the Soviets built a military airport at Shindand, 900 kilometers from the Strait of Hormuz. NATO took note.

The threat to the USSR's southern flank could not excuse the scattering of anti-personnel mines indiscriminately around Afghanistan. Nor could it justify the use of napalm, helicopter gunships, tanks, and heavy artillery against villagers equipped until 1985 with Enfield rifles and the Holy Koran.

The Kremlin did not have to contend with an informed public opinion. But neither could it bury thousands of Soviet soldiers in secret, hide the wounded and disabled, or convince the young generation that its "international class duty" was to die in Afghanistan.*

AFRICA

In its first diplomatic victory in Black Africa, in 1974 the USSR persuaded Somalia to sign a treaty of friendship and cooperation. Arms and a little economic aid flowed into the desperately poor country, and Soviet crews built naval and air installations. Entrenched in Southern Yemen and influential in Djibouti and the breakaway Ethiopian province of Eritrea, the Soviet Union dominated the Gulf of Aden and the Strait of Bab al-Mandab. It could choke off the flow of Persian Gulf oil. Hoping to solidify its position and counterpose a Marxist federation to the anti-Soviet Egypt–Sudan alliance, in March 1977 the Kremlin despatched Fidel Castro to the region.

The centuries-old enmity between Muslim Somalia and Christian Ethiopia had not evaporated under their Marxist regimes, and it did not wither under the impact of Castro's charm. Shortly after the Cuban leader's visit to the Gulf of Aden, however, the military regime in Addis Ababa broke with the United States and asked for Soviet military and economic assistance. Promising $500 million worth of

---

*The Soviet regime inscribed the words "Died while fulfilling his international class duty" on the grave markers of the soldiers who fell in Afghanistan.

arms to Ethiopia, the Kremlin plunged into the Ethiopian–Somali quarrel. In July 1977 Somalia invaded Ogaden, an Ethiopian province inhabited by Somali tribespeople. When Moscow sided with the Ethiopians, Somalia broke relations and turned to the West.

With the aid of 10,000 Cuban troops and Cuban pilots flying Soviet aircraft, Ethiopia drove the Somalis out of Ogaden but halted at the frontier. That enabled Havana and Moscow to keep their promise to limit intervention to the defense of Ethiopian territory.

Gains in Ethiopia offset losses in Somalia. Reopened in June 1975, the southern approaches to the Suez Canal remained under close Soviet surveillance. One major goal in Africa achieved, the Kremlin also wanted to seize control of some of the continent's strategic minerals. Neither Ethiopia nor Somalia had any such resources, but other nations did. The cordial ties with the Addis Ababa regime gave Moscow a base from which to compete for African resources.

The Soviets and Cubans intervened in the 1975–1976 civil war in Angola, and from that tormented country Soviet influence percolated throughout West Africa. Moscow also had good relations with Nigeria, which permitted Soviet ships to use its ports. Guinea served as a Soviet military staging area. In Zimbabwe, the USSR and Cuba backed Joshua Nkomo's guerrilla faction, which a Beijing-backed rival group eventually defeated. A Marxist party ruled in Mozambique. In North Africa the emotionally unstable Libyan dictator, Colonel Muammar Qaddafi, welcomed Soviet arms and served Soviet interests by training and financing terrorists. By early 1984 Soviet and Cuban military and technical advisers were serving in 14 African nations, and Moscow had treaties of friendship with Angola, Mozambique, Ethiopia, and Congo.

And yet the position that seemed so strong in 1978 appeared far less impressive a few years later. Only a half-dozen of Africa's 50 countries espoused Marxism-Leninism as official ideology. Soviet influence remained roughly on a par with that of the United States but was eclipsed in North Africa by that of Libya and in West and Central Africa and Madagascar by that of France. The defiantly racist Republic of South Africa, which enjoyed profitable relations with the USSR and Israel, remained the dominant power in the south.

LATIN AMERICA

Some of the same factors that facilitated Soviet penetration of India also applied to Latin America, where communism's best allies were poverty, disease, ignorance, corruption, economic imperialism, and despair. The success of the Castro revolution in Cuba vitiated the Monroe Doctrine and opened the door to expansion of Moscow-financed roguery. The USSR delegated direction of revolutionary insurgencies to Fidel Castro.

No one could convince the Washington hysterics that the Soviets did not mastermind every guerrilla insurgency and land-reform movement in Latin America. The United States toppled a democratically elected, left-leaning government in Guatemala in 1954. The FBI's J. Edgar Hoover denied the existence of organized crime in the United States but discovered 53 Communists in the Dominican Republic. That prompted President Lyndon Johnson to send in 20,000 American troops. Moscow did have some influence—less than Washington believed—on the regime of Salvador Allende, a Socialist elected President of Chile in 1970 despite massive American support of his conservative rival. An erratic reformer unquestionably naive about his Chilean Communist allies and their Moscow masters, Allende died in the 1973 *coup* that brought to power the very model of a modern fascist dictator, American-sponsored Augusto Pinochet.

In the 1980s the USSR provided extensive economic and military aid to the leftist Sandinista regime in Nicaragua. The Sandinistas took control after overthrowing another American puppet, Anastasio Somoza. Through Cuba, the Kremlin supported a leftwing insurgency in El Salvador against the landed oligarchy and its American-trained "death squads."

This activity in Latin America reflected a decision to step up pressure on the United States, which had lost its enthusiasm for foreign misadventures after Vietnam. The Soviets calculated each move carefully, however, and did not consider sending troops to the Western Hemisphere.

THE WEST

Khrushchev's successors compiled an uneven record in dealing with Eastern Europe, China, and the Third World, but on the whole they managed their relations with the West cleverly. Obliging the West to recognize the USSR as its military equal was the greatest political triumph in Soviet history. The Kremlin achieved another major goal when 35 heads of state signed the Final Act of the Conference on Security and Cooperation in Europe (CSCE) in Helsinki on August 1, 1975. The signatories promised to respect one another as equals, refrain from using force to settle disputes, and recognize each nation's territorial integrity. This legitimized the postwar division of Europe—hence the Soviet empire.

A "second basket" of agreements pledged the nations of Europe, the United States, and Canada to expand cooperation in trade, scientific and technological exchanges, protection of the environment, and tourism. The "third basket" promised an increase in human contacts, including an increase in the exchange of information, improved working conditions for foreign correspondents, exten-

sion of cultural and educational exchanges, and reunification of families.

The Kremlin touted the security provisions of the treaty as the great Soviet victory they were, found nothing controversial in the "second basket," and ignored the third. The CSCE became a permanent institution. The West did succeed in placing the human rights issue on the table, and in time that would bear fruit in Europe. It failed to grow in the Chinese climate, even after the 1989 Tiananmen Square massacre.

NATO and especially the United States found it difficult to accept the loss of military superiority; East–West relations turned sour. When a new administration came to power in Washington in 1981 pledging to restore western supremacy, political observers in NATO and the Warsaw Pact nations warned of a new Cold War.

Having failed to stop the Federal Republic of Germany from joining NATO, the Kremlin drew a nonnegotiable line: Nuclear weapons in West German hands would mean war. When the German Social Democrats—whom both Hitler and Stalin had tried to destroy—took power in October 1969, there came about a partial reconciliation between Bonn and Moscow, and between the two German states. Formally renouncing the nuclear weapons a few demented Westerners had wanted to give them, the new West German government signed the Nonproliferation Treaty. That paved the way for the bilateral USSR–West Germany treaty of August 1970. Abandoning all claims to German territory lost in the war, the Bonn regime accepted the Oder–Neisse line as Germany's—whether GDR or reunited—eastern frontier.

The warming of the Central European political climate continued. In October 1971 a Quadripartite Agreement on Berlin regulated access and codified the four-power understanding of West Berlin's relationship to the Federal Republic. The two German states established diplomatic relations in May 1973 but exchanged "representatives" rather than ambassadors. In September 1974 the United States formally recognized the German Democratic Republic.

West Germany became a major Kremlin trading partner. In 1977, annual bilateral trade reached $5 billion and stabilized around that figure. The largest deal involved a Bonn contract for Soviet natural gas over a 25-year period. West German firms supplied much of the equipment for the construction of a Siberia–Germany pipeline.

There was benefit for Poland here. In 1968, the Bonn Christian-Democratic regime had openly supported the Czechoslovak reformers, feeding Kremlin paranoia and contributing to its decision to invade. This experience in mind, in 1980–1981 the German Social-Democratic government scrupulously avoided meddling in Poland and even persuaded the Dresdner Bank to extend a $675 million loan to Warsaw. That helped Solidarity and Poland escape the fate of Czechoslovakia.

Following the deaths of dictators in Spain and Portugal, the USSR established diplomatic relations with those nations. Communists entered the cabinet in France in 1981. Britain expelled more than a hundred Soviet diplomatic personnel for espionage in 1971, but four years later it granted Moscow $2.39 billion in low-interest credits to purchase British goods. European interests financed and helped construct a huge automotive plant at Naberezhnye Chelny—"Brezhnevsk" 1982–1988—on the Volga after Washington denied the Ford Motor Company permission to participate. Principle came before profit, except in Latin America, Africa, and China. France and Italy joined West Germany in making long-term contracts for Soviet natural gas. All three, plus Britain and Japan, defied the United States and supplied pipeline equipment to the USSR.

Unable to seal the cracks in its own far-flung empire, the USSR adroitly exploited differences within the capitalist camp. When American firms withdrew under U.S. government pressure, Japan agreed to join in several huge projects in Siberia and to help develop an oilfield off Sakhalin. Argentina and Canada filled huge orders for grain when political developments curtailed deliveries from the United States.

East–West trade developed in spurts, notably between 1973 and 1976, when the value of Soviet imports from the industrialized nations increased 101 percent. The USSR imported $3 billion worth of goods from the West in 1970, $26 billion in 1980. In June 1983 the Soviet hard-currency debt to the West stood at more than $28.7 billion. For 40 months following the invasion of Afghanistan the West refused to grant any substantial loans to Moscow; then, in May 1984, an international consortium led by Germany's Dresdner Bank agreed to lend $250 million. No U.S. bank participated; no U.S. bank profited; no one understood the logic.

The USSR normally received preferential treatment from Western bankers. However inefficient, the country's huge economy could absorb reasonable debt, and after 1973 its hard-currency reserves increased dramatically as the world price of oil and gold soared. The Soviets managed their debt carefully; in the early 1980s they kept the ratio of debt-service to current earnings at about 16 percent.

American business leaders were no less eager than their foreign counterparts to participate in the Soviet market, but shifting political winds in Washington made it difficult to establish stable trade, especially in commodities. Then in June 1972 President Richard Nixon announced the largest grain transaction in history. The USSR would purchase a minimum of $750 million worth of American wheat, corn, and soybeans over three years; in fact, it bought much more. The following spring Leonid Brezhnev predicted a long-term need for American grain and proposed a 30–40-year pact. The USSR would receive permission to buy millions of tons of grain annually and would pay with raw materials, oil, and certain specialized equipment.

The 1972 grain deal constituted a by-product of "détente." Bracing for confrontation during a Nixon presidency, Moscow encountered cordiality and cooperation. Unprincipled cynicism reigned in both Moscow and Washington. Advised by Henry Kissinger, Nixon widened the war in Vietnam; sanctioned Cambodia's destruction; took steps to give Pakistan and Israel a nuclear capability; sold everyone everywhere all the arms they needed to kill anyone who needed killing; encouraged Iran's bloodstained shah to increase the price of oil; and initiated a rapprochement with Beijing that nullified everything Nixon had ever said about China. Allowing the USSR to overtake and surpass the United States in terms of military strength, Nixon and Kissinger proclaimed the birth of détente. Later, President Gerald Ford and Kissinger legitimized the USSR's East European empire.

Slow to comprehend this dazzling sequence of acts, the American public rather more quickly grasped the increase in food prices that followed the "great grain robbery"—the 1972 Nixon-Kissinger-Brezhnev deal. Nixon fell before he could negotiate a second deal. In October 1975 his successor, Ford, signed a five-year pact that *obligated* the Soviets to buy six million tons of wheat or corn annually and *permitted* them to purchase up to eight million tons. This promised to help solve the perennial Soviet agricultural crisis. It also benefited American grain companies, but not American consumers. From 1976, when it took effect, through 1979, the United States controlled 70 percent of the Soviet grain trade.

The most dramatic if not necessarily meaningful fruit of détente, the 1972 Anti-ABM Treaty, brought SALT I to a conclusion. The following year Kremlin leaders expressed relief when President Ford announced he would retain Kissinger as Secretary of State; the

Soviets knew a friend when they found one. Brezhnev and Ford–Kissinger sustained the cordiality. At a November 1974 meeting in Vladivostok they outlined a new agreement to regulate the nuclear arms competition. Ford's critics charged him with making too many concessions to Moscow.

The Soviets wanted to trade; some American politicians demanded that Washington extract concessions in the area of human rights. Passed over the strenuous objections of Ford and Kissinger, the Jackson–Vanik Amendment to the 1974 Trade Act linked most-favored-nation status and special trade credits to the emigration of Jews and other citizens. Calling this interference in its internal affairs, the Kremlin refused to give public assurances. Trade continued to increase; emigration remained at low levels until 1979. In that year the Soviets signaled their satisfaction with the SALT II treaty and a new grain agreement by permitting a record 51,320 citizens to leave. Because of the events in Afghanistan and other issues, however, trade declined after 1979, and emigration virtually ceased.

The administration of President James Carter injected a confrontational Evangelical Christian morality into diplomacy: The world had not seen anything quite like this since Alexander I of Russia sponsored the Holy Alliance. Was this another Crusade? The Brezhnev regime denounced criticism of its human rights record and threatened to break off arms-control talks. Negotiations and trade, however, went forward. The two sides signed the SALT II agreement in 1979. Sophisticated American computers and other high-tech items went to the USSR in increasing quantities, sometimes through third countries. The United States imported such strategic commodities as enriched uranium, titanium, manganese, and oil from the Soviet Union.

The Soviets managed to deal with Carter until 1979. In that year, responding to the Soviet emplacement in Belarus and Ukraine of nuclear-tipped rockets aimed at Western Europe, NATO decided to deploy American nuclear missiles in Europe. Until the "Euromissile crisis" was resolved, NATO and the USSR would hover on the brink of war.

Responding to the Soviet invasion of Afghanistan, which "shocked" him, Carter embargoed all but the minimum grain shipments required by the 1975 contract. He could not halt sales by other countries; the 1980 harvests were good around the world and the Kremlin found other sources. The American share of the Soviet market fell to 20 percent. The November 1980 election of Ronald Reagan led to the unraveling of many ties between Moscow and Washington, the grain trade not among them. Drawing a sharp distinction between technology—sales of which he sought to halt—and food, Reagan lifted the grain embargo early in 1981.

Zealous proponents of a grotesque ideology they neither understood nor believed, the old men in the Kremlin could not adjust to the century's most ideological American president. Accustomed to denouncing the West with reckless abandon, and to forecasting a universal Communist victory, the Soviets howled when Reagan referred to their "evil empire" and predicted the overthrow of the Soviet regime.

TWO DECADES OF STAGNATION DIPLOMACY

The Kremlin proclaimed its contempt for both Carter and Reagan, whom it charged with responsibility for the sharp rise in international tensions. Perplexed when their own threatening words and actions strengthened the resolve of the West, the Kremlin leadership tried to rally the Soviet people. In the spring of 1984 Radio Moscow began broadcasting the ultra-patriotic popular songs of 1939–1941.

The USSR championed revolutionary change everywhere save in its own empire. The West tended to resist change everywhere *except* in that empire. Neither side would compromise; each probed constantly for weakness. Miraculously, the serious clashes took place through surrogates on at least one side and did not lead to superpower war.

The USSR and the United States had less control over events than each other's propagandists, and the world media, liked to claim. Middle Eastern and Persian Gulf developments moved at a pace far beyond the capabilities of any strategic planners. Volatile Black Africa gave the USSR more defeats than victories and the United States few successes. The Kremlin did not dare count such dictators as Colonel Qaddafi of Libya as friends. The problems of Latin America antedated the Soviets and Fidel Castro by generations. Nothing could justify the blatant aggression in Afghanistan, yet even there, on its southern border, the Kremlin confronted genuine dilemmas.

There seemed little danger that either side would deliberately launch an attack on the other. The real threat was war by accident or uncontrollable terrorist incidents.

SUGGESTED ADDITIONAL READINGS

GERVASI, TOM. *The Myth of Soviet Military Superiority.* New York: Harper & Row, 1986.

GOLAN, GALIA. *Soviet Policies in the Middle East: From World War II to Gorbachev.* New York: Cambridge University Press, 1990.

HASLAM, JONATHAN. *The Soviet Union and the Politics of Nuclear Weapons in Europe, 1969–1987.* Ithaca, NY: Cornell University Press, 1987.

HOLLOWAY, DAVID. *The Soviet Union and the Arms Race.* New Haven, CT: Yale University Press, 1983.

MCCGWIRE, Michael. *Military Objectives in Soviet Foreign Policy.* Washington, DC: Brookings Institution, 1987.

SAKHAROV, ANDREI D. *My Country and the World.* New York: Knopf, 1975.

22

RELUCTANT REVOLUTION
Gorbachev, Glasnost, and Perestroika

Around midnight on March 11, 1985, the CPSU Central Committee announced that Mikhail Sergeyevich Gorbachev would succeed Konstantin Chernenko as general secretary. With publication the next day of Andrei Gromyko's nominating speech, the world learned that Gorbachev had actually governed the country much of the time during Chernenko's prolonged illness. Three years later, one of the new leaders, Yegor Ligachev, revealed that the vote had not been unanimous.

GORBACHEV

Born into a Russian peasant family in the Stravropol (North Caucasus) region in March 1931, Mikhail Gorbachev grew up knowing the land and politics. His grandfather and father, both Communists, worked on a collective farm. Gorbachev attended local schools and remained in his village during the 1942–1943 German occupation; his mother later revealed that at one point he had to miss school because he had no shoes.

Gorbachev's mother—like those of Stalin and Khrushchev—had her son baptized and raised in the Russian Orthodox Church. State atheism soon knocked that out of him, but when he became general secretary of the Communist party he lifted the restrictions on the Christian sects and later on Muslims. In 1988 he sanctioned a nationwide celebration of the millennium of Christianity in Russia and Ukraine.

Working on the *kolhoz* after the war, Gorbachev won the Order of the Red Banner of Labor at the unusually early age of 18. That plus the silver medal as salutatorian of his secondary-school class, and an unblemished Komsomol record, won him admission to Moscow State University. Opting to study law, he read Marx, Engels, Lenin, and Stalin—but also St. Thomas Aquinas, Hobbes, Locke, and Machiavelli. He studied Latin. In 1954 he married a sociology student, Raisa Titorenko, who would become the most detested woman in modern Russia after the Empress Alexandra.

One of Gorbachev's university classmates, Ždenek Mlynař, later an official in the 1968 Czechoslovak reform regime, told an interviewer that even in the early 1950s Gorbachev had expressed doubts about Stalin and Stalinism, and had spoken of the need for decentralization. At the 1988 Nineteenth CPSU Conference, Gorbachev used a phrase the "Prague Spring" made famous, "socialism with a human face."

The new General Secretary of the CPSU, Mikhail Gorbachev (right), with Foreign Minister Gromyko (center) and Premier Tikhonov on the day of Konstantin Chernenko's funeral, March 13, 1985. (AP/Wide World Photos)

Gorbachev joined the Communist party in 1952 and served as a Komsomol organizer; that marked him as *nomenklatura* material. Evidence of the state's trust in a faithful son came in the 1960s when the KGB permitted him to travel abroad with official delegations and even to drive through France and Italy with his wife.

After graduation from the university, Gorbachev returned to Stavropol, worked his way up through the party ranks, and became a delegate to Khrushchev's second "de-Stalinizing" Party Congress, the Twenty-Second in 1961. But he applauded the overthrow of Khrushchev three years later and smoothly transferred his loyalty to the Troika leadership, then to Leonid Brezhnev. In 1970 he became regional party first secretary—a set-for-life member of the *nomenklatura*.

Gorbachev had powerful patrons in Fyodor Kulakov, Yuri Andropov, and Mikhail Suslov. Andropov was born in the Stavropol area, and the others had served there. They all regularly vacationed nearby, and Andropov took a sentimental interest in local party affairs. In 1971 Gorbachev became a full member of the national party Central Committee without having served the customary probationary period.

When Kulakov died suddenly in 1978, Gorbachev took his agriculture portfolio on the Secretariat and, although he did not initiate it, became identified with the "Ipatovsky method" of harvesting grain: As in the United States, huge squads of combines followed the harvest across climatic zones. This enjoyed success in some regions, and *Pravda* published a front-page interview with the dynamic young man from Stavropol. In a move reminiscent of Khrushchevian "from the asphalt to the land," Gorbachev began transferring responsibility from the bloated Moscow bureaucracy to regional bodies. He reintroduced a cooperative brigade system on some *kolhozes:* The brigade's income depended solely on performance. Incentives reappeared in scattered areas.

In regions—including the North Caucasus—where the climate was mild, the soil fertile and the reforms popular with the locals, the yields increased. Nationally, however, the harvest declined from 1978's record 237 million metric tons to 179 million tons in 1979, and it nose-dived to 158 million tons in 1981. In 1983, Gorbachev's last year in charge of agriculture, the farms produced 192 million metric tons. The usual factors of mismanagement, waste, and bad weather were at work, and the party had always demanded a scapegoat. Only Andropov's protection saved Gorbachev, who became a candidate member of the Politburo in 1979 and a full member a year later.

Gorbachev acted as the dying Andropov's grand vizier from November 1982 until February 1984. Nominally in charge of ideology and—through part of 1983—agriculture, he also took charge of experiments to loosen state control of industry. That job normally would have gone to one of the chief claimants to the throne, Grigori Romanov, party secretary in charge of heavy industry. Gorbachev also played a major role in the attempt to eradicate corruption. He was Andropov's indispensable aide, and ultimately his only link to the Politburo.

To Machiavelli's observation that no man ever killed his successor we may add that no Soviet leader ever picked him. Andropov wanted Gorbachev, but in February 1984 the Brezhnev machine suppressed a paragraph in one of Andropov's letters—shades of the Lenin "testament"—in which he asked the party to take that step. Gorbachev would have to wait for Konstantin Chernenko to die.

THE BITE OF THE IRON TEETH

After the perfunctory obsequies for Chernenko, Gorbachev unveiled a platform he summed up as *glasnost* ("openness") and *perestroika* ("restructuring"). The two words entered the international political vocabulary almost overnight; the new Soviet leader had struck a nerve. At an April 1985 Central Committee plenum he called for "revolutionary" changes, and a year later he equated *perestroika*

with revolution. No Soviet political leader used the word "revolution" lightly.

Gorbachev spoke for the younger *nomenklaturshchiks* who acknowledged the system's problems, admitted its mistakes, and planned major repairs—but remained wholly committed to Soviet communism. Guarding their flanks against the remnants of the old guard and a generally conservative public opinion, they called for more socialism even as they were dismantling it. In June 1988 Gorbachev took on the growing number of his critics:

In all spheres of life, including the spiritual, we must overcome a very basic factor, alienation, which unfortunately occurs when socialism is deformed by authoritarian-bureaucratic distortions. Alienation, bureaucratism, and formalism can be overcome only along lines of democratization and openness . . . of a moral cleansing of our society.

The dismissal of Stalinism as a mere "authoritarian-bureaucratic distortion" almost amounted to an endorsement, and "formalism" has no meaning. What was the general secretary up to?

By the time Gorbachev came to power, the dreaded step from which the Communist party had recoiled in 1956 and 1961, attesting to its own illegitimacy,* had become unavoidable. No myth could rescue the party; nothing could salvage the economic nonsystem; no mere apology could atone for the indiscriminate slaughter of the Soviet people. The country required a frontal assault not only on Stalinism but also on Leninism—the "If only Lenin [or Bukharin] had lived!" syndrome.

Gorbachev inherited an understrength Politburo of 10 members, of whom he alone did not owe his position to Brezhnev. Even after he filled three of the four—or six, if the 16-member body be the standard—vacancies in April 1985, the old guard maintained a majority. The promotion of Yegor Ligachev, secre-

---

*See Chapter 16.

tary for personnel and ideology ("second secretary"); Viktor Chebrikov of the KGB; and Nikolai Ryzhkov, secretary in charge of the economy, only temporarily strengthened Gorbachev. These three interpreted *glasnost-perestroika* conservatively.

Between April 1985 and October 1988 Gorbachev fashioned a shaky Politburo majority. The only Brezhnev-era holdovers were Ukrainian party boss Vladimir Shcherbitsky and Vitaly Vorotnikov, prime minister and later president of the RSFSR. Gorbachev forced Grigori Romanov and Viktor Grishin into ignominious retirement. Dinmukhamed Kunayev, who like Heidar Aliyev had retained his Central Committee seat after being dismissed from the Politburo, conveniently died before the state could indict him for corruption. Eduard Shevardnadze, a Georgian and a close Gorbachev ally, succeeded Andrei Gromyko at the foreign ministry.

A September–October 1988 Central Committee plenum left Ligachev and Chebrikov, who were acting as a brake on Gorbachev, on the Politburo, but it sent Ligachev into the minefield of agriculture and removed Chebrikov as head of the KGB. Chebrikov did retain some influence in security matters and ideology as head of a commission on legal affairs.

In July 1985 Gorbachev gave Gromyko an honorable transition into retirement by making him titular head of state. Three years later he threw him out, took the office for himself, and redefined its powers. Now officially called "president," the holder of the position had broad authority in legislative initiative, foreign policy, and defense.

The November 1988 USSR Supreme Soviet session that had approved these changes created a 2,250-member Congress of People's Deputies as a kind of superparliament. It elected the president, who reported to it. The Congress elected a 422-member working parliament, the Supreme Soviet, from its own ranks. Always in session, the smaller body reviewed legislative and administrative acts. The president and members of the Supreme Soviet and Congress were limited to two five-year terms.

For the first time since November 1917, voters went to the polls on March 26, 1989, in relatively free elections. Not surprisingly, the sole legal party, the Communist, won 87 percent of the seats in the new Congress. But some nonparty candidates, and maverick Communists such as Boris Yeltsin of Yekaterinburg (Sverdlovsk), scored impressive victories. Andrei Sakharov won an Academy of Sciences seat despite fierce Communist opposition. Many entrenched high-level Communists were defeated; the voters turned 20 percent of the regional party secretaries out of office. An independent political movement, Sajudis, won three-quarters of the seats in Lithuania; the independent Popular Front won 25 of Latvia's 29

(Map by Larry Fogel, © 1989, *The Washington Post*). Reprinted with permission.

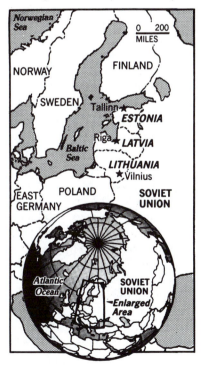

seats. Many Communists won only because local officials kept their opponents off the ballot.

Though deeply flawed, the March 1989 elections represented a crucial step forward. They gave some promise of remaking the political system into a hybrid between the Fifth Republic in France, with its strong presidency, and Mexico, a one-party democracy with a weak legal opposition.

THE ECONOMY

Gorbachev's worst foe was his own irredeemably corrupt Communist party, in power for more than 65 years. But he also had to contend with a drop in world oil prices, the 1986 nuclear catastrophe at Chernobyl, the 1988 earthquake in Armenia, and generally miserable weather that reduced the harvests. A well-intentioned but poorly planned anti-alcohol campaign cost the state 37 billion rubles in lost revenues between 1984 and 1987.

By spring 1989 *perestroika* had registered only modest success. Blocked by managers wedded to smokestack industry and collectivized agriculture, the Gorbachevites decided to eliminate central planning. They would decentralize and modernize the outmoded industrial base first, then turn to agriculture. In the Russian manner they debated endlessly, wrote position papers, drew up programs, talked some more, argued—and succeeded in polishing their speaking and writing skills. They also unsettled the country. Sensing an upheaval, those in charge of production at all levels either cut back or withheld their products from the market. This recalled 1928, when the peasants sensed the approaching end of the NEP and kept their grain in the villages. The ubiquitous lines of consumers grew longer.

Gorbachev could not reform the 18-million-member central bureaucracy. As Nikolai Shmelyov said,

there are three million bureaucrats in our Ministry of Agriculture. Think of it. These people know nothing except how to carry their briefcases. All . . . these bureaucrats are afraid of losing their jobs, and they are anathema to a healthy economy.

Shmelyov pointed out that "[r]esistance to *perestroika* . . . no longer comes from the top levels of our bureaucratic pyramids." By early 1989 Gorbachev had replaced more than two-thirds of all ministers, more than three-fifths of all provincial party first secretaries, three-quarters of all first secretaries of city and district party committees. Putting new people in jobs that themselves had no raison d'être was merely to postpone the reckoning and in some respects was worse than doing nothing. The resistance to reform of middle- and lower-level bureaucrats was unshakable.

The country had no one trained in Western management techniques. High-level delegations went to America to observe business-school training; when they returned home, most produced talk and paper. As always, enterprise managers excelled above all in giving the appearance of executing Moscow's orders. They had no interest in anything but gross output—the sole index of success. They requested the largest possible budgets and work force, as much time as possible to fulfill contracts, and the lowest possible quotas. They feared computerization and cost accounting like the plague. Were *perestroika* to succeed, they were doomed.

THE THIRD DEATH OF STALIN*

Mikhail Gorbachev had been in power 21 months when Anatoli Marchenko died in the Gulag; conflicting reports about the autopsy lent weight to the widespread suspicion that

---

*The phrase comes from Elena Joly, *La troisième mort de Staline* (Arles: Editions Actes Sud, 1989).

Marchenko had suffered yet another savage beating. The release of Andrei Sakharov, Yuri Orlov, Anatoli Shcharansky, Iosif Begun—all but a small handful of political prisoners and detainees—could not conceal the deaths in the Gulag of more prisoners in Gorbachev's first two years than during the entire Brezhnev era. Those lonely deaths—Marchenko's was one of the few the world noticed—must factor into an evaluation of Mikhail Gorbachev.

An editorial board announced in 1988 that the twelfth and last volume of a general history of the USSR could not be published: *Glasnost* having made honesty legal, the twelfth volume would necessarily negate the previous eleven. A year earlier Gorbachev had declared that there should be "no forgotten names or blanks either in history or in literature." This and similar invitations opened the sluices; Yegor Ligachev and other conservatives tried to reclose them. In June 1988 the government canceled high-school examinations in history. Like genetics, the discipline had to have time to recover from Leninism–Stalinism.

Carrying "de-Stalinization" to its highest level yet, the Supreme Soviet and the courts overturned the convictions of all defendants in the "show trials" of the 1930s. Despite vigorous and at times fanatical conservative and fundamentalist opposition, the CPSU posthumously exonerated and reinstated Bukharin, Kamenev, Zinoviev, Radek, Rykov, and thousands of lesser-known victims of the "troikas" and "special boards" of 1934–1953. In the spring of 1988, Vasili Selyunin and the historian Nikolai Popov published articles critical not only of Stalin and Feliks Dzerzhinsky but also of Lenin, whom Selyunin identified as the father of the Gulag. Gorbachev disputed this latter charge.

The general secretary and his chief ideologist, Aleksandr Yakovlev, wanted to exploit the rehabilitation and glorification of Bukharin to legitimize *glasnost–perestroika* as the reincarnation of the NEP. Gorbachev presided over what Elena Joly has called the "third death of Stalin," but he would not sanction the dethroning of his idol, Lenin.

Even Trotsky returned to acceptance, if not favor. The court historian to Gorbachev and later Boris Yeltsin, Dmitri Volkogonov, wrote in *Pravda* in September 1988 that "Trotsky was not an enemy of the revolution or of socialism . . . [but] of Stalin." That judgment surprised no one outside the Soviet Union.

•

THE ARTS

The state itself, and new private enterprises, published the works of once proscribed writers and poets such as Bulgakov, Zamyatin, Akhmatova, Mandelstam, Nikolai Gumilyov, Nabokov, Brodsky. The Writers' Union posthumously reinstated Pasternak, whose *Dr. Zhivago* appeared in many editions. Anatoli Rybakov's *Children of the Arbat,* a study of the Terror suppressed for two decades, reached the public in 1987. The editor of *Novy Mir,* Sergei Zalygin, persuaded Gorbachev to allow publication of Aleksandr Solzhenitsyn's monument to the victims of Leninism–Stalinism, *The Gulag Archipelago.*

Yuli Daniel lived to see publication of his poems and even one of the stories that had cost him five years in the Gulag. He died in December 1988. Andrei Sinyavsky, who had gone to prison with him and had been allowed to emigrate after serving most of his sentence, received a visa to attend the funeral. But Soviet remained Soviet: The embassy in Paris issued the visa too late. When Sinyavsky finally reached Moscow, it was to visit his friend's grave.

In the cinema, Tengiz Abuladze's trilogy of anti-Stalinist works, of which *Repentance* became a classic, won the 1988 Lenin Prize. The Latvian director Juris Podnieks took an unflinching look at the problems of modern youth in *Is It Easy to Be Young?* Director Vasili

Pichul and scenarist Mariya Khmelik portrayed unvarnished anomie in *Little Vera.* In 1990 Stanislav Govorukhin—at heart an arch-reactionary—directed *You Can't Live Like This,* a searing indictment of Communist rule.

NATIONAL MINORITIES

Unleashed by *glasnost–perestroika,* ethnic antagonisms burst into the open in 1986. A nation of 130 different peoples, of which only Ukrainians and Belarusians are ethnically and linguistically close to the Russians, officially lived in peace: The Lenin regime declared in 1923 that it had solved the "nationality question." But Ukrainians had paid a terrible price for resisting communism and Russian domination, and collectivization had decimated the nomadic Kazakhs. The Turkic and Iranian Muslim peoples of the USSR had endured cruel persecution. The Estonians, Latvians, and Lithuanians knew the heavy hand of the Terror.

Khrushchev had permitted most, but not all, of Stalin's "punished peoples" to return to their homes. For the most part the process unfolded peacefully, but in 1958 riots in the Chechen-Ingush ASSR took a number of lives as Georgians, Dagestanis, Avars, and others resisted eviction from the Chechen-Ingush homes and farms they had taken with the state's blessing.

In 1967 the Kremlin "rehabilitated" the Crimean Tatars but denied them the right to return to the Crimea. This left them, like the Kurds and some others, a people without a home. In 1987 and early 1988 the police and KGB broke up peaceful demonstrations in Moscow in which the Crimean Tatars demanded restoration of their property and their civil rights.

In June 1988 a Kremlin commission reported that there were "no grounds" for reestablishing a Crimean Tatar ASSR; *glasnost–perestroika* had limits. The population of

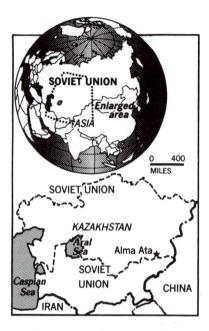

(Map by Larry Fogel, © 1989, *The Washington Post*). Reprinted with permission.

the peninsula had tripled since the war, and the urban areas were populated by Russians and Ukrainians. Most collective farmers were of those nationalities. Spas catering to the Russian–Ukrainian trade dotted the landscape, and the *nomenklaturshchiks* had luxurious villas set in park-like estates. This left no room for the descendants of Chingis Khan, who had called the Crimea home for five centuries.

Under Khrushchev and Brezhnev, the CPSU had tried to make good on its threat to create a new, purely "Soviet" nationality. That meant forcing a Communist anti-culture and the Russian language on all nationalities. The Communists struck especially hard in Ukraine, where they outlawed the Ukrainian Catholic Church and made Russian the language of higher education. In 1975 the local KGB forbade Kiev firemen to fight a fire of suspicious origin that destroyed a major part of an ancient Ukrainian library and archive. Pyotr Shelest and his successor as Ukrainian party boss, Vladimir Shcherbitsky, slavishly did Moscow's bidding to the point of speaking Russian at public functions in Ukraine.

Wherever Russians lived, they had their own schools. Sent by the millions to work in other republics, they diluted the native populations and threatened the survival of native cultures, especially in Kazakhstan, Yakutia, and Estonia. Outside Slav-speaking Belarus and Ukraine, fewer than 2 percent of Russians learned the native language of the republic to which they migrated. Russian was the exclusive language of all federal-level and inter-republic official business.

In December 1986, thousands of Kazakh young people rose up in the capital, Alma-Aty, when the Politburo fired the aged, corrupt Dinmukhamed Kunayev as Kazakh Communist leader and appointed Gennadi Kolbin, an ethnic Chuvash,* to succeed him. Few Kazakhs wasted any love on Kunayev, but they had prodigious collective grievances against the Communist party-state. The 1926 population had counted four million Kazakhs; collectivization reduced the number by more than a million. Not content with genocide, the Communists suppressed the Kazakhs' language and their Sunni Muslim culture. By 1950 the republic had more Russians than Kazakhs. The Soviet Army buried Kazakh soldiers who fell in the Second World War, in Hungary in 1956 and Czechoslovakia in 1968, and in Afghanistan, in Soviet military cemeteries rather than in Muslim sacred ground. The persecution of other Muslim peoples in the USSR differed only in degree.

Using the passive voice bureaucrats cherish, Gorbachev wrote in his *Memoirs* that "[f]orce was used" in Alma-Aty "to teach a lesson to

---

*The Chuvash are a people of mixed Finnic and Turkic descent who live along the Middle Volga in the Russian Federation.

Kazakhstan and the others [the Soviet Muslim republics]." As it happened, Kazakhstan taught *him* a lesson. Within a few months the Politburo called off its campaign against Islam in the belief that alienating 50 million Soviet Muslims would help win the war in Muslim Afghanistan.

With regard to the national minorities, the Communists had always tried to divide and rule. For centuries, there has been bitter enmity between Turkic Muslims and Christian Armenians. In 1923 Stalin gave control of the mountainous, Armenian-populated enclave of Nagorno-Karabakh to Soviet Azerbaijan, home of the Turkic, mainly Shiite Muslim Azerbaijanis (or Azeris). The Armenians had long lobbied unsuccessfully to overturn Stalin's decision. Now, with power slipping away from Moscow under *glasnost–perestroika*, the dispute exploded. Riots in Yerevan and Nagorno–Karabakh provoked a violent counterreaction in Baku and elsewhere. There were several thousand casualties. Television broadcasts of these events forever shattered the myth of the "great friendship of Soviet peoples."

A government commission hastily examined the problem. It reported that nearly 80 percent of the Nagorno-Karabakh population were Christian Armenians but recommended the area remain under Azerbaijani control. Stung in Kazakhstan, Moscow now sacrificed the Armenians of Nagorno-Karabakh in the name of better relations with Azerbaijan and the other Muslim republics, and the Islamic world in general. When the rioting intensified, the Kremlin ousted the party leaders in both feuding republics and placed Nagorno-Karabakh under its direct rule.

Rioting in Baku took the lives of many Armenian residents. In January 1990 Gorbachev sent in several thousand troops ostensibly to "restore order" but in fact, as Marshal Dmitri Yazov acknowledged at the time, to save the Azerbaijani Communist party and with it the Soviet colonial empire. Alexander Lebed, a

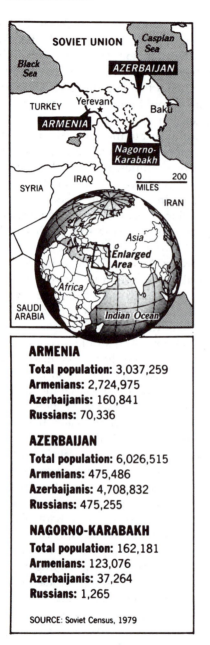

ARMENIA
Total population: 3,037,259
Armenians: 2,724,975
Azerbaijanis: 160,841
Russians: 70,336

AZERBAIJAN
Total population: 6,026,515
Armenians: 475,486
Azerbaijanis: 4,708,832
Russians: 475,255

NAGORNO-KARABAKH
Total population: 162,181
Armenians: 123,076
Azerbaijanis: 37,264
Russians: 1,265

SOURCE: Soviet Census, 1979

(Map by Brad Wye, © 1988, *The Washington Post*). Reprinted with permission.

hero of the Afghan War, commanded the Tula Airborne Division. Only military force could keep Azerbaijan in the USSR.

According to the way the Kremlin customarily kept the books, the Soviet Army's slaughter of several civilians in Yerevan five months later during a "pacification" operation balanced the score. In reality, it once again demonstrated Gorbachev's fatal weakness. He did not shrink from a traditional Communist party show of force, but after showing it he lacked the will to take it to the limit. He would not last long.

Other nationalist movements that threatened the Soviet federal structure blossomed. Unfurling their long-forbidden black-blue-white flag, the Estonians established a People's Front. That body proclaimed its independence from the CPSU, still the only legal political party in the USSR. The Front called for abolition of Moscow's control and the "Estonization" of industry. It wanted to make Estonian the republic's official language, restrict immigration, and disenfranchise those who could not speak Estonian. It demanded the right to veto the application of USSR legislation in Estonia. In November 1988 the Estonian Communist party leadership itself proclaimed the supremacy of Estonian Supreme Court decisions over the laws of the USSR.

FOREIGN AFFAIRS

The pressing need to restructure the economy from the ground up stemmed not only from the system's internal contradictions but also from the militarization of the entire society. The USSR had achieved nuclear parity with NATO and had built a military machine that could, on paper, match NATO and China combined. The crushing burden of military spending, which some experts estimated at 40 percent of GDP, had bankrupted the nation. The architects of *glasnost–perestroika* resolved to reduce defense expenditures, but the only way to do that was to reexamine the premises that had guided Soviet foreign policy since 1920.

The Gorbachev Kremlin agreed to a humiliating withdrawal from Afghanistan. Unleashed by *glasnost,* public opinion almost unanimously opposed the conflict, which had sapped the blood and morale of the nation and further depleted the treasury. Not only that: The Afghan guerrillas—the mujahadeen—now had CIA-supplied surface-to-air missiles. The war that was never winnable was now lost. Gorbachev secured a U.S. agreement to stop supplying weapons, and Soviet troops began withdrawing. The last Soviet soldier left early in 1989.

By fortuitous coincidence, Soviet–American negotiations aimed at reducing the numbers of short- and intermediate-range nuclear weapons in Europe began the day after Gorbachev became general secretary. He revamped the Soviet delegation and gave it fresh instructions. The new men in the Kremlin understood that the United States would accept nothing less than the "zero option": The Soviets would remove the nuclear missiles aimed at Western Europe, and NATO would then withdraw from Europe the American nuclear weapons targeted on the USSR. Meeting in Washington in December 1987, Gorbachev and Ronald Reagan signed a treaty embodying this agreement.

The first meeting of the two presidents had taken place two years earlier in Geneva, the second in Reykjavik, Iceland, in October 1986.

New York, December 1988. (Paul Hosefros/NYT Permissions)

Reagan went to Moscow in May–June 1988 for the fourth and last. Despite the accord on the shorter-range missiles, fundamental disagreements remained. The American side insisted on proceeding with research and development of a "space shield" despite Soviet protests that it would violate the 1972 Anti-ABM Treaty.

The Afghanistan war and the Soviet–Cuban intervention in Angola were winding down, but regional conflicts still burned in Cambodia, Nicaragua, the Middle East, and elsewhere. The Soviets continued to finance a North Korean military buildup that went far beyond legitimate defense needs. But Soviet thinking was changing. Like General Charles de Gaulle a generation earlier, Gorbachev frequently spoke of a Europe "from the Atlantic to the Urals." In December 1988 he went to the United Nations to announce the USSR's intention to withdraw 50,000 troops and 5,000 tanks from bases in Eastern Europe as part of an overall plan to reduce the Soviet Army by 500,000 men and 10,000 tanks.

Gorbachev and his people realized that, with American short- and medium-range nuclear missiles leaving Europe, the Continent no longer posed any serious threat to Soviet security. A NATO inferior in conventional weapons could hardly mount an invasion; Napoleon and Hitler would likely be the last invaders for some time—at least from the West. Needing Europe—for technology and loans—far more than it needed him, Gorbachev appeared to appreciate the symmetry of simultaneous rapprochement with the Americans and, for the first time since 1917, reintegration into Europe.

The great puzzle in Soviet foreign affairs remained China, where Soviet military cutbacks were even more welcome than they were in the West. Between them, Moscow and Beijing spent enormous sums each year to guard their common border, sums more profitably employed elsewhere. A modest warming trend in Moscow–Beijing relations developed in 1987–1988. In May 1989 Gorbachev would go to Beijing to meet Chinese leaders—an encounter followed by a great atrocity.

SUGGESTED ADDITIONAL READINGS

BROWN, ARCHIE. *The Gorbachev Factor.* New York: Oxford University Press, 1996.

BUCKLEY, MARY, ed. *Perestroika and Soviet Women.* New York: Cambridge University Press, 1992.

GORBACHEV, MIKHAIL S. *Memoirs.* New York: Doubleday, 1996.

GORBACHEV, MIKHAIL S. *Perestroika.* New York: Harper & Row, 1987.

PALAZCHENKO, PAVEL. *Gorbachev and Shevardnadze: The Memoir of a Soviet Interpreter.* University Park, PA: Penn State Press, 1997.

YELTSIN, BORIS N. *Against the Grain.* New York: Summit Books, 1990.

23

THE NEW TIME
OF TROUBLES

Crisis of the Gorbachev
Revolution

Four years of *glasnost*, Andrei Sinyavsky remarked, had freed the intellectuals to
say there was nothing to eat. *Perestroika* had not relieved the shortages. Queues
for food and fuel grew longer, the public mood increasingly hostile toward
a general secretary regarded as all talk and no action. The liberated media
chronicled the economic distress in exhaustive detail. One infallible index
of a nation's political morality—crime—climbed toward American levels.
Adrift at home, Gorbachev tried to find his moorings abroad.

FOREIGN AFFAIRS

Following well-publicized April visits to Cuba
and Great Britain, Mikhail Gorbachev went to
China in May 1989 looking for another foreign pageant to shore up his sagging position
at home. Locked in their own reformers-vs.-
conservatives battle, the Chinese leaders welcomed the opportunity to discuss bi-lateral issues.

Talks between Gorbachev and the semi-re-
tired Deng Xiaoping, Chinese Communist
party Chief Zhao Ziyang, and Prime Minister
Li Peng produced agreements to resume local
trade along the frontier and to reduce military
forces to a "minimum level commensurate
with normal good-neighborly relations." Beijing and Moscow would upgrade talks on territorial and border disputes to the foreign-
minister level and restore relations—which
Mao Zedong had suspended—between the
two Communist parties. They could not find a
mutually acceptable formula to end the war in
Cambodia; Moscow supported Vietnam's intervention and Beijing opposed it.

Demonstrations that had begun in Beijing
a few weeks earlier spread to other cities. Appealing for democratic reforms, the protestors
escalated their rhetoric while the authorities
were preoccupied with Gorbachev. Because of
the huge crowds of demonstrators, the Soviet
leader could not get to Tiananmen Square to
lay a ceremonial wreath. The next day, more
than a million peaceful protestors paralyzed
central Beijing. To the relief of Chinese Communist hardliners, Gorbachev left on May 18.

Thirty years of hostility between the two Communist giants appeared to be ending, but domestic events in China now overshadowed that.

On June 3–4, 1989, the world watched on television as tanks and armored personnel carriers entered Tiananmen Square and rolled over thousands of young people armed only with ideals and hopes. Deng and Li ordered the soldiers to show no mercy. Back in Moscow, Gorbachev expressed "regret" over the loss of hundreds of lives and the injuring of roughly 10,000 people. Neither then nor in his *Memoirs* did he draw any parallel between Tiananmen Square and what Soviet troops had done in Tbilisi a few weeks earlier, on a much smaller scale but leaving the Georgians no less dead.

Gorbachev went to Berlin early in October for the GDR's fortieth anniversary celebration and angered his hosts by publicly calling for reform. Masses of anti-Communists promptly took to the streets to demand the resignation of Erich Honecker, head of the East German party and government. Honecker fell. Within days, Soviet Foreign Minister Eduard Shevardnadze called for dissolution of the Warsaw Pact. On November 9 East German security forces stood by as crowds tore holes in the Berlin Wall: *Moscow did not intervene.*

This moment in modern history ranks with the fall of the Bastille, Waterloo, the Austro-Hungarian decision to go to war in 1914, the Bolshevik seizure of power, Munich. With one order, Mikhail Gorbachev could have plunged the world into a crisis of stupendous dimensions. That he did not do so assures Gorbachev, whatever his shortcomings, a place of great honor in history. By calculated action and uncalculated inaction, he had set in motion the events that led to the dismantling not only of the Berlin Wall but of the Soviet empire and the Soviet Communist system itself.

On a state visit to Italy in late November, Gorbachev enunciated a vision of a "common European home." Sincere though he may have been, he also wanted to diminish American influence in Europe and eliminate NATO. The general secretary continued on to Malta for a modest if seasick meeting with President George Bush; the encounter reinforced awareness that the Cold War was ending.

The dizzying tempo accelerated. In November the Supreme Soviet granted economic autonomy to the Baltic republics. The leaders of five Warsaw Pact nations condemned their own 1968 invasion of Czechoslovakia and began negotiations with Moscow for the withdrawal of Soviet forces from Eastern Europe. Along with his sadistic wife, Elena, the Romanian dictator, Nicolae Ceaușescu—whom Elizabeth II and Richard Nixon had wined and dined—went before a firing squad in the bloodiest East European revolution. In Romania as in most countries, however, Communists relabeled "Social Democrats" remained in power.

Perplexed as to why he was much more popular abroad than at home, Gorbachev continued his travels, his wife, the elegant, free-spending, opinion-dispensing Raisa, at his side. May 1990 found him in the United States for a second meeting with George Bush. Gorbachev paraded a natural talent for American-style public relations that delighted America but outraged Russia, where millions saw him as a better-dressed Khrushchevian chatterbox. He and President Bush signed major arms control agreements; one banned production of chemical weapons and limited existing stockpiles to 5,000 tons. Seeking to reduce strategic offensive weapons by 50 percent, the leaders initialed protocols and joint statements that further confirmed the dramatic relaxation of tensions.

Pandering to American officialdom's low regard for his rival, Gorbachev denigrated Boris Yeltsin's election as chairman of the Russian Supreme Soviet (president). This displayed appalling lack of decorum, not to mention taste. Gorbachev overestimated the value of his American popularity in Russia—and underestimated Yeltsin.

In a move that heralded reunification, on the first day of July 1990 the East German government relinquished control of its fatally diseased economy to West Germany. Gorbachev had expressed vague support for German unity, on a gradual basis and with ironclad safeguards for Soviet interests. But he was now in the habit of making strategic policy by pulling tricks out of his hat, and he could not stop. Two weeks later he and West German Chancellor Helmut Kohl met in the USSR, where over beer and sausages they agreed on German reunification. When he conceded that the new Germany would remain in NATO, the Soviet leader shattered a pillar of Kremlin foreign policy and sealed his own political demise.

Gorbachev persuaded himself he had gotten a good deal. The GDR (East Germany) had long been an expensive luxury that would provide few advantages in the event of conventional war in Europe, none in a nuclear conflict. Kohl pledged to finance the withdrawal of Soviet forces from Germany and provide massive financial and technical aid to the USSR. Gorbachev thought he could sell this package to his own military and to conservative Communists. But there was no military or civilian housing in the USSR for the troops who would be coming home from Germany, and Germany did not have the money to rebuild a Russia seven decades of communism had ruined. The military, the CPSU, and a large cross section of the Soviet public believed that Gorbachev had sold the USSR's strategic strength, prestige, and honor for a mess of pottage.

A few days later, the East and West German leaders promised to guarantee Poland's frontiers by treaty immediately after reunification. On September 12, the wartime Allies surrendered their occupation rights in Germany.

East Germany ceased to exist on October 3; the last barriers separating one part of Germany from another came down. The astronomical cost of rebuilding the East—and paying off Moscow—promised to reduce the German standard of living for at least two decades. But Germany, already the fourth largest economy, was poised to assume an even greater political and economic role on the world stage—and to dominate Central Europe. Their ranks swelling by the day, Gorvachev's enemies jotted this down.

The 1990 Nobel Peace Prize went to Gorbachev, who was still presiding over the most spectacular diplomatic revolution in history. NATO and the Warsaw Pact signed a Conventional Forces in Europe Treaty that reduced non-nuclear arms. Further infuriating Gorbachev's opponents, the USSR and its allies made much bigger arms cuts. On November 21, members of the Conference on Security and Cooperation in Europe* signed the Charter of Paris for a New Europe. Not since 1815 had prospects for an enduring peace appeared so bright.

Gorbachev had made this possible. But his own country was coming apart, and he lacked the skills to hold it together.

THE CENTRIFUGE

The Soviet Communists had destroyed the culture of more than two dozen numerically small ethnic groups and threatened to make extinct the Kazakhs, Estonians, and some other peoples. The attempt to create a Frankensteinian "new Soviet man and woman" failed, but the antireligious campaign did great harm to every culture in the USSR beginning with Russia's. It had a pernicious effect in the Muslim and Buddhist areas and in Siberia and the Far

---

*Later renamed Organization for Security and Cooperation in Europe (OSCE).

North, where shamanism and other ancient belief systems clung precariously to life. Russian-Communist chauvinism alienated the five million "Volga" (or "Kazan") Tatars, the largest ethnic group denied a Union republic, allegedly because Tatarstan did not border on a foreign state. Russian-Communist arrogance earned contempt in Transcaucasia and Siberia and strengthened nationalism in the Baltic states, Armenia, Georgia, and elsewhere.

The erosion of central authority and Gorbachev's own willful ignorance of the nation's ethnic problems took a toll. Suppressed nationalist sentiments resurfaced in many areas; primitive tribalism run amok in others.

In March 1989 the Abkhaz, a Caucasian people whose ASSR was surrounded by Georgian territory, demanded independence. The Georgians refused—but insisted on their own freedom from Moscow. In April, on the eleventh anniversary of the restoration of Georgian as that republic's official language, tens of thousands of people paraded through the streets of Tbilisi behind "Free Georgia" activists demanding independence. Panicking, the local officials called in the Army, whose Russian commander, General Igor Rodionov, equipped his troops with rifles, sharpened entrenching tools, hardwood cudgels, CS (chlorine and sulphur) tear gas, a stronger gas (chloroacetophenone [*cheryomukha*]), and chloropicin, an agent last used in the First World War. When Rodionov gave the order, the soldiers attacked the peaceful demonstrators, among whom were many children and women. About 40 deaths and several hundred injuries resulted. For nearly three weeks Rodionov refused to disclose the chemical composition of the gases, forcing physicians to treat the victims by trial and error. Gorbachev denied knowledge of and responsibility for the incident. A Kremlin enquiry blamed the demonstrators and exonerated General Rodionov, the military command, Kremlin authorities, and, of course, Mikhail Gorbachev.

Using the bureaucratic passive, Gorbachev wrote of Tbilisi that "the decision to use force was taken without consulting me." Later, he would not know about Vilnius, Baku, and other, similar episodes. He left for Tiananmen Square a few weeks after what he called the "events" in Tbilisi.

A Ukrainian nationalist group, *Rukh* ("The Movement"), urged that the USSR become a confederation of autonomous republics. Kazakhstan's new leader, Nursultan Nazarbayev, announced support for Gorbachev's reforms but insisted on political and economic autonomy. Moldova, Kyrgyzstan, Ukraine, and Uzbekistan all made the native language the official language. Among the Tatars, some citizens demanded Union republic status, but others now called for complete independence. In the Ferghana region of Uzbekistan, and in Osh Province of Kyrgyzstan, violent struggles took place in 1988–1989 between the native populations and "immigrants" who were in fact peoples from the Caucasus whom Stalin had forcibly resettled in Central Asia. Several thousand people died in this, the area Marco Polo—or whoever wrote the work ascribed to him—called the loveliest on earth.

Baltic deputies in the Congress of People's Deputies agitated for autonomy and briefly walked out when Gorbachev tried to silence them. The Latvian parliament proclaimed that republic's independence. In a show of contempt for Moscow, Estonia passed laws that relegated its Russian and Ukrainian minorities to second-class citizenship.

Late in 1989, the Lithuanian Communist party voted to separate from the CPSU. A few months later, the Sajudis party won a comfortable majority in both local and republic elections, and the musicologist Vitautas Landsbergis became president. When the Lithuanian Supreme Soviet proclaimed the republic's independence, the Kremlin initiated a military crackdown and ordered all diplomatic consular personnel to leave Vilnius. The Army took control of Communist party property and began hunting down deserters and draft-dodgers. Moscow shut off the flow of oil. Gorbachev avoided further humiliation when Lithuania suspended—but did not revoke—its declaration of independence in return for a promise to negotiate. He did not understand that Vilnius would discuss only the mechanics of the break, not the break itself.

Declarations of independence from Uzbekistan and Moldova on the eve of the Twenty-Eighth CPSU Congress in July 1990 did not gladden conservative delegates, and, shortly after the Congress, Ukraine announced it would quit the Union. Armenia, Turkmenistan, and Tajikistan followed in August, Kazakhstan in October. The question was not whether the remaining republics would follow, but when.

RUSSIAN NATIONALISM

The largest, most populous, richest, militarily strongest republic was of course Russia. Early in June 1990, with Boris Yeltsin presiding, the RSFSR Supreme Soviet claimed sovereignty over Russian territory and natural resources.

Yeltsin and most Russians* saw the power struggle as between a renascent Russia and a terminally ill, deformed-from-birth USSR. Russian institutions, notably the Orthodox Church, emerged from decades of repression and neglect, but the Communists had so polluted the Church that cleansing it would take generations. It was not simply that Lenin and Stalin and Khrushchev and their successors—until Gorbachev—had arrested, imprisoned, and executed thousands of priests and nuns, and dynamited or bulldozed monasteries,

---

*English cannot convey in one word the distinction between *russkie*, Russians, and *rossiyane*, all citizens of Russia whose homeland is that nation whatever their actual nationality or ethnic group. Here, "Russians" refers to *rossiyane*.

cathedrals, churches, and chapels. Since 1922 the Communist regime had total control over the Church hierarchy, seminaries, institutions, and property. The Communist party invaded the sacrament of confession and required priests to inform on parishioners. Every single church had to surrender at least 50 percent of the funds it received—the kopecks of an impoverished people—to the KGB; sometimes the secret police "take" was 100 percent. The "tax" persists to this day; and in the cities organized crime also takes its share.

In a small town northeast of Moscow is Holy Trinity Monastery, founded by the fourteenth-century monk Sergii Radonezhsky. With its seminary and churches, it is a kind of Russian Orthodox Vatican. In 1989 it resumed its historic name of Sergeyev Posad; the Bolsheviks had called it Zagorsk. The Sarovskaya Pustyn (Hermitage) in Tambov Province once again began to receive both the pious and the curious, but the state discouraged this: Nearby was the atomic complex "Arzamas-16," dedicated to destruction. Optyna Pustyn near Kaluga, the Donskoi Monastery in Moscow, the Aleksandr Nevsky Monastery near St. Petersburg, and many other complexes, cathedrals, and churches returned to the Russian Orthodox Church.

In the 1920s, the Communists converted a five-altar, nineteenth-century Orthodox cathedral at Ramenskoye south of Moscow into a combination pasta factory and brewery. In 1989, Father Valentin Dronov and the local community began to restore it. In the village of Yerakhtur in Ryazan Province, the tiny local congregation met—still meets—in a wooden shed as it tried to renovate the large brick church built by nineteenth-century grain merchants. There are several thousand such stories in Russia and Siberia. But many more thousands of holy sites—this is true of all religions in the old USSR—lay utterly neglected, testimony to Bolshevik barbarism.

As the Russian people awakened to the physical and moral despoilation of their homeland, pro-independence sentiment burgeoned. Civil society reemerged in unsanctioned clubs and groups that represented every conceivable national interest—patriotic societies, descendants of the gentry and the aristocracy, environmentalists, students of Russian history and culture, and so on.

Freedom of speech and assembly, for which Russia must thank Gorbachev, made all this possible. In such mass-circulation weeklies as *Argumenty i fakty* (*Arguments and Facts*) the Russians could at last read the truth—or at least the closest approximation since 1917—about their past, and their present. There appeared a profusion of historical monographs, new ones and hundreds that could not have been published earlier. While only sensational works such as *Kremlin Wives* won wide popularity, the public did slowly learn its history and unlearn the Bolshevik myths.

The independence movement represented the most moderate tendency in Russian nationalism; chauvinism and even fascism had substantial support. Vladimir Zhirinovsky's ludicrously misnamed Liberal Democratic party demanded restoration of "Great Russia" within the borders of 1865; those borders had included Alaska. Modeling himself on Adolf Hitler and supported by CPSU–KGB factions, Zhirinovsky ran a strong race for the Russian presidency in 1991, finishing third. An anti-Semite who was himself half Jewish, he said, "My mother was Russian, my father a lawyer."

Another Hitler devotee, Dmitry Vasilyev, also an anti-Semite and also partly Jewish, headed a "national-patriotic front" movement, *Pamyat* ("Memory"), which advocated restoration of the monarchy, reestablishment of Russian Orthodoxy as the state Church, and *narodnost* (here, "Russians first"). Praising the hoary forgery *The Protocols of the Elders of Zion,* Vasilyev condemned Jewish Bolsheviks—including "the half-Jew Lenin"—for persecuting Russian Orthodoxy and destroying Russia. But *Pamyat*

faded rapidly, and in 1991 its 25,000 members switched allegiance to Zhirinovsky.

Rival nationalisms and ethnic violence were tearing at the fabric of the state. In late July 1990 the Kremlin invited representatives of the republics to Moscow to discuss the draft of a new treaty that would, Gorbachev promised, meet demands for devolution yet preserve the union.

POLITICS

In April 1989 Gorbachev purged 110 "Dead Souls"* from the Communist party Central Committee to clear the decks for a debate on reform. Beginning May 25, for 13 days a mesmerized public watched the televised proceedings of the new Congress of People's Deputies (CPD). As the first order of business, the Congress elected Gorbachev president. Communists controlled 85 percent of the seats.

But Boris Yeltsin, dismissed as Moscow party boss in November 1987 and then from the Politburo, had won an at-large Moscow seat with 89 percent of the vote. Still a Communist, he helped forge a quasi-democratic opposition to Gorbachev and the party regulars. Andrei Sakharov, whom most Communists saw as the Anti-Lenin, sided with Yeltsin on most issues and focused debate on the necessity for a speedy transition to democracy and the institutionalization of civil and human rights.

Barely able to make himself heard above the crude shouting of the Gorbachev claque and the Communist fundamentalists, Sakharov demanded abolition of Article 6, the constitutional guarantee of the Communist political monopoly. Reds of all shades hated Sakharov for that, his opposition to the Afghan War, his denunciation of the Communist system, and for his renunciation of the nu-

---

*Title of the classic comic novel by Nikolai Gogol.

clear weapons he helped create. But Sakharov, Yeltsin, Gavriil Popov,* Anatoli Sobchak,** other reform Communists, and independents set out to rein in the lawless CPSU.

Conservative and fundamentalist Communists still controlled most levers of power. When the Congress elected the Supreme Soviet, it excluded Yeltsin. The reformers called for a nationwide strike—not on Gorbachev's agenda. A seat for Yeltsin materialized when Deputy Valentin Kazannikov of Omsk stepped down on condition Yeltsin take his place.

Yeltsin's supporters had not spoken casually: A wave of strikes hit the coal mines in the spring and summer of 1989 and threatened to bring the economy to a standstill. Prime Minister Nikolai Ryzhkov appointed a commission, which promptly announced support for the strikers. This and other concessions greatly increased the budget deficit and generated demands for equal treatment. The Gorbachev regime resisted here, gave in there, printed more money.

At the end of July 1989, Sakharov, Yeltsin, Popov, Yuri Afanasyev, and others formed an Inter-Regional Group of several hundred deputies. The Gorbachev regime, as committed to hanging onto power as it was to reform, attacked these people in the media, tapped their telephones, and kept them under physical surveillance.

Mistaking their own confused, often contradictory ideas for coherent programs, the Gorbachevites insisted on setting and carrying out their agenda even when they were not sure what it was. Party General Secretary Gorbachev sought to camouflage attacks on the reformist opposition by removing Ukrainian Party Boss Vladimir Shcherbitsky, former KGB Director Viktor Chebrikov, and other hard-liners from the Politburo in September 1989—

only to appoint three KGB officials including Director Vladimir Kryuchkov as replacements.

THE END OF ARTICLE 6

In November 1989 the conservative-fundamentalist factions in the USSR Supreme Soviet barely defeated a motion to debate Article 6. At the second USSR Congress of People's Deputies (CPD) in December, Gorbachev sidetracked the issue. The most influential opponent of the Red monopoly, Andrei Sakharov, died two days later; his passing impoverished Russian democracy. Gorbachev paid only tepid respects at the bier of the man whom he had liberated from exile, then brutally hounded in the parliament.

Sakharov would play no role in the 1990 "February Revolution" he had done so much to bring about. The largest unofficial crowd in Russia since 1917—half a million or so—gathered in Moscow on February 4 to honor his memory and cheer demands for democracy and the repeal of Article 6—which Gorbachev conceded "would not be a tragedy." On March 13, 1990, the CPD voted to end the monopoly, thus legalizing a multiparty system. But the Communist party retained control of the political mechanism, and that tempered the joy.

To arrest the obvious decline in his political fortunes, Gorbachev asked the Congress to create a stronger executive presidency and elect the first president. What he could not have won from the citizenry, he would take from the Communist-dominated Congress. The voters would choose *future* presidents.

The CPD elected Gorbachev, but nearly 500 votes out of 1,824 went against him. Party discipline was collapsing. In his acceptance speech, Gorbachev concentrated on the economy. He promised to "liberalize" prices, end state industrial and agricultural monopolies, permit free trade in surplus commodities, establish a stock market. A few days later he

---

*Popov became mayor of Moscow in 1990 and not coincidentally a millionaire.

**Sobchak was elected mayor of Leningrad in 1990.

named a 16-member "presidential council," a kind of cabinet. As was his habit, he hooked reformers and reactionaries to the same wagon, ensuring it would go nowhere.

In the March 4, 1990, elections—the first that were truly free—for local offices and for *republic* Congresses of People's Deputies in Russia, Ukraine, and Belarus, adherents of a new movement called Democratic Russia and superficially like-minded candidates won 70 percent of the seats. As one of the winners, Boris Yeltsin quickly became a central figure in the Russian CPD and Supreme Soviet.

THE POWER STRUGGLE

Democracy and freedom mystified Gorbachev. From atop the Lenin Mausoleum, where Stalin and Beria and Khrushchev and Brezhnev had once stood, he watched May Day marchers parade through Red Square carrying banners that read LET THE CPSU LIVE IN CHERNOBYL! GORBACHEV—CHIEF PATRON OF THE MAFIA! TO HELL WITH THE POLITBURO! DOWN WITH THE EMPIRE AND RED FASCISM! FREE LITHUANIA! A few days later he proposed to make it a crime to insult the president.

The jibes were the least of his worries. Over CPSU opposition, Boris Yeltsin won the chairmanship (presidency) of the Russian Supreme Soviet, the republic's highest office. Declaring that Russia's interests outweighed those of the USSR, he pledged to fight for radical reform. The power struggle entered a more serious stage. The KGB denied rumors that it had sabotaged airplanes carrying Yeltsin and staged traffic accidents involving his vehicle. In the CPD, the "dark [sinister] colonels" of the "Union" (Soyuz) faction demanded an end to democratic reform and institution of a dictatorship. Party fundamentalists pushed the candidacy of the neo-Stalinist Ivan Polozkov for general secretary.

Democratic Russia, which embraced broad sectors but by no means all the anti-CPSU opposition in the Russian republic, held its founding congress only in October 1990. Disillusioned by Gorbachev's vacillation and fearing a right-wing coup d'état, its members had coalesced around Yeltsin. Composed of both genuine democrats and opportunists betting on Yeltsin and Russia, Democratic Russia's leadership had a mottled political complexion but agreed on one premise: For all his service to the cause of freedom and democracy, Mikhail Gorbachev had failed.

CPSU DEATHBED: TWENTY-EIGHTH PARTY CONGRESS

Gorbachev returned from Washington in June 1990 to assist in preparations for the Twenty-Eighth Party Congress. Unimpressed by his foreign successes, a dispirited party hemorrhaging from millions of resignations could no longer support the patchwork experiments that constituted his program, but it lacked the will to oust him. Many members looked to Ivan Polozkov and the Russian Communist party—independent of the CPSU since June 20—to overthrow Gorbachev.

But Gorbachev manipulated the agenda, won reelection as general secretary by 3,411 votes to 1,116, and promptly expanded the Politburo to include representatives from all Soviet republics. That pleased the non-Russians but did not enhance his standing in Russia. He alienated almost everyone by dismissing the liberals Eduard Shevardnadze and Aleksandr Yakovlev, and the conservatives Nikolai Ryzhkov and Vladimir Kryuchkov. He engineered the defeat of his former rival, Yegor Ligachev, for the new post of deputy general secretary, equivalent to the old unofficial "second secretary." But where did Gorbachev stand?

Humbling himself almost to the point of groveling, Boris Yeltsin asked for political rehabilitation, thinking he needed party backing to be effective as president of the RSFSR. He still hoped for the reform of the CPSU. But when the delegates greeted him with jeers and catcalls, Yeltsin lost his last illusions: He called on the Communists genuinely to reform themselves into Democratic Socialists. He demanded that the CPSU relinquish all state functions in Russia and abolish its cells in the military, the KGB, and other state agencies. Russia, he declared, would neither obey Communist orders nor be frightened by Communist threats.

A lifelong Communist and atheist, Yeltsin experienced something of a Calvary or at least a journey to Damascus at this Party Congress. In any event he found liberation. He resigned from the Communist party, and Gavriil Popov, Anatoli Sobchak, Sergei Stankevich, and others quickly followed his lead.

The CPSU now consisted of a dwindling handful of disoriented Gorbachevites; a powerful fundamentalist faction; the holders of perhaps 250,000 key posts in government, industry, armed forces, and KGB; and 14 million to 15 million—down from 21 million—rank-and-file members. Many Communists sensed that the Twenty-Eighth Party Congress would be the last.

Mortally wounded though the CPSU obviously was, Yeltsin's demonstrative break with it left him vulnerable to KGB machinations likely to be more successful than previous ones. As strong as his own electoral mandate was, he had, as Gorbachev—of all people—sneered, won the Russian presidency by a bare majority. Yeltsin would need caution, and luck.

THE ECONOMIC CALAMITY

Russia now confronted the USSR, and an agreement between the two most powerful politicians emerged in late July 1990. Yeltsin would support Gorbachev's economic reform, while Gorbachev would accelerate that reform

and accept devolution of central government powers to the republics.

Gorbachev signed a decree "rehabilitating" all victims of Stalinism from the 1920s to the early 1950s. The document made no mention of people persecuted under Lenin between 1917 and 1924, Khrushchev, Brezhnev, Andropov, Chernenko, or Mikhail Gorbachev. A second decree restored citizenship to some dissidents, notably Aleksandr Solzhenitsyn and Yuri Orlov, whom Brezhnev had forcibly exiled. Gorbachev neither explained why he had waited five years to do all this nor accounted for the omissions.

All the competing economic plans recognized the carnage of the "vodka economy" and the necessity of cutting military spending. But what would replace alcohol revenue, and what would become of the military-industrial complex? If the means of production came under private control, what would happen to the 45 to 60 percent of the work force that labored in hopelessly outmoded factories and plants? What would the tax structure be? How could the state eliminate subsidies on food, housing, transportation, and medical care, yet ward off civil war?

A solution that seemed to make painful sense involved (1) steep price increases—only partially offset by higher wages—on food, housing, medical care, and energy; (2) rapid privatization of most state property, excluding defense and strategic natural resources; (3) fair taxation of privatized production, property, and incomes; (4) major reductions in state expenditures; (5) budgetary and accounting reform; (6) devaluation of the ruble, which would eventually become convertible; and (7) foreign assistance.

In late August a team of economists under Stanislav Shatalin and Grigori Yavlinsky presented a "500-Days Program" that embodied these measures, acknowledging that it would bankrupt entire industries and throw millions of people out of work. Prices would rise steeply, and inflationary pressures would test political resolve. The *nomenklatura* would take all its privileges—political and economic influence, high wages in good jobs that often involved no work, excellent housing, private medical care—with it into the market economy. A safety net would give some protection to the lowest-paid workers and retirees, but the standard of living of at least three-quarters of the population would deteriorate sharply and remain low for at least 18 to 36 months. That was the optimistic view.

Yeltsin accepted the Shatalin-Yavlinsky program. USSR Prime Minister Nikolai Ryzhkov and his economists, however, proposed an alternative that would in effect preserve the existing system. On Yeltsin's initiative, the Russian Supreme Soviet adopted a resolution demanding Ryzhkov's resignation and formation of a government of national unity. Ryzhkov threatened to resign if the Shatalin plan became law.

Gorbachev announced he would accept the bitter medicine of the "500 Days"—but in the same breath expressed confidence in Ryzhkov. Three days later he unveiled a draft "presidential plan" concocted by the once-respectable Abel Aganbegyan. The outlandish hodgepodge would offset price increases in some sectors with reductions in others; privatize some enterprises but leave most in the state sector; continue huge subsidies to the defense; lease land to farmers but retain state ownership.

When even Ryzhkov rejected this nonsense, Gorbachev persuaded the restive USSR Supreme Soviet to grant him special executive powers to run the economy by presidential decree until March 1992. He began at once: A November 1990 order required enterprises to turn over 40 percent of their hard-currency earnings to the central government. Private businesses could not survive this confiscatory step. At the end of December a *secret* decree instituted a 5 percent sales tax on consumer goods and services. Even if forthcoming, the proposed revenues would cover only a small fraction of state expenses.

On November 1, 1990, the Russian Supreme Soviet voted 155–9 to begin implementing the original "500 Days Program" in Russia immediately. The disintegration of the USSR had become irreversible.

SOCIAL TENSION

The rancorous debate among the economically illiterate frayed the public's nerves, and in summer–autumn 1990 civil disturbances shook many cities. Exercising his power to ensure public safety, at the end of December Gorbachev ordered joint Army-police patrols in Moscow and other major cities to control crime—and to monitor demonstrations.

Once again the spectre of 1928 appeared. Knowing price increases were imminent, people began hoarding food and everything else they could buy and store. Managers of retail stores, bakeries, food-processing plants, collective farms, steel mills, and oil fields slowed production, waiting for prices to rise. For the first time in decades, bread lines appeared in Moscow in August 1990. Smokers rioted when tobacco supplies dried up. American makers thoughtfully stepped in with emergency supplies priced below cost, and handsomely packaged; one bogus-macho brand of cigarettes virtually replaced the ruble as standard currency. Soap and detergents disappeared from the stores—a major grievance of the coal miners. In the free peasant markets, prices rose beyond the means of most citizens. Most of the billions of rubles the state printed, and the foreign currency now widely circulating, ended up in the hands of the *nomenklatura* and other criminal elements.

When the media tried to interpret some unannounced Army maneuvers near Moscow, Marshal Dmitri Yazov denied rumors that preparations for a military takeover were under way, but he did so in such a way as to leave the question hanging. Food rationing began in thousands of villages and towns in October and in December reached Leningrad.

In this tense situation, the Gorbachev regime received little credit for permitting religious education in the schools and enacting a law guaranteeing freedom of conscience. This, the "rehabilitations," and the publication of banned literary and political works, gratified the intellectuals but left most people indifferent. Preoccupied with the ever more difficult task of making ends meet, and numbed by decades of Communist propaganda about "speculators," many citizens saw the end of controls on petty private trade not as freedom but as a license for the unscrupulous to enrich themselves. Security loomed larger than freedom in the minds of citizens long hostile to private enterprise and accustomed to a low, but guaranteed, standard of living—the "poorfare" state. Opinion polls indicated a sizable majority believed life had been better under Brezhnev. In 1989 the USSR deficit surpassed 100 billion rubles—11 percent of GDP. The government acknowledged an inflation rate of 10 percent in mid-1990; at the end of the year it reached 25 percent *per week*. By 1991 the gold reserve had fallen by a factor of 10, to 240 tons. The *nomenklatura* was sending it to Switzerland to keep it safe for the *nomenklatura*. The Union of Swiss Banks was happy to cooperate.

In December 1990 Gorbachev declared "law and order" his top priority, threw in his lot with the fundamentalists, stepped up his courtship of the military, and named the Latvian Stalinist Boris Pugo minister of the interior. KGB chief Vladimir Kryuchkov threatened to retaliate against government opponents "financed by the West" and to close down "destructive" newspapers. Challenged to cite his authority for suppressing publications that had not violated the Press Law, Kryuchkov replied, "The law can't provide for everything."

On December 20, Foreign Minister Eduard Shevardnadze suddenly resigned. In an emotional speech, he attacked the "dark colonels" and others who had accused him of destroying the Soviet position in Europe and of giving away too much in arms-control agreements. Shevardnadze warned that dictatorship lurked around the corner. The astonished Gorbachev declined to criticize the colonels, who had demanded that he restore order or face removal, and he scoffed at Shevardnadze's prediction. Two days earlier he had said on television,

Everyone knows I won't be a dictator. I could have been . . . had I kept all my power vested in the leadership of the Communist party. . . . The old party leaders wielded power like no one else in the world. Not even Pinochet had such power!

The demon of Augusto Pinochet haunted the dying nation's politics. Gorbachev had sanctioned—ex post facto, he invariably claimed—the bloodshed in Tbilisi and other cities but was psychologically incapable of emulating Pinochet, the American-sponsored fascist dictator of Chile (from 1973 to 1989), at least on the scale required to shore up the Soviet regime. Gorbachev's hand-picked team was not so squeamish.

Gorbachev had named Marshal Yazov defense minister in May 1987. In October 1988 he installed Anatoli Lukyanov, who had a sinister record in Czechoslovakia in 1967–1968, as vice president under the old Brezhnev system, and Vladimir Kryuchkov as KGB director. Then came the Pugo appointment. On December 26 Gorbachev shocked the Congress of People's Deputies by nominating Gennadi Yanayev to be vice president under the new system. A notorious alcoholic and satyr, Yanayev had no qualifications for any responsible post at any level, even in the Communist party. The Congress of People's Deputies rejected him, then reversed itself when Gorbachev threatened to resign.

Prime Minister Nikolai Ryzhkov suffered a heart attack on December 26, 1990. In mid-January 1991, immediately after the Vilnius massacre,* Gorbachev replaced him with Valentin Pavlov and made Aleksandr Bessmertnykh foreign minister. Save for a few supporting players, a new presidential team was in place, ready to do its patron's bidding or betray him, as the situation warranted.

––––––––

*See the following chapter.

SUGGESTED ADDITIONAL READINGS

DODER, DUSKO, and LOUISE BRANSON. *Gorbachev: Heretic in the Kremlin.* New York: Penguin, 1991.

FESHBACH, MURRAY, and ALFRED FRIENDLY, JR. *Ecocide in the USSR.* New York: Basic Books, 1992.

LIGACHEV, YEGOR. *Inside Gorbachev's Kremlin: The Memoirs of Yegor Ligachev.* New York: Pantheon Books, 1993.

MATLOCK, JACK F., JR. *Autopsy on an Empire.* New York: Random House, 1995.

YELTSIN, BORIS N. *Against the Grain: An Autobiography.* New York: Summit Books, 1993.

24

DEATH OF THE USSR

In November 1990, Russian Communist Boss Ivan Polozkov gloated that "public committees for national salvation and the defense of socialism" were springing up in many localities. In December, KGB Director Vladimir Kryuchkov and other USSR officials began planning "extraordinary measures."

BLOODY SUNDAY II

In January 1991, Lithuanians learned through the state-controlled media that a "national salvation committee" was taking over the functions of the republic's legally constituted government. The announcement did not mention any names because no such committee existed; Kryuchkov and USSR Interior Minister Boris Pugo invented it. On the night of January 12–13, Pugo's OMON* ("black beret") forces stormed the headquarters of Vilnius TV, killing 14 unarmed occupants and wounding more than 200. Vilnius's blood now mingled with that of Alma-Aty, Tbilisi, Yerevan, Baku, Stepanakert, and Sumgait.**

Mikhail Gorbachev protested that he had learned of this new "Bloody Sunday" only after the fact. Explaining nothing and apologizing for nothing, he left the public to draw one of two conclusions: He had lost control of the security forces, or he had decided after all to emulate Augusto Pinochet.

Six days later, Riga television broadcast without commentary a "national salvation com-

mittee's" declaration that it had taken power in Latvia. Pugo was trying to provoke a confrontation with democratic forces. When that did not take place, he sent a "black beret" detachment to seize the Interior Ministry in Riga. Four civilians, including the noted cinematographer Andris Slapins, were killed.

Gorbachev remained unperturbed. Like the Latvians, he said, the Lithuanians had brought this on themselves. A flippant expression of regret reinforced the growing conviction that he would spill as much blood as necessary to preserve the USSR and, equally important to Gorbachev, his personal power. Not until late March of 1991 would he dissociate himself from the "national salvation committees."

Pugo's promotion to colonel general was but one sign of the impending return to neo-Stalinism, or maybe even Stalinism. Another was Gorbachev's authorization for Kryuchkov's KGB to enter any business or enterprise, confiscate documents, remove evidence, question employees. Still another was Prime Minister Valentin Pavlov's sudden withdrawal from circulation of 50- and 100-ruble banknotes, one-third of the nation's active currency.† This

---

*An acronym for "militia [police] special mission squad." There were then about 30,000 men in OMON forces under interior ministry control.

**The violence actually began in Yakutsk, but no deaths were recorded there.

†Citizens had to account for all savings beyond one month's salary when exchanging old notes.

Boris Yeltsin, Moscow Mayor Gavriil Popov, and Russian Orthodox Church dignitaries at the ceremonial laying of the first stone for the reconstruction of Kazan Cathedral, November 4, 1990, which Stalin destroyed in 1936. (ITAR-TASS)

peculiar "reform," like those of Stalin and Khrushchev, confiscated the savings of millions of citizens.

Gorbachev had appointed Pugo, Kryuchkov, and Pavlov. Now he tried to put his chief of staff for party affairs, Valeri Boldin, on the new National Security Council.* The Supreme Soviet—no friend of *perestroika,* much less of democracy—rejected the nomination. Everyone save the man who nominated him knew Boldin served two masters: Gorbachev, and Gorbachev's enemies. Not even the Communist-dominated Supreme Soviet could stomach him.

---

*Yanayev, Pavlov, and Foreign Minister Aleksandr Bessmertnykh—who would remain neutral during the putsch—also served on this body, which Gorbachev created on March 7, 1991.

TO PRESERVE THE UNION

When the Russian Republic Supreme Soviet debated the Vilnius and Riga massacres, state television—on Kremlin orders—at first denied Boris Yeltsin live airtime. A vociferous public outcry changed bureaucratic minds. Yeltsin accused Gorbachev of seeking "absolute power" and—predicting he would never grant the republics independence—called for his resignation and the transfer of power to a "collective body."

In his counterattack, Gorbachev charged the democrats with attempting to destroy the USSR. That, he said, would kill reform and produce chaos, civil war, perhaps even world war. The Gorbachevites drafted an agreement that would give the republics the right to secede under strict conditions. The democratic opposition and many nationalists rejected this as a device to maintain centralized power.

Fundamentalist Communists condemned a priori any change in the 1922 document—largely Stalin's work—that created the USSR. Kazakhstan's Nursultan Nazarbayev favored a compromise involving political devolution and a common market. Scoffing at Gorbachev's boast that Russia would sign the treaty, Yeltsin called for a "declaration of war on the country's leadership, which has led us into this morass." Critics accused Yeltsin of siding with Pugo and Kryuchkov. In fact, it was a calculated risk to save embryonic democracy.

The Baltic states, Georgia, Armenia, and Moldova boycotted the March 17 referendum, which asked, "Should the USSR continue to exist or not?" In the nine other republics, about 75 percent of those voting answered affirmatively. But what did "or not" imply? The Kremlin had announced in advance that the vote would have no legal consequence, yet Gorbachev called it a victory. Far more significant was the Russian electorate's overwhelming approval, in a companion referendum, of direct popular elections for the office of RSFSR president.

ETHNIC VIOLENCE

Defenders of the Union pointed to violence on the periphery as proof of the need for a firm central authority. Animosities held in check for seven decades indeed menaced the nation with civil war.

The conflict in Nagorno-Karabakh continued unabated. The Azerbaijani minority sought support from other Turkic peoples and Muslims outside the USSR, while the Armenian majority relied on aid from Armenia, Moscow, and the Armenian diaspora. This ancient ethnic-religious-cultural-historical animosity united the Shiite Muslims of Azerbaijan—and Iran—with Islam's dominant Sunnis. Turkey offered to mediate the conflict; but Turkey was Armenia's hereditary foe.

In Moldova, the roughly 55 percent of the Romanian-speaking population rode a wave of national-ethnic expression and Slavophobia. The Ukrainians and Russians—about 30 percent—naturally tried to stem this tide. Moldovan overtures to the post-Ceaușescu regime in Bucarest made reunion with Romania a distinct possibility. This alarmed all minorities; ethnic violence erupted in 1992. General Aleksandr Lebed's Russian Fourteenth Army quickly subdued the Romanian-speaking separatists, but Lebed could not remain in Moldova forever, and the victory was only temporary.

Looming above every other minority problem was Ukraine. Desperately trying to prevent that republic's secession, the Gorbachev regime legalized the Uniate (Ukrainian Catholic) Church, which Stalin had outlawed; that merely generated new demands. The separatist movement faltered when the Ukrainian Communists, then still serving Moscow, infiltrated *Rukh* ("The Movement") and seized control. Miraculously transformed into respectable nationalists, the Communists under Leonid Kravchuk temporized, hoping the USSR would survive, then after the August 1991 "vodka putsch" announced that only total independence would satisfy them.

Communists remained in control of the Central Asian republics and Kazakhstan, where generations of Slav colonialism and Soviet Communist misrule had stunted the growth of the intelligentsia and inhibited the formation of even proto-political parties. Most nationalist movements remained weak, but some party bosses exploited the center's collapse to edge toward independence. A serious effort to oust the Moscow-leaning Communists came in Tajikistan. The great majority of the population was Sunni Muslim by tradition and heritage. Militantly *Shiite* Iran, however, sponsored a religious revival that threatened the Communist regime in Dushambe. In 1992, scattered violence became a civil war in which Russia inevitably became involved. In late 1996 and early 1997 a tenuous truce emerged.

Lacking a strategy, Gorbachev again changed tactics. In April 1991 he persuaded Yeltsin and the leaders of eight other republics to join him in a "nine plus one" plan to preserve the USSR. No realistic observer doubted that the Baltic states, Georgia, Armenia, and Moldova would go their separate ways. Under the proposed agreement, the other nine republics would gain considerable autonomy in return for remaining in the USSR—the "one" that would control foreign policy, defense, and much fiscal policy.

YELTSIN'S MANDATE

In the RSFSR presidential election campaign, Boris Yeltsin was clearly the favorite. In return for his support of "nine plus one," he won the Kremlin's agreement to transfer control of the Kuzbas and Rostov-on-Don mines to the RSFSR and tried to placate the striking miners with higher wages and increased benefits. He renewed his pledge to work with Gorbachev.

Party conservatives favored Nikolai Ryzhkov, the former prime minister. Vadim Bakatin, who had served briefly as interior minister, hoped to win voters who considered Ryzhkov too conservative, Yeltsin too radical. Vladimir Zhirinovsky cultivated the "Stalin class"—the *Lumpenproletariat,* mindless chauvinists, Communist fundamentalists, street thugs—which demanded iron-fisted rule in a Russian-dominated USSR free of Jews and a belligerent foreign policy. General Albert Makashov promised cheap vodka and the recovery of Alaska.

The KGB and the fundamentalists attacked Yeltsin viciously, but a month before the election Kryuchkov and Yeltsin agreed to establish a quasi-independent *Russian* KGB. Deter-

mined to protect the secret police, Kryuchkov was hedging his bets. For his part, Yeltsin knew he could not defeat the KGB—and could not conceive of Russia without it.

Yeltsin won with 60 percent of the vote. Ryzhkov lagged far behind with 16 percent; Zhirinovsky finished third with 7.27 percent. The great prize Gorbachev had made possible but did not understand, democratically conferred power, went to a former protégé become mortal enemy. Gorbachev had come to office because fewer than 300 Central Committee members confirmed a secret decision of nine old men. More than 45 million citizens of Russia had voted for Yeltsin.

TOWARD FIASCO

Yeltsin's victory set in motion the second phase of the plot to return the older, more conservative wing of the *nomenklatura*—the Soviet equivalent of the Mafia's "men of respect"—to power. Never comfortable with Gorbachev, it had lost faith in his ability to be its Pinochet.

In mid-June Valentin Pavlov demanded that the USSR Supreme Soviet transfer to his Cabinet some emergency powers earlier given the president. Supreme Soviet Chairman Anatoli Lukyanov, a longtime Gorbachev associate, supported Pavlov, as did Kryuchkov. Calling "emergency measures" necessary to "save the country from ruin," the KGB chief pledged to "preserve the [Communist] social system, not protect somebody's power." Gorbachev denounced this attempt to curb his powers, and by a 262–24 vote the Supreme Soviet rejected Pavlov's plan. A legal transfer of power eluded the conspirators.

Incredibly, Pavlov remained in office. Gorbachev had lost control of events, his government, and, it seemed, his senses. Marshal Yazov and Kryuchkov publicly denied planning "some sort of *coup.*"

The Pugo-Kryuchkov-Pavlov-Boldin-Yazov conspiracy also served notice on Yeltsin. Pavlov bribed Yakut (Sakha) officials to give the USSR government exclusive rights to mine and market the ASSR's diamonds and other minerals. That would deprive the Russian republic of more than a billion dollars annually in tax revenues.

On June 20, 1990, Moscow Mayor Gavriil Popov called on American Ambassador Jack F. Matlock at the latter's official residence. As the two chatted, Popov wrote a note in large letters: A COUP IS BEING ORGANIZED TO REMOVE GORBACHEV. WE MUST GET WORD TO BORIS NIKOLAYEVICH [YELTSIN]. Then in Washington, Yeltsin would see President George Bush later that day. Writing back, Matlock asked for names. Popov scribbled "PAVLOV, KRYUCHKOV, YAZOV, LUKYANOV." Later he added Valeri Boldin and some others.

Washington informed Matlock that President Bush would pass the message along to Yeltsin and identify the source.* Matlock was to inform Gorbachev only that the United States had received an unconfirmed report of an imminent attempt to overthrow him.

There would be no coup. Matlock did not reveal the names on Popov's list. Gorbachev heard Matlock out and asked him to convey his thanks to President Bush. But he, Gorbachev, had the situation under control: The "plot" was nothing more than the belligerent grumbling of the "dark colonels" in Soyuz (Union). In his 1995 *Memoirs,* Gorbachev continued to insist on this interpretation. In his own book, *Autopsy on an Empire,* Matlock called him a "somnambulist."

Gorbachev departed on July 7 to ask the "Group of Seven" (G-7) capitalist states then meeting in London for economic aid. He left

routine government operations to the traitor Boldin; Byzantine intrigue now descended several levels. A conservative newspaper claimed Gorbachev was staging a charade to obtain agreement on the Union treaty and favorable treatment from the G-7. Warning that the G-7 were out to enslave the Soviet Union, Valentin Pavlov denounced the highly publicized "grand bargain"—tentatively approved by both Gorbachev and Yeltsin—according to which the West would extend $30 billion in aid in return for a Kremlin pledge to continue on the road toward democracy and the free market.

THE COUNTDOWN

Late in June 1991, an OMON detachment occupied and shut down the Vilnius telephone-telegraph-radio-television center, then mysteriously withdrew after two hours. There were no casualties; reaction in the USSR and abroad was muted. The dress rehearsal had been successful.

Signs of an impending mutiny multiplied, not least because Marshal Yazov, Gennadi Yanayev, and Valentin Pavlov drank and talked too much and—like Gorbachev—relied on unreliable subordinates. Pugo was relatively sober and close-mouthed. The shooting in May of the Latvian OMON chief had shaken the entire organization's morale, however, and the smooth Vilnius rehearsal had not restored it. Shocked by the failure of the "national salvation committees" to attract any support beyond Communist fundamentalists and Russian chauvinists, KGB head Vladimir Kryuchkov had become more cautious. The creation of a Russian KGB, he realized, had been a mistake. Many agents and administrative employees had transferred their loyalties from the USSR to Russia. Organizational gossip flowed across jurisdictional lines and jeopardized the chances of achieving surprise in any major operation.

---

*Matlock later wrote that, ignoring the KGB's total control of all Soviet communications, Secretary of State James Baker proved "thoughtless" and President Bush "reckless" in their subsequent handling of the extraordinary situation. *Autopsy on an Empire,* p. 545.

Anatoli Lukyanov did not consider himself disloyal to Gorbachev, with whom he had long worked closely. He attended secret meetings that debated introduction of a state of emergency, but never—he later maintained—the overthrow of the president. Lukyanov was not alone in believing drastic measures imperative. He and others reasoned that, with Gorbachev incapable of decisive action, the heads of key state agencies were obliged to save the nation.

THE DEMOCRATIC FORCES

Early in July, Eduard Shevardnadze and other prominent figures formed a Democratic Reform Movement. Nucleus of a mass citizens' rally rather than a political party, the movement sought to play an educational role and prepare the free citizenry to fill the vacuum left by the CPSU's disintegration. Among the leaders were Mayors Popov of Moscow and Sobchak of Leningrad, Russian Vice President-elect Aleksandr Rutskoi, Russian Prime Minister Ivan Silayev, Stanislav Shatalin, and Aleksandr Yakovlev.

Boris Yeltsin was not a member. He took the oath of office as president of Russia in a July 10 Kremlin ceremony, and 10 days later he ordered the Communist party banned in the workplace throughout the republic. There would be no leniency toward those responsible for ruining a great nation. Gorbachev attacked the decree as unconstitutional.

Disagreements between the two presidents notwithstanding, the conspirators Lukyanov, Kryuchkov, Pavlov, Pugo, Boldin, and Yazov believed Gorbachev and Yeltsin were conspiring to destroy the USSR. On July 23 the conservative *Sovetskaya Rossiya* published a menacing article, titled "A Word to the People" from right-wing writers and officers who called on the military and all "healthy forces" to save the country.

"How we could have given power," the statement asked, "to people who do not love this country, who enslave themselves to foreign masters and seek advice and blessings overseas?" The signers—among them General Aleksandr Rutskoi and Gennadi Zyuganov—warned that the "Motherland is dying, falling apart, sinking into darkness and nothingness." Virtually identical language would resurface on the first day of the putsch.

Gorbachev, Yeltsin, and Nursultan Nazarbayev met in Novo Ogaryevo near Moscow on the night of July 29–30 to refine the proposed Union treaty, the signing of which they planned for August 20. They agreed that the republics would have greater control over fiscal policy, and that respect for human rights would be a "highly important principle" of the new USSR. On July 30 the Pavlov Cabinet rejected these points and took steps to curtail the republics' economic autonomy.

Gorbachev's opponents rejected human rights, decentralization, and economic reform. In the realm of foreign policy, their near-hysterical arguments did not prevent Gorbachev and President Bush from signing history's most sweeping strategic arms-reduction agreement in the Kremlin on July 31, 1991. Although retaining thousands of nuclear warheads, the two sides had taken a step toward sanity. Coupled with the liberation of Eastern Europe and the reunification of Germany, the 1990–1991 arms accords definitively ended the Cold War.

Clinging to his illusions, Gorbachev proposed a new CPSU program. It foresaw democratization of the party along European Social-Democratic lines and finally acknowledged the magnitude of the horrors: "The Communist Party unconditionally condemns the crimes committed by the Stalinists, who broke and mutilated the lives of millions of people, of entire nations." The Stalinists whom Gorbachev had appointed to the highest offices in the land did not take these words kindly.

Three days after publication of the draft, the last survivor of Stalin's inner circle, Lazar Kaganovich, died peacefully in his apartment across the Moscow River from the Kremlin. A few years earlier he had pledged to live until the return of Stalinism. Had he lived three weeks longer, he would have gone out with a smile.

THE "VODKA PUTSCH"

Gorbachev left on August 5 for a vacation at Foros in the Crimea; no Crimean Tatars allowed. He continued to work on state papers and finally moved against Prime Minister Valentin Pavlov: By an August 10 presidential decree Gorbachev transferred all property owned by the central government to a USSR State Property Fund. As lessor, the Fund would oversee the privatization of state enterprises, real estate, and other holdings worth trillions of rubles. The president would appoint the Fund chairman, who would report only to him. This stripped the Cabinet of control over state property; Pavlov would be powerless to preserve the old system.

The conspirators had to move. Marshal Yazov entrusted operational planning to Major General P. S. Grachev, commander of airborne assault troops. Grachev put his troops on high alert, but once the putsch was under way did not lose contact with the Yeltsin forces. Vladimir Kryuchkov edited the list of people to be arrested and increased the already-existing surveillance; he called Gorbachev several times during the week of August 10–16. Although he did not reveal all his moves, Kryuchkov warned that a crisis was at hand and urged declaration of a state of emergency. Gorbachev refused. When the conspirators later claimed that the president had known everything, they were not wholly truthful, but neither were they wholly fabricating their defense.

On August 17, Kryuchkov summoned the plotters to the KGB's luxurious, vodka- and scotch-stocked "ABC Complex" in Moscow. He and Yuri Plekhanov—head of the KGB Ninth Directorate, which was supposed to protect the leadership—told the others that an armed uprising against the government was imminent; it was linked to the new Union treaty, the signing of which was set for August 20. They did not know, or could not reveal, who was involved, but they claimed the rebels had already taken up strategic positions in Moscow and elsewhere.

If only it were so, from their point of view. Imagination enhanced by vodka and scotch, the conspirators signed a declaration for broadcast a few hours later: Owing to the illness of President Gorbachev, a "State Committee on the State of Emergency" (SCSE) was taking power.

Marshal Sergei Akhromeyev and several other high-ranking officers conveyed the military establishment's approval. The committee assigned Boldin, Plekhanov, General Valentin Varennikov, and a subordinate to fly to Foros and present the fait accompli to Gorbachev. The KGB would take 60 or so leading democrats and liberal publicists into custody; a grateful nation would applaud the decisiveness.

Recognizing Plekhanov, the head of the presidential security force at Foros admitted him and his colleagues late in the afternoon on August 18. Gorbachev listened briefly, then attempted to telephone Moscow, only to discover that the lines had been cut. Cursing, he told the delegation that neither he nor the USSR Supreme Soviet had appointed any such committee. Valeri Boldin—risen from what he later claimed was his deathbed—read the SCSE declaration and demanded Gorbachev sign it. Accusing his commander-in-chief of weakness in the face of "extremist, nationalist, and separatist forces," General Varennikov screamed at him to resign. According to his own account, Gorbachev told his visitors to "go to Hell." Raisa Gorbacheva began burning the family's private papers.

The Russian "White House" (James Trott)

The delegation returned to Moscow bearing neither Gorbachev's signature nor his head. Gorbachev, his family, and three dozen loyal members of the guard remained in Foros under house arrest. For the next three days minor functionaries stationed near Foros, but not inside the compound with Gorbachev, had possession of the nuclear-attack codes.

The state of emergency ostensibly went into effect at 4:00 A.M. Moscow time on August 19. Justifying it on the basis of the Constitution and the referendum on the USSR's fate, eight SCSE members* swore to resolve the "profound and comprehensive crisis, the political and civil confrontation, the confrontation between nationalities, chaos and anarchy."

Having just returned from Kazakhstan,

Boris Yeltsin heard the SCSE statement on the radio. He immediately went to the Russian "White House," the parliament building, barely eluding the KGB detail sent to arrest him. Assisted by loyal police and civilians, his guards began constructing barricades.

At 9:00 A.M. Yeltsin, Russian Prime Minister Ivan Silayev, and Acting Chairman of the RSFSR Supreme Soviet Ruslan Khasbulatov issued an appeal "To the Citizens of Russia." They denounced the SCSE's act as "right-wing, reactionary, and unconstitutional" and urged citizens to rebuff the "putschists" and return the country to "normal constitutional development." They insisted that Gorbachev be allowed to address the nation and called for the convening of an extraordinary session of the USSR Congress of People's Deputies. They proclaimed a general strike.

The Russian "White House" is in the Kras-

---

*Yanayev, Pugo, Yazov, Kryuchkov, Pavlov, A. I. Tiyazkov, Vasili Starodubtsev, Oleg Baklanov. The terrified Boldin was trying to hide.

nopresnensky borough. That morning, the borough council could not contact it and did not know Yeltsin's fate. At 10:00 A.M. borough council members published their own declaration:

RESPECTED KRASNOPRESNENSKY RESIDENTS!

At dawn today a coup d'état took place in our country. The lawful president, M. S. Gorbachev, was removed from power. The free media have ceased functioning. We are deprived of the possibility of learning the reaction of the population, the Supreme Soviets, and the republic governments to these events.

Power is in the hands of the Army, KGB, Interior Ministry.

We protest the introduction of the state of emergency and abolition of the constitutional rights of citizens.

We demand an extraordinary session of the USSR Supreme Soviet and M. S. Gorbachev's appearance before it.

We call on all citizens to maintain calm and order, to refrain from giving grounds for provocations, and to remember that an incautious step could lead to bloodshed.

The return of the legal power can only be accomplished by lawful means. The lives of your relatives, friends and neighbors depend on your restraint and calm.

For the coordination of our efforts, wait for information from your councilmen.

Written by historian Yuri N. Zhukov,* the document reflected the harmony between the democratic intelligentsia and the RSFSR leadership.

The conspirators proved dazzlingly inept. After instructing the Army to "maintain order," Marshal Yazov—"I won't be a Pinochet," he said—told his subordinates to watch televi-

---

*Son of Olga Ovchinnikova, the Red Army commander pictured on page 31.

sion and listen to the radio. Vladimir Kryuchkov and Boris Pugo shut down most newspapers and took control of the official broadcast media, but foreign television and radio continued uninterrupted, as did three small print news services. International telephone lines, though as always monitored by the KGB, functioned normally. Beamed by satellite to Munich, London, and Atlanta, information came back to the RSFSR "White House" via TV signals, telephone, e-mail, and fax. Several low-power radio stations operated intermittently. The defenders of the infant democracy had adequate information and could coordinate with each other.

On August 19, Yeltsin signed three decrees that pronounced the putsch unconstitutional and branded its perpetrators outlaws. He warned that if anyone obeyed SCSE orders he would be prosecuted, and he guaranteed legal protection to military, security agency, and prosecutorial personnel who opposed the SCSE. At a tense noon press conference he asked Muscovites to come to the "White House" to defend democracy.

At 1:00 P.M., Yeltsin climbed atop a Taman Division tank—elements of that unit had opted to defy the SCSE—and exhorted the crowd to prevent the overthrow of the legally constituted regime. Like his unhesitating decision to back Gorbachev, this was a defining moment: The courageous gesture heartened the supporters of democracy and confounded its enemies. One of Yeltsin's decrees authorized RSFSR officials and agencies to carry out functions of the USSR government in Russia.

General Varennikov repeatedly called Kryuchkov demanding to know why Yeltsin had not been shot. Convinced of the passivity of the public and the weakness of the democrats, the plotters had anticipated a quick and easy victory. Kryuchkov and Pugo would make arrests, of course, but there was no great hurry: Who would dare disobey the KGB?

Many thousands of people did. The unexpected resistance at the "White House," where the crowd continued to grow throughout the day, appeared to call for activation of a backup plan: KGB "Alpha Group" would storm the building.

At 5:00 P.M., Gennadi Yanayev, Boris Pugo, and three other conspirators gave one of the modern era's strangest press conferences. Yanayev had been drinking steadily for 36 hours; hands shaking uncontrollably, he announced that he had assumed the duties of the presidency. Gorbachev was ill, but after a "long rest and treatment in a safe place" he might be able to return to work. The SCSE had taken power to combat the disastrous economic slide, ethnic violence, and general anarchy. There would be a temporary suspension of some civil liberties including the right of assembly and freedom of the press. Communist newspapers including *Pravda* would continue to publish.

A journalist asked, "Did you seek any suggestion or advice from General Pinochet?" Yanayev did not answer.

The SCSE intended to bury *glasnost–perestroika* and restore a tough KGB regime—at a minimum. The conspirators sensed the population had had enough of vacillation, jungle capitalism, and humiliation in Afghanistan and Eastern Europe. They believed people were disgusted with a free press that embarrassed public officials and dredged up the past, and were outraged by the pornography on sale everywhere. The endless political bickering, the plotters believed, had exhausted people who had had no role in politics since 1920; politics was best left to the Communist party! A move to end all this would surely have popular support. The CSCE cause was just, its forces invincible. It had unfurled its colors; all patriotic citizens would salute them.

These propositions proved false in Moscow, Leningrad, and most other large cities. The plotters had more support in small towns and villages, where conservative views usually pre-

vail. The chief enemy of both SCSE and democrats, however, was apathy. Even in the urban areas, a population weary of worthless promises generally remained aloof. Pro-democracy crowds surrounded the "White House" and flooded Palace Square in Leningrad, where Mayor Anatoli Sobchak and other democrats denounced the conspirators, but most citizens went calmly about routine business in both cities. In Samara, Nizhni Novgorod (formerly Gorky), Astrakhan, Irkutsk, Novosibirsk, Yekaterinburg (formerly Sverdlovsk), Vladivostok, and other cities, most people neither knew nor cared what was going on in Moscow.

Toward the end of the day on August 19, several vehicles of the airborne forces drove up to the "White House" flying the white-blue-red Russian flag, which Peter the Great had copied from the Dutch. Disobeying Marshal Yazov, General Grachev had despatched them to protect RSFSR leaders. The SCSE had cracked. There was hope.

Communication between the two sides developed in the early morning hours of August 20. As news came in from around Russia of pledges of support—including the military—for Yeltsin, and almost incidentally for Gorbachev, the democratic leaders came to realize the strength of their position. By mid-morning, Aleksandr Rutskoi, Prime Minister Ivan Silayev, and Ruslan Khasbulatov met Anatoli Lukyanov— who feigned great surprise at it all—and presented the Russian government's demand for the immediate liquidation of the SCSE.

At noon an enormous crowd listened outside the "White House" to Rutskoi, Shevardnadze, Popov, Sergei Stankevich, and other speakers: Liberty still lived, and the SCSE "state criminals" had 24 hours to surrender. But at 5:30 P.M., anticipating the Alpha Group assault, Yeltsin's lieutenants ordered women to leave the "White House." The defenders braced themselves. Loyal Army units had provided weapons, gas masks, and fatalistic advice; no one had any illusions about the chances of the two thousand civilians and a few soldiers inside the "White House." The Alpha Group commander estimated he could annihilate them and take the building in 20 minutes.

Several hundred tanks, armored personnel carriers, and heavy trucks now clogged central Moscow. Civilians bantered with the soldiers, brought food and flowers, pleaded with them to hold their fire. As bewildered as everyone else in Russia, the troops protested that they had no intention of shooting.

The hours passed and the situation at the "White House" remained peaceful. All over the country, agencies and individuals who had initially supported the putsch began to have second thoughts. After a nasty scolding from his wife, Marshal Yazov resigned from the

SCSE. Pavlov and Yanayev drank themselves into insensibility, a process which, given their head start, did not take long. KGB head Vladimir Kryuchkov's worst fears about divided loyalties among KGB personnel came true.

But the logic of events demanded blood. A revolution, as Mao Zedong had said, is not a tea party; neither is a comic-opera putsch. Nerves were frayed. Neither the SCSE nor the defenders of the "White House" had had much sleep. Fraternization with civilians had confused the soldiers and compromised discipline; the absence of clear-cut orders made a tense situation worse. The military vehicles that careened around Moscow were occasionally hit by Molotov cocktails and paving stones, and sometimes the occupants fired back. In the

September 29, 1991, "Russian Requiem" concert at the Bolshoi Theatre, Moscow, in honor of the three young martyrs to democracy. From left: Ruslan Khasbulatov, Raisa Gorbacheva, Mikhail Gorbachev, Ludmila Rutskaya, Aleksandr Rutskoi, Ivan Silayev. (ITAR-TASS)

end, three young civilian men were killed: Dmitri Komar, Ilya Krichevsky, and Vladimir Usov would rest among Russia's honored dead.

On the afternoon of August 21, the plotters realized their gamble had failed. It was just a misunderstanding, they said—they thought they were doing what the president *wanted*. Yazov, Lukyanov, Kryuchkov, Politburo Member Oleg Baklanov, and other officials flew to Foros, where Gorbachev refused to see them until they restored his communications. They complied. He denounced them as traitors.

Early in the morning of August 22, Gorbachev returned to Moscow, but not before naming General Mikhail Moiseyev, a SCSE sympathizer, as the new defense minister. That appointment stemmed from inadequate information, but Gorbachev's decision not to go to the "White House" reflected stupendously bad judgment. Tens of thousands of people were waiting for him. His ordeal had been no worse than theirs, his bravery of a lesser magnitude. And he had handpicked every single one of the conspirators. This whole business, as Martin Malia wrote, was "an act of the Soviet government"—which Gorbachev headed.

Gorbachev went home. Vladimir Kryuchkov and Marshal Yazov went to prison. The crowd at the "White House" drifted away, its exaltation tempered by the suspicion that courage and democracy needed a worthier champion.

DEATH OF THE USSR

A handful of people had put their lives in jeopardy to defend the Russian White House; millions celebrated their victory. The great myth of secret-police omnipotence exposed, an enormous crowd jammed the square in front of KGB headquarters and refused to disperse until a crane removed the statue of "Iron Felix" Dzerzhinsky, Lenin's first deputy butcher. It is not clear who summoned the crane. The

square resumed its old name, Lubyanka. The people inside KGB headquarters continued their work, which included videotaping the demonstration.

Gorbachev rescinded the appointment of Defense Minister Moiseyev on August 23, but he promptly made two more of the same ilk. He referred to himself loftily as "the president" and defended the CPSU. A public opinion poll revealed an approval rating of 4 percent for him, 77 percent for Yeltsin.

On August 23, Gorbachev came to the Russian parliament to thank it and give his version of events; the deputies heckled and jeered him. Humiliated almost beyond endurance, he complied like a chastised schoolboy when Yeltsin commanded him to read aloud documents proving the treason of his appointees. The USSR deathwatch had begun.

Boris Pugo, who had ordered the "black berets" to kill unarmed civilians, shot and seriously wounded his wife, then committed suicide. Marshal Akhromeyev hanged himself. Still smarting from his wife's tongue-lashing, Marshal Yazov wept as he apologized for disgracing his uniform. Protesting their innocence, Anatoli Lukyanov and Valeri Boldin joined the other surviving plotters in prison.

Yeltsin temporarily banned Communist party newspapers, then on August 23 "suspended" the party in Russia. Struggling to catch up, Gorbachev resigned the next day as CPSU general secretary, transferred control of CPSU property to the state, and ordered the party out of the government, KGB, judiciary, and military.

Ignoring a warning from Armenian President Levon Ter-Petrosian—himself no democrat—not to try to "reanimate the cadaver," Gorbachev fought on. He persuaded the USSR Supreme Soviet to dissolve itself, then carried the battle to the USSR Congress of People's Deputies. On September 5 that body transferred legislative power from the Kremlin to the 10 republics still—despite declarations of independence—formally in the Union. There was nothing left of the USSR but the shell.

The *Russian* Congress of People's Deputies approved plans for the kind of drastic economic reform Gorbachev had rejected. In mid-November 1991, Boris Yeltsin moved to take control of all USSR economic resources in Russia, which would absorb all USSR ministries beginning with those involved in the economy. This reduced the federal government to beggary. The USSR had a deficit of 153 billion rubles through the first three quarters of the year, and to deal with it Gorbachev appealed to the Supreme Soviet to print more money. On November 30, Yeltsin agreed to bail out Gorbachev's bankrupt regime—by taking over the USSR budget.

Meeting at Nikita Khrushchev's former dacha at Belovezhskaya Pushcha near Minsk on December 8, Yeltsin, Belarus President Stanislav Shushkevich and President Leonid Kravchuk of Ukraine signed a treaty creating a Commonwealth of Independent States (CIS). The USSR, they announced, was dead.

According to several aides who were present, Boris Yeltsin was thoroughly intoxicated at that meeting, and he remained so for the next couple of weeks. That explains, in part, why he called the American secretary of state with the news before telephoning Gorbachev, who immediately asked the USSR Congress of People's Deputies to overturn the Belovezhskaya Pushcha act.

Still soliciting the views of the other Muslim republics, President Nazarbayev of Kazakhstan did not attend the Belovezhskaya Pushcha meeting. After a fortnight of hectic negotiations, the leaders of all the Soviet republics except the Baltics and Moldova met in Alma-Aty on December 21 and approved the general principles agreed on at Belovezhskaya Pushcha: "With the formation of the Commonwealth of Independent States," they announced, "the USSR ceases to exist."

On December 24, Russia took over the USSR seat in the United Nations. On Christmas Day, 1991, Mikhail Gorbachev resigned as president of a nation that had not existed for four days, and at midnight the Russian flag replaced the hammer and sickle over the Kremlin. When Gorbachev returned the next day to clear out his office, the man who had changed the world found that Yeltsin had changed the locks.

SUGGESTED ADDITIONAL READINGS

BOLDIN, VALERI I. *Ten Years That Shook the World: The Gorbachev Era as Witnessed by His Chief of Staff.* New York: Basic Books, 1994.

DOBBS, MICHAEL. *Down with Big Brother: The Fall of the Soviet Empire.* New York: Knopf, 1997.

GORBACHEV, MIKHAIL S. *Memoirs.* New York: Doubleday, 1996.

GRACHEV, A. S. *Final Days: The Inside Story of the Collapse of the Soviet Union.* Boulder, CO: Westview Press, 1995.

KRYUCHKOV, V. A. *Lichnoe delo.* (2 vols.). Moscow: Olimp, 1996.

LIGACHEV, YEGOR. *Inside Gorbachev's Kremlin: The Memoirs of Yegor Ligachev.* New York: Pantheon, 1993.

MATLOCK, JACK F., JR. *Autopsy on an Empire.* New York: Random House, 1995.

REMNICK, DAVID. *Lenin's Tomb: The Last Days of the Soviet Empire.* New York: Random House, 1993.

25

THE TIME OF TROUBLES: SECOND CONVULSION*

Q: *What are the lessons [of the putsch] for the West?*
A: **I suppose: Don't exclude exotic possibilities from your scenarios of the future of Russia—or of anywhere else. If you are a student, switch from political science to history.**
—**Robert Conquest in** *The Wall Street Journal,* **August 22, 1991**

The sudden disappearance of a superpower has no precedent in modern history and only the vanishing of Atlantis offers a parallel in Western mythology. Among the millions of uncomprehending Russians were the "vodka putschists" now lodged in Sailors' Rest Prison in Moscow.**

THE POLITICAL ANTI-STRUCTURE

Boris Yeltsin dismissed the senior Gorbachev appointees but could do nothing about the *nomenklatura,* the "men of respect" who embodied the state of which he was the head. Most secret-police personnel remained in place. Those in foreign intelligence-gathering merely changed their identification cards from KGB to SVRR, an acronym for Russian Foreign Intelligence Service. The new chief was the career KGB General Yevgeni Primakov, later foreign minister. The Russian ministry of security took over domestic KGB functions—and Alpha Group—and kept the same personnel, as did the interior ministry. At the foreign ministry, where many top officials had supported the putsch, there took place the greatest reorganization since Molotov's time.

Army General Pavel Grachev, whose refusal to follow the putschists' orders had swung the battle against them, became defense minister. He forced senior generals who had supported the putsch to retire and demoted or transferred many other officers. Commander of Soviet paratroopers in Afghanistan between 1985 and 1988, Grachev now had to oversee the humiliating withdrawal of the Russian Army from the former Soviet republics, the largest such operation in history. In a spring 1992 comment aimed as much at the Yeltsinites as at their opponents, Grachev said the armed forces "would not be dragged into bloody chaos."

---

*After the death in 1584 of Ivan IV "The Terrible," Russia entered a chaotic period that lasted until the accession of the Romanov dynasty in 1613. Some scholars date this "Time of Troubles" from 1584, others from 1598, when Boris Godunov—de facto ruler from the time of Ivan's death—became tsar.

**Valeri Boldin was released in December 1991 on grounds of ill health.

Russia had almost no experience of democracy. The 1977 Brezhnev Constitution, which did not clearly define the powers of the three branches of government or their relations with each other, remained in effect, but more than 300 amendments had rendered it incomprehensible. To be sure, the original document had been a fraud not meant to be taken seriously save for Article 6, which guaranteed the Communist political monopoly. Nevertheless it was technically the basic law of Russia. "Supreme power" resided in the 1,041-member Congress of People's Deputies, which met twice a year. It elected a standing parliament, the 250-member Supreme Soviet, from within its own ranks. The Supreme Soviet had the right to reject presidential nominees for prime minister and the ministries of defense, foreign affairs, and security ("power ministries"). In 1990, the voters had elected the Congress of People's Deputies through a Soviet-era system that emphasized the *nomenklatura's* interests.

The executive branch was under a president who was also head of state. Directly elected by popular vote and limited to two four-year terms, he or she appointed the government, subject to the parliament's approval of "power ministry" nominees. Both president and parliament had the right of legislative initiative.

At the apex of the third branch of government was a 13-member Constitutional Court

Learning capitalism, Moscow, September 1992. (James Trott)

that ruled on the constitutionality of any issue brought before it. The Congress of People's Deputies created the Court in 1991. The Supreme Soviet proposed candidates, on whom the Congress then voted. Membership on the Court was for life.

The press was free chiefly because the politicians, most of whom wanted some degree of censorship, could not agree on how to limit it. The executive and legislative branches fought between themselves as to how to exercise state control of radio and television. Regional state television, especially in St. Petersburg and Siberia, sometimes had greater programming flexibility than did the central operations in Moscow. In St. Petersburg, the KGB helper Aleksandr Nevzorov's nightly "600 Seconds," which mercilessly pilloried first Gorbachev, then Yeltsin, was one of most popular shows in the country. In 1994, the state sold a 49 percent interest in the largest TV network, ORT, to private interests. The second largest state-controlled network was RTR. After the events of early October 1993 the privately financed, nongovernmental Independent Television came into being.

THE REPUBLICS AND REGIONS*

As the central power disintegrated in the old USSR, that of the 89 republic and regional councils (soviets) and their leaders had grown. In March 1992, three hastily drawn documents collectively known as the Federation Treaty sought to decentralize power. The accord between the federal government and the 15 na-

tional republics,* (in which non-Russians usually predominated, *appeared* to give the latter considerable autonomy including control over the land and natural resources. But one article specified that exercise of such control was subject to both federal and republic laws. This treaty would prove especially divisive in Checheno-Ingushetia, where the Yeltsin regime's crude attempt to enforce federal dominance would degenerate into the bloody conflict of 1993–1996.**

The federal government concocted another recipe for disaster with the treaty defining its relations with the *Russian* regions—the *oblasti* and *kraiya.*†The central authorities insisted on keeping the regions subordinate to the center. This virtually guaranteed the active opposition of the regional leaders, most of them members of the old Communist *nomenklatura* who now belonged to the CPRF or the Agrarian Union.

POST-PUTSCH POLITICS

It was impossible for a multiparty political system to emerge overnight. The largest wing of the old CPSU had undergone rebirth as the Communist Party of the Russian Federation (CPRF),†† while the rest split into several factions across the narrow band between neo-Stalinism and Stalinism; the noisiest were the Russian Communist Workers' Party, the All-Russian Communist Party of Bolsheviks, and Working Moscow. Only the CPRF had the ex-

---

*Autonomous republics: Bashkiria (Bashkortostan), Buryatia, Dagestan, Kabardino-Balkaria, Kalmykia, Karelia, Komi, Mari, Yakutia (Sakha), Chuvashia, Checheno-Ingushetia, Udmurtia, Tuva, Tatarstan (Tataria), North Ossetia, Mordovia. **Autonomous provinces**: Adyge, Jewish (Birobidjan, where there were very few Jews), Gorno-Altai, Karachai-Cherkess, Khakass. **National districts**: Koryak, Chukot, Taimyr, Evenk, Khanti-Mansi, Agin-Buryat, Yamalo-Nenets, Komi-Permyak; Nenets; Ust-Ordyn Buryat.

****See Chapter 26.

†Singular *oblast* and *krai*. These administrative subdivisions are roughly equivalent to American states or French *départements*. According to the Constitution that existed to October 1993, the regional councils served as the primary channel for governing the country. Ethnic Russians predominate.

††In April 1992, the parliament voted to change the name of the republic from Russian Federation to Russia. The Communists, however, clung to the word "Federation."

perience, organizational structure, discipline, and inside knowledge of the existing bureaucratic-constitutional structure to exploit the new political rules to the fullest.

Out of the depths of troubled times came many strange creatures to flop around on the political beach. Having served Brezhnev and Andropov with equal fidelity, Arkady Volsky now headed Civic Union, which urged "reform at a slower pace" and the continuation of subsidies to smokestack industries. Under its umbrella were Volsky's own Russian Union of Industrialists and Entrepreneurs (which gained no parliamentary seats); Nikolai Travkin's center–right Democratic Party of Russia; and Aleksandr Rutskoi's Free Russia Party, which concentrated on the career of Aleksandr Rutskoi. Some *kolhoz* managers established Agrarian Union as a CPRF ally. A "red–brown" (Communist-Fascist) alliance reminiscent of KPD–Nazi cooperation in Weimar Germany brought together some extremist enemies of democracy. Brown "Russian Unity" formed the core of the "National Salvation Front." Advocating a military–KGB dictatorship, it claimed that Jews controlled Yeltsin's government and that Yeltsin and Gorbachev, on the orders of an international Zionist conspiracy, had destroyed the USSR. The red "Fatherland" of some active-duty and retired KGB and military officers operated at about this level. The Fascist clown Vladimir Zhirinovsky led his Liberal Democratic Party and what was left of Pamyat in an assault on civilization. General Albert Makashov—he of the cheap vodka and the recovery of Alaska—led the small, deeply embittered Union of Officers.

These were not Western-style political parties, partly because the words "party" and "politics" had a sinister ring. Competing were the fragmented but still powerful Communists and various camps, factions, personal organizations, clans-of-opportunity (e.g., Civic Union), organized crime and free-lance criminal organizations, labor associations, the Russ-

ian Orthodox Church, women's-rights organizations, military associations, thuggeries, and others. Looming over the entire process were the "men of respect," among whom the most important subgroup was the "Red directors"—the senior bosses of economic sectors and managers of large industrial operations and major collective farms.

Boris Yeltsin built a ramshackle, barely serviceable political machine composed of ex-Communists like himself, independent Communists, Left and center intellectuals, newly churched Social Democrats, and others. Serving as his own prime minister from the August 1991 putsch until June 1992, he found himself frustrated at every turn by the Constitution, parliament, and Constitutional Court.

Some of Yeltsin's problems were of his own creation. His behavior at Belovezhskaya Pushcha* was all too characteristic, and, like Gorbachev, he often misjudged character. He promoted his bodyguard and constant companion, Aleksandr Korzhakov, formerly a major in the KGB's Ninth Directorate and before that an automobile mechanic, to be chief of the 20,000-man presidential security service. Korzhakov transformed it into his private army. Renowned as an unscrupulous adventurer, he would become Yeltsin's chief adviser on all issues including the war in Chechnya and Russia's relations with the World Bank. He made a fortune when Yeltsin granted his ostensibly philanthropic National Sports Foundation the right to import liquor and tobacco free of duty.

Another influential Yeltsin adviser, Yuri Skokov, was known for his ruthless low punches in the political infighting. The Yeltsin aide Oleg Soskovets privatized a Siberian tin foundry without any help at all from the law. Yeltsin appointed Vyacheslav Bragin, innocent of any knowledge of television or journalism, to head national television at Ostankino; Bragin

---

*See the preceding chapter.

would compound the October 1993 disaster.

Still more ominously, Yeltsin had sponsored the political career of Ruslan Khasbulatov, an ethnic Chechen and an economist, as a gesture to the national minorities. Khasbulatov too had displayed great courage in defying the putschists, but victory unleashed in him a lust for power and luxury. He interpreted his position as chairman (speaker) of both Congress and Supreme Soviet as constitutionally the most powerful in Russia. Under his expert manipulation, a willing Supreme Soviet—where 87 percent of the deputies were CPRF or Agrarian Union members—insisted on exercising "supreme power." The Soviet saw the presidency as being "like the Queen of England"—wholly ceremonial.

Khasbulatov protected and glorified himself and the Supreme Soviet with an army of more than 5,000 guards, aides, servants, and sycophants. He treated himself to chauffeured Mercedes and BMW limousines, handmade Italian clothes and shoes, Havana cigars, fine wines and liquors, and Brezhnev's apartment on fashionable Kutuzovsky Prospekt. On alighting from his limousine, Khasbulatov liked to flick two or three centimeters of cigar ash in the direction of the huddled masses. By Christmas 1991, he was predicting Yeltsin's imminent fall from power.

Another costly Yeltsin misjudgment gave Khasbulatov a powerful ally. Attempting to reassure the demoralized military establishment, Yeltsin selected General Aleksandr Rutskoi, a decorated Afghan War fighter pilot, as his partner in the 1991 Russian elections. In office, Vice President Rutskoi had nothing resembling a political program, but his gruff demeanor and blunt manner of speaking appealed to some people who longed for "law and order." After standing with Yeltsin against the putschists, Rutskoi rapidly distanced himself from his patron and let it be known that political intrigue disgusted him. But it soon became clear that his goal was the presidency,

with Aleksandr Rutskoi as dictator-president. To achieve that, he had first to join Khasbulatov in asserting the primacy of the parliament, then bring down Boris Yeltsin.

ECONOMIC REFORM

The already sharp rate of decline in industrial output increased after the putsch and the breakup of the USSR. Private stores were well stocked—with goods priced far beyond the means of 95 percent of Russians. Highlighting the distorted nature of the infant free market, many items were imported: Their production generated no wages in Russia, and only foreign producers and Russian middlemen profited. Not even import duties and fees came into the Russian treasury: The importers bribed the lowly paid—sometimes even unpaid—customs agents and transport workers to look the other way. Contrasting starkly with the imported opulence, the food supply in state stores was lower than at any time since 1946. The poorest of the poor foraged through garbage dumps, or begged. Mortality rates climbed and life expectancy diminished, especially for males. Undernourished children studied in unheated schools.

Servicing the gigantic foreign debt devoured funds desperately needed at home to rebuild the country and construct a social safety net for the defenseless—orphans, the homeless, the disabled, widows, pensioners. The debt came from the loans the West had granted the Gorbachev regime in the 1980s in a misguided attempt to prop it up. Russia defaulted in 1991.

A December 1991 treaty fixed Russia's share of the $68 billion USSR debt at 61.34 percent. In 1992, bilateral agreements provided for Russia to assume the entire debt and for five other former republics to relinquish claims to many USSR assets. Russia proved unable to pay more than a fraction of the amounts due in 1992, and in 1993 the creditor nations rolled the debts over. The Russian foreign debt stood at $113 billion in the spring of 1996, $10 billion less by December.

Yeltsin gathered around him what Serge Schmemann of *The New York Times* called a "small clutch of articulate, English-speaking [economic] reformers." Yegor Gaidar, Boris Fyodorov, Anatoli Chubais, and Grigori Yavlinsky persuaded him to administer "shock therapy" to the desperately ill patient by rapidly dismantling the centralized economy, thus producing a social revolution that would, in Martin Malia's words, "disperse power and create the pluralism of interests requisite for democracy."

On January 2, 1992, the government removed price controls on 90 percent of all goods and predicted price increases of 300 to 400 percent. In fact, there was a 250 percent leap (on average) the first day, and by year's end prices stood 1,000 to 1,500 percent above those of December 1991. Like the Stalin, Khrushchev, and Gorbachev–Pavlov "currency reforms," the decontrolling of prices destroyed the savings of tens of millions of citizens. But the shops were full, as the economists had promised they would be, and the "men of respect" and the *nouveaux riches* flocked to them.

To minimize social unrest, the reformers limited price increases on—i.e., continued to subsidize—bread, potatoes, cabbage, and some dairy products. Charges for rent and public transportation rose but remained far below free-market value. Some, but by no means all, workers received modest wage increases that did not remotely keep pace with inflation, and by the spring of 1992 three-quarters of the population had fallen below the official poverty line.* A year later, inflation reached 1 percent per day, close to hyperinflation.

Beginning in 1992, the *nomenklatura,* non-

political organized crime, and the senior bureaucracy spirited away an estimated $25 billion *per year* to the Swiss Bank Union's no-questions-asked vaults. In 1996, 250,000 Russians flew to Dubai and spent a billion dollars on goods destined for resale in Russia. Barely semiproductive, Russia had become a mere consumer and transferrer of wealth.

PRIVATIZATION

The privatization of state assets accompanied the lifting of price controls. In charge of the program was Anatoli Chubais, a St. Petersburg economist. As head of the State Property Committee, he began by issuing each of Russia's 150 million citizens a free voucher with a face value of 10,000 rubles (then about $33). The voucher represented one "share" of the total national wealth the Communist regime had accumulated. Aleksandr Solzhenitsyn, no economist but well informed, claimed early in 1997 that the "total value of all the vouchers represented only a small fraction of 1 percent of that wealth."

The citizen could use the voucher to buy shares in privatized enterprises. But if one bought shares in, say, Azov Steel or Ural Machinery or Volga Automotive, what did one have? Even if the program had been fair, which it manifestly was not, a Russia just one year removed from communism did not and could not understand the market. Millions of citizens sold the certificates for next to nothing (a couple of bottles of vodka was a common price), traded them for food or clothing, gave them away, misplaced them, forgot about them, tore them up. Many people named pets "Voucher."

Early in 1992 the parliament approved the privatization of 14,000 large nonmilitary enterprises employing 15 million people. Because an operation of that magnitude required—so it would seem—the most careful planning and coordination, through most of 1992 the gov-

---

*Then set at 342 rubles per capita; in December 1991 that sum would buy 1.5 kilograms of meat.

ernment limited this to trade and service enterprises, beginning with 4,500 retail stores in Moscow. By the end of the year the reformers had auctioned off about 100,000 such stores and shops—70 percent of the consumer marketplace. Over the next two years the Kremlin transferred a third of all industrial enterprises, and two-thirds of the trade and service sectors, to private owners.

After the privatization of that first third of state property, Russia theoretically had about 40 million stockholders. But that was deceptive: In practice, 70 percent of all stock ended up in the hands of the *nomenklatura* and the senior bureaucracy, who reaped the greatest financial windfall in history. All Russia was for sale. As befitted their position, the "men of respect" were first in line and paid kopecks for property worth trillions.

This came about for three principal reasons. First, centrally planned Soviet corruption had created the requisite institutional-bureaucratic-information apparatus. The *nomenklatura* constituted a cabal of "insider traders" who simply could not lose. On February 28, 1992, Chubais denounced "privatization by *nomenklatura*" even as he fueled the flames of the process.

Second, there were no precedents. It took Margaret Thatcher's Conservatives seven years to sell off 43 state-run companies even though the British had the technical and financial skills and institutions, democracy, an ancient constitutional system, and an honest bureaucracy. Russia had none of these. The privatization of Russia, like the disappearance of the USSR, was unique in history.

Third, Russia was still in the early stages of creating an informal network of nongovernmental organizations and influential individuals who shape and monitor public policy and public opinion—a civil society. Thus, the new reformers and the old "men of respect" could plan the sale without interference and overwhelm the public with a propaganda campaign.

The United Nations, the United States and other Western nations, and Japan supplied technical advice and funds. The International Finance Corporation (IFC), a specialized UN agency affiliated with the World Bank, played a major role. It worked out a plan for "corporatization" whereby workers in a medium- and large-scale enterprise would receive up to 35 percent of all shares in the enterprise either free or at a discount—but only one of every 3.5 shares that went to the workers carried voting rights. The manager of the enterprise could buy 5 percent of the shares—also at a discount—and all carried with them the right to vote on company policies. The IFC justified this gift to the *nomenklatura* on the grounds that privatization could not succeed without its support. The government retained the remaining 60 percent of the shares until they could be auctioned off or exchanged for vouchers.

Foreign financial institutions profited handsomely. It was necessary to estimate the value of the enterprises, organize the auctions, supervise the preparation and distribution of the certificates, and so on. Foreigners moved in to handle the immense task, and to train Russians. The Communists and the extremist fringe parties charged that foreign intelligence agencies, notably the CIA, were deeply involved in the privatization process, but they did not present concrete proof. In 1992, the United States Congress voted to give Russia $2.5 billion in aid.

Determined not to provoke the generals or the top-most rank of the *nomenklatura,* the government proceeded slowly where privatization and "downsizing" of the military-industrial complex were concerned. Defense-related enterprises* employed roughly half the work force and accounted for more than half of

---

*In addition to bombs, tanks, military aircraft, and so on, some such enterprises produced bicycles, small appliances, and other items far removed from defense.

GDP. This skew, turned in on itself and knotted, is what ultimately ruined the Soviet economy, which could conceivably have stumbled on a few more decades. Khasbulatov, Rutskoi, and the parliament argued vociferously in favor of continued state subsidies. Their stated goal was to avoid mass unemployment and social dislocation. What they in fact feared was the market, the success of which would doom their relabeled communism.

No one in the Kremlin thought the reforms would be popular. Most of the criticism came down on Yeltsin, who was still serving as his own prime minister, and the strain began to affect his health. He wanted Yegor Gaidar in the post, but Gaidar had long been cruelly mocked in the Supreme Soviet: Imitating Gaidar's nervous mannerism, deputies smacked their lips loudly, and sometimes made barking noises or displayed photographs of St. Bernard dogs—Gaidar had one—when assailing the government. In June 1992 Yeltsin made Gaidar acting prime minister.

While accusing ex-President Gorbachev of living like a king, Yeltsin built himself a luxurious villa on an official salary that might have financed a modest dacha. General Rutskoi lived on a similarly lavish scale, and he too liked Mercedes limousines. Former Mayor Gavriil Popov of Moscow became a multimillionaire. We have seen Khasbulatov at work and play. All Congress and Supreme Soviet members enjoyed high salaries, lucrative perquisites, and—if they were right with Khasbulatov—Moscow's best apartments and first-class trips abroad. Some deputies who had suffered persecution and imprisonment for their opposition to the Communist regime now sent their children to expensive private schools in the West.

All but the richest and most powerful 2 or 3 percent of the population looked on helplessly as the stacked-deck "free" market replaced the Soviet poorfare state. The CPRF and other opponents of reform coined the slogan, *It's not privatization—It's grabification!* (Ne privatizatsiya—a prikhvatizatsiya!) and plastered it all over Russia. The fact that Vladimir Kryuchkov and other unlaudable types agreed could not alter this ugly truth. One gang of above-the-law people had replaced another, with this difference: The new one was more acceptable to the West and Japan.

Yeltsin and the reformers insisted that a free-market "trickle-down effect" was taking hold: A few were living well today; tomorrow others would join them; soon all Russia would prosper. Khasbulatov and Rutskoi denounced the government as babies-for-breakfast capitalists, Wall Street stooges, gangsters, pornographers. On the street there was talk of "Tsar Boris" and his "time of troubles."

State affairs ground almost to a halt. When in December 1992 Yeltsin demanded a nationwide referendum to decide between him and parliament, the Congress accused him of treason and without debate changed the Constitution to forbid such referenda. Ostensibly to break the impasse, Constitutional Court Chairman Valeri Zorkin brokered an agreement: There could be a referendum if Yeltsin were to dismiss Acting Prime Minister Gaidar.

There were 13 judges on the Constitutional Court, and Zorkin and nine others had made the transition from the CPSU to the CPRF without skipping a beat. In the Byzantine-Mongol-tsarist-Communist tradition, the Communist judges, Khasbulatov, and Rutskoi interpreted every attempt at compromise as weakness.

Weary of the incessant accusations that he was seeking to impose a dictatorship, in December 1992 Yeltsin dismissed Gaidar. Khasbulatov and Zorkin triumphantly announced that there would be no referendum after all. The nation had become ungovernable.

Yeltsin named a prominent "Red director," Viktor Chernomyrdin, to replace Gaidar. Knowing him as one of their own, the Supreme Soviet gleefully approved.

As head of Gazprom, the natural-gas monopoly that controls a third of the world's reserves, Chernomyrdin had received a large chunk of its privatized stock, the total value of which was set at a shockingly conservative $100 billion. In 1996, Gazprom sold 1.15 percent of its equity to foreign investors for $429 million, and in that year privatized Gazprom supplied about 30 percent of Europe's natural gas. What this means for the value of the Chernomyrdin shares remains a Russian state secret.

Having gone to bed one evening an ordinary salaried bureaucrat, Viktor Chernomyrdin awakened the next morning in a changed economic situation. What is more, he became prime minister, a post that entitled him to speak out against the "mechanical transfer of Western economic methods to Russia." That is what endeared him to the Supreme Soviet. Campaigning for Yeltsin in the 1996 presidential election, he would tell one female voter that he refused to believe she had only the equivalent of $50 a month to live on.

One day, a new Nikolai Gogol will explain all this.

TOWARD THE SHOWDOWN

On March 11, 1993, the Congress of People's Deputies voted overwhelming to curtail Boris Yeltsin's powers, scrap his economic program, and cancel the proposed referendum. Nine days later, Yeltsin went on television to announce he was assuming "special powers" in order to stabilize the political situation. But he did not proclaim presidential rule, nor did he spell out what he intended to do beyond ordering an April 25 referendum on his leadership.

Two crucial developments dictated this indecision that passed for strategy. First, the republic and provincial leaders, whom Ruslan Khasbulatov had courted more successfully than had Yeltsin, made clear their opposition to presidential rule. Second, Yeltsin had failed to obtain the support of the republic and regional leaders, and of his minister of security, Viktor Barannikov, for a plan to disband the Congress and its Supreme Soviet and rule by presidential decree pending introduction of a new Constitution. Yeltsin lost his opportunity; Barannikov lost his job. Viktor Yerin became minister of security. The regional leaders appeared to hold the balance of power.

Both first and second plans veered sharply in the direction of dictatorship, but what that would have replaced is difficult to say: No one was really governing Russia. Valeri Zorkin condemned Yeltsin's March 20 action as a "state coup" before seeing the text of the speech. Khasbulatov and Aleksandr Rutskoi issued strident appeals for Yeltsin's overthrow. When that did not happen, they extracted yet another compromise. There would be a second question on the ballot: "Do you approve of the social and economic policies the president and his government have pursued since 1992?" They suspected Yeltsin might win personal approval but believed the voters would reject his reforms.

Khasbulatov, Rutskoi, the CPRF–Agrarian Union-dominated parliament, and the Zorkin Constitutional Court suffered a humiliating loss as the Russian electorate backed Yeltsin 57.4 to 39.9 percent, his reform program by 53.7 to 45.5 percent. Moreover, 70.6 percent called for early elections for the Congress of People's Deputies. On the question of an earlier date for the presidential election, 49.8 percent voted in favor; 49.1 percent was opposed.

Caught off-guard by the self-inflicted defeat, parliament prepared for the next round. Encouraged by Yeltsin's failure to follow up his second victory, his opponents stepped up their efforts to topple him. That brought renewed marches and street demonstrations, and in May OMON troops—of Vilnius and Riga infamy—broke up several pro-parliament rallies in Moscow that either were or were not threatening to get out of hand. In any event OMON was not known for gentle behavior.

Yeltsin would later acknowledge his error in not exploiting the referendum. Instead of dissolving parliament and setting new elections, he convened a Constitutional Assembly in July and entrusted it with formulating a new Constitution. Increasingly desperate for support, he was prepared to offer the devolution of considerable central government authority to the republic and regional governments.

Most of the delegates to the Constitutional Assembly, however, were Communists whose sympathies lay with Ruslan Khasbulatov and the Supreme Soviet. Knowing Yeltsin's position was becoming untenable, they agreed in principle to change the Federation Treaty to permit devolution of much central government power to the regions, and to make the republics "sovereign states." But then they declined to vote on these amendments. To weaken Yeltsin further, the delegates, Khasbulatov, and Rutskoi opted for the status quo.

The increasingly frustrated Yeltsin then called on the leaders of the republics and regions to form a Federation Council, which he hoped would become an estates-general, a rival to the parliament that might draft and adopt a new Constitution. Again he promised devolution; again the republic and regional leaders declined to accommodate him.

Khasbulatov and Rutskoi adamantly rejected new parliamentary elections absent a simultaneous election for the presidency. But Yeltsin had won a four-year term in June 1991, an unequivocal vote of confidence in April 1993. In a November interview he revealed that, in July, he had written out an order dissolving parliament. He kept it in his office safe, and he alone had known of its existence.

On August 10, 1993, Yeltsin warned—or promised—that September would be "super-tense." His meaning became clear on September 1, when he suspended Vice President Rut-

skoi and evicted him from his Kremlin office. A prosecutor had charged Rutskoi with corrupt practices involving the Swiss corporation Seabaco. In a still greater gesture of defiance, on September 18 Yeltsin brought Yegor Gaidar back into the Cabinet as first deputy prime minister and acting economics minister. Gaidar replaced Oleg Lobov, a Yeltsin crony from the Sverdlovsk (Yekaterinburg) bureaucracy who maintained close ties to the Communist Party of Russia.

Also on September 18, Russian television broadcast picture and sound as Khasbulatov called Yeltsin a "drunk" and made some crude gestures. For better or worse, no one could make a political living in Russia by attacking vodka. Educated Russians recalled Mikhail Lermontov's "Cossack Lullaby" (1838):

The evil Chechen climbs the riverbank,
    sharpens his dagger;
But your father's a veteran warrior
    and he's got the guts for the fight:
Sleep, little one, and rest easy . . .
    Baiiii-yush-kyyy . . . baaaii-yuuu. . . .

When a second attempt to win support from the provincial leaders also failed, Yeltsin increased the rate at which he was replacing those officeholders with his own people. He set a meeting of the Federation Council for October 9, then made a final attempt at compromise: He would agree to another presidential election in June 1994—after the election of a new parliament. The opposition dismissed the offer.

DECREE NO. 1,400

On September 21, 1993, citing the authority bestowed on him by the 1991 presidential election and the April 1993 referendum, Boris Yeltsin went on television to announce Presidential Decree No. 1,400: "[A]s of today, the implementation of the legislative, executive, and supervisory functions of the Congress of People's Deputies and the Supreme Soviet of the Russian Federation ceases. Meetings of the Congress will no longer be convened."

This marked the death of the Brezhnev–Gorbachev Constitution. Yeltsin said that, on December 11–12, 1993, the nation would elect deputies to a bicameral Federal Assembly, which would become the "highest body of legislative power."* He lashed out at his tormentors, saying, "More competent, educated, and democratic people should fill the Russian Parliament. I believe such people exist in Russia. I believe we shall find them and elect them."

He declared he "favored early presidential elections"—*after* the convening of the Federal Assembly. He pledged not to resort to violence to enforce his actions but warned that attempts to thwart them would be punished. Pending the outcome of the parliamentary elections, he would govern by presidential decree. (Two days later he decreed a new presidential election for June 12, 1994.)

The toughness belied a tenuous position. Defense Minister Pavel Grachev issued a terse statement reaffirming the neutrality of the armed forces in politics. Knowing he did not control the generals, Grachev was going to wait and see. The ministers of interior and security, Viktor Yerin and Nikolai Golushko, respectively, remained noncommittal.

Ruslan Khasbulatov chaired an emergency meeting of the Supreme Soviet on the night of September 21–22, 1993. Proceeding in accordance with the CPRF–Agrarian Union majority's reading of the Constitution, the Supreme Soviet deposed Yeltsin and called on him to "surrender to the appropriate authorities or leave the country." It appealed for a nationwide general strike and named Aleksandr Rutskoi interim president. The 10 Communists on

the Constitutional Court pronounced Decree No. 1,400 unconstitutional and grounds for impeachment.

Rutskoi began forming a new government from his headquarters in the "White House," where the Supreme Soviet held its sessions. He and Khasbulatov appealed to the population, and more urgently to the Army and the security agencies, for support. Rutskoi supervised the stockpiling of small arms and ammunition. The parliamentary forces drew up plans to seize the Kremlin, the Lubyanka (secret-police headquarters), the mayoral offices, the TV broadcasting center at Ostankino, and other key points. Full of excitement, they prepared lists of people to be arrested. The fanatical Viktor Anpilov of Working Moscow—affiliated with Working Russia—promised Bolshevism and a bloodbath. The Fascist Ilya Konstantinov of the National Salvation Front just promised blood. Reports from the provinces were encouraging. Few provincial governors would lift a finger to save Yeltsin; even Anatoli Sobchak of St. Petersburg and Boris Nemtsov of Nizhny Novgorod (formerly Gorky) offered only tepid support for the president.

It would appear that a clear majority of high regional officials did in fact oppose Decree No. 1,400. But once again the extreme centralization of power came into play: Everything hinged on events in Moscow.

Rutskoi made a critical error when he named candidates to fill the "power ministry" posts. Particularly egregious was the nomination of Viktor Barannikov, whom Yeltsin had ousted, as security minister. Barranikov's replacement, Viktor Yerin, controlled Alpha Group—the KGB commando force that did *not* storm the "White House" in August 1991. Informed of Rutskoi's selections, Pavel Grachev, Yerin, and Nikolai Golushko pledged support for Yeltsin and appeared demonstratively at his side during a televised walk around the Kremlin grounds. The commanders of five

---

*On the new parliament, see Chapter 26.

elite Army divisions* stationed around Moscow followed suit, as did the head of the Central State Bank, Viktor Gerashchenko.

Ruslan Khasbulatov had unwittingly made his own contribution to Grachev's decision. In April 1993, he had accused the defense minister of malfeasance, specifically of profiting from the sale of Soviet military property in Germany. Whatever the merit of that charge, Grachev had remained in office and had not forgotten anything.

As Peter Frank of Essex University wrote at the time, "Beyond any shadow of a doubt, Yeltsin's action [in disbanding the parliament], in terms of Russia's outdated and anachronistic [C]onstitution, was illegal. Whether it was morally justified or not is a question . . . ."

THE OCTOBER COUNTERREVOLUTION

There could be no peaceful resolution. The stakes were too high, the egos too large. Khasbulatov and Rutskoi continued to believe they had sufficient support in the Army, secret police, and the Moscow mob to overthrow Yeltsin even after the "power ministers" proclaimed their support for him. Having demonized Yeltsin, they had left themselves no avenue of escape: They now had to establish a neo-Communist dictatorship or sink into oblivion, perhaps face a firing squad.

The government ringed the Moscow "White House" with a cordon of police. Sympathizers, curious passers-by, and people looking for excitement converged there, and some slipped through the lines. Khasbulatov, Deputy Speaker Yuri Voronin, Aleksandr Rutskoi, and others periodically appeared on the steps to harangue the crowd. Moscow Mayor Yuri Luzhkov, whose support was no less crucial

_____
*Kantemirov, Taman, Tula Airborne, 119th Airborne, and the ministry of the interior's Dzerzhinsky Division under General Anatoli Kulikov.

than that of Grachev and the generals, obeyed Yeltsin's order and cut off electricity, heat, water, and telephone service to the "White House." A majority of the Moscow City Council, however, backed the parliament.

Rallies, demonstrations, and marches, nearly all of them pro-parliament, took place all over Moscow. The marchers carried Soviet flags and large photographs of Joseph Stalin, and some gave the Nazi salute—in a land that had given 20 million to 40 million victims to the Lenin–Stalin Gulag, 27 million dead in the Hitler–Stalin war.

Valeri Zorkin of the Constitutional Court again graciously offered to mediate. This time, only parliament agreed. Zorkin's prayers remained unanswered but the Patriarch of the Russian Orthodox Church, Aleksii II, returned from a visit to the United States and presided over negotiations at the Danilov Monastery. A shaky truce emerged: The parliamentary forces would surrender their weapons, the government would restore utilities. Mayor Luzhkov threw the switches and opened the valves. The opposition kept its weapons and increased its demands.

Yeltsin issued an ultimatum: Evacuate the "White House" by Monday, October 4.

Demonstrators around the White House and elsewhere in the central city attacked the police with rocks, street signs, sticks, debris, and fists. Lacking clear orders and poorly trained in crowd control, the officers retreated in disarray.

Emboldened by a gigantic demonstration and march on Saturday, at noon on Sunday, October 3, Rutskoi exhorted the "White House" mob to seize power. As Khasbulatov screamed for the capture of "the criminal Yeltsin," the videocamera—this footage was shown a week later—zoomed in on his hands, which were shaking uncontrollably, like Gennadi Yanayev's at the "vodka putsch" news conference two years earlier.

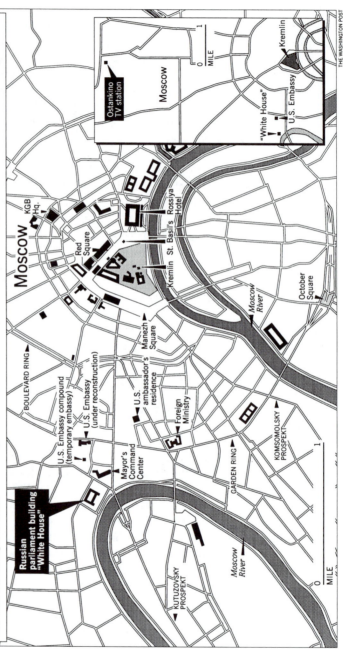

CHRONOLOGY OF VIOLENCE IN MOSCOW

(All times are local, seven hours ahead of EDT):

Sunday 12:30 p.m. Several dozen hard-line supporters of parliament attempt to rebuild barricades on the Garden Ring Road but are dispersed by police.

2 p.m. Thousands of parliament supporters gather at October Square under a giant statue of Soviet state founder Vladimir Lenin. Riot police attempt to block the demonstration but are overwhelmed by protesters.

2:20 p.m. Demonstrators leave the square and head down Garden Ring Road toward parliament, known as the White House. They punch through police lines with clubs, metal pipes and wooden planks, and pelt officers with a steady rain of rocks and bottles. Dozens of people are injured.

4 p.m. Demonstrators reach the White House, and volleys of gunfire erupt. Much of the firing is in the air. Volunteer parliament guards storm the nearby city government building.

6 p.m. At the urging of parliamentary Speaker Ruslan Khasbulatov, thousands of parliament supporters gather at the main television complex and attempt to storm the building, which is guarded by elite government troops stationed inside.

6:30 p.m. Yeltsin declares a state of emergency in Moscow.

8 p.m. Three television channels go off the air after demonstrators fire rocket-propelled grenades at the television center, starting a fierce gun battle. Dozens of protesters storm the building but are repulsed by the troops inside. Government forces at the television center are reinforced by troops in 12 personnel carriers.

Monday a.m. Yeltsin orders troops to retake buildings.

6:45 a.m. A column of armored personnel carriers breaks through barricades outside White House and opens fire.

THE WASHINGTON POST

Moscow, October 3–4, 1993. (*The Washington Post*). Reprinted with permission.

By any standard, this constituted a summons to the violent overthrow of the legally constituted government and marked the personal point of no return for Rutskoi and Khasbulatov.

At 2:00 P.M. on October 3, a pro-parliament rally of seven or eight thousand people at October Square overpowered the police. That transformed a crowd into a mob, which went on a rampage, made its way the five kilometers to the Moscow "White House," broke through police lines, and began erecting makeshift barricades.

At 4:00 P.M., Yeltsin declared a state of emergency in Moscow and placed General Aleksandr Kulikov in charge. Defense Minister Pavel Grachev issued orders to the elite divisions. Thirty-five minutes later, Khasbulatov and Rutskoi appeared on a "White House" balcony. No one could hear Khasbulatov, but Rutskoi's exhortation to seize the mayoral offices and the Ostankino TV center came through clearly. Within minutes, the mob broke into and sacked the mayoral offices and several other buildings.

Commandeering buses, trucks, and private automobiles, General Albert Makashov led elements of the mob, several hundred men, in an assault on Ostankino. Most were equipped only with street-gang projectiles, but a few had AK-47 rifles, machine pistols, and grenades from the "White House" arsenal. At Makashov's side were Viktor Barannikov, Rutskoi's security minister-designate, the crazed Viktor Anpilov of Working Moscow, and the National Salvation Front's Ilya Konstantinov. Once inside Ostankino, the TV building, they would announce that the Yeltsin regime had fallen and that President Rutskoi had declared martial law.

When the Ostankino defenders refused to surrender, the Makashov mob blasted the front doors with a rocket-propelled grenade and drove a truck through the gap. Makashov cried out, "This is the free territory of the USSR!" At 7:38 P.M., the four TV programs at Ostankino went off the air, and within an hour Khasbulatov, speaking to the 1,500 people—including 75 journalists—inside the "White House," announced the capture of Ostankino.

That, as Mark Twain said on reading his own obituary, was premature: About a hundred *spetsnaz* troops had arrived a few minutes ahead of Makashov. Unable to prevent his entry into the building, they did secure the upper floors. About 90 minutes later, interior ministry troops arrived, and from then on it was no match. In the fighting, which lasted several hours, 62 people including seven journalists were killed, and several hundred were wounded.

Ostankino did not cease broadcasting because of General Makashov, whose invaders never got above the ground floor: The director of television operations, Vyacheslav Bragin, had simply panicked. As the American journalist Jamey Gambrell wrote at the time, "The city went into shock: almost everyone I talked to spoke of the terror they felt when the airwaves went dark that night. That was when people realized the country might really be on the brink of civil war."

Channel 1 (Ostankino) did not return until the next morning. The news staff of Channel 2 (RTV, or Russian Television) moved to a remote location and resumed broadcasting at 8 P.M., the newsreaders frequently apologizing for their lack of information. Yegor Gaidar went on radio an hour later to appeal for supporters of President Yeltsin to assemble at the Moscow City Council Building. Fifty minutes later he repeated his statement on RTV, and other government officials broadcast similar terse messages. Yeltsin did not speak publicly; his aides later claimed he had simply decided to wait until the next morning.

A pro-government crowd—or mob, in the Rutskoi-Khasbulatov-Zorkin view—that eventually numbered about 40,000 gathered at the City Council building on Tverskaya (formerly Gorky Street). Gaidar addressed the crowd

The "White House" is Burning, October 4, 1993. (Agence France-Press/Vladimir Mashati)

shortly before midnight and said the government forces were beginning to get the upper hand. In fact, those forces lacked coherence and direction.

Rutskoi had earlier warned the police and troops around the "White House" that he would punish them if they did not defect to him. There were virtually no takers.

In the early hours of Monday, October 4, Yeltsin tightened the noose. Troops encircled the Kremlin and the defense ministry General Staff building, where the nuclear-weapons command center was located. At 6:45 A.M. a column of armored personnel carriers broke through Rutskoi's makeshift barricades around the "White House" and opened fire on the building. Those inside responded with rifle fire and rocket-propelled grenades. Both Russ-

ian and international television broadcast the images, interrupting at 9:00 A.M. for President Yeltsin, who vowed to crush the "armed Fascist-Communist putsch."

Journalists relayed Rutskoi's call for negotiations; Prime Minister Viktor Chernomyrdin demanded unconditional surrender. When a white flag appeared at one window, Pavel Grachev ordered the military to cease firing at that section. Ruslan Khasbulatov announced he was ready for talks, but not surrender. The armored personnel carriers and a dozen T-72 and T-80 tanks continued the shelling.

In mid-afternoon, Rutskoi telephoned Valeri Zorkin of the Constitutional Court: "I'm asking you to have somebody call the embassies . . . make the foreign ambassadors come here. . . . I implore you, Valera—you're

Khasbulatov (center foreground) and Rutskoi (second from right) under arrest. (Archive Photos/Reuters)

a believer ... you'll have this sin on your soul!'*

THE END

The exchange of fire continued. Shells from the tanks rocked the "White House" and sent up vast clouds of black smoke. Thousands of spectators gaped at this *son et lumière* display and some were killed or wounded by stray bullets and sniper fire. The latter came from the "White House" and from its champions hiding

*Veronika Kutsylo (Kutsillo), a reporter for the Moscow *Kommersant,* was present in the room and taped the conversation. Valera is a nickname for Valeri.

on the roofs of nearby buildings. Small groups of people, some with their hands clasped behind their heads, began emerging from the "White House" under white flags. The tank fire concentrated on the thirteenth floor.

At 3:02 P.M., Pavel Grachev arrived at the "White House" and talked with a group of men who had surrendered. About 40 minutes later, journalists still inside the building reported that Rutskoi and Khasbulatov were ready to capitulate if Yeltsin would guarantee their safety. In quick succession, Yeltsin ordered a curfew in Moscow and suspended all Communist, Fascist, and super-nationalist publications. More groups of people left the building, hands clasped behind their heads. Khasbula-

Izmailovsky Park, Moscow. (James Trott)

tov and Rutskoi surrendered at 6:05 P.M. An hour later, a government spokesman announced that they had been removed to a "safe place." That would be Lefortovo Prison, which dated back to the time of Peter the Great.

Boris Yeltsin admired Tsar Peter, who had also crushed a rebellion against his personal authority that evolved into an attempt to reverse a social and economic revolution. As Martin Malia observed, "The cost in lives was high and the symbolism starkly negative, but at least . . . [Yeltsin's] actions cleared the air of pseudo-constitutional ambiguities and removed the last institutional debris of Soviet power."

SUGGESTED ADDITIONAL READINGS

BLASI, JOSEPH R., ET AL. *Kremlin Capitalism: Privatizing the Russian Economy.* Ithaca, NY: Cornell University Press, 1996.

COLTON, TIMOTHY J. *Moscow: Governing the Socialist Metropolis.* Cambridge: Harvard University Press, 1995.

KNIGHT, AMY. *Spies Without Cloaks: The KGB's Successors.* Princeton, NJ: Princeton University Press, 1996.

SELIGMAN, ADAM B. *The Idea of Civil Society.* New York: Free Press, 1992.

WHITE, STEPHEN, RICHARD ROSE, and IAN McALLISTER. *How Russia Votes.* Chatham, NJ: Chatham House, 1997.

YELTSIN, BORIS. *The Struggle for Russia.* New York: Times Books, 1994.

Author's Note: I wish to pay tribute to the courageous, immensely skilled people who wrote and broadcast from Moscow in those fateful days of September–October 1993. I have relied heavily on their first draft of history: Fred Hiatt, Lee Hockstadter, and Margaret Shapiro of the *Washington Post*; Celestine Bohlen, Steven Erlanger, and Serge Schmemann of *The New York Times;* Matthew Campbell and Peter Millar of the *Sunday Times* (London); Adi Ignatius, Claudia Rosett, and Elisabeth Rubinfien of *The Wall Street Journal*; Jamey Gambrell in the *New York Review*; Paolo Valentino of *Corriere della Sera*; Veronika Kutsylo of *Kommersant*; Dmitri Ostalsky and *Segodnya*; Vitali Tretyakov and *Nezavisimaya Gazeta*; the staffs of *Izvestiya*, *Komsomolskaya Pravda*, *Moskovsky Komsomolets*, Interfax (especially Vyacheslav Terekhov), ITAR-TASS, AP, UPI, Agence France-Presse, Radio Russia, Moscow Echo (radio); Steve Hurst and Claire Shipman of CNN.

26

THE TIME OF TROUBLES: THE NEW RUSSIA

When the Spassky Tower chimes struck 4:00 P.M. on October 6, 1993, the two soldiers standing motionlessly at Lenin's tomb pivoted and disappeared into the mausoleum, which is connected to the Kremlin by a tunnel, for the last time. Boris Yeltsin had closed Russian Army Post No. 1. The same day, Mayor Yuri Luzhkov announced that the Lenin Museum would become a Moscow City Council office building. Then he dissolved the City Council.

THE AFTERMATH

The official death toll of October 3–4, 1993, climbed from 118 to 198, then fell back to "about 150." Yeltsin went on television on October 6 and appealed to Russia to "put the nightmare of these black days behind us. Do not say someone has won and someone has lost. That would be inappropriate, blasphemous. The deadly breath of fratricide has scorched us all." He extended the state of emergency for a week.

Albert Makashov, Ilya Konstantinov, Viktor Anpilov, and about 350 mob rank-and-file joined Aleksandr Rutskoi and Ruslan Khasbulatov in prison. Valeri Zorkin yielded to pressure to step down as Constitutional Court chairman but remained a member; Yeltsin "suspended" the Court. Procurator-General Valentin Stepankov, who had bungled the "vodka putsch" investigation, and had hesitated to support Yeltsin, lost his job to Aleksei Kazannik, the Omsk lawyer who had yielded his parliamentary seat to Yeltsin in 1989.

Censorship ended, but the Supreme Soviet's semi-official newspaper *Sovetskaya Rossiya*, along with *Pravda*, other Communist journals, and several chauvinist, Fascist, and anti-Semitic organs such as Aleksandr Prokhanov's* *Den* (The Day) remained proscribed, as did Aleksandr Nevzorov's rabid "600 Seconds" on St. Petersburg TV. A week later the Kremlin ruled that *Pravda* and *Sovetskaya Rossiya* could resume publication under certain conditions.

Procurator-General Kazannik filed charges against the insurrectionists. That neither they nor the "vodka putschists" faced the death penalty marked another stage on Russia's journey away from Stalinism.

Claiming the right to appoint local governors, Boris Yeltsin began settling accounts outside Moscow. He dismissed the governor of Novosibirsk, who had sided with parliament, and a month later fired Governor Eduard

---

*Prokhanov wrote the notorious 1991 "A Word to the People." See above, Chapter 24.

Yeltsin and Metropolitan Yuvenali of Kolomna and Krutitsi, dedicating a statue of Yaroslav the Wise, Yaroslavl, October 23, 1993. (Reuters/Gennady Galperin/Archive Photos)

Rossel for "exceeding his authority" in Yekaterinburg Province: Rossel had proclaimed an independent "Urals Republic." President Kirsan Ilyumzhinov of Kalmykia called Yeltsin a dictator and pledged to keep oil revenues at home.

The bloated municipal and lower-level councils (soviets), a key feature of the Soviet Communist system, fell by the wayside. The St. Petersburg boroughs had 3,500 deputies; Moscow had three times that many, and all received good salaries. The Khasbulatov–Rutskoi parliament had expertly manipulated this political patronage: No one wanted to lose a job that involved no work.

Yeltsin ordered a special commission to create a system of smaller regional legislatures to replace the councils. He scheduled new elections for the regional councils in Siberia, the Maritime Provinces, and the North, and urged reform of republic legislatures and new elections. The Supreme Soviet in Siberia's diamond- and oil-rich Yakutia (Sakha), where Russians slightly outnumber Yakuts, voted itself out of existence.

In November, Yeltsin abrogated his promise to hold early presidential elections, saying the presidential mandate "should be fully used and exercised until 1996." But it made little sense to schedule *parliamentary* elections for December; Russia needed more time to recover from the shock and sort out her priorities. Nevertheless, Yeltsin pressed ahead, and he appointed a commission to draft a new Constitution.

POLITICS

The old *nomenklatura* and its "democratic" offspring manipulated the levers of power. The government banned Working Russia, the parent organization of Working Moscow, and the National Salvation Front; Yeltsin pointed out defensively that Germany and other countries

prohibited extreme Left and Right parties and movements. Notable among the 91 groups that registered by late October were:

1. Pro-Reform

(a) Yegor Gaidar, Finance Minister Boris Fyodorov, Foreign Minister Andrei Kozyrev, Anatoli Chubais, and Chief of Staff Sergei Filatov founded *Russia's Choice,* the main reform party. At the first convention on October 16 there loomed behind the podium a giant reproduction of an equestrian statue of Peter the Great—one of Yeltsin's heroes—and the inscription "Russia's Choice—Freedom, Private Property, Lawfulness." The party's signature song was "Russia Is Risen," which of course has powerful Christian overtones. Yeltsin himself was not a member.

(b) Deputy Prime Minister Sergei Shakhrai and some Yeltsin aides established *Russian Unity and Accord* (acronym PRES), which advocated reform "at a slower pace," an expanded social safety net for the poor, and devolution.

(c) *Yabloko* ("Apple") was an acronym of the surnames of Grigori Yavlinsky, former Yeltsin Aide Yuri Boldyrev, and Vladimir Lukin, Ambassador to the United States. Yabloko backed reform, but because Yavlinsky had vast presidential aspirations, it called for a gradual approach, and for devolution.

(d) The *Democratic Reform Movement* of Anatoli Sobchak and Gavriil Popov stood for rapid economic reform. But Sobchak's once-brilliant star had faded, and it was widely known that Popov had parlayed the Moscow mayorality into a fortune. He would not be the last municipal executive to do so.

2. Centrist

(a) The main vehicle of the "Red directors" was Arkady Volsky's *Civic Union.* The aging "men of respect" continued to produce low-grade steel for which there were no buyers. As long as the old plants and factories remained in operation, the directors could keep their jobs.

(b) The *Democratic Party of Russia*, led by Nikolai Travkin, Oleg Bogomolov, and Stanislav Govorukhin, eluded description but favored "sensible reform."

(c) The name of *The Future of Russia—New Names* reflected the stilted political language and culture. Lacking any coherent program, these former Komsomol officials staged rallies that featured hard-rock music and a soft political line.

3. Legal Opposition

(a) Under the leadership of the anti-Semitic Gennadi Zyuganov,* the *Communist Party of the Russian Federation* (CPRF) retained the hammer and sickle symbol but added ROSSIYA (Russia) in the old script. Voters were free to interpret the juxtaposition. Opposed to the reforms, the CPRF promised to renationalize state property and reestablish the USSR. Like Ruslan Khasbulatov, Zyuganov pledged to respect democracy, and he wore Versace suits.

(b) The stars of the *Agrarian Party* were Aleksandr Zaveryukha, Yeltsin's deputy prime minister in charge of agriculture, and Vasili Starodubtsev, a leader of the "vodka putsch" released from prison in 1992. The party advocated collectivized agriculture.

(c) The *Liberal Democratic Party* consisted of Vladimir Zhirinovsky and his unstable ego, disgruntled citizens, and street thugs. A master orator and TV star, Zhirinovsky specialized in chauvinist, racist, law-and-order, anti-Semitic harangues.

4. Issue-based Groups

(a) E. F. Lakhova and Alevtina Fedulova founded *Women of Russia*, the first such independent group. Perfunctorily defending women's interests, it called more forcefully for the strengthening of family values and a Soviet-style welfare system. It demanded continued subsidies for light industry, especially those in which women workers predominated—for example, food-processing and textiles. The group condemned the closing of day-care centers and the practice of dismissing pregnant women and mothers of small children from their jobs. It protested Moscow's decision to shut down the baby-food industry.

(b) Self-proclaimed champion of the victims of pollution, the *Constructive Ecological Movement* (CEM) was not really "green" but rather an old-fashioned Communist front. Huge areas of European Russia, Siberia, and the North were indeed disaster zones; the Aral Sea was all but dead, Lake Baikal severely threatened. The CEM, however, savored only the money-making opportunities in "save-the-environment" campaigns.**

THE DRAFT CONSTITUTION

Ordered to create a powerful presidency, the Constitutional Commission labored nonstop. Claiming that all who stood for office implicitly accepted its legitimacy, Yeltsin forbade criticism of the draft Constitution it published in November 1993.

In 137 articles and nine "transitional provisions," the draft Constitution guaranteed human, civil, and property rights, and freedom of speech and assembly. It established the pre-

---

*In his 1995 book *Beyond the Horizon*, Zyuganov claimed that Jews had had a "controlling interest in the entire economic system of Western civilization" in the 1930s.

**The 1986 Chernobyl catastrophe hit hardest in Ukraine, Belarus, Poland, and Lithuania. The Kursk, Oryol, Bryansk, and Smolensk areas of Russia also suffered from radioactive fallout, as did Sweden, Norway, and Germany as far south as Bavaria.

sumption of innocence as a fundamental principle of law and provided for a social safety net patterned after Germany's. It sought to fragment the KGB successor organizations, and it specified that federal law would decide questions of land ownership.

Federal Assembly (Parliament)

1. *Federation Council:* The upper house would be the bulwark of presidential power. Because the reorganization of the republics and regions remained incomplete, the first Federation Council would be appointed and serve only until December 1995. Thereafter it would have two elected members from each of the 89 republics and regions and would sit for four years. It could impeach the president by a two-thirds' vote.

The Federation Council could override presidential vetoes with a two-thirds' majority, if the Duma voted likewise. The Council alone could ratify deployment of the armed forces abroad and confirm presidential declarations of martial law or a state of emergency. It alone could approve internal boundary changes.

2. *State Duma:* The lower house would have 450 members, half elected in geographic, single-constituency districts, half on a proportional, party-slate basis. Each voter could cast two ballots: One for an individual candidate, a second for a party slate. A political party that won 5 percent or more of the total vote would gain seats based on relative electoral support; 10 percent would translate into 22 to 23 seats. The first State Duma would serve two years until new elections in December 1995, thereafter for four years or until dissolved by presidential decree.

The State Duma could confirm or reject presidential choices for prime minister, director of the Central Bank, and senior judges, and it shared with the president the right of legislative initiative. A Duma bill became law if the Federation Council and the president approved or took no action within 14 days. If the Federation Council disapproved a Duma bill, a two-thirds' Duma majority could override.

The Duma could approve or reject the budget and could bring down a government by a vote of "no confidence." It could file impeachment charges against a president; the Federation Council would adjudicate. Only the State Duma could grant amnesty.

The Presidency

Limited to two four-year terms, the president was head of state and commander-in-chief of the armed forces, guarantor of the Constitution and the integrity of the state, articulator of the principles of domestic and foreign policy. Subject to Duma confirmation, the president nominated and could dismiss the prime minister and the director of the Central Bank. Presidential nominations for the Constitutional Court required Federation Council approval. The president appointed the judges of the Supreme Court and the Higher Court of Arbitration.

Under certain conditions, the president could dissolve the State Duma and rule by decree for up to a year. Presidential decrees automatically became law unless the Constitutional Court found them unconstitutional, or parliament nullifed them with new legislation, which would be subject to presidential veto.

The president could call a referendum at any time on any issue, declare martial law or a state of emergency, propose and veto legislation. Only treason or a similarly "grave crime" constituted grounds for impeachment.

The Succession

There would be no vice presidency. Were the president to become incapacitated, the prime minister would govern temporarily. Should the president die in office, the prime minister would govern pending an election within three months.

The Government

It carried out the president's policies under a prime minister, who chose the other ministers subject to the president's approval. The government prepared the state budget for the Duma to accept, modify, or reject.

Constitutional Court

Appointed by the president subject to Federation Council confirmation, 19 independent judges served for life and could be dismissed only for cause. The Constitutional Court would rule on the constitutionality of laws and decrees, review cases submitted by the Procuracy or other state agencies, and act on citizen complaints. It could approve or block impeachment proceedings against the president.

Should the voters approve it, this Constitution would give Russia a far stronger presidency, and a much weaker parliament, than France. General Charles de Gaulle had shaped the modern French structure; he was no democrat, but neither was he a Pinochet.

THE DECEMBER 1993 ELECTIONS

Boris Yeltsin ruled that, for the draft Constitution to become law—that is, the basis for a definitive document—at least 50 percent of eligible voters had to approve it. Thus, if a bare majority voted, Yeltsin and his Constitution would be diminished; if fewer than half voted, Russia would have a parliament grounded only in a strong-man decree.

When he finally appeared on television on December 9, 1993, Yeltsin merely asked for approval of the draft Constitution and the election of "responsible and honest" candidates. He assailed "hatemongers," meaning Communists and Zhirinovskyites. He had earlier banned two other hate groups, and several fringe organizations.

Beginning on November 22, Ostankino television Channels 1 and 2 broadcast "Voters' Hour" before the evening news. The news itself and programming in general conveyed a strongly pro-government, pro-reform line.

Many candidates displayed a talent for negative campaigning. The Communists attacked the government, Russia's Choice, and the draft Constitution. Centrist and opposition parties blamed the government for crime and the desperate economic situation. Promising to bring the faith healer Anatoli Kashpirovsky and the pornographer Eduard Limonov into his Cabinet, Vladimir Zhirinovsky assailed the government, Jews, Yeltsin, and Mikhail Gorbachev for betraying Russia. But he supported the draft Constitution because he intended to make use of it:

There's nothing like fear to make people work better. The stick, not the carrot. I'll do it all without tanks on the street. Those who need to be arrested will be arrested quietly, at night. I may have to shoot 100,000 . . . but the other 300 million will leave peacefully. I have the right to shoot these 100,000. I have this right as president.

In the first two weeks of televised campaigning, the opposition parties broadcast 39 political advertisements accusing Yeltsin and Yegor Gaidar of creating Russia's misery. Only three commercials blamed the Communist Party. Russia's Choice featured Gaidar in a domestic situation, St. Bernard dog at his feet. This impressed viewers. The Sobchak–Popov Democratic Reform Movement required its candidates to submit to interviews with the rock star Oleg Gazmanov, whose political qualifications remained hidden. The Future of Russia—New Names produced a bizarre commercial: Its candidates took off their jackets, loosened belts, toasted "the new Russia" with champagne, and offered the bottle to the moderator, who was not in on the joke. Civic Union candidates appeared as the old-style Communist bosses they were, promising to end the reforms and uphold the interests of "workers and peasants."

Attempting to win over religious and conservative voters, two weeks before the election Yeltsin ordered the State Tretyakov Gallery—the main collection of Russian art—to turn over the two most venerated Russian icons to the Orthodox Church. The Bolsheviks had seized them in 1920 and miraculously had not used them for bayonet practice.*

Only 57 million citizens voted. At least 50 million stayed away from the polls, and *Izvestiya* claimed the government forged nine million pro-reform ballots. Chechnya and Tatarstan boycotted the elections, although the Tatars did elect deputies in 1994.

---

*The twelfth-century Byzantine Virgin of Vladimir icon came to Kiev and later Moscow from Constantinople. Andrei Rublyov, the greatest master of the art, painted the Holy Trinity icon about 1415. Yeltsin's order specified that these icons, though now physically in the Church's possession, would remain state property and part of the Tretyakov collection.

The entrenched, well-organized Communists and Agrarians naturally won substantial representation. Women of Russia made a surprisingly good showing. The emergence of the Liberal Democrats as the strongest single political party stunned everyone but Vladimir Zhirinovsky and the Liberal Democrats. Russia's Choice won 17 percent of the vote.

The makeup of the State Duma elected in December 1993 was as follows:**

Pro-Reform	(seats)	Anti-Reform	(seats)
Russia's Choice:	76	Liberal Democratic party	63
Yabloko	25	Communist party	45
Unity and Accord (PRES)	30	Agrarian party	55
TOTAL	131	TOTAL	163

Non-aligned	(seats)
Democratic Party of Russia	15
Women of Russia	23
Independents and representatives of small parties	112

Thus ended the referendum Yeltsin had sought, with Zhirinovsky taking nearly a quarter of the vote. The draft Constitution narrowly passed and *Izvestiya*'s charges of ballot-box stuffing rang true. Two leading "vodka-putsch" conspirators, Anatoli Lukyanov and Vasili Starodubtsev (who in 1997 became governor of Tula province), would be in the new parliament, as would the KGB's St. Petersburg TV personality Aleksandr Nevzorov and scores of other KGB types and dyed-in-the-wool Communists.

BYZANTIUM-ON-THE-MOSKVA

The humiliated Yegor Gaidar compared Zhirinovsky—who was flattered—to Hitler and called for an "anti-Fascist coalition." But the ri-

---

**Because Tatarstan and Chechnya did not participate in the election, this Duma began with 444 members.

Reconstruction of the Cathedral of Christ the Savior, Moscow, 1996. (Lena McClellan)

On Guard: Reconstruction of the Cathedral of Christ the Savior. (Lena McClellan)

valry between Gaidar, Grigori Yavlinsky, and Boris Fyodorov had produced the debacle.

Yeltsin's draft Constitution was now the basic law of the land, even though the final version would not be completed until 1995. The attacks on Zhirinovsky as a "Russian Hitler" diluted the charge that Yeltsin was a Pinochet. Media attention on Zhirinovsky highlighted his chauvinist-Fascist ideas and KGB connections.

The election having watered reformer stock, Gaidar and Boris Fyodorov resigned in mid-January 1994. Of the original team, only Anatoli Chubais—who had even more enemies than Gaidar—remained in government as a deputy prime minister and chief of the privatization program. Declaring "the period of market romanticism over," Prime Minister Viktor Chernomyrdin promised to slow down the reforms, prop up smokestack industries, and "if necessary" reimpose price controls.

When the new parliament convened in 1994, Ivan Rybkin of the Agrarian party, who had led the Communist faction in the Supreme Soviet, became chairman (speaker). He promised to work with Yeltsin for an "Accord on Social Harmony" that would renounce violence in the resolution of political and social conflicts. Yeltsin, Chernomyrdin, Chairman Vladimir Shumeiko of the Federation Council, and a host of others signed, but the Communists and Rybkin's own Agrarians, and the Zhirinovsky Liberal Democrats, refused.

On February 23, 1994, the Duma imposed its own kind of social harmony when it overwhelmingly approved amnesty for the October 1993 insurrectionists and the dozen "vodka putschists" still awaiting trial. The Agrarians, Communists, and Zhirinovskyites pushed through the resolution without serious debate.

Yeltsin told Minister of Security Nikolai Golushko, a KGB dissident-basher, to delay the release. Golushko refused to acknowledge receipt of the order.

The reorganization of the security ministry into the Federal Counterintelligence Service—in 1995 renamed Federal Security Service (FSB)—was then under way. Security ministry control of the KGB prisons including Lefortovo had passed to the interior ministry. When Procurator-General Aleksei Kazannik received the order to delay the paperwork, he cited the new Constitution: The Duma's action had to stand. Kazannik and four deputies resigned, and a minor functionary filed the papers. Aleksandr Rutskoi and Ruslan Khasbulatov drove away from prison in their Mercedes sedans. Viktor Anpilov, Ilya Konstantinov, General Makashov, Vladimir Kryuchkov, and Gennadi Yanayev took more modest transportation, and hundreds of petty thugs disappeared into the Moscow night.

The elections, the amnesty, and the national mood obliged Yeltsin to distance himself from the reforms even as he pledged to continue them. Andrei Kozyrev adopted an aggressively nationalist stance at the foreign ministry. In the spring of 1994 Nikolai Travkin, who had become almost as conservative as Stanislav Govorukhin, entered the Cabinet.

The most influential Kremlin adviser remained Aleksandr Korzhakov, who was positioning the presidential security force—as large as two Army divisions—for something; it was not clear what. Next in line was Oleg Soskovets, genuinely a former steelworker but unconvincing as an ex-Communist. A first deputy prime minister, he was Viktor Chernomyrdin's senior executive assistant and personal friend. Soskovets headed a "Commission on Urgent Questions," which regulated the cost of electricity, fuel, and rail transport and was thus, an American journalist noted, the "key command slot over the Russian industrial economy." Soskovets detested Gaidar, Chubais, and the reforms.

Mikhail Barsukov was director of the Federal Intelligence Service, which reveled in a new law the Duma passed in February 1995 and Yeltsin signed in April. The FSB could search private homes without warrants; infiltrate all foreign organizations and domestic ones suspected of criminal activity; create "fronts" under cover of other government departments; establish electronic and other surveillance with a court order; conduct wholly independent criminal investigations; decide what constituted state secrets and exercise control over them; provide security for the armed forces and the federal government; and operate its own jails. Yeltsin and the Duma thus reestablished the KGB as the FSB.

Chief of Staff Sergei Filatov, who controlled access to Yeltsin and deferred only to Korzhakov and Soskovets, pursued a private agenda aimed at sabotaging the reforms. The deputy prime minister responsible for nationalities and regional policy, Nikolai Yegorov, bore much responsibility for the Chechnya disaster.

These men tried to destroy Anatoli Chubais, whose faith in the free market Chernomyrdin likened to Stalin's defense of collectivization. Although he temporarily lost his place in the inner circle, Chubais cultivated a political alliance with Tatyana Dyachenko, Yeltsin's younger daughter, and would make a spectacular comeback.

As the politicians, economic reformers, new and old *nomenklaturas*, entrepreneurs, criminal bosses, secret-police leaders, and others butted heads in this ruthless struggle for power, Viktor Chernomyrdin developed a mild respect for reform. His Gazprom stock having made him one of the richest men in the world, he slowly distanced himself from the old "Red directors." He courted the World Bank, the International Monetary Fund (IMF), the Export-Import Bank, the Overseas Private Investment Corporation, the United States Trade and Development Agency, and the G-7 nations. Money poured into Russia in the form of investments, credits, loans, and grants; it became possible to contemplate the country's reintegration into the world market.

The *nouveaux riches* had an even faster timetable. At the peak of the financial-techno-logical-entrepreneurial-profiteer élite were such men as Boris Berezovsky, director of the enormous LogoVAZ holdings; Vladimir Gusinsky, chairman of Most ("Bridge") Group; Mikhail Khodorkovsky of the Menatep Group (investment banking); Aleksandr Smolensky, chairman of Stolichny Savings Bank; Vladimir Vinogradov of Inkombank; Vladimir Potanin of the Interros conglomerate and Uneximbank, Russia's largest private lender.

Nearly all the directors of Russia's 2,500 banks (October 1995) had become overnight millionaires. Not one could have had a legally amassed net worth of more than a few thousand dollars in 1989, but now, between them, they were sending at least $25 billion a year to banks in Switzerland and Cyprus. They enjoyed the protection of their own extensive private security services and the blessing of the state. They made billions on the 1994–1996 war in Chechnya, more with the coming of peace; *someone* had to get the state contracts.

When the value of the ruble fell 25 percent on October 11, 1994, "Black Tuesday," the entrepreneurs increased their deposits in foreign banks and sent their wives and children to live abroad. In 1995 the Russian GDP shrank 4 percent, in large measure because the entrepreneurs were producing nothing but a good impression on foreign governments and financial institutions. Russia was being plundered by a handful of her own citizens as no nation in history. This enhanced the possibility of a return to power of the Communists, probably in temporary alliance with the Zhirinovskyites.

THE 1995 PARLIAMENTARY ELECTIONS

Boris Yeltsin was hospitalized in October 1995 with what proved to be major cardiac problems. During his illness, Korzhakov, Soskovets, and Barsukov plotted to cancel the parliamentary elections scheduled for December 1995. As a first step, they ordered the Central Election Commission to disqualify Aleksandr Rutskoi's Derzhava (Great Power) party and Grigori Yavlinsky's Yabloko.

Prime Minister Chernomyrdin, and Gennadi Zyuganov and the Communists, protested vigorously when they learned of this scheme. Yavlinsky observed that "some people do not want a presidential election next year." Aleksandr Lebed asked rhetorically who could take Russia seriously, "if this is the way our system treats legitimate political parties?" The World Bank, the IMF, and other international lenders threatened to withhold loans.

The Supreme Court restored Derzhava and Yabloko to the ballot. In the summer of 1996, Korzhakov and Soskovets would try again to subvert democracy.

More than 60 percent of the electorate participated in the December 1995 elections. Russia was becoming accustomed to democracy, but the vote indicated that the Communists remained formidable. The CPRF won about 22 percent of the vote, double its 1993 share, and would have twice as many deputies as the progovernment parties. Altogether, the core opposition of Communists, Agrarians, and Zhirinovsky's Liberal Democrats garnered 38 percent. That, however, was down from 44 percent in 1993, and indeed the CPRF gains came at the expense of the Liberal Democrats, whose vote fell to 11 percent, less than half that of 1993. The Communists also picked up support from the Agrarians, who did not get 5 percent of the popular vote and thus failed to qualify for party-slate seats. Some Agrarians did win in single-constituency districts. The now anti-reform Women of Russia fell short of the 5-percent barrier but did win seats in single-constituency districts, as did the hard-line Communist Labor party.

Of the three main pro-reform parties, Prime Minister Chernomyrdin's Our Home Is Russia* won just under 10 percent; Yavlinsky's Yabloko party about 8.5 percent. With only 4.8 percent, Gaidar's Russia's Choice did not qualify for party-slate deputies. The combined total fell short of the 29 percent of the vote that reformist groups had won in 1993.

Independents and small-party deputies rounded out the composition of the new Duma, which met in January 1996. Gennadi Seleznyov of the CPRF succeeded Ivan Rybkin as speaker of the Duma.

THE ECONOMY

In 1993, more Mercedes automobiles were sold in Moscow than in any other European city, most of them for cash. In Berlin, Zürich, Geneva, Lausanne, Munich, Vienna, and Copenhagen, Russian citizens purchased—almost always with cash—more than half all new Mercedes and BMW vehicles sold in 1994 and 1995. Like the narcotics traffic, such commerce can only proceed with high-level official connivance.

The Russian GDP declined 12 percent in 1994 and 15 percent—adjusted for inflation—in 1995. The 1993 inflation rate had been 900 percent. That fell to 220 percent in 1994, 133 percent in 1995, and 21.8 percent in 1996. The Chernomyrdin government attributed the steady drop to its new "tight money" policy.

Prices increased tenfold in 1993, fourfold in 1994, and doubled in 1995. Industrial production fell 25 percent in the third quarter of 1993, nearly as much in the first quarter of 1994. Presidential decrees reduced taxes on business, cut export quotas, and promised aid to companies dependent on foreign investment. Twice in 1996 the IMF withheld loan payments because the Russian government had failed to collect more than a fraction of

---

*The media and the public jeered, "Our home is Gazprom."

the taxes due it; Gazprom was the biggest single offender. The ex-Gazprom boss Chernomyrdin cracked down a little, more revenues came in, and loan payments resumed. But the GDP fell an inflation-adjusted 6 percent in 1996.

The fall 1995 harvest was the worst in 30 years. As usual the weather played a role, but most important was the legacy of collectivization. The Constitution sanctioned the sale of land to private owners, but only according to a land code mandated by federal law. Not until the summer of 1995 did the Duma approve a bill, and even then it "froze" Chapter 17, on the conditions of land sales. Communist and Agrarian deputies demanded a continued major role for state ownership role in land, but through parliamentary subterfuges the privatization forces outflanked them.

Then in March 1996 Yeltsin, whose Constitution gave federal lawmakers jurisdiction over the land question, unilaterally decreed that *all* land would be privatized. Wary of the resurgent Communists, he sought to regain the initiative for the presidential election; the Constitution meant what he said it meant.

THE WAR IN CHECHNYA

The Soviet-era politicians of Checheno-Ingushetia, a Muslim enclave in the foothills of the Caucasus, had supported the 1991 "vodka putsch." After that fiasco, they yielded power to a spontaneously organized Congress of the Chechen People, which elected former Soviet Air Force General Dzhokar Dudayev president and proclaimed Chechnya independent.

The Chechens seized some Soviet airliners and went into business. Frederick Cuny, who would be assassinated in Chechnya, wrote in April 1995 that "Opium, heroin, and hashish were among the more profitable commodities sent northward"—to Russia. The Dudayev regime also bought Russian Army weapons on

the black market, kept some for its own use, and sold the rest abroad, some to Bosnia.

The struggling Yeltsin regime ignored the problem until November. Then, acting on the advice of Vice President Rutskoi and Aleksandr Korzhakov, Yeltsin sent a thousand troops to impose martial law. Dudayev's forces blocked them at the Grozny Airport for three days until Yeltsin recalled them. Rutskoi blamed Gaidar and other Yeltsin cronies for the humiliation.

Ingushetia split off from Chechnya in June 1992 and rejoined the Russian Federation. The arms and narcotics traffic through Chechnya continued unabated, and many Russians blamed soaring crime rates in European Russia on "dark"—swarthy—people of the Caucasus in general and the Chechen "mafia" in particular. Something had to be done. Yeltsin, however, preoccupied with the reforms, had to contend with a demoralized Russian Army, the incompetent and corrupt Defense Minister Pavel Grachev, Aleksandr Korzhakov, and Oleg Soskovets. Violent clashes on the Russia–Chechnya frontier in the fall of 1992 produced casualties.

In the spring of 1993 Dudayev dissolved the Chechen parliament, which Russia had not recognized, and—as Frederick Cuny wrote—began "courting Muslim radicals in the Middle East, toying with declaring an Islamic state and imposing Shariah law." Mystical Sufi Islam flourished. The fate of the 200,000 ethnic Russians in Chechnya became a matter of concern for Moscow.

Backed by Korzhakov, Soskovets, Security Minister Mikhail Barsukov, and Interior Minister Anatoli Kulikov, Defense Minister Pavel Grachev bragged that a few hundred Russian paratroopers would take Grozny, the Chechen capital, in two hours. On December 11, 1994, Yeltsin gave the order. Russian bombers leveled the center of Grozny. This and subsequent raids, and a protracted artillery bombardment, reduced the city to rubble. Thousands of el-

Chechnya. (*The Washington Post*). Reprinted with permission.

derly Russian pensioners were among those killed.

The Chechens retreated to the hills and harassed the Russian forces with hit-and-run guerrilla attacks. The Russian soldiers fought back blindly, often turning their weapons on civilians. General Aleksandr Lebed, who opposed the war, attacked Yeltsin for sending "unprepared, untrained boys to face bullets" and declared that only a "criminal power" would send "hundreds of citizens to certain death."

In 1995 a Chechen chieftain, Shamil Basmayev, seized a hospital and took more than a thousand hostages in the town of Budyonnovsk, Russia. Refusing to negotiate, the local Russian commander shelled the hospital and killed about 150 patients. A public outcry forced Moscow to step in. Permitted to return

to Chechnya in triumph, Basmayev later became a candidate for the Chechen presidency.

Early in 1996 Chechen guerrillas took 3,400 hostages in the Dagestani (Russian Federation) town of Kizlyar. More than 200 Dagestanis and Russians were killed, nearly a thousand wounded. Kizlyar, which produced Russia's finest brandy, was destroyed. The guerrillas again went free. Three months before the Russian presidential elections, Yeltsin dismissed Grachev, Korzhakov, Barsukov, and Soskovets.

Dzhokar Dudayev died in battle in April 1996. His successor, Zelimkhan Yandirbayev, renamed Grozny (Russian for "Terrible") Dzhokar-Ghala (Dzhokarville).

After his own reelection, Boris Yeltsin appointed General Aleksandr Lebed to negotiate a peace settlement in Chechnya. Lebed signed a truce with Aslan Maskhadov, the Chechen prime minister and chief of staff of the armed forces. The Russian Army would withdraw, the Chechens would hold elections, and the question of Chechnya's status in the Russian Federation would be discussed "at a later date."

On November 23, 1996, Yeltsin ordered the last two Russian military units, which together had about six thousand men, to withdraw from Chechnya. The political status of the area was left vague.

The Chechens went to the polls on January 27, 1997, to choose between Yandirbayev, Shamil Basmayev, Aslan Maskhadov, and several minor candidates, all of whom advocated independence. Maskhadov won by a comfortable margin and declared that "our independence must be recognized by all states, including Russia." The Kremlin lamely explained that the Chechen elections cleared the way for "serious negotiations."

FOREIGN AFFAIRS

Chechnya's attempt to secede, coupled with the arms and narcotics traffic that flourished with the blessing of Chechen leaders, presented Russia with a terrible dilemma, and no one could argue that right lay exclusively on one side or the other. Yeltsin's war brought shame and disgrace on Russia, but business continued as usual. The IMF approved the second largest loan in its history—$10 billion—to Russia, and the Council of Europe, purportedly dedicated to preserving human rights, welcomed Russia into its ranks.

In January 1993 Yeltsin and President William Clinton signed the START II Treaty in Moscow, which provided for the reduction of existing strategic nuclear arsenals to one-third the 1993 levels within a decade. The U.S. Senate approved the accord in 1996, but as of the

spring of 1997 neither the Supreme Soviet nor its successor, the State Duma, had ratified it. The Communists, Zhirinovskyites, and nationalists of all parties criticized START II as a further humiliation of Russia. But the cutback in mass-destruction weapons that began in 1990 continued. By 1997 Russia had reduced the number of its strategic warheads from 11,000 to 7,000. The United States had cut its arsenal to 8,000, down from 13,000.

Russia had been defeated by the Afghan mujahadeen and humiliated by the Chechen guerrillas. She frequently could not pay or feed or house her own soldiers, let alone equip and train them. At least for the time being, no Russian strike to the west with conventional forces was possible. Nevertheless, Poland, Hungary, the Baltic States, and the Czech Republic, traumatized by the events of 1944–1989, demanded protection from Russia, and NATO began the process of expanding into an Eastern Europe vacated by the Soviet military.

What Eastern Europe really needed was not membership in NATO, a defensive alliance against a nation that no longer existed, but association with the European Union. The Union, however, refused to open its common market to the cheap labor and agricultural produce from Eastern Europe. To placate the Americans, who would as usual pay all the costs involved, and calm the Poles and Hungarians, the European Union unenthusiastically assented to NATO expansion. Like the mobilizations of August 1914, this process took on an irresistible momentum, and the first steps to admit Poland and the Czech Republic came in July 1997.

In the late 1930s some Europeans joked that the USSR would adhere to the Anti-Comintern (Axis) Pact. Sixty years later there was some not entirely frivolous speculation that Russia would join NATO. Western politicians spoke of a "partnership for peace," but defining the guarantees to be given Russia by an alliance directed against her proved difficult.

Although various polls showed the Russian public more interested in pocketbook issues than in NATO, the plans to expand that military–political alliance encountered strong hostility in Russian political circles and generated a new cohesiveness among the military leadership. The prospect of massive defense contracts united the remnants of the old *nomenklatura* and "Group of 13." Aleksandr Lebed once declared that NATO's move into Eastern Europe could lead to World War III, only to reverse himself in September 1996: "If they want to expand, let them waste the money. Who is Russia going to fight now? We are a poor country. We have nothing to fight with."*

In the mid-1990s, Ukraine and Kazakhstan completed the transfer to Russia of the Soviet nuclear weapons on their territories. In November 1996 the last 18 Soviet SS-25 nuclear-tipped strategic missiles in Belarus were transferred to Russia, and Yeltsin and Belarus President Aleksandr Lukashenko soon began negotiations on reunion.

Russia now had the "China card" the United States had played in the 1970s. Moscow and Beijing had resumed normal relations in 1989, and in 1995 and 1996 officials spoke publicly of a "strategic partnership" that would give NATO and the world some food for thought. Prime Minister Li Peng came to Moscow in December 1996 to purchase military hardware, sign an agreement expanding trade, and arrange for the settling of the border problem.

Russia continued to sell military aircraft, warships, armored personnel carriers, and other weapons to China, cryogenic rocket engines to India, submarines to Iran, and advanced military hardware to other coun-

_____
New York Times Magazine, October 13, 1996, p. 56.

tries. The West charged that this heightened international tensions; in reality, Western manufacturers did not like the competition. In 1994 the United States peddled $12.4 billion worth of arms around the world, 56 percent of the total trade. Great Britain came second with $3.4 billion, Russia a distant third at $1.3 billion.

THE 1996 PRESIDENTIAL ELECTION

Boris Yeltsin bore responsibility for Russia's economic distress and the existence of enormous ill-gotten wealth alongside mass near-destitution. The blood of Chechnya was on his hands, and corruption of colossal dimensions began in his office. By the winter of 1995–1996 his popularity had plummeted to single digits in every public-opinion poll. Yeltsin responded by dismissing the ablest—if also most controversial—member of his Cabinet, Anatoli Chubais. The Communist Gennadi Zyuganov seemed destined to become Russia's next president—*if* the election took place as scheduled.

Because a Zyuganov victory would cost them their jobs and miraculous fortunes, the Yeltsin cronies and Pavel Grachev decided to cancel the presidential election. They began floating rumors of their intentions in November 1995.

After his victories in the 1991 "vodka putsch" and the October 1993 showdown with the Supreme Soviet, Yeltsin had sunk into lethargy. Once again his will seemed to fail, and his health declined. He left Korzhakov, Soskovets, Barsukov, and Oleg Lobov—head of the Security Council, which Yeltsin had created by decree—to run the government.

But when Tatyana Dyachenko warned her father that he would likely finish far behind Zyuganov and even Zhirinovsky in the presidential contest, Yeltsin began to stir. In February 1996 he dismissed Oleg Soskovets as his campaign manager, but left him in place as a first deputy prime minister. He named Anatoli Chubais, Soskovets's arch-enemy, to run the campaign. Chubais's ally was Tatyana Dyachenko.

The blatantly unconstitutional March 1996 decree privatizing land made it even easier for the Communists to attack Yeltsin as a dictator. But it was the Communist presidential candidate, Gennadi Zyuganov, who had written in his 1995 book, *Beyond the Horizon,* that "Stalin needed five to seven more years to make his ideological perestroika irreversible and ensure the revival of the . . . interrupted spiritual and statist tradition of Russia." Zyuganov claimed there were more people in Russian prisons in 1996 than there had been in Stalin's Gulag.

Zyuganov would forbid private ownership of land; return the means of production to state control; institute censorship; remove all restrictions on the KGB; and re-create the USSR, by force if necessary. A Communist spokesman told a group of former Soviet officers that Zyuganov's "moderate stance" was for electioneering purposes only; the Communists had "an unpublished 'maximum agenda.'"

Federal law specified that campaigning cease at midnight Friday, June 14. Nevertheless, the state-owned networks ORT and RTR, the private NTV, and Cosmos, a private "superstation" in Moscow, having conducted a "weeklong anti-Communist extravaganza," concluded on June 15 with some powerful documentaries on the "maximum agenda" of the Stalin years. ORT showed Nikita Mikhalkov's 1995 anti-Stalinist film *Burnt by the Sun* in prime time.

There was nothing subtle or fair about this, and Zyuganov, Zhirinovsky, Lebed, and the other candidates did not have equal access to television. That they had any access at all rep-resented progress of the kind Zyuganov and Zhirinovsky vowed to reverse.

On June 16, nearly 70 percent of those eligible cast ballots:

	Percent
Boris Yeltsin	35.28
Gennadi Zyuganov	32.04
Aleksandr Lebed	14.52
Grigori Yavlinsky	7.34
Vladimir Zhirinovsky	5.70
Svyatoslav Fyodorov	0.92
Mikhail Gorbachev	0.51
Martin Shakkum	0.37
Yuri Vlasov	0.20
Vladimir Bryntsalov	0.16
None of the above	2.96

Vladimir Zhirinovsky stood exposed as a marginal figure whom only a great crisis—NATO expansion?—could restore to real prominence. But the widespread support for Stalinism of the combined Zyuganov–Zhirinovsky vote came as a shock to the democratic and semi-democratic forces. Grigori Yavlinsky of Yabloko succeeded chiefly in uniting other reformers against him. General Lebed, who had earlier flirted with the Communists, emerged with enhanced stature. He had campaigned on a simple "Truth and Order" platform. He opposed the war in Chechnya, favored "careful reform," and was unequivocally anti-Communist.

Two days after the election, Yeltsin fired Defense Minister Pavel Grachev, only to replace him with Colonel General Igor N. Rodionov, butcher of civilians in the 1989 Tbilisi massacre. On June 20, 1996, Yeltsin dismissed Korzhakov, Soskovets, and Federal Security Service* Chief Mikhail Barsukov, who had schemed to cancel the election. Yeltsin barely averted a second attempt at a coup d'état.

No candidate having received an absolute majority, the two top vote-getters would meet

---

*Another branch of the old KGB.

in a runoff. Zyuganov courted the Zhirinovsky voters, few of whom were likely to switch to Yeltsin. The key to the second round, however, was Aleksandr Lebed, who announced he would support Yeltsin. That won him appointment as head of the Security Council, and Yeltsin assigned him to bring a definitive end to the war in Chechnya.

Almost as important as Lebed's support was the "Group of 13's" denunciation of Zyuganov and the CPRF. An ad hoc association of Aleksandr Smolensky, Boris Berezovsky, Vladimir Gusinsky, and 10 other super-rich bankers and "industrialists," in April 1996 the "13" had called for political reconciliation—on condition their holdings be left untouched. The Communists swiftly declined. Now, after the first round, the "Group of 13" charged that the Communist plan to restore a Soviet-style econ-

omy would ruin Russia. It financed Yeltsin's campaign, leaving operational control to Anatoli Chubais and Tatyana Dyachenko.

On July 3, 1996, after a strenuous campaign that found him boogeying in Rostov-on-Don, folk-dancing in Siberia, and gyrating to rock music in Moscow, Boris Yeltsin defeated Gennadi Zyuganov by a margin of 54 to 40 percent. With a better candidate and equal access to the media, the Communists might have made a stronger showing. But in any event Russia voted against a return to the past.

TWILIGHT OF THE YELTSIN ERA

Aleksandr Lebed immediately went to Grozny, arranged a cease-fire and then a truce, boasting that "The Chechens put Allah first, me sec-

General Aleksandr Lebed and Ina Lebedeva leave polling station surrounded by bodyguards, Moscow, July 3, 1996. (Agence France Press/Aleksandr Nemenov)

ond." It was a remarkable accomplishment, but Lebed overreached, and he began responding to journalists' questions not because he had answers but simply because he was asked. He would solve the economic crisis, stop crime, restore Russia's international standing, and be a candidate for the presidency. Uniquely among Russian politicians, he did not drink alcohol.

All this was certain to infuriate Yeltsin, Prime Minister Chernomyrdin, Chubais, Dyachenko, and others; Yeltsin dismissed Lebed as suddenly as he had appointed him. But Lebed—the name means "Swan"—was now the country's most popular politician. Only 46 and evidently in good health, he seemed likely to have a second opportunity to run for the highest office before the next scheduled election in the year 2000.

In the beginning Lebed courted such strange allies as Aleksandr Korzhakov, the Travkin-Govorukhin Democratic party of Russia, and the Congress of Russian Communities. He went to Washington, New York, and NATO headquarters in Brussels in search of international respectability. It was difficult to determine where he stood on many important issues, but he demonstrated a capacity for growth, and his straightforward manner appealed to many people. During a January 1997 visit to New York he said there was not a single honestly made fortune in Russia:

When I greet a group of entrepreneurs, I shout, "Hello, crooks!" If they take it O.K.—they're not hopeless. If they beat their chests and deny it—they're incorrigible.

Early in 1997, Lebed and some associates founded the Russian People's Republican party, which promised a "third course" between "totalitarian socialism" and "criminal capitalism."

When Yeltsin collapsed shortly after his electoral victory, the political maneuvering became frantic. Viktor Chernomyrdin, whom Lebed called "so inarticulate he needs a translator from Russian into Russian," hoped to persuade Chubais to serve as prime minister in a Chernomyrdin presidency. At 41, Chubais was 17 years younger than Chernomyrdin and—a *New York Times* correspondent wrote—"lethally smart and extremely well-organized." The "Group of 13" and Western financial and political circles praised Chubais as a genius; the public, and his political enemies, detested him. In October 1996 Chubais received an assignment to oversee the collection of overdue taxes from corporations and state monopolies including Gazprom. The Chubais commission had an ominous name, "Cheka." But had Yeltsin appointed him, or had Chubais and Tatyana Dyachenko signed his name to the papers?

Yeltsin appeared only twice in public before announcing on September 5 that he would soon undergo heart surgery. That operation, a quintuple bypass, took place in November 1996. The surgeons pronounced the procedure a complete success and promised that Yeltsin could resume a full work load after an appropriate period of rest and recovery.

Late in December 1996 Yeltsin received Chinese Prime Minister Li Peng in a formal ceremony in Moscow, but Chernomyrdin and Foreign Minister Yevgeni Primakov, who replaced Andrei Kozyrev in 1995, conducted the negotiations. When German Chancellor Helmut Kohl arrived in January 1997, Yeltsin exhausted what strength he had left and was obliged to return to the hospital, this time with pneumonia. By February 1997 he had spent only two weeks in his office since the July 1996 presidential election; one of his physicians said that Yeltsin was suffering from asthenia (debility).

On January 22, 1997, the Duma voted 229 to 63 to remove the president from office on grounds of ill health. But Yeltsin briefly appeared at his Kremlin office the same day, and the chamber nullified its own vote, which in any event had no legal force. On February 1, Yeltsin turned 66—nearly eight years beyond the life expectancy of Russian males.

In February–April 1997, Yeltsin appeared to make yet another remarkable comeback. Radiating some of his old vigor, he appointed a solidly pro-reform government dominated by two first deputy prime ministers. Anatoli Chubais, who also occupied the post of finance minister, would have overall responsibility for the day-to-day management of the economy. Yeltsin also charged him with revamping the governmental structure and with coordinating relations with the mass media. The other first deputy prime minister, the 37-year-old Boris Nemtsov, governor of Nizhni Novogorod, was entrusted with regulating the energy monopolies, Gazprom included, which owed trillions of rubles in back taxes, and with reforming the pension system. One of the first regional leaders to privatize industry and land, Nemtsov agreed to come to Moscow at the urging of Tatyana Dyachenko.

The presence in the new Cabinet of Anatoli Kulikov as deputy prime minister, and Yevgeni Primakov as foreign minister, constituted obeisance to the security organs, which remained almost as powerful as in Soviet days. Among the six new deputy prime ministers were Yakov Urinson, who as economics minister was in charge of the macroeconomy, and Alfred Kokh, who headed the State Property Committee.

Yeltsin met the American president, William Clinton, in a March 1997 "summit" in Helsinki. In return for promises of increased aid, Yeltsin bowed to the fait accompli of NATO's expansion into Eastern Europe. He obtained Clinton's pledge that NATO would not deploy nuclear weapons in Poland, the Czech Republic, or anywhere else in Eastern Europe. That did not satisfy such authoritarian nationalists as Zyuganov and Zhirinovsky, who immediately charged Yeltsin with selling

out Russia. Some great political battles lay ahead.

THE NEW CRUSADE

The Russian reformers have repeatedly insisted that the transition from Soviet communism to freedom and democracy cannot be accomplished without pain. The distribution of the suffering, however, has been grossly unfair: About three quarters of the population live close to or below the poverty line, while perhaps 1 percent have not only not suffered but have also reaped enormous profits with the blessing of the hopelessly corrupt bureaucracy.

Russia's new rulers have sanctioned the importation of an extraordinarily vulgar Western and Japanese commercialism that threatens to swamp traditional Russian culture and values already distorted by seven decades of spiritual depravity under Lenin and his successors. The culture that provided a moral refuge, a sanctuary, after the events of 1917–1920, may be fading. The bookstores are full of Western pulp fiction, self-help guides, and pornography. There are many buyers for that, relatively few for the classics of Russian literature. It is difficult to find Russian or any other classical music on radio or television, impossible to get away from the generic international heavy metal sound, even in the villages.

But Russian democracy resembles the ilexes draped in Spanish moss that the British writer-diplomat-Member of Parliament Harold Nicolson saw in Charleston, South Carolina, in 1937: "In detail ugly and untidy, in the mass strange and impressive." Russia treasures democracy and freedom as much as any nation and has suffered more than most for it. Democracy has survived against great odds since 1991 and may yet prove tough enough to prevail against the tug of Russia's tragic past, and the lure of barren materialism.

SUGGESTED ADDITIONAL READINGS

BARANOVSKY, VLADIMIR, ED. *Russia and Europe: The Emerging Security Agenda.* Oxford: Oxford University Press, 1997.

GOULD, JENNIFER. *Vodka, Tears, and Lenin's Angel.* New York: St. Martin's Press, 1997.

HEWETT, ED A., with CLIFFORD G. GADDY. *Open for Business: Russia's Return to the Global Economy.* Washington, DC: Brookings Institution, 1992.

HOGAN, MICHAEL, ED. *The End of the Cold War: Its Meaning and Implications.* New York: Cambridge University Press, 1992.

KHAZANOV, ANATOLY M. *After the USSR: Ethnicity, Nationalism, and Politics in the Commonwealth of Independent States.* Madison: University of Wisconsin Press, 1995.

LINDEN, CARL, and JAN S. PRYBYLA. *Russia and China on the Eve of a New Millennium.* New Brunswick, NJ: Transaction Publishers, 1997.

MANDELBAUM, MICHAEL. *The Dawn of Peace in Europe.* New York: 20th-Century Fund Press, 1997.

MOSS, WALTER G. *A History of Russia.* Vol. 2: *Since 1855.* New York: McGraw-Hill, 1997.

Author's note: This chapter rests heavily on reporting by the Russian press, especially *Segodnya, Nezavisimaya Gazeta, Izvestiya,* and *Kommersant,* and in the news agency Interfax, and by the late Frederick Cuny in the *New York Review*; Thomas Friedman, Michael R. Gordon, Michael Specter, and Alessandra Stanley in *The New York Times*; Lee Hockstadter and David Hoffman in the *Washington Post*; Steve Liesman, Betsy McKay, and Claudia Rosett in *The Wall Street Journal*; Martin Sieff in the *Washington Times*; Phil Reeves in the *Independent* (London); and James Meek in *The Observer* (London).

INDEX